D1499597

FIELD MARSHAL

FIELD MARSHAL

THE LIFE AND DEATH OF

ERWIN ROMMEL

DANIEL ALLEN BUTLER

CASEMATE
Philadelphia & Oxford

Published in the United States of America and Great Britain in 2015 by
CASEMATE PUBLISHERS
908 Darby Road, Havertown, PA 19083
and
10 Hythe Bridge Street, Oxford, OX1 2EW

Copyright 2015 © Daniel Allen Butler

ISBN 978-1-61200-297-2
Digital Edition: ISBN 978-1-61200-298-9

Cataloging-in-publication data is available from the Library of Congress and
the British Library.

10 9 8 7 6 5 4 3 2 1

Printed and bound in the United States of America.

For a complete list of Casemate titles please contact:

CASEMATE PUBLISHERS (US)
Telephone (610) 853-9131, Fax (610) 853-9146
E-mail: casemate@casematepublishing.com

CASEMATE PUBLISHERS (UK)
Telephone (01865) 241249, Fax (01865) 794449
E-mail: casemate-uk@casematepublishing.co.uk

CONTENTS

ALSO BY DANIEL ALLEN BUTLER

*"Unsinkable"—The Full Story
of RMS* Titanic

The Lusitania*: The Life, Loss, and Legacy
of an Ocean Legend*

Warrior Queens—the Queen Mary *and*
Queen Elizabeth *in World War Two*

The Age of Cunard—A Transatlantic History, 1939–2003

*Distant Victory: The Battle of Jutland
and the Allied Triumph in the First World War*

*The First Jihad: The Battle for Khartoum
and the Dawn of Militant Islam*

*The Other Side of the Night:
The* Carpathia, *the* Californian, *and
the Night the* Titanic *was Lost*

*The Burden of Guilt—
How Germany Shattered the Last Days of Peace,
Summer 1914*

*Shadow of the Sultan's Realm:
The Destruction of the Ottoman Empire
and the Creation of the Modern Middle East*

To
Robert C. Lendt

who is the exemplar
of all that a teacher should be . . .

and who helped me to understand
that wars are ultimately decided by men,
not merely by the numbers of their tanks and guns. . . .

AUTHOR'S NOTE

FIELD MARSHAL ROMMEL.

Those three words instantly conjure up images of tanks, half-tracks, and armored cars jockeying their way across a desert landscape, while footsore infantry slogs its way into defensive positions and hidden antitank guns suddenly reveal themselves in furious bursts of fire. The name invokes the memory and reputation of the German Afrika Korps and its nemesis, the British Eighth Army.

Erwin Rommel was a complex man: a born leader, a brilliant soldier, a devoted husband, a proud father; intelligent, instinctive, brave, compassionate, vain, egotistical, and arrogant. In France in 1940, then for two years in North Africa, then finally back in France once again, in Normandy in 1944, he proved himself a master of armored warfare, running rings around a succession of Allied generals who never got his measure and could only resort to overwhelming numbers to bring about his defeat. And yet he was also naive, a man who could admire Adolf Hitler at the same time that he despised the Nazis, dazzled by a Führer whose successes blinded him to the true nature of the Third Reich. Above all, though, he was the quintessential German patriot, who ultimately would refuse to abandon his moral compass, so that on one pivotal day in June 1944, he came to understand that he had willingly served an evil man and an evil cause. He would still fight for Germany even as he abandoned his oath of allegiance to the Führer, when he came to realize that Adolf Hitler had morphed into nothing more than an agent of death and destruction, and in that moment he chose to speak Truth to Power. In the end Erwin Rommel was forced to die by his own hand, not because, as some would claim, he had dabbled in a tyrannicidal conspiracy, but because he had committed a far greater crime—he dared to tell Adolf Hitler the truth.

This was the man who has beguiled me for almost my entire life, initially as the dashing, daring leader of the Afrika Korps whose exploits in Libya seemed to be a curious admixture of German martial prowess, British doggedness, and anachronistic chivalry, with a dash of *Beau Geste* thrown in for good measure. Then, as I matured and my study—and comprehension—of warfare simultaneously broadened and deepened from adolescent fascination with the tools and weapons of war to developing insights into how and why men fight wars, I sought to understand why someone as essentially decent and honorable as Erwin Rommel would willingly, even enthusiastically, offer the services of his sword to the likes of Adolf Hitler and the Third Reich. It was not until the twenty-first century dawned and the distinctions between nationalism and patriotism began to crystallize as they had never done before that I felt I had found the key that would unlock that mystery. The end result was *Field Marshal—The Life and Death of Erwin Rommel*.

The title suggested itself almost instantly: I discovered that when asked what was the first name to come to mind when they heard the words "Field Marshal" people who would have been hard-pressed to name a single general from any of the warring nations of the Second World War—aside from, perhaps, George S. Patton, Jr.—would blurt out "Rommel!" This was a phenomenon I encountered in locales as geographically and culturally diverse and distant as Los Angeles, California, rural Minnesota, South Florida, Philadelphia, Pennsylvania, suburban Grand Rapids, Michigan—even Ottawa, Ontario, Canada and Belfast, Northern Ireland. It was then that I realized that the time had come to create a biography of Erwin Rommel that was at once a military history and an honest portrait of the man who bore that name.

Unlike many biographies of great or famous soldiers, *Field Marshal* is not simply a military history onto which a biography has been grafted. It is an examination and exploration of the life of a fascinating soldier and a remarkable man. A plethora of fuller, far more detailed accounts of military operations in the Second World War in Europe are available to someone seeking out such works. I have made a deliberate effort to limit the intrusion of events outside of the immediate experience or knowledge of Erwin

Rommel in both the First and Second World Wars, especially those away from the front or theater where Rommel was serving, save where the presentation of such events is necessary for context or perspective or where they will have significant, though not always direct, impact or consequences for Rommel. This is not an attempt to marginalize those events, but rather a conscious decision of perspective. I have also striven to, whenever possible, allow Rommel to speak for himself. This, then, is Erwin Rommel's story, as he lived and died, no more, no less.

———————

HAVING MADE THE decision to write a biography of Rommel, I had to confront the embarrassment of riches in available sources about his life and times. The simultaneous starting points for anyone intent on more than the most superficial introduction to the man are two books written by Rommel himself, *Infanterie Greift an*, and *Krieg ohne Hass*, along with a collection of his letters and memoirs edited by Basil Liddell-Hart and titled *The Rommel Papers*. Unlike the majority of soldiers throughout history, Rommel was a lively and engaging writer, and rarely can the immediacy of his words be improved upon, so whenever possible, Rommel should be allowed to speak for himself.

There are extensive official German, British, and American archives on Rommel. The single most important collection is found in the National Archives in Washington DC: primary Rommel material; the war diaries of the Führer's headquarters, the German General Staff, and the Oberkommando des Wehrmacht (O.K.W.); the diaries of Col-Gen. Alfred Jodl, the Chief of Operations for the O.K.W.; and the war diaries of the German forces in Africa, from Afrika Korps to Heeresgruppe Afrika, along with the war diaries and files of various units and formations in France with which Rommel was at one level or another associated. (The war diary of Army Group B in France in 1944 is part of the Rommel files themselves.)

At the Bundesarchiv in the Federal German Republic, specifically the Militararchiv at Freiburg-am-Breisgau, there can be found Rommel's personnel file, and a collection of unpublished manuscripts by officers who served with or under Rommel. Most of the primary documents held by the Imperial War Museum are, in fact, exact copies of files in the possession of either the National Archives or the Bundesarchiv. Nonetheless, the Museum is a priceless resource for anyone studying the Desert Fox, as it can provide a near-inexhaustible supply of information about the 1940 campaign in France, the war in North Africa, and the invasion of France in 1944, especially biographical information on the Allied generals who had, for the most part, the misfortune to cross swords with Rommel. Likewise the Museum and its staff are a fountain of knowledge about the details of day-to-day living in and dying in France or Libya, which any author worth his salt will draw upon in order to add immediacy and authenticity to his narrative.

A fourth archive, the microfilm collection of EP Microfilm Ltd., in Wakefield, Yorkshire, England, is particularly useful in that its contents fill in significant gaps in the documentary records of other archives. A word about this collection is necessary here, however: it was assembled by the historical writer David Irving, a figure of considerable controversy due to his opinions regarding the nature of the National Socialist regime, the character and deeds of the man who created and led it, and reality of the Holocaust, as well as questions about the accuracy of the content of some of his writings. Irving is a polarizing figure and can be a source of discomfort to historians who wish to make use of his research but desire to distance themselves from the man and his opinions. (An uneasy parallel can be drawn to the data collected during the medical experiments conducted by the SS—the information is there, but is it hopelessly tainted because of who collected it?) I will say this much in regard to this dilemma: Irving has proven to be a tireless researcher, and as such has been of immense value to the historical community that studies and writes about the Second World War in Europe. None of the original documents he has discovered has ever been impeached, and thus their reliability can be accepted. As for his opinions regarding the truth about the Holocaust, the nature of the Third Reich, and the character of Adolf Hitler, however, I am in utter and total disagreement with them: the utility of his research does not lend automatic confirmation to his conclusions. And as for the body of Irving's work as a whole, well, let's just say *caveat emptor* and leave it at that.

The experience of visiting The Tank Museum in Bovington, Dorset, England, as a researcher is one without parallel, for not only does the Museum possess the single largest collection of the tanks, half-tracks, armored cars and miscellaneous vehicles that fought on both sides in France and North Africa, but the staff is possessed of a detailed knowledge of these vehicles which is staggering, priceless to a dedicated and determined author. Just as important is the simple experience of standing alongside, sometimes touching, these vehicles, from the tiny Panzer I to the behemoth of the Panzer VIa, the Tiger I. Being so close to such vehicles, or even better, having an opportunity to clamber inside one, imparts an understanding of that intoxicating mix of power and vulnerability which makes these vehicles so fascinating, something that can never be adequately conveyed through the written word.

These four institutions were at the heart of the research done for *Field Marshal—The Life and Death of Erwin Rommel*. Other sources were used, of course, but they merely added to the foundation laid at Freiburg, Washington, London, and Bovington. The only flaw inherent in conducting research in such institutions is the infinite variety of distractions and digressions offered by the sheer volume of information immediately to hand about so many diverse and fascinating subjects. A pity, that: so many archives, so little time. . . .

———————

TURNING TO STRICTLY personal concerns, once again my heartfelt gratitude goes out to David Farnsworth, president of Casemate Publishing, for having confidence in yet another of my projects; Steven Smith, my long-suffering managing editor, for his patience and encouragement as he oversaw the development of the manuscript; Ruth Sheppard, whose perception, insight, and meticulous attention to detail allowed her to perform an outstanding job editing the manuscript; and Tara Lichterman, executive assistant at Casemate and the person who really keeps all of their ducks in a row.

The ever-reliable Trish Eachus-Crabtree once again took on the task of being one of my first readers, along with her husband, Leonard Crabtree, USMC (ret.); Trish also did her usual yeoman service as my proofreader. And she notched up another engagement in her never-ending battle with my run-on sentences. The woman has the patience of a saint.

Scott and Wendi Bragg provided technical, moral, and intellectual support. Wendi in particular deserves mention for helping me unravel an exceptionally thorny moral problem regarding Erwin Rommel: dissecting the ethical process by which Rommel finally came to conclude that breaking faith with Hitler was not merely the right thing to do, it was the only choice he had if he were to remain true to himself. It was Wendi who pointed out that to a truly moral individual, an oath like the *Fahneneid* was binding only so long as both parties lived. By 1944 it was evident to all that Adolf Hitler no longer "lived," in that he was not at all the same man to whom Erwin Rommel had sworn his personal loyalty 10 years earlier. The oath had been dissolved by Hitler himself, in his descent into madness. It was a moment of epiphany when she laid this out for me, as it made so much of Rommel's thoughts and actions in late 1943 and 1944 far more comprehensible and purposed.

A few more of the Usual Suspects deserve thanks for showing up: Maureen Haley for periodically bending my ear—and letting me bend hers in turn—when I needed a break from the Libyan desert or the Normandy beaches to return for an hour or two to the real world. Captain Michael Guardia, United States Army, for encouragement, lively discussion and debate, and the insight of a serving tank officer into the nuts and bolts of tank operations. Mike is also an accomplished military author in his own right—like me, he's published through Casemate, you can find his books in their online catalog: http://www.casematepublishing.com. My first readers deserve a tip of the hat: once again Trish and Len Crabtree, along with Michael Guardia; also Tom Lynskey and David Weber. My friends from LHS and Hope College—you know who you are—who check in periodically if only to say hello and encourage me to keep on keeping on: it always means so much more than many of you probably realize. Thank you!

And finally, the last word of gratitude goes out to the man to whom this book is dedicated: Robert C. Lendt. As a high-school teacher (he's now retired), Bob first introduced me to Erwin Rommel as a man, not simply some semi-mythical figure of television and film. It was he who spurred my interest in the Afrika Korps, showing me how to see it as more than just a bunch of spiffy tanks running around in the desert, and then using it as an introduction to a much wider world of history. It was Bob Lendt and another teacher, George Beecher, now long deceased, who in all of my public school days had the most profound effect on me and my willingness to embrace my vocation. "Thank you" just isn't sufficient, but it will have to do.

For all of these people and institutions, "gratitude" seems to be a somewhat inadequate word; however, mine is deep and abiding, and very genuine. If this book has become greater than the sum of its parts—and I fervently hope it has—it is because of the selflessness with which so many of those parts were provided by the people mentioned here. Whatever information, support, or encouragement they offered me, they did so without any qualification whatsoever. So while it is my name only which appears on the cover, I can never hope to claim sole credit for bringing this work into existence.

What I can and will do, however, is own all of the content and conclusions, especially in light of the fact that many of those conclusions will fly in the face of conventional wisdom and long-accepted historical explanation. To paraphrase from David Lloyd George, my friends will not be allowed to let themselves be converted into an air-raid shelter to keep the splinters from hitting me. The conclusions—there are many—and the errors—if there be any—are mine and mine alone. That's the way it is, because, as always, I wouldn't have it any other way.

Daniel Allen Butler
Atlantic Beach, Florida
October 15, 2014

A FOX IN THE DESERT

H e stood staring out into the seemingly endless and empty landscape of the North African desert, a short, stocky man in desert-brown tunic and trousers, the usual polished gleam of his jackboots dulled by a dusting of yellow-brown sand. The peaked hat he wore marked him as an officer, the gold-spangled crimson collar tabs and matching shoulder-boards with their elaborate gilt knotting and pips marking him as a *generalleutnant* (lieutenant general). On his left breast he wore the silver wreath of the Combat Wound Badge, signifying that he had bled in battle on at least two occasions; above that was the stark, distinctive black-and-silver *cross patée* of the Iron Cross, First Class, an award for valor which he had the curious distinction of having won once in each of two world wars. At his throat were two more decorations, one the Knight's Cross of the Iron Cross, Nazi Germany's highest award for gallantry in action. Yet, beside it, incongruously, hung the blue-and-gold-enameled Maltese cruciform of the *Pour le Mérite, Imperial* Germany's highest award for valor in combat.

He stood straight, as befitted a soldier, but without the affected stiffness typical of a German General Staff officer. Hands clasped at the small of his back, his feet spread at shoulder width, it was the stance of man alert yet deep in thought. The face was handsome, with a profile that was all straight lines and angles; the cheekbones were broad and prominent. Above them sat a pair of alert, intelligent eyes that were a cool, measuring gray; the nose was strong and slightly prominent. A thin-lipped mouth, clearly prepared to easily move between compressed concentration and a broad grin, sat above an angular jaw with a hint of a cleft in it. All in all it was a face well suited to projecting the confidence and determination—and ambition—of the man who wore it: it was the face of a leader.

It was March 23, 1941. Up until this moment, few people outside of

16

Germany would have recognized his name or his face. But as he stood in the Libyan desert just outside the small coastal town of El Agheila, lost in thoughts and plans, he was about to change all of that. Soon his name would be repeated over and over by the prime minister of the British Empire, as part of a ringing declaration that he was the one man the British Army *must* defeat in order to win the Second World War. Within a matter of weeks almost the entire world would come to know of Erwin Eugen Johannes Rommel, the man his British foes would call "The Desert Fox."

No one knows who actually coined the name and first applied it to Erwin Rommel; it simply, somehow, came to be and sprang into common usage among Allied and Axis soldiers—in German it is rendered *Wüstenfuchs*—and then among their respective newspapers and newsreels, more or less simultaneously. It was a title fairly earned on a dozen battlefields stretching across the wastes of North Africa's Western Desert from Tunisia, across Libya, almost to the gates of Alexandria. It was the complete summation of the wily though impulsive tactician and shrewd, but not infallible, strategist who, sharply outnumbered and poorly supported, bedeviled British and American armies and ran rings around a succession of Allied generals for almost three years.

Like his namesake, when on the attack Rommel struck swiftly and sharply, and when on the defensive was never more dangerous than when at bay. Like a fox, he was elusive, swift, and almost always on the move; sitting passive and immobile was not in Rommel's nature. And like far too many foxes, he would be hunted relentlessly by his enemies until at last he was run to earth by a pack of baying hounds whose collective moral worth vanished into insignificance when measured against his own. He would die, not in battle, but by his own hand, a few miles from his home, as part of a bargain struck with a psychopath in order to protect his wife and teen-aged son from homicidal retribution, one last act of courage in a life filled with courageous deeds. And it was an action filled with irony, for Erwin Rommel was a man of unimpeachable integrity, and his suicide had been decreed not as a consequence of an act of treason, as so many would one day be misled to believe, but because he had done the only thing he knew how to do: he told the truth—to Adolf Hitler. In the end, he was compelled to take his own life because he was a patriot.

His death was a tragedy, not only for Rommel and his family, but for the nation he loved as well. The shadow cast by the monstrous Nazi regime stained the character and reputation of the German people for generations—whether rightly so or not is still the subject of debate. When the Second World War ended in Europe in May 1945, there were far too few men who had held any senior post of leadership in Germany during the years of the Third Reich who had not been tainted by the foulness of that regime. Had he lived, Erwin Rommel would have been one of that rare breed; what he might have become, what role he might have created for himself, in a postwar Germany is impossible to say. Yet it can be assumed without fear of reasonable contradiction that whatever the part he played, it would have been large and profound: Germany—and the Germans—would have been the better for it. Anyone who takes the time to regard the man at length will soon see past the skilled military technician and recognize in Rommel's moments of insight and introspection the flashes of brilliance that are proof of a truly great mind and character.

It is a self-serving conceit of the liberal elite of the late twentieth and early twenty-first centuries that military leaders are essentially second- or third-rate intellects, unable to successfully compete with their alleged betters and find a place in the "real" world. It is an ill-informed opinion, for it flies in the face of all contemporary evidence as well as historical experience. No American university, for example, offers a curriculum as mentally and physically demanding as that of any of the United States' service academies. More to the point, all of history's Great Captains have been men of extraordinary intelligence and wide-ranging ability. Julius Caesar, who never knew defeat when commanding Roman legions, was equally successful as an author, explorer, businessman and politician. Frederick the Great wrote poetry and philosophy, composed music that is played to this day, and reformed his kingdom's monetary and legal systems, while at the same time winning a succession of wars that transformed Prussia from a minor central European state into a major Continental power. Goethe considered Bonaparte to possess the most powerful mind in human history; the French emperor's nemesis, Wellington, who, like Caesar, never lost a battle, closed his public career after serving as Great Britain's prime minister. In the twentieth century, Douglas MacArthur, after a series of brilliant campaigns in the Pacific, served as proconsul in occupied Japan, during which time he personally drafted a new, democratic constitution for Dai Nippon that is still regarded six decades later as a legal masterpiece. Dwight Eisenhower oversaw the strategy that allowed the Allies to crush the Third Reich, then went on to serve two terms as president of the United States. Rommel was part of this tradition, for while it would have been inappropriate to deem him an "intellectual," his was a first-class intellect. He disdained the intelligentsia, with their self-important posturings and pretenses; at the same time, he was always articulate, often insightful, and possessed not only the capacity to rationally analyze any given situation but also gifts of intuition that bordered on the uncanny. It was a point of particular pride with Rommel that he was often able to outmaneuver an opposing commander because he was able to outthink him. It was a capacity that he repeatedly demonstrated in two world wars, in the First as a junior officer, in the Second in command of a panzer division, then a *panzerarmee*, and ultimately an entire *heeresgruppe*.

There were no premonitions of greatness, though, no portents when Rommel came into this world that he would one day become the most famous soldier his homeland would ever produce, that his tactics and strategies would be studied and emulated by generations of soldiers to follow, most especially those of his former enemies. No one could have suspected that he would one day rise to the rank of field marshal while leading the most celebrated armored corps of the Second World War, or that his name would one day be known—even familiar—to millions of people yet unborn when his own life ended 54 years later. He did not spring up the scion of a distinguished family of German officers, the embodiment of Teutonic militarism and *obrigkeit*. Erwin Rommel was the son of a schoolteacher, deeply rooted in the German middle class, imbued with all of his social strata's caution where the Junker aristocracy was concerned. All of his life he would hold, and sometimes openly exhibit, even flaunt, a sense of contempt for German aristocrats, particularly for those "professional" officers with a *von* in their names who seemed to regard martial prowess and skill at arms as a birthright, their especial reserve, and who in turn regarded him as a lucky amateur. For his part, Rommel would gleefully knock all of their strategies into a cocked hat, as for nearly two years in North Africa he won his victories against a revolving door of Allied generals who never seemed to be able to get his measure, all the while doing so while being outmanned, outgunned, and outsupplied. In the end, he was defeated at El Alamein by a foe whose numerical and material superiority was so great as to be overwhelming; even then, he almost won the battle. And it would be in his final battlefield, Normandy, with his hard-won knowledge and understanding of the dreadful material superiority possessed by the British and Americans, that his strategy would prove to be Germany's only hope of victory, and the plans and theories of the General Staff officers of whom he was so contemptuous would be exposed for the houses of cards that they were.

But all of that lay in the future. Now, as the sun set on the Mediterranean Sea rippling up to the North African shore, he had readied his Afrika Korps, which at this moment mustered a strength of little more than a single division, to strike the next morning toward a British armored corps which just a few months earlier had routed an entire Italian army nearly a quarter-million strong, driving it from the Egyptian border westward across almost the whole of Libya. Rommel's coming attack was an act of the sort of pure audacity that had always been his hallmark combat; by doing so—though there was no way he could have known it at the time—he would dramatically, decisively alter the entire strategic picture of the Second World War. And in doing so he would take the first steps down the road that would ultimately lead to his own destruction. . . .

CHAPTER ONE

THE BIRTH OF A SOLDIER

But the Lacedaemonians, who make
it their first principle of action to serve
their country's interest, know not
any thing to be just or unjust by
any measure but that.
—PLUTARCH, *Lives of the Noble Greeks*

E rwin Rommel was a German.

Deceptively simple and self-evident, this single fact would be found at the core of all that would define him as a man. He would be many things in his lifetime: dutiful son, diligent student, would-be inventor, clandestine lover, determined teacher, loyal husband, devoted father, apt instructor, aspiring aviator, best-selling author, and, above all, dedicated soldier and brilliant field commander. But overarching all these achievements was the defining, essential truth of Rommel's life—and his death: he was a German.

Recognizing this as the cornerstone of Erwin Rommel's character allows everything about the man to be understood with astonishing clarity, including the final decision of his life—the manner in which it would end. From it, every facet of the man proceeds; without it, he would be inexplicable. Emphasizing that Erwin Rommel was a "German" is not to identify him with some vague but convenient Teutonic stereotype; rather it makes a particular point of how Rommel viewed himself and his place in the world. He was born into the first generation of Germans for whom the noun "Germany" no longer defined some vaguely delimited region of Central Europe but now identified a sovereign state—the German Empire. That identity would in turn define his life. And though that life began, naturally, with Rommel's birth in 1891, it can be fairly said that his story began fully two decades earlier, just outside of Paris, France, in the Hall of Mirrors at the Palace of Versailles. . . .

The consequences of the eighteenth day of January 1871 would loom large over, and at times cast a shadow across, the continent of Europe for fully three-quarters of the century that followed. That was the day when, in the Hall of Mirrors, Otto von Bismarck, chancellor of Prussia and the architect of German unification, declared the creation of the German Empire. His pronouncement was the culmination of three aggressive wars, coupled with a series of diplomatic alliances, that, under the leadership of the Kingdom of Prussia, subordinated and unified into a single nation a motley collection of petty Teutonic sovereigns, aristocrats and their states: four kingdoms, five grand-duchies, six duchies, seven principalities, three free cities and the imperial domain of Alsace Lorraine, the remnants of medieval feudalism that had bedeviled the German people since the Middle Ages. It marked the end of the centuries-long political morass in north-central Europe, where "Germany," much like "India" before the Raj, had long been a geographical notion rather than a cohesive nation.

That the Germans had failed prior to 1871 to produce a unified "Germany" was not the fault of the German people. Germany's greatest tragedy, at least until 1933, was the series of conflicts in Europe collectively known as the Thirty Years War. Fought between 1618 and 1648 by a handful of royal and noble houses, the war had begun as an armed religious struggle pitting Protestants against Roman Catholics, and ended as an open confrontation between coalescing powers of France, Austria, Denmark, Spain, the Netherlands, and Sweden, that were developing distinct identities as nation-states. What made this series of wars a German calamity was that the Protestants and Catholics, and later the French, Austrians, Danes, Spanish, Dutch, and Swedes, all used the region known from Roman times as "Germania" as their battleground.

Such was the nature of seventeenth-century warfare that the innocent inhabitants across whose land the opposing armies marched and fought were the war's true victims, as their monies, livestock, crops, and sometimes children were carried off as plunder to pay for the mostly mercenary forces—very few of them German—actually fighting. Rapine, pillage, and looting were the order of the day, and it was customary for a retreating army to burn a farm, a village, or a town, slaughtering the inhabitants in the process, rather than allow it to fall into the hands of the enemy. The result was to leave the Germans physically, financially, and morally exhausted when an end to the hostilities was finally negotiated via the Peace of Westphalia in 1648—it is estimated that at least half of the population of the region died during the war; in some areas, barely one person in ten survived.

Starved in both body and spirit, those Germans left alive at the end of the war focused what little energy and few resources they possessed on mere survival. As foreign armies tramped to and fro across the land, there was scant opportunity for the growth of the sort of ethnic cohesion that was taking place in France, Sweden, or England at the time, or to rally around a ruling house in the manner of the lands owned by the Austrian Hapsburgs, making nations out of what had previously been agglomerations of feudal holdings. The result was that "Germany" emerged from the Thirty Years War as the same motley collection of petty domains ruled by minor nobles it had been when the war began.

One of the larger of these small states, Brandenburg-Prussia, was, in the century that followed the Thirty Years War, fortunate in having a succession of talented, if not particularly likeable, rulers who steadily improved its finances and organization, while at the same time raising an army of moderate size but formidable quality. Simultaneously, through clever diplomacy and shrewd marriage contracts, Brandenburg-Prussia expanded its holdings, until by the year 1740, now known as the Kingdom of Prussia, it was *primus inter pares* among all the small German states. In that year King Friedrich II, who would be remembered as Frederick the Great, began the succession of wars with the Austrian House of Hapsburg that would culminate in the Seven Years War, fought from 1756 to 1763. The ultimate result of these wars was that Prussia emerged almost doubled in size and population, second only to Hapsburg Austria among the German states, and was now the acknowledged leader of those states which were not bound by marriage, formal alliance, or some other treaty, to Austria. A showdown for primacy in Germany between the two seemed inevitable, but it was forestalled by the aggressive wars of Revolutionary France and later the French Empire under Bonaparte.

Prussia's role as Britain's partner in the final defeat of the French emperor at Waterloo caused the kingdom's political stock to rise sharply in value among the smaller German states, and Prussia's monarchs began to work toward a unification of these minor states under Prussian leadership, only to be repeatedly thwarted by Prince Klemens von Metternich, Austria's Machiavellian foreign minister of the day. Von Metternich, architect of the "Concert of Europe" and ardent disciple of the principle of a "balance of power" between the larger European nations, saw Prussia's aspirations as rightly threatening Austria's German primacy, and perceived that threat as a danger to his carefully maintained balancing act between the Great Powers of Europe. Inevitably then, he was determined to rein in Prussian ambition, and worked tirelessly to do so.

There were, as the diplomats of the day saw it, two solutions to the "German Question" of which power would dominate the smaller German polities: the *Grossdeutschland*, or "Big Germany" solution, and the *Kleinedeutschland* or "Little Germany" solution. In the former, the northern German states would be unified in a German Empire under the auspices of Prussia, while the latter simply maintained the petty—and pettyfogging—status quo. Naturally, von Metternich vigorously advocated for a *Kleinedeutschland*, as a united German Empire would threaten Austria's power and position as the leading "German" state in Europe. For more than thirty years he was able to coerce, cajole, and sometimes outright bribe one or more of the smaller northern German kingdoms—Bavaria, Württemburg, or Saxony—to block Prussia's exertions toward unification. Even after the upheavals of the revolutions of 1848, which saw von Metternich ousted from public life, German unification remained an apparently chimeral dream.

That dream finally began to move closer to reality in 1861, when King Wilhelm I ascended to the Prussian throne. Unification was the overarching goal of Wilhelm's reign, and to achieve it he was assisted by his chancellor, Prince Otto von Bismarck, arguably the most adroit diplomat of the nineteenth century, and his army Chief of Staff, General Helmut von Moltke, who was unquestionably an operational and logistical genius. Together, the three men led Prussia to victory in three short, decisive wars—the German-Danish War against Denmark in 1865, the Seven Weeks War against Austria in 1866, and the Franco-Prussian War in 1870—which allowed von Bismarck to negotiate the assimilation of the smaller German states into a great German empire under Prussia's leadership, a process which culminated in the proclamation in the Hall of Mirrors on January 18, 1871.

These feats of arms gave the newborn empire military and political supremacy in Central and Western Europe, while a penchant for hard work and efficiency allowed German workers and industrialists to spawn an economy that at the time was second only to that of the British Empire. Equally impressive were the Germans' accomplishments in science, medicine, and the arts: in the years following the proclamation of the German Empire, the world would be given the final—and best—operas of Richard Wagner, the first works of Richard Strauss, the dramas of Gerhart Hauptman, the novels of Theodor Fontane. The realm of medicine would see the development of cell theory through the work of Schwann, Schleiden, and Virchow, and the introduction of Karl Bayer's pharmaceuticals. Science and engineering in their turn would introduce the names Benz, Röntgen, von Zeppelin, von Helmholtz, Diesel, Bosch, and Daimler to the world.

And yet, with unification came complications: for all their achievements and abilities, the Germans felt that the other European powers weren't giving their new nation its due respect. It was a sense of insecurity as real as it was illogical, for while the German Empire was new, the German people were not—rather, they were a familiar part of the European landscape. While the unrelieved enmity of France was an inevitable consequence of her defeat in the Franco-Prussian War, none of the rest of Europe's powers, great or small, demonstrated anything but goodwill to the empire. Still, the Germans persisted in acting as if the rest of the European community was treating them as parvenus.

Almost by way of reaction to this mistaken belief, the philosophies of Nietzsche and Treitschke, that of the *Übermensch* and the arch-nationalist, fed a growing belief among the Germans that Teutonic blood was superior, and that by right Germany was entitled to primacy of place in the world order. German diplomacy became characterized not by endeavors at cooperation and conciliation but by outright threats and blandishments of force intended to extract concession through intimidation. Barbara Tuchman succinctly described it this way: "In German practice [Theodore] Roosevelt's current precept for getting on with your neighbors was Teutonized to, 'Speak loudly and brandish a big gun.'"[1]

It was an attitude predictably guaranteed to alienate rather than endear, and the more overtly it was displayed, the more swiftly the goodwill of Germany's neighbors began to fade, as they began to believe that one byproduct of the easy victories of 1865, 1866, and 1871 was a form of national self-delusion regarding Germany's proper place in the world. The frequent German assertions of superiority became ever more strident with each iteration. When the Boxer Rebellion broke out in China in 1900, the German troops dispatched by Wilhelm to relieve the besieged European embassies in what was still called Peking were charged by the Kaiser to model their conduct on Attila's ancient Huns when they met the Chinese in combat. (It was a poor choice, as "Hun" became a pejorative that would haunt the Germans for the next half-century.) Clamoring for their "place in the sun" when Germany entered the last mad scramble for colonies in Africa and the Far East, ultranationalistic societies such as the Alldeutscher Verband (Pan German Union) and the Navy League believed that the other European powers were obligated to simply concede to Germany on demand what those nations had acquired through outpourings of blood and treasure. It appeared to her neighbors that Germany was determined to deliberately affront even those powers that had been disposed to be friendly. Beguiled by their own bluster, neither the German people nor their leaders understood the antagonisms their actions and attitudes were provoking. The only explanation that seemed acceptable to the German people was that the nations surrounding Germany were formulating a policy of political and military encirclement (*Einkreisung*) of Germany in order to deny the Germans their rightful place as masters of the world.

This, then, was the Germany into which Erwin Johannes Eugen Rommel was born on November 15, 1891. . . .

He was born in the town of Heidenheim, a few miles north of the university city of Ulm, in the Kingdom of Württemburg, one of the small German states that now formed the German Empire. Ulm and the towns and villages which surround it sit close to Württemburg's eastern border, squarely in the middle of the region known as Swabia. The people there are called Swabians, and even among Germans have something of a distinct identity. For almost the whole of its history, Swabia was an agrarian region, and in the last decade of the nineteenth century, most Swabians would have cheerfully identified themselves as peasants. ("Peasant" has never been a perjorative term in German, as it means simply a farmworker, rather than holding any implication of being a dull, unlettered rube.) Swabians are often characterized as being cunning, canny, and clever. They are typically hard working, usually sensibly frugal, and often exasperatingly stubborn. In a way, Erwin Rommel would prove to be a Swabian writ large, for all of these traits he would possess in abundance.

But his roots did not lie in agriculture. His father, also Erwin Rommel, was a one-time artillery officer who became the headmaster at the Protestant secondary school in Aalen; his mother, Helene von Lutz, was the daughter of the *regierung-präsident*, the head of the local government council. Helene's somewhat distant ties to the minor nobility of Germany notwithstanding, the Rommels were a typical middle-class German family of the day: respectable, responsible, resourceful, and reverent—in the case of the Rommels, solidly if quietly *Evangelische*, Lutheran.

Erwin Rommel was not born to be a soldier; that is, it is not impossible to imagine him in some dynamic career other than that of an army officer, for there was no military tradition in the Rommel family. True, there was more than enough precedent to establish that soldiering has long been a respected aspiration among the Germans. The annals of Prussia and the German states are filled with a whole litany of "vons" who have served the Fatherland ably and proudly—Mellethins, Kleists, Treskows, Rundstedts, Stübens, Schwerins, Mansteins, Stauffenbergs, Kluges, Zietens and such— but military service was not the only path for social advancement in the new German Empire, nor was the possession of a patent of nobility requisite to success. Erwin Rommel, Senior, demonstrated this when he resigned his commission as a lieutenant of artillery in the XIII (Royal Württemberg) Army Corps at the end of his obligatory service in order to follow in his father's footsteps and become a professor. A not inconsiderable factor in his decision was that the prestige accruing to a career in education was comparable to that accorded to an *offizier*, while the pay was more attractive, especially for a young man in his mid-20s with a new wife and a family on the way.

Erwin, Junior, would be the second of five children in that family, having an older sister, named Helene, and two younger brothers, Karl and Gerhard. (A third brother, Manfred, died in infancy.) Details of Rommel's childhood are sparse; he rarely spoke of it himself, a reticence not, apparently, born of bitterness or unhappiness, but rather because it was pleasantly unremarkable. The elder Erwin Rommel was described by one would-be biographer as strict and pedantic, harsh and overbearing, the implication being that he was something of a petty tyrant. But evidence of such is absent, apart from, perhaps, that writer's wishful thinking; it can be reasonably assumed that the elder Rommel was a typical German head-of-the-household in Wilhelmine Germany: legally, he was *Herr im eigenen Haus*—the master of his house—whose word, will, and whim were law and could not be gainsaid by anyone living under his roof. No doubt the words *"Es wird um hier zu sein!"* ("There will be order here!") were heard from time to time (especially in a house with five children in it!), but even so, that is a far cry from a distant and forbidding father figure.

In any event, the variety of careers and professions chosen by the Rommel siblings speaks against it: the aspirations which led to such choices could not have flourished in the cold and stifling regime of a petty tyrant. Erwin, Jr., of course, became a soldier—with his father's enthusiastic blessing—while sister Helene, who would never marry, carried on the family tradition and became a teacher. Karl learned how to fly and served as a pilot in the Luftstreitkräfte, Germany's first air force. He would serve as an advisor to the Turks in the Great War, and be awarded the Iron Cross First and Second Class in the process, but eventually a severe case of malaria would cause him to be invalided out of the service before the war's end. Gerhard, the youngest brother, became an opera singer. The same biographer asserts that Rommel was "a pale and often sickly youth," but again, like the comments about Rommel's father, there seems to be little to substantiate the claim. Rommel himself once remarked that "my early years passed quite happily," and there is no reason to doubt him.[2]

The handful of incidents and recollections from Rommel's childhood and adolescence that have survived are noteworthy because they demonstrate that many of those particular personality traits and facets of character which would one day make Erwin Rommel an extraordinary wartime officer began to clearly manifest themselves during his formative years. Rommel was 12 years old when the Wright brothers flew the first successful heavier-than-air craft at Kitty Hawk, North Carolina, but unpowered flight—gliding—had been all the rage in Germany since before Erwin's birth, due primarily to the pioneering aerodynamic work of Otto Lilienthal, the first truly successful designer and pilot of manned gliders. It is hardly surprising, then, to learn that when he was 14, inspired by Lilienthal's work, Rommel and a childhood chum built a glider of their own and tested it in the open fields around Aalen. Even Rommel had to admit that it didn't fly very far—but it did fly, which was no small feat for a pair of teenaged boys with no formal education in glider design or construction. About this same time, young Rommel purchased a motorcycle, and no sooner had he brought it home than he began to completely disassemble it, down to the last nut, bolt, washer, and screw, the better to understand how all of its various systems worked. More impressively, when he reassembled it, the motorbike ran perfectly, a remarkable display of mechanical aptitude even in a society already known for its love of and fascination with machinery.

Incidents like these made it unmistakable to the elder Erwin Rommel that his namesake was gifted with a sharp, agile brain, and, being the schoolmaster that he was, he did his best to encourage it. He discovered that in addition to a natural talent for engineering and mechanical work, his second son shared his own talent for mathematics, and he encouraged the boy to, among other things, attempt to memorize the table of logarithms. As young Erwin approached his middle teens, when German boys traditionally begin to give serious thought to the vocations and professions they will follow as adults, he decided, for a time, to follow in his father's footsteps and become a teacher; later, he considered engineering at the Zeppelin works at Friederichshafen. Ironically, perhaps, he would become both a teacher *and* an engineer during his career as a soldier, excelling at each.

What happened next can only be attributed to the workings of fate, or perhaps destiny. As Erwin Rommel, Jr. approached his 18th birthday without having made a firm decision about a career, his father began urging him, rather forcefully, to consider a stint in the German Army. Rommel would have been subject to conscription in any case when he reached the age of 18, but whether it was because the elder Rommel simply thought that a term of military service which actually involved a degree of responsibility would be a good thing for his son, or if he saw something in young Erwin which hinted that the army might be the boy's true calling, no one will ever know. Whatever his reasons for them, the father's arguments must have been persuasive, for in the fall of 1910, Erwin Eugen Johannes Rommel, Junior, future field marshal, one day to be known as "the Desert Fox," enlisted in the 124th (6th Württemberg) Infantry Regiment, part of the 26th Infantry Division, as a *fähnrich* (cadet ensign).[3]

The terms of his enlistment were that of an *advantageur*, that is, an officer candidate. Originally he had hoped to become an artillery officer like his father, but after an initial interview with the commanding officer of the 49th Artillery Regiment, his application was denied, as was, surprisingly, his application to the Engineers.

In retrospect this may well have been the decisive moment in Rommel's career, as well as one of history's great "what-ifs." Had Rommel served as an artillery officer during the Great War instead of as an infantryman, would he have evolved into the dashing and dynamic officer he became—would there have been any opportunity for him to do so? Or would he have become an unimaginative plodder? Such was certainly the fate that befell Britain's General (later Field Marshal) Alan Brooke, Chief of the Imperial General Staff and Churchill's senior military advisor from 1941 to 1945. Brooke had been an artillery officer in the First World War, and spent as much time in the Second bewailing the need to avoid another Western Front slaughterhouse as he did expending effort to find the means of doing so. Hindsight makes it very difficult to imagine Rommel as pedantic, dull, and stodgy, but it is a fascinating alternative to consider, nonetheless.

Having neither the desire nor the money to become a cavalryman—officers were required to purchase their own mounts and uniforms, both of which were expensive—the only choice remaining was the infantry, to which Rommel duly applied and was accepted. He completed his cadet training at the end of March 1911, his performance being good enough to earn him a posting to the Königliche Kriegsschule, a sort of finishing school for promising young officers, in Danzig. The course there lasted eight months; it was demanding, as it was meant to winnow out those who were intellectually or temperamentally unsuited for the responsibilities of leadership. Rommel had to work hard, of which he had never been afraid, and when he finished the course, his marks on his final report, while not outstanding, were uniformly good. The school's commanding officer, in reviewing Rommel's file, noted that the young man in question was an intense, sometimes overly serious young man, inclined to be reclusive, who neither smoked nor drank; in his opinion, Rommel had the makings of "a useful soldier," as solid an endorsement as the German Army gave in those days. On his 20th birthday, November 15, 1911, Rommel formally graduated; the following January he was promoted to lieutenant and posted to back to

Württemburg, reporting to his father's old regiment, the 124th Infantry, posted in Weingarten.

During his months in Danzig, Rommel gained more than a commission: he also acquired a monocle and a fiancé. The former was an affectation, the latter would prove to be the love of his life. Lucia Maria Mollin (Rommel would call her "Lucie" or "Lu" to the end of his life) was 16 years old, slender, vivacious, her dark hair and dark eyes evidence of her Polish and Italian ancestors; as graceful as she was pretty, she was a prize-winning ballroom dancer. They met at one of the formal balls regularly given by the officers' mess at the Kriegschule to allow the cadets the opportunity to polish their social skills. For parents in Danzig's middle class these affairs presented a chance for their young, marriageable daughters to meet young men of suitable social standing and good prospects. In this respect the Danzig Military Academy was very much like officer training schools around the world since time immemorial.

Like Erwin, Lucie's father was a schoolmaster, although he had died some years before their meeting. She had come to Danzig to study languages, and learned to speak Italian, French, Spanish, English, and Polish. As can be expected, she was thrilled to be seen walking out in Danzig on the arm of the dashing young Leutnant Rommel, although it was a source of endless amusement for her how he had to quickly pop the monocle out of his eye and into his pocket whenever they came in sight of a senior officer, in order to avoid a reprimand: junior lieutenants were forbidden to wear monocles. By the time Erwin was transferred to Weingarten, the two young people had what was called in those days "an understanding," though exactly when it would come to fruition was vague: junior officers were forbidden by tradition from marrying before the age of 25, and after that still required permission from their commanding officers.[4]

The love story between Erwin and Lucie nearly came to an end, however, before it well and truly got started, because of a romantic detour taken by Rommel while he was posted to Weingarten, one with unexpected consequences. What happened reveals much that is telling of both the character of Erwin Rommel and the innate snobbery of Wilhelmine Germany's middle class. A pretty young fruit seller in Weingarten named Walburga Stemmer caught Rommel's eye; Lucie Molin, more than 700 miles distant, was momentarily forgotten, and they fell in love—or at least in lust. Such a thing was unremarkable even in those days—Rommel wrote charming love letters to her, calling Walburga his "little mouse"—but what happened next had an almost soap-opera-like quality to it. Walburga became pregnant and gave birth to a daughter, named Gertrude, on December 8, 1913. While middle-class Wilhelmine Germans were more relaxed about sexual intimacy outside of wedlock than were, say, their English Edwardian contemporaries, they were every bit as strict about paternal responsibility.

For Rommel, this unexpected turn of events created a moral dilemma fraught with profound personal and professional consequences. However attractive Walburga might be, and whatever she and young Rommel felt for one another, the stigma of her working-class origins made her socially unacceptable as a potential wife for an ambitious young officer. The *offizierkorps* had long abandoned any pretense to being composed solely of men of noble birth: by the time Rommel received his commission, the vast majority of German officers were, in fact, of thoroughly middle-class stock. That did not mean snobbery and elitism had been banished from the ranks of the *offiziere*; on the contrary, such sentiments were, perhaps predictably, even more rampant than they might have been in a wholly aristocratic body. Presuming that working-class men were incapable of conducting themselves with discretion and integrity, the self-appointed middle-class guardians of the *offizierkorps'* honor roundly refused to accept such men—or their wives. Working-class origins for either spouse were grounds for ostracism and a sure path to unpopular assignments and glacial advancement—the antithesis of what a young man of the character and temperament of Erwin Rommel wanted from an officer's life. Marriage to Walburga Stemmer would mean that Erwin Rommel could bid farewell to his military career just as it was beginning.

At the same time, Rommel could not simply turn his back on Walburga and their daughter: perversely, the same unwritten code of honor that deemed Fraulein Stemmer as unworthy to be an officer's lady demanded that Rommel acknowledge his responsibility toward her and little Gertrude. Rommel, who would never, in written or spoken word, publicly comment on the affair or its consequences, had little choice but to acquiesce. In the summer of 1913, he returned to Danzig, there to face the music with Lucie Molin. Somehow he explained the entire situation to Lucie in such a way that her response, if she didn't exactly forgive him, made it clear she understood what had happened. It could well be that Lucie found herself respecting the earnest young officer who was brave enough to face a scorned woman's wrath; certainly Rommel's impulsive nature wasn't unknown to her (and if this situation was not the product of impulsive behavior, it would be difficult to describe one which was!), so some allowance for that might have been made as well.

And a certain degree of calculation on Lucie's part cannot be dismissed as impossible. Until the twentieth century was well-nigh to being on its way out, German women were expected to embrace as the compass of their lives the role of the keeper of the three Ks: *Kinder, Küche, Kirche*—children, kitchen, and church. Dancing may have won her prizes in her teen years, but, as the remainder of her life would demonstrate, Lucie Molin was too much the traditional German woman to ever imagine it as more than a youthful diversion. In Erwin Rommel she had found "her" man, and she was, clearly, determined to keep him. Precisely how it was all explained and settled between remains unknown, all those who had intimate, first-hand knowledge of them having long since taken those secrets to the grave. In any event, Walburga would be regarded as an informal member of Rommel's family until her death in 1928, while Gertrude would live with her father until his death in 1944.

With something approximating a settlement between Erwin, Lucie, and Walburga being reached in the summer of 1913—and the "understanding" between Lucie and Erwin, an informal betrothal of sorts, now firmly in place—Rommel was next posted to Ulm, very close to home, where he would spent the next year teaching and training new drafts of soldiers and officer cadets called up to the colors by Germany's wide-ranging conscription laws. It was a task Rommel enjoyed immensely (he would affirm later in life that nothing gave him as much satisfaction as he instructed young men on how to be soldiers), and he was given the responsibility of training not only new recruits, but also of supervising the refresher courses given to returning reserve officers. What made it all so pleasant, at least for the instructors, was the knowledge that, while the training was being done in deadly earnest, the deterring power and might of the Imperial German Army was such that the possibility of these thousands of young men ever hearing so much as a single shot fired in anger was almost hopelessly remote. None of them could have imagined, in that golden summer of 1914, that in the span of five short weeks, their entire world would start to unravel, or that just over four years later, it would vanish forever.

It began on June 28, in a street in Sarajevo, Bosnia, when a young man named Gavrillo Princzip shot and killed the Archduke Franz Ferdinand, heir to the throne of Austria-Hungary, along with the archduke's wife, Sophie. The assassination served as the trigger that released tensions that had been building in Europe for nearly a century, and what should have been a private quarrel between Vienna and Belgrade quickly spiraled out of control into a continent-wide conflagration. A little more than a month after the shootings, a tragedy of errors saw Russia, Germany, Austria-Hungary, and France go to war as a complex and tangled skein of alliances and diplomatic maneuvers quickly and irretrievably unraveled, for, as Winston Churchill's apocalyptic allusion put it, "The vials of wrath were full."[5]

As unimaginable as Europe's rush toward self-destruction may seem, what is still all but impossible to truly comprehend more than eighty years later is how enthusiastically the peoples of Germany, France, Austria-Hungary and Russia rushed to war, the ecstatic crowds thronging the Unter den Linden, the Champs-Élysées, the Ringstrasse, or Red Square cheering as their respective governments declared war, or how readily the young men were prepared to march off to the sound of the guns, to the strains of *Deutschland uber Alles, le Marseillaise* or *Bozhe, Tsarya khrani*. What should have been an isolated quarrel between Austria-Hungary and Serbia instead became the means to an end for settling old scores, asserting new hegemony or confirming existing preeminence.

But as all of these interlocking dramas and ambitions were unfolding in the weeks after the assassinations in Sarajevo, Great Britain stood apart from it all. There was no reason for the British to become involved in what essentially was a quarrel in Eastern Europe that posed no threat to Great Britain or her national interests. That was to change, abruptly and irrevocably, however, on August 3, when German troops invaded Belgium, surging forward in a huge mass of *feldgrau* (field-gray) toward the fortress city of Liège. A five-power treaty formalized in 1839 had guaranteed Belgium's neutrality—Prussia and Britain had been two of the signatory nations; now a formal protest was sent to Germany over this violation of Belgian neutrality, and an ultimatum issued to Berlin, announcing that if German troops had not begun their withdrawal from Belgium by noon on August

4, a state of war would exist between Great Britain and Imperial Germany. The German chancellor, von Bethmann-Hollweg, however, assured everyone that Britain would never go to war over a 75-year-old treaty that was hardly more than "a scrap of paper."

The Germans didn't even bother to respond. Instead they kept pouring more and more troops into Belgium, along with mammoth cannon, specially designed years before by Krupp and Skoda, to reduce the Belgian forts that ringed Liège and blocked their advance. For the Germans were bound by that strategic dogma that has become enshrined in the lexicon of popular history as the Schlieffen Plan: the rigid and inflexible deployment of Germany's armies, designed to crush France in six weeks, before the mobilization of Russia's huge army could be completed, allowing the whole of German might then to be massed in the east to face the expected Russian onslaught, eliminating Germany's worst nightmare—fighting a two-front war.

The provisions of the plan necessitated the violation of Belgian neutrality to guarantee the success of the German army, allowing three-fourths of the German forces—a million and a quarter men—to swing behind the French armies positioned along the Franco-German border and descend on them from the north, rolling up the French lines like a bloody carpet. Twelve noon passed on August 4 without word of any intention of a German withdrawal, and so the orders went out to dispatch the British Expeditionary Force, the B.E.F., to Belgium, there to take up positions on the left of the French Seventh Army, and prepare to meet the German juggernaut.

The catastrophe that had overtaken Europe was now complete. It was given a name and it would be called the Great War.

CHAPTER TWO

THE GREAT WAR

*The war was a mirror; it reflected man's every virtue
and every vice, and if you looked closely, like an artist
at his drawings, it showed up both with unusual clarity.*
—GEORGE GROSZ

The world had never seen anything like the clash of armies meeting each other in the West and in the East.

To the German General Staff, the B.E.F. was so small as to be almost not worth consideration, but, German derision notwithstanding, those six divisions were, man for man, the finest troops Europe had ever seen or would ever see again. When they finally met the oncoming waves of *Feldgrau* on August 22, they handed the advancing Germans setback after bloody setback for the next month, retreating only when their exposed flanks were threatened, their numbers slowly but irrevocably dwindling, as the supporting French armies, bleeding and demoralized, reeled from the shock, surprise, and sheer weight of the German assault.

While the French armies desperately sidestepped to the west in the hope of forming a line which would finally stop and then throw back the German invaders, the courage and tenacity of the B.E.F. inflicted fatal delays and diversions on the German's unforgiving schedule for advance. Despite the dire predictions of Schlieffen himself, the plan appeared to be about to hand Germany the crushing victory she was seeking, for the French had been overextended to the east in their thrust into Lorraine. Had the B.E.F. not taken up its position on the extreme French left, the Germans would have swept in behind the French Army, encircling it, exactly as von Schlieffen had hoped it might.

But when the German Army was within sight of Paris, hastily assembled French forces—not letting the time bought so dearly by the B.E.F. go to waste—launched a devastating counterattack into the German right flank, while the Tommies turned about and lunged at their *Feldgrau*-clad pursuers. These blows threw the now more-than-weary Germans back some 40 miles, with the exhausted armies all finally coming to a halt on September 22.

By the end of the year, after a series of sidesteps called the "Race to the Sea" had ended, two thin, snake-like lines of opposing trenches, growing more and more elaborate with each passing week, had been dug from the Swiss border to the Channel, depriving each side of the opportunity to maneuver, as the armies began looking for a way to break the enemy's lines. Strategically, the Allies were faced with the task of forcibly ejecting the Germans from occupied Belgium and France. Tactically, it was a bloody and almost hopeless undertaking, as time and again the French and British armies surged forward against the waiting German defenses—and each time found some hellish new innovation that cut them down by the thousands.

Mud, blood, gore, long days or weeks of boredom punctuated by hours of absolute terror, were the frame for the sights, sounds, and smells of men living a nightmare where they and their comrades were shot, torn, gassed, pulverized, immolated and obliterated in ways that human beings had never before suffered and endured. In the First Battle of Ypres, in October 1914, where wave after wave of German infantry, many of them university students advancing arm-in-arm singing patriotic songs, were cut down by deadly accurate British rifle fire, one German division lost over 9,300 men dead out of strength of 12,000—*in a single morning*. Later, when the Allies were on the offensive, time and again the Tommies and *poilus* would clamber over the top of their trenches after artillery bombardments that had lasted for hours, sometimes days, or even weeks, attacked across the shell-torn mudscape that stretched between the opposing lines of trenches known as no man's land. The Germans, having weathered the barrage in the relative safety of their deep dugouts, would emerge to assume their prepared positions and bring down a withering hail of rifle, machine-gun, and artillery fire on the advancing troops. The results were inevitable: more often than not, there would not be enough soldiers left alive among the attackers to take the objective and hold it, or if the Allied troops did reach their goal, the cost was prohibitive—at the Somme, one attack that advanced barely 700 yards took three weeks at a cost of nearly 30,000 lives. Even on days when the public communiqués would read "All quiet on the Western Front" (the German read *"In dem West ist nicht neuen"*), nearly 5,000 men were becoming casualties, victims of sniper fire and random shelling. It was as if a small town was being methodically wiped off the face of the earth each day. The British, who in some ways were becoming even more methodical than the Germans, referred to such losses as "normal wastage."

July 1, 1916, the first day of the Somme Offensive, would forever be remembered as the Black Day of the British Army. At 6:00 A.M. 120,000 Tommies went "over the top" to attack the Hindenburg Line. By nightfall, barely more than 12 hours later, half of them had become casualties, 20,000 of them dead. The Somme attack had been launched in order to take pressure off the French Army, which was locked in a death struggle with the German Army around the fortress city of Verdun. In the 10 months of that battle, each army would lose more than 350,000 dead in an area little more than 10 miles square.

The Somme did not end on the first day; the battle continued with a fury that ebbed and flowed until November, eventually gaining a 7-mile advance, at a cost of 420,000 British soldiers killed, wounded, or missing; the Germans losses totaled nearly a quarter million men. But while the British Army's hopes for a breakthrough had perished in mud and barbwire, the strategic horizons for the German Army seemed bright with promise. While no one was winning the war on the Western Front, by all appearances Germany and her allies were winning it everywhere else.

The Central Powers (as Germany and Austria-Hungary now styled themselves) began their string of strategic victories in the autumn of 1915, when Bulgaria joined the alliance and helped the Austrian armies overrun Serbia. Even before the Serbs collapsed, an attempt by the Allies to knock the Ottoman Empire out of the war by a coup de main had failed at the Dardanelles: over the next two years the Turks would fight the British Empire to a strategic draw. The Kingdom of Romania, sensing an opportunity to aggrandize itself at the expense of Austria-Hungary, declared war on the Central Powers in August of 1916; by December the Romanians were suing for peace.

Italy, who had not earned and did not deserve the Great Power status she accorded herself, had ignored her alliance with Germany and Austria-Hungary in the crisis of the summer of 1914. The theme of the Italian prime minister, Antonio Salandra, during those crucial weeks was endless repetitions of "Compensation! Compensation!" letting it be known that Italy was available to the highest bidder; there had been no takers. However, by the spring of 1915 the Italian government perceived an opportunity to exploit the Dual Monarchy's preoccupation with the Serbs to the south and the Russians to the north, and declared war, hoping to annex Trentino and the Tyrol, and seize the Adriatic port of Trieste. Instead her attacks were stopped cold by the Austro-Hungarian forces, and a bitter stalemate had imposed itself along the Isonzo River, where the Italians attacked and the Austrians repulsed them with bloody regularity.

To be sure, there were moments of alarm for the Central Powers. When a German U-boat sank the British passenger liner *Lusitania* in May 1915, the ensuing diplomatic confrontation with Washington DC left Berlin with the realization that sooner or later the United States would be added to the list of Germany's foes. And the Brusilov Offensive, launched by the Russian Army in the summer of 1916, was perhaps the most skillfully executed operation of the war, and came perilously close to routing the Austro-Hungarian Army. Only swift German reinforcement stiffened the sagging morale of Franz Josef's troops, and the Dual Monarchy fought on.

The Allies took the offensive again in 1917, and it would prove to be an *annus horribilis*. The overture came in April, along a sector of the Western Front known as the Chemin des Dames, where the French, who believed that they had discovered a tactical "formula" which would break the stalemate, opened their great attack. The abortive "Nivelle Offensive," named after the French commanding officer who conceived and executed the plan, lasted three weeks, cost 187,000 casualties, and gained less than a mile. Thus the burden fell once more on Great Britain. A carefully developed plan, strategically sound but betrayed by weather, geology, and—worst of all—politicians, resulted in the British Army's collective Golgotha. Officially known as the Third Battle of Ypres, it would be forever immortalized as Passchendaele, after a village which stood squarely in the center of the British line of advance. Five months of fighting gave a gain of 5 miles and a casualty list 315,000 names long. It had been the Tommies' supreme effort: they had no more to give. If France was morally and spiritually exhausted,

Britain had become physically so: there were, quite literally, no more fit men to replenish the ranks of His Majesty's regiments. Scraping the bottom of the barrel accomplished nothing, for there was nothing there: it is a matter of record that draft notices were sent to men who were maimed, or mentally ill, or even, in a few instances, already dead.

On the other side of the trenches, the human cost for Germany in each of these battles was equally horrible as that of the Allies. Ultimately, German losses at Verdun, the Somme, and Passchendaele exceeded those of France and Great Britain; and for Germany, with a much smaller population relative to the Allies, replacements were harder to muster. Nor were the losses merely numerical: by the end of 1916 whatever qualitative superiority over the Allies' soldiers the German *soldaten* once possessed had dissipated, and only the German Army's technical superiority kept it ascendant. By the end of 1917, even that was being eroded.

And there was another force, its results less readily visible or immediately obvious, insidiously eroding German and Austrian strength. Neither nation was self-sufficient in food production, and before the war close to a third of Germany's foodstuffs had been imported from overseas. Now the Royal Navy's blockade of Germany cut off altogether those sources of supply, and by the summer of 1916 shortages became increasingly frequent, while as 1916 turned into 1917, starvation began to loom over the civilian populations of the Central Powers. One way or another, 1918 would be the decisive year of the war.

In the east, battles equally costly in lives but even greater in scope than those of the Western Front would be fought between the Central Powers and Imperial Russia, bearing names like Tannenburg, the Masaurian Lakes, Tagenrog, Gorlice-Tarnow, Lake Naroch, and the Brusilov Offensive; only the immense distances of the Eastern Front prevented these battles from being individually decisive—it would be their cumulative effect which would play into the hands of the Bolsheviks and other revolutionaries which eventually brought down the Romanov dynasty and then toppled the provisional government. Eight decades of Soviet meddling and "revision" have left the reliability of the records of those years suspect, but at the very least it can be stated with certainty that close to four million soldiers, Russian, Austro-Hungarian, and German, died in battle on the Eastern Front between August 1914 and November 1917. How many more, mostly Russian, died of disease and malnutrition is impossible to calculate, although the total could easily be double the number of combat deaths.

Yet, if 1918 was to be the decisive year of the war, 1917 was the pivotal one, and during it the hinge of fate turned against the Central Powers. The moral affront of the resumption of unrestricted submarine warfare and the blundering attempt at "diplomacy" which became known as "the Zimmermann telegram" had pushed the forbearance of the American people and their government past the breaking point, and on April 6, 1917, the United States declared war on Germany. Almost a year would pass, however, before the weight of American manpower and industry would begin to make itself felt; when it did so, the Allies would be invincible. Germany's only hope of victory now lay in forcing the French and British to come to terms before the American juggernaut materialized. The collapse of Imperial Russia released 60 German divisions to be redeployed in the West, where for the first time since the opening weeks of the war the Kaiser's army would enjoy a numerical superiority over the Allies. It was an opportunity that the German General Staff did not intend to waste.

As 1918 dawned, it was clear to the political and military leadership on both sides that the armies of all the warring nations were approaching exhaustion—the question was who would falter first. Germany's position was, on the whole, the worst, for the British blockade had been slowly starving the German Empire to death for more than three years. Meat and milk were all but non-existent; turnips had replaced potatoes as a dietary staple; flour for making bread often contained as much sawdust and chalk as wheat. With its new-found numerical superiority on the Western Front, the German Army High Command believed that it had the strength for one last great offensive, but after that there would be no hope of victory: Germany was as exhausted as her foes.

The result was a succession of hammer-blows thrown against the Allied lines, collectively known as the *"Kaiserschlacht"*—the Kaiser's Battle—beginning in late March 1918, with a new offensive opening with each passing month until July. The first, landing on the British Army, was the most successful, for it had the advantages of superiority in manpower and materiel as well as strategic surprise; yet in the end it failed, for while the British Army fell back, the Tommies held their line, and dreadful losses were inflicted on the attacking German divisions. It would prove to be a decisive development, for each of the four German offensives which followed were launched with diminishing numbers and declining morale, while the Allies were marshaling their strength and regaining a measure of confidence as each following German offensive was contained and then repulsed.

By the end of July the Germans had lost more than 600,000 killed, wounded, and missing—irreplaceable losses—in this succession of offensives with little to show for it: some territory had been gained, but no strategic breakthrough had been achieved, no decisive result attained, and the German Army was finally exhausted. At the same time, the Allies, infused with new strength in manpower, materiel, and morale as the American Army began to arrive in France in significant numbers, went over to the offensive. In August and September, their numerical superiority regained, the Allies attacked the German line relentlessly; moreover, by this time they were also gaining a tactical and technological ascendency as well. One by one, through the month of October and into November, Germany's allies fell away, and finally, in the first week of November, revolution swept over the Reich, the monarchy was dissolved, and the German government, now a republic, asked the Allies for an armistice. At 11:00 A.M. on November 11, 1918, the fighting ceased.

The Great War would be the defining event of the twentieth century, even more so than the larger war which followed 20 years later. It was what historians deem a "world-historical event": it fundamentally altered how humanity viewed itself, its societies and institutions, its values and morals. The world which emerged from the war in 1918 was far, far different than that which entered it in 1914; the Great War was (and remains) the greatest cataclysm in Western history since the fall of Rome.

Materially, the cost of the war was staggering: it has been estimated that the monetary expenditure of the war exceeded $186,000,000,000 (at 1918 values). But the human cost was almost beyond measure, for it embraced not only casualty lists, which were almost mind-numbing in their length, but also the toll extracted on Western civilization, one which could never be repaid or replaced. The total dead and missing for uniformed soldiers of all services of all the combatant nations surpassed 10 million; the number of wounded was twice that. Every soldier who fought in the First World War who survived the experience would be marked—and often scarred—

by the weeks, months, or years they spent fighting. Each one brought away his own distinct memory and legacy from his experience, though not all had experienced it the same way. For those men who had who made soldiering their career before the war and sought to continue in that profession afterward, many of the scars were intellectual—not in some detached, academic fashion, but rather in the sobering consideration that, for all of the desire that the Great War truly might be "the war to end all wars," the likelihood of some future conflict on the continent of Europe was all but inevitable. The incidents and events of the war taught lessons and provided insight, both into their vocation and into themselves: they, more than anyone else, had no desire to ever see the Western Front repeated.

Erwin Rommel would prove to be one such. By chance or fortune, he missed the worst horrors of the Western Front, and the mental and emotional scarring it left on the minds and spirits of a generation of French and British officers. These would be the men who, when called upon to lead divisions, corps, and armies in the next war, would often become more focused on avoiding a reprise of Flanders, Verdun, or the Chemin des Dames than they were on winning the battles at hand. That Erwin Rommel would prove to be a very different general than the French or British officers who opposed him would be due in no small part to the simple fact that Erwin Rommel had experienced a different war than did they.

His posting to Ulm in March 1914 put Rommel in command of the half-dozen 77mm field guns of No. 4 Battery, 49th Field Artillery Regiment. A significant portion of his duties was devoted to training conscripts, fresh off the farms and out of the shoppes, who had been assigned to the regimental artillery for the duration of their term of service. Naturally, all throughout July, Rommel, along with all of his fellow officers, paid close attention to the developing crisis in Central Europe which followed the assassinations in Sarajevo, and when French reservists were called to the colors on the last day of July, it was clear to all that the chances for peace were rapidly diminishing: should Berlin decide to mobilize the German Army, war would be unavoidable. Orders for mobilization were posted the following day, August 1; war was declared on France and Russia a day later.

Immediately Rommel asked his commanding officer for permission to return to the 124th Infantry, a request that was readily granted. The regiment was assigned to the 53rd Infantry Brigade, itself part of the 27th (2nd

Royal Württemberg) Division, which was sent into the tiny principality of Luxembourg, along with the rest of the Royal Württemberg Army, now the XIII Corps, subordinated to the Fifth Army under the command of Crown Prince Wilhelm, the heir apparent to the Imperial throne. The mission assigned to the Fifth Army under the cast-iron dictates of the Schlieffen Plan was to take up a position in the Ardennes Forest, near the spot where the borders of Luxembourg, Belgium, and France converged. There it would act as the pivot-point for the massive wheeling movement of the First, Second, Third, and Fourth Armies marching across Belgium as they sought to outflank the French Army in one grand, sweeping strategic maneuver. The reservists reported to their depots, where they were parceled out to their units; uniforms, weapons, and equipment were issued; troops trains were formed and loaded; and the whole panoply began rolling toward the frontier. Acording to Rommel's account of the journey to the front, there was an almost festive air about the mobilization:

> The trip to the front on August 5, through the beautiful valleys and dells of our native land and amid the cheers of our people, was indescribably beautiful. The troops sang and at every stop were showered with fruit, chocolate, and rolls. Passing through Kornwestheim, I saw my family for a few brief moments.[6]

Once at the German border, the men left the trains behind and began marching, arriving on August 18. Four days later, Leutnant Erwin Rommel, Jr., in command of a rifle platoon, had his baptism of fire.

It was near a village called Bleid, just inside Belgium, itself intrinsically unimportant to either side. To the south, however, down along the border separating France from the Imperial German territories of Alsatia and Lothringen—Alsace and Lorraine, France's coveted "lost provinces"—Germany's 6th and 7th Armies were facing four attacking French armies determined to take back those provinces. It was vital to the German strategy that the attention of France's *Grand Quartier Générale* be kept firmly focused on those attacks, and not allowed to wander to the north, where three-quarters of a million *soldaten* were marching first west, then south, prepared to fall on the rear of the French Army and envelope it in a titanic Cannae. The village of Bleid only mattered insofar as driving out the French would aid in the effort to continue masking the massive movement of the German armies to the north. The events of that day in that place were little more than a skirmish, little different than 100 similar encounters that had already occurred, or thousands more which would take place over the course of the next four years. But because it was Erwin Rommel's first action, the scrap in and around Bleid deserves a careful look, because of what it would reveal about Rommel as a combat soldier.

The dawn of August 22 was foggy, and the mist made the French soldiers who had taken up positions in and around Bleid nervous. They could hear the unmistakable sound of infantry moving along their front, but exactly how far distant and in what direction was impossible to tell. A few ragged, ineffective volleys of rifle fire reached out in the direction of the Germans as Leutnant Rommel lead his platoon forward. The whole of II Battalion was advancing, its four companies deployed in line abreast. Two days earlier, Rommel had led his men in clearing the village of Conses, "with fixed bayonets, fingers on triggers, and all eyes studying doorways and windows for telltale evidence of an ambush," but all they encountered was an old woman who assured them that the French soldiers had already left. This time, there was no mistaking where the French were.[7]

Bleid was the centermost of three villages, with Gevimont to the north and Senieux to the south. The French pickets had been methodically withdrawing in good order as the Germans approached the outskirts of the village, and Rommel halted his platoon in the cover of a hedgerow that surrounded a cluster of farm buildings, sending out small detachments to his left and right to make certain that in the fog the platoon had not become separated from the rest of the company.

Taking a sergeant and two privates with him, Rommel, who had wisely exchanged his pistol for a rifle before going into action, moved forward to scout out the farm itself, which proved to be deserted. Peering around the corner of a building which opened on the main road running past the farm, he saw 15 or more French soldiers, chattering over their breakfast, oblivious to the fact that German soldiers were less than 50 feet distant from them. Counting on the element of surprise, Rommel decided that he and his three men would be sufficient to handle this situation, and at a nod from the young *leutnant*, the four of them opened fire on the startled Frenchmen.

Some of the enemy soldiers went down, never to rise, before they could get off a shot in return; others scuttled behind cover and began shooting back. Estimating that there were around 10 French soldiers left alive, Rommel and his trio of myrmidons charged them, only to be greeted by a fusillade of rifle fire coming from windows and doors in buildings on either side of the road. The four Germans beat a hasty retreat whence they came, and once back with the rest of his platoon in the shelter of the hedgerow, the youthful lieutenant did a quick assessment of the situation. What happened next was a decisive moment in the life and career of Erwin Rommel.

> Should I wait until other forces came up or storm the entrance of Bleid with my platoon? The latter course of action seemed proper. . . . The strongest enemy force was in the building on the far side of the road. Therefore we had to take this building first. My attack plan was to open fire on the enemy on the ground floor and garret of the building with the 2nd Section and go around the building to the right with the 1st Section and take it by assault.[8]

Rommel's platoon then began to clear the village house by house. The rest of II Battalion rushed up in support, and the French were driven out of Bleid in an hour. Casualties were heavy, though: nearly a quarter of the battalion's officers and one in every seven men were killed, wounded, or missing. At the end of the fight, Rommel passed out, a reaction brought on by the stress of his first combat, exhaustion from the long journey to the front, and an unspecified stomach ailment. (This latter problem would plague him for the next several months, and Rommel would continue to have intermittent problems with his health throughout his career.)

The action at Bleid, while all but inconsequential to the overall course of the war, looms large in the life of Erwin Rommel, beyond it being his introduction to combat. Courage, decisiveness, an understanding of the power of tactical surprise as a force multiplier—a skill that would receive the necessary honing in the years to come—and boldness. (Some might say "impulsiveness," yet what is boldness but impulse leavened by calculation?) Also prominent was Rommel's acute awareness that war, while it might be a grand adventure, was not one without cost or suffering. "Bleid presented a terrible sight," he would later write. "Among the smoking ruins lay dead soldiers, civilians, and animals. The troops were told that the opponents of the German Fifth Army had been defeated all along the line and were in retreat; yet in achieving our first victory, our success was considerably tempered by grief over the loss of our comrades." Rommel would prove in two world wars that he possessed a rare talent for warfare, but he would never grow fond of it.[9]

Over the course of the next month, Rommel fought in a half-dozen similar small actions as the Fifth Army began advancing, pressing hard on the French, who were reeling back under the immense weight of the right wing of the German Army which had swept across Belgium. Only a combination of tenacious defensive stands by the B.E.F.—coupled with timely, though not always orderly, withdrawals—prevented the whole of the French Army from being enveloped and then destroyed in detail. Even when the German advance toward Paris was stopped at the Marne River, the minor attacks continued, as the rest of the German Army continued to bear down on the French: the Schlieffen Plan had failed but victory still seemed possible, as the Germans believed that there was yet a chance that the morale of the French armies would break.

In yet another such attack, this one on September 24, near Varennes-en-Argonne, a small town about halfway between Rheims and Metz, Rommel had his second major personal encounter with the enemy, though this time it would not be as fortuitous as that at Bleid. Leading his platoon in an assault against French infantry holding a line along the old Roman road leading southwest of Varennes, he was suddenly confronted by five French soldiers. Snapping off two quick shots from his rifle, Rommel dropped a pair of them, but when he squeezed the trigger a third time, he was rewarded with only a dry "click": the magazine was empty. Again, not waiting to give his enemies time to gather their wits, he rushed forward, bayonet in hand (wiry and strong for his size, Rommel prided himself on the skills in hand-to-hand fighting he'd acquired in peacetime), only to be knocked off his feet when a rifle bullet hit his left thigh, blowing out a fist-sized chunk of flesh. Seeing their officer go down, the men of Rommel's platoon pressed home their attack, and soon he was safely behind German lines and on his way to a field hospital. Transferred to a corps hospital two days later, he underwent surgery to repair some of the damage to his leg—none of which was, fortunately for him, permanent—which was followed by three months of recovery and limited duty. The wound also earned Rommel his first combat decoration, the Iron Cross, Second Class. Years later, when he was writing of the tactical lessons to be learned from this encounter, he would comment wryly that "In a man-to-man fight, the winner is he who has one more round in his magazine."[10]

It would be the middle of January 1915 before Rommel was sufficiently fit to return to his old unit, II Battalion of the 124th Infantry Regiment. Upon arrival, he was given command of the 9th Company, at once recognition of his experience and leadership, and an unspoken acknowledgment of the casualties already suffered within the ranks of the German Army's junior officers. It was also the occasion of his introduction to trench warfare, for by this time both the Allies and Germans had begun digging in along the positions which they would hold—more or less—for almost four more years. Already certain patterns of operation were taking shape: the German General Staff chose to concentrate the bulk of Germany's manpower and resources in the east, against the Russians, where the sheer scale of the front made impossible the sort of unit density which stifled any kind of maneuver or strategic movement on the Western Front. Offensive action in the West would be limited to raids on enemy positions and small-scale attacks designed to disrupt Allied plans and preparations for offensives of their own.

Rommel found himself leading his company in one such attack on January 29, on a stretch of front in the Argonne Forest just east of Verdun. Using the sparse undergrowth to conceal his men as best he could, Rommel deployed them in open order and the company began crawling toward a French line of entrenchments sited on the opposite side of a small, shallow valley, hoping to reach a small hollow which would offer a "dead zone" immune from enemy small-arms fire. Before his men were halfway there, the French opened up with rifles and machine guns, and though they could hide in the near-barren bushes, Rommel's men had no cover. Seeing no alternative but to rush the French, he ordered his bugler to sound the charge: 9th Company leaped up, cheering, and dashed forward toward the French, who promptly decamped from their position. In short order 9th Company had advanced close to a thousand yards from their own entrenchments, and a reserve company moved up to help consolidate the position. Rommel now led his company westward, to the edge of the forest, where he and his men encountered a barbwire entanglement denser and more extensive than any of them had ever before seen.

Ahead, beyond the wire, lay a small hill which if occupied would offer a commanding position of the open ground to the south. There was heavy enemy small-arms fire to the left and right, but 9th Company was presently sheltered from it in yet another hollow. The only way forward was through the wire barricade and into open, exposed ground. Rommel didn't hesitate:

> I ordered the company to follow me in single file, but the commander of my leading platoon lost his nerve and did nothing, and the rest of the company imitated him and lay down behind the wire. Shouting and waving at them proved useless. I found another passage through the obstacle and crept back to the company where I informed my first platoon leader that he could either obey my orders or be shot on the spot. He elected the former, and in spite of intense small-arms fire from the left we all crept through the obstacle and reached the hostile position.[11]

A message was sent to battalion headquarters—"9th Company has occupied some strong French earthworks located one mile south of our line of departure. We hold a section running through the forest. Request immediate support and a resupply in machine-gun ammunition and hand grenades."—but the new position proved untenable: the earthworks ran parallel to any line of attack from the east, and the ground was so frozen that Rommel and his men were unable to dig defensive positions of their own. When a strong French counterattack materialized from that direction, Rommel began looking for a more defensible position. Two hundred yards to his right a quartet of French blockhouses sat unoccupied, and he immediately ordered his men to move to them. For almost two hours Rommel and his fifty-odd men held out against increasingly fierce French attacks, but ammunition began to run low and the perimeter around the blockhouses was shrinking, with the possibility that 9th Company would be cut off increasing with every passing minute. Finally word from headquarters arrived: "Battalion is in position half a mile to the north and is digging in. Rommel's company to withdraw, support not possible." What would happen next was up to Rommel.

Now for a decision! Should we break off the engagement and run back through the narrow passage in the wire entanglement under a heavy cross fire? Such a maneuver would, at a minimum, cost fifty percent in casualties. The alternative was to fire the rest of our ammunition and then surrender. The last resort was out. I had one other line of action: namely, to attack the enemy, disorganize him, and then withdraw. Therein lay our only possible salvation.[12]

Amazingly, the brash tactic worked, and the startled French attackers were thrown back in confusion long enough to allow Rommel to extricate his men through the barbwire entanglement and back to the German lines, losing only five men along the way. For this action, he was awarded the Iron Cross First Class, and was the first *leutnant* in the 124th Regiment to be so honored. II Battalion's 9th Company was now known as "Rommel's Company," a singular, if informal, honor, as it was rare in the Imperial German Army for a unit to be identified, even casually, by its commander's name. For his part, Rommel found company command exhilarating:

> For a 23-year-old officer there was no finer job than that of company commander. Winning the men's confidence requires much of a commander. He must exercise care and caution, look after his men, live under the same hardships, and—above all—apply self-discipline. But once he has their confidence, his men will follow him through hell and high water.[13]

Rommel spent the next six months in the Argonne, most of the time occupied with the same sort of low-level bickering with the French. In mid-May command of the 9th Company was taken away from him and given to a lieutenant with more seniority who had yet to lead a company in battle, the same sort of supersession still familiar to modern combat commanders when a chair-warmer is in need of having his "ticket punched." Rommel, having no desire to leave his men, remained as the company's second-in-command. A second German attack on the position Rommel had captured and briefly held in January went in on June 29, and in that action Rommel suffered his second wound when he was struck on the shin by a piece of shrapnel; this time around the injury was sufficiently minor that hospitalization wasn't necessary. For the time being he remained with 9th Company, though he would be given temporary command of 2nd then later 4th Company when their commanding officers were ill or absent on leave.

In any event, his remaining time with the 124th Infantry was short, as promotion to *oberleutnant* at the beginning of September was followed a month later by a posting to the newly formed Württembergische Gebirgs-bataillon (Württemberg Mountain Battalion). The French *Chasseurs Alpins*, highly trained light infantry skilled in mountain fighting, had offered up some serious headaches for the German Army in the opening battles in the Vosges Mountains of Alsace and Lorraine in August and September 1914. The German response was the formation of dedicated mountain units of their own, something the German Army had never previously possessed. The first move in that direction was made by the Bavarian Army, which created Schneeschuhbataillon I & II (the 1st and 2nd Snowshoe Battalions) on November 21, 1914, with a third formed in April 1915, followed by a fourth in May. That same month all four were brought together into a single regiment, while two more such regiments were created out of independent Prussian and Bavarian *Jäger* battalions. Originally organized during the Napoleonic Wars to serve as scouts and provide screens of skirmishers for the regular infantry regiments, by the time the Great War began, they had lost most of their distinctive tactical functions, though their uniforms and higher standards of discipline continued to distinguish them from ordinary infantry battalions. Now, the *Jäger* were to once again become specialized units and soldiers.

The Württembergische Gebirgsbataillon was the Army of Württemberg's contribution to the *projekt*. Soldiers from almost every one of the kingdom's regiments were transferred to the new unit, those who before the war were avid skiers or had experience climbing mountains being the first selected. In addition to such skills, officers considered for posting to the Mountain Battalion had to be proven leaders in combat. Rommel was, of course, a natural for selection, and given command of 2nd Company. He initially regarded his new commanding officer, tough, ambitious Major Theodor Sprösser, as something of a martinet, an opinion that would gradually change once the major led the battalion in combat. Training was rigorous but not harsh, and when, at the beginning of December 1915, the battalion moved to western Austria for ski training, it became something of a holiday for men like Rommel who had been skiers since childhood or adolescence.

The Mountain Battalion spent almost a month billeted at the St. Christoph's Hospice near the Aarlberg Pass, but just before New Year's Day, officers and men boarded troop trains which took them, not south to the Tyrol and the Italian front as they had hoped, but west to the Vosges Mountains. There they took up a position on the South Hilsen Ridge, 25 miles north of the Swiss border. In stark contrast to the Argonne or Flanders, where units were packed together like sardines in a tin, the front was sparsely held: the Mountain Battalion was assigned to hold a 5-mile-long line of strongpoints, a frontage that along the Somme, for example, would have been covered by at least two divisions. The terrain so grossly favored the defense while complicating supply problems that not even the French, still hopelessly enamored with the offensive, were foolish enough to attempt a major attack in this sector. Various strongpoints and local terrain features were assigned picturesque names—the Little Southern, the Whip, the Picklehead, the Little Meadow, and so on, and much of the time there was spent in training, particularly for newly commissioned officers. There were periodic raids on French positions, but hardly on the scale or with the frequency that occurred in the trenches.

Such masterful inactivity couldn't last forever, and at the end of October, the Mountain Battalion was withdrawn and sent east, to do battle with the Romanian Army. On August 27, 1916, in what can only be described as an act of monumental stupidity, Romania had declared war on Austria-Hungary, and within five days the other Central Powers responded in kind. Romania was essentially surrounded by her enemies—Germany to the north, Austria-Hungary to the west and southwest, Bulgaria to the south; Russia, to the east, would do its best to provide whatever assistance it could, but Russia's successful Brusilov Offensive, which had been the impetus behind Romania's rash decision, was beginning to lose momentum and the Russian Army had problems of its own. With its army outnumbered, ill-equipped, and poorly trained, Romania's strategic position was hopeless.

Within hours of the declaration of war against the Austrians, a half-million Romanian soldiers rushed through the frontier passes and threatened the region the Germans called "Siebenbiirgen"—"Seven Fortresses"—after seven castles built there centuries earlier by the Saxons, but that the rest of the world knew as Transylvania. Despite some initial successes, within a matter of two weeks, the Romanian forces were stopped in their tracks. The rugged Transylvanian Alps and Carpathian Mountains were precisely the sort of country in which the Württemburgische Gebirgsbataillon—along with the newly formed Alpenkorps, a German division specially organized from *Jäger* battalions taken from the Prussian and Bavarian armies—had been created to fight. On September 18 the Germans and Austrians began their counterattack, and over the next 10 days, the Romanians were tumbled pell-mell out of whatever gains they had made and back into Romania itself. By the middle of October, however, they were able to stop the Germans at the passes of Vulcan and Szurduk.

The Alpenkorps, to which the Mountain Battalion was now attached, was initially deployed to force these passes. Though the Romanian mountains were far removed in every sense from the mire and carnage of the Western Front, the march forward from the railhead near Petroceni left no doubt that mountain fighting possessed its own catalogue of hardship and peril.

> We climbed over a narrow footpath and our packs with their four days' uncooked rations weighed heavily on our shoulders. We had neither pack animals nor winter mountain equipment, and all officers carried their own packs. We climbed the steep slopes for hours.
>
> It began to rain as we started to climb without benefit of a guide. The rain grew heavier as night began to fall and it was soon pitch black. The cold rain turned into a cloudburst and soaked us to the skin. Further progress on the steep and rocky slope was impossible, and we bivouacked on either side of the mule path at an altitude of about 4,950 feet. In our soaked condition it was impossible to lie down and as it was still raining, all attempts to kindle a fire of dwarf pine failed. We crouched close together, wrapped in blankets and shelter halves and shivered from the cold. . . . After midnight the rain ceased, but in its stead an icy wind made it impossible for us to relax in our wet clothes.
>
> When we reached the summit, our clothes and packs were frozen to our backs. It was below freezing and an icy wind was

sweeping the snow-covered summit. Our positions were not to be found. Shortly after our arrival a blizzard enveloped the elevated region and reduced visibility to a few yards. . . . [T]he surgeon also warned that a continued stay in the snowstorm in wet clothes, without shelter, without fire, and without warm food, would result in many sick and much frostbite within the next few hours. We were threatened with court-martial proceedings if we yielded one foot of ground.

Numerous cases of high fever and vomiting were reported, but renewed representations to sector were without effect. . . . When day broke the doctor had to evacuate forty men to the hospital. Captain Gossler had decided to move off with the remainder of the companies, come what may; ninety percent were under medical treatment because of frostbite and cold.[14]

Bickering among army and corps headquarters prevented the attack on the passes from going forward; instead the Mountain Battalion was moved northward, where it staged a near-textbook attack on the Romanian positions atop the Lesului massif on November 11. A set-piece frontal assault, the attack on Lesului should have been a bloodbath, but here the Germans demonstrated what the hard-won tactical lessons taught them in the trench-raiding and local attacks of the Western Front could accomplish in open warfare. Skillful use of terrain for concealment along with coordinated fire-and-movement by infantry sections, coupled with effective, concentrated covering fire to keep the Romanians' heads down, resulted in the capture of Mount Lesului with astonishingly light casualties; in Rommel's company, which had been part of the decisive flanking movement forcing the Romanians off the mountaintop, the only casualty was a single wounded *soldat*.

Rommel was allowed to show his own mastery of these lessons the next evening, on the approach to the village of Kurpenul, on the far side of Mount Lesului. In a dense fog, 2nd Company began descending toward the village, Rommel having posted scouting detachments on both flanks as well as sending an advance guard forward. Romanian troops could be seen in the village, and somewhere in the fog an artillery battery was shelling the German positions down in the Vulcan Pass. Having only the vaguest idea of the Romanian positions and not wanting to risk having his company cut off from the rest of the battalion, Rommel halted in place, set up a screen of sentries, and waited for the rest of the battalion to catch up with 2nd Company. By that time the last Romanian soldiers had left the village and the Mountain Battalion moved in.

First light brought more fog, and with it a Romanian counterattack. Visibility was down to a few score yards, and the enemy's advance was somewhat tentative, as both sides were equally vague as to the other's deployment. Rommel, for whom the tendency to move to wherever the action was the hottest was becoming instinctual, moved forward.

I went with the advance guard, consisting of one squad, and the remainder of the company followed 160 yards to the rear. The fog swirled hither and yon and the visibility varied between a hundred and three hundred feet. Shortly before the head of the column reached the south end of the village, it ran into a closed column of advancing Romanians. In a few seconds we were engaged in a violent fight at fifty yards range. Our opening volley was delivered from a standing position and then we hit the dirt and looked for cover from the heavy enemy fire. The Romanians outnumbered us at least ten to one. Rapid fire pinned them down, but a new enemy loomed on both flanks. He was creeping up behind bushes and hedges and firing as he approached. The advance guard was getting into a dangerous situation. It was holding a farmhouse to the right of the road, while the remainder of the company appeared to have taken cover in the farms some five hundred feet to the rear. The fog prevented it from supporting the advance guard. Should the company move forward, or should the advance guard retire? Since it was a question of asserting ourselves against a powerful superiority, the latter appeared to be the best thing to do, especially in view of the extremely limited visibility.

I ordered the advance guard to hold the farmhouse for an additional five minutes, and then to retire on the right side of the road through the farms and reach the company, which would furnish fire support from its position a hundred yards to the rear. I ran back down the road to the company; dense fog soon concealed me from aimed fire by the Romanians. I quickly ordered a platoon of the company and a heavy machine gun to open fire on the area to the left and the advance guard began to drop back under this fire protection.[15]

The Romanians, now firmly in contact with the Württembergers, pressed their attack hard; Rommel estimated that his company was out-numbered ten-to-one, and there is little reason to doubt the accuracy of his assessment. At one point, 2nd Company's 1st Platoon had driven back the Romanians facing them, and impulsively edged forward, leaving its place in the line. Now that platoon was in danger of being cut off, and Rommel was faced with a commanding officer's most feared dilemma.

> I was none too elated with this course of events. Why did the platoon fail to stay in its place as ordered? Should I commit my last reserves, as requested by the platoon leader? Under these conditions all of us might have been surrounded and crushed by superior numbers. Would such a loss have crippled the left flank of the Württemberg Mountain Battalion? No, as little as I liked it, I could not help the 1st Platoon.
>
> I ordered the 1st Platoon to disengage immediately and fall back along the village road. The remainder of the company was disposed to cover the retirement of the platoon.[16]

Rommel cooly adjusted his positions and continued to hold off the Romanians until Major Sprösser could bring up reinforcements, after which the Romanians gave up on their attack and withdrew, although exchanges of rifle fire continued throughout the morning. Another Romanian attack materialized in mid-morning, but by this time the fog had burned off, and the Romanian advance was halted in its tracks well short of the German lines. With the Vulcan and Skurduk passes now in the hands of the Germans and Austrians, the overall strategic situation in Romania stabilized somewhat, for the moment at least, as both the Central Powers and the Romanians paused to catch their breath. This was the perfect opportunity for Erwin Rommel to slip away on leave for a brief visit to his home in Ulm, but first he had a much more important appointment to keep in Danzig.

On November 27, 1916, Oberleutnant Erwin Eugen Johannes Rommel married Lucia Maria "Lucie" Mollin. The young officer Lucie once thought overly serious had become the love of her life, and she the love of his. Exactly when their engagement became formalized remains something of a mystery, as does the reason why they chose this particular time to make their union a reality, but certainly all of the old restrictions and prohibitions concerning junior officers marrying that had been in place before the war began were now so much rubbish. Whatever arrangements had been made regarding Walburga Stemmer and her daughter were evidently acceptable to Lucie: there isn't the slightest hint of jealousy or insecurity in any of her letters to Erwin, before or after their wedding. Rommel had begun writing her on an almost daily basis back in 1912, and continued to do so throughout the war—indeed, for the remainder of his life, whenever they were separated, he would try dash off at least a few lines to her every day, even when in the middle of a desperate battle.

The newlyweds had a bare two weeks together before Rommel had to return to the Mountain Battalion, though it wouldn't be until mid-January 1917 before he again saw any significant action. Bucharest fell to the Germans on December 6, two-thirds of Romania was now in the hands of the Central Powers, and the remnants of the Romanian Army retreated into northeastern and eastern Romania, behind a line of rugged ridges on the west bank of the Siret River, a defensive position of tremendous natural strength. Holding on like a thorn in the Central Powers' flesh, just to the west of the ridgeline, was a strong Romanian force dug in around and atop Mount Cosna, southeast of the town of Targu Ocna. The ridge behind Mount Cosna was the key to the entire Siret River Line; before the Germans and Austrians could mount any sort of attack on the enemy's main position, they first had to drive the Romanians off Cosna. To take Cosna, they first had to capture the village of Gagesti (modern-day Paragesti), which sat just below Cosna's southern slope.

Rommel, though still only an *oberleutnant*, was given command of an *abteilung* ("detachment") of two rifle companies and a heavy machine-gun platoon, the sort of ad hoc formation which was the precursor to the *kampfgruppe* (battle group) concept which the German Army would employ with such success a quarter century later, and on January 7, 1917, ordered to take and hold Gagesti.[17] A foot of snow lay on the ground, there was a swirling fog that played hob with visibility, and temperatures were below freezing—all in all, precisely the sort of conditions to encourage an enemy's complaisance. (The effects of the cold cut both ways, however: at a critical moment in the coming action, Rommel's machine-gun platoon would be using alcohol to clear away ice that had jammed its weapons' firing mechanisms.) Moving out after sunset, Rommel's plan was to seize a few outlying buildings around Gagesti which would serve as jumping-off points for a morning attack on the village proper; but as his men moved through the snow and mist, encountering isolated groups of Romanian soldiers who apparently had little stomach to this fight and readily surrendered, Rommel saw an opportunity to take the village by coup de main. After giving his troops a few hours' rest, he ordered them to charge the village, making as much noise as possible (Rommel recalled that his two companies were "as loud as a battalion") to create the impression of greater numbers. The Romanian defenders, surprised and demoralized, meekly surrendered—a total of 360 prisoners of war were taken.[18]

What happened next was pure Rommel: from somewhere he had acquired a horse he named "Sultan," and in the gray morning light Rommel and Sultan rode out to reconnoiter the Romanian positions beyond Gagesti, accompanied only by Mess Sergeant Paffle. A half-mile outside the village, the two Germans accidentally rode straight into a Romanian patrol, about 15 men strong. The range was too short for there to be any chance of Rommel or his sergeant dashing off unseen; Rommel being Rommel, he rode forward and in a calm, reasonable, but firm voice, explained to the Romanians that, since Gagesti was lost, they were, in fact, prisoners of war, and should lay down their arms and head into the village to join the other POWs. The already demoralized Romanians, though probably not actually understanding one word in three Rommel said, comprehended his meaning and readily complied. The incident taught Rommel a lesson about the value of a bluff well played against a discouraged opponent that he would never forget.

What happened after that was a slice of military life the sort of which every soldier and ex-soldier from the Sumerians onward has known all too well. Major Sprösser brought forward the rest of the battalion, formally relieving Rommel's battle group at midnight. Rommel marched his men back to the Mountain Battalion's regular billets, 7 miles to the west of Gagesti, where they cleaned their weapons and gear, then settled in for some well-deserved rest. No sooner had they done so than an urgent message from the front arrived: "Enemy has broken through in mountains north of Vidra. Rommel detachment to move to Hill 625 north of Vidra, where it is to join 256th Reserve Infantry." Rommel and his men wearily trudged back to the front, only to learn upon arrival that the situation was well in hand and their presence was not required. Finding mail from home awaiting them when they returned to their barracks (after yet another 7-mile march) compensated somewhat for the fiasco.[19]

The incident outside Gagesti revealed a new facet of Rommel's maturing persona as a combat leader—the force of his personality. He was becoming a leader, not just by virtue of his rank, but by nature as well; it was as if warfare was the crucible and combat provided the heat which unexpectedly created the alloy of Rommel's emerging character. His first biographer, Desmond Young, tellingly makes the point that "[Rommel] was a young man of 25, looking even younger than his age, and in rank only an *oberleutnant* from a not-particularly distinguished line regiment [the 124th Württemberg]." Theodor Werner, who first met Rommel in 1915, recalled him as being "slightly built, almost schoolboyish, inspired by a holy zeal, always eager and anxious to act. . . . Anybody who came under the spell of his personality turned into a real soldier. However tough the strain he seemed inexhaustible. He seemed to know just what the enemy were like and how they would probably react. His plans were often startling, instinctive, spontaneous and not infrequently obscure." Now, a year and more later, that energy, drive, and imagination combined to imbue Rommel with a confidence and self-assurance that was rapidly approaching arrogance, only made tolerable by the accomplishments behind it.[20]

In early February, the Württemburgische Gebirgsbataillon was withdrawn from Romania and sent back to the Western Front, taking up its old position near Hilsen in the Vosges Mountains. As before, the difficult terrain coupled with the lack of any significant strategic objective behind either army's lines ensured that the same degree of "live-and-let-live" activity prevailed during the five months the Mountain Battalion spent deployed there. It was time well spent on training replacements and developing new tactics: on August 1, 1917, the Mountain Battalion departed the Vosges and was once again deployed to Romania. There, beginning on August 9, Erwin Rommel would lead his *abteilung* into action in what would be one of the most hard-fought battles of his life, storming Mount Cosna.

The Germans and Austrians had failed to take and hold the whole of Mount Cosna the previous December, and the Romanian Army, once all but left for dead, experienced something akin to a resurrection in the spring and early summer of 1917. The Russian Army had taken control of the defensive line along the Siret River, behind which the Romanians reequipped, reorganized, and retrained, helped by 150,000 rifles, 2,000 machine guns, 1,300,000 grenades and 355 artillery pieces provided by France and Great Britain. By mid-summer the Romanians had once more manned the Siret River Line, assuring their Russian allies that they could now hold it. It was absolutely vital to the Russians that the Romanians stay in the fight. From the Allies' perspective, the Romanian government's decision to go to war had been a colossal blunder: a neutral Romania had protected the southern flank of the Russian Army in its struggles with the Germans and Austrians—now, a Romanian defeat along the Siret would lay that flank bare to the Central Powers, and the consequences for Russia would be disastrous. For the Germans and Austrians, capturing Mount Cosna would be the key that unlocked the entire Siret River Line: taking it would split the Romanian front in two, and that line was the Allies' last truly defensible position, for behind it was only open rolling plains, the beginnings of the Ukrainian steppe.

The Alpenkorps was given the mission of taking Mount Cosna; the Württemburgische Gebirgsbataillon would lead the assault. Although Rommel was still only an *oberleutnant*, he was one of the battalion's most experienced combat officers, and Major Sprösser tasked him with planning and leading the initial attack, giving him command of three rifle companies as well as two machine-gun companies. Sprösser knew his man, for Rommel had developed an uncanny sense of terrain, what was once called *coup d'oeil* in the Great Captains of the eighteenth and nineteenth centuries. Marlborough had it, so did Bonaparte in his early campaigns; General Helmut von Moltke (the Elder) proved at Sadowa and Sedan that he possessed an eye for good ground as well; Wellington was probably history's absolute master of the art of the tactical use of terrain. Now it was Rommel's turn, though he would be operating on a much smaller scale.

The Mount Cosna massif would provide plenty of opportunity for Rommel to display his skill, with steep, heavily wooded slopes and undulating ground. The massif runs almost due north to south in two long, parallel ridges, the western ridge longer and and slightly lower than its eastern counterpart. At the center of the west ridge is a secondary summit connected by a saddle, or cwm, to the peak of Mount Cosna proper. The Romanians set up their defenses at the end of both ridges and on the adjacent heights of Mount Piciorul. Attacking uphill is always an exceedingly dangerous operation, as normally the defenders can observe everything the assaulting force is doing, all the while remaining more or less safely under cover. Rommel exploited the folds and furrows along the slopes of the ridges to minimize this advantage, and when his attack went in, Rommel's troops, despite being outnumbered and outgunned (something that would become characteristic of his forces in a later war), acting on his instructions, made as much noise as possible, so that

> . . . the enemy . . . was deceived as to our main attack by a lively fire, shouting and hand grenades, and was induced to dispose his reserves incorrectly. The thrust by the 3rd Company against the flank and rear then led to a quick success. In the same way five . . . positions were taken one after another, though the final garrison was two companies strong. The attacks followed each other so quickly that the enemy had no time for regrouping.[21]

Rommel continued to push his men forward until they had turned the enemy's flank on the south end of the western ridgeline, almost a mile behind the Romanians' main position. When one of the machine-gun companies moved up, Rommel's troops took up positions for an all-around defense—Rommel likened it to a hedgehog—drove off a counterattack and held their ground, which forced the Romanians to abandon the whole of the ridge during the night.

Not wanting to give the enemy any respite, the Alpenkorps' attack continued the next day, August 10, this action bidding fair to be even more difficult than that of the previous day. The Romanian defenses were heavier, and there would be no artillery support for Rommel's *abteilung*—the only fire support he would have would be that of the two machine-gun companies. Rising to the challenge, Rommel made textbook use of them, using one company to put concentrated, constant fire on the point of the attack, forcing the Romanian troops to keep their heads down until the German infantry was almost on top of them; the other machine-gun company kept up an interdicting fire that prevented enemy reinforcements from moving up. Careful reconnaissance before the attack allowed Rommel to find the most advantageous rout to the Romanians' main line of resistance, minimizing the exposure of his troops when moving across open ground.

As was his wont, Rommel was leading from the front, and for the third time in this war, paid a price for his boldness:

> I was close behind them and was just crossing a small depression when I was forced to hit the dirt by a burst of machine-gun fire coming from the right. The bullets dug small holes in the turf and their source seemed to be a slope some nine hundred yards southeast of Hill 674, nearly thirteen hundred yards away. I had only pitiful cover behind a small mound and I intended to dash on when the machine-gun fire lifted. Suddenly, I received a bullet from behind in the left forearm and the blood spurted. Looking around, I discovered a detachment of Romanians firing on me and a few men of the 1st Company from some bushes about ninety yards behind us. In order to get out of this dangerous field of fire I made a zigzag dash to the knoll in front of us where some elements of the 1st Company had to defend themselves for about ten minutes until the Romanians to the west had been taken care of in hand-to-hand fighting by the men following us. The French officer commanding the Romanian unit kept shouting "Kill the German dogs" until he took a bullet at close range.

Rommel was lucky: the bullet passed cleanly through his arm, missing both bones completely, though the wound bled profusely; he made do for the time being with a rough-and-ready bandage from the battalion surgeon then went forward again to resume commanding the attack.

The Romanians fought bravely and they fought hard, and immediately launched a counterattack to drive the Germans off the ridge. Their lack of proper training, despite the best efforts of their French advisors, coupled with their lack of combat experience, led to clumsy, uncoordinated attacks. They might have done well against the armies of 1914, but courage and tenacity were no match for men who already seen three years of war. The Romanians fell back yet again, this time to the slopes of Mount Cosna itself.

During the night of August 10–11, the Mountain Battalion was moved to the far left of the German position, on the west side of Mount Piciorul. Two *abteilungen* were formed, one under Rommel, the other under Hauptmann Gossler. Rommel performed a personal reconnaissance of the objective, Hill 674, the secondary summit of Mount Cosna, and, still enjoying the confidence of Major Sprösser, drew up a plan of attack that called for his detachment to move first, sweeping around to the north and attacking the Romanians' right flank, drawing their attention—and reserves—to Hill 674. Once Captain Gossler judged that the enemy was fully engaged, his detachment would attack the summit of Mount Cosna from the south.

Rommel deployed some of his infantry and most of his machine guns to directly face the enemy lines, where they would lay down a hot and heavy fire on the Romanians, and hopefully hold them in their trenches. Meanwhile, he led three rifle companies and part of one machine-gun company to the left, ready to take the Romanians in the flank. By noon, everyone was in position and the German troops directly facing the Romanians opened up a furious fusillade, which was the signal for Rommel to begin his attack. The Germans' lead elements broke through the enemy defenses, but a surprisingly swift response by the Romanians had them quickly pinned down by heavy small-arms fire. Stymied, Rommel was unable to find a way out—at one point he even considered withdrawing—until one of the company commanders, taking his cue from Rommel's own methods, initiated an attack that began to roll up the Romanian lines, and by mid-afternoon the entire enemy position on Hill 674 was in German hands. Rommel's *abteilung* began advancing on Mount Cosna's northwest slopes while Captain Gossler's *abteilung*, having infiltrated around the enemy's left flank on the southwest slope, pressed its own attack hard. The Romanians dithered, unable to decide which attack to stop first, and were driven off Cosna for their pains.

The uncharacteristic hesitation Rommel displayed at the top of Hill 674 may well have been a consequence of the extreme pain and loss of blood caused by the wound he had taken in his left forearm the previous day. On the night of August 12 he requested permission to report to the battalion's field hospital to have the wound properly dressed—he could have, with justification, requested evacuation further to the rear; predictably, he was back with his *abteilung* within 12 hours.

Over the next three days the Romanians launched a series of strong, determined counterattacks, trying to retake the mountain; they fought fiercely and gave the German mountain troops all that they could handle, more than one company coming near to exhausting its ammunition supply in trying to hold back the Romanians. But again, superior training and bitter experience won out over *élan* and grit; the Romanian attacks were driven off every time. Rommel's stark accounting of his own physical condition on the morning of August 14 is eloquent testimony to ferocity of the fighting:

> I tried to get some sleep, but it was so cold that I gave up the idea; so I took Lieutenant Werner and inspected the night's work in the early dawn light. I had not had a chance to remove my shoes for more than five days and, as a result, my feet were badly swollen; also, I had had no opportunity to renew the bandage on my left arm or to change the bloodstained overcoat hung around my shoulders and my likewise bloodstained trousers. I felt very debilitated, but the weight of responsibility was such that I did not consider going back to the hospital.[22]

The Romanians continued their attacks on the Germans holding Mount Cosna for the next week, Rommel remaining with his detachment the entire time. There is something admirable about his determination to remain with his men, but there is, at the same time, something disturbing about his unwillingness—or inability—to recognize that he was not indispensible. It's a far from uncommon quality among good combat officers at almost any level of command, but there is an inherent danger in it, as exhaustion can impair good judgment and lead to poor command decisions, threatening the lives of the very men toward whom the officer feels such loyalty. Fortunately for Rommel, the whole of the Alpenkorps was withdrawn from Mount Cosna on August 25. It was not a moment too soon:

> In the afternoon, because of a high fever, I began to babble the silliest nonsense, and this convinced me that I was no longer capable

of exercising command. In the evening I turned the command over to Captain Gossler and . . . after dark I walked down the ridge road across Mount Cosna, back to the group command post, a quarter of a mile southwest of Headquarters Knoll.[23]

On September 1 the Alpenkorps was sent to Carinthia, in southern Austria, where it spent six weeks resting and refitting—and preparing to lead an offensive against the Italians. Rommel, meantime, was able to spend part of this time in Danzig with Lucie, recovering from his wound and exhaustion.

Like the Romanians, the Italians had entered the war on the side of the Allies motivated by pure, unadulterated self-interest. After abandoning her Triple Alliance partners, Germany and Austria-Hungary, in August 1914 (with some good reason, admittedly), the Italian government had been offered what was, in its most basic terms, a huge bribe by the Allies in early 1915. In secret clauses of the Treaty of London signed on April 26, Italy was promised the Austrian county of Tyrol and most of the Austrian coast along the Adriatic Sea in exchange for a declaration of war against Austria-Hungary, which was readily forthcoming on May 23, 1915. The Allies' plan was to compel the Austrians to withdraw a sizeable portion of their troop strength from operations against the Russians and the Serbs in order to defend against an Italian offensive into the Tyrol.

The result was nothing like the French and British had planned. Eleven battles were fought more or less along the line of the Isonzo River (known imaginatively as the First through Eleventh Battles of the Isonzo), which for decades had been the traditional border between the Dual Monarchy and the Kingdom of Italy. Scraps of territory changed hands, hundreds of thousands of soldiers were killed, wounded, or went missing, but the line of battle had barely moved after more than two years of fighting. Like some macabre caricature of the Western Front, trenches and dugouts were carved out, but rather than being dug out of the mud, chalk or clay of Flanders and France, these fieldworks were hacked out of ice and snow. (Some bodies are still being found, almost a century later, frozen in mountain glaciers where soldiers on both sides fought and died in below-freezing conditions.) By the autumn of 1917, however, Austria-Hungary's ability to sustain her war effort had begun flagging, while the morale of the Italian Army, suffering from inadequate supplies, inferior weapons, and a regimen of near-brutal discipline, was close to collapse. The German General Staff, which in practical terms meant Generalfeldmarschall Paul von Hindenburg and his Quartermaster General, Erich Ludendorff, concluded that with the assistance of German troops on the Italian Front, the Central Powers could mount one last offensive, one sufficient to knock Italy completely out of the war and relieve the pressure on the Austrians.

To accomplish this, however, von Hindenburg and Ludendorff had no intention of repeating the failed tactical formula of the Western Front—artillery bombardments days or weeks in length, followed by close-serried ranks of soldiers marching in lockstep across no man's land, where they would be met by massive barbwire entanglements and a hailstorm of machine-gun fire, the advance halting every time an enemy strongpoint was encountered and not resuming until each one was overcome. Instead, a new tactical doctrine, known as "infiltration tactics," would be employed. Infiltration tactics were not so far different from those the Württemburgische Gebirgsbataillon had been using for over a year, and which Oberleutnant Erwin Rommel had been refining in action. The fundamental elements of these tactics were a short, sharp, but extraordinarily heavy artillery bombardment along a relatively narrow front, followed immediately by an assault by specialized infantry units, called "storm troopers" by the Allies, but better defined by their German nomenclature: *Stosstruppen*—shock troopers. These soldiers, often operating in semi-independent units as small as individual companies, would probe the enemy defenses, finding and flowing around strongpoints and heavily defended positions, bypassing them—they would be overcome by succeeding waves of conventional infantry after the *Stosstruppen* had cut them off from their support. The storm troopers would continue to move forward, always probing for the weak spot, driving as deep as possible into the enemy's rear areas, disrupting communications, reinforcements, and supplies.

Seven German divisions, 750 guns and mortars, and over 100 aircraft were withdrawn from the Western and Eastern Fronts and sent to reinforce the Austrians; chlorine and phosgene gas would be employed for the first time on the Italian front. Four German and Austrian armies, all told 350,000 strong, were about to square off against three Italian armies that between them mustered just over 400,000 soldiers. The Fourteenth Army, a mixed bag of 18 German and Austrian mountain divisions, was the largest of the four, and would spearhead the attack; the Alpenkorps would be the point of that spear. The offensive began on October 24, 1916; the Italians would call it the *Twelfth* Battle of the Isonzo, the rest of the world would know it as the Battle of Caporetto.

The Mountain Battalion deployed just east of the town of Tolmino, which was, along with the small city of Caporetto, Fourteenth Army's immediate objective. Conceptually, the plan formulated by von Hindenburg and Ludendorff was the assault on Mount Cosna writ very large. The massive, rocky heights along the Isonzo River between Caporetto and Tolmino were the keystone of the entire Italian defensive line; once past those heights, in particular Monte Matajur, Monte Kuk, and the Kolovrat ridge the Fourteenth Army could sweep down onto the broad plain of the Veneto and the Tagliamento valley, and straight on to its ultimate objective: Venice.

At 2:00 A.M. on October 24, a thousand German and Austrian guns, firing as fast as they could be reloaded and re-registered, erupted in a four-hour bombardment of the Italian defenses along the Isonzo. In a pouring rain the infantry moved out just after 6:00 A.M., the Württemburgische Gebirgsbataillon following just behind the initial assault wave, then, once the river crossing was accomplished, passing through them to take on the role of the advance guard for the Alpenkorps. Rommel's *abteilung*, once again composed of three rifle companies and a machine-gun company, took the point. The ground was reminiscent of Mount Costa, steeply sloped, heavily wooded, with visibility rarely more than a few yards in any direction. The detachment first encountered Italian troops when the lead section all but walked into an enemy strongpoint and the Italians opened fire. This was the second of the three Italian defensive lines; Rommel saw immediately that, with its heavy barbwire obstacles and deep trenches, even a half-hearted defense by the Italians would make direct assault akin to suicide. While pondering his next move, Rommel noted a steep-sided gully (he called it a "camouflaged path") running off to his left just below the Italian line. What happened next was pure Rommel.

> The well-camouflaged path along the wood's edge gave me an idea.
> This path probably constituted the means of communication with
> the forward Italian line. . . . The path was winding and the camou-

flage on the south side gave such good concealment toward the up-slope and in the direction of the Italian positions that it would be difficult to identify friend or foe using it. Without enemy interfer-ence we could move over the path and be in the enemy positions inside of thirty seconds. If we moved rapidly then we might cap-ture the hostile garrison without firing a shot. I singled out Lance Corporal Kiefner . . . gave him eight men, and told him to move up the path . . . with a minimum of shooting and hand grenade throwing. . . . [L]ong, anxious minutes passed and we heard noth-ing but the steady rain on the trees. Then steps approached, and a soldier reported in a low voice: "The Kiefner scout squad has cap-tured a hostile dugout and taken seventeen Italians and a machine gun. The garrison suspects nothing."

Thereupon I led the whole Rommel detachment . . . up the path and into the hostile position. . . . Assault teams noiselessly widened the breach until we had fifty yards on either side of the path. Several dozen Italians, who had sought shelter in their dugouts from the streaming rain, were thus captured by the skillful mountain troops. Thanks to the heavy cover the enemy farther up the slope did not perceive the movement of the six companies.[24]

Rommel and his men continued to move forward, by this time well in advance of the timetable set by the original operational plan. There was a very real hazard in this as German and Austrian artillery was still intermit-tently falling around them, the presumption being that there wouldn't yet be any friendly forces in that area, and the shelling would serve to keep the Italians' heads down until the German infantry arrived. Fortunately, Rom-mel's *abteilung* suffered only a single casualty to friendly fire; of the Italians, there was little to be seen, aside from a handful of small patrols and out-posts that were handily overcome. The advance up the slope was tough going, especially for the machine gunners, whose loads averaged around 90 pounds each, but by mid-afternoon Rommel's band of mountain war-riors had moved up another thousand yards and made contact with the 3rd Battalion of the Bavarian Life Guards, who had been moving up on the Mountain Battalion's left flank. By this time the rain had stopped and the overcast was breaking up; Rommel and his men could clearly see ahead of them the Kolovrat ridge, dominated by Hill 1114, which marked the position of the Italians' main line of resistance. The ridge was the next day's objective, and from every indication they could see, the enemy was alert and well prepared. It was not an encouraging sight.

That evening, Rommel was called to the 3rd Life Guards Battalion command post, where he met

> Major Count von Bothmer, the Life Guards commander, who had just arrived on the scene. . . . I reported the disposition of my six mountain companies and he then demanded that my units be attached to his command. I took the liberty of remarking that I took my orders from Major Sprösser, who, as far as I knew, was senior to the commander of the Life Guards, and that I expected Major Sprösser to arrive at my command post at any moment. Count von Bothmer replied by forbidding me to move any part of my detachment to the west or against Hill 1114, saying that this was work for the Life Guards only. Then, as a sop to us, he allowed that the units of the Württemberg Mountain Battalion would be permitted to occupy and secure Hill 1114 after the Life Guards had captured the position on October 25; or we could follow the Guards Regiment in the second line behind their thrust to the west. I told him that I would inform my commander of his actions. Then I was dismissed.[25]

The encounter with Major von Bothner left Rommel "none too happy," as he put it, although it's unclear whether his anger was the consequence of being ordered to "hold the horses" for the Bavarians in the morrow's attack, or von Bothner's arrogance and aristocratic condescension. Given how dismissive—and even contemptuous—Rommel would be of aristocratic officers later in his career, and how much, even now, he thrived on combat, it could have equally been either—or both. In any event, when Major Sprösser arrived early the next morning, Rommel immediately presented him with a plan he had concocted overnight that would both thwart Major von Bothner and put the *Gebirgsbataillon* right in the thick of the fight.

Rommel proposed that the battalion separate itself from the Bavarians by moving a half-mile west, and from there conduct its own assault on the

Kolovrat ridge. Sprösser gave a conditional approval to the plan—Rommel would be given the 2nd and 3rd Rifle Companies and the 1st Machine-Gun Company to undertake his maneuver, with further support promised if he were initially successful. It's fairly clear from reading "between the lines," as it were, of Rommel's account of this incident that while Sprösser had no interest in an open confrontation with Major von Bothner over the Bavarian's presumption, he was less than pleased at having another, junior officer, issuing orders to his battalion, hence his willingness to endorse Rommel's plan, however conditionally. Even with those conditions, the young *oberleutnant* now had what he wanted. It was October 25, 1917: what followed would be, without a doubt, the most amazing single day in the whole of Erwin Rommel's remarkable life.[26]

Rommel and his three companies moved out at first light, traversing the slope to the right so that they could come at the Italians from an unexpected direction. Using the skill he'd acquired in Romania at using dead ground to conceal movement, Rommel brought his detachment to a point less than 200 yards from the top of the ridge. Below and to his left, a firefight broke out between the Bavarians, who were moving up to their own assault line, and the Italian defenders atop Hill 1114. It proved to be a welcome diversion: a five-man patrol led by a junior lieutenant went forward to inspect the Italian wire obstacles and came back with not only the information Rommel required, but with a handful of prisoners as well. The Italians directly above Rommel and his men seemed little concerned by the small-arms fire off to their left and instead were content to remain in their dugouts. Hearing this, Rommel ordered the rest of his three companies to follow the same route the patrol had taken to the Italian trenches. Moving along a saddle that ran into the Korlovrat ridge proper, the entire detachment was inside the enemy defenses within minutes, and cheerfully set about taking prisoners, several hundred of them by Rommel's count.

The 5,400-foot peak of Monte Matajur, to the west, was the objective, and Rommel began pressing in that direction as hard and as fast as he could, exploiting the surprise of his unexpected appearance in the Italian trenches to overrun and disarm as many of the enemy troops as possible, enlarging his foothold on the ridge in anticipation of the promised support from Major Sprösser. Suddenly, the entire detachment came under heavy rifle and machine-gun fire as Italians in a support trench, along with troops farther up the ridgeline, opened up on Rommel and his men—enemy infantry could be seen massing for a counterattack a hundred yards ahead—and Rommel's 2nd Company, sent forward to keep up the pressure on the Italians, was in danger of being overrun. Time was limited—and so were options.

Outnumbered and outgunned—again—Rommel quickly realized that there were no good defensive solutions to his dilemma, so he did what came most naturally to him—he attacked. Once more he used his particular talent for evaluating terrain to good advantage, noting a patch of dead ground on the slope approaching the Italian trenches, where the Italians would be unable to see or fire on his troops. While his two machine guns directed a steady suppressive fire on the Italians in the lateral trench, and trusting 2nd Company to be able to hold off its attackers long enough for him to get 3rd Company into position, Rommel moved his men into that dead ground, and waited for the Italians to make another rush toward 2nd Company.

> I gave the attack signal to the 3rd Rifle and the 1st Machine-Gun Companies. While the first heavy machine gun opened up a steady fire on the enemy from its concealed position on the right, where it was soon joined by the second, the mountain troops on the left stormed the enemy flank and rear with savage resolution. Loud shouts resounded. The surprise blow on the flank and rear hit home. The Italians halted their attack against the 2nd Company and tried to turn and face the 3nd Company. But the 2nd Company came out of its trench and assailed the right. Attacked on two sides and pressed into a narrow space, the enemy laid down his arms. . . . An entire battalion with 12 officers and over 500 men surrendered in the saddle three hundred yards northeast of Hill 1192. This increased our prisoner bag on the Kolovrat position to 1,500.[27]

By 9:15 A.M., just over three hours after leaving the Mountain Battalion's lines, his detachment was in possession of a half-mile segment of the Kolovrat ridge. From there, however, Rommel could see Italian troops forming up to his left and right, preparing to attack his three companies.

What Rommel did next went beyond bold into the brash, and possibly slightly crazy. But again his eye for terrain showed him something unusual:

the support road that ran behind the Italian defenses on the ridgeline was mostly dead ground. The engineers who had blasted and excavated the road saw no reason, since it was on the side of the ridge opposite the enemy, to ensure that there were clear fields of fire onto it from the defenses above. Now Rommel saw the road as an opportunity, and was faced with a decision: should he go up or down? Up meant clearing out the Italian defenders all the way to Hill 1114, a not-at-all-impossible proposition, for those defenders were currently quite thoroughly distracted, being heavily engaged against the 18th Bavarian Life Guards. Apparently the Italians were giving the Bavarians all they could handle, as the Guards had so far made no progress whatsoever toward the summit of Hill 1114. Down meant into valley on the far side of the ridge, into the village of Luico, where a large number of Italian soldiers could be seen milling about and the trucks of a recently arrived supply convoy sat waiting to be unloaded. Up meant achieving the day's objective, the capture of Monte Kuk; down meant blocking the retreat of the entire defending force holding the Kolovrat ridge. Rommel headed down.

Brushing aside a few scattered groups of enemy soldiers, Rommel and 150 or so men from 3rd Company outpaced the rest of the *abteilung* and burst into the center of the village, scattering startled Italians in every direction. Standing in the crossroads at the center of Luico, Rommel realized that he was effectively 2 miles behind the Italian main line of defense, and the Italians up on the ridge had no idea he was there! In the supply trucks he and his men found bread, fruit, eggs, and wine, which the hot, thirsty, and tired Württembergers happily "liberated." Then, pulling back out of the village into what Rommel felt was a more secure position astride the road leading down from the ridge, he had his men set up an all-round defense, knowing that an Italian riposte in some form was inevitable, but from which direction was anyone's guess.

Meanwhile, on the other side of the ridge, after several hours of hard, confused fighting, the Bavarians had finally pushed the Italians off Hill 1114. It was captured by a company under the command of Leutnant Ferdinand Schörner, who reported—erroneously—that he had captured the summit of Monte Matajur, when in fact he had done no such thing. Through neither man knew it at the time, this particular feat of arms, not a small accomplishment in its own right, in view of the determination shown by the Italians in defending the hill, would ignite a long-running, often bitter, sometimes petty, rivalry between Schörner and Rommel. Feldmarschall Karl von Bülow, commander of the Fourteenth Army, had promised the *Pour le Mérite*, the "Blue Max," Germany's highest (and naturally most coveted) award for gallantry in combat, to the officer commanding the unit which captured the summit of Matajur—Rommel had been determined to be that officer, but it would be Schörner who would be receiving the medal.[28]

It was just as well that Rommel had no idea what was transpiring up on the ridge above him, as it was not long before a column of Italian soldiers, *Bersaglieri* to be precise—Italy's elite light infantry—came marching through Luico, utterly confident that all of the German and Austrian troops were on the other side of the ridge. They were understandably startled when they stumbled upon Rommel's small detachment; Rommel tried to bluff them into surrendering without a fight but an exchange of rifle and machine-gun fire began, which lasted for about 10 minutes. Finally the shooting from the Italians began to taper off, then ceased altogether, and the *Bersaglieri* commander signalled his willingness to surrender. Evidently believing that the presence of Rommel's "advance party" signaled the collapse of the ridgeline defenses and that the bulk of the Fourteenth Army was about to descend on them, the Italians chose the better part of valor and laid down their arms—50 officers and 2,000 men of the 4th Bersaglieri Brigade meekly marched into captivity. By now the rest of Rommel's *abteilung* was beginning to catch up with him, while Major Sprösser was bringing the rest of the Mountain Battalion over the ridge and moving into Luico from the opposite direction; Monte Kuk was now in German hands.

Two peaks along the ridgeline were still in Italian hands, Monte Cragonza and the actual summit of Matajur, and as long as they remained so, the Alpenkorps' hold on the rest of the ridge couldn't be considered secure. The Italians would be able to observe every move the Alpenkorps made, bring down machine-gun fire on units that strayed into range, and call in fire missions for Italian artillery batteries sited to support the defenders. As the afternoon faded into evening, Rommel allowed his men to rest while he studied the ridgeline through a pair of binoculars. He then went to Major Sprösser and expressed his confidence that with the proper artillery support and maximum surprise he could take Cragonza (also known as

Hill 1096). Doing so would cut the road by which the Italian positions atop Matajur were supplied, as well as being the only route of retreat available to the defenders.

As the moon rose in the small hours of October 26, Rommel's heavily reinforced *abteilung* of three rifle and three machine-gun companies began working their way back up the ridge, making for the summit of Monte Cragonza. It was still dark when the village of Jevszek, which sat on the shoulder of Cragonza, was taken without a fight, another 1,600 Italian POWs, including 37 officers, being gathered in later that morning. The position atop Cragonza was not to be taken so easily: for once Rommel could see no tactical alternative to a frontal assault, and so he went forward fast and hard with his three rifle companies and stormed the peak.

> Flanking machine-gun fire from the north struck amongst us. We rushed on. . . . For a while on the Matajur road I myself provided a target for an Italian machine gunner. There was no cover against his fire. I escaped the well-laid cone of fire by running upslope around a bend of the road about seventy yards away.
>
> The losses only increased the fury of the mountain troops. Trench after trench was taken and nest after nest of machine guns was wiped out. The hard job was completed about 0715. The valiant 2nd Company . . . had captured the peak of Monte Cragonza.[29]

Now all that lay between Rommel's *abteilung* and the Alpenkorps' ultimate objective was the Mrzli, the secondary summit of Monte Matajur, connected to the peak itself by a saddle which was thick with Italian infantry.

> . . . Already during our attack we had observed hundreds of Italian soldiers in an extensive bivouac area in the saddle of Mrzli between its two highest prominences. They were standing about, seemingly irresolute and inactive, and watched our advance as if petrified. They had not expected the Germans from a southerly direction— that is, from the rear. . . .
>
> . . . The number of enemy in the saddle on Mrzli was continually increasing until the Italians must have had two or three battalions there. Since they did not come out fighting, I moved near

along the road, waving a handkerchief, with my detachment ech-eloned in great depth. The three days of the offensive had indicated how we should deal with the new enemy. We approached to within eleven hundred yards and nothing happened. Had he no intention of fighting? Certainly his situation was far from hopeless! In fact, had he committed all his forces, he would have crushed my weak detachment and regained Monte Cragonza. Or he could have re-tired to the Matajur massif almost unseen under the fire support of a few machine guns. Nothing like that happened. In a dense human mass the hostile formation stood there as though petrified and did not budge. Our waving with handkerchiefs went unan-swered . . .[30]

What happened next was akin to a scene out of a Dürrenmatt play: as Rommel approached to within 150 yards of the Italians, they suddenly broke and ran in all directions, scores of them rushing forward to greet him, hoisting him on their shoulders amid shouts of *"Enviva Germania!"* An entire regiment—1,500 men—of the Salerno Brigade threw down their weapons and surrendered to the handful of riflemen who had kept pace with Rommel. The road to the Matajur summit—the true summit—lay wide open, with only a single regiment of enemy infantry defending it.

What followed was almost equally strange: a message from Major Sprösser arrived, directing Rommel's *abteilung* to withdraw from the ridge and return to Luico. The major, seeing the enormous number of prisoners coming down from the slopes of Monte Cragonza and the Mrzli—more than 3,000 Italian officers and other ranks—assumed that Monte Matajur itself had fallen, and wanted the Mountain Battalion reassembled so that it could rest and refit before renewing the offensive—there was no purpose to occupying the Kolovrat ridge now that the Italian defenses had been breached or taken. The whole of Rommel's *abteilung*, save for the under-strength rifle company and the machine company that were with him at the moment, were already moving down toward Luico. Rommel, of course, did not know the reasons for Sprösser's order, but he did know it was a mistake.

Should I break off the engagement and return to Mount Cragonza?

No! The battalion order was given without knowledge of the situation on the south slopes of Matajur. Unfinished business remained. To be sure, I did not figure on further reinforcements in the near future. But the terrain favored the plan of attack greatly and every Württemberg mountain trooper was in my opinion the equal of twenty Italians. We ventured to attack in spite of our ridiculously small numbers.

We kept attacking. The heavy machine guns were moved up in echelon. From Hill 1467 a hostile battalion tried to move off to the southwest by way of Scrilo. But the fire of one of our machine guns, delivered at sixty yards from the head of the column, forced the battalion to halt. A few minutes later, waving handkerchiefs, we approached the rocky hill six hundred yards south of Hill 1467. The enemy had ceased firing. Two heavy machine guns in our rear covered our advance. An unnatural silence prevailed. Now and then we saw an Italian slipping down through the rocks. The road itself wound among the rocks and restricted our view of the terrain to a few yards. As we swung around a sharp bend, the view to the left opened up again. Before us—scarcely three hundred yards away—stood the 2nd Regiment of the Salerno Brigade. It was assembling and laying down its arms. Deeply moved, the regimental commander sat at the roadside, surrounded by his officers, and wept with rage and shame over the insubordination of the soldiers of his once-proud regiment. Quickly, before the Italians saw my small numbers, I separated the 35 officers from the 1,200 men so far assembled, and I sent the latter down the Matajur road at the double, toward Luico. The captured colonel fumed with rage when he saw that we were only a handful of German soldiers.[31]

At last it was the turn of the Matajur summit itself, 400 yards ahead and 300 feet higher up. While his six heavy machine guns directed suppressive fire on the summit, Rommel carefully led his riflemen across the open ground, as always using every wrinkle, fold, and undulation to best advantage for cover and concealment. Just as he got his men in position to storm the garrison on the pinnacle of Monte Matajur, the enemy commander surrendered. Either the man had not realized just how small was

Rommel's band of attacking infantry, or else, seeing that the rest of the Kolovrat ridge had fallen and that the only road by which reinforcements could have reached him or he and his men could have withdrawn was in enemy hands, concluded that the Matajur summit would fall no matter what he did. Whichever it was, he evidently decided that getting his men (and quite possibly himself) killed for no purpose was the height of folly, so he gave it up as a bad job. At 11:40 A.M., October 26, 1917, Rommel's signals section fired the prearranged pattern of flares that announced that the Alpenkorps' objective was secured.

In 52 hours of near-continuous operations, Rommel and his men had covered a horizontal distance of almost 18 miles (and the vertical equivalent of another 2), much of the time under enemy fire, broke through the center of the Italian defenses along the Isonzo River Line, took in rapid succession one enemy village and four summit positions, and captured almost nine thousand enemy soldiers. Though Rommel would remember by name every man killed or who had suffered a severe wound, the human cost of these achievements had been astonishingly small—six dead and 30 wounded. Though he was denied the *Pour le Mérite*, Rommel and his accomplishments were singled out for mention in the Alpenkorps' Order of the Day on October 27, a measure of professional recognition which was no small salve to the ego of an ambitious and rather vain young infantry officer.

With the line of the Isonzo River defenses split wide open, the Italians had no choice but to retreat. The Alpenkorps was shifted to the Fourteenth Army's right flank, where its mountain-fighting skills could be put to best use as the Army's advance trailed its right wing along the foothills of the Dolomite Mountains. A string of short, sharp delaying actions marked the Württembergers' progress westward, and it was in one such engagement on November 7 that Rommel's *abteilung*, once again at its usual strength of three rifle companies and a machine-gun company, was given the task of clearing an Italian blocking force from the Klautana Pass, approximately 12 miles east of the town of Longarone.

For the first time since the early days of the war, Rommel's attack failed. Throughout the war, he had been careful to examine every action in which he'd been engaged, in order to root out and absorb whatever tactical lessons could be drawn from them. For all of his undeniable arrogance and vanity, Rommel could be remarkably self-honest when necessity de-

manded: the knowledge that, while death and injury were inevitable consequences of warfare, men's lives would be wasted through carelessness or
over-confidence repeatedly drove home that necessity. In this case, Rommel
readily acknowledged that over-confidence had played a part in the failure
of his attack, coupled with a degree of over-complication in the planning
and execution.

Though they had driven off their German attackers, the Italian troops
holding Klautana Pass were spooked by the attack, and decamped a few
hours later. The road to Longarone was wide open. While not a large town
by any definition, Longarone had a tremendous strategic importance: the
single rail line which was the sole supply route for the Italian Fourth Army
and 12th Corps ran through the town, while the Piave River valley was the
only practical route by which the 12th Corps, already in danger of being
isolated and cut off by the Fourteenth Army's advance, could withdraw from
its positions to the north, in the Carnic Alps. At noon on November 9 the
Germans reached Longarone.

> The Piave valley lay before us in the brilliant light of the midday
> sun. Five hundred feet below us the bright green mountain stream
> rushed over its broad, multi-branched, stony bed. On the far side
> was Longarone, a long and narrow town; behind it lofty 6,000-foot
> crags soared up to the heavens. The automobile of the Italian dem-
> olition crew was crossing the Piave bridge. An endlessly long hos-
> tile column of all arms was marching on the main valley road on
> the west bank. It was coming from the Dolomites of the north
> [12th Corps] and was heading south through Longarone. Lon-
> garone and its railway station, as well as Rivalta, were jammed with
> troops and stalled columns.[32]

Here was an opportunity that a solider of Erwin Rommel's caliber
could not resist. Rommel's *abteilung* was the advance guard for the Mountain Battalion, which in turn was the lead element of the whole of the
Alpenkorps. Knowing this, Rommel found that the tactical situation offered
him three choices as to what action he would take. The first was to simply
wait for the rest of the Mountain Battalion to catch up before engaging the
Italians; by now, anyone who knew anything about Erwin Rommel would

understand that this was about as likely as having the sun rise in the west. The second, which would create considerable destruction and confusion among the Italian forces in Longarone, would be to remain on the east bank of the Piave, and have all four of his companies—the machine-gun company in particular—open fire on the long columns of Italian soldiers until such time as the remainder of the battalion arrived. The third alternative was to find a way across the Piave and *attack* Longarone. It would be a bold, almost foolhardy move; Rommel himself would later hold it as a maxim that "A risk is a chance you take; if it fails you can recover. A gamble is a chance taken; if it fails, recovery is impossible." Attacking Longarone would clearly fall in the category of a gamble; nevertheless, it would be a *calculated* gamble. His experience in France and Romania had taught him that, much like Sir Isaac Newton's notional body in his First Law, an army in a state of retreat tends to remain in a state of retreat unless something compels it to do otherwise. While interdicting the withdrawal of the 12th Corps from the east bank of the Piave would certainly have been costly to the Italians, actually blocking their line of retreat would create chaos that could produce potentially decisive results. Gamble or no, for Rommel there was no other choice to make.[33]

A mile down-river from Longarone was the village of Dogna, and there the Piave was fordable to infantry on foot. The machine-gun company remained on the east bank directly across from Longarone and set up its half-dozen heavy machine guns, while Rommel took the two rifle companies down to Dogna and crossed the river, then moved north. It was dusk before all of his riflemen were across and he was able to bring them up to the outskirts of Longarone. The Italians were surprised but responded with alacrity, and returned such a heavy volume of fire that Rommel was forced to retreat, his men taking whatever cover they could find inside buildings and behind stone walls and fences. Meanwhile Major Sprösser had brought up the rest of the battalion and sent a company across the Piave at Dogna with orders to cover Rommel's rear by taking up positions to block any Italians coming up the road from the south.

When darkness fell a column of Italian infantry that Rommel later estimated to be at least a thousand strong surged down the road out of Longarone, overrunning isolated German soldiers and nearly capturing Rommel himself. Running as hard as he could, Rommel reached the blocking force by Dogna and was able to turn them around before the Italians arrived. The Germans then put up such a heavy fire that the Italian attack was halted in its tracks; Sprösser continued to send reinforcements, and sometime around 2:00 A.M. the Italians gave up and withdrew back into Longarone. At dawn, with his *abteilung* back to its full strength, Rommel began a cautious advance north toward Longarone; a hundred yards outside the town he was met by one of his own men, Leutnant Schoffel, who had been captured in the attack out of Longarone the previous evening. Schoffel handed Rommel a handwritten letter from the commanding officer of the Longarone garrison.

> Headquarters, Fortress Longarone
> To the commander of the Austrian and German forces:
> The forces in Longarone are not in any condition to offer further resistance. This Headquarters places itself at your disposal and awaits your decision as to the disposition of our troops.
> Major Lay[34]

Momentarily stunned, Rommel quickly had the men of his detachment fall in and they marched into Longarone, where Rommel formally accepted the surrender of the town and the garrison: the entire 1st Italian Infantry Division, 10,000 strong; 200 machine guns; 18 pieces of mountain artillery; 600 draft animals; 250 wagons; 10 trucks and two ambulances. Leutnant Schoffel, it turned out, had convinced his captors that Rommel's small force was considerably larger than in truth it was; unexpected "confirmation" of his story came from an Italian soldier, who had been taken prisoner early the previous day, told by Major Sprösser that an entire German division had surrounded the town, and later allowed to elude his captors and return to Longarone. Rommel had been right all along—a retreating army tends to cling to an attitude of defeat. Rommel's losses since the capture of Monte Matajur were six men killed in action, two severely wounded, 19 slightly wounded, and one missing.

The victory at Longarone would be the high-water mark of the Battle of Caporetto: despite their best efforts, the Germans and Austrians were unable to maintain their momentum, while French and British divisions, rushed up to northern Italy from Salonika, began shoring up the once-crumbling Italian army. Rommel and Sprösser would each be awarded the *Pour le Mérite* for their respective parts in the capture of Longarone, which would be remembered as one of the Italian Army's greatest humiliations. For Rommel it was unexpected but very welcome compensation for the "Blue Max" he was denied at Monte Matajur. Awarded by Kaiser Wilhelm personally, the citation accompanying the medal specified that it was given for breaching the Kolovrat line, storming Monte Matajur and capturing Longarone. In the years to come, Rommel would only acknowledge that it was for the Monte Matajur action alone—unless he found himself in Italian company, at which time he would find an opportunity to mention that it had been given to him for Longarone. It also, to his dismay, marked the end of his service with the Württembergische Gebirgsbataillon: sent on a well-earned leave in the first week of the new year, when he returned to duty he was promoted to *hauptmann* (captain) and posted to the headquarters staff of the XLIV Army Corps, the new designation for the Army of the Kingdom of Württemberg. He would remain a staff officer for the remainder of the war, until Germany signed an armistice with the Allies on November 11, 1918 and the hostilities of the Great War ceased. He would return home to Ulm, there to be reunited with Lucie just before Christmas 1918, in time for what promised to be a bleak Yuletide throughout the Fatherland. Almost 22 years would pass before he would once again lead men into battle.

CHAPTER THREE

AN OFFICER OF THE REICHSWEHR

*Against the Republic's enemies, the
Constitution was no protection.*
—GORDON CRAIG

So in December 1918, Hauptmann Erwin Rommel, one-time commander of an *abteilung* of the Königliche Württembergische Gebirgsbattalion, Württembergische Armee, holder of the *Pour le Mérite* and the Iron Cross First Class, three times wounded in battle, returned home from the war. It was far from the sort of homecoming which he had anticipated when his regiment marched out of Ulm more than four years earlier: bold confidence in victory had been replaced by the stark reality of defeat, while the events of November 1918 had shifted the foundations of the German nation and shaken the soul of the German people. When the war ended, so too did the era of true German greatness.

When it came, the end came swiftly, though there had been signs of its approach for those willing to see them as early as November 1917. The quality of life in Germany had been in steady decline since the summer of 1915 as the debilitating effects of the Royal Navy's blockade began to be felt in ever-widening circles in German society. By the end of 1916 food was being carefully rationed, and for all but the wealthiest families, what had once been staples—white bread, butter, milk—were rapidly becoming luxuries. The winter of 1917–18 would be remembered as the "Turnip Winter," when potatoes, before the war one of the cornerstones of the German diet, became all but unobtainable and Germany's civilians were forced to turn to the less appetizing and less nourishing alternative. Malnutrition became the norm, and infant mortality soared. Before the blockade was lifted in June 1919, at least a quarter-million Germans of all ages would have died of starvation. The soldiers at the front fared slightly better, as they were usually able to draw on local supplies and sources for food, but by the summer of 1918, the cupboards of the German Army's quartermasters were bare—uniforms and accoutrements were no longer issued, as the sources of cloth and leather had vanished. All the German Army possessed in material abundance were weapons and ammunition.

The German people accepted these hardships with a surprising stoicism, for it was an article of faith with them that if the war had rendered their lives so miserable, conditions must be equally terrible in the Allied nations, and the *Volk* were grimly determined to prove that they could tough it out longer than the effeminate French or the hopelessly sentimental British. Briefly, there was an illusory sense that they would succeed. Though a formal peace treaty with Germany would not be signed until March 1918, the collapse of Russia's provisional government in the wake of the wake of the Bolshevik coup in early November 1917 effectively took Russia out of the war, and gave a real sense of hope to the German Supreme Army Command that, despite the suffering and hardship, victory was on the horizon. But when, that same month, the Caporetto offensive failed to compel either an outright surrender by the Italians or at least a ceasefire on the Italian Front, the handwriting was on the wall. Another 10 months would pass, however, before Wilhelm and his generals were willing to read it.

Imperial Germany's simultaneous military and civil dissolution came to pass in relatively short order. On September 29, 1918 Field Marshal von Hindenburg and General Ludendorff presented themselves at the Imperial Army Headquarters in Spa, in occupied Belgium, where for the time being the Kaiser had taken up residence. Together they bluntly told Wilhelm, along with the chancellor, Count Georg von Hertling, that Germany's military situation was irretrievable: there were no longer any reserves, morale was crumbling, and the supply situation was beyond redemption. Ludendorff, who for all of his façade of Prussian bellicosity and bluster was a high-strung neurotic, was in near-hysterics proclaiming that the Western Front was in imminent danger of collapse; this was far from true, but together von Hindenburg and Ludendorff were adamant in their demand for a ceasefire with the Allies. They were not prepared, they assured Wilhelm, to countenance outright surrender, and yet they also advised that Chancellor von Hertling announce that President Wilson's "Fourteen Points" were acceptable as the basis for peace talks. Since Wilson's supposedly "equitable" peace program required the abdication of the Kaiser, the abolition of the monarchy and the empire, and at least a partial territorial dismemberment of the German nation, in practical terms it was tantamount to surrender. This was too much for Chancellor von Hertling, who resigned three days later; the appointment as his successor on October 3 of Prince Maximilian of Baden, who was widely recognized as a genuine liberal, was intended to be a conciliatory gesture to the Allies.

In spite of Ludendorff's dire predictions, the German Army managed to hold on for another month, but there was no disguising that it was steadily retreating, the number of desertions grew daily, and loyalty to the Kaiser was evaporating. Ludendorff was dismissed as chief of staff and replaced by General Wilhelm Gröner (von Hindenburg was not permitted to resign), who now focused solely on getting the army back onto German soil reasonably intact. Wilhelm, who technically still ruled, though he had long ago abandoned any pretense of exercising real authority over the war, clung to the delusion that even if he would no longer be Kaiser, he would at least be permitted to keep his throne as king of Prussia. The Allies were intransigent, there could only be one possible outcome, but still Wilhelm dithered, and as he did, thousands of men died needlessly every day on the Western Front.

Finally the decision was taken out of his hands. When the sailors of the High Seas Fleet learned that Admiral Franz von Hipper was planning one final sortie against the British Grand Fleet, with the intention of turning it into a death-ride that would produce a suitably glorious—and gory—*götterdämmerung* for the German Navy, they mutinied in Kiel and Wilhelmshaven on the night of October 29, setting up soldiers' and sailors' soviets modeled after those created in Russia a year before. Like dry tinder to which a match had been set, their revolt spread like a flash fire across the whole of Germany and the Imperial edifice began to crumble. The Allies made it absolutely clear that they would not negotiate with Wilhelm or any of his ministers—they would treat only with the representatives of a German republic. Still Wilhelm refused to act—abdication, he declared, was out of the question. Finally, Max von Baden had enough, and took it upon himself to force the issue: on November 9 he announced that the Kaiser had abdicated. Wilhelm, presented with a *fait accompli*, boarded his imperial train and rode it into permanent exile in the Netherlands. Two days later, at 5:00 A.M. on November 11, at Compiègne, just behind the French lines, a small German delegation, military and civilian, signed an armistice with the Allies. While technically only a ceasefire, the agreement was effectively a recognition of Germany's military defeat. Six hours later, at "the eleventh hour of the eleventh day of the eleventh month," the armistice went into effect.

After four years of carnage the like of which the world had never before seen, the war was over and the soldiers could go home. But the Germany which Rommel, along with five million other German soldiers, sailors, and airmen, had called home, and to which they now hoped to return, the Fatherland from which the German Army had erupted, east and west, in August 1914, was no more. The German Empire vanished the moment the Kaiser's train crossed the border into Holland; in its place it left the bastard child of military defeat and political humiliation, what was possibly the most confounding national government of the twentieth century, a schizophrenic Rube Goldberg-esque contrivance that seemed to be dedicated in equal part to self-destruction and self-preservation—the Weimar Republic.

The "German Republic" was proclaimed in Berlin, just hours after the announcement of the Kaiser's abdication on November 9, 1918, by the left-leaning Social Democratic Party, the largest single political party in Germany, led by Friedrich Ebert. The Imperial chancellor, Prince Max of Baden, had feared that without a central government a defeated Germany would fall into chaos, and recognized that peace with the Allies could only be reached by a central authority which was at least semi-functional. Facing these painful realities, the same day that he announced the Kaiser's abdication, he authorized a formal transfer of powers to Ebert's republic, although he technically lacked the legal authority to do so. That afternoon, a few hundred communists who openly declared their intent to emulate the Russian Bolsheviks and styled themselves the Spartakusbund (Spartacist League), announced the formation of a rival "Socialist Republic."

Ebert, like Prince Max, feared a breakdown of law and order, quickly sought an accommodation with the Spartacists, and oversaw the formation with them of a "Council of the People's Deputies." At the same time, in order to guarantee that his fledgling government held on to the reins of power, Ebert came to terms with General Wilhelm Gröner, Ludendorff's successor as the army's *de facto* Chief of Staff, agreeing to keep the government out of army affairs in exchange for Gröner's pledge that the army would protect the new German state. Lacking continuity with any part of the Imperial regime, its legitimacy was suspect; a republic had simply been foisted onto the German people, the question of a constitutional monarchy or a republic never having been put before the Reichstag or any other national assembly.

Meanwhile, at the front, relief more than exultation or despair initially prevailed among the Allied and German as more than four years of fighting came to an end. Over the next two weeks, as per the terms of the armistice, the German Army evacuated the territory it occupied in France, Belgium, Alsace-Lorraine, and Luxembourg, and withdrew into the Fatherland. While Allied armies would occupy the west bank of the Rhine River by year's end, and the British naval blockade of Germany would continue until a formal peace treaty was signed, peace, for the Allies at least, had come last.

But while the Great War itself may have ended with the armistice, for Germany and the German people fighting would continue uninterrupted, in one form or another, and in wildly varying levels of intensity, for another 15 years, as German *soldaten* went from combating Tommies, Yanks, and *poilus* for *Kaiser, Reich, und Volk*, to killing each other in the name of political causes. For the three years immediately following the sudden quiet on the Western Front, Germany stood on the knife-edge of open civil war, as ultraconservative Freikorps and their sympathizers battled Socialists and Communists in the streets of German cities and towns. Even when the imminent threat of *Brüderkrieg*—civil war—had passed, the looming presence of the *femen* (political assassins), as well as bloody, sometimes murderous, street brawls between rival gangs of political thugs, sustained a measure of simmering terror throughout Germany that the *Volk* had never before imagined, let alone known. The peaceful, orderly political processes of the empire were gone, replaced by the politics of the bludgeon, the knife, the gun, and the grenade. It is only when this tragic truth is recognized and accepted that the eventual rise of the Nazi Party, and with it Adolf Hitler, to the pinnacle of power in Germany becomes explicable.

Erwin Rommel would spend the 1920s as an officer of the Reichswehr, the remnant permitted by the Treaty of Versailles of the once-mighty German Army which had gone to war in 1914. Germany's political upheavals during that decade would, as they occurred, barely touch him or his family, but their consequences would drive the forces which in the decade that followed shaped his life and career, sometimes leading, sometimes directing him to decisions which would bring him to the moment where he would die by his own hand. For this reason they demand to be explored and examined, in order for sense to be made of a fatal choice Rommel would make in June 1944.

From November 1918 to January 1919, the Council of the People's Deputies, the self-appointed, makeshift committee cobbled together from members of the Fatherland's largest political parties, left, right, and center, governed Germany more-or-less by decree. It was self-evident to all, however, that the council was very a temporary measure, hardly representative of the German people as a whole and unpalatable to the Allied powers. The Allies, intent on eradicating all traces of militarism in Germany, decided that the Hohenzollern monarchy and warmongering were synonymous, and were determined to see a popular, elective government take shape in post-Wilhelmine Germany. A Nationalversammlung (National Assembly) was elected in mid-January 1919 to write a new German constitution; in order to avoid the increasingly violent political climate in Berlin, the assembly convened in the town of Weimar. By August 11 the last debates were resolved and the constitution ratified: the newly minted document created a federal republic, governed by a president and parliament. Though it was called *Die Verfassung des Deutschen Reichs* ("the Constitution of the German Reich"—the same title borne by the old Imperial constitution) it would be forever identified by the German people and the world at large with the town where it was drafted, and so be known as the Weimar Constitution, the government it created, the Weimar Republic.

By whatever name it would be known, the new government would never be truly popular with the German people, and it almost immediately came under attack from right, left, and center. To the millions who were still loyal to the monarchy, if not the Kaiser himself, the very idea of a republic was anathema, and the social agenda initiated by the government— a sweeping reform of labor laws establishing better hours, conditions, and pay for workers, along with the abolition of class-based social institutions— was openly regarded as the thin end of the wedge that would open the door to a radical, openly socialist state, and eventually an outright communist regime. At the other end of the political spectrum, the new government's social policies, however enlightened they might have been, weren't seen as being sufficiently sweeping and radical. The conservatives felt that the Republic invested too much power in the common people, the liberals and socialists maintained that for all its egalitarian pretensions, the government still favored those with money and titles at the expense of the working class. And for many Germans, regardless of their particular political persuasion, the Weimar Republic was inextricably linked to the humiliation of Compiègne: the men who accepted the terms of the armistice were the same men who created the German Republic, and who would soon be denounced as the men by whose actions "the German Army was stabbed in the back." Seven months later those same men would set their signatures to the Treaty of Versailles, accomplices in the national shame that accompanied Germany's compulsory acceptance of it.

The anger created by the Versailles document originated with the fact that it was not "negotiated" in the sense that it was a consensus among equals, an international contract drawn up between all signatories; there had been no give-and-take, no compromises, no synthesis of differing ideas or goals. The Allies merely decided what terms they would present to Germany, then handed the finished draft to the German delegation, along with the choice of either signing it without question, or resuming hostilities. Allied armies, nearly a million strong in total, already held bridgeheads across the Rhine: fighting was not an option for the Germans, for they no longer had anything like a cohesive army with which to conduct a defense. Even had one been to hand, the strategic situation was hopeless: without tanks, artillery, or an air force, Germany was indefensible. The German people would come to regard the treaty as a *diktat*, an ultimatum. Yet in practical terms it was no harsher than the settlement the new-minted German Empire had imposed on France in 1871, while the treaty of Brest-Litovsk, concluded in December 1917 between Germany and Bolshevik Russia, had been far more punitive. However, the popular perception would prove critical, for it fostered a receptive audience to the lie, put about by the defeated German generals, that the German Army, fighting valiantly at the front, had been stabbed in the back by pacifists and revolutionaries at home. The legend of the *Dolchstoss*, the "dagger shock," the "stab in the back," had begun.

Versailles methodically stripped Germany of nearly a fifth of her territory, reduced the German Army to a strength of 100,000 men, barely more than a glorified police force; all but abolished her navy, dispossessing the High Seas Fleet of all of its ships but an obsolescent handful; and banned the existence of a German air force. Additionally, the German armed forces were prohibited from possessing modern heavy weapons, including tanks and heavy artillery, while also being forbidden the capacity to develop and produce them in the future. All of this was humiliating to a people who had bestowed an inordinate degree of national pride in their armed forces. If those conditions weren't sufficiently punishing, the treaty imposed a crushing indemnity—"crushing" in that no specific amount was stipulated; the Germans would continue to pay until the Allies grew tired of taking their money—intended to repay the Allies for their costs in four years of carnage. The victorious powers were determined to ensure that Germany would never again wage an aggressive war.

Adding insult to injury was the treaty's Article 231, which read: "The Allied and Associated Governments affirm and Germany accepts the responsibility of Germany and her allies for causing all the loss and damage to which the Allied and Associated Governments and their nationals have been subjected as a consequence of the war imposed upon them by the aggression of Germany and her allies." In other words, Germany was to bear the sole blame for the war.

It was no small point: Germany's "guilt" provided the legal underpinnings, the legitimacy, for dismembering the German Reich—Silesia, sections of East Prussia and the Rhineland were all taken away from Germany and either demilitarized or given to one of the newly formed nations in Central Europe—as well as the imposition of crippling reparations and the dissolution of Germany's armed forces. More than any other of the Allies' punitive provisions in the treaty, this would be the most deeply resented by the German people, an open wound for which there was to be no healing. It would become a grudge which the German people bore against the Allies, and which demagogues and agitators would use as a weapon to hack away at the limitations and provisions of the Versailles treaty, claiming that it was unfair to saddle the German nation and people with the total guilt for a conflict for which, they insisted, all the warring nations, victors and vanquished, bore some degree of responsibility.

Nonetheless, the Allies were unyielding: unquestioning acceptance of the terms of the Versailles treaty was the price of peace for Germany, and yet there would be no peace for the Germans. Even as Gustav Bauer, Weimar's chancellor, affixed his signature to the document on June 28, 1919, right-wing Freikorps led by General Rüdiger von der Goltz were summarily executing leftists in Germany's Baltic districts. For that matter, violence had erupted between armed gangs of every political persuasion in the weeks that followed the Kaiser's abdication, a lamentable but predictable byproduct of the confusion of those days. But the formal introduction of murder and terror as ineradicable parts of Germany's new political process can be said to have taken place on January 4, 1919, in what became known as the "Spartacist Uprising." For reasons never fully explained, a large group of workers spontaneously began erecting barricades in the newspaper quarter of Berlin; the Socialist and Communist political leadership at first refused to cooperate, but within days saw a political opportunity and called for a general strike throughout the city—some half-million Berliners complied. The co-founders of the radical Spartacus League, Karl Liebknecht and Rosa Luxemburg, both ardent and dedicated Communists, were the most visible political leaders in the strike, and their faction inadvertently lent its name to the uprising. On January 7, the Socialists and Communists, loudly unhappy with what they perceived as collusion and collaboration between Friedrich Ebert's government and the conservatives, decided that the moment had arrived to stage a coup which would topple the fledgling republic.

The defense minister, Gustav Noske, acting on Ebert's orders, had already brought several Freikorps units into Berlin to suppress the radicals; once the general strike was announced, Ebert ordered them to clear the streets. The Freikorps, all ex-soldiers, well-armed and to a man determinedly anti-socialist and anti-communist, quickly re-took the barricaded thoroughfares—by January 15 the rising was over. About a hundred strikers were killed in confrontations with the Freikorps, whose casualties were a fraction of that number; but, more sinister in its implications for the future of the Weimar Republic, even as the actual fighting died out, thousands of Socialists, Communists, and Spartacists were being hunted down throughout Berlin and executed by Freikorps troopers, including Liebknecht and Luxemburg.

As early as December 1918 it had been obvious that the infant German

Republic needed an army of its own, if only to be the instrument that imposed order onto a nation daily falling further into chaos. As the German Empire had disintegrated in November 1918, so did the German Army. Like the Prussian Army, the armies of Bavaria, Saxony, and Württemberg marched home to their respective kingdoms. Except that, like the Kingdom of Prussia, none of those monarchies any longer existed: in Munich, Ludwig III actually anticipated Wilhelm II in abandoning his throne, abdicating on November 7, 1918, bringing an end to the 738-year rule of the House of Wittelsbach in Bavaria, while Friedrich August III of Saxony surrendered his crown six days later. Friedrich of Baden abdicated on November 22; the last holdout was Wilhelm II of Württemberg, who finally gave up his throne on the last day of the month. With the dissolution of the five kingdoms that composed the German Empire, their respective armies were left leaderless, their chains of command broken, with no one and no institution empowered to issue orders. On March 6, 1919 the Weimar government issued a decree which established the Vorläufige Reichswehr ("Provisional National Defense Force"), with a nominal strength of 400,000 officers and other ranks. This lasted until January 1, 1921, when a new Reichswehr was officially established according to the limitations imposed by the Treaty of Versailles.

The new provisional army proved to be anything but reliable, however. On Christmas Eve 1918, in a bloody confrontation in Berlin with a group of armed revolutionaries, made up mostly of sailors from Kiel that called itself the Volksmarinedivision ("the People's Naval Division"), the provisional army was humiliated. Brought in to clear out the Stadtschloss ("State Castle"—the Kaiser's former residence), where the sailors had billeted themselves, the soldiers were instead driven off, but not before large numbers of them were seen leaving their units to openly join the sailors. The Volksmarinedivision withdrew from the castle later that same day, but the provisional army's reputation and the government's prestige had both suffered severely in the wake of the incident. The skirmish at the Stadtschloss led Major Kurt von Schleicher, the protege of General Wilhelm Gröner and something of a political opportunist, to create the Freikorps to prevent the occurrence of another such incident.

Schleicher's idea was to recruit Army veterans and former Imperial officers to create paramilitary volunteer units which could be used to suppress any organized opposition to the Republic—but most particularly radical Socialists and Communists. The plan was a stroke of evil genius. After the Armistice, there had been no orderly, systematic demobilization of the German Army: it withdrew from France and Belgium in reasonably good order, but once inside Germany's borders, the corps, divisions, and regiments simply dissolved, and most German soldiers made their way as best they could to their homes, individually or in small groups. Others, who had no real home to which they could return—or, given the looming specter of massive unemployment, no prospects for a stable future once they arrived—felt disconnected from civilian life, and sought the reassuring, stable familiarity of military life found in the Freikorps. These paramilitary bands also exerted a powerful attraction on those disillusioned veterans, angry at Germany's sudden, apparently inexplicable defeat, who sought some form of revenge against political and social enemies they held responsible for Germany's failure to win the war. This melange of arch-nationalistic paramilitary units would be involved in nearly every act of political violence in Germany between 1919 and 1923.

It should be noted that the explicit purpose of the Freikorps was not the protection of the Weimar Republic, per se, rather it was the repression of the left-wing elements of Germany's political processes. The Freikorps were essentially indifferent to the survival of the Republic, seeing it only as a placeholder to eventually be supplanted by some form of arch-conservative, autocratic government. This was openly demonstrated in March 1920, in a near-comic opera incident known as "the Kapp Putsch." Also known as the Kapp-Lüttwitz Putsch, after its leaders Wolfgang Kapp and Walther von Lüttwitz, the affair was an attempt to overthrow the Weimar Republic and establish a military regime. Kapp was a career politician of an ultranationalist bent who viewed Germany's defeat in the Great War as a national humiliation and who was one of the most ardent evangelists of the "Dolchstoss myth"—the "stab in the back" betrayal of the German Army by liberal politicians who made peace with the Allies. Von Lüttwitz had been a general in the Imperial Army who currently held command of the Berlin military district; his loathing of the Treaty of Versailles equaled that of Kapp's. He had been the commanding officer of the Freikorps units that had put down the Spartacist Uprising, and apparently this gave him a taste for military coups.

On March 11, 1920 von Lüttwitz, who was maneuvering behind the backs of his nominal civilian superiors, sent instructions to Hermann Ehrhardt, a Freikorps leader who commanded the eponymous Marinebrigade Ehrhardt, to enter Berlin, secure the Reichskanzlie—the Chancellery—and depose the Republican government. By mid-morning on March 13, joined by a battalion of provisional Reichswehr troops, the Freikorps held all of the major buildings in the city, and the government fled first to Dresden then to Stuttgart. Kapp announced the creation of a provisional government, with himself as *Reichskanzler* (chancellor) and von Lüttwitz as minister of defense; they believed their position was secure, as they had the open support of several Reichswehr units and senior officers, along with the Freikorps and other conservative, nationalist and monarchist groups.

What Kapp and von Lüttwitz did *not* have was support of the majority of the old aristocracy, the civil service, the labor unions or the general populace, all of whom, for various, sometimes contradictory reasons, had no love for Kapp, von Lüttwitz, or their goal. Two days after the putsch, Ebert struck back, confident that, no matter how indifferent were most Germans to the Republic, they were not prepared to accept a military dictatorship in its place, issuing a decree from Stuttgart that called for a general strike all across Germany. William Manchester memorably described the response: "When Germans obey, they really obey; next day, not a single water tap, gas range, electric light, train or streetcar would function." The nation was paralyzed, and so was the bureaucracy: most of the civil servants refused to report for work, making it impossible for Kapp to govern. He resigned on March 17 and immediately fled to Sweden; Lüttwitz held out for another day before he, too, gave up and departed for Hungary.[35]

The indifference of the Freikorps to the fate of the Weimar Republic was unmistakable in their refusal to evict Kapp and von Lüttwitz from the Reichskanzlerie. What should have been equally disturbing to any objective observer was the matching indifference of the Reichswehr, under the command of General Hans von Seeckt. When asked by Reich President Ebert and Chancellor Bauer where the Reichswehr stood in the crisis, von Seeckt, at once evasive and revealing, famously replied, "The Reichswehr stands behind me!" He then refused an order from Ebert, Bauer, and Defense Minister Gustav Noske to put down the putsch by whatever means necessary, claiming that "There can be no question of sending the Reichswehr to fight these people." (Later he would declare that "Reichswehr do not fire on Reichswehr!") At this point Ebert asked von Seeckt straight out "Is the Reichswehr reliable?" The general replied, "I do not know if they are reliable, but they do obey me!"[36]

Von Seeckt regarded the Reichswehr as "a state-within-a-state" and took the position that as such it was dedicated to the defense of Germany, rather than any particular German government. Whatever the Weimar Constitution might say about the *Reichspräsident*'s authority over Germany's military, Ebert understood that had the Reichswehr as a whole openly sided with Kapp and von Lüttwitz, the Weimar Republic would have died in its infancy. In practical terms Ebert could exercise little if any control over the Reichswehr without von Seeckt's active cooperation. The price of that cooperation would be for the Weimar regime to merely turn a blind eye to the Reichswehr's evasions, deceptions, and at times outright defiance of the terms of the Treaty of Versailles, through which von Seeckt planned to reduce that document to utter impotence; it was active collusion in such undertakings Ebert, even as he was genuinely dedicated to a popular, responsible government for Germany, was far from immune to the sense of national humiliation heaped upon Germany by the Allies with their peace treaty: he saw no reason why a German republic should not be permitted to be as proud and powerful as the German Empire. Weimar had survived the Kapp Putsch—barely. There was no guarantee that it could survive another such challenge to its legitimacy and existence without the support of the Reichswehr, and so Ebert gave a tacit consent to cooperation with von Seeckt's goals and ambitions.

Admittedly, the Reichswehr was an unusual institution, placed in peculiar circumstances. On September 30, 1919, the Vorläufige Reichswehr was reorganized as the Übergangsheer ("Transitional Army") numbering about 400,000 men. On January 1, 1921, the Transitional Army was, in turn, supplanted by the Reichswehr officially sanctioned in the Treaty of Versailles. The terms of the treaty were rigorous and detailed, drawn up to ensure that Germany would never again possess the capacity to wage an aggressive war. Technically, the name Reichswehr now referred to the unified defense organization composed of the Reichsheer, the army, and the Reichsmarine, the navy, but "Reichswehr" quickly came to mean the army in the minds of most Germans and foreigners alike. The strength of the new army was limited to a maximum of 100,000 men—4,000 officers and 96,000 other ranks—organized into seven divisions of infantry, and three of cavalry. The elaborate reserve system of the old Imperial Army, which allowed it to more than treble the army's peacetime strength when mobilized, was abolished; there would be no army reserve of any description. The navy's strength was established at 15,000 men of all ranks, its ships limited to six pre-dreadnought battleships, a half-dozen light cruisers, and a minor assortment of destroyers, minesweepers and gunboats—submarines were absolutely *verboten*. There would be no German air force of any kind or description.

Heavy weapons such as artillery with a bore larger than 105 mm (205 mm for naval guns), were banned, as were any tanks or armored cars; when, where, and how replacements for worn-out equipment would be procured—and in what numbers—was strictly regulated. The establishment of an army general staf, regarded by the allies as the embodiment of Teutonic aggression, over which the Kaiser's government had, they believed, exerted far too little control, was prohibited. Compliance with all of the terms and restrictions imposed by the Versailles treatywould be monitored until at least 1927 by the Military Inter-Allied Control Commission.

Hans von Seeckt was the man responsible for putting into effect all of these restrictions on what was left of the German military. He had become the commanding officer of the Reichswehr on October 11, 1919, succeeding Wilhelm Gröner as Chief of the General Staff; he would be the last man to hold that position. When the articles in the Versailles treaty which applied to the German armed forces went into effect, the office of chief of staff was abolished, along with the General Staff itself, and von Seeckt assumed the more pedestrian title of *Chef der Heeresleitung* ("Chief of the Army Command"). The responsibilities of some branches of the General Staff were taken over by civilian departments of the Weimar government, others by new bureaus created to conform the new army command structure to treaty requirements; the purely operational functions of the General Staff, however, were deliberately devolved upon the Truppenamt ("Troop Office"), a deceptively mild name that hid its true function. Working hand-in-glove with the newly created Weapons Office and the branch inspectorates, the Truppenamt, under von Seeckt's careful guidance, set about reshaping and rebuilding Germany's postwar standing army.

Slender, ram-rod backed, always impeccably turned out, with the inevitable monocle screwed firmly in place, von Seeckt came from a military family and first served in the elite Emperor Alexander Guards Grenadiers of the Prussian Gardekorps. He was no military genius, at least not as a fighting soldier: he never led a unit in combat, having spent almost his entire career as a staff officer. In that capacity, however, he displayed a remarkable talent for planning and organization: the great German victory over the Russians at Gorlice-Tarnow in the summer of 1915, which came near to causing the collapse of the Russian army, was made possible by von Seeckt's planning and staff work as chief of staff to Field Marshal August von Mackensen. Later he was transferred to the German military mission to the Ottoman Empire; while there, von Seeckt sent a communiqué to Berlin which gave a chilling insight into the set of his moral compass. Reporting on the massacre of Armenian civilians by units of the Turkish Army, the news of which was raising a storm of outrage among the Allies and Central Powers alike, he declared that when faced with an impossible choice between morality and necessity, as he believed the Turks to be, morality must give way. Put another way, to von Seeckt the end always justified the means.

In the aftermath of the Armistice, von Seeckt was given the task of overseeing the withdrawal of German forces in Eastern Europe, in the formerly Russian territories occupied under the terms of the Treaty of Brest-Litovsk. He was then posted as part of the German delegation to the Versailles peace conference, where he argued unsuccessfully for a 200,000-man Reichswehr. Succeeding General Wilhelm Gröner as the Chief of the General Staff in October 1919, he became responsible for the creation of Germany's new national defense force, the Reichswehr. It was a task that would have overmastered a lesser man; for someone with von Seeckt's organizational skills, it was the quintessential professional challenge.

Even before the final terms of the Treaty of Versailles were set down, von Seeckt was determined that the Reichswehr, in whatever size and form permitted by the Allies, would be a thoroughly professional fighting force, prepared to serve as the framework, the cadre, of a greatly expanded German army. Only an officer who had displayed extraordinary ability either as a combat leader or in a staff position, would be permitted to become an officer of the Reichswehr. Limited to a strength of just 4,000 men, there was no room for placeholders in the new *offizierkorps*. A similar standard was applied to the non-commissioned officers and other ranks. Officers signed on for a minimum term of 25 years, rankers enlisted for a minimum of 12—there was to be no conscription, each man was a volunteer.

Officers and men were to be thoroughly trained in not only the skills required of their current postings, but also to be prepare to take command of at least the next higher unit—i.e., privates could take command of squads and platoons, platoon sergeants would be competent to command companies, battalion commanders to lead regiments or even brigades, as need be. Von Seeckt had no illusions that, at a strength of 100,000 men of all ranks, the Reichswehr would be able to defend Germany from a foreign attack; he was confident, however, that in the event of a national emergency, young German men in the tens of thousands would willingly, even eagerly, answer a call to the colors to provide the manpower with which a much, much larger army would be swiftly created. The officers, NCOs, and other ranks and men of the Reichswehr would provide the knowledge of strategy and tactics, along with the specialized, technical skills needed to properly employ modern weapons. Unspoken by anyone but understood by all was the assumption that, in the event of a war, the Freikorps would serve as the immediate ready reserve for the Reichswehr, buying time for those eager young men to be properly trained before being packed off to do battle. The *Stahlhelm Bund der Frontsoldaten* ("Steel Helmet League of Frontline Soldiers"), yet another unofficial nationalistic paramilitary organization composed of former soldiers, could have readily provided another half-million experienced men.

At the same time, while von Seeckt was prepared to speak candidly of his plans for the Reichswehr to anyone who would listen—and there were many, many Germans so willing, while the Allies seemed determined to turn a deaf ear to the general—he held the officers and men of his tiny army to very high standards of conduct. They were, he declared, expected to set an example for all German men—indeed, for all German people—by their conduct, deportment, speech, and above all, character.

If fate once again calls the German people to arms, and who can doubt that day will come, then officers should not have to call on a nation of weaklings, but of strong men ready to take up familiar and trusted weapons. The form these weapons take is not important as long as they are wielded by hands of steel and hearts of iron. So let us do our utmost to ensure that on that future day there is no lack of such hearts and hands. Let us strive tirelessly to strengthen our own bodies and minds and those of our fellow Germans. . . . It is the duty of every member of the general staff to make the Reichswehr not only a reliable pillar of the state, but also a school for the leaders of the nation.[37]

An apt student of history, von Seeckt repeatedly made the point to his officers that since the fall of Rome Western civilization had known far more years of war than of peace; in this he was not a warmonger of any shade, but a supreme realist. Peace was always the most desirable state of affairs between nations, he believed, but he also doubted that a perpetual, worldwide peace between modern, industrial nations was something which mankind could ever achieve. "My own training in history," he wrote, "prevents me from seeing in the idea of permanent peace anything more than a dream whereby it remains an open question whether one can consider it, in Moltke's phrase, a 'good dream' or not." War at some point then being inevitable, the Germans would have to defend themselves; therefore, it was the duty, he held, of every German soldier—officer or ranker—to be as thoroughly prepared to fight as he could make himself.[38]

An essential part of that preparation was, as von Seeckt saw it, the requirement that Reichswehr officers be more than mere military martinets: intelligence and imagination were often as valuable in war as rifles and artillery. In many ways he set the bar himself: polite, thoughtful, and reserved—in utter contrast, say, to the boorish, crude, and obstreperous Ludendorff—his education and experience were quite broad. He spoke English and French fluently, art, science, and culture found their way into his conversation as frequently as did military matters, and before the Great War he had traveled widely in Africa and India; he knew Europe as well as he knew the back of his hand. He was also a keen student of modern technology and its applicability to warfare. While he was determined to see the regimental traditions of the old Imperial Army maintained by the battalions of the Reichswehr, von Seeckt was equally intent on assuring that the intellectual traditions of the new German Army were firmly rooted in the twentieth century.

The training standards were high and exacting. Von Seeckt himself wrote several of the manuals which laid down tactical and operational doctrines for the Reichswehr: "Leadership and Combined Arms Combat," "Training of the Rifle Squad," "Individual Training with the Light Machine Gun," "Training Regulations for the Infantry." The necessity of combined arms tactics was continually emphasized, along with the idea that every unit commander understand the larger operational goal of his parent unit, because he "will oftentimes be obliged to act upon his own initiative . . . during the course of the engagement. . . . Quick decision and clear desire of the leaders guarantee to us the advantage in an encounter." Von Seeckt also foresaw the need for Reichswehr *soldaten* to be prepared to fight against weapons which Germany had been forbidden to possess: during the 1920s mocking photos would often appear in the foreign press showing the Reichswehr on maneuvers with motorcars bearing placards announcing that they were tanks and soldiers standing by wooden logs pretending to be heavy artillery. Such displays were taken as proof that the teeth of the German Army had once and for all been well and truly pulled—a perception encouraged in Berlin. What such supercilious commentators failed to see was that what the Reichswehr was accomplishing made actually possessing such weaponry unnecessary, at least for the moment: it was creating in its officers and men the ability to think of how to defend against such weapons—and how to employ them when the time came for Germany to rearm herself. Von Seeckt was assuring that even though the Reichswehr could not field modern weapons, that would not mean the Reichswehr would not know how to use them.[39]

It was into this professional world that Erwin Rommel was accepted on October 1, 1920, when he was posted as a company commander, Reichswehr Infantry Regiment 13, based in Stuttgart. He would remain there, an infantry captain, for the next nine years. It was hardly durance vile, however: in many ways, the nine-year interlude as a company commander was almost a lark for Rommel. Von Seeckt had little use for officers who were merely intellectuals—a role to which Rommel never pretended—but he was determined that Reichswehr officers be intelligent, inquisitive, and energetic—all characteristics which Rommel possessed in abundance. As von Seeckt expected his officers to develop a mastery of all the tools of warfare, mechanical and mental, Rommel was able to give free rein to his fascination with engineering and his gift for tinkering with machinery. One of the first tasks he set about for himself was to learn everything he could about internal combustion engines, a skill which would pay unanticipated dividends in the future.

For Rommel, the return to the familiar routine of garrison duty was reassuring. The transition from war to peace for him had been not been violent, but it had been unsettling. Released from the Army of the Kingdom of Württemburg when the monarchy was dissolved, he was accepted into the Vorläufige Reichswehr that temporarily replaced the now-defunct Imperial Army. One of his first postings was command of the 32nd Internal Security Company, in Friedrichshafen on the Bodensee—Lake Constance— a motley collection of ratings and petty officers from the old Imperial Navy who had little to do, and whose food and living conditions were poor. The sailors were in a mutinous mood, sullen, uncooperative, and resentful of being placed under an army officer, openly mocking of Rommel for wearing his decorations, including his *Pour le Mérite*. Rommel, for whom the camaraderie of the bivouac and the battlefield had erased any sense of superiority that his commission might once have imparted, replied while fighting at the front, he had at times prayed to Almight God to spare the men of the German Navy. "My prayers were heard," he declared, "because here you are!" It was a response at once ingenuous and disarming, but it worked: disciplinary problems among the sailors in Rommel's charge declined dramatically.[40]

With civil disturbances occurring all over Germany at the time, Rommel found himself ranging to and fro, being called out to variously put down riots in Westphalia, in the south of Bavaria near the Swiss border, and within Württemberg itself. He was keen on keeping violence and the use of force against civilians to a minimum, usually doing his best to find a way to diffuse a tense situation through the sheer force of his personality. He wasn't adverse to using force to impose order when confronted with ugly, threatening crowds, but he was loathe to resort to lethal force; in an incident in Münsterhausen, he used fire hoses in a manner similar to the way he had employed machine guns in Romania and Italy to disperse an angry mob. Despite his relative youth—he was not yet 34—years of leading soldiers in combat had imbued Erwin Rommel with a considerable command presence, and he put it to good use. Alternately authoritative, conciliatory, cajoling, or persuasive as need be, he was able to avoid embroiling himself in the sort of bloodshed that was becoming all too common across Germany. It was undeniably his good fortune that he was never required to cooperate with any of the Freikorps, who had already acquired a reputation for extraordinary ruthlessness in dealing with those whom they regarded as enemies; Rommel was not asked to compromise his moral compass. Many of his fellow officers would not be able to make the same claim, with tragic consequences for themselves and Germany two decades hence.

Rommel had remained with the army when the Vorläufige Reichswehr was reorganized as the Übergangsheer, and was one of the first junior officers to apply for admission to von Seeckt's Reichswehr. With the dissolution of the Imperial Army, the pool of officers from which the Reichswehr could choose its cadre was large: while more than a quarter of the German Army's regular officers had been killed in Great War (nearly 12,000 out of 46,000), the Reichswehr had only 4,000 postings for commissioned officers under the terms of the Versailles treaty. This, of course, ideally suited von Seeckt's purposes, with his emphasis on quality personnel, allowing him to select only the best candidates available: there would be no deadwood among the Reichswehr's officer corps. With his outstanding combat record and his awards for bravery, Rommel was a natural choice, and was one of the first candidates selected; the result was his posting to the 13th Infantry Regiment.

Now that he was back in Germany, and in a secure employment situation, Erwin and Lucie had the time—whenever duty did not take him out of Württemberg—and opportunity to begin to create a home for themselves in Stuttgart. It was during the years in Stuttgart that Rommel learned how to be a husband and, in due course, a father. There had been precious little time to spend with Lucie during the war, so that, when he returned home in November 1918, although they had been married for over two years, they were in a very real sense newlyweds. Rommel, conscious of the obligation he had made before the war, saw to it that Walburga Stemmer was brought into the household, along with little Gertrude, who was now six; Walburga was presented as Rommel's cousin. Apparently no one inquired too closely about Gertrude's actual status—in the years that immediately followed the war, there was a heartbreaking number of young widows with small children, and it can be comfortably assumed that such a circumstance was implied to explain the presence of Walburga and her daughter under Erwin and Lucie's roof.

If Erwin had changed during the war—the overly serious and self-important post-adolescent had been superceded by a usually cheerful, occasionally thoughtful, always self-confident adult— the same can also be said of Lucie. No longer the just striking woman-child of the days in Danzig when she won Erwin Rommel's heart, she had grown into a lovely young woman in the full bloom of her beauty; during Erwin's absence during the war she developed a very firm, almost domineering personality, and she ran the Rommel household with a whim of iron. Erwin remained smitten— he would do so for the rest of his life—and happily jumped to do Lucie's bidding whenever she called for him.

Rommel's service in the Great War had seen a remarkable degree of activity and action, and the experience imparted a certain restlessness that became an inescapable part of him—even away from his company, he seemed to have a compulsive need to always be *doing* something. The Bodensee became a frequent excursion destination for Erwin and Lucie: he was a strong swimmer and an avid boater. Lucie, though taken with the scenery, was less enthusiastic about both: she once told him "I swim just about as well as a lead duck!", a claim which was apparently borne out when she capsized her boat and Erwin had to rescue her. She enjoyed skiing far more, although she also had her limits there: she would tire far more quickly than her husband, whose years with the Württembergische Gebirgsbataillon had left him a skilled skier with enormous stamina. On one skiing outing, Lucie decided she'd had enough and plopped down in the snow, refusing to budge unless it was to return to the warmth of the ski lodge. Unimpressed, Erwin told her "You'd best get up—I don't recommend death by freezing!" Lucie was adamant, however, and Rommel was compelled to concede and call it a day.

Rommel would spend four years as the officer commanding an infantry company in II Battalion of the 13th Reichswehr Regiment; on the surface quite a comedown for a captain who as an *oberleutnant* had been commanding detachments that at times were near battalion strength. But such an appearance would have been deceiving: while he was performing the duties of a company commander, Rommel was being taught the fundamentals of battalion and regimental command, in accordance with von Seeckt's organizational doctrine for the Reichswehr. In the autumn of 1924, he was moved over to the staff of II Battalion, there to learn the nuts and bolts of battalion operations and begin preparing himself for battalion—and eventually, regimental—command. After three years on the battalion headquarters staff, he was given command of the unit's machine-gun company, a posting he would hold until October 1929. Regimental records show that Rommel quickly became highly proficient at not merely employing heavy machine guns, but actually firing and maintaining them—unlike most prewar officers, he was never afraid to get his hands dirty.

All of this presents Rommel as being a somewhat one-dimensional individual, so thoroughgoing a soldier that there was little room or time in his life for anything unrelated to the profession of arms, and, objectively, such a depiction would be true—to a degree. He was the consummate professional soldier, who had very little enduring interest in disciplines or pursuits which lacked a relevance or applicability to some aspect of military life. Even his holidays had military overtones: sometime during his posting in Stuttgart, Rommel acquired a motorcycle and sidecar, and in the summer of 1927, he and Lucie set off for Italy, where he retraced his footsteps during the Caporetto campaign. Never the soul of tact, while visiting Longarone, he let it be known that he had led the German soldiers who had taken the town and forced the surrender of an entire division of Italian infantry; he was asked to leave in short order.

All of which can be said to superficially bear out the description of Rommel afforded him by Ronald Lewin as being "dour, self-reliant, and unsophisticated." And yet that is an unbalanced, oversimplistic depiction of the man. There are far too many photographs taken throughout his life of a grinning Rommel for there to be any justification for calling him dour, and while he was indeed self-reliant, that was a characteristic he developed on the battlefields of the Great War, where life-and-death decisions had not lent themselves to rapid resolution by higher authority. As for being unsophisticated, that was exactly the sort of soldier which von Seeckt prized most highly, the sort of soldier not given to over-elaborate dialectics and rationaization, but a man who saw and understood his duty and set about to fulfill it to the best of his ability. And yet, while he took an unmistakable pride in his wartime accomplishments and clearly loved—and thrived on—the military life, he was no warmonger. "Thoughtful" and "philosphical" are two words which are rarely associated with Erwin Rommel, but whenever he was asked about the Great War, he would always describe it as a foolish endeavor, a folly that should never be repeated. Though he might have been a highly skilled practitioner of warfare, it was not something he loved.[41]

No doubt part of that attitude was shaped by one of the happiest events of Rommel's life: on December 24, 1928, his first—and only—child with Lucie was born, a son, Manfred. The boy would be a source of joy to Rommel for the remainder of his life, and while the elder Rommel never surrendered one iota of his authority as the father figure—this was Germany, after all—nowhere in Manfred's recollections of his father would there be memories of the elder Rommel being harsh, condescending, or patronizing. Manfred would eventually prove to be as headstrong as his father, and their occasional clashes of will would be memorable, for Rommel could be a demanding father and Manfred would, inevitably, fail to meet all of his father's expectations, but his love for Manfred would never be conditional.

Manfred's birth overshadowed and eventually eclipsed a singularly unhappy event that had occurred in the Rommel household two months earlier. In October, Walburga Stemmer died unexpectedly at the age of 36. The cause of death was recorded officially as pneumonia; 75 years later, her grandson, Josef Pan, would claim that she had actually committed suicide. Before Manfred was born, he asserted, Walburg clung to the hope that somehow Rommel would eventually choose to leave Lucie and return to her; the imminent arrival of a child with Lucie removed all such hope, and Walburga ended her life by taking poison. While such a scenario is not entirely implausible, it remains pure hearsay: all of the principals are now dead, and apart from Walburga's death certificate, no documentary evidence of any kind exists. Gertrude, though, would remain a welcome member of the Rommel household until she reached adulthood, and would visit her father whenever possible when he was home on leave. Manfred would grow up believing her to be his older cousin.

In many ways, Rommel treated his son as he did one of his young recruits: inexperienced, unfocused, wanting for shaping and molding, requiring that combination of sternness and camaraderie which builds mutual trust, and above all, in need of an example. Rommel would sometimes be exasperated and frustrated by Manfred, an intelligent lad who possessed a very independent mind and who proved when necessary that he could be every bit as stubborn as his father. Like fathers everywhere, Erwin Rommel had perhaps overly ambitious hopes for his son: years later, Manfred would recall that his father "had three ambitions for me: he wanted me to become a fine sportsman, a great hero, and a good mathematician. He failed on all three counts." More important would be the fact that although Rommel would be largely absent physically during some of the most critical years of Manfred's youth, the son would remember that the father had been able to impart enduring life lessons, not only through his words, but through his deeds.[42]

Awareness of the importance of example was something Rommel brought to the command of his soldiers as well. Addressing officer cadets, he would exhort them to

> Be an example to your men, in your duty and in private life. Never spare yourself, and let the troops see that you don't in your endurance of fatigue and privation. Always be tactful and well-mannered and teach your subordinates to do the same. Avoid excessive sharpness or harshness of voice, which usually indicates the man who has shortcomings of his own to hide.

That Rommel was setting an excellent example himself is borne out in the fitness reports on him submitted by his superiors. The most telling was written at the beginning of September 1929 –it is notable because it was prepared just before Rommel took the next significant step in his military career. The evaluating officer noted that Rommel was possessed of a "quiet, sterling character, always tactful and modest in his manners. . . . He has already demonstrated in the war that he is an exemplary combat commander. He has shown very good results training and drilling his company. There is more to this officer than meets the eye." The report also remarked on Rommel's talent for evaluating terrain, one of his "very great military gifts." The report concluded with the recommendation that Rommel was well suited to serve as a military instructor.[43]

That next rung up the professional ladder for Rommel came a month later, on October 1, when he was posted to the Reichswehr's Infantry Training School in Dresden. There he would have a four-year tenure and begin to make his mark, however minor at the time, upon the German army. He was given the task of teaching small-unit infantry tactics to junior officers, a textbook case of fitting a round peg into a round hole. Energetic, animated, Rommel often spoke without notes, relying on his excellent memory instead, frequently—and justifiably—drawing on his own experiences in the Great War to drive home hard-won truths. Rommel had always had a fondness for drawing, and was in fact quite good at it: he put that talent to good use in his lectures, frequently dashing off a sketch or diagram to clarify or emphasize a particular point or detail. He also had a knack for a pithy turn of phrase that summed up great insight in a few words, one of the most popular being "Shed sweat, not blood."[44] It was a posting from which Rommel derived tremendous satisfaction, some years later confiding to a friend, "I was never happier than when working with young soldiers."

It was also good for his ego; peace did nothing to diminish Erwin Rommel's vanity, and the professional validation that accompanied his appointment as an instructor at the Infantry School had to have been profound. Rommel was not—nor would he ever be—a graduate of the War Academy, nor was he ever recruited for a General Staff appointment. While there are clear indications in remarks he made in passing to friends, or confided in letters, that he resented what he took to be deliberate slights on the part of the artillerymen and aristocrats who dominated the General Staff, he was able to take a perverse pride in what he regarded as his first priority at the Infantry School: "I want to teach them first how to save lives!"[45]

Rommel was, for the most part, exceedingly content with life in the Reichswehr. He was useful, fulfilled, and was given a strong sense of purpose; in this he was distinct from the millions of men, German, French, British, Austrian, Italian, American, who found themselves part of what Gertrude Stein would christen "the Lost Generation." As with most wars, the Great War was the defining moment of the lives of the men who fought it: it had imparted to most of them a narrow, intense purpose during those years, unlike any they had ever known before, whether they saw it as a great crusade to defeat an enemy, or simply day-to-day survival in an environment which was usually indifferent to their continued existence and often actively hostile to it. The abrupt yet ambiguous end to which the Armistice brought the war left the victors with little real sense of having won anything, while the vanquished felt a greater sense of betrayal than they did defeat. The moral exhaustion created by the war did not occur in the trenches, it manifested itself when the soldiers returned home and found nothing awaiting them that required the same manner of commitment, the same degree of intensity that they had known at the front. At the end of the Second World War, victorious Allied soldiers, sailors, and airmen were able to rebuild their countries, or build them anew; the Germans and the Japanese were presented with the opportunity to work toward redemption. In November 1918, peace offered only a sense of business unfinished and destinies unfulfilled.

Rommel knew none of that: he had established himself as a distinguished soldier and leader of men in wartime, now he was proving that he could be equally proficient in the duties of a peacetime instructor, teaching, not merely drilling, creating leaders, not cannon fodder. He fully embraced General von Seeckt's professional philosophy, with its emphasis on professionalism, whereby enlisted men as well as officers were trained not only for their current postings, but were simultaneously being prepared for higher levels of command. It only made sense that the Reichswehr would someday be the cadre of a much larger German army, though it was generally accepted that any such expansion would be the result of a national emergency rather than a peacetime program. For Rommel, that was sufficient, he felt no need to know more, to look too closely at what the men who commanded the Reichswehr were doing behind closed doors. Had he done so, he certainly would have been startled, he might well have been shocked.

From the day the Reichswehr was established, von Seeckt had been dedicated to two bedrock principles: the first was an unshakable commitment to Germany's eventual rearmament; the second was an adamant insistence that the officers and other ranks be apolitical, that they be *"überparteilichkeit"*— that is, above party politics. Indeed, from various incidents and public pronouncements, it was unmistakable that von Seeckt ideally hoped for a Reichswehr that was above the state, or at least above any national government, its ultimate loyalty given only to Germany.

That was a dangerous concept, for it implied that the Republic was irrelevant, that von Seeckt, or his successors as commanding officer of the Reichswehr, possessed the authority to arbitrarily decide what would be the rightful form of government for Germany, as well as who would and would not be permitted to govern. It was a belief that was at best ethically ambiguous, as it arrogated to the commander of the Reichswehr an authority that had never been, explicitly or implicitly, legally acceded to him. In short, it was a very thinly disguised prætorianism. And while there may have been nothing inherently immoral about von Seeckt's goals, the means he chose to accomplish them and the consequences of those choices tainted the character of not only the German Army, but the whole of Germany's leadership, civil and military, as well.

It began more-or-less innocently enough, depending on how broadly "innocence" is defined, in 1921, when, at von Seeckt's direction, a special secret department was created in the Reichswehr, Sondergruppe (Special Group) R; the R stood for Russland—Russia. Sondergruppe R's primary mission was clandestine cooperation and coordination with the government of the Soviet Union in the development of tanks, heavy artillery, poison gas, and aircraft, as well as creating and refining tactical and operation doctrines for their employment, all of it in clear violation of the Treaty of Versailles. Though its existence was never made public at the time, Sondergruppe R and its mission were no secret to the highest levels of the German Republic: the minister of defense, Otto Gessler, actively participated in its creation and oversaw its ongoing activities. Responsibility for the detailed operations of the group was given to Generalmajor Kurt von Schleicher, Major Eugen Ott, and Generalmajor Kurt von Hammerstein-Equord.

To protect the secrets and secrecy of Sondergruppe R, another organization was created, this one styled the Arbeits-Kommandos (Work Commandos), under the command of Major Ernst von Buchrucker. Ostensibly a sort of public-works undertaking whereby Reichswehr soldiers were organized into labor companies which would assist with civilian construction projects, they were, in fact, assassination squads working under the direction of Sondergruppe R, charged with the elimination of German citizens who passed information to the Allied Control Commission. The Control Commission was the oversight body created to ensure Germany's compliance with the disarmament clauses of the Versailles treaty; Arbeits-Kommandos branded as traitors anyone who went to the commission with information about forbidden activities. Also targeted were known or suspected socialists and communists, or simply anyone that von Seeckt or the triumvirate of officers directing Sondergruppe R deemed treasonous. Collectively Sondergruppe R and the Arbeits-Kommandos became known as the "Black Reichswehr"; historians generally agree that between 1920 and 1923 over

350 political murders were carried out by the Arbeits-Kommandos.

While the effrontery—as well as the chilling ruthlessness—of such an organization and its activities might be startling, it pales in comparison with the sheer gall of Sondergruppe R's operations in Russia. In late 1921, at von Seeckt's direction, von Schleicher met Leonid Krasin, the Soviet Union's People's Commissar for Transport, and arranged German financial and technological aid for the development of the Soviet arms industry in exchange for Soviet support in helping German efforts to evade the disarmament clauses of the Treaty of Versailles. All told, some 75 million Reichmarks (nearly $19 million, equal to $250 million in 2015) was directed into the Soviet arms industry through the Reichswehr. What makes this noteworthy is that it was done with the active participation of the government of the German Republic: in 1919 and 1920, cabinet laws, which roughly corresponded to an American president's Executive Orders, were passed by the Ebert government which specifically permitted clandestine and illegal armament programs by the Reichswehr as well as German industries.

This is where the great riddle of the Weimar Republic originates: just what was the breadth and depth of the government's collusion in evading the spirit and the letter of the Versailles treaty, despite the repeated public assurances by every one of the Republic's chancellors that the treaty was an integral part of the law of the land? The answer remains a mystery eight decades later, one that is likely never to be solved: obviously, millions of Reichsmarks were expended over several years, but just how many remains unknown, as everyone involved was keeping more than one set of books. But even more baffling is the degree of complicity between the government and a Reichswehr which was at best openly indifferent to the Republic's continued existence, and would, under the right circumstances, be actively hostile to it. While Supreme Court Justice Robert H. Jackson may once have opined that the United States' Constitution "was not a suicide pact," evidently the Weimar Constitution was. History is hard-pressed to offer up an example of a government so willingly complicit in its own dissolution.

Even so, regardless of how absurd the idea might seem to a rational mind, there was nothing illegal or immoral about a government facilitating its own demise. What permanently besmirched the Reichswehr's honor was its sponsorship of the *femen* who carried out political murders at the behest of the "Black Reichswehr"; what thoroughly discredited the integrity of the German Republic was the systematic and methodical deception of the German people as well as of the Allies by the men who created it, when they offered repeated reassurances of the Republic's commitment to disarmament while it was in the very act of creating the weapons and doctrines with which the next war would be fought. It is a truism that all governments lie: they lie to each other, they lie to their own people, they frequently lie to themselves. But a fundamental premise of functional government is that such deception, at least on such a monumental scale, must be an exception rather than a norm: to rule effectively, a government must be able to maintain at least a minimum level of credibility; by the same token, it must inevitably fail when it chooses to function on plausible deniability alone. Adolf Hitler might have been the master of the Big Lie, but his whoppers would not have been as successful by half had not the German people already been prepared for them by the Republic.

It can be little wonder then that by the end of the 1920s, with the industrialized world in the iron grip of the worst economic depression in history, nearly one out of every three German workers unemployed, inflation so severe that "rampant" and "runaway" do not even begin to describe the debacle, and the Allied powers still demanding that Germany make good on her reparations payments, the German government came to be increasingly regarded by the German people as irrelevant—or at least hopelessly dysfunctional. To the *Volk*, the politicians, having so distorted the truth for so long that they became unable to recognize reality for what it was, had more interest in playing an endless game of ministerial musical chairs in the Reichstag and the Chancellery than in working to bring Germany out of her nightmare. It could hardly be surprising then that when a stirring, eloquent, charismatic outsider presented himself, declaring that he had solutions to Germany's problems, he would be widely regarded as a savior. While the Reichstag deputies engaged in round after round of meaningless committee meetings and empty resolutions, the German people turned to someone who was prepared to *act*. They had never before in their history sought a man on horseback, but never since the Thirty Years War had Germany been brought to such dire straits. Through a combination of circumstance, guile, violence, bluff, shrewd political maneuvering, and public acceptance, Adolf Hitler secured his appointment as the chancellor of the German Republic.

CHAPTER FOUR

THE THIRD REICH

Power resides only where men believe it resides. . .
a shadow on the wall, yet shadows can kill. And
ofttimes a very small man can cast a very large shadow.
—GEORGE R.R. MARTIN

The rise of the Nazi Party, its leader and his apostles from wide-eyed fanatical splinter party to the absolute masters of Germany is the most thoroughly chronicled political phenomenon of the twentieth century. Explanations of and apologists for how it came about are rife, and there is hardly room, let alone need, for yet another accounting of those events, although it should always be borne in mind that the phenomenon which was Adolf Hitler came about not through a coincidence and confluence of exceptional economic, social, and political circumstances which will likely never again recur, but rather because a sufficiently ruthless individual possessing a genuine will to power—a true Nitzschean *Wille zur Macht*—can always exploit a people who, feeling betrayed by their institutions and bereft of leadership, will be willing to embrace a demogogue who offers what appear to be answers and solutions to their fears and problems.

For Erwin Rommel, the Nazis were fundamentally irrelevant to him, personally and professionally, until January 30, 1933; at noon that day, Adolf Hitler took the oath of office as chancellor of the German Republic. Prior to that moment, the irrelevance of both Hitler and the Nazis to Rommel was not due to any postured disdain for or inherent disapproval of the National Socialists or their leader; instead it was the product of Rommel's dedication to being the perfect non-political Reichswehr officer, as conceived of by von Seeckt.

This is not to say that Rommel was unaware of Hitler, or that he held no political views or opinions whatsoever; either idea is patently absurd. But until Hitler became chancellor, he was only the leader of a political party, one that was, admittedly, rising and which was, month by month, exercising greater and greater influence over the German people as well as the government's policies; but Hitler remained a party leader without office nonetheless. Elevation to the chancellorship meant that, at whatever remove it might be, Adolf Hitler would now be an influence on Erwin Rommel's career and life. If the rumors were true, and Hitler was prepared to combine the office of the *Reichskanzler* with that of the *Reichspräsident* upon the death of the clearly ailing and failing Paul von Hindenburg, Hitler's influence would grow even more direct.

That Hitler only became relevant to Rommel upon taking office shades the entire relationship which would spring up between the two men. It would be in the main a relationship—to call it a friendship would be unrealistic—of expedience, for the most part mutually beneficial, but ultimately doomed to falter and fail in acrimony. In order to comprehend how that relationship came about, its nature and its limits, it is essential to have an understanding of Erwin Rommel's politics, such as they were and what there were of them—no simple undertaking where the person in question was not known for being introspective or openly philosophical.

At core, Erwin and Lucie Rommel were quintessential middle-class Germans, and their political views reflected this—intellectuals, socialists and Marxists would have seen them as hopelessly bourgeoisie. Erwin tended to lean a little to the left of center in his attitudes, essentially reflecting the politics of Erwin Rommel, Sr. Had he been required to identify himself with any one party, it would have most likely been the Social Democrats. This should come as a surprise to no one, given the younger Rommel's extroverted, intellectually unassuming nature. As he approached adulthood, he had merely adopted his father's political views as his own and never found sufficient cause to change them as he grew older. All evidence goes against the idea that Rommel ever embraced or endorsed any sort of right-wing political dogma or doctrine. There is nothing in any of Rommel's correspondence, or in any recollections or records of his conversations, for example, to indicate that he ever favored the sort of proscriptions on individual rights and liberties which are so dear to the hearts of totalitarian regimes, or would have even regarded such as necessary if unwelcome evils.

At the same time, it can be said that it is highly unlikely that Rommel ever gave more than a passing thought to such concepts: the works of Rousseau, Burke, Paine, and Jefferson would never have been found on his nightstand. Because, outside of the profession of arms, Rommel was not a great abstract thinker, there was the strong tendency within him to dismiss whatever did not touch him, his family, or his immediate circle of friends and colleagues as being somewhat less than valid. If the excesses of the Third Reich did not happen to him personally, or to someone he knew, then, in a way, they hadn't really happened. In this, Rommel was unarguably naive; he was also hardly alone.

Lucie tended to be more overtly nationalistic, Erwin not so much. (Soldiers as a rule tend to shy away from nationalism as opposed to patriotism.) Unquestionably, she found Hitler, personally, far more interesting than did Erwin—she was certainly less critical of the new *Reichskanzler* than was her husband. There was a touch of something close to hero-worship in her attitude toward Hitler. She seemed considerably less impressed with the Nazis overall, however—it can be fairly said that she merely tolerated them.

The most significant event in Rommel's life during 1933 was not the accession of Hitler to the chancellorship, or the National Socialists' takeover of the Reichstag. It was his promotion to major on October 1 and the accompanying transfer out of the Infantry School at Dresden and into the 17th Infantry Regiment in Goslar, in the Harz Mountains. There he would take command of III Battalion—the regiment's *Jäger* battalion. Once again the round peg was slipped effortlessly into the round hole: his years as an instructor in Dresden taken together with his wartime experience bid fair to combine into a particularly dynamic battalion commander.

There was no Alpenkorps, there were no mountain battalions, in the Reichswehr: the drill and parade-ground traditions of such units were carried on by a handful of *Jäger* ("Hunter" or "Stalker") battalions. But aside from a few distinctions in uniform and insignia, the *Jäger* battalions were, in fact, ordinary line units; they lacked any specialized training, and had no higher physical standards than did the Reichswehr's other infantry battalions. That was an unsatisfactory state of affairs to Major Rommel: if his battalion was going to call itself a *Jäger* battalion, it would *be* a *Jäger* battalion, and no sooner had he arrived in Goslar than he set about making it one.

In a small, closed professional community such as was the Reichswehr, everyone knew everyone else by reputation, if not by name or even personally. Rommel, then, was not exactly an unknown quantity coming to the 17th Infantry: he had already acquired something of a reputation for his dynamic classes and lectures at the Infantry School; then there was his well-known ego, which would hardly have been a secret among his new colleagues at Goslar. Despite the *Pour le Mérite* and the Iron Cross First Class that he wore, his officers, likely believing that he had gone soft in four years as a classroom instructor and was no longer up to the rigors of commanding a combat unit, thought to take him down a peg. Not long after he had reported to his new posting, they invited him to climb to the top of a nearby mountain and then ski to the bottom. Rommel readily agreed, then invited them to repeat the excursion with him—three more times. The officers demurred at the suggestion of a fifth round trip and Rommel had made his point.

Rommel insisted, in the finest *Jäger* tradition, that all of his officers learn to hunt and shoot. He was firmly convinced that developing such skills improved junior officers' tactical skills, by giving them a better, more practical appreciation of terrain and cover. He also insisted on a higher level of marksmanship for the other ranks, and made physical fitness a top priority for everyone. And he led by example, becoming a familiar sight every morning, jogging along the side of the road, his arms held up against his chest, his breathing deep and rhythmic, putting in his requisite 2 miles. And while he was strict, he was no martinet: he encouraged his men to seek him out when they encountered problems that could not be resolved through regular procedures and channels, or ask his counsel on personal issues. It was almost, but not quite, a paternalistic approach to command. He had learned in four years of warfare that young soldiers can readily come to regard their officers, who often were at best just a few years older, as father figures. The half-derisive, half-affectionate appellation "the Old Man" soldiers everywhere have given their commanding officers since the days of Leonidas' hoplites has always been a many-layered one. Experience had taught Rommel that mutual trust and confidence between officers and men often meant the difference between life and death for both, and that in peacetime or war, maintaining an Olympian detachment from his men was not the way a good officer created such a bond.

Rommel would spend two years in command of III Battalion, and they would be two of the happiest years of his life. Secure in his profession, happy in his home and family, Rommel's world remained largely insular, with little time for and even less interest in politics. But for all of his focus on his profession, Rommel could no longer ignore Hitler and the Nazis; events would conspire to ensure that he would be unable to remain the fundamentally apolitical officer he had been in the Reichswehr. Whereas it can reasonably be asserted that the Weimar Republic had ever entered his life, the Third Reich would positively intrude on it. In this he was no different than sixty-five million other Germans.

Immediately upon becoming chancellor, Adolf Hitler began to accrue power and alter the nature of the office. Virulent anti-Communism was part of National Socialist dogma, and the claim that Germany was on the brink of a Communist revolution had been one of the cornerstones of Nazi electioneering. When the Reichstag building was destroyed by arson on February 27, Hitler immediately blamed the German Communist Party and used the incident as a pretext for the suspension at will of habeas corpus throughout Germany. A month later, the Reichstag, controlled by Nazi-dominated coalition of extreme right-wing parties, passed the *Gesetz zur Behebung der Not von Volk und Reich* ("Law to Remedy the Distress of People and Reich") a blatant enabling act which allowed Hitler, as chancellor, to rule by decree for four years. Paul von Hindenburg, the former field marshal of the old Imperial Army, who had been elected the Republic's second (and last) president, succeeding Friedrich Ebert, signed it without comment. Eighteen months later, in August 1934, Hindenburg was dead, and the last obstacle between Hitler and absolute personal power was removed; Hitler used the Enabling Act to merge the chancellorship with the presidency to create a new office, "*der Führer.*"

The summer of 1934 was filled with momentous events in Germany. In May, the soon-to-be-dreaded People's Court, presided over by Roland Freisler, was established. On June 14, Benito Mussolini, Il Duce of Fascist Italy, and Adolf Hitler met for the first time; two weeks later, a non-aggression pact between Germany and Poland was signed. But one incident that summer would send tremors reverberating across Europe: the Night of the Long Knives, the systematic purge of the Nazi Sturmabteilung—the SA—which, by the time it was done, would bind Adolf Hitler and the German Army together in an insoluble bond of blood.

The SA was the spawn of the Freikorps, the quasi-military reactionary bands of ex-soldiers who fought gun-battles with communists, socialists, and liberals in the streets of German cities in the first years of the Republic, and the Nazi Party. Like the Freikorps, the SA filled its ranks with disillusioned and disgruntled ex-soldiers who despised the Republic, along with a leavening of beer-hall brawlers and street thugs. Known as the Brownshirts for the distinctive color of their uniform, the SA was the official brute squad of the National Socialist German Workers Party, tasked with silencing dissenters and hecklers at Party rallies and gatherings, usually through the liberal use of fists, boots, brass knuckles and blackjacks. Originally small in number, as the Party grew, so did the SA, led by Captain Ernst Röhm, a one-time officer in the Bavarian Army and later the Reichswehr; he had been dismissed from the latter for his political activities. By the late 1920s, as the Nationalsozialistische Deutsche Arbeiterpartie grew from a regional political curiosity in Bavaria to a nationwide organization, to the point where popular reference to it had been reduced to merely its initials—the NSDAP—or contracted into simply the Nazi Party, the SA grew apace, until by 1930, it numbered a million members. By now it was the Nazis' "official" militia, its mission to intimidate into impotence by whatever means necessary the Party's political opposition. In keeping with National Socialist doctrine, communists, socialists, liberals, and Jews were the priority targets of such actions—which included vandalism, arson, assault, and murder. Gun battles in the streets of Berlin, Munich, Hamburg, and other major German cities with Communists and their sympathizers, usually the Rotfrontkämpferbund (the Red Soldiers' Front—a Communist Party-supported counter to the SA) became commonplace. June 1932 saw the worst single month of political violence prior to the Nazi assumption of power: there were more than 400 street battles all across Germany; 82 people were killed, some of them innocent bystanders. The violence served two purposes: one was the suppression of organized political opposition to the Hitler and the Nazis, the other was coercion of the population into supporting the Nazis by persuading the German people that the violence would end when Hitler came to power.

It was not to be. The SA had always been a semi-autonomous organization within the Nazi Party structure, and by January 1933 it was suffering from a severe case of divided loyalties as a consequence. While Adolf Hitler, now Reichskanzler Hitler, was the titular head of the Sturmabteilung, its true leader was Röhm, who was becoming increasingly dissatisfied with Hitler and unhappy with what he regarded as the National Socialists' "unfinished revolution." With the Nazis' political opponents all sufficiently cowed, or having been eliminated outright, in the weeks which followed Hitler's appointment as chancellor, the Nazis' requirement for the SA's strong-arm tactics evaporated; the SA seemed blithely unaware of this fact. Now ordinary German citizens, police officers, or even in some cases, foreign diplomats, became targets of SA violence, as the "Storm Troopers," as the SA men styled themselves, gave vent to the habits of violence they had followed for the previous decade. Rather than rein in his thugs, Röhm encouraged them, seeing the potential for instability their actions represented as an opportunity to press for a "second revolution," its objective being the dispossession of the businessmen and industrialists, the same conservative elements of German society which had financed the rise of the Nazi Party, seeing it as a potential bulwark against communism and radical socialism.

There had always been a genuinely "socialist" wing of the Nazi hierarchy, the most prominent among them being the propaganda minister, Joseph Göbbels, Gottfried Feder, one of the founders of the original Deutsche Arbeiterpartie who had pretensions of being an economist, Walther Darré, one of a handful of Nazis possessed of a PhD and who could at least make a claim to being an intellectual, and Röhm. With their generally feeble grasp of economics, these distinctly "socialist" National Socialists spurned capitalism, advocating instead nationalizing most industries, worker control of the means of production, and the confiscation and redistribution of property and wealth of the upper class. The Brownshirts, whose beer-swilling seems to have blinded them to political reality, regarded themselves as the spearhead of the "*Nationalsozialistische* revolution," never realizing that the true purpose of the National Socialist movement was solely to elevate Adolf Hitler to power. The Nazis never truly possessed a coherent political or economic doctrine, an awkward fact for Röhm and his cronies, as it rendered any pretensions to a true revolution meaningless. Nevertheless, the self-deception continued, with Röhm publicly declaring to the ranks of the Sturmabteilung that once the Nazis' grasp on the levers of power was sufficiently firm, even more radical changes would take place in the German political and social landscape, with the SA being the chief beneficiary.

Natürliche, this was alarming to the German industrialists, particularly the firms of Krupp, Thyssen, and I. G. Farben, who had been the key financial backers of Hitler's rise to power, and they demanded assurances that the "second revolution" rhetoric of Röhm and company was just that— hot air. Hitler, whose position was not yet absolutely secure, and who knew that he needed the continued support of the industrialists, now and in the years immediately ahead as he rearmed Germany in preparation for settling with the Allies once and for all the hash of Versailles, soothed their worried brows. He would act, he reassured them, long before Röhm could begin to bring about his "second revolution."

By the beginning of 1933, Röhm was exploring ways to expand the power of the SA, if need be at Hitler's expense, to make that revolutionary dream come true. Having been given a seat on the National Defense Council, he soon began to demand a more expanded role for the SA in the German armed forces, envisioning a day in what he was confident would be the not-too-distant future when his storm troopers, now over three million strong, replaced the Reichswehr as Germany's national army. In a letter sent to General Walther von Reichenau, the chief of the Reichswehr's Ministerial Office, the liaison between the army and the Nazi party, on October 2, 1933, Röhm declared: "I regard the Reichswehr now only as a training school for the German people. The conduct of war, and therefore of mobilization as well, in the future is the task of the SA."[46]

The army was justifiably alarmed, as it regarded, and with good reason, the SA to be an undisciplined mob, brawlers well-versed in breaking heads in street fights but little else, hardly a combat-trained, let alone combat-ready, army. There were also open allegations of widespread corruption and immorality within the ranks of the SA which the Reichswehr found intolerable. Hitler, who had attained only the rank of *gefreiter* (corporal) during the Great War, and knew that he would have never risen out of the non-commissioned ranks in the old Imperial Army, privately shared much of Röhm's animosity toward the army's traditionalists, with their aristocratic pretensions and preferrences, as the army would one day discover to its cost. But for Hitler, the support of the Reichswehr (and to a lesser extent the Reichsmarine) was vital to his ultimate ambition: the (illegal under the German constitution) succession to the ailing Paul von Hindenburg as *Reichspräsident*. A compromise of sorts was offered to Röhm, whereby in exchange for his formal acknowledgment that the SA was subordinate to the Reichswehr, it would announced that the SA was now an auxiliary arm of the Reichswehr, transforming Röhm's private militia into an official arm of the government. Röhm, however, despite what he might say publicly, was far from satisfied with what he regarded as less than half a loaf, and declared to his comrades that he did not feel at all bound to accept orders "from that ridiculous corporal."[47]

The deciding moment for Hitler apparently came on April 11, 1934, when he met with the senior officers of the Reichswehr and the Reichsmarine aboard the navy's new flagship, *Deutschland*. It was here that he first openly sought the support of the armed forces for his plans to unify the offices of *Reichskanzler* and *Reichspräsident* following von Hindenburg's imminent demise. There would be a price, he knew, but he was confident it would be one he was willing to pay. It was: the assembled generals and admirals required that Hitler pledge to expand the Reichswehr and Reichsmarine; recognize their primacy as Germany's only land and naval armed forces; emasculate the SA; and marginalize Ernst Röhm. Hitler, seeing that such a pact would leave himself and the *offizierkorps* mutually indebted, and counting on an opportunity arising in the future by which he could call his half of the debt due, agreed without reservation.

The last day of June was set for the beginning of what would become known as the Night of the Long Knives, and lists of SA members marked for summary execution—along with particularly bothersome opponents of Hitler and the Nazis, as well as a handful of individuals with whom particular Party members had long-standing grudges—were drawn up. At dawn on June 30, Röhm was arrested by Hitler personally at the SA leader's home in Bad Wiessee; this act was the signal for the rest of the Nazi assassination squads to begin their work. Between June 30 and July 2, 1934, the whole of the SA leadership was purged; at least 85 people were done to death, including General Kurt von Schleicher and his wife—von Schliecher had been Hitler's predecessor as chancellor; a born intriguer, von Schliecher was a staunch opponent of Hitler, if only because the new chancellor stood in the way of his own ambitions. Gustav Ritter von Kahr, a Bavarian state commissioner who put down Hitler's abortive 1923 coup—immortalized as the "Beer Hall Putsch"—and Gregor Strasser, a one-time Nazi who had broken with Hitler were also among the victims. When the slaughter was over, the power of the SA was broken forever: although the organization would only cease to exist when the Third Reich itself was extinguished in 1945, it would never again play any meaningful role in German politics.

There was a high irony in purging the SA leadership and marginalizing the SA itself: Hitler had removed from the scene the only force in Germany which could have protected him from the army, should the *offizierkorps* choose not to follow him. The nascent SS, though numerous, was still too poorly armed and organized to ensure that Hitler would or could remain in power. Yet such was Hitler's own belief, rightly as it turned out, that he had the measure of both the officer corps and the mass of the German people: in their relief at the removal of the threat of an SA-led revolution, they would rally to him, military and civilians alike binding themselves to Hitler in a horrible parody of a blood oath. His moral ascendency over the army was now all but complete.

In this Hitler was the beneficiary of Germany's experience with the Freikorps and the *Femen*: however despised it was, the violence which they had introduced into German politics in the half-decade following the Great War had gradually become an accepted part of the political process in the Weimar Republic. Thus the German people had not merely resigned themselves to the sort of street thuggery the Nazis had carried on in the successive election campaigns leading up to their triumph in January 1933: they had by this time come to accept as natural that this was the way things were done, especially by the myrmidons of the New Order. The Night of the Long Knives would prove to be the cats-paw of the whirlwind that would be reaped by the Third Reich, sown by the wind of the Second. Otto von Bismarck had assured the Germans more than sixty years earlier that "The great issues of the day will not be settled by speeches and majority resolutions, but by iron and blood. . ." but the Iron Chancellor had been speaking of how irreconcilable differences between nations would be settled, not the manner in which the *Volk* would decide disputes among themselves. Yet his words had set the stage for exactly that, and it was precisely what the Germans had chosen to do: having accepted violence as not merely the ultimate but the preferred arbiter between nations, it was inevitable that they should embrace *"eisen und blut"* in settling their own affairs.

But if the German *offizierkorps* had made a deal with the devil—and it had—in its defense it could be fairly said that it did not truly know the identity of the contractor. It was much the situation to which the Prince of Denmark gave voice: "For the Devil hath power to assume a pleasing shape"; that is precisely what Hitler did. The swift and decisive action he took in purging Röhm and his henchmen while simultaneously marginalizing the SA—and by implication removing the threat of a genuine revolution and a German civil war—effectively obscured the fact that the selfsame ruthlessness could one day be applied to the army and its officers, or even the entire nation. Only a very perceptive few saw this terrible truth at the time; it was with a chilling prescience that Erwin Planck, a retired infantry officer, wrote to his friend General Werner von Fritsch, saying, ". . . if you look on without lifting a finger, sooner or later you will meet the same fate."[48]

Consequently a measure of caution must be exercised before categorically castigating the German generals for their wholehearted endorsement of Hitler: it was impossible for them to see that Hitler was leading them—and Germany—into a moral and physical abyss from which none of them would escape intact, and most of them never escape at all. No one, possibly not even Hitler himself even in his worst psychotic dreams, truly knew what would be the full reach of the Stygian darkness which lay ahead. Only a select few were ever allowed even a peek at the wide-eyed, raving lunatic that lurked behind the composed façade which in these years Hitler presented to the world, and they were in their own ways so malignant and perverse that Hitler and his "philosophies" did not seem at all unusual, or a cause for alarm. Understandably, then, the army applauded the Night of the Long Knives, while the ailing President Hindenburg, Germany's highly revered military hero, sent a telegram saying, "From the reports placed before me I learn that you, by your determined action and your brave personal intervention, have nipped treason in the bud. He who would make history must also be able to shed blood. You have saved the German nation from serious danger. For this I express to you my most profound thanks and sincere appreciation." There were no protests forthcoming from the Reichstag, already settling comfortably into its role as Adolf Hitler's rubber stamp. The German press, having already undergone the first waves of suppression and censorship under Göbbels' Propaganda Ministry, maintained a judicious silence. Among the German people, however, there was shock at the violence of the Nazis' actions against some of their own, but of openly expressed anger or outrage there was little. No doubt some of this could be ascribed to fear of the new secret police apparatus, the Gestapo, but for most Germans, there was a sense that the SA had earned their punishment. The Brownshirts had been arrogant, vulgar, and violent, too many innocent Germans had suffered physically or financially from their gangster-like depredations so sympathy was decidedly limited. Victor Klemperer, a Dresden-born Jew who converted to Protestantism before the Great War, recorded in his diary how one close friend praised Hitler's "personal courage, decisiveness and effectiveness;" another matter-of-factly summed up his feelings: "[Hitler] simply sentenced them"—the guilt and the deserved punishment of Röhm and the SA were already foregone. Historian David Fraser neatly encapsulated the attitude of the German public: "Hitler—dependent as he had been on the SA in his early years and owing them much affection—had acted with moral courage and saved Germany. . . . A sickness seemed to have passed, and the physician—persuasive, optimistic, and successful—was Adolf Hitler."[49]

For his part, Rommel's reactions to the events of June 30 to July 2 were ambiguous. It was impossible for him to have remained ignorant of what happened to Röhm and the other SA leaders—every officer and ranker in the Reichswehr knew what had happened to them. Undeniably the Nazi house had required a good cleaning, and the looming presence of the SA, along with Röhm's thinly veiled hints about a German civil war, his "second revolution," were too immediate to be dismissed as mere bluster. Yet it also seemed to Rommel that Hitler had gone too far, had overreacted, in the degree of brutality he exercised in punishing Röhm and his SA henchmen. "The Führer didn't have to do that," he told his battalion adjutant. "He doesn't realize how powerful he is, otherwise he could have exercised his strength in a more generous and legitimate way."[50]

The comment is unsettling, for it conveys an essential naivety as to Adolf Hitler's true character, which Erwin Rommel would retain until barely a year before his own death. Whether or not it was necessary for Hitler to carry out such a bloody and brutal purge of the SA leadership was immaterial: all that mattered to Hitler was that he could do so, without let or hindrance. He had now defined the fundamental nature of his regime: when addressing the Reichstag on July 13 in a speech broadcast nationwide, he declared:

In this hour I was responsible for the fate of the German people, and thereby I became the supreme judge of the German people. I gave the order to shoot the ringleaders in this treason, and I further gave the order to cauterise down to the raw flesh the ulcers of this poisoning of the wells in our domestic life. Let the nation know that its existence—which depends on its internal order and security—cannot be threatened with impunity by anyone! And let it be known for all time to come that if anyone raises his hand to strike the State, then certain death is his lot.[51]

Implicit in Hitler's speech was his self-identification with the state— *"L'état, c'est moi!"* as it were—with the explicit assurance that anyone who threatened the state—and in so doing, Hitler—would meet the same fate as Röhm. He did not even find it necessary to offer the fig leaf of declaring that he and Germany were one; henceforth the only loyalty which mattered in Germany was not to Germany, but to Adolf Hitler.

A month later the idea became a codified reality. On August 20, two weeks after President von Hindenburg finally shuffled ponderously off to Valhalla and Hitler decreed the unification of the offices of *Reichskanzler* and *Reichspräsident*, the cabinet decreed the "Law On The Allegiance of Civil Servants and Soldiers of the Armed Forces" (*Gesetz über die Vereidigung der Beamten und der Soldaten der Wehrmacht*), requiring all soldiers and civil servants to take an oath of personal loyalty to Hitler. Previously soldiers had sworn the *Reichswehreid*, pledging their loyalty to "the People and the Fatherland" (*Volk und Vaterland*); civil servants were further required to swear that they would uphold the constitution and laws of Germany. Now every man and woman in government service was required to make a new pledge, one which vacated any previous oaths sworn, no matter to whom:

Ich schwöre bei Gott diesen heiligen Eid, daß ich dem Führer des Deutschen Reiches und Volkes Adolf Hitler, dem Oberbefehlshaber der Wehrmacht, unbedingten Gehorsam leisten und als tapferer Soldat bereit sein will, jederzeit für diesen Eid mein Leben einzusetzen.

I swear by God this sacred oath that to the Leader of the German empire and people, Adolf Hitler, supreme commander of the armed forces, I shall render unconditional obedience and that as a brave soldier I shall at all times be prepared to give my life for this oath.

This would be known to history as the *Fahneneid*.

The oath was not Hitler's idea, as is commonly believed: it was drafted by Defence Minister General Werner von Blomberg and General Walther von Reichenau, the chief of the Ministerial Office, who both held very strong Nazi sympathies (von Reichenau was a Party member, in open defiance of Reichswehr regulations), and who were both thoroughgoing toadies. When presented with the new oath of allegiance, however, unlike Caesar at the Lupercal when thrice "offered a kingly crown, which he did thrice refuse," Hitler in no way demurred. Historically, Germans have always taken oaths of any kind with utmost solemnity—in this the Germans of the 1930s were no different than their ancestors who swore fealty to Teutonic knights, petty barons, or Hohenzollern princes. The *Fahneneid* was yet another chain by which Hitler could bind the German people to him and his fate, this one perhaps more significant than the others, as it was a spiritual binding. Erwin Rommel for one would hold firmly to this oath— until the pivotal day in June 1944 when he came to realize that not he but Adolf Hitler had dissolved it.

The first meeting of Major Rommel and der Führer came about on September 30, 1934. The occasion was an impromptu inspection of an honor guard provided by Rommel's *Jäger* battalion while Hitler was in Goslar to lend his presence to Goslar's Harvest Festival, an enormous open-air gathering of peasants and farm workers from all over Germany—upwards of a million of them. A photograph of the event exists, showing Hitler, hat in hand, marching down a line of assembled soldiers standing rigidly at "Present arms!" while beside him walks Major Rommel, who is bearing a ceremonial sword and wearing a slightly outsized (on him) coal-scuttle helmet, looking for all the world like an ambulatory, *feldgrau* mushroom. Rommel appears to be frowning, and there is a particularly grim set to his mouth, as if he were angry. If so, he had good reason to be: just a few moments earlier he had been involved in a row with the SS major commanding Hitler's personal bodyguard. When called upon to have his battalion fall in for the Führer's *inspektion*, Rommel was told that a rank of black-uniformed SS troopers would be interposed between his troops and Hitler, allegedly for the latter's "protection." Infuriated, Rommel refused to turn out his battalion, declaring that if his soldiers' oaths of loyalty weren't sufficient guarantee of der Führer's safety, then they would remain in their barracks. Flustered, unaccustomed to such open defiance, the SS officer backed down and the "asphalt soldiers" were dismissed. There is no record of whether Hitler heard anything of the incident, or if he did, what he thought of it. Two years would pass before Hitler and Rommel again crossed paths.

The incident with the SS was indicative of how little regard Rommel had for most of the Nazi apparatus. The SS might be better disciplined than the SA—they were undoubtedly sharper dressers; the SA uniforms had come from surplus pre-Great War stocks of tropical issue—but they were not what Rommel would have ever regarded as real soldiers, and the psuedo-mystical mumbo-jumbo with which Heinrich Himmler attempted to surround his "new order of Teutonic Knights" was, to Rommel, beyond laughable. The hard-headed, practical Swabian in him saw that it served no purpose, but served only to draw personnel and resources away from the Reichswehr, or, as it became known on May 21, 1935, the Wehrmacht. On that date Hitler decreed that peacetime conscription, hitherto barred by the Versailles treaty, would be resumed; he had already announced that Germany would begin openly rearming on March 16. The immediate goal was the creation of an army of 36 divisions; further expansion would follow as Germany's industries regained the capacity to adequately supply and equip them.

This momentous announcement was greeted with an outpouring of patriotic sentiment all across Germany. Hitler was playing a cagey game, as the realities of rearmament were more complex than merely putting a third of a million young German men in uniforms and passing rifles out to them. A rearmament program would virtually assure full employment throughout Germany, and revitalize several industries that were failing in the economic morass of the Great Depression. This, combined with vast public works projects, such as the construction of the *autobahnen* (which had its own military significance), would see the fulfillment of the promises which Hitler had made to the German people that he would restore prosperity to the Fatherland. It was yet one more example of that perverse magic which Hitler was able to work on the Volk in those years before Germany again went to war. Little wonder then that the Germans' sense of loyalty to their Führer continued to grow.

But there was more to that loyalty than only fat pay envelopes and full lunch pails. It was a loyalty produced of genuine feeling, not the product of coercion by the Gestapo. For the German people, the swastika did not begin as a representation of evil, it was a symbol of hope and change.

The key to comprehending the "why" behind the loyalty offered to Hitler by the German people is understanding what is actually meant by that shopworn phrase "he restored the German people's national pride." What Hitler did, bluntly, was make Germany—and with the nation the German Army—relevant to the affairs of Europe and the world once again. What shone so brightly for the German people in all that Hitler was telling them—indeed, shone so brilliantly that it dazzled them to much of what else he was saying, particularly the most sinister truths about his intentions—was his dedication to Germany's rearmament. After the three-quarters of a century of near-continuous violence since 1939, the concept is difficult to grasp for most people—that a large standing army, a powerful navy, a strong air force should be the source of passionate national pride, and that someone preaching, promising, tanks, guns, aircraft and warships should be regaled as a national savior rather than dismissed as a dangerous warmonger. But Mao Zhe Dong's best-known aphorism holds—quite correctly—that "All political power proceeds from the barrel of a gun." And there is where Hitler turned armaments into magic.

He was fond of repeating to the German people that the Versailles treaty had left Germany *"Heerlos, Wehrlos, Ehrlos"*—without an army, without power, and without honor. The words stung, not because they were true, but because the Germans *believed* them to be true. What is almost always overlooked by observers—then and now—trying to explain the phenomenon of Adolf Hitler and the Nazi Party is that the Treaty of Versailles formalized, codified, and institutionalized a perpetual marginalization of Germany. For the century following the Peace of Westphalia in 1648, moral, physical and financial exhaustion, helped in no small part by Hapsburg ambitions, prevented the German states, a motley collection of baronies, counties, duchies and princedoms, from marshaling the resources as well as the political will necessary to coalesce into a unified German nation. When Prussia began to rise as power under Frederick the Great, Louis XV of France embraced the "Reversal of Alliances" in 1756 in large part to thwart the Prussian king's ambitions, and Bonaparte, while reducing the number of petty German states from more than three hundred to fewer than forty, still adroitly employed a policy of "divide and conquer" in order to continue to keep the Germans marginalized, a principle to which Metternich of Austria adhered well into the middle of the nineteenth century. When Wilhelm I and von Bismarck achieved the unification of the several German states into the German Empire in 1871, they created a nation which was the military, political, and economic juggernaut of the Continent—proof, to the German people, of their previous repression—a juggernaut which would be spitefully rendered militarily, politically, and economically irrelevant by Germany's defeat in November 1918. It was worse than impotence, and it was humiliating to a people as proud as the *Volk*.

Versailles had formalized that irrelevance: with her army diminished in size and power to little more than a national gendarmerie, her navy reduced to a glorified coast guard, forbidden any form of air force and denied modern weapons, burdened with a throttling reparations debt that was literally incalculable, Germany was reduced to abject impotence, her very security dependent on the continued goodwill of smaller, weaker neighbors. This was the same Germany whose military strength had for almost fifty years required that she be a part of every calculus in international politics.

Three-quarters of a century later, looking back at the monstrosity—and monstrousness—of the Third Reich, it requires a prodigious feat of simultaneous imagination and sympathy to be able to remember that in 1935 all the excesses of the Nazi regime lay in the future, and that no one at the time truly knew they were coming. The Nuremburg Laws, the betrayal of Czechoslovakia, the rape of Poland, the Sonderkommando and Einsatzgruppen, the *Nacht und Nebel* decrees, the Wannsee Conference, the *Endlösung*, the death camps, medical experiments, slave labor—not to mention the second devastating European war in less than a generation—all seem inevitable in retrospect, as innumerable decisions and actions, large and small, whether by Hitler, his henchmen, or petty, anonymous bureaucrats, are seen to conspire and converge to produce such a monstrous edifice. And yet all of it was far from being so when Hitler and the Nazis assumed power in 1933: while in retrospect that inevitability may seem as a given, the stark truth is that none of it was visible as such before the events took place—inevitability is only obvious after the fact.

And even as Hitler's malignity began to manifest itself, the magic he worked on the German people still held. Even men like Erwin Rommel would be splattered, if not actually tarred, with the brush of National Socialism because he found Hitler fascinating. And that was precisely the problem: Hitler *was* fascinating. William Manchester best summed up how the Führer accomplished this feat when he made the point that

> . . . National Socialism at its height was one of the most potent political medicines the world has ever known. For xenopobic Germans the tug was irresistable; whatever their reservations about *die Neuordnung*, they joined ranks behind Hitler whenever the Reich seemed threatened. He knew that they would, and he made certain that the threat was never far off. That was part of the Führer's genius. His foreign policy made war inevitable, yet each link in the chain of aggression toughened the loyalty of the *Herrenvolk*. . . .[52]

It would be utterly unrealistic to expect that senior German officers, who were entrusted with the safety and security of the Reich, would respond with less alacrity than the general populace to such provocation. And Hitler knew his audience all too well: in perpetuating the sense of impending danger to *Vaterland* and *Volk*, he preyed on that peculiarly Teutonic fear of encirclement, an apprehension that first took root in the Germanic tribes of the Teutoburgerwald. It was a fear that became such an inseparable part of the German character that the language itself cast anyone who was not of the *Volk* into a single, vast collective noun, with all of its subtly dreadful implications—*Auslander*, outsiders.

The Nazis were an authoritarian regime, true, but the Germans were a people comfortable with, even embracing of, living under an authoritarian government. How could they have been otherwise? The Germans had never known anything but life under authoritarian rule—aside from the brief experiment of the Weimar Republic, the nature of German government changed only in degree, never in fundamental form. The Germans followed—obeyed—Hitler and the Nazis because it was their nature as a people to obey: they had never any example, any experience, to follow in order to do otherwise. Recognizing the truth of the German people's experience does not exonerate them, for the Nazi regime was history's greatest exercise in immorality, and morality is—and must be—based on more than experience; but it does explain them, and so makes them comprehensible, if not understandable.

And yet, explanation is not excuse. It was here that the German people willingly deferred to their national, ethnic, and cultural heritage, and in doing so became, as Daniel Goldhagen unforgettably labeled them, "Hitler's willing executioners." Historically, though they were neither docile nor stupid, the Germans were a people accustomed to and comfortable with being led. Choosing their own destiny through consensus was unfamiliar to them, they had no tradition of self-determination. The *motifs* of *autorität* ("authority") and its handmaiden *obrigkeit* ("duty") ran through every strata of German society, from the *Vater* ruling his household with a (hopefully) benign paternalism, to the *Konzernherr* directing his business with a single-minded purposefulness, to the Kaiser, whose title was a Germanic rendering of Cæsar, with all of the authoritarianism that implied. The Reichstag, established by the constitution of 1871, had, for all of its bluster and occasional rebelliousness, been little more than a rubber stamp for Imperial polices; from the day of its founding the German Empire was dominated by the Kaiser and the chancellor, sometimes individually, sometimes in tandem, depending on who sat on the throne and who occupied the office.

It had been Germany's fortune or misfortune, depending on point of view, that in the first decades of the empire its destiny had been guided by men of powerful character possessed of strong, if sometimes somewhat maleable, moral authority. Its first chancellor, Prince Otto von Bismarck, was at once a passionate patriot and a consummate practitioner of *Realpolitik*, who imbued his office with an air of *gravitas* and *dignitas* that would wrap around his successors like a mantle, however ineffectual they may have been. Likewise, the first Kaiser, Wilhelm I, was a strong-willed monarch who was unshakable in his belief that he ruled by divine right—with an implicit obligation to rule wisely. He was also no mere figurehead who unquestioningly endorsed his chancellor's policies, though he has at times been portrayed as such: his disagreements with von Bismarck, though few and far between, were positively Olympian when they did occur. Together these two men, whose leadership was generally sage and, though undeniably ultraconservative, rather tolerant by the standards of the day, set high the bar by which their successors would be measured. Perhaps too high, for none of those who followed would come near to measuring up to their gauge.

Nonetheless, so great was their stature within the Reich that their successors could bask in the reflected glory of the first Kaiser and chancellor and appear to be just as wise and strong. It was a lie, though not a conscious, deliberate one— ironically, perhaps, the German people's first exposure to the *Grosse Lüge*, "the Big Lie"—and so the Germans continued to believe that men who were not chosen by the *Volk*, nor directly (or even indirectly) answerable to them, were somehow naturally imbued with genuine leadership qualities. Disaster came when, with the advent of the Weimar Republic, the German people were expected to choose from among themselves men who possessed such *führungsqualitäten*: they simply did not know how to recognize them. What could they be expected to do, then, when a man who seemed to be so gifted appeared on the stage of German national politics? Adolf Hitler was not the man they needed, but he convinced them, by playing on their desire to be convinced, that he was the man they wanted.

Thus, when the Third Reich was looming upon them, the Germans never saw it coming. Accustomed as they were to governments that were authoritative in nature but which had always recognized the necessity of some degree of self-restraint, their experience never gave them cause to imagine the malicious abuses of power which an authoritative regime which deliberately abandoned all restraint could commit. Indeed, there was nothing in Germany's national experience that could have given them reason to believe that such a terrible regime could exist, let alone that they would welcome it with open arms.

Eventually the scales would fall from Erwin Rommel's eyes and all of the worst of the Third Reich would be manifest to him, but that moment was still years in the future. In early 1936, he was a freshly minted *oberstleutnant*—lieutenant colonel—the rapid expansion of the Wehrmacht having accelerated promotions for all of the former Reichswehr officers. He was no longer a battalion commander in Goslar: in September 1935, when his promotion was posted, he was transferred to the War Academy in Potsdam, the cradle of German militarism. He exultantly shared the news by letter with Lucie: "I have been earmarked as a full-blown instructor at the new Potsdam school of infantry! Top secret! So make tracks for Potsdam, but keep it under your hat!" There was a delicious irony to this posting, as

Rommel had never been invited to attend the academy to supposedly learn the arcana of warfare—now he was an instructor there, assigned to teach those very mysteries to young officers and officer cadets.[53]

Those young men found Rommel to be as dynamic and entertaining a lecturer as he had been at Dresden. He had a calculated disdain for officers who wore the coveted double crimson stripes of the General Staff, regarding them as mere theoreticians rather than real soldiers—an attitude which endeared him to his students, as soldiers everywhere enjoy seeing pompous superiors taken down a peg, especially when it is done by someone wearing credentials of the sort Rommel displayed with his Iron Cross and *Pour le Mérite*. As always, he insisted on physical fitness being a top priority—again, the voice of his experience in the Great War, thrice wounded but never evacuated out of his unit, giving an especial validity to this conviction. In keeping with his irregard for General Staff officers, he had little patience for textbook answers to tactical problems posed to his students. He was known to bark out, when someone would begin to quote some long-dead military authority in response to a classroom exercise, "I don't want to hear what Clausewitz thinks, tell me what *you* think!"[54]

Erwin, Lucie, and Manfred lived quietly in Potsdam; Rommel was never much for socializing—again the Swabian in him manifesting itself in his preference for his home life. He spent much of his time riding, shooting, swimming, giving free rein to his passion for keeping physically fit. Always a bit puritanical—the influence of his Lutheran upbringing, no doubt—he never smoked and only occasionally drank alcohol; he was no prude, however: he never demanded that his men adopt his own habits, though he did expect them to accept the consequences and responsibilities that came with whatever lifestyles they chose—just as, in fact, he had done himself. He also worked to keep his mind agile, finally accomplishing what had been one of his childhood goals, memorizing the table of logarithms. The unfulfilled engineer in him would always fuel that passion for mathematics. It was a passion he tried to share with Manfred, but apparently whatever engineering genes Rommel had inherited he never passed on to his son. Meanwhile, Manfred, now eight years of age, was beginning to become aware of a larger world around him, which included an imperfect understanding of some aspects of National Socialist dogma. One day while out walking with his father he happened to see a local physician who had a rather large, hooked nose. He innocently asked, "Papa, is he a Jew?" Rommel was, in Manfred's words, "highly indignant." To him, Nazi racial theories were so much claptrap; they would always remain so.[55]

Other ideas put forward by the Party were not so absurd, though not all of them were well executed. One such idea sprang up in February 1937 and Rommel was tapped to put it into action. Someone—it's unclear exactly who—at the War Ministry proposed that the young men of the Hitler Jugend, the Hitler Youth, be given rudimentary military training as part of their summer educational program. And why not? The Führer himself had declared in *Mein Kampf* that the army was to be the ultimate school of patriotic education! Hitler, who had a phenomenal memory, recalled having heard that Lieutenant Colonel Rommel was regarded by his colleagues and superiors as an outstanding instructor. Accordingly, he suggested that Rommel take over this new program. Since suggestions from Hitler were tantamount to orders for his subordinates, soon Erwin Rommel and Baldur von Schirach, the director of the Hitler Youth program, were working together to implement the concept.

The results were not happy. Learning who exactly was responsible for the idea's failure would depend on who was recounting the program's history. According to von Schirach's version of events, Rommel wanted to spend an inordinate amount of time on military instruction; Rommel, the son and grandson of distinguished educators, maintained that there was an excessive emphasis on paramilitary instruction and not enough time spent on traditional education. In his opinion, military instruction could wait until these young men were past adolescence; during the formative years of their teens they should be given as much traditional education as possible. Whatever the truth was, Rommel and von Schirach quarreled incessantly for the better part of a year before the whole program was abandoned as a bad job.

The most likely reason why Hitler remembered Rommel's name was because of an incident that took place some six months before the Hitler Youth scheme was hatched. In September 1936, Rommel was assigned to Hitler's military escort while the Führer was taking part in that year's Reichsparteitag at Nuremberg (better known as the 1936 Nuremberg Rally). It was a routine, almost boring assignment, until the afternoon when Hitler suddenly announced that he would be taking a drive through the countryside south of the city. Rommel had drawn the traffic control duty that day, and Hitler gave specific instructions that no more than six vehicles be allowed to accompany his Mercedes. Rommel dutifully ticked off the first six cars to pass, then quickly stepped out into the street and barred the way for the rest of the would-be entourage. Senior officers and Party *bonzen* (bigwigs) alike railed at Lieutenant Colonel Rommel, who remained unmoved and unmoving, faithful to the Führer's orders. When Hitler returned a few hours later, the furious officials complained vociferously about what they regarded as Rommel's high-handed behavior; Hitler made a point of coming directly to Rommel and personally commending him for the strict execution of his orders.

Rommel came to Hitler's attention yet again in the summer of 1937—and commanded the attention of a good many other Germans as well. While he had been an instructor at the Dresdener Infantry School, Rommel had taken the time to write down and annotate his recollections of his wartime service, adding detail and perspective supplied by official reports from the Army archives; they served as the basis for his lectures on small-unit tactics. While he was at Potsdam, he took these notes, rewrote them to produce a dramatic narrative which he called *Infanterie Greift an—Infantry in the Attack*—and submitted it to Voggenreiter's, a local publisher, who further polished the manuscript and turned it into a proper book, illustrated with maps and diagrams in Rommel's own hand. To Rommel's surprise, the book not only sold, it sold phenomenally, and went through multiple editions. Rommel was simultaneously flattered and embarrassed by the attention the book garnered for him, remarking to a fellow Potsdam instructor that "It's astounding the money there is to be made from such books! I just don't know what to do with all the cash that's flooding in. I can't possibly use it all. I'm happy enough with what I've got already. And I don't like the idea of making money writing up how other good men lost their lives."[56]

It was a pleasant problem to have, but it was a problem nonetheless. Ostentation had never appealed to Erwin and Lucie, and they had always been happy to live within their means. Now, however, the royalties from Rommel's book were adding up, and each fresh royalty check added to a new headache: income taxes. Like any good Swabian, Rommel detested paying taxes on the principle of the thing; the added income from *Infanterie Greift an* simply added to the amount he was obliged to give the government. Careful consultation with the accountants at Voggenreiter's came up with an ingenious solution, however: every year, the publisher would pay whatever royalties the book earned, up to a total of 15,000 marks. Anything over that number was kept on account by the publisher and earned interest, to be paid out if and when Rommel's royalties fell below 15,000 marks. It was all legal and above board—and very, very canny.[57]

The humility Rommel expressed in his confidence to his colleague at the War Academy was far from feigned. False modesty was not one of Rommel's besetting faults—anyone entitled to wear the *Pour le Mérite*, the Iron Cross First Class, and the Silver Wound Badge certainly had no call for such posturing. He was possessed of a streak of vanity of near-epic proportions, and he was not at all adverse to self-promotion. But the concern that he was somehow profiting from other men's deaths or disfigurements was genuine; a reading of *Infantry in the Attack* is memorable in no small part for the recollections about the casualties suffered during the various actions in which Rommel was engaged. Whenever possible, he mentions them by name and rank, they are not mere faceless ciphers or interchangeable parts to him. The straightforward, matter-of-fact accounting he gives for each man's demise bestows a dignity on them, and conveys a sense of genuine loss on Rommel's part. They are the accounting of a man who would never permit the demands of war to overwhelm his humanity.

That the events and incidents described in his book might not, after all, turn out to be Erwin Rommel's only experience with war seemed to be an ever-growing possibility as Germany passed through the latter half of the 1930s. Events were moving with unsettling speed: on October 25, 1936, a Rome–Berlin Axis was declared between Italy and Germany, the much ballyhooed "Pact of Steel," the language of which left no doubt that it was directed at France and Great Britain. Germany had already withdrawn from the League of Nations and the World Disarmament Conference in October 1933. A plebiscite held in January 1935 in accordance with the terms of the Treaty of Versailles and conducted under the auspices of the League, returned a vote whereby more than over 90 percent of the people of the Saarland declared their wish to be reunited with Germany. In the same speech in which Hitler decreed the return of conscription and the expansion of the Wehrmacht to a strength of 600,000 officers and men, he also announced that Germany would create an air force—the Luftwaffe—and expand her navy far beyond the limits set by Versailles; the Anglo-German Naval Agreement, which permitted the Kriegsmarine a total tonnage in warships equal to 35 percent of that of the Royal Navy was signed on June 18. Versailles was becoming increasingly irrelevant.

At dawn on March 7, 1936, acting on instructions from the Führer himself, 19 German infantry battalions marched into the Rhineland, which by the terms of Versailles was to be kept demilitarized in perpetuity. This was the most blatant challenge yet to the treaty; it was also a colossal bluff: should the French Army units stationed to the west of the Rhineland countermarch and offer the least resistance to the encroaching Germans, those same 19 battalions had specific orders to immediately about face and march right back out again. Hitler himself later confessed that "The 48 hours after the march into the Rhineland were the most nerve-wracking in my life. If the French had then marched into the Rhineland we would have had to withdraw with our tails between our legs, for the military resources at our disposal would have been wholly inadequate for even a moderate resistance."[58] But the French did nothing, and as the sun set that evening, Versailles was a dead letter. A few months later, Hitler flexed his growing military muscles for the first time by sending German tanks, artillery, troops, and aircraft to Spain to support General Francisco Franco and his *Falangistas* in the Spanish Civil War. At each new provocation, however blatant, the leaders of the Western democracies, men like Leon Blume and Stanley Baldwin—and later Eduard Daladier and Neville Chamberlain—scowled fearsomely, uttered a few empty phrases about the sanctity of solemn international treaties, issued dire warnings of the consequences should some future violation occur, and then, satisfied that the obligatory motions had indeed been gone through, did nothing more. Hitler was confident that he now had the measure of his opposition: for them, no burden was too heavy, no price too great to pay for peace. In March 1938, Hitler chose to put his conclusions to the test.

CHAPTER FIVE

BLITZKRIEG

Battles are won by slaughter and maneuver.
The greater the general, the more he contributes
in maneuver, the less he demands in slaughter.
—WINSTON CHURCHILL

O n the morning of March 12, 1938, three infantry divisions, a panzer division, and the supporting units of the Wehrmacht's Eighth Army crossed the German border into Austria. Almost twenty years had passed since German soldiers last stood on foreign soil, although this time they came—and were welcomed as—an army of liberation, or at least, unification. This was the beginning of the Anschluss, the union of Austria and Germany, the first step down the road to Adolf Hitler's dream of *Grossdeutschland*, the "Great Germany" which would gather all of Europe's ethnic Germans into the bosom of the Reich.

Not a shot was fired as the dark-gray tanks and trucks rolled along Austria's mountain roads, and if any voices were raised in anger, they were drowned out by the cheers of thousands of Austrians lining the roadsides, waving swastika flags, arms out-thrust in the *Hitlergrüsse*, tossing bouquets of flowers at the passing German troops until the blossoms were heaped on bonnets, hoods, and turret tops. This was a *blumenkrieg*, a war of flowers. It was all extraordinarily *heiter*, that curious, jaunty German word that compounds cheer, brightness, and festivity.

It hardly resembled an invasion, though that is precisely what it was. Called "*Unternehmen Otto*"—Operation *Otto*—Germany's annexation of Austria, however peacefully achieved and warmly received, was an irrevocable breach of not one but two multinational treaties concluded 19 years earlier. The Anschluss violated Article 80 of the Treaty of Versailles, which established that

> Germany acknowledges and will respect the independence of Austria within the frontier which may be fixed in a treaty between that State and the principal Allied and Associated Powers; she agrees that this independence shall be inalienable. . . .[59]

In a similar vein, the Treaty of St. Germain-en-Laye, drawn up simultaneously by the Allies and presented to the Austrian delegation to the peace conference on the same day that the Germans were handed the final draft of the Versailles treaty, declared that

> The independence of Austria is inalienable otherwise than with the consent of the Council of the League of Nations. Consequently Austria undertakes in the absence of the consent of the said Council to abstain from any act which might directly or indirectly or by any means whatever compromise her independence, particularly, and until her admission to membership of the League of Nations, by participation in the affairs of another Power.[60]

Hitler had, of course, made abundantly clear his disdain for Versailles, so it was hardly surprising that he should be ready to reduce the St. Germain treaty to just one more of those "scraps of paper" of which the Germans had become so fond. Almost from the moment that he was certain the French had conceded the *fait accompli* of the remilitarized Rhineland, Hitler systematically bluffed, bullied, threatened, and lied to the Austrian chancellor, Kurt Schuschnigg, in order to create the precise circumstances which would allow the Wehrmacht to march into Austria and be greeted with a nationwide celebration. It was gangster diplomacy, pure and simple, and through it Hitler was able to add Austria to the German Reich without so much as a single shot being fired by either side.

Erwin Rommel played no part in the Anschluss operations: he was still dividing his time between his duties as an instructor at the Staff College in Potsdam and trying to make a go of the Wehrmacht liaison with the Hitler Youth. The Anschluss would have a considerable effect on his next posting, however. His promotion to *oberst* (colonel) went up on August 1, 1937; a year later he was named the commandant of the Theresian War Academy at Wiener Neustadt, just outside of Vienna. The annexation also seems to have encouraged him to be more open in acknowledging his regard for Hitler. Rommel would always find the Nazis as a whole repugnant, however well he might get on with individuals who happened to be Party members or functionaries; Hitler, however, he saw as somehow standing apart from and above the Party and its various apparati. Though hardly inexplicable—Hitler was striving mightily these days to present himself to Germany and the world at large as a statesman, for whom the bigoted, violent rantings in *Mein Kampf* were left behind, the products of a passionate patriot caught up in turbulent times now past—it was certainly naive, particularly for a man of Rommel's intelligence. Unquestionably Hitler's charisma had worked its magic on Rommel, just as it had, and would continue to do, on so many Germans who encountered Hitler face-to-face. It was also a charm which would continue to be spellbinding long after its bearer had morphed into a creature which bore little to no resemblance to the national leader to whom Rommel had sworn personal allegiance. But in 1938, it was still remarkably potent and still bore some passing resemblance to reality.

There were small, superficial changes in Rommel's habits which gave evidence of his shifting attitude—he would frequently close his letters with "*Heil Hitler!*" for example—but more unsettling were the increasingly uncritical nature of his admiration for Hitler, and the bits and pieces of Party jargon that began creeping into his vocabulary. In a confidential report submitted to Berlin following a series of speaking engagements he undertook at the invitation of the Swiss army, he noted that "The young [Swiss] officers, particularly expressed their sympathies with our New Germany. Individuals among them also spoke with remarkable understanding of our Jewish problem."[61]

Germany *did* have a Jewish problem, just as did France, Poland, Belgium, Hungary, and, to a lesser extent, Great Britain. The problem, however, was not the Jews themselves, but rather how they were regarded in their own homelands by their own countrymen. Centuries of teaching by Catholics and Protestants alike that the Jews had put to death Jesus Christ stigmatized an entire people, while the common view held that, because Jews often lived in closed communities, distinct and separate from the surrounding Gentiles, the Jews regarded themselves as a superior people—conveniently ignoring the fact that they "lived apart" because they had been forcibly segregated by secular or Church decree. No amount of fidelity, courage, or assimilation could ever completely put to rest the belief that Jews felt a greater loyalty to themselves as a people than they did to the nations and states where they were born, lived, worked, and died. A people so regarded make easy and convenient targets for angry men and women seeking scapegoats on which blame for their own sufferings can be laid. Angry people are rarely rational and considerate—they are, however, easily misled and manipulated by demagogues and charlatans. Such were the Germans in the 1920s and early 1930s, and Erwin Rommel, who *was* a rational and considerate man, was not entirely immune to the passions that were swirling about the Fatherland during those years. There is a wealth of evidence demonstrating that Rommel thought the Nazis racial and ethnic dogmas and doctrines so much rubbish, and yet even he could not escape expressing himself in the idiom of the times, hence his reference to the "Jewish problem." He would do nothing in the whole of his military career to directly aid and abet the Nazis in carrying out their racial crimes, their genocides, their reign of terror. But that does not mean that Erwin Rommel was entirely innocent.

For where Rommel did aid and abet Hitler and the Nazis, however indirectly, was in countenancing first the Anschluss, followed by the annexation of the Sudentenland six months later, and the occupation of the rump of Czechoslovkia six months after that. While these acts cannot be equated with the crimes against humanity as a whole that were later perpetrated by the Third Reich, they were crimes nonetheless. Rommel and his fellow officers aided and abetted Hitler and his henchmen in the casual, almost contemptuous demolition of the entire edifice of international law, of dealings in good faith between statesmen, of solemn agreements among nations being accorded the same weight and gravity as national law. The enabling acts passed by the Reichstag had rendered the German constitution impotent, the rule of law within the Reich meaningless; little wonder then that the Nazis were convinced that *outside* the Reich international covenants and conventions could be dismissed with an equal lack of regard and a commensurate ease. Crimes against nations became commonplace, even trivial; from there it was an almost trivial step to the commission of crimes against humanity.

It could be argued, reasonably if not compellingly, that Hitler, in abrogating the specific articles of the Versailles treaty which limited the size and scope of the German armed forces, forbad conscription, and prohibited the possession of any advanced armaments, was merely casting aside restrictions on Germany's internal policies which the Allies had no real right, moral or legal, to impose in the first place. It could be further argued that remilitarizing the Rhineland was a rightful assertion of sovereignty over territory that had never ceased to legally be a part of Germany. Given that there had been a strong groundswell of support in a truncated Austria for the idea of a union with Germany in the weeks and months following the Armistice, a case could even be made, although it would be significantly weaker in its moral authority, that with the Anschluss Hitler was merely carrying out the will of the German and Austrian people. But what happened next was, beyond question, a crime, one that no degree of rationalization or pettifogging could excuse or disguise: the rape of Czechoslovakia.

When Hitler vowed to gather all of Europe's ethnic Germans into the Fatherland, his pledge was taken to be as much an exercise in rhetoric as statement of intent. Not so: he was speaking literally. Once Austria was comfortably absorbed into the Reich, Hitler turned his attentions to Czechoslovakia, and in particular the lands that shared a common border with Germany, collectively known as the Sudetenland. The Sudetenland, which was more of a geographical notion than a defined region, had never been part of the German Empire: it had been ruled by the House of Hapsburg since the early sixteenth century. When the Allies carved up the Austro-Hungarian Empire after the Great War and created the state of Czechoslovakia, the Sudetenland was incorporated into the new nation. Through a carefully stage-managed campaign of propaganda, intimidation, bluster, and threats of war, Hitler altered the world's perception of the Sudetenland from that of a region where the inhabitants had for the past 18 years been living prosperously and contentedly in their new homeland, into a hotbed of ethnic dissention and rebellion on the verge of a civil war. He then systematically browbeat the prime ministers of Great Britain and France, Neville Chamberlain and Édouard Daladier, into consenting to a German annexation of the region, without either of them so much as asking for the Czechoslovakian government's permission to do so.

In the fantastically complex psychology of Adolf Hitler, the lust for vengeance was one of its most powerful compulsions. Czechoslovakia represented nearly everything that he hated most deeply: the bastard child, as he saw it, of Versailles, Czechoslovakia was a prosperous popular republic where its Jewish population was a loyal, integral part of the national fabric. By its very existence Czechoslovakia gave the lie to nearly the whole of Nazi dogma, therefore that existence could not be tolerated. As such, then, the little country cried out to be, in one of Hitler's favorite words, "*zerschlagen*" ("smashed") in an act of vengeance for violating what Hitler believed should have been the natural order of things.

The Czechs, for their part, had long been suspicious of Hitler and the Nazis, and had constructed a belt of strong fortifications along the Czech-German border which, once manned by their well-armed and well-trained army, would have readily repulsed any military incursion by Hitler's new-fangled Wehrmacht. In order to neutralize those defenses, Hitler manufactured the Sudetenland Crisis of the autumn of 1938, probably the single most perfect expression of his calculated cynicism. By annexing the Sudetenland, Germany would take over those border fortifications, leaving the rest of Czechoslovakia essentially defenseless. The fate of the Sudeten Germans was of little or no real interest or consequence to Hitler: they were merely tools, the means by which he would effect the obliteration of a country which he felt had no right to exist.

On the last day of September 1938 Hitler met with Chamberlain and Daladier at Munich, where they assured him that Britain and France would forego their treaty commitments to defend Czechoslovakia, and the Führer in turn reassured them that he had no further territorial ambitions in Europe. Hitler ordered the Wehrmacht into the Sudetenland the next day; by 10 October all of the contested districts were occupied. Then followed almost six months of relative calm, but on March 10, 1939, Hitler presented the Czech government with an ultimatum: accept the forcible incorporation of what remained of Czechoslovakia into the Reich as a protectorate, or face immediate invasion. To sweeten the pot, Hitler offered to give the Luftwaffe permission to indiscriminately bomb Prague. The Czechs had no choice: abandoned by their erstwhile allies, shorn of their defenses, with openly hostile neighbors to the north and south in Poland and Hungary, their situation was hopeless. They acceded, and on March 15 Hitler drove triumphantly into Prague.

Erwin Rommel was still commandant at the Theresian War Academy when the German Army marched into the Sudetenland. He still enjoyed being an instructor and overseeing the training of young officers, while his domestic life with Lucie and Manfred was pleasantly uneventful. He was not ignorant of the Sudetenland Crisis—no officer of the Wehrmacht could be—but he was sufficiently removed from the events as to not immediately be touched by them. But when Hitler arrived in Prague and announced his intention to drive straight into Hradcany Castle, the seat of the Czech government in the heart of the city, Rommel could not distance himself from the events, as he was there right beside der Führer, in command of Hitler's personal escort.

No one has ever been able to explain how or why Adolf Hitler took a personal interest in the career of Erwin Rommel. True, they were both veterans of the Great War, where each had repeatedly demonstrated his personal courage under fire. (Hitler, a *gefreiter*—corporal—had been awarded not only the Iron Cross Second Class, the usual decoration for bravery in combat given to non-commissioned officers, but also the Iron Cross *First* Class, which was almost exclusively reserved for officers.) But there were other officers who had also proven their courage under fire, contemporaries of Rommel, such as his one-time rival Ferdinand Schörner, who would ultimately prove himself to be a sycophantic toady. The Hitler Youth military training program had been a failure, in no small part because Rommel was unable to get on with Baldur von Schirach, one of Hitler's favorites, hardly a recommendation. At the same time, Rommel was well known throughout the Wehrmacht for his disdain for aristocratic stuffed-shirt officers, a contempt Hitler shared. In the end it may have been nothing more than a case of the biter bit, Hitler for once being charmed by this charismatic infantry colonel.

Whatever the precise details may have been, Rommel was detached from the Theresian Academy and placed in command of the Führer's escort when Hitler entered Prague. Hitler, who had a flair for heavy-handed showmanship, wanted to drive straight to the gates of the Hradcany, making an emphatic statement as to the totality of Czech subjugation. The SS, including Himmler, were aghast at the idea, fearing for Hitler's safety, but General Erich Hoepner, commander of the XVI Panzer Corps, urged Hitler to make the gesture. When Hitler hesitated, Rommel barked at him to "Get in an open car, and drive straight to the Castle!" just as he would have done himself. A week later, the political melodrama in Prague concluded, Rommel was back in Wiener Neustadt.[62]

The Western democracies, France and Great Britain, had not bestirred themselves in the slightest to save what had been left of Czechoslovakia when Hitler delivered his ultimatum, and the Führer was certain now that he had the measure of those who would have been his enemies—henceforth he would have a free hand in Central Europe, for it seemed perfectly clear now that there was nothing east of the Rhine for which the French or the British would be willing to go to war. Indeed, during the Munich Crisis, Neville Chamberlain, in a radio address to the British people, had declared, "How horrible, fantastic, incredible it is that we should be digging trenches and trying on gas masks here because of a quarrel in a far-away country between people of whom we know nothing." But unknown to Hitler, a line had been crossed: Chamberlain and Daladier were no longer in any mood to compromise or be compromised. Both were statesmen of the old school, when a national leader's given word was binding. At Munich both men had sacrificed an ally in exchange for Hitler's solemn promise that he had made his final territorial demand in Europe, doing so in the mistaken belief that they were averting a wider crisis, hoping that by surrendering a few they would save many by averting another world war. In Prague Hitler had shown that he felt no more bound by his own pledges than he did by the treaties to which Germany was partner. Together France and Britain declared that should Hitler seek to expand Germany's borders again at the expense of her neighbors, there *would* be a war. Hitler dismissed their new-found resolve as so much rhetoric, and set about creating a pretext for an outright war against Poland.[63]

"The Polish Question" had been a festering wound between Germany and her neighbor to the east since the Versailles peace conference, when Poland had been created out of what had been mostly Russian and German territory. Russia, now the Soviet Union, had been in the throes of a civil war and unable to so much as lodge a protest. Germany, however, saw two entire provinces ripped away and given to the Poles, and the German people refused to be reconciled to their loss. (The parallels with the French attitude toward Alsace and Lorraine in the years following the Franco-Prussian War are unavoidable.) The province of East Prussia was completely cut off from the rest of Germany by the "Polish Corridor," a swath of territory carved out of Prussian land to allow Poland access to the Baltic Sea, while the great port of Danzig had been declared a "free city" under Polish administration. While the German people had cheered lustily when the

Wehrmacht rolled into Austria, the Sudetenland and Czecholslovakia, there had been little real enthusiasm for open warfare, whatever Hitler might have wanted to believe. A war with Poland, on the other hand, was a different story: there were millions of Germans, many of them dispossessed following the creation of the Polish state, who would welcome an opportunity to settle a few old scores with the despised nation to the east.

Throughout the summer of 1939, tensions between Berlin and Warsaw were methodically ratcheted higher, as Hitler pushed events closer to the tipping point and the Polish government maintained a belligerence which in light of the state of Poland's army and her strategic situation was utterly unrealistic—encouraged, tragically as it turned out, by assurances from Paris and London that if Germany invaded Poland, it would also mean war with France and Britain. When on August 22 Rommel was summoned to Berlin for a special briefing, he was convinced that its purpose was to assign to him some special mission in a war he expected to begin any day. He was quite right on both counts. On August 23 the Molotov–Ribbentrop Pact was signed, a mutual non-aggression pact between Nazi Germany and Soviet Russia which contained secret clauses that provided for the partition of a conquered Poland; on August 25, Rommel was promoted to *generalmajor* ("I left the Reichs Chancellery a brand-new general wearing a brand-new general's uniform," he wrote ecstatically to Lucie that night), and given a new, totally unexpected posting: when the war with Poland began, Rommel would command the Führerbeglietbataillon, responsible for the protection of the Führer's headquarters and Hitler himself.[64]

The German attack on Poland began in the pre-dawn hours of September 1, 1939. Germany's Anschluss with Austria, the annexation of the Sudetenland, and the occupation of the rump of Czechoslovakia, while carried out bloodlessly, had been tantamount to dress rehearsals for the mechanized warfare which the Wehrmacht was about to unleash against Poland. The operations in Austria, the Sudetenland, and Czechoslovakia had served as a "proof of concept" for its organization, machines, equipment, and doctrines. The German Army was developing a new form of warfare, and there were still plenty of kinks to work out, bugs to eradicate, as the mobility of mechanized forces, the reach of air power, and the flexibility of infiltration tactics were brought together in a form of warfare that the West would come to call "Blitzkrieg."

The Poles' situation was essentially hopeless: surrounded on three sides by German territory, their only chance at stemming the German advance was to abandon the western third of Poland, withdraw into the center of the country and make a stand along the Vistula River and before Warsaw, hoping that the French and British would intervene in the west and draw off enough of the German Army's strength to allow the Poles to keep fighting. This strategy was soon in tatters as the speed with which the German spearheads advanced gave the Poles no time in which to organize defensive lines. The problem was not the shopworn cliché of cavalry charging columns of armor—a scenario that actually occurred but once—rather it was the Poles' lack of comparable mobility: the Germans were simply moving faster than the Poles were able to respond. Even had they been able to stand on the Vistula and at the gates of Warsaw, the Poles were doomed, as they were stabbed in the back by the Soviets, who invaded from the east on September 17. The German and Soviet armies met at Brest-Litovsk on September 22, and though isolated fighting continued until October 6, the Polish campaign was essentially over. It was a staggering, lopsided victory for the Wehrmacht, whose losses in killed, wounded, and missing totaled just under 50,000, while the number of Polish dead and wounded alone was four times that number. In a speech given in Danzig a month after the campaign began, Hitler assured the world that "Poland never will rise again in the form of the Versailles treaty. That is guaranteed. . . ."[65]

Hitler had made only a slight miscalculation in his assessment of the Allies: Britain and France had indeed honored their pledges to Poland and declared war on Germany, but then immediately thereafter the British Prime Minister, Neville Chamberlain, began to dither and blither, constantly finding new excuses for not striking at Germany across her western border, which during that sad September was held by a mere six divisions. Daladier of France followed Chamberlain's lead, and the western front, such as it was and what there was of it, was a scene of masterful inactivity, a situation the French press soon dubbed "le Drôle de Guerre"—the Funny War—while their British counterparts called it the "Phoney War."

Rommel saw no actual combat while commanding the Führer's bodyguard in Poland, although on more than one occasion Hitler seemed determined to get as close to the fighting as he could, roaming as he did across Poland behind the advancing Wehrmacht, sometimes aboard the *Führerson-*

derzug, the "Führer's Special," incongruously named "*Amerika*," or in a small armored column. When the 2nd Panzer Division forced a crossing of the San River under heavy fire from the Polish defenders, they were also under the watchful eye of Adolf Hitler, who wanted to personally see his tanks in action. (Hitler had played a decisive role in the creation of the first panzer divisions.) At the Baltic port of Gydnia, which the Poles had defended ferociously, Hitler decided to personally inspect the ruins of the last Polish bunker, which sat almost literally at the water's edge at the bottom of a steep incline. Rommel, charged with traffic control, announced that only the Führer's car and one other vehicle would be allowed down that grade— everyone else would have to remain behind. When Martin Bormann, Hitler's private secretary and personal gatekeeper, attempted to follow in a third car, Rommel stepped into the street and blocked the way, responding to Bormann's obscenity-laced demand to be allowed to pass by bellowing back at him, "I am the headquarters commandant and this is not a kindergarten outing! You will do as I say!" Humiliated, Bormann silently vowed retribution, though it would be years in coming.[66]

The wreckage of Polish tanks and artillery, along with crashed Polish aircraft, were of special interest to Hitler, who had a lifelong fascination with machinery. Less attention was paid to the long columns of Polish prisoners of war, or, for that matter, the casualties suffered by the German Army. One disturbing incident took place in East Prussia, when a train filled with wounded German soldiers was eased onto a railway siding next to Hitler's *Amerika*. The bloody and maimed young men were clearly visible to those aboard—Hitler ordered the shades on the windows lowered to block them from view. Rommel was present for this display of Hitler's indifference to the plight of the soldiers who fought and bled for him, an incident which only much later would begin to signify.

What Rommel immediately gained from his presence at the Führer's headquarters was an eagle's eye view of how the campaign was being fought; it was highly educational. This was his first experience of seeing war from a higher command perspective, and he took away a keen understanding of how mechanized and motorized units utilized speed and surprise to create a "force multiplier"—producing favorable results from their maneuvers and attacks that were disproportionate to the numbers of men and machines involved. The applicability of his own command style and combat experiences in the Great War, especially those in Romania and Italy, quickly became obvious to him, and he began to wonder how he might gain command of one of the coveted panzer divisions. He was uniquely positioned for such a possibility: in one letter to Lucie, he wrote, "I was able to talk with [Hitler] about two hours yesterday evening, on military problems. He's extraordinarily friendly toward me. . . . I very much doubt that I will be at the Kriegsschule much longer, when the war is over."[67]

Rommel was wrong on both counts: he would remain the titular commandant of the Theresian Academy for another six months, albeit temporarily posted to Berlin should it be necessary to reactivate the Führer's escort battalion; and the war was far from over. With military operations in Poland complete, he was able to secure a few days' leave to spend with Lucie, but returned to Hitler's headquarters on October 2 in order to prepare for the German Army's victory parade through Warsaw on October 5. The city was a smoldering, reeking ruin, much of it reduced to rubble by Luftwaffe bombs and Wehrmacht artillery shells; Hitler stood for two hours on a specially constructed temporary reviewing stand while units of the army and air force marched past, Rommel standing behind him and to his right throughout. Hitler and company returned to Berlin that night, and on October 6 Hitler delivered a speech to the Reichstag in which he offered to make peace with Britain and France. Poland no longer existed, he argued; the entire reason the French and British had gone to war had evaporated. In a private conference with his senior officers the following day, Hitler let it be known that if his peace overtures were rebuffed, he was determined to invade the west at the earliest possible opportunity.

Rommel would never return to Poland, and he departed the country just as the SS Einsatzgruppen, the special purpose commands, were moving in, so he remained unaware of what happened in Poland in the wake of the Wehrmacht's triumph. The systematic, methodical extermination of Poland's aristocratic and intellectual elite, along with her Jews, as well as anyone else the Nazis deemed unfit to live, along with the simultaneous deportation of all able-bodied men to factories in the Reich where they would become slave labor, began almost as soon as the last panzer came to a halt. It was the leading edge of a stormfront of death and despair that would sweep across Central and Eastern Europe in the wake of the Wehrmacht for the next six years. Protected by a conspiracy of silence that all but assured disappearance and death for anyone who was too assiduous in their effort to pierce it, the Nazis' liquidation of their various "problems"—the Jewish problem, the Gypsy problem, the Slav problem, the homosexual problem, the aged or infirm or mentally ill problem—in the east would rot the morals and poison the honor of an entire generation of German officers, as well as far too many of Germany's soldiers, who served there. Prepared, willing, to look the other way, to invoke the principle, so popular with the Germans throughout their history, of "*Not kennt kein Gebot!*"—"Necessity knows no law!"—millions of ordinary, decent *Volk* became, in the words of Daniel Goldhagen, "Hitler's willing executioners."[68]

Had he been paying closer attention, Rommel would have had an inkling that something seriously amiss was happening in Poland. Not long after the invasion began, Lucie contacted Rommel, asking him to make inquiries as to the fate of her uncle, a Catholic priest named Edmund Roszczynialski. Initially Rommel was fobbed off with bureaucratic excuses; more than a year would pass before he would have to inform her that there were no records of any kind regarding Father Edmund. Nor was there likely ever to be—he had simply vanished, almost certainly just one more anonymous victim of the SS execution detachments.

But by then, so much had happened to Rommel in particular and the world as a whole that the fate of a single Catholic priest became all but insignificant. In the months of October and November 1939 a titanic battle of wills was being fought between Hitler, who wanted to invade France and the Low Countries immediately if not sooner, and the Army High Command and General Staff, who, for a variety of reasons, some sound, others born of a hesitance that bordered on cowardice, sought to postpone any new offensives for as long as possible, preferably forever. The Polish Army, no matter how hard or how bravely it fought, had been not only outnumbered but also outclassed in its confrontation with the Wehrmacht. In 1939 the French Army, despite its current lethargic posture on the Western Front, was widely regarded as one of the finest, if not the finest, armies in the world. And however much the French may have lost their fondness for offensive action, no German officer who fought against them in the Great War could forget their tenacity on defense, especially at Verdun, where, undeniably, a rational army would have run away. The French Army would, of necessity, bear the brunt of any German attack in the west, and the German generals feared another prolonged, indecisive bloodbath of the sort they had fought from 1914 to 1918.

The truth is, if the German Army *had* attacked in the west in the late autumn of 1939, that sort of stalemate almost certainly would have been the result. Showing a singular lack of imagination, the O.K.W. (Oberkommando des Wehrmacht—the Armed Forces High Command) had developed a plan for attacking the western Allies that was little more than an elaborate rehashing of the Schlieffen Plan of 1914—precisely what the French and British army commands were planning to defend against. The plan called for the German Army to anchor its left flank on the Ardennes Forest, and advance in a gigantic wheeling maneuver across Holland and Belgium with the objective of outflanking the French and British forces arrayed against it. (The two significant departures from the Schlieffen Plan was that first, there would be no battle of the frontier this time round— the Maginot Line defenses were too formidable to make any such action feasible—and second, Holland would be invaded along with Belgium; leaving Holland neutral in 1914 ultimately came to be regarded as a poor strategic decision.) The Anglo-French defensive plan, known as the "Dyle Plan," called for the French Army and a British expeditionary force to advance into Belgium and take up a defensive position along the Dyle River, denying the Germans any opportunity to outflank them.

Weather and logistics ultimately combined to make any offensive operations in late 1939 impossible, and during the winter of 1939–40, Generalleutnant Erich von Manstein, the Chief of Staff of Army Group A, one of three such commands assigned to the attack on the west, began to rethink the O.K.W. plan. Turning the basic concept of the plan on its ear, he proposed that rather than simply marking time in the Ardennes, the German Army deploy its panzer divisions there, giving them the mission of breaking through the French defenses and then using their speed and mobility to move behind and cut off the Allied forces that had advanced into Belgium, drawn there by a large-scale feint by the right wing of the German Army.

The plan was imaginative, bold, daring, and risky, and for all of those reasons the most senior officers of the Wehrmacht vehemently opposed its implementation. But it appealed to Hitler, who recognized that, by its inherent risk, von Manstein's plan, which he likened to the cut of a sickle, hence the unofficial name it bore, "*Sichelschnitt*," offered a victory the size and scope of which had never before been seen in any European war. He ordered further elaboration and development of the plan, much to the chagrin of Generaloberst Franz Halder, the O.K.W. Chief of Staff, who had been largely responsible for the O.K.W.'s original plan.

In its final form, *Sichelschnitt*, now known as "Fall Gleb"—Case Yellow—called for two Army Groups, A and B, to carry out the offensive in the west. Army Group B on the German right, would move first, its 19 infantry divisions and three panzer divisions moving across Holland and Belgium, to serve as the bait for the trap to be sprung by Army Group A. Comprised of 37 infantry and seven panzer divisions, Army Group A would rush into and through the Ardennes Forest, which the French Army regarded as too dense to allow the passage of armored units, and force a crossing of the Meuse River, after which the panzer divisions would drive hard and fast for the English Channel, bypassing tough opposition and fixed fortifications, leaving them to be reduced by the infantry divisions which followed. The infantry units would also shore up the flanks of the corridor created by the panzers on their way to the Channel. The bulk of the French Army, along with whatever forces the British sent to France, would be trapped in Belgium cut off from their supply lines, with nowhere to retreat.

No doubt all of this would have been of great professional interest to Erwin Rommel under any circumstances, but it became of far more personal interest in February 1940, when he was given command of the 7th Panzer Division, one of the units to be assigned to Army Group A for the dash to the English Channel. He had spent the winter still in command of the Führerbeglietbataillon, and was present at the Reich Chancellery on November 23 when Hitler gave a violent dressing-down to his senior generals, damning their foot-dragging and obstructionism, questioning their fighting spirit and stopping just short of open accusations of cowardice. Rommel hung on every word, as he agreed with almost everything Hitler said: he enjoyed seeing these generals, many of them titled aristocrats who had spent most of their active careers in comfortable staff postings, taken down a peg. They had grown a bit too fond, in Rommel's eyes, of the ease and routine of a peacetime army; now the Führer was putting them on notice that he expected them to be fighting soldiers rather than simply strutting martinets in high-collared uniforms.

None of the disdain, even contempt, which Hitler displayed to his other generals ever found its way into his relationship with Rommel. (It would be a stretch to call it a friendship—it's improbable that Adolf Hitler ever formed a true friendship as an adult.) One of the reasons for Rommel's extended tenure as commander of the Führerbeglietbataillon—a post more suited to a lieutenant colonel or colonel rather than a brigadier general—was undoubtedly Rommel's reputation as a frontline soldier. None of Hitler's cronies could claim the sort of shared experiences which linked Hitler and Rommel. None of them had fought in the trenches on the Western Front—Hermann Göring, commander-in-chief of the Luftwaffe, had been a fighter pilot during the war, Bormann, Hitler's secretary, and Heinrich Himmler, Reichsführer-SS and chief of the Gestapo, had been too young to serve in the army during the war. Almost alone on Hitler's staff Rommel knew what it was like to go through combat multiple times and survive—he and Hitler could claim equally with Winston Churchill that there was something exhilarating in being shot at by an enemy who missed.

The strange camaraderie shared by Hitler and Rommel did not go unremarked upon by the rest of Hitler's coterie, notably by Colonel Rudolf Schmundt, Hitler's chief Wehrmacht adjutant, who developed a strong dislike for Rommel and thought he had altogether too much ready access to der Führer. Ironically, Schmundt would come to appreciate what an outstanding soldier Rommel truly was and the two men would become good friends, with Schmundt often providing a back-channel to Hitler when Rommel's need to speak with the Führer was particularly pressing. At the moment, however, ". . . relations with Schmundt are strained," he wrote in a letter to Lucie. "Don't know why: apparently my position with Hitler is getting too strong. Not impossible that a change will be insisted on from that quarter. . . ." Regardless of whatever might be the attitude of Hitler's staff, Rommel had already made it known that he was chafing in the relative confinement of being the Führerbeglietbataillon commander, and was angling for a divisional command—and not just any division: he was openly lobbying for command of a panzer division.[69]

There were only 10 such divisions in the whole of the German Army, and after the Polish campaign they were considered among the plum assignments of the Wehrmacht. Rommel, having only donned his general's shoulder boards and collar tabs a few months earlier, was extraordinarily junior to be considered for such an appointment, but Hitler chose to indulge his favorite soldier, and on February 10, 1940 Rommel arrived in Bad Godesberg, headquarters of the 7th Panzer, and formally assumed command five days later. With him he brought 10 copies of *Infanterie Greift an*, to be given to his regimental and battalion commanders, the better for them to understand how Rommel planned to lead his division. Actually it was not that hard to discern: at a formal dinner in Berlin on February 17, while waiting in the reception line for Hitler to arrive, Rommel found himself standing next to Generalleutnant Rudolf Schmidt, who had been his commanding officer in the Reichswehr's 13th Infantry Regiment, and led the 1st Panzer Division in Poland. Leaning close to Schmidt, Rommel asked, "General, what is the best way to command a panzer division?"

"You'll find that there are always two possible decisions open to you," Schmidt replied crisply. "Take the bolder one—it's always best."[70]

The 7th Panzer had only been operational for five months when Rommel assumed command. It had fought in Poland as the 2nd Light Division, one of four hybrid, experimental units that were not quite infantry divisions and not quite fully fledged panzer divisions. A light division had only a single two-battalion panzer regiment on its strength—in this case the 25th Panzer Regiment—unlike a proper panzer division which had two. Combat experience in Poland showed that this left these divisions seriously deficient in firepower, which led to higher casualties. A second panzer regiment (the 66th in this case) was subsequently added to each of the light divisions, though these would have only a single tank battalion, and the units renamed and renumbered as panzer divisions. (Eventually 66th Panzer Regiment's tank battalion was folded into the larger 25th Regiment, and the 66th was dissolved.) Over half the 7th Panzer's tanks were the Czech-designed and -built Pzkw 38t model, an agile, rugged, fast vehicle that, while not as heavily armored as the Pzkw III, the German Army's main battle tank at the time, carried as powerful an offensive punch. The division also included two regiments of motorized infantry, an artillery regiment of three battalions with 12 guns each, an antitank battalion and a pioneer (engineer) battalion.[71]

Rommel, who knew better than most division commanders what was to come in the spring, was of the opinion that both he and the 7th Panzer had grown soft in the months of inactivity following the Polish campaign, and set about changing that. He renewed his own dedication to being physically fit at the same time that he started whipping the division into shape. He threw himself into learning everything he could of the day-to-day operations, the "nuts-and-bolts" as it were, of a panzer division; one battalion commander was sent packing less than two weeks after Rommel's arrival for what the new commanding officer regarded as slackness, and the entire division was instilled with the lessons Rommel had learned in his own four years of warfare. Rommel had learned in Romania and Italy that firepower or movement alone were rarely decisive, but when combined were almost invariably irresistible, a lesson that mostly been lost in the memories of the quagmire of the Western Front—now he taught it to the 7th Panzer. Battalion and company commanders were expected to show initiative in carrying out the division's overall plan of operations. Robbing the enemy of the will to fight could be more devastating than merely depriving him of the means to fight, and that there was more to victory than gaining mere useless ground. "Don't fight a battle if you gain nothing by winning it" was one of his favorite maxims; so was his injunction to "Shed sweat, not blood." To Rommel, the only acceptable definition of victory was an enemy beaten and an objective taken, while needless loss of life was not only the hallmark of bad generalship, it was the height of stupidity. Events would prove that on occasion Rommel would fall short of his own standards—not unexpected, considering that they were set so high.[72]

The three months between Rommel's assumption of command of the 7th Panzer and the beginning of *Fall Gelb* were filled with intensive training and preparation at every level in the German Army. Everyone, Allied and German alike, knew that an attack in the west was coming, especially after Germany occupied Denmark and invaded Norway in late April 1940. Hitler got lucky in Norway, there is no other way to put it. The German objective for the invasion was to secure the Norwegian port of Narvik, which could be used year-round to ship the precious iron ore dug from Swedish mines to the insatiable maws of the Ruhr's weapons factories— Sweden's Baltic Sea ports were locked shut by ice for six months every year. But the British, anticipating a German move against Norway, stole a march on Hitler, getting their naval forces into position before the German invasion fleet sailed. Yet, despite inflicting near-crippling losses on the German Navy, the British then bungled the land campaign and the British troops sent to bolster the Norwegian defense against the Germans had to be withdrawn; the Wehrmacht eventually occupied the whole of Norway and set up a puppet government by the middle of June, though the Norwegians never formally surrendered.

By that time, however, the world's attention had shifted to France and the Low Countries, where on May 10 the Wehrmacht finally began its offensive. The date had been kept a very close-held secret, Rommel not receiving his orders to deploy the 7th Panzer until the evening of May 9— some of his rifle companies didn't reach their start lines until 20 minutes before they were scheduled to jump off. Nonetheless, meticulous planning beforehand kept the inevitable confusion to a minimum: army, corps, and divisional boundaries were set, objectives clearly defined, phase lines drawn, roads assigned, and supply and support troops organized, all of their pre-attack movements behind the front lines well-rehearsed. Contingency plans had been drawn up for every major unit, and coordination with the Luftwaffe for close support firmly established. The planning for *Fall Gelb* was as thorough and meticulous as that of the Schlieffen Plan a generation earlier; while spectacular in execution, that plan had also been a spectacular failure. The Germans were anxious that history not repeat itself: just hours before the offensive began, Rommel had an opportunity to dash off a quick letter to Lucie, where he wrote, "We're packing up at last. Let's hope not in vain. You'll get all the news for the next few days from the papers. Don't worry yourself. Everything will go all right."[73]

Army Group B, under the command of Generaloberst Fedor von Bock, invaded Holland and Belgium at dawn on May 10, and the French and British obligingly responded by moving the First and Seventh Armies, along with the British Expeditionary Force, eight divisions strong, forward to the Dyle River, exactly as von Manstein had anticipated. Accordingly, Army Group A, led by Generaloberst Gerd von Runstedt pushed through the rugged hills and narrow roads of the Ardennes. There Generalleutnant Hermann Hoth's XV Corps—the 5th and 7th Panzer Divisions and the 32nd Infantry Division—was positioned on the right flank, where it was to protect the army group should the French or British launch a counterattack from the north while Generaloberst Heinz Guderian's XIX Corps was forcing a crossing of the Meuse River.

The decisive moment of the 1940 campaign came on the third day of operations, when Guderian's three panzer divisions (the 1st, 2nd, and 10th) as well as Rommel's 7th Panzer all forced crossings of the Meuse River, behind which the French had drawn up their main line of defense. (The much-vaunted—and truly fearsome—Maginot Line was sited to the south of where the battles of France in 1940 would be fought. Built to protect France's frontier with Germany, it had never been envisioned as extending north along the Franco-Belgian border. *Fall Gelb* had been planned specifically to avoid any need to attack the Maginot Line directly: properly supported the line would have been all but invulnerable and German casualties catastrophic.) The 7th Panzer had met very little opposition on the first three days of the offensive: roads had been cratered by French and Belgian engineers, and large trees felled across roadways to create roadblocks, but few of these obstacles were defended, so that for the first two days of the division's advance, Rommel's troops were shedding far more sweat than blood. He quickly adapted a tactic his *abteilung* had frequently used with success in Romania and Italy, liberally spraying suspected enemy positions with machine-gun fire: this had the simultaneous effect of "knocking" to see if "anyone was home," while also forcing an enemy to keep his head down. As Rommel's tanks, half-tracks, and armored cars moved forward, short, sharp bursts of fire were going out left and right. It was expensive of ammunition, but it was also very effective.

Rommel's lead unit reached the towns of Dinant and Houx on the Meuse River the afternoon of May 12, hoping to take the bridges there "on the bounce," but the French blew up them up just as the lead panzers were beginning to cross. Rommel came forward and saw that his infantry was about to attempt to cross the Meuse using inflatable rubber boats, but the French defenders were well concealed, and heavy, accurate shellfire was falling on the Germans. Improvising—he had no smoke generators with him—Rommel ordered several houses sitting upwind on his side of the river to be set afire, creating a smokescreen that allowed his infantrymen to paddle across the river and begin firing into the French right flank. The divisional artillery was called in, while several Panzer IVs were brought forward to provide close support. The defenders were still determined to make a fight of it, and the German infantry company which had crossed the river at Dinant was now pinned down by heavy small-arms and artillery fire. (At one point in the battle for Dinant, Rommel was shot at by a trio of French

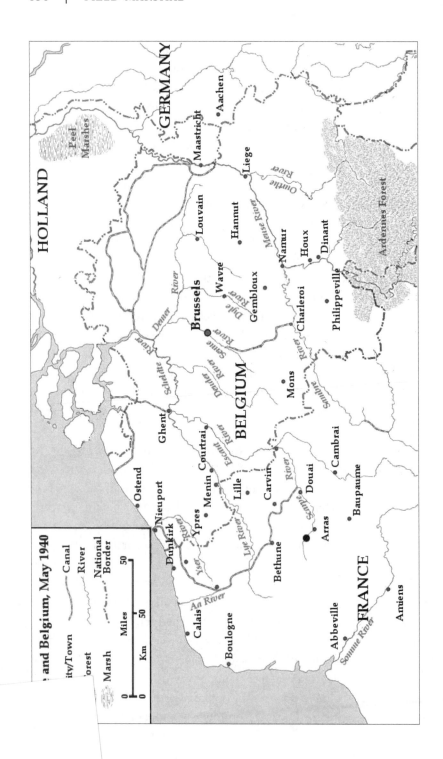

soldiers who had only moments before surrendered. They all missed, and a burst of machine-gun fire cut them down.) A platoon of French tanks came up to support the defenders, but a flurry of small-arms fire drove off the enemy armor, who apparently imagined the German force on the west bank of the river to be much stronger than it was. To the north, Rommel's 7th Motorcycle Battalion had successfully crossed the Meuse at Houx, but was making only slow progress clearing the French off the west bank. The French were fighting with such a degree of skill, and their defensive positions had been so well prepared, that Rommel eventually decided that the issue was not going to be decided by the infantry: more tanks were brought up and eventually their fire silenced the French. (One tank commander, Leutnant Karl-August Hanke, a rabid Nazi whom Göbbels had foisted on the 7th Panzer, brought his Panzer IV so far forward that he was firing at French positions at the near-point-blank range of 50 yards. A few weeks later, Hanke, who believed that his Party membership exempted him from strict army discipline, was relieved for insubordination and sent home by Rommel, who also rescinded a recommendation for Hanke to be awarded the Iron Cross First Class.)

After nearly 24 hours of continuous fighting, with a bridgehead across the Meuse secured, Rommel now showed his true colors. Without bothering to inform anyone in the 5th Panzer Division, he appropriated that unit's portable bridging equipment and added it to his own, then embarked on a monumental act of insubordination. While the finer details of *Fall Gelb* were being worked out, Franz Halder, who imagined himself to be a far greater general than he was, and whose gifts for spite exceeded his military talents, had tinkered with von Manstein's plan in such a way that its most aggressive elements were muted—or eliminated altogether. (Halder and von Manstein personally detested one another; Halder's pettiness was such that he was prepared to abet the failure of a major German offensive if it meant blackening von Manstein's reputation.) The daring armored thrusts to the English Channel had been reduced to mere reconnaissance in force, the whole operation being then reduced to the same foot-slogging pace that had doomed the Schlieffen Plan in 1914.[74]

But General Guderian, rightly known as the father of the Panzerkorps for his vigorous and visionary advocacy of armored warfare in the 1930s, along with Army Group A's other panzer leaders, tacitly agreed to adhere to von Manstein's original planning and once they had broken through the French defensive lines, drive their panzers as hard and fast as they could straight for the Channel. This was meat and drink to Erwin Rommel, with his thrusting, aggressive style of command, and he readily agreed. Now, having purloined his neighbor's bridges, he took dead aim on Calais. The commanding officer of the 5th Panzer Division, Generalleutnant Max von Hartlieb-Walsporn, protested Rommel's high-handed action to General Hoth, to no avail. Hoth understood that Rommel would know what to do with such equipment, while von Hartlieb-Walsporn clearly did not. A diffident man who made an excellent peacetime general but who was sadly out of place commanding a panzer division in wartime, von Hartlieb-Walsporn would be relieved two weeks later and would never lead combat troops again.

As soon as a bridge was in place on May 14, the 7th Motorized Rifle Regiment, under command of Colonel Georg von Bismarck, pushed forward, moving west of Dinant, where strong French forces were mustering for a counterattack. Rommel went forward with his tanks to reinforce von Bismarck and so had his first bit of excitement in the campaign. Unexpectedly coming under enemy antitank fire, Rommel's panzer was hit twice and knocked into a ditch, where it sat canted steeply on its right side, with bullets and shells flying about from all directions. More panzers moved up and Rommel was able to extricate himself from the disabled vehicle and commandeer another, following behind the commander of the 25th Panzer Regiment, Colonel Karl Rothenberg, to where von Bismarck's regiment was fighting. The 7th Panzer Division was now 65 miles beyond its start line.

The division reached Philippeville and continued westward through Avesnes and Landrecies on May 15. This day was the tipping point for the French Army, for it never again fought as well or as hard as it did at Dinant and Houx. A gaping hole 60 miles wide had been torn in the front of the French Ninth Army, and in order to restore the situation, a general order to retire was issued by the French commander, General André Corap. Materially, doctrinally, and above all, mentally, the Allies were neither equipped nor prepared to deal with the German panzer divisions. It was not a matter of numbers—the Allied armies actually fielded more armor than did the Germans, 3,400 Allied tanks compared to 2,500 German panzers—rather it was their inability to use them as effectively as the Germans. Tank for tank, most Allied vehicles were equal or superior to their German counterparts, but even in those Allied units that were styled as "armored" divisions, the prevalent tactical and operational doctrine was to use them to support the infantry, while German doctrine held exactly the reverse. This meant that the Allied generals thought in terms of operations defined by the speed at which a foot soldier moved, while the German generals thought in terms of operations conducted at the speed at which their panzers moved. It was a difference as fatal—to the Allies—as it was profound.

In the north, the Allies began to fall back, even though they outnumbered Army Group B, as General von Bock's three panzer divisions were wreaking havoc of their own, forcing the French First Army to fall back, which compelled the British to follow suit, or else leave their right flank dangling in the open. In the south, the French Army began to unravel, as Corap's order to withdraw—meant to reestablish a solid front against the Germans, a sensible operational necessity—was seen by the average *poilu* as something akin to an admission of defeat. When Rommel realized just how fragile was French morale, the effect on him was like blood in the water to a shark. Possibly the most enduring and deep-seated lesson he had learned in the Great War was the need to attack an enemy's will to fight: rapid movement, flanking attacks, concentrated firepower, surprise—all of which Rommel was a past master—conspired to amplify the erosion of an enemy's will that inevitably accompanied the noise and stench of combat, the killing and maiming. Rommel found neither glory nor satisfaction in the destructiveness of war: he was a professional soldier, not a mindless killer; his job was to attain objectives, not take lives. Anything that could expedite accomplishing the first without needless resort to the second would be his preferred method of waging war.

Philippeville was to have been one of the strongpoints on a new French "stop line"—a collection of bunkers, dugouts, and entrenchments that the men of the 7th Panzer mistakenly thought were part of the Maginot Line—where the German advance was to be contained. Rommel simply had his tanks and armored cars roll straight through the town without a halt, advancing with turrets traversed alternately left and right, spraying any suspected enemy positions with machine-gun fire, an occasional 75mm shell from a Panzer IV being thrown in for good measure. On the way into the town Rommel had already seen the road littered with trucks, gun tractors and artillery pieces abandoned by the French at the approach of the German tanks, clear evidence that the morale of the Ninth Army, at least, was collapsing. Leutnant Braun of the 25th Panzer Regiment, commanding one of the Panzer IIIs, memorably described his unit's arrival in Philippeville:

> General Rommel orders me to take the lead and in a village square, where I have a feeling there must be Frenchmen, I shoot into houses with my pistol and yell, "*Soldats français, venez!*" and on that command the doors of every house open and a great crowd of Frenchmen, perhaps several companies, flock into the square with their hands up![75]

On the way to Avesnes, Rommel and his men encountered more of the same, scores, sometimes hundreds, or even thousands of French soldiers surrendering without so much as a shot being fired.

> Soon we began to meet refugee columns and detachments of French troops preparing for the march. A chaos of guns, tanks, and military vehicles of all kinds, inextricably entagled with horse-drawn refugee carts, covered the road and verges. . . . The French troops were completely overcome by surprise at our sudden appearance, laid down their arms and marched off to the east beside our column. Nowhere was any resistance attempted. . . . Hundreds upon hundreds of French troops, with their officers, surrendered at our arrival. . . .[76]

Now and then there would be a hard case, such as the steely-eyed lieutenant colonel who, his unit overrun, furiously refused to surrender. Three times Colonel Rothenberg called on the Frenchman to give himself up, three times the brave but foolhardy officer refused—in the end, he was shot. A courageous death, but an unnecessary one; there was literally nothing more the unfortunate Frenchman could have done for his country.[77]

At Avesnes, Rommel had reached his assigned objective for the first phase of *Fall Gelb*: strictly speaking he was to stop now and await further orders, but the quiet little cabal among the panzer division commanders dictated otherwise. Already Rommel was planning to push straight into Landrecies where there was a bridge across the Sambre River, the last major obstacle between the German Army and the Channel coast. The masses of French refugees fleeing the German advance, choking the road from Avesnes, did more to slow the 7th Panzer Division's progress than did the French Army. At twilight on May 16, Rommel's tanks rolled straight across the bridge over the Sambre and right up to a French barracks on the far side of the river, where the garrison meekly formed up on the parade ground, laid down their weapons, and marched off into captivity. The lead elements of the 7th Panzer drove west in the darkness, and at dawn on May 17 stopped atop a hill overlooking Le Cateau—60 miles west of where the division had crossed the Meuse River, 175 miles from where the division had started just seven days earlier. In that time, the division had accounted for roughly 10,000 French prisoners of war, had captured 27 artillery pieces, and destroyed 130 French tanks and armored cars. The human cost had been startlingly low: the 7th Panzer had suffered, to that point, only 35 dead and 59 wounded, more than sufficient justification for Rommel's tactics, expensive in ammunition, but parsimonious of lives.

The pace was terrific, though, and the strain was beginning to tell. The division was strung out along a narrow, finger-like corridor almost 30 miles long; the 12th Infantry Division, on the left flank, whose troops were mostly advancing on foot, simply wasn't able to keep up, while the 5th Panzer, on the right, was suffering the consequences of its commanding officer's uninspired leadership. Communications between individual units within the division were sporadic as atmospheric conditions and equipment breakdowns interfered with radios, the lead elements were beginning to run short of fuel and ammunition, and there were thousands of disarmed French soldiers milling about inside the corridor, gradually being shepherded to the rear. The division was disorganized and running the risk of losing its unit cohesion.

This was a consequence of Rommel's free-wheeling style of command. His experience in the First World War (by now everyone was pretty much in agreement that this war was the second such) had taught Rommel that the proper place for a commanding officer was where the fighting was taking place, ready to act and react, a conviction he never entirely shook off even after the introduction of portable radio equipment. The need to be on the spot, to see for himself what was happening and direct the action, caused him to rush from flashpoint to flashpoint, dealing with regimental or even battalion tactics, rather than remaining with his divisional head-quarters, where his unit commanders and staff would be able to maintain regular contact with him and he could attend to divisional affairs. Remaining at divisional headquarters worked for other panzer commanders: while the gains of other panzer divisions led by more deliberate commanders might not be quite as spectacular as those of the 7th Panzer, they were still impressive, and wreaking almost equally great havoc on the French. The three divisions of General Guderian's Panzerkorps, the 1st, 2nd and 10th Panzer, had advanced almost as far as Rommel's 7th Panzer but were experiencing far fewer command and control problems, especially in resupply.

Rommel had absolute faith in his style of command, and given his uncanny knack for sensing exactly where a crisis would develop that required his attention, there was merit to his argument. Nonetheless, it was fraught with risk, not merely personal, although there was that: Rommel came under enemy fire almost as often during the campaign in France in 1940 as did any of his men. But it also posed a risk to those same men, whose lives were often dependent on decisions that only their division commander could make. This was a new style of warfare, this "Blitzkrieg," as the Allies were now calling it, one that seemed well suited to a man of Rommel's temperament and abilities, but it also had lessons to teach him.

One of those lessons was driven home on May 19 when Rommel was with the 25th Panzer Regiment just outside of Le Cateau, the remainder of the division strung out behind him for nearly 20 miles. The French were staging one of their local counterattacks, and because his panzers were low on gasoline, Rommel was being hard-pressed. The reason his fuel tanks were running dry was because his Chief of Staff, Major Otto Heidkamper, who was still with the divisional headquarters, had heard nothing from Rommel or Colonel Rothenberg all day: he assumed that the 25th Panzer had been overrun and they had been killed or captured; he refused to send fuel to a unit he was convinced no longer existed. As it happened, the French gave up on their attack, the 25th Panzer Regiment survived, and when Rommel eventually turned up alive, the ensuing row with Heidkamper was spectacular.

At this point even Rommel, usually impatient at the slightest delay when he was advancing, recognized the need to pause and sort out the division.

> It was now high time that the country we had overrun was secured by the division, and the enormous number of prisoners—approximately two mechanized divisions—was collected. I had kept the division staff constantly informed of our progress, but all messages had been transmitted blind from the [25th] Panzer Regiment's command tank, and there was no way of telling whether they had been received.[78]

There had been a few more uncoordinated local counterattacks on the flanks of the 7th Panzer's corridor which emphasized the division's vulnerability—with the following infantry divisions unable to keep up, a strong, determined attack could cut off the 7th Panzer and destroy it in detail. Mechanical breakdowns—trucks and armored cars as well as tracked vehicles—were becoming problematic; all of them needed fuel. The 7th Panzer spent the whole of May 17 replenishing and reorganizing—it would hardly do to call it "resting"—before resuming its westward march. Rommel gave the order: the line of advance was Le Cateau—Arras—Amiens—Rouen—Le Havre.

As the 7th Panzer advanced out of Le Cateau on May 18, the last remnant of French resistance, such as it was and what there was of it, began to evaporate. The French High Command adhered to the strategic doctrine of the "continuous front"—maintaining an unbroken line of resistance to the enemy; it was France's distilled experience and wisdom from the Great War. For four years the front had never been broken, save only in isolated local incidents and for brief periods of time. A grand strategic breakthrough by the Germans had never been achieved—the front always held, therefore, as long as a "continuous front" was maintained, it always would hold.

Army Group A's panzer divisions, however, had accomplished the impossible—not only was the French Ninth Army's front broken, it had been essentially obliterated. French doctrine and training—tactical, operational, and strategic—was completely ineffectual in stopping this kind of warfare. French armored divisions were organized and equipped to act as screens for massed infantry formations, but had little capability to launch and sustain attacks of their own. The only hope left to the French Army was that the panzer divisions would be forced to eventually halt through sheer exhaustion, giving the French enough time to rebuild another front.

The French prime minister, Paul Reynaud, who had replaced Daladier in April, saw the writing on the wall as early as May 15, when the news reached him that the Germans were across the Meuse in force. In a frantic phone call to his British counterpart, Winston Churchill, who had replaced Chamberlain on May 10, he exclaimed "We have been defeated! We are beaten; we have lost the battle!" Churchill flew to Paris the following day, and saw first-hand the incipient panic that was overtaking the French government: it was already preparing to evacuate the capital. Meeting the French commander-in-chief, General Maurice Gamelin, he studied the situation maps and asked bluntly, "Where is your strategic reserve?"

"There is none," was Gamelin's reply, and in that moment Churchill knew that Reynaud was right—the French had lost. In an instant the British prime minister's priority shifted from trying to stop the German advance to saving as much of the British armed forces in France and Belgium as possible.[79]

On May 20 Rommel reached Arras; it was here that he would be introduced to the British Army. On May 19, General John Verecker, Viscount Gort, commander of the British Expeditionary Force, was given explicit orders by General Edmund Ironside, the British Chief of the Imperial General Staff, to save as much of the B.E.F. as possible by withdrawing to the southwest, out of Belgium and into France, before the panzer divisions of Army Group A isolated it along with the French First and Ninth Armies; if that proved impossible, then it would be necessary to close on the Channel ports where, hopefully, the B.E.F. could be evacuated. It would not be an easy task, as seven of Gort's nine divisions were already engaged with Army Group B, the other two standing by as Gort's strategic reserve. To reach France, the B.E.F. would have to meet the panzer divisions head-on, as their line of advance lay directly across Gort's proposed line of retreat.

Rommel's reconnaissance battalion made the first contact with the British as it was trying to force a crossing of the La Bassée canal that ringed Arras; with the help of Luftwaffe dive-bombers, Rommel succeeded, but on the afternoon of May 21, the British counterattack began. The operation was supposed to be carried out by two infantry divisions, comprising about

15,000 men, but in the end just two infantry battalions, 2,000 men supported by 74 tanks—there would be no artillery or air support for them—actually made the attack. The British first ran headlong into the motorized SS regiment Totenkopf: the SS "supermen" watched round after round fired from their standard 37mm antitank guns bouncing like so many spitballs off the heavy armor of the advancing Matilda tanks, then promptly broke and ran. As they fled, they exaggerated the strength of the British forces and word reached Rommel, who was still south of Arras at this point, that at least five British divisions were attacking from the northwest. Rommel called up the 25th Panzer Regiment, told Colonel Rothenberg to get to Arras as quickly as possible, then rushed forward himself to take personal command of the defense.

> One of our howitzer batteries was already in position at the northern exit from the village [of Wailly, southwest of Arras] firing rapidly on enemy tanks attacking southward from Arras. As we were now coming under machine-gun fire and the infantry had already taken cover to the right, [Lieutenant] Most [Rommel's aide] and I ran on in front of the armored cars toward the battery position. It did not look as though the battery would have much difficulty in dealing with the enemy tanks, for the gunners were calmly hurling round after round into them in complete disregard of the return fire. . . . The enemy tank fire created chaos and confusion for our troops in the village. . . . We tried to create order. After notifying the divisional staff of the critical situation . . . we drove off to a hill 1,000 yards west of the village, where we found a light A.A. troop and several antitank guns. . . . With Most's help, I brought every available gun into action against the tanks. Every gun, both antitank and antiaircraft, was ordered to open rapid fire immediately and I personally gave each gun its target. With the enemy tanks so perilously close, only rapid fire from every gun could save the situation. We ran from gun to gun. The objections of the gun commanders that the range was still too great to engage the tanks effectively were overruled. All I cared about was to halt the enemy by heavy gunfire. Soon we succeeded in putting the leading enemy tanks out of action. . . .[80]

The crisis had not yet passed, however, as on Rommel's right flank the 6th Rifle Regiment was still hard pressed and taking heavy casualties. As the SS troops had learned, the Wehrmacht's standard antitank gun was powerless against the 3-inch thick armor of the Matildas, who in turn were wreaking havoc on the 6th Regiment's trucks and half-tracks. Weak as in truth it was, the British attack seemed to be on the verge of success. Only a last-ditch effort by the divisional artillery and a battery of 88mm antiaircraft batteries brought the enemy tanks to a halt. When Colonel Rothenberg's panzers at last reached Arras and caught the British in the flank, the issue was finally decided and the British withdrew.

The attack at Arras left Rommel shaken on a personal level: while helping rally the artillery, Leutnant Most was shot dead while standing right next to him. This was hardly Rommel's first encounter with death, nor was it his closest, but he was always upset when good men whom he knew were killed while under his command. He would go on to lose friends and staff members in North Africa, and again in France; to his credit as a man, he never became inured to it.

Of larger consequence to the current campaign in France, the action at Arras sent shock waves running up the German chain of command, all the way to Hitler's headquarters, where the Führer ordered a temporary halt in place for the panzer divisions while he, the O.K.W., and his army and corps commanders sorted out the situation. It was a moment of considerable mutual over-estimation by the Wehrmacht and the B.E.F.: Hitler and his generals were alarmed by the possibility that the British were significantly stronger than previously believed, which would necessitate a revision to the operational orders already issued to the panzer divisions; General Lord Gort was now convinced that his forces lacked the strength to drive through the German armored units and decided to fall back on the Channel ports where the B.E.F. would, hopefully, be evacuated.

The decision to halt the panzer divisions' drive to the English Channel was one of the most controversial of the entire war, as it would later be claimed that in doing so the Wehrmacht was denied the opportunity to take the Channel ports, trapping the encircled B.E.F. and compelling its surrender. At the time, however, it seemed to be military prudence: the panzers had been driven hard for two weeks, with breakdowns and equipment failures becoming more than problematical. The extent of the morale collapse of the French Army had yet to be fully appreciated at higher headquarters, so the threat of attacks on the still-vulnerable flanks of the armored thrusts west from the Meuse and Sambre Rivers seemed far greater than in fact it was. Balancing risks against opportunities, Hitler and his generals chose to minimize the risks: the order went out for the panzer divisions, wherever they were, to halt and take up defensive positions.

The stand-fast order from Hitler's headquarters thus afforded a few days of much-needed rest to the 7th Panzer Division and its commanding officer. While tank, vehicle, and artillery crews caught up on equipment maintenance and replenishing fuel and ammunition stocks, Rommel was able to resume his correspondence with Lucie.

23 May 1940

Dearest Lu,
With a few hours' sleep behind me, it's time for a line to you. I'm fine in every way. My division has had a blazing success. Dinant, Philippeville, break-through the Maginot Line, and advance in one night 40 miles through France to Le Cateau, then Cambrai, Arras, always in front of everybody else. Now the hunt is up against 60 encircled British, French, and Belgian Divisions. Don't worry about me. As I see it the war in France may be over in a fortnight.

26 May 1940

A day or two without action has done a lot of good. The division has lost up to date 27 officers killed and 33 wounded, and 1,500 men dead and wounded. That's about 12 percent casualties. Very little compared to what's been achieved. The worst is now well over. There's little likelihood of any more hard fighting, for we've give the enemy a proper whacking. Food, drink, and sleep are all back to routine. . . .[81]

Some of Rommel's comments to Lucie are intriguing for their prescience. The French government would seek an armistice with Germany on June 17, for example, just six days off from Rommel's prediction; likewise, there would be only two more incidents of hard fighting for the 7th Panzer before the French capitulation. The observation that a casualty rate of 12 percent in two weeks was "very little" sounds far more callous out of context than it truly was. Given how far and how fast the division had advanced—nearly 200 miles in less than two weeks, while taking thousands of prisoners of war and destroying nearly two divisions' worth of enemy tanks, vehicles, and guns—such losses were indeed light, especially when remembering that the German expectations, as were those of the French and the British, had been conditioned by the experience of the Great War, when tens of thousands of lives had often been sacrificed for incremental, indecisive gains.

The next letter Lucie received brought her the news that her husband would be adding to his already-impressive collection of medals: for his leadership under fire on May 13 at Dinant, a clasp to his Iron Cross Second Class; for the action on May 15 at Philippeville, a clasp to his Iron Cross First Class; and in recognition of what he had accomplished in leading the 7th Panzer Division, the award of the Knight's Cross of the Iron Cross. He was the first divisional commander to be so honored during the campaign.

> 7th Panzer Division
> Adjutant
> 25 May 1940

My Dear Frau Rommel,
May I be permitted to inform you that the Führer has instructed Lt. Hanke to decorate your husband on his behalf with the Knight's Cross.

Every man of the division—myself particularly, who has the privilege of accompanying the General—knows that nobody has deserved it more than your husband. He has led the division to success which must, I imagine, be unique.

The General is up now with the tanks again. If he knew that I were writing you, *gnädige Frau*, he would immediately instruct me to send you his most heartfelt greeting and the news that he is well.
. . .

May I close with the kindest regards from all members of the staff, and remain, *meine gnädigste Frau*,

> Your Obedient Servant,
> Schräpler[82]

"Schräpler" was Major Hans-Joachim Schräpler, Rommel's adjutant since mid-February, when Rommel took command of the 7th Panzer Division. He had already been wounded (in the arm) in this campaign, having returned to duty early after the untimely death of Lieutenant Most; he would remain with Rommel until his own death in North Africa in December 1941, during the retreat from Tobruk. This would not be the last time he would write to Lucie, standing in for her preoccupied husband; this letter, though, is one of his first to her, and is noteworthy as it clearly shows that Rommel had not lost his "touch." Despite its formality, it leaves no doubt of the high regard in which Schräpler held his commanding officer, a regard shared by the division as a whole. Soldiers, as a rule, always respect rank, if not necessarily the man holding it; in Rommel's case of the men of the 7th Panzer gave it to both—and soldiers will always fight well for an officer they respect.

The first of the two incidents of hard fighting remaining for the 7th Panzer began the day after Rommel wrote the second letter to Lucie. His division, now working along a new line of advance, turned north rather than west, headed for the city of Lille. The attack toward Lille began by establishing a bridgehead across the La Bassée Canal, one of the widest and deepest in northwest Europe. When a machine-gun battalion was pinned down by rifle fire from the well dug-in British rearguard, Rommel gave his men a tongue-lashing, standing atop a railway embankment running alongside the canal. As the divisional history told it,

> He complained that we were not doing enough to combat the British riflemen and climbed up on top of the railroad embankment, then, standing up right amid the enemy fire, proceeded to dictate targets to the antitank gun crews of Number Four and Number Seven companies. One by one their leading gunners and commanders were shot dead, clean through the head, but the general himself seemed totally immune to the enemy fire.[83]

Once the 7th Panzer was across the canal, General Hoth, Rommel's corps commander, despairing of the lethargic von Hartlieb-Walsporn, now gave Rommel command of the 5th Panzer Division as well as the 7th Panzer. He would need it, for his mission was to hold Lille's defenders in place until sufficient German infantry divisions arrived take the town. The 60 encircled Allied divisions Rommel mentioned to Lucie were the B.E.F., the French First and Seventh Armies, and the Belgian Army, which had joined the French and British forces on the Dyle River on May 10: they were all caught in the pocket created by Army Group B's offensive into Holland and Belgium, and Army Group A's drive westward from the Meuse. When the extent of the debacle that had developed once the panzers were across the Meuse and Sambre Rivers became clear, the French commander-in-chief, General Gamelin ordered the trapped armies to fall back and fight their way south, where they could join the French forces that would be pushing northward from the Somme River. The remnants of the French Ninth Army, reduced to some 40,000 men, occupied Lille, where they were to anchor the left flank of a defensive line responsible for holding back the Germans as the French retreated—the B.E.F. was already headed for the Channel ports. If they were to have any chance to avoid being completely cut off, that line had to be held. Conversely, taking Lille would allow the Germans to roll up the entire line and trap four enemy armies. The Germans were determined, then, that there be no mistake, committing seven divisions, three panzer and four infantry, to the attack on Lille.

The battle lasted four days, ending at midnight on May 31, when the French commander, General Jean-Baptiste Molinié, having done all he could, surrendered the town. It almost ended much sooner for Rommel, who, in his desire to be the first German officer to enter Lille (and collect whatever glory and fame would come with that accomplishment) drove straight into the city, only to find the streets swarming with French soldiers who were still willing to fight. A hasty gear-change into reverse and a mad scramble out of the town made good his escape. That same day he had a second close scrape, when the commander of 7th Panzer's reconnaissance battalion, Major Erdmann, was killed by friendly artillery fire just a few yards from Rommel. The following day General Hoth pulled both the 5th and 7th Panzer Divisions out of the attack—taking the city was now a job strictly for infantry. New orders were being drawn up and Rommel was told to ready his division to drive directly to the coast.

The Belgian army surrendered unconditionally on May 28, and the French First and Seventh Armies disintegrated, but the defense of Lille bought time for the B.E.F. to fight its way to Dunkirk, where between May 27 and June 4, 338,000 Allied troops were rescued from the beaches in what the British called Operation *Dynamo*. In London, Churchill would declare to the House of Commons and to the British public in general that "Wars are not won by evacuations," but the success in bringing out most of the troops of the B.E.F.—who nonetheless were forced to leave all of their tanks and artillery behind—allowed the British prime minister to convince his colleagues to fight on, whatever the French might choose to do.

While Churchill was anxiously waiting out the results of Operation *Dynamo*, Rommel had been summoned on June 2 to the Führer's presence at Hitler's temporary western headquarters near Charleville. He hurriedly drafted a report of the 7th Panzer Division's exploits thus far in the campaign and personally handed it to Hitler, who, after greeting Rommel with the words "We were very worried about your safety during the attack!" was duly impressed with its contents. Many of Rommel's colleagues were less so, viewing this as a blatant example of Rommel currying favor with Hitler. Privately, he was prepared to admit to having an ulterior motive, writing to Lucie, "I've got to act fast, or the same thing will happen as happened after Matajur." Having been robbed of glory once was one time too many for Erwin Rommel—it would never happen again if he had anything to say about it.[84]

Rommel was invited to attend the private conference which followed, the only divisional commander to do so, where Hitler outlined the O.K.W. plan for overrunning the remainder of France, *Fall Rot* (Case Red). The French Army's morale was fragile, its command structure shaky—Maurice Gamelin had been replaced as French commander-in-chief on May 19 by Maxime Weygand, a poor choice, as his dilatory nature had deprived his army of decisive leadership during the most critical days of the German offensive—and its best units had been sent to the First and Seventh Armies. *Fall Rot* called for two major attacks, the first on June 5 across the Somme River southwest towards Rouen and the Seine, the second four days later over the River Aisne to drive due south into the heart of France, splitting the French Army in two. Rommel returned to his division confident that the French would be compelled to give up in a matter of days, and feeling not a little bit cocky as well.

4 June 1940

Dearest Lu,

We're off again to-day. The six days' rest has done lot of good and helped us get our equipment more or less back into shape.

The new move won't be so very difficult. The sooner it comes the better fo us. The country here is practically untouched by war. It all went too fast. Would you cut out all the newspaper articles about me, please? I've no time to read at the moment, but it will be fun to look at them later.[85]

A few hours later, he was writing to Lucie again.

Today the second phase of the offensive begins. In an hour we shall be crossing the Somme. We've had plenty of time and so every-thing, as far as can be foreseen, is well prepared. I shall be observing the attack from well back in the rear. A fortnight, I hope, will see the war over on the mainland.[86]

At 4:00 A.M. on June 5, the 7th Panzer set out for Rouen, the entire division formed up in a huge, rolling armored "box" 2 miles wide and 12 miles long. Called a *flaschenmarsch* (literally an "area march") this formation was ideally suited to the open, gently rolling country the division now encountered. With the panzers forward, the flanks and rear protected by lighter armored vehicles, artillery, signals and support vehicles inside the box, every unit in the division could move to support any other unit in minutes. This way Rommel was able maintain a firm grip on the whole unit—there would be no repeats of the fiasco of May 19 outside Le Cateau.

Thus arrayed, the 7th Panzer Division advanced over 60 miles in two days, avoiding towns and villages which the French might have been em-ployed as defensive strongpoints, reaching Rouen on June 9, only to find the bridges across the Seine, which had been the division's objectives, blown up at the last moment by a handful of determined defenders. The approach to Rouen had been memorable: the division advanced day and night, stopping only when absolutely necessary and for the briefest amount of time possible, the troops, including Rommel himself, snatching a few hours' sleep here and there as best they could. Once, having paused briefly near a French farmhouse, Rommel was approached by a woman who lived there, who was clearly under the impression that she and her farm were still far behind the front lines. Seeing the unfamiliar uniforms, she blurted out, "Are you English?" Rommel shook his head. Horrified, the woman shrieked "Oh, the barbarians!" and fled back into her home. Rommel and his companions burst into laughter. Another day saw a British supply column, apparently as oblivious to the real military situation as had been the unfortunate Frenchwoman, captured intact and merrily plundered by the men of the 7th Division, who helped themselves to canned fruit, sweets, and tins of "bully beef" (canned corned beef) which for some reason German soldiers always regarded as a delicacy. At Rouen, Rommel and his men faced French colonial troops for the first time, the 53e régiment d'infanterie colonial mixte sénégalais (53rd Infantry Regiment Mixed Colonial Senegal, 53e RICMS), who ironically fought harder for France than did most Frenchmen. Resisting tenaciously, the Senegalese had to be dug out house by house, sometimes burned out with flamethrowers.

A dark cloud hangs over what happened next: there is evidence that some of the Senegalese troops who surrendered at Le Quesnoy, just outside of Rouen, were later shot out of hand. The question immediately arises: what did Rommel know of this and if he did, when did he know it? Such an incident was far from impossible, given the presence of dedicated Nazis like Lieutenant Hanke, who hadn't yet run afoul of Rommel, in the 7th Panzer's ranks: the Senegalese, who were "colored" troops, were, according to Nazi racial dogma, *Untermensch* who survived only at the sufferance of their racial superiors. It is not difficult to imagine Hanke or someone of his ilk encouraging soldiers still caught up in the fury and adrenaline surge of combat to kill their enemies outright, no matter how honorably those enemies fought or surrendered—there are after-action reports recounting just such incidents in the archives of every army to fight in the Second World War. The difference here would have been that Hanke's racial prejudices would have predisposed him to committing such a crime, making it a premeditated atrocity, with the 7th Panzer's soldiers serving as camouflage for his actions. For the Wehrmacht, the war had not yet assumed the stature of a racial crusade—that would have to wait until the Balkans and Russia—and given Rommel's attitude toward Nazi racial policies in general, and later his demonstrated treatment in North Africa of prisoners of war who were racially "inferior," it's almost impossible to conceive of Rommel authorizing such actions, or countenancing them after the fact. Some accusers have twisted a remark in Rommel's own account of the action in the village of Le Quesnoy as proof that he at least tacitly condoned the executions—"any enemy troops were either wiped out or forced to withdraw"—but the words themselves as well as the context of the passage hardly support the contention. Given the paucity of information about such executions by men of the 7th Panzer, compared to similar events in other German units at the time that are well-documented and attested, it could well be that, if they did in fact occur, a concerted effort was made to prevent him from gaining any reliable knowledge of such incidents. It is equally likely that the whole incident was a fabrication, an Allied propaganda ploy intended to suitably demonize the enemy. Nevertheless, the accusation was made and it has never been fully refuted, so there it must stand, at once unresolved and disturbing.[87]

Meanwhile, in the early hours of June 9, the 7th Panzer reached the valley of the Seine River, strung out along its northern slopes. An intact bridge across the Seine was found at the village of Elbeuf, but the division had become disordered in the darkness, and the battalion given the task of storming the bridge was delayed as it tried to move up to the river. Just as it was prepared to jump off for its assault, the bridge was blown up. Reconnaissance units reported that all of the other Seine bridges had likewise been demolished. The 7th Panzer would not take Rouen.

That task would fall to the 5th Panzer, as hardly had the dust from the fallen bridges settled than General Hoth had given Rommel and the 7th Panzer a new mission. A handful of relatively intact Allied units, including the British 51st Highland Division, separated from the First and Seventh Armies and the B.E.F., were trying to reach the coastal cities of Le Havre and Cherbourg, from where they hoped to be evacuated to England. Hoth told Rommel to set his sights squarely on the Channel coast and drive as fast as he could in order to cut the Allied line of advance and prevent those enemy units from reaching Le Havre. On the morning of June 10, Rommel was standing atop Colonel Rothenberg's command tank as Rothenberg ordered his driver to crash through the sea wall along the beach at Dalles, a small resort town halfway between Le Havre and Dieppe, and drive down to the water's edge. Rommel promptly signaled "Am at coast" to Hoth's headquarters; the panzers had reached the Channel: despite the naysaying of the likes of Franz Halder and the apprehension of Hitler and most of his senior generals, *Sichelschnitt* had achieved one of the swiftest, most decisive victories in history.

That same day, June 10, one of pivotal events in Rommel's life took place some six hundred miles distant from where he sat atop Oberst Rothenberg's Panzer IV. In Rome, Foreign Minister Count Galeazzo Ciano presented Italy's declarations of war to the British and French ambassadors. Hitherto, Fascist Italy had stood apart from the German war in Europe, decidedly non-neutral but very much non-belligerent. Now, however, Mussolini, who was even more of a political adventurer than Hitler, while possessing none of Hitler's calculated cunning, saw an opportunity for Italy's aggrandizement at France's expense: his goal was to gain Italy a voice in whatever peace negotiations took place, and with it the acquisition of part of France's colonial empire in Africa as Italy's share of the spoils. It was the single most stupid decision Mussolini ever made, for it would, in three years' time, lead directly to the collapse of Fascist Italy and his own downfall, and a little less than two years after that, his execution at the hands of his countrymen. It would also introduce the world as a whole to Erwin Rommel, who would be sent to North Africa to salvage what he could of Italy's collapsing colony in Libya from a British invasion, and in so doing so, brilliantly turn the tables on the invaders. But those events were more than eight months in the future, and no one at the time had the slightest inkling that they would so come about.

For the moment, Rommel had his hands full with the town of Sainte Valery-en-Caux, where the 51st Highland Division and a mixed bag of French units had holed up when the route to Le Havre was cut. For two days the ad hoc garrison held out under incessant artillery fire, the Highlanders fighting with particular tenacity as Rommel edged his panzers forward. When the German guns got within range of the harbor at Sainte Valery, any chance of further evacuation vanished, and the garrison's commander, General Marcel Ihler, ordered his men to surrender. The 51st Division's Major General Victor Fortune refused to do so, and continued fighting until his men, lacking tanks and artillery of their own, could no longer hold off the German advance into the town; he capitulated on the afternoon of June 12. In celebration, the 7th Panzer's divisional band gave a concert that night.

12 June 1940

Dearest Lu,

The battle here is over. Today one corps commander and four divisional commanders presented themselves before me in the market square of St. Valery, having been forced by my division to surrender. Wonderful moments!

16 June 1949

Before setting off south this morning (0530 hours) I received your dear letter of the 10th for which my heartfelt thanks. Today we're crossing the Seine for the second time and will, I hope, get a good step forward on the southern bank. With the fall of Paris and Verdun, and a wide break-through of the Maginot Line near Saarbrücken, the war seems to be gradually becoming a more or less peaceful occupation of all France. The population is peacefully disposed and in some places very friendly.[88]

After five days to rest and refit, the 7th Panzer was once again on the move, this time into the Cherbourg peninsula, its objective the port city of Cherbourg. By nightfall, having bluffed his way past a defensive position on the approach road, Rommel had deployed his division to attack. By this time, unconfirmed rumors of an armistice were flying about on both sides, and Rommel, sensing how easily soldiers could get careless—and thus needlessly killed—thinking the fighting was all but over, took considerable pains to make certain that his men did not lapse into such complacency. The attack began before dawn and the German tanks and infantry advanced with caution. At midday Rommel sent French civilians to the commander of the Cherbourg garrison demanding his surrender, and when no reply of any kind was received, Rommel called on Luftwaffe dive-bombers to begin pummeling the town. By 5:00 P.M., the Cherbourg garrison decided it had enough and surrendered.

It was then that Rommel learned that the rumors were true, an armistice was pending. Paul Renaud had stepped down as prime minister of France on June 16, to be replaced by Marshal Philippe Pétain, France's national hero of the First World War and a figure of great veneration by the French. Realizing that the military situation was hopeless—the French

Army was now outnumbered by more than two-to-one by Wehrmacht, with the Italian Army attacking in the south, morale was crumbling and with it the will to resist—Pétain immediately requested an armistice, which would be concluded on June 22, at Compiègne, on the same spot and in the same railway car in which the representatives of the German Army and the German Republic had signed their armistice with the Allies in November 1918. Rommel's war in France was over—for now.

The 7th Panzer Division immediately went into reserve in the Somme valley, where it was brought back up to strength and its equipment repaired or replaced as needed. In July, the division was designated as one of the units that would lead the amphibious assault in *Unternehmen Seelöwe* (Operation *Sea Lion*), the invasion of Great Britain, but when the Luftwaffe failed to gain control of the skies over England that summer, the plans for the invasion were quietly scrapped and the division was sent to Bordeaux, where it continued to train and where it was poised, if need be, to move swiftly into unoccupied France—there were rumors floating about of an impending revolt against the highly unpopular Vichy government, which had replaced the French Republic after the armistice with Germany was signed. Rommel would remain the division's commanding officer until early February 1941, and his officers and men would, by all accounts, well remember him and their service together in the Battle of France.

At the Charleroi conference on June 2, Hitler had told Rommel that the German press had christened the 7th Panzer the *"Gespensterdivision,"* the Ghost Division, because it moved so fast that no one, friend or foe alike, knew where it was, or where it would next appear. While the words were spoken in jest, there was an element of chiding in them, as, despite his obvious successes, Rommel's command style undeniably created problems for himself and his superiors. Effective command of a panzer division required that it be "led from the front," however, Rommel took the concept too literally. There was no need, for example, for the division commander to be so far forward that he could nearly suffer the same fate as the unfortunate Major Erdmann and be killed by a "short" from one of his own artillery batteries. Rommel was also too prone to leave his staff and sometimes even his radio vehicle behind while personally directing the actions of a single company or battalion, making effective coordination of the division's armor, infantry, and artillery problematic at best. General Heinz Guderian, when creating the panzer divisions, had developed a communication network that theoretically allowed command and control to be exercised from any unit in the division—Rommel never mastered the system during the 1940 campaign.

His impulsiveness sometimes led him to ignore his own staff officers, thus dsepriving him of their intelligence and initiative. He frequently failed to inform his Chief of Staff, the longsuffering Major Heidkamper, of his intentions or whereabouts, which led to uncomfortable moments such as the incident near Le Cateau when Rommel's tanks were running low on fuel and Heidkamper, having heard not a word from his commanding officer, assumed the worst had happened to him and held back the fuel bowsers. In short, Rommel was a combat commander *par excellence*, but temperamentally he was still very much the young *oberleutnant* leading a battalion of mountain troops up craggy slopes against Romanians or Italians; as a *generalmajor* and a divisional commander, he still had a lot to learn.

Whether he would have to time to complete his education became questionable as 1940 came to a close. Rommel was able to spend Christmas with Lucie and Manfred in Wiener Neustadt, but was forced to cut short his leave when yet another alarum went up in France over yet another rumored revolt against Vichy. He planned to take a second leave in February 1941 to make up for the time he lost with his wife and son at Christmas, but those plans were scrapped as well when orders arrived in Bordeaux for him to report to Berlin on February 6. Rommel reported to Generalfeldmarschall Walter von Brauchitsch in the morning, and to Hitler personally in the afternoon. He was informed that he was relieved as officer commanding of the 7th Panzer Division, and that he would instead be given command of a small, two-division corps which was being sent to North Africa, where it would be employed to bolster Italy's flagging fortunes in Libya. On February 9 he was promoted to *Generalleutnant*, on February 12 he flew to Tripoli to join his new command. The operation was code-named *Sonnenblume*—"Sunflowers"—his new command was called the Afrika Korps.

CHAPTER SIX

AFRIKA KORPS

It was a sideshow—the greatest of sideshows. . . .
—SIR CHARLES OMAN, on the Peninsular War

L
ate in the morning of February 12, 1941, Generalmajor Erwin Rommel
stepped off a Luftwaffe Junkers Ju-52 at the Castel Benito airfield outside Tripoli, Libya. That afternoon, he and Colonel Schmundt, who
by now had proven himself invaluable as an aide and adjutant, were flying
over the Libyan desert near El Agheila, giving Rommel the first look at the
landscape where he would become a legend. Two days later, he stood on
the quay as the troops and armored cars, motorcycles, trucks and artillery
of the 3rd Reconnaissance Battalion and 39th Antitank Battalion of the 5th
Light Division, the first German units to arrive in North Africa, were unloaded at the docks of Tripoli harbor. The port facilities at Tripoli, while
fairly modern, were not particularly extensive, their capacity limited, and
Rommel, anxious to get his men and equipment ashore as quickly as possible, demanded that the work continue throughout the night, the docks
bathed in the glare of floodlights, despite the very real possibility of an un-
friendly visit from the bombers of the Royal Air Force.

His urgency was driven by more than just his usual impatience: after
having made several reconnaissance flights, followed by conferences with
the senior Italian officers in Tripoli, Rommel had concluded that the only
way he could possibly accomplish the mission in North Africa given to him
by the Führer would be to pull off a bluff executed on a monumental scale.
For Rommel had not been sent to Africa to expand the reach of Nazi conquest along the far shores of the Mediterranean Sea. Despite the brilliance
of his unorthodox handling of the 7th Panzer Division in France—or arguably because of it —he had been tasked with containing the damage done

to the Axis' strategic position in the Mediterranean by Italian adventurism: in what would become something of a habit with him, Adolf Hitler, for reasons of political prestige, was trying to pull Benito Mussolini's irons out of the fire.

More than a handful of Roman emperors, various English and French kings, and even a few more recent heads of state—Idi Amin, Muamar Qadaffi, and the North Korean Kims, *pere et fils*, and the like—are remembered by history as little more than glorified buffoons. But rarely have any of them been in a position of sufficient power and influence to affect the course of world events, or alter the destinies of entire continents. And yet the one man of whom it could be said had a reasonable claim to being the greatest buffoon ever to become a head of state did exactly that: Benito Mussolini, Il Duce ("The Leader"), the dictator of Fascist Italy. Ignorant, arrogant, bombastic, and proud, his dreams of martial glory for Italy and fantasies of a revived Roman Empire would, by the time they had run their course, achieve nothing more than a few hundred thousand dead and wounded Italian soldiers, the complete loss of Italy's overseas empire, and an Italian nation left battered and broken by a war that by its end would run the length of the Italian peninsula.

Mussolini's first excursion into African adventurism occurred in 1935, when the Italians invaded Ethiopia, a conquest they could only accomplish through the use of tanks, bombers, and poison gas. He was distracted shortly thereafter by the Spanish Civil War, when he sent over 60,000 troops, along with several squadrons of the Regia Aeronautica, Italy's air force, to fight for General Francisco Franco's Nationalists. Shortly after that he began to develop closer military and diplomatic ties with Adolf Hitler, whom he had originally regarded with a measure of disdain. By 1938 and the Munich Crisis, Mussolini—and Italy with him—had fallen thoroughly into Hitler's orbit.

It wasn't until the summer of 1940 that Mussolini's attention returned to Africa. Italy had wrested away the Ottoman province of Tripolitania from the Turks in 1911, restoring its ancient Roman name of "Libya," and by dint of hard work and careful investment in the years that followed transformed what had been an Ottoman backwater into a fairly modern, reasonably prosperous Italian colony. Settlements and development were concentrated on the roadway that ran along the Mediterranean shoreline;

when Italy became an active belligerent in June 1940, work was already well under way to turn the towns of Benghazi and Tobruk into significant seaports. Tobruk in particular was heavily fortified in the months following the Italian declaration of war on France and Great Britain.

The Italian dictator soon saw that Libya's provincial governor-general, Marshal Italo Balbo, had over 215,000 Italian soldiers in Libya, while the British[89] forces right next door in Egypt numbered barely 35,000—an effective numerical superiority of better than six-to-one; likewise the disparity in strength between the Regia Aeronautica and the Royal Air Force units stationed in North Africa, while not as severe as that of the ground forces, also heavily favored the Italians. Mussolini, convinced that such apparently overwhelming superiority made an Italian victory inevitable, pressed Balbo to mount an offensive with the objective of simultaneously driving the British out of Egypt and seizing the Suez Canal.

Marshal Balbo was not nearly as sanguine as Il Duce about the prospect of an assured victory, however. He knew that his army was thoroughly modern and well equipped—for 1935, when Italy had invaded Ethiopia. But this was 1940, and in those five years weapons and warfare had evolved drastically and dramatically. Save for some 70-odd light and medium tanks, which were already obsolescent, Balbo had no armor. Only a few thousand of his infantry were motorized, that is, possessed their own truck transportation: the rest arrived at the battlefield in just the same manner as did the Italian regiments that had filled out the ranks of Bonaparte's Grande Armée—by marching to it. In the desert this translated into near-immobility, making the mass of Balbo's infantry more of a liability than an asset. Equally critical, the army's logistics were a shambles, in particular lacking the plans or means to guarantee an adequate supply of water for the troops as they advanced into Egypt. To have any chance of success, Balbo insisted, he needed at minimum one complete armored division, 100 water tankers, 1,000 trucks, and hundreds more antitank guns. Mussolini ignored Balbo's material demands and dismissed his misgivings out of hand: under heavy pressure, Balbo agreed to begin planning for an invasion of Egypt to begin sometime in late July or early August.

Those plans came to a temporary halt when Balbo was killed in a "friendly fire" incident where the Savoia-Marchetti bomber in which he was a passenger was mistakenly shot down by Italian antiaircraft gunners as it approached Tobruk on June 28, 1940. His successor, Marshal Rodolfo Graziani, despite voicing the same reservations and doubts as his late predecessor, was told by Mussolini to press on with the preparations for the offensive into Egypt, which finally began on September 13, 1940. After advancing for three days, Graziani's 150,000 troops, organized as the Tenth Army, stopped cold at the town of Maktila, 60 miles east of the Libyan–Egyptian frontier, and began to dig in, creating a line of fortified camps just east of the coastal town of Sidi Barrani which ran from the Mediterranean inland for roughly 40 miles, ending on the shoulder of a near-impassable escarpment to the south. From there Graziani refused to budge until he was reinforced and resupplied, although what little actual combat there had been with the British thus far had amounted to little more than skirmishes.

In Cairo, the British Commander-in-Chief Middle East, General Archibald Wavell, and the commander of the Western Desert Force, Major General Richard O'Connor, together concocted a plan, Operation *Compass*, to drive the Italians out of Egypt. Though badly outnumbered, the British forces were almost entirely mechanized, and thus highly mobile, while the British tanks were across the board superior to those deployed by the Italians, two crucial advantages the British commanders were determined to exploit to the fullest. Moving out on the night of December 7–8, having discovered a gap toward the southern end of the poorly sited Italian defensive positions, the British forces drove straight for Fort Capuzzo. Sixty miles behind the Italian lines, the fort dominated the coast road and was the key to the Italian defenses guarding the Libyan-Egyptian border. Capturing the fort would not only cut off the Italian army still clustered around Maktila from its supply base in Tobruk, it would block the Italians only route out of Egypt.

Graziani's army virtually disintegrated as every able-bodied officer and soldier fled westward in an effort to escape the British trap; a quarter of the Italian forces that had marched into Egypt were taken prisoner in the first five days of the British attack. Pressing forward with a speed and panache as impressive as any displayed earlier that summer by the Germans in France, the Western Desert Force, which deployed Australian and Indian divisions alongside British units, took Bardia on January 5, 1941, Tobruk on January 22, and Derna on February 3—some 400 miles from its starting line. Demoralized and off-balance, Graziani decided to abandon the whole of Cyrenaica, ordering his troops to fall back along the coast road to Beda Fomm, south of Benghazi.

Poor Italian communications security gave the game away to O'Connor, who detached a brigade-size column to drive straight west-southwest across the "bulge" of Cyrenaica and take Beda Fomm before the Italians arrived. Composed of tanks and infantry from the 7th Armoured Division, the justly famous "Desert Rats," this force, just over 2,000 strong, reached the Gulf of Sirte just north of Beda Fomm on February 4, took up strong defensive positions, and for three days fought off repeated attacks by the lead units of the retreating Italian army. With the British army to the front and rear, the Mediterranean Sea to the right and the empty waste of the Libyan desert to the left, the Italians simply gave up. Italian losses totaled around 3,000 killed, with 130,000 captured, out of the 150,000 men who had marched into Egypt. British, Australian, and Indian losses were 494 dead and 1,225 wounded, placing *Compass* among the most one-sided military campaigns in modern history.

While the British weren't able to drive the Italians out of North Africa entirely, they had, in a matter of weeks, upset the entire strategic situation in the Mediterranean. (They had no way of knowing that it would soon shift again, with equally dramatic consequences.) Only about 32,000 Italian troops, demoralized, lacking heavy weapons and all but the most basic kit, had escaped the disaster in Cyrenaica. There were still four Italian divisions in Tripolitania, the western half of Libya, which Graziani believed would be sufficient to stop any further British advance once they were positioned in the strong defenses prepared at El Agheila. Graziani himself had been among the first Italian officers to leave Tobruk when the British began sweeping westward along the Libyan coast, a situation which was not, despite appearances, an exercise in mere self-preservation. He was, after all, the governor-general of Libya, responsible for the entire province, not just the Tenth Army. He still had a job to do, namely preventing the rest of Libya from falling to the British.

Meanwhile, in a state of near-panic, Comando Supremo, the Italian high command in Rome, hurriedly shipped three fresh divisions, one infantry, one motorized, and one armored, across the Mediterranean to Tripoli, to further stiffen the defenses at El Agheila. They needn't have worried so much—O'Connor's forces, men and machines alike, were tired and worn, much in need of rest and refitting. Realizing he and O'Connor had taken their offensive as far as it could go, Wavell was, for the moment, prepared to call a halt. After all, *Compass* had exceeded even the most wildly optimistic expectations of the men who planned the operation. Ever the pragmatist, Wavell had confided to one of his senior officers on the eve of the attack that, "I do not entertain extravagant hopes of this operation but I do wish to make certain that if a big opportunity occurs we are prepared morally, mentally and administratively to use it to the fullest. . . ."[90]

This was Archibald Wavell at his finest: attuned to the possibilities of mechanized warfare; realistic, yet sufficiently flexible and imaginative to be prepared to seize and exploit unexpected opportunities. Born into a family of soldiers in 1883, Wavell was a man of formidable intellect, whom his headmaster at Summer Fields School said, in the classically understated English manner, had "sufficient ability to make his way in other walks of life"[91] than the army. Nonetheless, he chose to follow in his father's footsteps and was commissioned into the Black Watch when he graduated from Sandhurst in 1901. His first combat experience came in India in 1908, graduated from the Staff College two years later, and then spent a year as a military observer in Russia, learning the Russian language in the process; various staff positions followed, along with another stint in Russia, at one point running afoul of the Ohkrana, the tsarist secret police, who suspected him of being a spy.

When the Great War erupted, he went to France as a staff officer with the headquarters of the British Expeditionary Force, but within a few months was serving in the trenches, losing his left eye during the Second Battle of Ypres in 1915. Once he was pronounced fit for duty, he saw service once again with the Russians and then in the Middle East, rising to the temporary rank of brigadier before the Armistice. His service between the world wars was typical of that of most military men in Europe during those years—a succession of staff and command postings interspersed with brief stints on half pay, as there was a surplus of officers in the British Army during those years. In July 1939, he was named as General Officer Commanding-in-Chief of Middle East Command, with the local rank of full general; the title of his posting was changed to Commander-in-Chief Middle East in February 1940.

Despite his rather rocky relationship with Prime Minister Churchill—

Wavell was not given over to offering up pointless flattery to politicians—he was probably the ideal choice for the post. He had a firm grasp of the realities of desert warfare, especially the logistical challenges, as well as both the theory and practice of motorized and mechanized combined arms operations. He saw to it that the troops under his command were as well trained and thoroughly equipped for the desert as possible. And provided that he was allowed to exercise his command authority free from meddling by politicians, he had an excellent grasp of his strategic priorities: while overseeing Operation *Compass*, he was also directing a campaign in Ethiopia, where Major General William Platt was handily running the Italians out of the country.

When Wavell ordered the halt by the Western Desert Force outside of El Agheila in early February, his intent was that it would be as brief as possible, to give his troops some much-needed rest and allow them a chance to re-equip and refit their vehicles. He had the Italians on the run everywhere in northern and eastern Africa, and by now was supremely confident that he could drive them off the continent entirely, but on February 9, word came from London making the halt permanent and directing him to begin preparations for embarking at least one division for service elsewhere. The directive came straight from the prime minister, Winston Churchill, and though Wavell protested vigorously, he immediately set about to comply with his new orders.

As it turned out, events had anticipated Wavell's decision to halt before El Agheila: Mussolini had bungled yet another military adventure, this time in Greece. In April 1939, the Italians had invaded the tiny and essentially defenseless kingdom of Albania, on the eastern shore of the Adriatic Sea, forcibly incorporating it into the Kingdom of Italy; in late October 1940, Mussolini decided that Greece was a plum ripe for the picking. Jealous of the victories won by Adolf Hitler's Wehrmacht in France and the Low Countries, which had commanded the attention of the world, he declared, "Hitler always faces me with a *fait accompli*. This time I am going to pay him back in his own coin. He will find out from the newspapers that I have occupied Greece."[92] The resultant military laurels would burnish the reputation of Italian arms as well as Il Duce's stature as a would-be conqueror. The Greeks were of a different mind: when the Italian army attacked out of the Albanian hills, the Greeks fought back tenaciously and soon were counterattacking, driving the Italians pell-mell back across the Albanian border. By the end of January 1941, after having lost nearly a quarter of Albania, the Italians had finally stopped the Greeks, who were having severe supply problems in the rugged Albanian mountains.

There the situation might have stayed, in indefinite stalemate, had Winston Churchill not chosen this moment to intervene. Pugnacious and aggressive, Churchill saw the Italian attack on Greece as an opening where the British Army could once again have a presence on the European continent, eventually, it was hoped, striking directly at the Germans. Greece had been neutral in the European war until attacked by Italy: had Mussolini "stayed home," as it were, there would have been no opportunity for Britain to intervene. British intelligence was convinced—correctly—that the Germans were preparing to invade Greece, for reasons of political prestige as much as military necessity—an effort to help Mussolini "save face" and prevent repeated Italian embarrassments from splattering onto the Third Reich. Churchill saw a chance to steal a march on the Nazis by reinforcing the Greeks, and so directed Wavell to pull the Australian 6th Division out of the British position in front of El Agheila, and ready it to be transferred to Greece, the first of four British divisions to be sent there.

Mussolini now had two debacles on his hands, North Africa and Greece, which together could lead to the collapse of the Italian war effort; instead of gaining fresh conquests for his revived Roman Empire, victories which would earn the awe if not the admiration of the world, he had blundered into widening the war, creating awkward strategic complications for his German allies at the very moment when the O.K.W. was preoccupied with planning the pending invasion of the Soviet Union in the summer of 1941. Hitler decided that enough was enough—Mussolini, left to his own devices, was a liability, not an asset, and if the Führer couldn't abandon his fellow dictator, he could at least bring him to heel. In early October 1940 Hitler had met with Mussolini at the Brenner Pass and suggested sending a small contingent of German troops and tanks to North Africa to bolster the Italian effort against the British. The Italian dictator, in a fit of the same pique that drove him to invade Greece, had spurned the Führer's assistance; now, Hitler was no longer offering, he was telling Mussolini that the Deutsches Afrika Korps ("German Africa Corps"), which on January 11, 1941 was activated on his personal order, was going to Tripolitania with the express purpose of stopping the Italian collapse there.

It was this rather bizarre confluence of events and circumstances, then, that brought Erwin Rommel to North Africa. From the outset, Hitler had only meant for Afrika Korps to support the Italian defense of Libya; he neither imagined nor intended that North Africa would evolve into a major theater of the war. Meanwhile, senior officers of the ilk of Halder and von Brauchitsch considered it to be the perfect backwater in which to dispose of a rambunctious general who was insufficiently deferential to their caste. If they couldn't rid themselves of this troublesome officer, they could at least marginalize him.

Predictably, from the very beginning Erwin Rommel did not see it that way at all. Just as he had done in France, Rommel would write to Lucie daily while in North Africa, even if only a few lines, and the succession of letters she received in the weeks after Rommel's arrival in Tripoli creates a powerful impression of the energy, drive, and ambition he brought to his new posting. While careful not to give away the show, it was clear that he wasn't at all prepared to simply sit in place and wait for the British to do something.

14 February 1941

Dearest Lu,

All is going as well as I could wish. I hope to be able to pull it off. I'm doing well. There's nothing whatever for you to worry about. A lot to do. I've already had a thorough look around.

17 February 1941

Everything is splendid with me and mine in this glorious sunshine. I'm getting on very well with the Italian command and couldn't wish for better cooperation. My lads are already at the front, which has been moved about 560 kilometers [350 miles] to the east. As far as I am concerned [the British] can come now.

5 March 1941

Just returned from a two-day journey—or rather, flight—to the front, which has now been moved about 450 miles to the east. Everything going fine. A lot to do. Can't leave here for the moment as I couldn't be answerable for my absence. Too much depends on my own person and my determination. I hope you've gotten some of the letters from me. My troops are on the way. Speed is the one thing that matters here.

. . . Had a "gala" showing of *Victory in the West* here today. . . . I said [to the guests] that I hoped the day would come when we would be showing *Victory in Africa*.[93]

By the time this last letter was written, the whole of the 5th Panzer Regiment, the armored contingent of the 5th Light Division, around which the Afrika Korps would be organized, had been shipped across the Mediterranean and landed at Tripoli. It mustered a total strength of only 150 tanks, half of which were Panzer Is and Panzer IIs, vehicles more suited to reconnaissance and screening than to actual combat. Rommel, hoping to create an illusion of having greater strength than he actually possessed, staged an elaborate parade for his panzer regiment in Tripoli, rolling his tanks down the central boulevard of the city. Once they had turned off the main street, they raced back to the parade's starting point, and, like a stage army once again passed down the broad roadway, creating the illusion of a seemingly endless column of armor prepared to advance against the British. Rommel suspected, rightly, that Allied spies in Tripoli would take careful count of the numbers and types of vehicles in the procession, and pass their numbers on to the British intelligence services. After several such passes, the tanks, still painted in their dark *panzergrau*, roared off down the coastal highway toward El Agheila. At the moment, Rommel could have no idea just how effective had been his little ruse, or what unexpected dividends it would pay when he set into motion his own plans for the Afrika Korps. For what Erwin Rommel was about to undertake was nothing short of an act of audacious insubordination carried out on a truly massive scale.

The German General Staff's plan for the Afrika Korps, concocted under the name *Sonnenblume* ("Sunflowers"), was to do no more than hold the position at El Agheila, essentially accepting the status quo in North Africa. There were sound strategic reasons for adopting a more-or-less permanent defensive posture in Libya. Tunisia and Tripolitania were secure: the Vichy French regime in Algeria could be counted on to remain docile and cooperative, which meant that there would be no attacks from the west;

and by this time the Italians had pretty much had their fill of aggressive adventures. For their part, the upper echelons of the German high command were preoccupied with the planning for *Fall Barbarossa*, the invasion of the Soviet Union scheduled for the summer of 1941. Every aspect of Germany's military capability was to be subordinated to this titanic undertaking, and the General Staff officers of the O.K.W. were unwilling to consider any diversion or dilution of the forces available to the Wehrmacht with which to attack the Russians. In their eyes, that one armored division, the 5th Light, had been diverted to North Africa, and an entire Luftwaffe air corps, Fliegerkorps X, complete with fighters, dive-bombers, and level bombers, had been transferred to airfields in Sicily, all in support of a faltering "ally," was bad enough. Conventional strategic wisdom dictated that nothing more in the way of men or materiel be sent to Africa: Rommel's task was to hold the line against the British where he stood, nothing more.

Rommel took a very different view of the situation. In a memorandum analyzing the destruction of Graziani's Tenth Army, he concluded that

> Graziani's failure can be attributed mainly to the fact that the Italian army was delivered up helpless and un-motorized in the open desert to the weak but fully motorized British formations, while the Italian motorized forces, although too weak oppose the British successfully, were nevertheless compelled to accept battle and allow themselves to be destroyed in defense of the infantry. . . . Out of this purely motorized form of warfare which developed in Libya and Egypt there arose certain principles, fundamentally different from those applicable in other theaters.

In other words, immobility in the desert, whether the consequence of a lack of equipment and faulty organization, or inflicted by foolish orders from on high, was a recipe for disaster. Sitting at El Agheila waiting for the British to attack made defeat inevitable. As Rommel saw the situation, "defending" Libya by giving up half the province was foolishness—the best defense was one staged as far forward as possible. But by the time the Afrika Korps arrived in Tripoli, the Italians had withdrawn yet again, this time to Sirte, 100 miles further west, abandoning El Agheila to the British, with only screens of light units covering the distance in between. Therefore, rather than waiting for the British to come to him, he, Rommel, would take the war back to the British, and if given the opportunity, defend Libya by driving the British out of the province entirely. To accomplish this, though, Rommel would have to resort to evasion, deception, prevarication and outright lying to both his own German superiors and the Italian Comando Supremo. That he had to do so was the consequence of the bewildering—and often bewildered—command structure in North Africa.[94]

As the British—who have had more experience at it than any other nation on earth—could have told the Germans, coalition warfare is never easy. The peculiar, prickly, and paranoid personalities of Adolf Hitler and Benito Mussolini made joint military efforts between Germany and Italy rather more difficult than were such undertakings typically. The core of the problem lay in the very nature of the "Berlin–Rome Axis" itself. Formed in 1936, at a moment in European history when both Germany and Italy were feeling diplomatically isolated, it was never a proper alliance in the true sense of the word, as the military and political objectives of the two nations—and the two dictators—were too divergent to allow their military arms to develop a coherent joint strategy and command structures.

When Rommel arrived in North Africa, he was technically subordinate to the governor-general of Libya, which at the time was still Marshal Graziani, who would be replaced by Marshal Italo Gariboldi on March 25. The province was an Italian colony, the majority of the troops there were, and would remain throughout Rommel's African sojourn, Italian, and all of the Afrika Korps' supplies would be carried across the Mediterranean by Italian shipping. These three factors made the Germans *de jure* the junior partners in the North African venture. Rommel, from a combination of national pride and personal ego, was determined from the outset that he and his people would *de facto* take the lead in whatever campaigns lay ahead. To do so, he brazenly exploited the realities of the command structure for North Africa that had been cobbled together by Rome and Berlin.

Rommel's temper quickly chafed under Italian authority—his comment in his letter to Lucie that he was "getting on very well with the Italian command and couldn't wish for better cooperation" was disingenuous at best. Key to Rommel's frequent circumvention of Gariboldi and his successors—whom Rommel came to regard as a bunch of clucking old women—would be that as commanding officer of the German ground forces in North

Africa, he possessed the right to appeal any decision made in Rome with which he disagreed to the O.K.H., the O.K.W., or even Adolf Hitler himself. At the same time, when he disagreed with senior German officers on operational and strategic decisions in the Mediterranean theater, the Luftwaffe's General (later Field Marshal) Albert Kesselring, for example, he was not above playing a similar game with them. If Comando Supremo had issued a directive which Rommel could construe as being in support of his particular plans and objectives, he would simply point out that Rome had given him specific instructions and thus he had no choice but to obey orders.

Still, Rommel's attitude toward his Italian colleagues and superiors would remain one of mingled distrust and disgust. Understandably shaken by the rout of the Tenth Army by the Western Desert Force, the generals in Rome and Tripoli nonetheless seemed more intent on assigning—and avoiding—blame than on working to correct the defects in their army, and for this Rommel gave them little respect. During his time in North Africa, he would take an almost perverse pleasure, whenever asked by a senior Italian officer where he had won his *Pour le Mérite*, in blurting out "Longarone!"

At the same time, though, Rommel would discover that there was nothing fundamentally wrong with the typical Italian soldier—the problem was their *officers:* the higher the rank, the less competent they were. When under the leadership of German NCOs and junior officers, that is, men who knew what they were doing on a battlefield, Italian *soldati* could—and would—fight with tenacity and courage. Already the bravery of Italian artillerymen was legendary on both sides in North Africa: there would be more than one instance in the Libyan desert where British tanks had blood on their tracks after literally overrunning the positions of Italian gunners who stubbornly refused to give up their guns.

But even at their best the Italians would remain something of a liability for Rommel in North Africa, far less by way of any deficiencies of the Italians as soldiers than of the circumstances and reasons by which they were compelled to fight. Badly equipped, poorly trained, treated with indifference at best and disdain at worst by his officers, the typical *soldati* was hardly motivated to wage wars of conquest which brought glory to Mussolini and his cronies but did little to improve the material lot of the Italian people, and so could hardly be faulted for lacking in martial ardor. Rommel would have to do the best he could with them.

The stage was being set, the players were taking their places for Act I, Scene One of the great drama that would be the war in North Africa. After the grand production of its parade in Tripoli, the 5th Panzer Regiment was rushed forward, along with the 200th Rifle Regiment, an infantry unit, two reconnaissance battalions, an antitank battalion, a pair of machine-gun battalions and three batteries of artillery. Led by Generalmajor Johannes Streich, 5th Light Division's officer commanding, they first went to Sirte, then onward to El Mugtaa, just west of El Agheila. A late arrival was a "flak"[95]—antiaircraft—battalion, which included a dozen 88mm antiaircraft guns that could do double duty in an antitank role. Along with 5th Light came the Italian Ariete Armored Division and the 102nd Motorized "Trento" Division, while four divisions of Italian infantry followed as best they could. Hoping to deceive British aerial reconnaissance as to both his numbers and intentions, he gave orders for scores of dummy tanks to be fabricated out of canvas and plywood, some immobile, others mounted on the ubiquitous *kübelwagens* (a type of German jeep) so that they could be moved at will, and deployed in the desert, while real vehicles created a confusion of tracks in the sand.

Even as his preparations were still underway, Rommel began to consider the implications and potential of an offensive against the British in North Africa. In late February, when a young Italian officer reporting for duty on Rommel's staff lamented that his division had just been driven out of Ethiopia, his new commanding officer told him not to worry about it. "We're going to drive all the way to the Nile," Rommel declared with a grin, "then make a right turn and take it all back!" That was simply a bit of classic Rommel cockiness, but privately, giving his imagination free rein and allowing for a scenario where the best of all possible outcomes took place, he allowed himself to foresee such a possibility: once his second panzer division arrived in May, a quick, hard strike along the length of the Via Balbia, the Italian-built coastal highway, might drive the British all the way back into Egypt and across the Suez Canal. Drafting a letter to Berlin on March 9, he outlined what he believed should be the course of operations in North Africa: "My first objective will be to retake Cyrenaica; my second, northern Egypt and the Suez Canal." It is impossible to be certain whether Rommel regarded the concept as the basis for developing a detailed strategic plan for North Africa, or if this was simply a clever device he used in an effort to draw more of the O.K.W.'s—and Hitler's—attention to the Mediterranean theater in the hope of securing a greater commitment of reinforcements in the months ahead. In any event, at a command conference held in Berlin 10 days after sending off his letter, nothing was said to him about this idea for a wider war in North Africa.

By way of a prologue, the first encounter between German and British troops in North Africa occurred on February 24, when an armored car of the 8th King's Royal Irish Hussars was captured, along with its three-man crew. The three Englishmen and their vehicle yielded little in the way of useful information about British strength and intentions, but bits and pieces assembled by Rommel's intelligence section began to create the impression in the Afrika Korps commander's mind that what Rome and Berlin believed to be the strategic and operational situation in Cyrenaica was very different from the reality. He had been told that he faced two full-strength armored divisions, with at least one infantry division firmly dug in to support them. By the middle of March, though, Rommel began to suspect otherwise: however daunting the British defenses at El Agheila might appear, he was becoming more certain with each passing day that there was little strength behind them.

On March 18 Rommel flew back to Berlin, there to confer on the following day with Hitler and the O.K.W. about the future of operations in North Africa. Before he left, he directed General Streich to prepare a plan for the 5th Light Division to carry out a strong reconnaissance—essentially a probing attack—of the British position at El Agheila, the jump-off date set for March 24. In Berlin, he was received warmly by Hitler, who personally awarded Rommel the Oakleaves to his Knight's Cross, awarded in recognition of his leadership of the 7th Panzer Division in May and June of the previous year. Fulsome in his praise for Rommel's tactical and operational skills, Hitler also made lavish promises concerning the men, tanks, and equipment that would be sent to North Africa in the months to come.

A follow-on conference with von Brauchitsch and Halder delivered a cold dose of reality concerning the Führer's assurances of materiel largesse: as he was told when given command of the Afrika Korps, Rommel could indeed expect a second Panzer Divison, the 15th, as well as some additional artillery, antitank, and transport units by the end of May, but beyond that, aside from replacements to make good the inevitable combat losses, he could and should expect very little if anything in the way of reinforcement. Both Halder and von Brauchitsch were explicit in telling Rommel that he was expected to maintain a defensive posture in North Africa: under no circumstances was he to undertake a major attack against the British. As Rommel had no "need to know," as it were, they could not explain that the O.K.W. was hoarding its resources for the forthcoming invasion of the Soviet Union. To say that he was disappointed by this news would be an understatement; Rommel was convinced that a tremendous opportunity was being squandered, later writing that he was "not very happy at the efforts of Field Marshal von Brauchitsch and Colonel General Halder to keep down the number of troops sent to Africa and leave the future of this theater of war to chance."

AT DAWN ON March 24, the curtain went up on Act I, Scene One of Rommel's great adventure in North Africa, as General Streich sent out a strong reconnaissance in force to probe the British defenses at El Agheila. The tanks and armored cars of the 3rd Reconnaissance Battalion charged forward on a front 1,000 yards wide, their numbers augmented by many of the dummy tanks built on Rommel's orders in the last month. Behind the onrushing armor, the Afrika Korps' "soft-skinned" vehicles—lorries, gasoline bowsers, water tankers, staff cars and the like, so-called because they were unarmored—deliberately created a massive dust cloud, creating the impression that the attacking force was much larger.

The ruse worked. The British defenders, the understrength 2nd Armoured Division supported by a handful of infantry battalions, a force less than half the size of that which German intelligence in Berlin had assured Rommel was holding El Agheila, began abandoning their positions and moving northward just as the lead German tanks came into engagement range. The British, though surprised, having become accustomed to Italian passivity, retired quickly but in reasonably good order, withdrawing to Mersa el Brega, 40 miles north of El Agheila. Once there, the British began to dig in, stringing barbwire obstacles and laying minefields. Naturally, the longer they were allowed to work undisturbed, the stronger their position would become, as the terrain created an excellent defensive position: a ridge of low, sandy hills with the Mediterranean Sea on one flank and impassable salt marshes on the other formed a natural defile that all but compelled an attacker to resort to a frontal assault. Swinging wide to the east around the salt marsh in an effort to outflank Mersa el Brega would create more problems—especially supply difficulties—than it solved. If the British were going to stop the Afrika Korps, Mersa el Brega was the place to do it.

Rommel's holy trinity of warfare was "Sturm, Schwung, Wucht"—"attack, momentum, force," an intriguing variation on Bonaparte's dictum "Mass times velocity equals impact." All of his experience in Romania and Italy in the First World War, and in France in the Second, had driven home the lesson that once an enemy began to retreat, he would tend to keep retreating, particularly if a withdrawal route was to hand. Only with his back to the wall, with nowhere else to go, would an enemy turn and fight to the death. Rommel's natural inclination had always been to exploit that tendency to its fullest, and now he saw yet another opportunity to do so. The British in front of Rommel were far from panicked but definitely a bit off-balance, like a prizefighter caught on the wrong foot when hit by his opponent. They were disorganized by the retreat from El Agheila (no unit of any size in any army ever retreats in perfect order), plagued by equipment problems (most of the 2nd Armoured Division's tanks hadn't yet been properly modified for service in the desert), and suffering from the effects of a recently reshuffled command structure (the Western Desert Force had been designated XIII Corps at the beginning of January, only to have the corps deactivated in mid-February, with its units now under direct command of HQ Cyrenaica, all the way back in Tobruk). The very last thing the Rommel could allow the British was time to sort out their problems.

Accordingly, a plan for a frontal assault, something that Rommel was normally loathe to order, was drawn up, and on the morning of March 31 the 5th Light Division attacked Mersa el Brega. The British fought stubbornly, the Germans only slowly gained ground, and for a time it looked as if the defenders might hold on. But Rommel was once again doing what he did best, leading from the front, and he found a narrow track threading through the eastern edge of the sand hills, where they met the salt marsh, and sent the 8th Machine-Gun Battalion along it in a flanking move that threatened to cut the British line of retreat along the coast road. The British defenders saw this and immediately disengaged, this time somewhat more precipitously than they had done at El Agheila, making for the coastal town of Agedabia, another 50 miles up the Via Balbia. In their haste they left behind 50 Bren carriers—small, hardy, lightly armored, fully tracked infantry transports ideally suited to the desert, and a few dozen lorries, welcome additions to the Afrika Korps' inventory of vehicles.

Having taken Mersa el Brega and the British having fallen back to Agedabia, the Afrika Korps stood in what was the "front door" to the rest of North Africa's Mediterranean coast, but Rommel was now faced with a dilemma: whether or not to immediately press on to Agedabia. He was well aware that his orders from Berlin and Rome, as well as those of General Gariboldi, his nominal superior in Cyrenaica, forbade him to take any major offensive action—including any attack on Mersa el Brega—before the 15th Panzer Division arrived at the end of May. Technically, he was already in violation of those orders, something that, admittedly, had never been much of a hindrance to him when he believed he was faced with an opportunity to deal a defeat to the enemy, and he knew that he had before him a wavering foe, who, with one good hard push might be sent tumbling pell-mell all the way back to Egypt, reversing the decision rendered by Operation *Compass* only four months previously.

When he met with Hitler, Halder and von Brauchitsch on March 19, he had been emphatic in his belief that the British in North Africa were more intent on resting and refitting those units that had made *Compass*'s mad dash across Cyrenaica than on whatever the Germans and Italians were doing there. He pointed out that Luftwaffe reconnaissance flights had shown that XIII Corps was concentrating its armor near Benghazi, an ideal location for holding the Jebel Achdar, the rolling, fertile highlands of the Cyrenaica "bulge" just to the east of Benghazi. To Rommel, this was a mistake, for he was certain that he could lead the Afrika Korps across the base of that bulge, attacking toward Gazala, simultaneously threatening to strike at Tobruk and cut off the British garrison in Benghazi. To do this he needed the 15th Panzer sent to North Africa immediately, not in May. Halder and von Brauchitsch were adamant in their refusal: Rommel's second armored division would arrive as scheduled, not a day sooner. When it did, he was authorized to capture Mersa el Brega, strike at Agedabia, and possibly take Benghazi if the opportunity to do so presented itself, but in all events he was to exercise caution and be wary of overextending his forces. Rommel would later recount that he pointed out how *Compass* had shown that "we could not just take Benghazi, but would have to occupy the whole of Cyrenaica, as the Benghazi area could not be held by itself." Once back in Africa, Rommel was confident that he could explain away his decision to take Mersa el Brega as fulfilling the spirit if not the actual letter of his orders: the opportunity had presented itself, and he took it. Allowing the British another two months to improve the depth and breadth of their defenses would have made an attack in late May a far more difficult and costly operation, no matter what reinforcement he had received by that time. There was more than a bit of barracks-room lawyering in this rationalization, but it was far from unreasonable, and allowing officers in the field to use their judgment and initiative had been part of the German military tradition since the days of Frederick the Great. Driving on to attack Agedabia, however, was entirely another matter. . . .

Rommel being Rommel, he resorted to a tactical subterfuge, this one meant to deceive his own superiors. On April 1, Rommel drove to the 5th Light Division's headquarters company on the outskirts of Mersa el Brega, there to receive General Streich's report on the previous day's action. At one point in their conversation, Rommel asked in a voice that was half-bantering, half-serious, "So, when are we going to meet in Agedabia?" Streich, matching his commander's tone exactly, replied, "I don't know—we'll have to see about that." Already Streich was learning how to "read between the lines" in his conversations with his commanding officer: no sooner had Rommel left the command post than Streich began issuing orders for the 5th Light to begin moving northward at first light the following morning, its objective the capture of Agedabia.

For his part, Rommel busied himself with administrative details for most of the morning of April 2, not catching up with Streich until the early afternoon. Seeing the entire division rolling forward in combat formations, he made a theatrical display of being surprised, asking, "What's going on here?"

"I thought we ought not to give the enemy a chance to dig in all over again," Streich replied, "so, I'm moving my whole division forward, and I'm about to attack Agedabia."

Rommel nodded sagely. "Those were not my instructions," he said, "but I approve." The 5th Light Division took Agedabia that afternoon virtually without a fight.

The Italians were furious—not at having Agedabia retaken, but at Rommel's seemingly blithe ignorance of explicit orders from the governor-general, Gariboldi. Seeking out the Afrika Korps' commander, the portly Italian officer was blunt in confronting Rommel, declaring, "This is in contradiction to what I ordered! You are to wait for me before continuing any advance!" The O.K.W. expression of disapproval was more measured, Rommel being told that "Any limited offensive moves . . . are not to exceed the capabilities of your small force. . . . Above all, you are to avoid any risk to your open right flank, such as is bound to be entailed in turning north to attack Benghazi."

Fortune came down heavily on Rommel's side at this moment, contributing in no small part to his success at Mersa el Brega and Agedabia, as well as the continued relative freedom of action he would enjoy for the next few months. Unknowingly, he had attacked El Agheila and Mersa el Brega at exactly the moment when the British were at their most vulnerable in North Africa. The abortive Italian invasion of Greece had gone so badly that it soon became obvious to the political and military leaders on both sides that Hitler would have to intervene in order to prevent yet another strategic disaster overtaking his ally Mussolini. The Greeks had committed over three-quarters of their army's manpower to their northwestern frontier, where the Greeks were soundly trouncing the Italians. This left Greece's north*eastern* frontier almost denuded of troops, and there the Germans, along with their Bulgarian allies, began massing troops. German planning for this invasion had begun as far back as the beginning of November 1940, just days after a handful of small British detachments arrived in Piraeus. Hitler's objective was not simply saving Mussolini's floundering strategic situation, but, more importantly, denying the Royal Navy any possibility of establishing naval bases on the north shore of the Mediterranean.

For almost three months the Greek and British governments dithered in negotiations about the size and scope of British assistance until mid-February, when it was finally decided that a force of at least three divisions, including one armored, would be sent to Piraeus, and from there northward to the Bulgarian border. All three were drawn from Wavell's Middle East command; the Western Desert Force was particularly hard hit, giving up half its strength when the 1st Armoured Brigade, 6th Australian Division and 2nd New Zealand Division were tagged to be withdrawn to

Alexandria and from there sent to Piraeus. Thus his enemy's strength had been almost halved by the time Rommel attacked El Agheila, and many of those units that remained were new to the desert, suffering equipment and acclimation problems. Rommel's attack had caught the British out of position, flatfooted, unable to stage an effective riposte.

What would become an essential but sometimes overlooked element of the war in North Africa now came into play as Rommel moved north to Mersa el Brega, one which had no small part in how poorly the British were able to anticipate and prepare for Rommel's strike north. As the Axis forces began pushing up the coast of Cyrenaica, a shadowy, three-cornered, all-but-invisible intelligence battle was taking shape, one that began almost the same day that Rommel arrived in North Africa, steadily growing in intensity. For all that it was relatively bloodless, it was nonetheless waged as fiercely as any of the tank and infantry battles fought by the German, Italian, and British troops in the heat of the desert sun. It was a war of mostly, but not solely, signals intelligence, as radio operators, analysts, and cryptographers, along with spies in locales as distant and disparate as Lisbon, Rome, Cairo, and the suburbs of London, worked around the clock to provide their superiors with bits and pieces of information which, when properly pieced together, could produce operational and strategic advantages which could—and often did—prove decisive in the see-saw campaign in the Libyan desert.

Part of this shadow war of signals intelligence was Ultra, the British code name for their ultrasecret system of decrypting Wehrmacht and Luftwaffe radio messages sent via the Enigma device, an encryption machine that the Germans believed impossible to "crack," that is, once a message was encyphered by an Enigma machine, only someone possessing a similar machine with the proper settings could decypher and read it. In what was one of the two best-kept secrets of the Second World War (the other being the Manhattan Project), the British intelligence community was able to construct a machine that could do just that, however, and in early 1941, the radio traffic between Rome, Berlin, and Afrika Korps headquarters, intercepted and "unbuttoned" by Ultra, led the British to believe that Rommel would remain on the defensive at least until the arrival of the 15th Panzer Division in May. When Rommel advanced out of El Agheila, Churchill was convinced, based on the orders from Berlin that had been decyphered by

Ultra, that it was not a serious threat, cabling Wavell with the jocular comment, "I presume you are only waiting for the tortoise to stick his head out far enough before chopping it off." Wavell replied that, from his own reading of the Ultra intercepts, he was certain the Germans and Italians had no plans for any sort of major offensive, proof that he was, as he later admitted, "very much in the dark as to the enemy's real strength or intentions." Likewise, on March 30 Wavell informed Lieutenant General Phillip Neame, the General Officer Commanding-in-Chief and Military Governor of Cyrenaica and hence the commanding officer of the Western Desert Force, that Rommel would stay put in El Agheila for at least a month. Little did they know their man, nor would this be the only time when Rommel would choose to do exactly the opposite of what O.K.W. orders directed. Consequently, Rommel's panzers were rolling toward Benghazi even while the British in Cairo and London were still convinced that he was not yet ready to attack Mersa el Brega.[96]

Each morning for the next six weeks the cry would go out in the pre-dawn darkness, "*Aufsteigen!*"—"Mount up!"—and the panzer crews, having made whatever early breakfast they could, began to clamber into their tanks, prepared to advance and, if need be, fight yet another day. In the desert more than anywhere else in the world, the tank dominates the battlefield. A roaring, smoke-belching, flame-breathing steel box on treads, a tank is a remarkable combination of awesome power and surprising vulnerability. In the Panzer IIIs and IVs that were the fighting backbone of the Afrika Korps, five men served to crew each tank. The gunner, loader, and tank commander would, with a litheness born of long practice, slide through the hatches on the sides and top of the gun turret, while the driver and radio operator (who did double-duty by manning the hull-mounted bow machine gun if the tank was engaged by enemy infantry) took their places via hatches on the top deck of their machine.

The previous night, before they ate, slept, or attended to any personal business, all five crewman would have cleaned their tank's guns—the main gun, the machine gun mounted alongside it on a coaxial mounting, and the bow gun—topping off the fuel tanks, radiator, and engine oil, adjusting the tension on the tracks, and attended to whatever minor mechanical problems might have been produced by the day's action. Now, with the first faint light of dawn just beginning to touch the eastern sky, the driver started the engine (hoping that the batteries hadn't lost their charge overnight, always a possibility that would necessitate hand-cranking the engine), while the radioman warmed up his equipment and performed a quick signals check, after which he loaded his machine gun. In the turret, the loader did a quick visual inventory of the rounds available for the main gun—a 37- or 50mm weapon in the Panzer III, a short-barreled 75mm gun in the Panzer IV. Hopefully during the night the ammunition trucks had been able to fully replenish whatever ammunition had been expended the previous day, but if not, it was the loader's job to make the commander aware of how many rounds—antitank and high explosive—were available.

The gunner cleared the main gun for action, checking that there were no obstructions in the bore, and if necessary recalibrating the sights if the tank had seen hard use the previous day that might have skewed them. The commander tied his vehicle into the platoon and company radio nets and made sure that his maps were properly updated, then while the rest of the crew finished their work, he and the other tank commanders would hold a quick conference with their company commander to learn of any last-minute changes in plan. Once this was done, he would return to his vehicle, don his headphones, and wait for the crackle of static that would precede a slightly metallic-sounding voice giving the order to *"Weitergehen!"*—"Move out!"

Under way a tank is an impressive sight, if only because of its stark, uncompromising purposefulness. Its appearance is purely functional: there is no place for aesthetics on or in a vehicle designed expressly to destroy others of its kind, kill soft-skinned vehicles, and bring death to enemy infantry. How a tank is perceived on a battlefield is entirely subjective: an infantryman sees an armored behemoth, its armor seemingly invulnerable, possessing firepower that a mere footsoldier can never hope to wield. A tank is a mobile object offering friendly infantrymen cover and protection from enemy fire while it destroys enemy strongpoints and guns. Antitank gunners and artillerymen see enemy tanks as targets, one half of a kill-or-be killed duel, as rarely will gun or tank survive a direct hit from its opponent. Enemy tankers see their opponents in much the same way—a tank-versus-tank engagement has a more than passing similarity to an Old West gunfight: being quick on the draw isn't enough, to survive a tank crew has to be both fast *and* accurate.

It is the penalty for failure that is a tank crewman's worst nightmare. While the front armor of his vehicle may be as much as two inches thick, the sides are usually only half that, and the top and bottom armor only half that again. Inside that armor were fuel tanks which, in a Panzer III for example, could hold as much as 84 gallons of gasoline; up to 100 rounds of ammunition for the main gun would be stored in ready-use lockers on either side of the hull, adjacent to the turret. The result was that while a tank could hit hard and sometime be hit, to its crew it was always a rolling explosion waiting to happen if it took a hit in the wrong place.

If the crew of a tank struck by enemy fire were lucky, the incoming round might hit the transmission, blow off a part of the suspension, or knock out the engine, sufficient of course to immobilize the tank, but something the crew could readily survive. Worse were antitank projectiles that penetrated the armor and entered the crew compartment—fragments of red-hot steel would go whizzing about inside the tank at supersonic speeds with enough force to tear apart men and equipment with equal ease. The worst case was a hit in the fuel tanks or the ammunition storage: the result was what the men of the British 7th Armored Division, the legendary Desert Rats, called "brewing up"—either a searing flash as the ammunition exploded, or a swiftly spreading fireball that expanded out of every aperture in the stricken tank's hull as the fuel ignited. Either way, the fate of crewmen in such vehicles was grisly.

Even when there was no one shooting at them, there was more than sufficient discomfort and danger for the crew. Daytime temperatures in the North African desert often peaked close to 130° F in the summer months. Tanks would travel with every hatch and shutter open, in an effort to introduce even the smallest measure of a cooling breeze inside the vehicle. Once enemy action was in the offing, the hatches would be closed and the crew had to endure rising temperatures and limited ventilation. The stink of mingled sweat, gasoline fumes, hot motor oil, and the ammonia vapors from the burned propellant in spent shell casings made the air inside nigh unbreathable. Vision for all but the commander was limited to the narrow arcs offered by the vision blocks and ports of a crewman's position, while illumination came from one small light bulb in the turret and one in the hull for the driver and radio operator. Tank engagements usually were relatively brief, so that at the first opportunity a tank's crew would open the hatches to gulp down the fresh air, and even 120° F could seem blessedly cool after being shut up inside a sweltering steel box for as much as an hour at a time, fighting against an enemy just as determined to survive the encounter. Such was the life of a tank crew in the Afrika Korps.

This was the life that awaited the Afrika Korps' panzer crews when Rommel started his tanks rolling northward out of Agedabia. It was also at this moment that his signals intelligence section began to come into its own. Straining to capture every possible wireless message sent by the British, the Afrika Korps' radio intercept company, commanded by Lieutenant (later Captain) Alfred Seebohm, would sift through the signals to learn as much as possible about what enemy units were where, along with their strength, their orders, and their command structure. Ironically, the British themselves proved incredibly helpful in this, as the radio discipline of British and Commonwealth units alike was simply appalling. British radio operators chattered away like gossiping old women, and they were too prone to passing along messages, sometimes "in the clear"—that is, uncoded—up and down the chain of command that included the identity of every unit through which the message was sent, rather than specifying only the next to which a message was to be passed. From a single such message, Seebohm and his men could learn the identity of every unit in the chain of command through which that message had passed. Combined with captured British codes and painstaking traffic analysis, a picture of the entire British order of battle could be created.

So, on April 3, 1941, with his intuition that the British were ready to be tumbled out of Cyrenaica buttressed by the gleanings of his signals intelligence section, Rommel ordered his troops forward once again, dividing his forces into three columns. On the right, part of the 5th Light and a battalion of the Italian Ariete Division struck out across the chord of the Cyrenaican bulge, with the town of Derna as its objective: there it could block any British retreat along the Via Balbia. Command was given to Lieutenant Colonel Gerhard von Schwerin, a Prussian count whose family had been producing cavalry officers for three hundred years: Rommel could be confident that pursuit was in the *Oberstleutnant*'s blood. In the center, the bulk of the Afrika Korps' armor, the 5th Panzer Regiment, in company with the balance of the Ariete Division, set out for Msus, then Mechili, the site of an old Italian fort, to cut off any British forces that might make their own attempt at crossing Cyrenaica's bulge. On the left, the 3rd Reconnaissance Battalion and the Brescia Division drove up the coast road to Benghazi; just as this column set out, an Italian priest was brought to Afrika Korps' headquarters bearing the news that the British were already abandoning the town. With that, there was no holding back Rommel or his men: Benghazi fell that night, the British departure hasty and unorganized. (A few days later, when inspecting the port facilities, Rommel came across a blackboard where a cheeky Tommy had chalked an admonishment for the new owners: "Please keep tidy! Back soon!" Rommel grinned and then growled, "We'll see about that!")

That same night, his daily letters to Lucie still going out like clockwork, he wrote:

> Dearest Lu,
> We've been attacking since the 31st with dazzling success. There will be consternation among our masters in Tripoli and Rome, perhaps in Berlin, too. I took the risk against all orders and instructions because the opportunity seemed favorable. No doubt it will all be pronounced good later and they will all say they would have done exactly the same in my place. We've already reached our first objective, which we were not supposed to take until the end of May. The British are falling all over each other to get away. Our casualties are small. Booty cannot be estimated yet. You can understand why I can't sleep for happiness.[97]

Doubtless one of the sources of Rommel's mirth was an encounter late on the night of April 3 with General Gariboldi, Rommel's nominal commanding officer. Prickly and egotistical, furious that his orders to remain at Mersa el Brega had been ignored, Gariboldi stormed into the Afrika Korps' command post and confronted Rommel about this act of insubordination. Rommel dismissed his nominal superior's attempt to assert his authority, declaring that "One cannot permit unique opportunities to slip by for the sake of trifles." Voices were raised, angry words exchanged, and Gariboldi was well into mid-tirade when a signal from Berlin was handed to Rommel, who silently read it and then announced that Hitler and the O.K.W. had just given him complete authority to act as he saw fit.[98]

In fact, the signal handed to Rommel said exactly the opposite: it was a pointed reminder from Halder to advance no further than Mersa el Brega. Gariboldi, however, spoke and read little German, and couldn't challenge Rommel's version of the communiqué; even so, the Italian was not prepared to yield without a fight, and tried to resort to bluster. A second signal arrived, bearing the news (and Rommel, again being Rommel, wouldn't have been above stage-managing this) that Benghazi had fallen. Fuming, knowing his indignation had been trumped by events, Gariboldi turned and departed without a further word. Little more than two months later, he would be replaced, the primary reason cited for his relief being his inability to cooperate with Rommel.

A far more serious incident—and one very revealing of Erwin Rommel as commanding general—occurred on April 4, when he was told that problems with deliveries of fuel immobilized the 5th Panzer Regiment, a halt that would probably last four days. The problem began in the very abruptness with which Rommel had moved against Mersa el Brega, then on to Agedabia, and now out into the wilderness of Cyrenaica. Axis supply officers—German and Italian alike were caught flatfooted: with no forewarning of Rommel's intentions, there had been no opportunity to set up the fuel dumps, create the movement plans, and arrange the convoys required to carry fuel to the advancing armored columns. This was not France in May and June 1940—there were no local gasoline stations from which fuel could be commandeered for Rommel's thirsty panzers. Every drop of gasoline used by the Afrika Korps as well as the Italian armored and motorized divisions had to come from Europe, brought across the Mediterranean by tanker to Tripoli, and from there hauled by truck to the front. Further complicating the problem was a shortage of gasoline bowsers, tanker trucks with specially designed equipment that allowed them to refuel as many as a dozen tanks, trucks or armored cars simultaneously.

The blame for this supply fiasco fell squarely on the shoulders of Erwin Rommel: by failing to inform his *quartiermeister* (corps supply officer) that he was considering attacking the British ahead of the schedule laid down by the orders from O.K.W., Rommel gave his staff no reason to create contingency supply plans for such an operation—his staff naturally assumed that he would obey the orders from his superiors in Berlin and Rome. But while Rommel's impulsiveness was responsible for this blunder, it was his talent for improvisation which produced a solution: he ordered every truck in the 5th Light Division to halt in place, unload, and collect spare drivers from the tank crews. They were then sent back to El Agheila to collect gasoline and ammunition, driving non-stop, to replenish the fuel tanks and ammunition lockers of the Afrika Korps' panzers. Rather than a four-day delay, 5th Light had to halt in place for only one.

Such an experience was, naturally, part of the learning process through which any newly promoted corps commander had to go. Usually the corps staff were able to draw on their own experience to correct such oversights by their commanding general until he had a chance to settle into his new role, but in this instance, Rommel's staff was as inexperienced as he at this level of operations. Clearly, commander and staff both had a lot to learn; fortunately they were very quick learners. Nonetheless, while never being as ignorant of logistics as his critics both during and after the war would maintain, the limitations imposed by his supply situation would remain something of a blind spot for Erwin Rommel.

Nevertheless, the old cliché that "nothing succeeds like success" holds more truly in warfare than in perhaps any other form of human endeavor. Rommel presented Hitler, the O.K.W., and Comando Supremo with a *fait accompli* and defied any of them to call him out for his blatant insubordination. Gariboldi fumed, Cavallero (the Italian Chief of Staff) fulminated, and Halder and von Brauchitsch privately raged about insubordinate upstarts, but individually and collectively they did nothing. Hitler, normally never pleased by being gainsaid in any manner, was quietly delighted—because both men represented to him everything he detested about the German officer corps, he despised Franz Halder and held Walter von Brauchitsch in something close to contempt, so the spectacle of this stubborn young general who was one of his personal favorites showing up two of the General Staff's most senior officers was one to warm his lance-corporal's heart. Rommel made no effort to disguise his satisfaction when he wrote to Lucie that evening, saying, "Congratulations have come from the Führer for the unexpected success, plus a directive for further operations which is in full accord with my own ideas."[99]

The situation could well have turned badly on Rommel, nevertheless. The lack of an adequate fuel supply for the 5th Panzer Regiment was just one of a string of incidents in those first days of April which highlighted the confusion created within the Axis forces by the relative inexperience of both Rommel and his staff at this level of operations. When Streich's tanks set out eastward from Benghazi bound, hopefully, for Derna, they began bogging down in the soft mix of sand and rock once they left the Via Balbia, leaving the 5th Panzer Regiment strewn across the highlands behind the Jebel Akhdar when it ran out of fuel.

On April 5, worried that the delay would allow the retreating British time to escape and set up defensive positions along the coast road and at the old Turkish fort of Mechili, south of the Jebel Akhdar (which, in fact, was exactly what the new commander of the Western Desert Force, Lieutenant General Philip Neame, hoped to do), Rommel took the controls of a Fiesler *Storch* ("Stork") light observation plane, and flew back and forth between his widely separated units, issuing orders to resume the advance. He personally instructed Colonel Olbricht's machine-gun battalion to attack Mechili, then a few hours later countermanded that order, telling Olbricht to advance toward Derna, on the coast road, instead. Later that morning, meeting Streich and von Schwerin in the middle of the desert, he ordered an attack on Mechili to begin at 3:00 that afternoon. Von Schwerin said nothing, but Streich flatly refused the order, stating that with most of his tanks and armored cars still scattered across the desert as a result of the fuel fiasco, there was no hope of assembling a sufficiently strong force in time. Rommel, smarting at the implied rebuke over the fuel situation, shouted that Streich was a coward. The 5th Light's commander took his *Ritterskreuz* from his neck, held it out, and icily informed Rommel, "No one has dared to call me that before. Withdraw it or I'll throw this at your feet!" The Afrika Korps' commander muttered a half-hearted apology, but from that moment until Streich's relief two months later, there would be a distinct coolness between the proud Streich and the prickly Rommel.[100]

Late in the afternoon, Rommel returned, announcing imperiously that Streich and von Schwerin would together assault Mechili at 6:00 P.M., less than two hours hence; artillery support, he said, would be provided by the Italians. The Italians, however, were nowhere in sight, and aside from a handful of tanks and a few reconnaissance vehicles, the Germans had nothing with which to mount such an attack. The division and regimental commanders simply looked at each other and very pointedly said nothing; Rommel drove off, ostensibly to find the Italian artillery, which he never did. That night, he personally led a handful of infantry platoons in an attempt to take the fort: the British and Indian defenders in Mechili drove it off easily.

Rommel had his own personal share of near misadventures as well, flitting about the desert in his command car, or flying above it in his Fiesler. Having been mercilessly harried by the Royal Air Force before and during *Compass*, the Italians were prone to fire first on any aircraft they didn't immediately recognize, and ask questions later. So it was hardly surprising that Rommel should twice have come under fire from slightly trigger-happy Italian antiaircraft gunners who had never seen a Storch before. (They had shot down and killed their own Marshal Bagdolio the previous June because they misidentified his Savoia-Marchetti bomber as a British Blenheim.) On April 7, while trying to locate the German and Italian forces he believed should be converging on Mechili, Rommel almost landed beside a column of British trucks, noting his error only at the last minute and zooming away as fast as the little airplane could fly. Not long after, he spotted a lone 88mm gun in the desert and dropped in to land close by. As the Storch was taxiing over to the solitary gun, it hit a patch of soft sand and ground-looped, tearing away half its landing gear in the process. Jumping out, Rommel asked the gun crew if they had any transport handy. Assured that a truck was available, Rommel, recalling that the column of British vehicles was not far off, blurted out, "Then let's get the hell out of here—the British will be here in five minutes!"

Rommel, his copilot, and the gun crew clambered aboard, and, following Rommel's directions, set out to find the Afrika Korps' headquarters section, collecting a handful of stragglers and a trio of dispatch riders on the way. Hardly had they found the command vehicles than one of the notorious Libyan sandstorms swept over them, immobilizing the lot. A few hours later, as the wind began to ease, Rommel announced that he was going to Mechili to see if the attacks he had ordered had gone in. With visibility reduced to a matter of yards, it was necessary to navigate by compass and speedometer—and more than a little guesswork—but they managed to find a stretch of telephone wire, which they promptly followed on the presumption that it must lead *somewhere*. It did, bringing them directly and unexpectedly to the walls of Mechili, where General Streich was waiting patiently to inform Rommel that the fort had been taken a few hours previously, 1,700 enemy soldiers, some artillery, and most importantly a sizeable number of trucks having been captured in the process. The remains of the British 3rd Armoured Brigade—12 A-7 Cruisers, 20 light tanks and the same number of captured Italian tanks—and the 3rd Indian Motor Brigade had taken refuge in the old fort on April 6. Despite trying to brass it out by feigning a greater strength than they actually possessed—and twice refusing German calls to surrender—they capitulated after failing to break through the enemy perimeter on April 8.

With one of his two objectives in hand, Mechili, Rommel wasted no time in moving on the other, Derna. The previous day, Leutnant Hans-Otto Behrendt, who had come to North Africa so that Rommel could avail himself of the young man's skills as an Egyptologist and experienced desert traveler, had driven into Derna and found it deserted—the British had abandoned the town just hours before he arrived. Behrendt reported as much to Rommel, who immediately sent Ponath's 8th Machine-Gun Battalion packing with orders to occupy Derna as quickly as possible, von Schwerin's mixed force of Germans and Italians not far behind, Rommel himself in their train. This was a gamble on Rommel's part, forced on him by yet another mistake: when the 5th Panzer Regiment arrived at Mechili that morning, Colonel Olbricht asked permission to halt the unit long enough to clean the sand and grit that had accumulated in his tanks' guns and turret mechanisms during the sandstorm, a task that would take several hours at best to accomplish and leave the regiment immobilized. Rommel immediately agreed, then, when Behrendt's news of Derna reached him, regretted doing so. He had to hope that the British continued in their headlong plunge to the east, and didn't pause long enough to take a close look at the Axis forces pursuing them, for if they did, it would be readily apparent that those German and Italian units lacked the strength to stand long against a determined counterattack. The Western Desert Force, however, had not yet arrived at that inevitable moment when any retreating army stops to ask itself exactly from what is it running, and so the withdrawal continued. That moment was rapidly approaching, but for now fortune continued to favor the Afrika Korps, and Derna was occupied without incident.

For all of his mistakes, hardly a day passed in early April 1941 without some new plum figuratively falling into Rommel's lap. The German invasion of Greece began on April 6; by April 9 the Greek and British forces in the northeast were in full retreat; on April 15, the British began planning to withdraw their units from the mainland to Crete. The swiftly developing debacle in Greece occupied most of the attention and energy of Wavell and his staff, leaving them little time for Cyrenaica. The Royal Air Force had sent the best squadrons in the Middle East to support the operations in Greece, leaving the bombers and fighters of the Regia Aeronautica a free hand to harass the retreating British mercilessly. Bungled communications caused the main British fuel and supply depot at Msus to be put to the torch on April 6, leaving most of the British mechanized and motorized units with only whatever gasoline was left in their tanks—usually enough to run, rarely enough to turn and fight. And on April 7, Lieutenant General Neame and Lieutenant General Richard O'Connor were captured when their staff car ran afoul of one of von Schwerin's reconnaissance patrols.

As kind as fortune had been to Erwin Rommel in the first months of 1941, she was cruel to Philip Neame: like Rommel, Neame was newly promoted to corps command, but was forced to gather up the reins of the Western Desert Force as it was in the middle of yet another reorganization at the same time its most experienced units were being withdrawn. He'd barely had time to learn the names of his subordinates, let alone grow into his new command, when Rommel attacked, and the more experienced O'Connor, commander of the British forces in Egypt, was in Libya to assist and advise Neame in his new posting.

The loss of Neame and O'Connor, along with Brigadier John Combe, who was with them when the two generals were "bagged," was a sore blow to the British. The Western Desert Force was deprived of its commanding officer at the most critical moment of Rommel's offensive, temporarily paralyzing the British chain of command; O'Connor, Neame's predecessor, had led the Western Desert Force during *Compass*, and Combe was the commander of the flying column that had cut off the Italian retreat at Mersa el Brega in January. Philip Neame was unquestionably a good officer and a brave man (he had been awarded the Victoria Cross in the Great War), but he was new to the desert and had never before led armor. O'Connor and Combe were both "Desert Rats" who knew how to lead armor and motorized infantry in desert operations. Their experience might well have given the Western Desert Force a fighting chance at stopping the Afrika Korps west of Egypt; without it, only fate or chance could halt Erwin Rommel's advance.

Ironically, the British, who only a few short months earlier had proven themselves to be masters of desert warfare, were so impressed by the speed and skill, not to mention the sheer audacity, with which Rommel and his men had struck that the story was soon making the rounds within the Western Desert Force, and even in Cairo and Alexandria, that the Afrika Korps was a picked elite, specially trained and equipped for the war in North Africa. Had they known of this, Rommel's "Africans," as he would come to call them, would have convulsed with laughter. Far from being elite soldiers, they had to learn many of the basics of desert warfare "on the job." Much of their equipment was ill-suited for the desert: while the Wehrmacht's cotton "tropical" uniform was adequate for the climate, for example, the rubber-soled boots initially issued with it literally began to melt when they came into contact with rocks that had been baking in the desert sun. Even such basics as sand-colored paint were missing: when the 5th Panzer Regiment went into action for the first time its tanks and armored cars still wore the same *panzergrau* used in Poland and France. The crews had to resort to the temporary expedient of coating their vehicles with mud made from the local soils—good camouflage, but hardly durable.

A large portion of the Afrika Korps' success was attributable to two highly intangible factors, against which the British, for the moment, at least, had no effective counter: luck and Rommel. It was pure luck that brought the 5th Light Division to Cyrenaica at the moment when the Western Desert Force was being systematically stripped of its most experienced troops and its best equipment, which were being sent to Greece, where most of the men would become prisoners of war and their vehicles destroyed or abandoned. It was also the British misfortune that, just as the Germans were arriving in North Africa, Wavell's attention and energy were diverted elsewhere—specifically, to Greece. Again, it was simply bad luck that all of the available intelligence, including what was regarded as the most reliable source of all, Ultra, led everyone in the British chain of command, from Churchill on down, to believe that the Germans would sit passively behind the defenses at El Agheila. And again, it was pure luck that command of the Afrika Korps was given to an officer who possessed the imagination and moral courage to take advantage of such an extraordinary confluence of circumstances.

It was Rommel, of course, who was able to turn what would and should have been a succession of minor inconveniences for the British into something approaching a military calamity for them. For their bad luck was Rommel's good fortune, and he possessed not merely the temperament but also the tactical skill to recognize an opportunity and exploit it to the fullest. However Rommel may have fumbled about in the early days of April 1941, none of his mistakes were irretrievable, and they were made when the British were powerless to exploit them. However imperfectly, Rommel learned from those mistakes, and quickly got his legs under him, acting with the sort of boldness that General Schmidt a year previously had insisted was the essential characteristic of a panzer commander. The Afrika Korps was not an elite, it didn't need to be: it had an elite leader, and that made all the difference.

That the British might have thought their opponents to be a cut above the ordinary was an understandable mistake, as the Germans seemed to learn very quickly how to operate in the Libyan desert. The war in North Africa was fought across terrain and in conditions unlike those in any other theater of war, which, as Rommel emphasized in his critique of Graziani's advance into Egypt in the previous year, imposed their own set of rules on those who fought there. Unlike, say, Morocco, with its endless vistas of windswept sand dunes, the Libyan desert was mostly a rocky plain that rose from the Mediterranean, rather gently in some places, with startling abruptness in others. Steep-faced ridges called "escarpments" stretched parallel to the coast for most of the distance between Benghazi and the Egyptian frontier. The Via Balbia ran along these escarpments, or just below them: the handful of places where the road crossed through or over the crests created natural choke points where a determined defender could stop cold an attacking force many times its size. Behind the ridges of the escarpments stretched a stony, hardscrabble plain that reached south for as much as 200 miles before the vast, empty sands of the Sahara began.

Away from the coast, there were no permanent settlements; the only inhabitants were the Bedouin, Arab nomads who moved their flocks and herds between the widely scattered oases. Vegetation was sparse and stunted, save for the Jeb el Akdar, the Green Mountains of northwest Cyrenaica, which for a few weeks in the springtime lived up to their name. The ground was flat, hardscrabble, difficult—in some places impossible—for infantry and artillery to dig into. Typical of any desert, days were usually blindingly hot, while nights were uncomfortably chill. Hans von Luck, the major who commanded the 3rd Reconnaissance Battalion, remembered the heat vividly: "Everyone sought out a little patch of shade. Some men really did fry eggs on the overheated armor plating of their tanks. It is no fairy tale. I have done it myself." The heat of the day often was made worse by the blast furnace-like desert wind that the Bedouin called the "Ghibli." It frequently raised blinding sandstorms that made flying impossible and travel by land treacherous. With almost no landmarks to serve as guides and navigation points, a traveler who became disoriented in the Libyan desert was soon hopelessly lost, and unless incredibly lucky, dead shortly thereafter.[101]

Sand—or more properly, grit—was the never-sleeping enemy of anyone who would attempted to live and work in the Libyan desert and whatever tools or equipment they might possess. It got *everywhere*: in every crevice, crease, wrinkle, and orifice of the human body, in the works of every mechanism, device, and piece of equipment, no matter how simple. Aircraft engines required special air filters to keep out dust that would ruin piston rings and bearings; automotive engines needed the same, along with special oil filters. Sights and recoil mechanisms on artillery pieces and tank guns were especially prey to this grit, and required constant cleaning. Infantrymen had to clean the bolts of their weapons several times a day to keep them clear and functional, with only the lightest possible coating of lubricant on the actions, to prevent dirt from building up and causing malfunctions. And of course the grit constantly found its way into food and water.

All of this was more or less bearable, but then there were the flies, every bit as pervasive as the sand and grit. They were literally countless, creeping into everything with as much determination and efficiency as the sand—and with a special propensity for food. They were fond of human blood as well and when these flies bit they left welts and sores behind, which quickly festered. With them came disease: dysentery would be the constant bane of Rommel and his men. Adding insult to injury, in addition to the flies were the occasional venomous snake and an abundance of scorpions: there wasn't a man in the Afrika Korps or the Western Desert Force who didn't suffer from these vermin.

Fuel and water—the twin lifebloods of military operations in the desert—were particularly problematic for the Axis: every liter of gasoline had to be transported from a refinery in Europe to a Libyan port, usually

Tripoli, in an Italian tanker, running a gauntlet of British submarines and bombers in the process, and from thence to the front by truck. (It should be noted that the courage of the Italian tanker crews was on a par with that of the British and American merchant marine—there is no record of any Italian tanker, once it set sail for Libya, ever turning back.) As one side or the other advanced and so lengthened its supply lines, this sometimes created the almost comical situation where those trucks were burning more fuel than they were transporting, necessitating the creation of a succession of fuel dumps along the way, just to supply fuel to the fuel carriers. This was a tremendous handicap to operations, especially for the Afrika Korps, as objectives and operational planning frequently had to be tailored to available, often inadequate, fuel supplies. For the British, it was less of a problem, as much of their gasoline came from refineries in Iran, and was delivered to Cairo via pipelines rather than vulnerable tankers.

While water could almost always be found within a few miles of the coast, it was often brackish and saline, and there was never enough to supply the needs of more than a fraction of the soldiers on either side, necessitating tanker trucks to bring water forward from sources far behind the front. Again, the British had the advantage, Wavell having been the driving force behind the establishment of water pipelines and pumping stations in Egypt that carried clean fresh water westward, much closer to the troops than anything the Axis were able to set up. Whatever its source, the Afrika Korps purified all of its water, leaving it tasting heavily of chemicals. Some men tried to disguise the taste by mixing the water with reconstituted lemon juice, while others resorted to ersatz coffee, which they promptly christened "nigger sweat."

Food was yet another challenge for the Axis soldiers in North Africa. As any combat veteran from most any war can readily attest, the quantity and quality of service-issued rations can usually be described as "indifferent" at best, and the North African campaign was no exception to the general rule. The diet of the Germans and Italians in Libya was bland and unimaginative, with little variety. There was an abundance of Italian sausage, issued in tins stamped "AM" (for "*Administrazione Militare*"), which the Germans immediately christened "*Alte Mann*" ("Old Man"), but the Italians dubbed "*Arabo Morte*" ("Dead Arab"). The Germans had black bread, the Italians dry, hard biscuits, and both armies were provided with onions, oatmeal, and dried beans. German soldiers readily bartered with whatever Bedouin nomads were nearby for tomatoes, eggs, chickens, pretty much any fresh food the Arabs had to offer; the Italians, who despised the Bedouins and were despised in return, were less enthusiastic about such dealings.

What was always eagerly anticipated by both Axis armies were captured British supplies, especially "bully beef" (tinned corned beef), that staple of the British military diet, derided by generations of Tommies. The British also had white bread, a luxury in wartime Germany, as well as canned fruit—peaches were immensely popular with the men of the Afrika Korps. Captured British warehouses and supply dumps would always be thoroughly looted (in an orderly, efficient German manner, of course) of these prizes; frequently, parcels of bully beef would be sent home to Germany, where they were regarded as something approaching a delicacy.

All in all, the officers and men of the Afrika Korps had much to learn about desert warfare; to their credit, they learned quickly and, for the most part, well. The early mistakes apparently had a palliative effect on the Germans and Italians alike, for by April 8, everyone was moving in the right direction and quickly enough to satisfy Rommel. His letter to Lucie that day was openly exultant:

> Dearest Lu,
> I have no idea if the date is correct. We've been attacking for days now in the endless desert and have lost all idea of space or time. As you'll have seen from the communiqués, things are going very well.
> Today will be another decisive day. Our main force is on its way up after a 220-mile march over the sand and rock of the desert. I flew back from the front yesterday to look for them and found them in the desert. You can hardly imagine how pleased I was.[102]

His letter on April 10 informed Lucie that

> After a long desert march I reached the sea the evening before last. It's wonderful to have pulled this off against the British. I'm well. My caravan arrived at last early this morning and I'm hoping to sleep in it again tonight.[103]

The portrait of Rommel as a corps commander that emerges from those 10 hectic days between March 31 and April 9 is intriguing, though not always flattering. His ability to perceive the weakness of the British forces arrayed against him at El Agheila, based on nothing more than a few scattered bits of intelligence and his own instinct, was remarkable. Likewise was the swiftness and energy with which Rommel exploited that weakness: he saw a moment of tactical and strategic weakness on the part of the British where his nominal superiors, in Tripoli, Rome, and Berlin saw none, and understood that he was being presented with an opportunity the likes of which few generals are ever offered, and comprehended the fleeting nature of that moment; once past, it would never come again. His planning was bold and imaginative, relying on speed and surprise as much as violence in execution to ensure success.

But in that execution Rommel showed that he still had much to learn: for most of the problems encountered by the Afrika Korps in that first headlong rush into Cyrenaica, Rommel had no one to blame but himself. By his own admission, "Probably never before in modern warfare has such a completely unprepared offensive as this raid through Cyrenaica been attempted."[104] The word "unprepared" is key here, for though Rommel had the presence of mind and imagination to sense and seize the singular opportunity offered by the temporary vulnerability of the British forces opposite him, he reacted with much the same impulsiveness that he displayed as a young infantry *oberleutnant* leading a *Jägerbataillon* on the Isozo in 1918. His attack on Mersa el Brega was as much a surprise to his own staff officers as it was to the enemy, giving them no opportunity to calculate the supply requirements and create the detailed movement orders necessary to properly support the Afrika Korps' advance. When a lack of fuel or ammunition or both threatened to slow his advancing tanks' advance or even halt them in their tracks, Rommel expected his staff to immediately improvise solutions, or did so himself if necessary, and was frustrated by the delays created by such makeshift measures.

It was not that Rommel was ignorant of or indifferent to how vital was proper logistical planning for successful operations, although this would be a charge repeatedly laid against him by critics during and after the war. Few officers were, in truth, ever as conscious of their logistics as was Rommel in North Africa: rarely was his supply situation more than merely adequate; most of the time it barely approached that level of sufficiency. Rommel would, in the months to come, demonstrate an ability to execute daring, sweeping maneuvers on the most marginal sufficiency of fuel, ammunition, food, and vehicles. He refused, however, to become preoccupied with supply calculations, save in broad terms of what was and was not possible under the circumstances which obtained at a specific moment, believing that they were rightly the balliwick of staff officers possessed of specialized training in service and supply. Still, in order to function properly, a general's staff must know the mind of its commander and have a sense of his intentions and objectives, so that the commander's designs can best be carried out given the resources at hand. By failing to keep his staff informed of his plans in March and April 1941, Rommel handicapped them and himself; had the British been less disorganized than they were, the Afrika Korps could have been handed a nasty setback in its first confrontation with them, and the course of the war in North Africa—and the Mediterranean theater—drastically altered as a result. Rommel owed his success in that first dash to the Egyptian frontier in no small part as much to his enemy's disarray as to his own daring.

At the same time, his displays of temper and petulance showed Rommel hadn't fully exorcised the petty, bullying streak that had marred his character in the First World War. His working relationship with General Streich got off to a good start, by all appearances, but a frostiness set in between the two men when Streich made it clear outside Mechili that he would be neither intimidated nor marginalized when given what he regarded as pointless or foolish orders, invoking Rommel's wrath and a round of verbal abuse. Von Schwerin proved to be cut from the same bolt of cloth, and Rommel privately decided that both men would be replaced at the earliest opportunity by officers with more pliable personalities. Streich would be relieved at the beginning of June, von Schwerin would not live long enough for that to happen.

Overarching all of this is the question of whether or not Erwin Rommel should have obeyed his orders from the O.K.W. and General Gariboldi to remain on the defensive at El Agheila and not gone on the offensive at all against the Western Desert Force. In hindsight, the answer must be an unequivocal "Yes," yet to be categorical about it is to merely be wise after the fact. The chain of consequences resulting from his decision to attack in March 1941 were his first lunging advance to the Egyptian frontier; the retreat before the British offensive of Operation *Crusader*; his own subsequent counterattack which led to the Afrika Korps' triumph at Gazala—acknowledged to be Rommel's masterpiece—and the capture of Tobruk; his defeat at El Alamein; the long retreat to Tunisia and the bitter rearguard action fought there; and finally the loss of the whole North African theater in May 1943. Given the scale of the defeat which the Axis would ultimately suffer there, it is difficult to not acknowledge that a less dynamic and aggressive commander might well have better served the requirements of German and Italian grand strategy.

It was Rommel's first offensive that provided Churchill the opportunity to turn to North Africa as the seat of Britain's most important, indeed only, land campaign against the Germans and Italians for over two years. The need to restore British political and military prestige lost in the Grecian debacle compelled Churchill to turn a strategic backwater into a major theater of war, one where Britain must emerge triumphant, no matter what the cost: it was Rommel who provided the impetus for Churchill's decision. And yet, Rommel being Rommel, he could have done no other: passive defense was not for him, having developed his skillset of command and concepts of warfare during the years from 1914 to 1918 in a succession of postings where movement and maneuver were still possible. He never acquired the sort of passive bunker mentality possessed by men like Alan Brooke or Bernard Montgomery: dull, plodding, obsessively methodical, relying solely on overwhelming material superiority as the means to victory. Instead, his dynamism, his belief in the decisiveness of movement, stamped itself indelibly on the minds of friend and foe alike. Indeed, so thoroughly would this solitary German general dominate North Africa, that a year after Rommel's arrival, the prime minister of Great Britain would blurt out in a meeting of his War Cabinet, whilst attempting to direct global land, sea, and air campaigns, "Rommel! Rommel! Rommel! Rommel! What else matters but beating *him*?"[105]

But to imply that Rommel should have somehow known all of this was going to happen, and thus restrained himself from attacking at Mersa el Brega, is absurd. Rommel was no more prescient than any other man. His duty was to help Germany win the war, and, as he saw it, the best way to do so was to take advantage of the enemy's weakness and go on the offen-

sive. What would prove to be near-astonishing was not that he was ultimately defeated in North Africa, but rather the scale of the effort the Allies
had to mount in order to accomplish that defeat.

But all of this was in the future when, on April 10, 1941, Erwin Rommel gathered the Afrika Korps and two motorized Italian divisions, the 17th
Pavia and 27th Brescia, on the Via Balbia just east of Derna, preparing to
fling them eastward, take Tobruk by coup de main and drive the British
back across the Egyptian frontier. From there, at least according to the orders he issued that day, there would be no stopping before he and his men
reached the ultimate prize: "The enemy is definitely retreating. We must
pursue them with everything we have. Our objective is the Suez Canal,
and every man is to be informed of this!"[106]

Yet, even as he was issuing these orders, though he had no way of knowing, the same fortune whose fickleness seemed to tip every roll of the dice
in Rommel's favor during the first week of April was about to desert him.
When news reached Cairo on April 8 that Generals Neame and O'Connor
had been captured the previous day, Major General John Lavarack, the
officer commanding of the 7th Australian Infantry Division in Tobruk, was
placed in temporary command of all troops in Cyrenaica. His orders were
simple: hold Tobruk at all costs in order to buy time for the organization
of the defense of Egypt. To accomplish this, Lavarack had not only his own
division, but also the 9th Australian Infantry Division. He was a stolid, unimaginative type, in the best sense of both words: he wasn't prone to panic,
nor was he given over to exaggerating his enemy's strength or capability. He
calmly deployed two of his four infantry brigades, the 20th and 26th, in
blocking positions along the approaches to the fortress, while the other two,
the 18th and the 24th, occupied the defensive perimeter. He then placed a
fellow Australian, Major General Sir Leslie Morshead, in charge of the actual
defensive operations. Over the course of the next seven months, Morshead's
tactics would become literally a textbook example of how a primarily infantry force can successfully hold a position against an enemy armored
force of not only superior mobility but also superior numbers.

Initially, Rommel had thought to drive directly past Tobruk, bringing
his tanks around in a sweeping attack from the southeastern side of the
perimeter, a move that would simultaneously cut off the port from Cairo
and bring the panzers to bear on what was believed to be the weakest sec-

tion of the defenses. As the Afrika Korps and the Pavia and Brescia Divisions approached Tobruk, he changed his mind, believing that surprise and momentum would allow him to take the town "on the bounce," as it were. The first components of the 15th Panzer Division had just arrived in North Africa and made their way to Derna, a reconnaissance, a machine-gun and an antitank battalion, and Rommel ordered the 15th Panzer's commander, Generalmajor Heinrich von Prittwitz und Gaffron, to take them, drive straight ahead along the Via Balbia to Tobruk, and hit the defenders as hard as he could. But when the screen of German armored cars approached the perimeter, the Australians, manning Italian artillery captured when Tobruk fell during Operation *Compass*, drove them off in confusion; next the defenders blew up a bridge across a wadi (a dry gulch or river bed) at the outer edge of the defenses as the light tanks of the reconnaissance battalion attempted to take it. Seeing this, von Prittwitz tried to cross the wadi itself: his staff car drove down into the gulch despite the warnings of his own men, but before it could reach the opposite embankment, a captured Italian 47mm antitank gun opened fire, destroying the car, killing von Prittwitz and his driver. The general had arrived in North Africa just two weeks earlier.

The news that von Prittwitz had been killed very quickly reached the small white house in Derna where Rommel had set up the Afrika Korps' headquarters. Streich was furious: to him, the new general's death was the consequence of a foolish, wasteful decision by Rommel: only that morning, von Prittwitz had confided to von Schwerin, "Rommel has sent me to take command of the attack. But I've only just arrived in Africa, and I don't know the troops or the terrain." Still, like the dutiful Prussian officer he was, von Prittwitz had obeyed—and paid the price of obedience. Now, when Rommel returned to his headquarters, a furious Streich awaited him. "I informed [Rommel] that the general he had just sent up front was dead. That was the first time I saw him crack. He went pale, turned on his heel and drove off again without another word."[107]

Shaken by von Prittwitz's death, Rommel immediately gave up any thought of taking Tobruk by coup de main and instead reverted to his original plan of mounting a set-piece attack from the southeast. By April 11, Tobruk was surrounded with the 5th Light Division in position to the southeast, the three battalions of the 15th Panzer and the Brescia Division to the south, and two Italian infantry divisions along with Ariete Armored Division to the west. Inside the defensive perimeter were the Australian 9th Division, the 18th Infantry Brigade of the Australian 7th Infantry Division, HQ 3rd Armoured Brigade with roughly 60 working tanks and armored cars, a motorized regiment of Indian infantry, and several thousand British soldiers of various units, most of them artillerymen. All in all, the garrison of Tobruk numbered some 24,000 Australian infantry, organized in four brigades, along with roughly 12,000 British soldiers, mainly artillery, signals, and support personnel, and a few score tanks, some British-made, some captured from the Italians. There were also a few thousand Italian prisoners of war who hadn't yet been evacuated to Cairo, and the residents of the town. Rommel would spend the next seven months trying to take Tobruk in what is often styled a "siege," but was in fact nothing of the sort. The British continued to hold the harbor, through which supplies and reinforcements were continually fed into the town, while wounded soldiers and non-essential personnel were withdrawn. It would always be a dicey proposition, as the forward airfields that the Italians had built around Tobruk reverted to their original owners, and the Regia Aeronautica, along with several squadrons of the Luftwaffe's Fliegerkorps X, moved in and made life extremely uncomfortable for ships moving into or out of Tobruk's harbor.

Meanwhile, as his main units were taking up their positions around the town, Rommel threw together a *kampfgruppe* ("battle group") heavy on infantry, artillery, and antitank guns but with no tanks assigned to it, and pushed it further eastward, past Tobruk. Command of the *kampfgruppe* was given to Oberst Maximilian von Herff, who moved swiftly to capture key positions along the Libyan-Egyptian frontier. Before the month was out, Fort Capuzzo, Bardia, Sollum and the vital Halfaya Pass were in his hands. For the time being, Rommel's eastern flank was secure, and he could focus his attention on the capture of Tobruk. Against all conventional professional wisdom, he had pulled off one of the greatest bluffs in military history and through a combination of audacity, courage, guile, bluster, arrogance and insubordination recaptured almost the whole of Cyrenaica. What remained to be seen was how well he would respond when the British tried to take it all back.

CHAPTER SEVEN

TOBRUK

*Gentlemen, you have fought like lions
and been led by donkeys.*
—ERWIN ROMMEL, to Commonwealth
officers captured at Tobruk

Rommel's hopes of taking Tobruk "on the bounce" were thoroughly dashed by the death of von Prittwitz; when that effort failed, the fortress ceaselessly baffled his attempts to take it.[108] Tobruk—or more specifically, its harbor—was the great strategic prize along the Cyrenaican coast, the only port of any size other than Benghazi between Tripoli and Alexandria. Royal Air Force bombers had so badly damaged the harbor, docks, and cranes at Benghazi that the port could unload at best 750 tons of cargo a day, less than a third of its prewar capacity, while the sheer distance that supplies had to be moved from Tripoli created its own logistical nightmares for the Axis supply officers. (At one point Rommel's staff reckoned that for every liter of gasoline brought to the front, at least one liter was expended by the vehicles carrying it.) While at its best the capacity of Tobruk's port facilities was barely 1,500 tons a day, should the Afrika Korps take the port, the Axis supply lines would be shortened by almost 1,000 miles, eliminating the need (and waste) created by moving its supplies all the way from Tripoli. Not only would this have transformed the fuel situation for an army that seemed to be perpetually running on the ragged edge of fuel starvation, it would have eased immensely the strain on the Afrika Korps' motor pools and machine shops, which had to work round the clock to ensure that the endless truck convoys which carried the fuel, food, and ammunition to the troops continued to roll. Just as vital was the reduction in the amount of time Axis supply ships spent on the open sea between

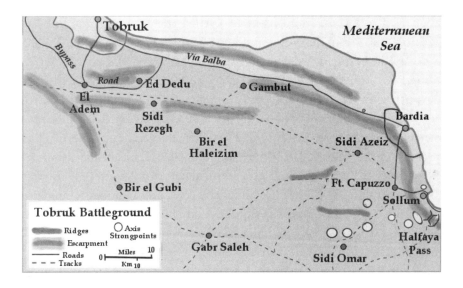

Italian and North African ports, exposed to British submarines, destroyers, and torpedo boats, as well as marauding RAF bombers and fighters. So narrow were the margins in the Axis supply situation between operational requirements and actual stocks of materiel on hand that the loss of a single cargo ship or tanker could cancel a planned operation, the destruction of a convoy could be catastrophic. It is no exaggeration, then, to say that Rommel *had* to take Tobruk, while it was equally imperative to the Allies that they hold it.

In addition to the transformation of his supply situation taking Tobruk would accomplish, Rommel was also well aware, as were General Wavell in Alexandria and Major General Morshead in Tobruk itself, that as long as the fortress remained in British hands, its garrison would remain a standing threat to the Afrika Korps' flank and rear, menacing Rommel's supply lines should he decide to move further east to threaten Cairo and Alexandria. This made taking Tobruk an imperative: time was not on Rommel's side, for even though the 15th Panzer Division was arriving as promised, there would be no further reinforcement from Germany, and while additional Italian units added to his numbers, they were mostly infantry divisions that lacked motor transport, and the poor quality of the tanks in the sole Italian armored division, Ariete, severely reduced the unit's effectiveness.

The strategic situation, then, that obtained in North Africa week of May 1941 was fundamentally a stalemate: given their current dispositions and strengths, at the moment neither the Axis nor the British were capable of forcing a decision. The Axis positions to the east of Tobruk, around Fort Capuzzo, Sollum, and especially Halfaya Pass just across the Egyptian frontier, were well-nigh impregnable, albeit thinly stretched, denying Wavell any chance—with the forces at his disposal at that moment—of attacking up the coast road to relieve the garrison at Tobruk. The strength of the Tobruk garrison, on the other hand, meant that Rommel could never risk withdrawing sufficient strength from around the fortress to renew his offensive into Egypt and drive on Cairo without inviting it to fall on his rear, cutting off his supplies and any possible line of retreat. Hence the stalemate. But Rommel knew that stalemate would only work in favor of his enemies, whose strength would grow, as Great Britain brought to North Africa not only more of her own army but Commonwealth forces as well. Eventually the Afrika Korps and the Italians would be overwhelmed by sheer weight of numbers if nothing else, while the best Rommel could hope for was merely to maintain his force levels. For his daring attack across Cyrenaica to be anything more than a glorified raid, he *must* take Tobruk.

Tobruk was going to be a tough nut to crack, however: in the 30 years they had occupied the town, the Italians had built an impressive defensive system. It was bounded east and west by rugged, rocky terrain, marked by no roads and few tracks; to the south the ground was flatter, more sand than rock. The Italians had done a textbook job in creating the fortifications that ringed Tobruk in no fewer than three concentric lines or belts. Strongpoints and bunkers were sited so that their fields of fire interlocked, and dug so that their tops were level with the surrounding ground, the better to not give away their location; the antitank gun and machine-gun emplacements were connected by tunnels rather than trenches, which made them difficult to spot even via aerial reconnaissance. Firing ports faced to the sides and rear, but not the front, reducing the vulnerability of each bunker to direct enemy fire; all were covered by antitank obstacles and deep barbwire entanglements. The perimeter, known as the Red Line, was defined by a broad antitank ditch, with sides too steep to be scaled by tracked vehicles, wire, and a double row of strongpoints, 150 in all, that included concrete bunkers for machine guns, infantry dugouts, and gun pits for artillery and mortars. Inside this perimeter were extensive minefields thickly sown with antitank and antipersonnel mines, and then two further defensive lines, the Blue (intermediate) Line, and the Green (innermost) Line.

All of these the Australians gladly co-opted for their own use, improving where and when they had the means, which meant building additional obstacles, laying minefields, and running additional lengths of barbwire. The defensive frontage that Morshead's Australians had to cover stretched for 31 miles; Morshead divided it into three sectors, assigning one of his infantry brigades to each. The 26th was given the western sector, the 20th Brigade the south, and the 24th the east. The fourth Australian brigade inside Tobruk, the 18th, was placed in reserve; it also did a measure of double-duty by manning the harbor defenses. Morshead ordered the entire telephone network installed by the Italian refurbished, and new wire laid as necessary: he wanted to be certain of an immediate and reliable flow of information and orders whenever and where the Germans attacked. Realizing that the best-laid plans—and wires—"gang aft aglee," he also instructed runner stations to be set up along the perimeter, manned around the clock. General Wavell told Morshead to expect to have to hold on to Tobruk for a minimum of eight weeks; Morshead planned and acted as if he would have to hold the town until hell froze over.[109]

The nickname "Ming" was given to Morshead by his Australian troops, who regarded him—with a mix of annoyance and affection—as something of a martinet, albeit one who was fair and who had a genuine regard for the welfare of his men and who was economical with their lives. The name was a play on the autocratic Emperor Ming "the Merciless" from the prewar Flash Gordon cinema serials: in addition to his authoritarian nature, Morshead bore a passing resemblance to Charles B. Middleton, the actor who played the fictitious tyrant. Two years Erwin Rommel's senior, Morshead, born in Ballarat, Victoria, in the extreme southeast of Australia, was not a professional soldier, a fact which, despite his courageous and distinguished service in the Great War, his superior, Lieutenant General Sir Thomas Blamey, commander of the Second Australian Imperial Force, irrationally regarded as a handicap. Morshead had been working as a teacher in Melbourne when Australia declared war on Germany and Austria-Hungary on August 5, 1914, and within days resigned his position, enlisted in the Australian Imperial Force, and was commissioned a second lieutenant within six weeks. He first saw action on the Gallipoli peninsula in April 1915, was wounded there, and invalided back to Australia; when he recovered, he took command of an infantry battalion posted to the Western Front, where he found himself and his unit in the thick of the battles at Messines, Passchendaele, Villers-Bretonneux and Amiens. By the end of the war, Morshead had been Mentioned in Despatches four times, named to the Order of St. Michael and St. George, and awarded the Distinguished Service Order. Here was a fighting soldier worthy of Rommel's mettle.

Between the wars, rather than return to teaching, Morshead became a businessman, working for the Orient Line, a steamship company, until 1939. Having remained active in the Australian militia, he was recalled to the colors when Australia declared war on Germany in September of that year, and given command of the 18th Infantry Brigade of the 6th Division in the Second Australian Imperial Force. The division was sent to the Middle East in early 1940, and January 1941 formed the infantry component of the Western Desert Force that tumbled the Italians out of Cyrenaica, taking Tobruk in the process. Two days after the fortress fell, Morshead was given command of the newly formed and half-trained 9th Division, which was almost immediately called upon to cover the British retreat when Rommel began his daring advance out of Mersa el Brega. Despite the division's lack of combat experience, Morshead's men fell back on Tobruk in good order, and when Lieutenant General John Lavarack, Morshead's immediate superior, was summoned to Cairo, he was utterly confident that he was leaving the defense of the vital port in good hands.

The death of von Prittwitz had had a sobering effect on Rommel who—at least privately—acknowledged that he was in for a fight if he was to take Tobruk. The original Italian bunkers and dugouts in which the Australians now sheltered had been well-sited and concealed, and during the short months in which the British held Tobruk, the Tommies had worked hard to improve them; now the Diggers were taking advantage of that labor. Rommel lacked detailed maps of the Italian positions—General Gariboldi insisted that they were nowhere to be found—and so good was the defenses' overhead camouflage, aerial reconnaissance yielded little useful information. The upshot was that the German and Italian soldiers tasked with assaulting the Tobruk perimeter had to conduct probing attacks to learn the strengths and weakenesses of each sector.

The first of the probing attacks began just after noon on April 11, 1941.

The 5th Panzer Regiment advanced, trying to draw fire, toward a section of the front just west of the El Adem road, which was held by the 20th Australian Infantry Brigade. It was a costly effort, five difficult-to-replace panzers left burning in front of the Australian lines before the German tanks withdrew. Two hours later, two companies of German infantry tried to infiltrate the Australian line in almost the exact same place, only to be met by ferocious small-arms fire. The Germans hastily withdrew, taking their dead and wounded with them; no Australian casualties were recorded for this action.[110]

The Germans got luckier, at least initially, on their next attempt, made the following day. Believing they now had the measure of the Australian defenses, Major Ponath's 8th Machine-Gun Battalion, totaling just over 600 men, began advancing on a section of the Aussie lines that seemed to be somewhat thinly held, exposed, and isolated. That position was held by a single platoon of Australian infantry, who saw the Germans begin moving forward just after 4:00 P.M. The defenders' arsenal was limited to a few score Lee-Enfield rifles, a pair of light machine guns, and some light antitank guns; their prospects for staging a successful stand against the Afrika Korps looked dim. But here the extensive preparations made by General Morshead paid their first dividend. Using the refurbished telephone network, the Australians were quickly able to, in their parlance, "whistle up" a few artillery batteries for fire support. Within minutes the ubiquitous British 25-pounder guns were dropping shells among the advancing Germans with frightening accuracy—most of the defenders' artillery units had registered their guns when they dug in, another product of Morshead's bag of tactical tricks.

Even though they were taking heavy casualties, the German soldiers continued to advance as three platoons of German panzers and one of Italian light tanks, some 20 vehicles all told, moved up to add their firepower to that of Ponath's advancing infantry. Moving through the artillery fire, the tanks came to an abrupt halt when they encountered a deep, broad antitank ditch, with sides too steep for any vehicle, wheeled or tracked, to successfully negotiate. This was, in fact, a continuation of the same antitank obstacle that had been fatal to von Prittwitz the previous day: the Italians had failed to inform Rommel that the ditch ran the entire length of the outer perimeter of the Tobruk defenses, and in the handful of aerial photographs he had it appeared to be a far less formidable obstacle than it turned out to be when encountered in person at ground level.

Now the situation became a case of the biter bit: the German and Italian armor milled about at the edge of the ditch, trying to find some way to negotiate it that didn't result in their tanks overturning in the attempt, or getting bogged down. As they did so, a quartet of British tanks arrived, heavily armored Matildas with 2-pounder (40mm) main guns that were more than powerful enough to penetrate the German vehicles' armor, and opened fire. Realizing that they were accomplishing nothing apart from providing the British tank crews with live target practice, the German panzer commanders quickly withdrew out of range. The heavy artillery fire continued, however, pinning the men of the 8th Machine-Gun Battalion in place, where they sought whatever cover they could find and did their best to dig into the rocky ground.

Grimly, Rommel informed Olbricht that his tanks would have to go "once more unto the breach," in order to either exploit whatever success Ponath's machine-gun battalion had in penetrating the enemy defenses, or to cover that unit's withdrawal. Olbricht bridled at this, and Streich, when he heard of it, refused to countenance any further action by 5th Panzer that was not part of a properly planned and coordinated operation, complete with air and artillery support. Streich understood the machine gunners' plight, but it was foolishness to throw away even more lives in yet another ad hoc attack—after all, it was just that sort of improvisation that brought the 8th Battalion to this impasse. Rommel, perhaps still stinging from the needless death of von Prittwitz and Streich's accompanying rebuke, bit off whatever reply he might have been inclined to make. Meanwhile, up in the front lines, the thinly clad German infantrymen were compelled to spend a very uncomfortable night in the open as the fearsome heat of the day gave way to near-freezing temperatures when darkness fell.

At noon the next day, April 13, Ponath extricated himself from his battalion's rather exposed position, and reported to Rommel in the commanding general's new mobile headquarters. This was an enormous British AEC armored command van, built with a heavy-duty suspension and riding on huge balloon tires that allowed it to travel off-road, one of three such vehicles captured at Mechili, which Rommel promptly commandeered and christened his "Mammut" ("Mammoth"). Inside this immense windowless bus, Ponath was informed that at 6:00 P.M., six battalions—24 batteries—of artillery would drop a fierce, five-minute "hurricane" barrage on the defenses in front of his battalion, giving cover to two platoons of *pionieren*, or combat engineers, who would move into the antitank ditch and place demolition charges at several points on both sides of the ditch, collapsing the walls and creating a path for the panzers to exploit. Ponath's men were tasked with moving across the ditch and creating a bridgehead within the enemy positions through which the German tanks could pass on their way to, hopefully, creating an outright breach in the defenses. Ponath returned to his men in mid-afternoon and did his best to spread the word about the new plan of attack.

As promised, at exactly 6:00 P.M. the German artillery opened an intense and accurate fire; the commanding officer of the 18th Antiaircraft Battalion, Major Hecht, went so far as to bring his 88mm Flak guns forward to engage the enemy dugouts and bunkers with direct fire. The engineers rushed into the antitank ditch, placed their charges, and set them off in a spectacular sequence of explosions. The 8th Machine-Gun Battalion rushed forward as night was falling, creating a gap in the Australians' lines roughly 500 yards wide and half that distance deep, then dug in as best they could and prepared to spend yet another night out in the cold. They soon learned that there were other perils in the night besides the cold. The dugouts originally built by the Italians had been constructed flush with the ground, and as such were difficult to see in broad daylight; at night they were invisible. Using the cloak of darkness, small groups of Australians crept out of their bunkers and quietly raided the attackers' positions, leaving behind them an indeterminate number of dead German soldiers.

At 3:30 A.M. on April 14, Rommel was already awake and writing to Lucie, informing her that "today may well see the end of the Battle of Tobruk. The British were very stubborn"—he was still unaware that Tobruk's defenders were primarily Australian—"and used a lot of artillery. However, we'll bring it off. . . ." An hour later, just before first light, Olbricht's tanks went roaring across the antitank ditch and into the gap created by Ponath's infantrymen. A dozen batteries of Italian field guns, along with Major Hecht's 88s, provided the fire support. Dawn was breaking as Rommel himself came forward to watch the attack progress, and for a brief while it seemed as if the string of luck created by Rommel's audacity would continue unbroken. But something he saw at the front seemed to spook Rommel, and he went dashing off to find the Ariete Division, to bring it up to reinforce Olbricht's 5th Panzer Regiment.[111]

Just what he saw—or thought he saw—remains a mystery, but what happened next is not. The Italian armored division had arrived at Tobruk only that morning, its tanks low on fuel and badly in need of servicing; it was in no condition to go directly into action. Nonetheless, Rommel insisted that whatever tanks and vehicles were in running order advance on the 5th Panzer's left flank, but as soon as the first British artillery shells began falling among them, the Italian troops broke ranks and fled. Disgusted, Rommel returned to El Adem and watched as the tanks of the 5th Panzer Regiment first came under fire from previously concealed Australian anti-tank guns, then were met by the garrison's contingent of Matildas. The Matilda had been designed as an infantry support tank, intended to wade directly into enemy fire, and as such was essentially immune to the shot or shells fired by the 37mm guns of Afrika Korps' panzers. The Matilda's own 2-pounder gun was more than sufficient to put paid to any of its opponents, and so the defenders began methodically picking off the German tanks one by one.

It was all over in less than three hours. While the British artillery worked over the 8th Battalion and the Matildas dealt with the panzers, the Australian infantry began pinching off the base of the German bridgehead, threatening to cut off the entire attacking force, armor and infantry alike. Major Hecht's Flak battalion fought ferociously, but eventually most of its guns were knocked out by enemy artillery. Having lost almost half his tanks and facing annihilation, Olbricht ordered the panzers to pull back, covering the withdrawal of the machine gunners as best they could while doing so. Not that there was much left to cover: by 8:00 A.M. three-quarters of the 8th Machine-Gun Battalion were dead, dying, or had been taken prisoner—among the dead lay the body of Major Gustav Ponath.

Furious at the failure of this last attack, Rommel demanded that Olbricht send forth his tanks yet again, this time at 4:00 P.M., and once more Streich demurred. He noted acidly to Major Karl-Otto Ehlers, Rommel's operations officer, that "had the British been the least daring, they could have pushed out of [Tobruk] and not only overrun the rest of my division but also captured the Afrika Korps headquarters. . . . That would have been the end of the German presence in Libya and of the Herr General's reputation as well." Apparently Streich's rebuke, while doing nothing to diminish Rommel's dislike for his outspoken subordinate, had a salutary effect: upon being informed of Streich's words, Rommel's only reply was a terse cancellation of the proposed 4:00 P.M. attack, the Afrika Korps instead being instructed to assume an "aggressive defense." Regrettably, Streich's reaction, if any, has been lost.[112]

The Australians had, for the time being, at least, beaten Rommel, and he gave up the idea that the El Adem position was a "weak" spot in Tobruk's defenses. In truth, what would become known in the Australian official histories as the "the Easter attacks" had revealed Rommel at his worst. Short-tempered, impetuous, and imperious, he refused to listen to the advice or counsel of his subordinates, underestimated his opponent even as he overestimated his own skills, all the while committing the worse offense possible by any commanding officer: he demanded more of his soldiers than they were able to give him. Not that the men of the Afrika Korps were unwilling, but rather the tasks he laid before them were superhuman.

Rommel's hand had been evident in each of these attacks, with their over-reliance on the same sort of speed and audacity that had been so successful in France the previous spring and summer. Having watched as French defenders repeatedly abandoned strong positions at the first display of determined opposition, he failed to recognize that the morale and cohesion of British Army, let alone that of the Imperial Forces—the Australian, South African, and Indian divisions deployed in the Middle East—were nothing like the fragile spirit of their erstwhile French allies. British forces might retreat, and do so in great haste and no little degree of disorder, but they rarely panicked. Rommel had absorbed the lessons of Dinant, Phillipeville, Avesnes, and Landrecies, but not those of Arras. The British, meanwhile, were prepared to supply further tutelage.

In the immediate aftermath of what can only be described as the fiasco at El Adem, something of a crisis in confidence occurred on the part of Rommel's immediate subordinates, together with a lapse in self-confidence. Streich in particular was especially bitter, as he had been adamant ever since the failure of the attack on April 11 which had cost von Prittwitz his life that only a methodically planned, carefully prepared set-piece assault stood any reasonable chance of breaking through the defenses of Tobruk.

Olbricht was fuming at what he considered to be the waste of valuable tanks and lives from his panzer regiment and the virtual destruction of the 8th Machine-Gun Battalion. Rommel himself couldn't disagree: suffering unnecessary tank losses was bad enough—the Afrika Korps would always be chronically short of tanks, particularly the precious Panzer IIIs and Panzer IVs—but enduring needless human casualties was worse. While he was not above spending his men's lives to gain an objective, Rommel was loathe to throw them away in exchange for something as mundane as the details of an enemy's defensive position. Nevertheless, through his own mistakes as well as circumstances beyond his control, he had been reduced to exactly that expedient.

The time had come to change tactics: boldness and dash having failed, he would now have to rely on deliberation and method if he were to succeed in capturing the town and, especially, the port. Rommel, after studying what information the Italian headquarters in Tripoli could provide about the three defensive lines around Tobruk, decided to attack the western sector of the perimeter around Ras el Madauar, a dominating hill which provided a matchless observation for British artillery spotters, and this time it would be the Italians who were to try conclusions with the Australians.

On April 15, an infantry battalion from the Brescia division, well supported by artillery fire, attacked the base of the hill and cracked the line of strongpoints. Again the Australians' communications net came to their rescue, bringing a hail of intense and accurate 25-pounder shells down on top of the Italians, who were forced to pull back to their starting positions. The next day it was the turn of the 1st Battalion of the Trento Division, with tanks from the Ariete in support, and yet again the ubiquitous British artillery broke up the attack.

Meanwhile, the Australians were being very aggressive in their own right; audacious Digger patrols were going out at night to infiltrate the enemy lines, bringing back whatever prisoners they could, and leaving dozens, sometimes hundreds, of dead German and Italian soldiers behind them. The fighting in the Libyan desert might have been remarkable for being less vicious than that of other fronts; that is not to say that it was any less lethal. These patrols served two purposes for General Morshead: it kept the Germans and Italians on edge, as they never knew where or when the next one of these nocturnal strikes would occur, and it prevented the men inside the Tobruk perimeter from developing the passive, purely defensive mentality that Morshead knew was usually fatal to a fortress garrison. They were the physical demonstration of what Morshead meant when he said, after seeing an article in a British newspaper headed "Tobruk can take it!", that "We're not here to take it, we're here to give it."[113]

Surprisingly, the setbacks experienced by the Italians did not raise a fraction of the ire or frustration in Rommel that he had expressed over the failure of the Afrika Korps to break through the Australian lines at El Adem. Nor did he place an inordinate amount of blame on the Italian troops for their lack of success, despite claims made by various critics at the time and later that the Italian army was Rommel's preferred whipping-boy when things went badly for him. Not that he wasn't above seeking out scapegoats: in a confidential report forwarded to the Kriegsministerium (War Ministry) in Berlin, he observed rather acidly that "During the offensive in Cyrenaica, and particularly during the early part of the siege of Tobruk, there were numerous instances where my clear and specific orders were not obeyed by my commanders," that "there were instances bordering on disobedience," and that "some commanders broke down in the face of the enemy." These were, unmistakably, references to General Streich, Colonel Olbricht, Major Ehlers (whom Rommel had shipped back to Germany in something approaching disgrace), and—to Rommel's shame—Major Ponath. He was more circumspect in giving voice to his anger and frustration in his letters to Lucie, telling her on April 16, for example, that "I don't get the support I need from my commanders. . . . I've put in for some of them to be changed."[114]

He was also careful to present a more optimistic face to her, one more consistent with the version of events being offered up to the German public by Göbbels' Ministry of Information. In that same letter he confided that "The battle for Tobruk has quietened down a bit. The enemy is embarking so we can expect the fortress to be ours very shortly." How much of this Rommel actually believed is impossible to say, although there is the impression that he was aware of writing to a larger audience, should Lucie care to share some of the less personal passages of his letters with friends. What comes next is rather surprising, given the candor mixed in with Rommel's obvious pride at his small army's accomplishments. Once Tobruk was taken, he wrote, ". . . then we'll probably come to a stop. Nevertheless our small force has achieved a tremendous amount, which has put a different picture on the whole campaign in the south." Regardless of what he might say to encourage his troops or provide as grist for Göbbel's propaganda mill, Rommel clearly understood that for the time being, the Afrika Korps and its Italian allies had reached the limits of their capabilities.[115]

Intriguing is his comment, almost an aside, that the Afrika Korps' advance to Tobruk "put a different picture on the whole campaign in the south," evidence that Rommel, for probably the first time in his career, was now thinking in strategic terms, however imprecisely at that moment. It serves as a benchmark for the remarkably rapid maturing as a strategist that Rommel would experience over the next three years. He might regard General Staff-trained officers with disdain, holding up his own combat experience and rapid rise to corps command as proof that intellectual credentials were not essential to a successful officer, yet that did not mean there were no gaps in Rommel's military education. The largest of such was his lack of strategic training: in Danzig, he was taught small-unit tactics and operations, along with the rudiments of logistics, the necessary tools for young junior officers. Strategy was not regarded as essential to their military education: it was assumed that, should they rise to higher command, they would at some point pass through the General Staff Kriegsakademie, where they would acquire a grounding in strategic theory. Rommel's abrupt—and highly irregular—rise from *oberst* to *generalleutnant* in the span of just three years knocked that assumption, and all of its implications, into a cocked hat. In the spring of 1941, Erwin Rommel was most assuredly *not* a strategist—but he was rapidly becoming one.

The need for him to do so would be ruthlessly driven home by the British in the months to come, as well as by events in Europe precipitated by the Wehrmacht. Rommel had not the slightest inkling when he ordered the Afrika Korps' lunge out of El Agheila that in doing so he would bring about a fundamental change in the grand strategy of the British Empire. Indeed, it is highly doubtful, given his use of the word "campaign" in his letter to Lucie, that Rommel even imagined North Africa could become a fully developed theater of operations. His candid admission to Lucie that at Tobruk the Germans and Italians had, for the short term, at least, reached the limits of their capabilities was an unspoken acknowledgment that, for all of his earlier grandiose pronouncements about taking Alexandria and capturing the Suez Canal, he truly understood that, for whatever reasons, to Hitler and the O.K.W. North Africa was only a sideshow.

Conversely, the Axis advance across Cyrenaica had been a godsend to Churchill, his War Cabinet, and his generals and admirals in their efforts to bring the war to the Germans. Forced to evacuate from France and Belgium in the first week of June 1940, followed by the withdrawal from Norway later that month, then run out of Greece even as the Afrika Korps was besieging Tobruk, nowhere in Europe itself or around the Mediterranean perimeter were British troops meeting German soldiers in combat. The Royal Air Force had won the Battle of Britain the previous autumn, but Britain's cities were now reeling under the nighttime bombing raids of the Luftwaffe that would become known as "the Blitz," while Britain's own bomber offensive against Germany had yet to truly hit its stride. At sea, the news was almost always bad: the German U-boat fleet was in the midst of their "Happy Time," sinking 282 Allied ships—1.5 million tons of shipping—in less than nine months, while losing fewer than a dozen submarines. And though commando raids on the coasts of occupied countries, along with the daring exploits of the Special Operations Executive (S.O.E.)—a highly irregular command created by Churchill and specifically directed by him to "set Europe ablaze,"—might, when suitably publicized and burnished, serve to boost the morale of Britain's civilian population, they were barely more than pin-pricks to the Germans.

With Rommel's headlong rush across Cyrenaica apparently stopped cold outside of Tobruk, Churchill and the War Cabinet were abruptly offered a place where the British Army could meet the Germans head-on with every reason to expect to a victory, and thus present the world, and in particular the United States, with the image of an empire still possessed of both the will and means to fight. Unwittingly aided by the Propagandaministerium's depictions of the handsome, dashing *Panzergeneral* who was making himself the master of desert warfare, Great Britain's own propaganda system began portraying Rommel as a noble nemesis, at once the moral antithesis of the stereotypical Nazi general and a commander of exceptional ability. Rommel would, in turn, and to the consternation of the British commanders in North Africa, repeatedly live up to that image. It would also come to have unexpected consequences for a surprising number of people on both sides.

The first indication Rommel had that the British were not prepared to accept being summarily kicked out of Cyrenaica came on the night of April 19–20, when 500 British commandos were put ashore on the outskirts of the minor seaport of Bardia, 30 miles behind the Afrika Korps' forward positions at Sollum and the Halfaya Pass. As darkness fell, a small task force—one submarine, three destroyers, and a light cruiser—brought the commandos to within a few hundred yards of the coast; from there men were brought ashore by landing craft—at least, that was the plan. The submarine failed to rendezvous with the other four ships, and so the Special Boat Section detachment it carried never arrived to join the rest of the commandos. Equipment problems set the operation behind schedule, and part of the raiding force landed in the wrong location; fortunately for them, there was no opposition at the beaches.

Faulty intelligence was to blame when the commandos either found their supposed targets to be non-existent or located in the wrong places. Minor damage was done to the port and its defenses before the approaching dawn compelled the commandos to withdraw; a communications error caused one company of the raiding force to be left behind when its transports did not show up. Though the British publicly hailed the Bardia raid as a victory, in material terms the raid was a dismal failure, and strategically it changed nothing in the disposition or balance of forces around Tobruk and at the Egyptian frontier. It was, however, a pointed message to Rommel that the British were rejecting any notion that they were resigned to doing nothing but standing on the defensive. Also, the raid caused Rommel some apprehension about the security of his lines of communication and supply to the German and Italian units holding Sollum and Halfaya, an anxiety that deepened significantly when, the day after the raid, April 21, his "Mammut" transport was strafed and damaged by a pair of RAF Hurricanes.

While Rommel was no stranger to physical peril, this was Rommel's first experience of being strafed, and it left him particularly unsettled. It was late in the day and he was returning from Bardia, where he had gone to examine the damage done by the British commando raid, to the German lines around Tobruk. The Mammut was hit 25 times as the Hurricanes made a pair of strafing runs. The vehicle's driver was wounded by a bullet that came through the vision slit in the armored visor that protected the windshield, while the driver of Rommel's armored half-track, Corporal Eggert, was killed, along with a dispatch rider, Private Kanthak. Rommel took over the wheel of the Mammut himself, intending to drive straight through to Tobruk, but he was unable to negotiate the unfamiliar route in the darkness, and was compelled to wait until sunrise before he could return to his command post.

Once there, he was greeted with the news that the detailed plans for the defenses of Tobruk—which just a week previously General Gariboldi had categorically stated were unavailable—had suddenly materialized at Afrika Korps headquarters. They arrived too late, of course, to be of any use to the nearly 2,000 German and Italian soldiers killed or wounded in the Easter attacks. Rommel was always convinced that Gariboldi had deliberately withheld them in the hope that Rommel's initial assaults on the fortress would fail—revenge for Rommel's defiance of Gariboldi's orders back in February to not advance beyond Mersa Matruh. Rommel's already low opinion of Italian senior officers—as opposed to Italian soldiers—plummeted further.

Examining these plans, Rommel immediately saw that the defensive lines protecting Tobruk were far more complex and sophisticated than he had originally believed, and that the individual strongpoints had been constructed with such skill and ingenuity that his original plans for breaking through those positions had been hopelessly optimistic. He also realized that taking Tobruk was a task which might exceed his resources, reporting to Berlin that the "Situation in Bardia [and] Tobruk [grows] graver day by day as British forces increase," and making the observation that the "Italians are unreliable," although this particular comment may have been directed more at the Italian Comando Supremo and General Gariboldi than at Italian troops as a whole. Then came a shopping list of requirements and demands: the immediate expansion of the 5th Light Division into a full-strength panzer division; the expedited arrival of the entire 15th Panzer Division; increased German and Italian submarine activity along the North African coast to interdict British reinforcements being sent into Tobruk; and an enormous increase in the number of Luftwaffe squadrons committed to the support of the Afrika Korps.

What stands out in these messages is their agitated and pessimistic tone. They are in marked contrast to the communications of the cool, confident commander who just weeks earlier had airily dismissed the instructions of the O.K.W. and followed his own lead, certain of his strength and ability to sweep the whole of the British Desert Force before him all the way to Alexandria and the Suez. While such a lapse of self-confidence was a rarity in Rommel, the interlude during the third week of April 1941 serves to illustrate that the fox had not yet fully come to terms with the desert.

Naturally, he put on a very composed face in his letters to Lucie (and, as always, understanding that he might indirectly be writing to a larger audience), telling her on April 21 that "Things have quieted down and I'm at last able to collect my thoughts after three weeks on the offensive. It's been very hectic for the last few weeks. We're hoping to pull off the offensive into Tobruk very soon. . . . At the moment we're lying in a rocky hollow, widely dispersed because of very active British aircraft. . . ." He went on to say that he was pretty sure Tobruk's defenders were being steadily reinforced, but he gave Lucie no reason to believe that he was anything less than fully confident of the outcome of the next attack. Aside from the passing reference to the "very active British aircraft," no mention was ever made about the strafing attacks. After all, a good husband didn't worry his wife with things over which she had no control.[116]

A few days later he provided more details for Lucie:

23 April 1941

Dearest Lu,
Heavy fighting yesterday in front of Tobruk. The situation was highly critical, but we managed to restore it. There's little reliance to be placed on the Italian troops. They're extremely sensitive to enemy tanks and as in 1917 quick to throw up the sponge. Newly arrived German units have now made the situation rather more secure. I had a meeting with Gariboldi and Roatta yesterday. . . . I was ceremonially awarded the Italian Medal for Bravery; I am also supposed to be getting the Italian *Pour le Mérite*. What a trivial business it all is at a time like this. I've been able to have my sleep out during the last few days, so now I'm ready for anything again. Once Tobruk has fallen, which I hope will be in ten days or a fortnight, the situation here will be secure. Then there will have to be a few weeks pause before we take on anything new. How are things with you both? There must be a whole lot of post lying at the bottom of the Mediterranean.

25 April 1941

Things are very warm in front of Tobruk. I shan't be sorry to see more troops arrive, for we're still very thin on the long fortress front. I've seldom had such worries militarily speaking as in the last few days. However, things will probably look different soon. . . . Greece will probably soon be disposed of and then it will be possible to give us more help. . . . The battle for Egypt and the Canal is now on in earnest and our tough opponent is fighting back with all he's got.[117]

Still clinging to the idea that a successful attack at Ras el Madauar, in the southwest, would open up the quickest, most direct route to Tobruk's harbor, the ultimate objective, Rommel began planning an attack that was more methodical and systematic than any of his previous attempts at taking the town. The start date was set for April 30. In the meantime, the Axis forces did their best to increase the pressure on Tobruk's defenders. Most of the Royal Air Force's strength in the Middle East was deployed to support the Allied withdrawal from Greece, and by April 25, all the remaining British fighters in Tobruk were withdrawn to Egypt, leaving the bombers and fighters of Fliegerkorps X free to bomb the town and harbor daily practically unopposed. Up at the Egyptian frontier, a hodgepodge of German and Italian units were contesting control of Fort Capuzzo with the British, while increasing the pressure on the defenders at the eastern end of Halfaya Pass, which the British were forced to abandon on the night of April 26, falling back another 20 miles to the coastal village of Buq-buq.

While all this was happening, Rommel was momentarily distracted— and considerably annoyed—by the latest antics of Dr. Göbbels' Propagandaministerium. Seeking to exploit Rommel's popularity with the German people by openly associating him with the Nazi regime, a featured article appeared in an early April issue of the government's newspaper *Das Reich* ostensibly presented the officially sanctioned version of Rommel's life story. In it, he was depicted as the son of a master mason, and was said—quite incorrectly—to have joined the NSDAP in the late 1920s. A copy appeared in Rommel's command van, and he promptly scrawled "*Unsinn!*" ("Nonsense!") across it before confronting Leutnant Alfred Berndt, his chief aide in North Africa and, not entirely coincidentally, a deputy *Reichspresschef* who reported directly to Göbbels. A fiery letter to the editorial staff of *Das Reich* quickly followed, in which Rommel made it clear that he was highly displeased at the falsehoods presented in the article. The editor of *Das Reich* replied, *"Wenn es auch nicht stimme, wäre es doch gut, wenn es stimmen würde"* ("Even were it not correct, it would nevertheless be good if it were," or more colloquially "Even if it is not true, it ought to be!"), sort of a Teutonic variant of "When the legend becomes fact, print the legend." Rommel was not mollified by this in the slightest, and demanded a correction be published. *Das Reich* complied, but grudgingly, and, in the time-honored tradition of newspapers everywhere, buried the retraction in an obscure section, on an inside page.

Alfred Berndt was a curious, intriguing individual. Unlike Rommel, he was a dedicated member of the Nazi Party and a firm believer in the National Socialist cause. He had been drawn to the Nazi movement while still a teenaged boy, largely due to Hitler's loud and repeated assurances that once in power he would right the wrongs done to Germany and her people by the Treaty of Versailles: in 1920 Berndt and his family had been forcibly dispossessed and expelled from their home in Prussia by the Poles when the new state of Poland was created by the terms of that treaty. Thirty-one years old when he became Rommel's aide, tall, powerfully built, with a strong jaw and a mass of wavy dark hair, he was intelligent, educated, literate, and personable. He was also every bit as blunt and outspoken as his commanding officer, and possessed a moral courage which Rommel admired; the two men instinctively liked one another. Berndt would fill much the same role for Rommel in North Africa as did Karl Hanke in France, that is, he was Rommel's publicist; after the war, Berndt would become widely regarded in Germany as the creator of the "Desert Fox" legend. He would also prove useful to Rommel in other ways: although only a mere lieutenant, because he had originally joined the Nazi Party in 1923, and was Göbbel's deputy, he was afforded an access to Adolf Hitler envied by many officers of vastly greater rank and seniority. Throughout the course of the entire North African campaign, whenever there was something to be said directly to Hitler which circumstances did not permit Rommel to say himself, Berndt would go in his stead to the Führerhauptquartier, bearing the message.

A distinctly more significant distraction for Rommel appeared on April

Field Marshal Erwin Rommel.
An official portrait taken in 1943;
note the *Pour le Mérite* worn alongside
the Knight's Cross of the Iron Cross.

Officer cadet Erwin Rommel with his sister Helen and brothers
Karl and Gerhard, in a photograph taken circa 1911.

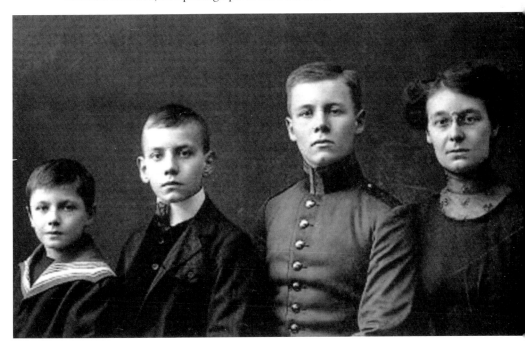

Leutnant Rommel with an unidentified comrade in France, 1915. In his buttonhole Rommel wears the ribbon of the Military Merit Order *(Militärverdienstorden)* of the Kingdom of Württemberg.

Taken shortly after the end of the Great War, possibly 1920 or 1921, Erwin and Lucie pose for a formal portrait as husband and wife.

Between the wars, a rare photo of Major Rommel, with his *Pour le Mérite*.

Below: Poland, the first week of September 1939; Rommel, commanding the Führer's bodyguard, stands to Adolf Hitler's immediate left.

Above: Generalmajor Rommel and the staff of 7th Panzer Division, near the River Seine, mid-June 1940.

Rommel standing next to a Panzer IVD outside of Dieppe. The camera was a personal gift of Propaganda Minister Josef Göbbels, who greatly admired Rommel.

Rommel at Saint-Valery-en-Caux on the Channel coast. The British officer on Rommel's left is Major-General Victor Fortune, Officer Commanding, 51st Highland Division, who has just formally surrendered the town to Rommel.

Erwin and Lucie Rommel in the summer of 1940. Rommel is wearing the Wehrmacht's summer white uniform tunic, and the Knight's Cross he was awarded during the Battle of France in June.

Rommel shortly after his arrival in Tripoli, February 1941.
He is standing with *Generalmajor* Stefan Frölich, who served
as the Luftwaffe's liason officer for the Afrika Korps.

Rommel with Italian Marshal Ettore Bastico, in North Africa,
spring 1941. Their professional relationship was tumultuous,
though it eventually evolved into one of mutual respect.

The Desert Fox. Rommel in North Africa sometime in 1941—the exact date is uncertain. Standing to Rommel's left is *Leutnant* Alfred Berndt, originally of Göbbels' Propaganda Ministry, who became an outstanding soldier, Rommel's friend, sometime confidant, and frequent unofficial messenger to Hitler.

The Afrika Korps on the move: 5th Light Division advancing toward Tobruk, April 1941.

The primary workhorse of the Afrika Korps, the Pzkw. *(Panzerkampfwagen)* III. This is the J model, which mounted a long-barreled 50mm gun, capable of defeating any British tank save the heavily-armored Matilda. This particular panzer was abandoned for lack of fuel outside of Tobruk in November 1941.

The Afrika Korps' other workhorse, the Panzer IV. This is the E model, which mounted a short-barreled 75mm cannon. This one has spare track on the rear deck and an improvised jerrycan rack atop the turret for storing extra fuel.

The much-feared 88mm Flak 36. Originally designed as an anti-aircraft gun, its extraordinarily long range (up to 8 miles) and remarkable hitting power made it the bane of Allied armor in North Africa.

British tanks, a study in contrast: to the left, the A-13 Cruiser, fast, somewhat unreliable, and vulnerable to any anti-tank gun in the Afrika Korps' arsenal; on the right the Matilda Mk. III, impervious to any German gun but the 88, thoroughly reliable, but slow, which was a handicap in the cut and thrust of desert warfare.

Left: Rommel in mid-May 1942, wearing an Afrika Korps sun helmet, having just been invested with Italy's Grand Officer's Cross of the Military Order of Savoy. He also wears Italy's Silver Medal of Military Valor.

Below: Rommel's Sdkfz. 250/3 command half-track, nicknamed *"Greif"* ("Strike"), somewhere in the Cauldron during the Battle of Gazala.

Right: Rommel, *Oberstleutnant* Fritz Bayerlein, and Field Marshal Albert Kesselring conferring during the Battle of Gazala, early June 1942.

Below: The "war without hate." Rommel and Berndt visiting a graveyard in Libya, where German and British soldiers lie buried side-by-side, equally honored.

Above: The "Rommel touch." Here Rommel awards the Iron Cross Second Class to one of his young tank crewmen. Whenever possible, Rommel preferred to make such awards in person. The young *schutzen* (private) and his commanding general both wear bandages over sores caused either by blisters or bites from sand flies.

Left: Rommel was immensely popular with the German people, and photographs such as this one, which bears his signature, were highly prized.

A rather stiffly-posed propaganda photo of Rommel inspecting a defensive position somewhere along the Atlantic Wall. When Rommel took command of the Channel coast defenses in 1943, the Atlantic Wall was little more than a joke; six months later it almost stopped the Allied invasion.

Rommel and the staff of Army Group B inspecting the Atlantic Wall defenses in April 1944. This photograph gives an excellent sense of how extensive were the anti-landing obstacles built along the French coast; at least five distinct types of obstacle are visible.

Rommel along with his chief of staff, General Hans Speidel, in late spring 1944. Behind them is Rommel's adjutant, Captain Helmuth Lang.

Rommel with his driver Daniel in the spring of 1944, in Rommel's Horsch sedan. Rommel habitually rode in the front seat to read maps for Daniel. After the invasion began, two or more officers rode with the Field Marshal to act as lookouts for enemy fighter-bombers.

Rommel on his return to his home in Herlingen, August 15, 1944. It can be clearly seen that his left eye is swollen shut—what is not readily visible is the deep depression in his left forehead, caused by the impact when his Horsch crashed after being strafed by Royal Air Force fighters.

Below: Rommel's funeral cortege, his coffin carried on the trail of a 105mm howitzer; his field marshal's baton lies atop the coffin. The stiff-armed *Hitlergrüsse* (Hitler salute) became mandatory for all military as well as civilian personnel in the wake of the attempt on Hitler's life on July 20, 1944.

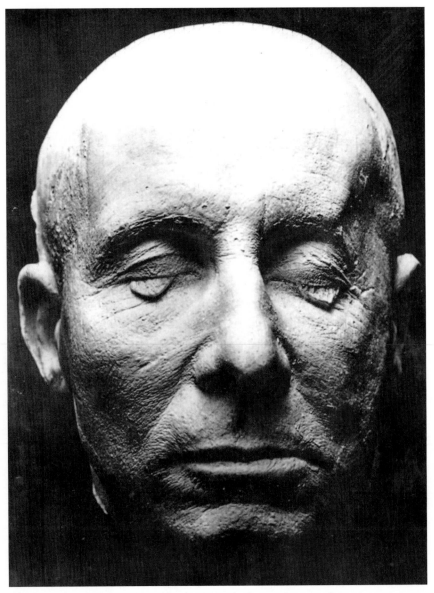

Erwin Rommel's death mask. Some observers have commented on the Field Marshal's expression of fatigue, resignation, and despair. His son Manfred regarded the expression as one of contempt.

25, with the arrival at the Afrika Korps' headquarters of Generalleutnant Friedrich Paulus, the Deputy Chief of the General Staff and Franz Halder's right-hand man. The O.K.W.'s cautious, conservative, highly traditional Chief of Staff was openly contemptuous of Rommel and his undeniably cavalier conduct in North Africa, confiding in his personal diary that "Rommel has not sent us a single clear-cut report in all these days, and I have a feeling that things are in a mess. Reports from officers returning from his command . . . shows that Rommel is in no way equal to his command. . . ." Halder had complete trust in Paulus' judgment, remarking that "He's probably the only man with sufficient personal influence to stop this soldier gone raving mad." Paulus' task was to provide proof of Halder's suspicions which the Chief of Staff could take to Hitler and with it demand that the Führer replace the maverick general in North Africa.[118]

But there was more to Paulus' mission than simply Halder's suspicion and envy of Rommel. It is worth noting that there is, in fact, a wealth of evidence in Halder's personal papers that he was, in varying degrees, naturally suspicious and envious not only of Rommel but of any German general *not* named Franz Halder. Paulus had been dispatched by the O.K.W. with the specific purpose of discovering exactly what was happening in North Africa: Halder's pettiness aside, Hitler and his generals *were* concerned about the dramatic shift in the tone of Rommel's signals to Berlin which followed the failure of the April 15 attack at Ras el Madauar. Operation *Barbarossa*, the invasion of the Soviet Union, was set to begin in less than two months, and the O.K.W. had to be certain that a debacle was not developing in North Africa that could only be redeemed through the diversion of men and materiel already assigned to that mammoth undertaking. Then there were the political issues—it would hardly enhance Germany's prestige if the general sent to North Africa with the mission of salvaging Italy's crumbling fortunes there in turn had to be rescued himself. Consequently, Paulus arrived in Africa with the full authority of the O.K.W. to approve or forbid any operation Rommel was planning or had already begun.

Paulus and Rommel had known each other for almost 15 years, both having been company commanders in Stuttgart in the late 1920s, although how well Rommel remembered Paulus from their days as company commanders in Stuttgart is unknown—certainly there was no evidence of any close friendship then or later. Given the fundamental differences in personality and temperament, it is hardly surprising: Paulus was an officer who led through the authority of his office, Rommel was a commander who led through the power of his personality; Paulus was the quintessential staff officer, Rommel the equally quintessential combat commander; Paulus viewed orders as inviolable and compulsory, Rommel saw them as mutable, subject to being modified or outright discarded on the basis of the knowledge and experience of "the man on the spot." In any event, Rommel was well aware of Paulus' purpose in North Africa, and made him familiar with all of his plans for the attack on Ras el Madauar; Paulus reserved judgment for the moment and allowed Rommel to proceed with his preparations.

Paulus could not fail to be aware of the tensions that were running high between Rommel and his senior officers, especially between Rommel and Streich. The Afrika Korps' commander was doing his best to continue to be the useful subordinate, while Rommel continued to treat him with something approaching contempt. At a planning conference on April 25, Streich, dubious about the terrain around Ras el Madauar, tried to offer some pertinent—and pointed—comments about the proposed nighttime advance on the Australian defenses there, and was pointedly ignored by Rommel; two days later, at another planning session, Streich remarked "A few days ago some of my officers and I had a look at the ground southeast of Tobruk. It is level and offers an excellent opportunity of moving our soldiers forward at night, right up to the fortifications; they can then attack at dawn." Rommel's reply was "I don't want to hear any of *your* plans; I want to hear how you intend to carry out *my* plan." As if this open rebuke wasn't a sufficient display of Rommel's displeasure with Streich, on April 27 General Heinrich Kirchheim, another newcomer to North Africa, was placed in command of the attack, now scheduled for April 30. At this, Streich knew beyond all doubt that his days in command of the Afrika Korps itself were numbered; the thought caused him little distress however, for the once-cordial relationship he'd shared with Rommel just two months earlier was irretrievably broken: Rommel's personality was, for Streich, simply too abrasive for the two men to work together in harness any longer.[119]

At dawn on April 30 a half-dozen artillery regiments, German and Italian, opened fire on the Australian positions in front of Ras el Madauar, their fire plan having been drawn up based on the Italian plans of the Tobruk defenses. At 8:00 P.M., the shelling shifted to targets further back from the front line of fortifications, and two *kampfgruppen* (battle groups), formed around the armored regiments of the 5th Light and 15th Panzer Divisions and a pair of *panzergrenadier* battalions, moved forward, breaking through the first line of defenses and overrunning the Australian bunkers and dugouts, driving nearly 2 miles into the Australian lines. As darkness settled, the attack continued, the Germans pressing forward well into the night until just after 2:00 A.M. on May 1, when a fog settled in around Ras el Madauar. Both sides worked to consolidate their positions, as around 8:00 A.M. the fog lifted and the Germans renewed their attacks. It stalled when the German tanks and half-tracks ran into a previously undetected minefield (yet another product of General Morshead's planning and preparations), which was covered by a combination of 2-pounder antitank guns and British tanks. A dozen Panzer IIIs and Panzer IVs were knocked out, a heavy loss for the Afrika Korps, as the stricken tanks were too far forward to be recovered and later repaired.

While "possession of the field" has always been one of the physical as well as psychological measures of victory in a battle, in the Libyan desert it offered a significant material benefit as well: tanks and vehicles that had only been put out of action, but not actually destroyed—broken tank treads, damage to engines, transmissions, or suspensions, or even hits which had done serious injury to the crew but had not done catastrophic damage to the vehicle itself—could be recovered, repaired, and returned to action by whichever side retained possession of the battlefield after the action. For the Afrika Korps in particular, which suffered from a chronic shortage of tanks, this could be a significant advantage—or handicap—depending on which way the battle had gone.

That evening, the Australians counterattacked but were thrown back with heavy casualties. But the Afrika Korps' attack had stalled, nonetheless, and rather than taking Tobruk as he had expected to do, Rommel had a salient 2 miles deep and 3 miles wide in the Australian lines, at a cost of over 1,200 killed and wounded, and the loss of almost half the armor committed to the attack. (Of 81 Panzer III and Panzer IV tanks engaged, 35 had been knocked out and could not be recovered.) Rommel was convinced that the Italian infantry had failed to do their job, remarking that

The Italians had acquired a very considerable inferiority complex, as was not surprising under the circumstances. Their infantry were practically without antitank guns and their artillery completely obsolete. Their training was also a long way short of modern standards, so that we were continually being faced by serious breakdowns [of morale]. Many Italian officers thought of war as little more than a pleasant adventure and were, perforce, having to suffer a bitter disillusionment.[120]

A sandstorm kicked up on May 2, effectively making any offensive action impossible. The next day, the Australians counterattacked again, this time striking directly at the Italian infantry that had moved up the previous day to bolster the German troops in the salient. Expecting the Italians to easily crumble and break, the Australians were unpleasantly surprised when the Italian infantry fought with skill and determination, losing only a single bunker to the Australian assault. In this action, many of the Italian troops were fighting under the direction of German junior officers and senior NCOs, giving weight to Rommel's earlier opinion that there was nothing fundamentally wrong with the average Italian soldier, but that he was too often let down by incompetent officers.

Meanwhile, Generalleutnant Paulus had seen enough. On the morning of May 4, he formally instructed Rommel to cease any further attempts to take Tobruk by direct assault, and instead lay siege to the town. Since Paulus' orders had the authority of an O.K.W. *behfel*, and his presence "on the spot," as it were, deprived Rommel of any chance to claim that distance had created a false or distorted impression in the collective mind of the General Staff, or any opportunity to creatively "intepret" those orders, Rommel had no choice but to comply. Paulus then departed North Africa, and once back in Berlin made his report to Halder. While it was hardly complimentary to Rommel, it was far from the scathing condemnation for which Paulus' chief had been hoping. Rommel was indeed, he said, a willful, arrogant officer, self-confident to a fault. At the same time, North Africa was and would remain a sideshow—there was no need to be overconcerned that it would become a distraction from *Barbarossa*, let alone a major theater for the Axis. Though not precisely what Halder wanted, Halder found Paulus' report reassuring—Rommel, mad or not, would remain properly sidelined. Intriguingly, it has been said that at some point Paulus considered suggesting that Rommel be relieved of command, with himself to be Rommel's successor, but that Paulus' wife, an incurable social-climber, persuaded him that North Africa was not the place where a senior general could make his reputation.[121]

No small part of Rommel's difficulties in taking Tobruk was the character of the Australians themselves: he would write in *Krieg ohne Haase* of an encounter with a group of about 60 Australians captured in the attack on Ras el Madauar, remarking that they were "immensely big and powerful men who, without question, represented an elite formation of the British Empire, a fact that was also evident in battle." They were tenacious in defense, and would guarantee that Tobruk remained Rommel's "*Dorn im Fleisch*" for the next seven months. At the same time, an equal degree of defensive determination, this one by Axis forces, was being displayed 100 miles east of Tobruk, on the Egyptian frontier, where a motley collection of German and Italian infantry, artillery, and antitank guns had been holding the Via Balbia at the narrow coastal defile of Sollum and the passage through Halfaya Pass.

The geography of the North African coast shared by Libya and Egypt was peculiar: a narrow strip of relatively level ground of varying width rose gently from the waters of the Mediterranean, then sheered abruptly upward into the slopes of a 600-foot high escarpment so steep that neither wheeled nor tracked vehicles could drive over it. The escarpment itself ran from a point about 70 miles east of the border westward all the way to Tobruk. At the coastal town of Sollum, the slopes of the escarpment approached to within a half-mile of the sea. A few miles south of Sollum was the Halfaya Pass, the only break passable to vehicles in the ridgeline of the escarpment, and the only means of bypassing the escarpment that did not require a long, tortuous detour inland. West of Sollum, and running inland to the southwest for 160 miles, was The Wire, a thick, dense, 6-foot high barricade of barbwire and wooden posts, built by the Italians as a border defense in the early 1930s. Together, Sollum and the Halfaya Pass created a natural bottleneck for any army advancing westward out of Egypt into Libya. Each position was a defender's dream: both offered numerous sites on the slopes of the escarpment for observation posts, along with positions for artillery and antitank guns with almost unlimited fields of fire. At Sollum, the coastal road, the Via Balbia, took a sharp 90-degree turn to the left, forced on the Italian engineers who built it by the terrain; at Halfaya, the road through the pass wound and twisted, again according to the dictates of the contours of the land. Any vehicle attempting to pass through either place was compelled to move at low speed, making itself a particularly vulnerable target. Sollum and Halfaya offered Erwin Rommel a golden opportunity to use the terrain against the British to make up for the Afrika Korps' inferior numbers.

In early April, as he was simultaneously bundling the motorized and mechanized units of the Western Desert Force across the Egyptian frontier and bottling up the Australian infantry in Tobruk, Rommel knew that if the garrison there were able to hold out even for a few weeks, a British attack, or even an out-and-out offensive, to relieve the beleaguered fortress would be inevitable. That knowledge had been no small part of the reason for the repeated attempts to take the town in mid- and late-April. With the O.K.W. having forbidden any further assaults, it was now the task of the Afrika Korps to contain the Tobruk garrison while at the same time blunting and ultimately defeating the inevitable British attack out of Egypt trying to break through to Tobruk and raise the siege. Rommel, anticipating that sooner or later the O.K.W. would give him permission to once more try to take Tobruk by storm, began redeploying his Italian infantry division to hold the perimeter around the fortress while his German units began training in the old-fashioned assault tactics that Rommel had employed so successfully in 1917 and 1918. In the reshuffling, he proposed to send two Italian divisions eastward to bolster the defenses at Sollum and the Halfaya Pass.

In the mad dash eastward from Mechili at the beginning of April, the 3rd Reconaissance Battalion had actually raced past Tobruk, occupied Sollum on April 15, and immediately dug in. In a few days it was joined by the 2nd Battalion of the 5th Panzer Regiment, and a battalion of motorized Italian infantry from the Trento Division, all under the command of Oberst Maximilian von Herff. Halfaya Pass was covered by two companies of *Bersaglieri* — tough, well-trained motorised infantry, the elite of the Italian army and justifiably regarded as formidable fighters by the Germans and British alike — with a half-dozen medium artillery batteries in support. Both positions were given a liberal sprinkling of German 37mm and 50mm antitank guns, but the key to the defense of either would be the thirteen 88mm Flak guns—seven at Sollum, six at Halfaya—sited and dug in to serve as antitank weapons. Originally designed as an antiaircraft gun, the Flak (*flugzeugabwehr kanone*) Model 36 and 37 guns (they differed only in the way their barrels were constructed) had proven able to defeat the armor of any tank in the Allied order of battle, including the heavily armored Matilda tanks of the British Army, as Rommel had discovered first-hand at Arras a year earlier. Now, in the flat expanses of the North African desert, the Flak 88 came into its own, as it possessed the range and power to knock out any vehicle its crew could see.

Colonel von Herff's tank battalion had roughly 40 Panzer III and Panzer IV tanks available (the actual number fluctuated daily, depending on how many tanks were actually running at any given moment), along with the armored cars of the 3rd Reconnaissance Battalion, ready to react to any British incursion toward Sollum or Halfaya. The Panzer III was a 25-ton tank armed with either a 37mm or 50mm main gun, designed before the war to be the Wehrmacht's main battle tank; its stablemate, the Panzer IV, was slightly heavier (27 tons), and armed with a short-barreled 75mm main gun, its original purpose being to support advancing infantry. Later the Panzer IV would be given successively longer 75mm guns as it took over the battle tank role from the Panzer III—in the spring of 1941, however, either vehicle was capable of taking on and defeating any tank currently put in the field by the British Army.

In addition to covering Sollum and the Halfaya Pass, von Herff, at Rommel's direction, also took his small armored force on frequent raids into British territory. The purpose of these raids was to simultaneously gather intelligence on British plans and intentions, destroy British supply dumps whenever possible, cause whatever casualties could be inflicted at minimal risk to his own units, take the odd prisoner or two, and generally inflict mischief and mayhem upon the British whenever and wherever possible, with an eye on keeping them off-balance. Wavell had ordered what remained of the Western Desert Froce's mechanized units to do their best to constantly press the Germans and Italians holding Sollum and Halfaya, and von Herff was returning the British in kind.

The intelligence-gathering aspect of von Herff's adventures was crucial to Rommel. Rarely has a commanding general become as adroit as did

Erwin Rommel during his years in North Africa in comprehending, inter-preting—and when necessary, intuiting—enemy plans and intentions from the information provided by his intelligence sources. Reconnaissance, both on the ground and from the air, was essential, of course, although it had its limitations: the British were the past masters of deceiving aerial observation and photography, a tradition begun by General Edmund Allenby in the Gaza campaign in the autumn of 1917. Prisoners of war often let slip critical bits of information, seemingly insignificant in and of themselves, but in-valuable when pieced together by intelligence officers with other sources of information, especially captured enemy documents. But in the Western Desert, it was signals intelligence—the interception and interpretation of wireless transmissions back and forth between headquarters and subordi-nate units, or between individual units themselves, which provided the richest source of intelligence about enemy capabilities and intentions, and which for Afrika Korps would become an essential element in the creation and continuation of the legend of the Desert Fox.

Signals intelligence in 1941 was still something of a dark art, for the Second World War was the first major conflict where significant amounts of essential communications by combat units took place via wireless radio. In the First World War, nearly all communications on land were sent and received via telephone lines, or, when those failed, via runner or even car-rier pigeon. Wireless equipment was still far too bulky and balky to be any-thing like an apparatus transportable in a battlefield, thus its tactical and operational usefulness was essentially nil. It would not be until the 1920s that radio transceivers became sufficiently compact and reliable to be mounted in tanks, armored cars, and command vehicles. Benefitting from two decades of naval experience with wireless, armies immediately under-stood that, unlike telephone lines, where any would-be eavesdropper had to physically tap into a cable in order to hear what it was transmitting, it was impossible to secure a wireless signal from the prying ears of anyone with a tunable radio receiver. Codes and coding systems were quickly de-veloped and adopted, but in practice, as most of the codes and code ma-chines were time-consuming and clumsy to operate, many armies were lax, sometimes egregiously so, in employing them consistently. (One of the ad-vantages of the German "Enigma" system, which turned out to be a vulner-ability that the British were ultimately able to exploit in their development of "Ultra," was the ease with which messages could be encoded or decoded. This led to the generation of a huge number of Enigma-encoded messages passing back and forth among and between units of the Wehrmacht, the Luftwaffe, and the Kriegsmarine, and as any cryptographer would readily acknowledge, the larger the volume of messages with which a code-breaker has to work, the more likely that code will, in fact, be broken. That is, in a greatly simplified form, exactly what happened with Ultra.)

British units in Egypt, from corps headquarters down to battalion level, were frequently guilty of very poor radio discipline, often transmitting messages partially or even fully "in the clear," that is, uncoded, or spending time in idle chit-chat among units. Even when coded, the volume of messages sent and received by a given unit, their length, and the identifiers used by the sender and receiver could offer priceless bits of information about those units, reveal their overall organization and chain of command, and offer significant clues as to strengths and supply situations. An astute intelligence officer—and there were several such in the Afrika Korps—eavesdropping on his enemy's radio net could readily deduce patterns and habits in those communications, and so recognize that when those patterns changed, it almost invariably signified something important was about to happen.

That was precisely what happened on the night of May 14, when Leutnant Alfred Seebohm, commanding officer of the 3rd Company, 56th Signals Battalion and the Afrika Korps' best signals intelligence specialist, heard the word "Fritz" broadcast to all British units in Egypt, and listened as the Tommy radio net then went silent—something that had never before occurred. Seebohm, who had a small liaison detachment assigned to Rommel's staff, immediately passed the word along about this unusual incident, and Rommel, sensitive to the vulnerability of the Sollum–Halfaya position, alerted Colonel von Herff, and reinforced the southeastern sector of the Tobruk perimeter as a precaution against a sortie by the Tobruk garrison. At 6:00 A.M. on May 15, the British attacked at Sollum and Halfaya in what was to be the aptly named Operation *Brevity*.

Ultra intercepts had provided London and Cairo with at least part of the report that Paulus had made to Halder, including observations he made about the Afrika Korps' shortages of fuel and ammunition. General Wavell immediately understood that the Axis forces around Tobruk and at the Egyptian frontier had for the time being shifted to the defensive and saw an opportunity to relieve Tobruk. In London, Churchill read the same intercepts, and from them somehow concluded that the Germans were on the verge of collapse; before long, he was pestering Wavell to launch a major attack to relieve Tobruk and rout the Afrika Korps.

Wavell was already planning such an operation, to be called *Battleaxe*, but the forces needed for such an effort were far from ready: tanks, guns, and equipment lost or worn out in the retreat from Cyrenaica had to be repaired or replaced, while new brigades and regiments arriving from Britain had to be trained, and often their tanks and vehicles—fresh from the factory—had to be modified and adapted to the conditions of the Egyptian and Libyan desert. Wavell had no reasonable expectation of mounting the sort of offensive Churchill was demanding before mid-June, but he did believe that he had the means to lay the groundwork for it, by taking Sollum and the Halfaya Pass, capturing Fort Capuzzo if practicable, and, as far as possible, "writing down" Rommel's strength. This would be Operation *Brevity*. Brigadier William Gott, who had been harrying the Germans and Italians at the Egyptian frontier for weeks, was given command of the operation, and on the morning of May 15, he attacked in three columns, with infantry and armor more-or-less working together. The battle was essentially over in two days.

Gott's southern column, composed of elements of the 7th Armoured Brigade, was to take the long way around behind the escarpment, moving up to Sidi Azeiz and cutting off the retreat of the Axis units at Sollum and Halfaya. The center column, made up of the 22nd Guards Brigade, was tasked with taking the southern (upper) half of Halfaya Pass along with Fort Capuzzo, a ramshackle fortification that dated back to Italy's first occupation of Libya in 1911. The northern column, comprised entirely of infantry, was given the lower half of Halfaya Pass and the town of Sollum as its objectives.

The breadth of the British advance at first created no small confusion for Rommel, who believed that the enemy had committed two full divisions to the attack. He reacted by dispatching a second *kampfgruppe* from Tobruk, this one formed around a tank battalion from the 8th Panzer Regiment, under the command of Lieutenant Colonel Hans Kramer, with orders to link up with Kampfgruppe von Herff south of Fort Capuzzo that afternoon. Meanwhile, Gott's center column ran into strong opposition from the *Bersaglieri* at the top of Halfaya Pass. Rather than fight it out with the Axis antitank guns, the Guards moved on to Fort Capuzzo. The fort's defenders, however, put up a stout resistance, and it wasn't until early afternoon that Capuzzo was taken—briefly. The northern column found itself held up by the understrength *Bersaglieri* company at the entrance to Halfaya Pass; it needed the entire day to force the stubborn Italians to abandon their positions. As a consequence, the planned British threat to Sollum never materialized.

Von Herff pulled his *kampfgruppe* back behind Sollum, to where the coastal road runs along the top of the escarpment, and from there he launched a counterattack on Capuzzo, taking it back from the British just hours after they had captured the fort. Meanwhile, on the desert flank, German reconnaissance patrols shadowed the 7th Armoured Brigade, but mistook the thin-skinned British cruiser tanks for the heavily armored Matildas. Colonel von Herff at first considered swinging wide into the desert to strike the 7th Armoured in the flank but was understandably chary of taking them on without antitank guns in support. Instead he chose to remain near Capuzzo and link up with Kampfgruppe Kramer in the morning, where the combined strength of the two battle groups could deliver a knockout punch to the British armored columns.

Gott, meanwhile, saw that his center column, the 22nd Guards Brigade and its accompanying infantry, was now left sitting in the open around the oases of Bir Wair and Mussaid, vulnerable to a German counterattack. In the early hours of May 16, he pulled the column back to the top of Halfaya Pass, possibly with the idea of trying to take the remainder of the pass later that day; at the same time, waiting for the Germans to make the next move, he ordered the 7th Armoured Brigade group to halt in place somewhere west of Fort Capuzzo.

Kramer's battle group reached Fort Capuzzo at 6:30 A.M., and at 8:00 A.M., he made contact with Kampfgruppe von Herff. At this point the British missed an opportunity to deal Rommel, the Afrika Korps, and the entire Axis adventure in North Africa a crippling blow: by mid-morning both *kampfgruppen* ran out of fuel and were immobilized. Had Gott known of this and immediately ordered an attack by the 7th Armoured Brigade and the 22nd Dragoons Guards, he could have destroyed almost half of the Afrika Korps' tank strength. As it was, none of his reconnaissance units divined the reason for von Herff and Kramer's immobility, and the opportunity passed. It would be almost 4:00 P.M. before both panzer battalions could move again, setting off to the west of Capuzzo in pursuit of the British armor seen there the previous day, von Herff now confident that he possessed sufficient strength to deal with whatever the British had there. Tanks from the 5th Panzer Battalion bickered briefly with a company of cruiser tanks from the 7th Armoured Brigade, then both sides withdrew, each convinced they had driven off a powerful enemy attack. During the night the Germans and British tankers repaired damaged vehicles, replenished ammunition stocks, and prepared to once more try conclusions in the morning, but at dawn General Gott, unwilling to leave the 7th Armoured sitting unsupported in the middle of the desert, ordered the brigade to pull back to its starting point at Bir el Khireigat. Operation *Brevity* was over.

For the British, *Brevity* could only be regarded as a failure: only a single objective had been attained, and that only in part, the capture of the northern, lower end, of Halfaya Pass. The British operations never truly came close to accomplishing Wavell's primary objective, acquiring positions from which to launch an offensive to relieve Tobruk. In terms of personnel and materiel lost, casualties for both the Germans and the British were remarkably low for all the fighting that had actually taken place. Each lost a handful of tanks and a few hundred men killed, wounded, or captured—there was no Italian armor involved in the entire battle, and Italian records of killed and wounded have been lost; the British later claimed to have taken almost 350 Italian prisoners, a not unrealistic figure given the determined *Bersaglieri* defense of Halfaya.

At the same time, *Brevity* was unquestionably a victory for the Axis, although it would be an exaggeration to call it significant. It has sometimes been viewed as the first real battle Erwin Rommel fought as a commanding general—as opposed to what were little more than glorified pursuits of a disorganized enemy in France and across Cyrenaica—but to characterize it as such is misleading. Once he had sent Lieutenant Colonel Kramer's battle group forward to join Colonel von Herff, Rommel had very little influence on the outcome of the fighting around Capuzzo, Halfaya and Sollum. The battle was fought and won by Kampfgruppen von Herff and Kramer, and the *Bersaglieri* companies at Halfaya. The significance of *Brevity* for Erwin Rommel lay in its aftermath, rather than what happened during the battle itself; his lack of exercising direct command during the battle did not prevent his learning from it.

The first lesson Rommel immediately drew was tactical: he took note of how von Herff's movements around the upper part of Halfaya Pass seemed to validate his own ideas about the coordination of tanks and anti-tank guns. At this point in the desert war, and well into the summer of 1942, the overall quality of the Panzer III and IV models in firepower, protection, and reliability was superior to anything the British could field. But that superiority was not absolute: most of Rommel's tanks were still vulnerable at combat ranges to the ubiquitous 2-pounder gun that was the main armament for all British tanks at the time. Indeed, the 2-pounder was so effective that its presence on the battlefield had relegated the Panzer I and II to reconnaissance duties and actions against "soft" targets, such as infantry formations. The Matilda frankly frightened German panzer crews, because its heavy armor was completely impervious to the 37mm Pak 36 (*panzerabwehrkanone*—antitank gun) and could shrug off hits from the 50mm Pak 40 at medium and long ranges—its own 2-pounder could, in turn, put paid to any of the Afrika Korps' tanks. The only German weapon that could defeat the Matilda at any range were, of course, the 88mm Flak guns.

This reality spurred Rommel to develop more flexible tactics for his antitank guns, tactics which would allow him to employ them aggressively, by advancing a screen of armor and moving up a line of guns behind it. At the proper moment, having drawn their British counterparts into an engagement, the panzers would fall back, drawing the pursuing British tanks into the fire of the previously hidden 37mm and 50mm Paks. A handful of Flak 88s, with their long range, would be sufficient to take on and take out any Matildas that might be among the British attackers—the lighter guns would be able to finish off anything else. This ploy would become the standard Axis tactic for the remainder of the war in North Africa.

The success of Kampfgruppen von Herff and Kramer spurred Rommel into thinking more deeply about the use of small, battalion-sized ad hoc units assembled for particular actions and operations. This offered a far greater degree of flexibility in reacting to or taking advantage of specific tactical and operational situations, which might be relatively fleeting, and to which larger formations would be too ponderous and unwieldy to swiftly respond. Rommel did not invent the *Kampfgruppe*, or battle group; elements of the concept date back to the *Stosstruppen* of 1918, and it would be the cornerstone of Wehrmacht operations on the Eastern Front throughout the war. He brought the idea to the Western Desert, however, and in employing it he gave the Afrika Korps, and, to a lesser extent, the Italians, an operational flexibility which the British were never able to equal, and which often made up for the Axis inferiority in numbers of men, vehicles, and equipment.

The first opportunity for Rommel to put this developing concept into action came just 10 days after *Brevity* came to an end. Rommel knew that the British would soon return, and in greater numbers, and he was determined to take back the lower half of the Halfaya Pass before they did so. His solution was *Fall Skorpion*, an attack by three *kampfgruppen* made up of tanks, artillery—including antitank guns—and infantry from the 5th and 8th Panzer Battalions, the 104th Infantry Battalion, the 3rd Reconnaissance Battalion, and the 33rd Artillery Regiment, all under the command of Oberst von Herff. On the morning of May 27, they struck at Halfaya Pass, which was held by a single battalion of the Coldstream Guards, supported by a handful of Matildas and a single battery of 25-pounder guns. The Coldstreams were in an untenable position, as there were no other British units close enough to provide support or reinforcements, and they were overrun in less than two hours. As soon as news of the German attack reached him, General Gott ordered the Halfaya garrison to abandon the pass, which they did, leaving behind 173 soldiers killed, wounded, or taken prisoner, along with the wrecks of five Matildas, four field guns, and eight antitank guns. The last British gains from *Brevity* had been eliminated.

Relieved now that the whole of Halfaya Pass was back in his possession, Rommel significantly reinforced its defenses, giving the responsibility for holding the pass against the inevitable British offensive to one of the most colorful—and beloved—characters in the whole of the Afrika Korps, Hauptmann Wilhelm Georg Bach. Just a year younger than Rommel, Bach was cheerful, outgoing, cigar-chomping, slightly myopic Bavarian who had been awarded the Iron Cross, First and Second Class, in the Great War, and who walked with the aid of a cane courtesy of a severe leg injury incurred in that conflict. He had joined the Imperial German Army in the first week of August 1914, was so highly regarded as an enlisted man that he was marked for officer training, being commissioned a lieutenant of Reserves in August 1915. He served at the front for just over a year before being wounded in combat at the Somme and taken prisoner by the British. When he was repatriated to Germany after the war, he enrolled in an *Evangelische* (Lutheran) seminary, became an ordained Christian minister, and took up a position as the pastor of a church in Mannheim.

He never resigned his commission, however, and so found himself— clerical collar, cigars, cane and all—recalled to reserve duty in the summer of 1936, when Hitler began his vast expansion of the German Army. In September 1939, with Germany again at war, Bach was posted to a reserve regiment stationed along the Moselle River, where the German and French armies went through the motions of the Phoney War. February 1940 saw him assigned to command a company in the 104th Infantry Regiment, which went into action for the first time in May, when the Wehrmacht invaded France. Then when the 104th Regiment's parent unit, the 33rd Infantry Division, was dissolved in November 1940, the regiment became part of the newly created 15th Panzer Division, which was promptly sent to North Africa. The 1st Battalion of the 104th was Kampfgruppe von Herff's infantry component when Halfaya Pass was retaken; heavily reinforced, it was immediately assigned to defend the recaptured defile, with Bach temporarily in command. Under his direction, most of the battalion's strength—including five batteries of antitank guns, one of them the deadly 88mm Flak guns—was placed on the heights at the top of the pass, while the entrance down by the coastal road was covered by a machine-gun company and heavily mined.

At first, Rommel was unsure what to make of Hauptmann Bach; the clergyman-turned-infantry officer was habitually addressed by his soldiers as *"Vater"* ("Father"), and it was unclear whether it was a reference to his former profession or to his paternal nature, for Bach had a reputation for taking very good care of his men. While Rommel was also held in high regard by his soldiers, his invariably punctilious nature discouraged that sort of familiarity. Also, Rommel, though not given over to requiring his rankers to waste time and effort on needless "spit and polish," expected his officers to *look* like officers; given his own streak of vanity, he was almost always immaculately turned out. (When Rommel finally conceded defeat to the desert heat and began wearing short trousers in early May, it was an occasion for much comment by his staff and subordinates—out of his hearing, of course.) Bach, however, looked like nothing so much as a walking bundle of military laundry, all rumples and wrinkles—a less "soldierly"-looking officer would have been hard to find. Consequently Rommel took an initial dislike to Bach, and presumed that the Hauptmann's military talents were on a par with his appearance. It would be only a matter of weeks, however, before Rommel would find himself numbered among *Hauptmann* Bach's admirers, for, despite his unprepossessing countenance, Bach could fight like a lion.

At the same time that the Halfaya garrison was strengthened, reinforcements were sent to Sollum and Fort Capuzzo, backed by a handful of strongpoints (*stützpunkten*) that were well armed with antitank guns, mortars, and machine guns. In constructing these positions, Rommel unashamedly drew on the hard-won experience his soldiers had earned in attacking the Tobruk defenses, and his engineers openly copied their best features. Rommel also seized whatever plums fortune chose to drop into his lap: while driving along the coast road on one of his inspections of these new defenses, Rommel happened across dozens of artillery pieces of varying caliber, along with piles of ammunition, sitting abandoned in the desert northwest of Bardia. These were the guns abandoned six months previously by Marshal Graziani's army in its headlong flight westward during Operation *Compass*. As Rommel told the tale,

> This materiel was just waiting to be used, and I therefore gave immediate instructions for all unclaimed Italian guns to be collected up and used to strengthen the Sollum–Halfaya–Sidi Omar front. A substantial number of these guns was put in order by one or two of our German workshops and then installed in the strongpoints. But the Italian High Command did not agree at all, and General Gariboldi had me informed . . . that the guns were Italian property and were only to be used by Italians. They had been perfectly content up till then to stand by and watch this materiel go to wrack and ruin, but the moment the first guns had been made serviceable on our initiative, they began to take notice. However, I was not to be put off.[122]

During his years in Africa, Rommel would more than once remark on what he called "Italian treachery," usually in reference to some intelligence failure or imagined betrayal by unnamed Italian spies, but incidents like this gave an added fillip to his suspicions that, however loyal may be the Italian soldiers at the front, doing the actual fighting, their superiors in Rome and Tripoli were more interested in political infighting and *machismo* posturing than in actually winning the war; to Rommel that was the ultimate treachery.

Though not completely satisfied—he was still chronically short of men, vehicles, and equipment, especially artillery, despite the unexpected and involuntary Italian largesse—Rommel could now feel a bit more confident in the security of the approaches to Tobruk. Rightly certain that *Brevity* had not been a serious effort at relieving the besieged fortress, he now turned his hand once again to training his infantry units, especially the Italians, in tactics he devised to defeat and capture the defenses of Tobruk. His hope was that he would have an opportunity to storm the town before the British began the offensive to relieve the Australian defenders.

At the same time, he had to set his own military house in order, not the most pleasant of tasks. The first priority was to bring some sense of order to the supply situation. The Axis forces in Africa were experiencing their first significant supply crisis: superficially, this was the consequence of Rommel's mad but inspired dash across Cyrenaica and his less-than-inspired attacks on Tobruk; more realistically, it was the combined fault of O.K.W. and Comando Supremo. The chronic supply difficulties that plagued the Afrika Korps and the Italian Army resulted from fundamentally flawed strategic thinking in both Berlin and Rome. Admittedly Rommel's drive across Libya had placed a near-breaking strain on the already inefficient Italian supply system, yet the harsh reality was that Italy's North African ports barely possessed the capacity to meet the peacetime requirements of the Italian army and the Italian civil population in Libya. Even had Rommel obeyed his original orders and remained on the defensive at El Agheila, the addition of the Afrika Korps' two panzer divisions and their supporting units pushed the supply requirements far beyond the total capacity of Libya's ports still in Axis hands. Now, with the addition of a handful of squadrons from Fliegerkorps X flying out of bases west of Tobruk, the situation only became worse: despite the best efforts of the Italian navy, the Italian merchant marine, and the Luftwaffe, the Axis armies in Africa were steadily being starved of fuel and supplies—and the war in North Africa would be first and foremost a war of supply.

There is an old—and misleading—bit of conventional military wisdom which holds that "amateurs study tactics, while professionals study logistics." The truth is that amateurs study only tactics *or* logistics, while professionals study both simultaneously. The most brilliant tactics ever devised are pointless when the supplies needed to execute them do not exist, while all the supplies in the world are useless when a commanding officer has no idea how to effectively employ them. Of course, in modern mechanized warfare, there is far more involved in the term "supplies" than the classic "Three Bs" of black-powder days—Bullets, Beans, and Boots. The problems are considerably more complex than simply securing sufficient gasoline to power the tanks and trucks, or shells for the artillery. To properly function a mechanized army is dependent on an astonishing range of articles and materiel, ranging from spark plugs, piston rings, gaskets and seals, bearings and bearing grease, engine oil, transmission fluid, special recouperator oil for recoil mechanisms, tires for trucks and armored cars, rubber road wheels for tanks, replacement links for tracks, tubes for radios, maps, compasses, lens cleaner, bore cleaner, medical supplies and equipment, to items as mundane but utterly essential as socks, uniforms, and boots. In all, just the two divisions of the Afrika Korps alone required over 700 tons of supplies per day in order to be able to conduct basic operations—when they were on the attack, that figure doubled.

None of this should have come as a surprise to the O.K.W. or Comando Supremo: the supply requirements ought to have been calculated before the first German unit sailed for North Africa, and the constraints imposed by the limitations of the Libyan ports understood with perfect clarity by the General Staff officers whose professional responsibility it was to oversee and, if possible, overcome such difficulties. Rommel, for his part, blamed the Italians for deliberately misleading their German allies, and if his censure is taken as being limited to the upper echelons of the Italian command structure, he was exactly right. In Rome, Mussolini, along with General Ugo Cavallero, chief of Comando Supremo, Admiral Arturo Riccardi, undersecretary of the Regia Marina, Italy's navy, and, to a lesser degree, General Graziani in Tripoli, all airily reassured Hitler, Halder, Field Marshal Walter von Brauchitsch (the commander-in-chief of the German Army), and General der Flieger Otto von Waldau, who commanded Fliegerkorps X, that the Italian navy and merchant marine would be able to transport more than enough tonnage to Libya to keep the Afrika Korps properly supplied. Hitler and his officers, in turn, simply took the Italians at their word, and planned accordingly.

Consequently, in March 1941, when Franz Halder asked Rommel how he expected to solve the Afrika Korps' looming supply problems, Rommel rightly shot back, "That's your pigeon!" The implication was that had Halder and the General Staff properly done their jobs, they would have foreseen the near-insurmountable obstacles to adequately supplying a *panzerkorps* in North Africa, and advised Hitler, who at the time was still amenable to taking the advice of his senior officers, against committing any ground forces to shoring up the sagging Italian war effort in Libya. Halder never forgave him for the barb, and began circulating the rumor among his fellow senior officers that Rommel's grasp of logistics was weak, if not positively feeble, the beginnings of a myth that continues to persist.

Yet Rommel was correct: the German high command had blithely taken its Italian counterpart at its word without question, with the result being a logistical disaster waiting to happen in North Africa. Rommel, in the last days of May, found himself compelled to decide how often Paul was to be robbed to pay Peter, and of how much. The supply situation of the entire North African campaign—until only a matter of weeks before its conclusion—would be run as a makeshift, improvised proposition, the Afrika Korps at times as much dependent for its existence on captured enemy supplies and equipment as that provided by its own quartermaster branch. At the same time, lest the mendacity of the Comando Supremo be taken as representative of the whole of the Italian armed forces, it should be remembered that, despite the best efforts of the Allied naval and air forces in the Mediterranean to prevent it, 84 percent of all the fuel, food, and munitions shipped to the Afrika Korps reached North Africa, all of it carried in Italian ships. The fault was not with the men responsible for delivering the supplies, but rather with those who made impossible promises and those who acted on them.

It has to be said that Rommel sometimes made the situation more difficult than it actually was with the risks he took, but in May 1941, at least, Rommel knew he had to fight with one eye figuratively on his divisions' fuel gauges and ammunition stocks: he had no room for error, and any risks he might take in countering the coming British offensive would have to be very finely calculated indeed. He was also acutely aware that both O.K.W. and O.K.H. (Oberkommando des Heers—the General Headquarters of the Army) would be peering over his shoulder during any operation to come in Libya. General von Brauchitsch had already sent Rommel a rather tart signal (in a letter to Lucie dated May 26, Rommel called it "a considerable rocket") about the messages from Rommel received in Berlin in regard to the situation around Tobruk and at the Egyptian frontier. From all appearances, the General Staff and the Army Command minimized the severity of the difficulties Rommel faced, while overestimating the degree of whatever advantages he held over his British opponents. It is not at all difficult here to detect the influence of General Paulus' report to Halder, made earlier that month. Paulus had thus far spent his entire military career, save for a few months in France in the autumn of 1914, in various staff positions: he never truly experienced and so never understood (as he would demonstrate at the cost of his entire army at Stalingrad just 18 months later) the profound differences between theoretical staff work and the harsh practical realities of life at the front. Paulus had downplayed the severity of Rommel's supply problems, citing prewar statistics and theoretical studies which demonstrated, to his satisfaction—and Halder's—that Rommel's concerns were exaggerated.

For his part, Rommel was unimpressed by the O.K.H. missive. His reaction was exactly what would be expected from someone who scorned career staff officers like Paulus, Halder, and von Brauchitsch. As he wrote to Lucie, "the result will be that we'll keep our mouths shut and only report in the briefest forms." A few days later he was telling her that "Either they have confidence in me or they haven't. If they haven't then I'm asking them to draw their own conclusions"—a thinly veiled threat to resign his command. He then cut to the heart of the matter: "It's easy enough to bellyache when you aren't sweating it out here." With that, as far as Rommel was concerned, the whole issue was closed.[123]

A somewhat thornier problem was of more immediate concern to Rommel at that moment, as he was undertaking a very thorough reorganization of his own officer corps—it might almost be called a purge. He was determined to create a command structure staffed by officers who he knew would obey his orders rather than debate them. The first to go was, of course, Generalleutnant Streich, commander of the Afrika Korps, who had long known that he would be replaced. Neither Rommel nor Streich handled their final exchange with any particular grace: on May 16, Rommel telephoned Streich's headquarters and announced, "Streich, I have asked for you to be replaced. You will continue in command, however, until your successor arrives!"

"Does the General have any further orders?" Streich replied drily, then broke the connection before Rommel was able to reply. When his replacement arrived on the last day of May, Streich said goodbye to Rommel in a stiffly formal leave-taking. Rommel attempted to explain that he could no longer tolerate Streich's habit of questioning orders, and that he believed the departing general's performance of his duties had lapsed at times because he had been too interested in the welfare of his men. Streich simply retorted, "Herr General, I can imagine no greater words of praise for a division commander." And with that, he was gone.[124]

Streich's words stung, for Rommel, as he had demonstrated in the First World War, and then in France in 1940, held the well-being of the soldiers under his command as one of his highest priorities. What Streich failed to grasp—and Rommel failed to make clear to Streich—was that now, as a corps commander and *de facto* commander of the Axis forces in Libya, Rommel's priorities had shifted. He was compelled to take a broader, longer view of everything that was happening in North Africa, to better understand and plan the campaign for which he had been given the responsibility of fighting. He was being compelled, by his position, to think like a strategist, and strategy, however subtle, requires a willingness to be ruthless in its execution which is rarely demanded at the tactical or operational level; this was a burden Streich, as a division commander, never had to shoulder. The misfortune of the two men, who had begun their time in Africa by working so well together, was that both were right, according to the perspective given them by their levels of command, but the realities of war demanded that Rommel's point of view prevail.

The man who replaced Streich was Generalleutnant Johann von Ravenstein, the scion of a distinguished military family and, like Rommel, the recipient of the *Pour le Mérite*. In France, in May 1918, he had successfully led a few dozen soldiers into an attack that captured an important railway and took 1,500 prisoners. At the end of the Great War, von Ravenstein left the army and became an electrician, rejoining the army in 1934; he was promoted to colonel in October 1936. Von Ravenstein had spent almost all of his time in the First World War at the front, where he was wounded in action three times; like Rommel, and in spite of his aristocratic heritage, he was a fighting soldier with little time to waste on staff officers.

Lieutenant Colonel Herbert Olbricht, commanding officer of the 5th Panzer Regiment, was the next to go. Like Streich, he too was prone to argue with Rommel rather than simply obey—unlike Streich, this seemed to be the result of clashing personalities, rather than differing command styles and priorities; his place was temporarily taken Major Ernst Bolbrinker. The commander of a panzer battalion, whose nerve broke during the April 30 attack on Tobruk, was given a court-martial and sent back to Germany in disgrace. Colonel von Herff, whose handling of his battle group during *Brevity* had impressed Rommel mightily, was given temporary command of the 15th Panzer Division, which was rapidly being brought up to full strength as all of its component units were finally arriving, a position he would hold while the division's commander, Generalmajor Walter Neumann-Silkow, was becoming acclimated to the desert. There was an element of fear behind the speed with which the Afrika Korps' command structure was ruthlessly rebuilt: intelligence briefings made Rommel uneasy about how the strategic situation in the Mediterranean was shifting, and could force General Wavell's hand to begin his offensive to relieve Tobruk at the earliest possible moment.

On the morning of May 20, 1941, three regiments of German *fallschirmjäger* (paratroopers) were dropped on the island of Crete in an airborne invasion under the code name Operation *Merkur* (*Mercury*). By the second day, miscommunication among a bumbling Allied command allowed a vital airfield to fall to the Germans, who then flooded the island with reinforcements. In 10 days the battle was over—the British and Greek defenders were evacuated by sea, with nine Royal Navy warships sunk, while another dozen were heavily damaged, among them an aircraft carrier and two battleships. Just as critical to Britain's strategic position in the eastern Mediterranean, the Germans immediately deployed several of Fliegerkorps X's bomber squadrons to Crete, dramatically increasing the Luftwaffe's ability to provide close support for the Axis forces in Libya as well as interdict British troop movements.

Rommel correctly suspected that, as a consequence of this latest Allied debacle, Wavell was under considerable pressure from London to produce a counterbalancing Allied success, specifically by striking at the Afrika Korps and relieving Tobruk. On May 12 a convoy arrived at Alexandria, having survived the gauntlet of passing the length of the Mediterranean, subjected almost the entire time to intense bombing attacks by the Luftwaffe and the Regia Aeronautica. Among masses of vital supplies for the Western Desert Force—now XIII Corps—it brought 238 new cruiser tanks for the 7th Armoured Division, which had worn out its vehicles in Operation *Compass* and thus been out of action since February. No sooner had the convoy, which had been code-named "Tiger," arrived in Alexandria than Churchill began pestering Wavell as to when his "Tiger cubs" would go into action. For all of his admirable pugnacity Churchill knew next to nothing about desert warfare, while Wavell was a past master of the art; despite the prime minister's unsubtle urgings, Wavell adamantly refused to simply throw tanks, guns, and their crews at the Germans and Italians, trusting to luck to acquire a victory. Everything had changed in North Africa since the heady days of November 1940, whether or not Churchill understood this to be so: this time around, Wavell could not count on being aided by the inferiority of his opponents' equipment, the fragility of their morale, or the incompetence of their leaders. Indeed, while he had every confidence in the morale and leadership of his own troops, the question of technical inferiority gnawed at him. In a confidential report sent to London on May 28, he admitted that "Our infantry tanks are really too slow for a battle in the desert, and have been suffering considerable casualties from the fire of the enemy's powerful antitank guns. Our cruisers have little advantage in power or speed over German medium tanks. Technical breakdowns are still too numerous." His comments should not be construed as pessimism, however: Wavell was simply being realistic, a far more desirable characteristic in a commanding officer than that of "painting pictures" (in Bonaparte's *mot*) or "taking counsel of his fears" (which General George S. Patton, Jr. regarded as a commander's worst possible sin). Wavell had to hand the freshly re-equipped 7th Armoured Division, the 4th Indian (Motorized) Division, and the 22nd Guards Brigade; their 250 tanks should outnumber the armored strength of the Afrika Korps by at least two-to-one, and with them Wavell would, as he said in closing that report, "succeed in driving the enemy west of Torbruk."[125]

The Tiger convoy was hardly a secret to either side, and so Rommel knew that when the British began their offensive, they would almost cer-tainly have a large, even dangerous, numerical superiority over his two panzer divisions. He positioned the 15th Panzer's tank regiment just west of Fort Capuzzo, where it would be able to readily respond to any British armored units that broke past the Halfaya or Sollum defenses, while the 5th Panzer Regiment was posted just east of Tobruk, where it could keep an eye on the garrison there and take action in the event that the Australians tried to break out to the east in order to link up with advancing British units. His signals intelligence section warned him on June 6 that British armor was moving into positions just east of Halfaya where they could scale the coastal escarpment. He wrote to Lucie that evening, saying "The British have moved forty miles into the desert. The problem is I don't know if they're falling back or preparing for a new attack."

His greatest worry was fuel: every move he made against the British would be influenced in some way by the Afrika Korps' limited stocks of gasoline. Nevertheless, he assured Lucie, "We're ready for them."[126]

British radio discipline had noticeably improved since *Brevity*, and the wizards of Leutnant Seebohm's signals interception unit were nowhere near as certain of the details of the British order of battle, chain of com-mand, and unit strengths as they had been before the first, abortive British attack. Still, they did their best, and even under such constraints their best was very, very good indeed. Perhaps their single most important contri-bution to the battle to come was made on the night of June 14, when the "Peter" was transmitted to all British units, after which the radio net went silent. Seebohm's subordinates immediately recalled the identical use of the name "Fritz" immediately before *Brevity*, and Rommel was immediately informed. The alert went out to the German and Italian units at both the Egyptian frontier and the Tobruk perimeter, and a prearranged artillery bar-rage was fired to keep the Australians preoccupied. At 4:00 A.M. on June 15, the British attacked. Operation *Battleaxe* had begun.

Wavell's plan for *Battleaxe* broke the operation down into three stages. The first was to capture the German defensive positions at Halfaya, Sollum, and Fort Capuzzo, while engaging and defeating the Afrika Korps' panzers in the area around Sidi Aziez. Once this was accomplished, XIII Corps would drive along the Via Balbia and link up with the Australians defending Tobruk; together the two forces would then push westward to retake Derna and Mechili. Wavell was confident that there he could establish a strong position to hold against any possible Axis riposte, and use Mechili as a staging area for any further advance into Cyrenaica. To accomplish the first part of the plan, XIII Corps was divided into the "Coast Force" and the "Escarpment Force." The Coast Force would take Halfaya Pass, the Escarpment Force would cross the escarpment ridge while still behind British lines, at a point south of Buq Buq, then move westward around behind the German defenses, capturing Fort Capuzzo, Musaid and Sollum in the process. Meanwhile, the 7th Armoured Brigade Group was specifically tasked with engaging and destroying Rommel's panzers. If this part of Wavell's plan succeeded, the rest of *Battleaxe* would fall into place like clockwork. What Wavell was not to know was that his plan was based on intelligence (which was poor due to shortages of proper equipment and trained pilots needed for photographic reconnaissance) which incorrectly indicated that two-thirds of the Germans' tank strength was situated around Tobruk; this would have placed him at a decisive material advantage on the frontier region.

Overall command of the British ground forces was given to Lieutenant General Noel Beresford-Peirse; Air Marshal Arthur Tedder, in command of the Royal Air Force in the Middle East, the "Desert Air Force," as it styled itself, was working hand-in-glove with Wavell and Beresford-Peirse in order to provide all possible air support for *Battleaxe*, even to the point of diverting squadrons of fighters and bombers from other part of the eastern Mediterranean to Egypt. Air operations actually began three days before *Battleaxe* commenced, as the Desert Air Force concentrated on destroying or at least disrupting any Axis traffic moving along the Via Balbia east of Benghazi. On the morning of June 15, fighter patrols hovered over the advancing columns of British armor, ready to drive off any attempts at interdiction by *German* fighters or dive-bombers; their efforts were so effective that only six sorties were completed by the Luftwaffe that day. Rommel had frequently complained to both Berlin and Rome about the poor, sometimes almost non-existent cooperation between the Axis air forces and ground forces. He particularly resented the fact that the Luftwaffe set its own mission and target priorities, with minimal reference to the needs of the ground forces, a very different situation than that which had obtained in France the previous year; the surprising degree of coordination achieved between Beresford-Peirse's armor and Tedder's air support only served to make more biting the validity of Rommel's complaints.

The first action between the British and Axis forces began at 6:00 A.M., June 15, when the Coast Force moved into Halfaya Pass; two battalions of Indian infantry, supported by a half-dozen Matilda tanks, attacked the lower half of the pass, while a company of a dozen Matildas and a battalion of Highland infantry tried to overrun the defenders at the top. By noon all but two of the tanks had been knocked out, while the Indian infantry were pinned down by heavy and accurate machine-gun fire from *Vater* Bach's men and intermittent shelling by the Italian field guns covering the pass. Although the defenders at Halfaya were cut off and effectively bottled up by the British forces at each end of the pass, the battle for the pass itself progressed pretty much as Rommel expected it would; Bach and his men could clearly, for the time being, take care of themselves. The central thrust of the British armor, the 7th Royal Tank Regiment's attack on Fort Capuzzo, was of more immediate concern to Rommel. After six hours of hard fighting around the fort, the German and Italian defenders were forced to fall back on the *stützpunkt* west of Bardia, where they joined up with the 15th Panzer Division.

It was here for the first time that Rommel showed the deft touch that would characterize so many of his tank battles in North Africa. Using I Battalion of the 8th Panzer Regiment, he began a series of counterattacks against the 4th Armoured Brigade, which was soon joined by the 22nd Guards Brigade. None of these attacks were pressed very hard, instead they were something more akin to very aggressive feints, where the German tanks would briefly bicker with their British counterparts, then withdraw in apparent disorder in hope of luring pursuing British tanks into a concealed line of antitank guns. In this way, Rommel accomplished two goals: he was able to somewhat reduce the number of the Matildas, which despite their slow speed were still the bane of the German medium tanks, and he kept the British armor occupied while the 5th Light Division moved east from Tobruk to Sidi Azeiz, northwest of Capuzzo, where it could join the 15th Panzer in properly coordinated counterattacks. As night fell on June 15, three of the *stützpunkten* were taken by the British, along with almost 700 German and Italian soldiers captured and eight field guns taken out of action. This would be their last significant success during *Battleaxe*.

To the west of Capuzzo was the Hafid Ridge, also called Bir Hafid, which was actually a series of wave-like ridges that dominated the local landscape and offered an excellent defensive position while also serving as a potential jumping-off point for any armored forces advancing toward To-bruk. The 7th Armoured Division was given the mission of taking and holding the ridge, which it approached at around 9:00 A.M. on June 15. As the tanks of the lead battalion crossed over the crest of the first ridgeline, carefully concealed German antitank guns opened fire at point-blank range. The two tank regiments had no supporting artillery with them, and the 2-pounder guns carried by the A-9 and A-10 Cruiser tanks, along with the new Crusader, which was supposed to be Wavell's "secret weapon" in *Battleaxe*, lacked a high-explosive (HE) round: the British tanks had no way to effectively return fire, as the only way they could suppress the enemy guns was to destroy them with direct hits. The supporting artillery, which could have driven the German gunners to ground in short order, had failed to keep pace with the tanks and so were still well out of range. The British armor pulled back over the ridge and moved to turn the flanks of the ridge-line. The Axis gun crews were caught looking the wrong way, and before they could get their antitank guns swung round, the British tanks were among them, chewing them up with machine guns the tanks had been un-able to bring to bear earlier. Only when a pair of 88mm Flak guns began picking off the A-9s, A-10s and Crusaders at long range did the carnage among the gun crews come to a halt.

A report from a Desert Air Force reconnaissance plane warned the 7th Armoured that enemy armor was approaching, so they pulled back across the ridge to await the panzers in favorable terrain. The expected attack never materialized, and instead the antitank guns on the reverse slopes of the ridge were seen limbering up and being towed away. The division went charging after them, only to be greeted as they broke the crest of the next ridge by yet another wrinkle in Rommel's evolving bag of tricks. A second line of antitank guns was waiting—the withdrawal had been a ruse, and within minutes nearly a quarter of the 7th Armoured's surviving tanks were either destroyed or heavily damaged. Another reconnaissance report, this time accurate, warned the British of the approach of a battalion of tanks from the 5th Panzer Regiment. The two armored forces engaged each other at long range as dusk approached and the 7th Armoured Division slowly withdrew from the Bir Hafid ridge.

The first day of *Battleaxe* was over, and the British had attained only one of that day's objectives: taking Fort Capuzzo. The Halfaya Pass garrison was safely bottled up, but as long as Hauptmann Bach and his gunners held their positions within the pass, possession of Halfaya's upper and lower ends was a hollow victory. The British armored columns had lost close to a third of their strength, and while something like a third of those tanks put out of action were repairable, the ones lost at Bir Hafid had to be written off entirely, as they fell into German hands at the end of the engagement there. Despite the day's successes, Rommel knew the battle was far from over, writing to Lucie in the early hours of June 16 that

> There was heavy fighting in our eastern sector all day yesterday, as you will have seen from Wehrmacht communiqués. Today—it's 2:30 A.M.—will see the decision. It's going to be a hard fight, so you'll understand that I can't sleep. These lines in haste will show you that I'm thinking of you both. More soon when it's all over.[127]

The Germans and Italians had suffered serious losses in infantry and among their antitank guns and gun crews at both Capuzzo and Bir Hafid, but the harsh calculus of desert warfare was such that men were more easily replaced than equipment. Rommel, for his part, had played masterfully on British aggressiveness, repeatedly drawing British armored units into range of his antitank guns, "writing down" British tank strength while avoiding a tank versus tank engagement before he had his armor sufficiently concentrated. By sunrise he would have to hand two nearly complete panzer divisions, and he was not about to let them sit idle.

When Rommel's intelligence section warned him on the night of June 14 that Wavell's attack was expected the next day, it could provide only limited information about British strength and intentions. In the wake of *Brevity*, XIII Corps had, for the time being at least, improved its wireless security, leaving Leutnant Seebohm and his people very much in the dark. Fortune, however, once more smiled on the Afrika Korps, as just after midmorning on June 15, a complete list of XIII Corps' call-signs and unit codenames was found in a knocked-out British armored car. Straining to catch every enemy signal they could, Seebohm and his signal boffins used the list to put together a remarkably accurate estimate of British unit strengths and intentions. It was with this information that Rommel first demonstrated his extraordinary tactical sense, what the Germans call *fingerspitzegefühl*—the "tingling of the fingers," or tactical intuition.

With the 7th Armoured Division having for the time being abandoned their effort to take the Bir Hafid ridge and moved closer to Capuzzo, Rommel saw an opportunity to send the 5th Light Division south, almost to Sidi Omar, then turn east until it was southwest of Halfaya Pass. This would put it in position to strike the 22nd Guards Brigade from the rear and relieve the Axis units defending Halfaya. To prevent the Guards from being reinforced, the 15th Panzer Division would launch an all-out attack of its own against Fort Capuzzo, pinning the 4th Armoured Brigade in place around the fort. Seebohm had deduced that the British intended to begin their own operations that day at dawn, so Rommel decided to get his own punch in first, and directed Neumann-Silkow, 15th Panzer's commander, to begin moving against Capuzzo in the pre-dawn darkness.

Going the opposite way, Beresford-Peirse decided that, since Fort Capuzzo was already in XIII Corps' hands, the best plan of action was to maintain *Battleaxe*'s original objectives. To this end, he ordered the 11th Infantry Brigade to continue its attack on Halfaya Pass while the 22nd Guards Brigade stood in place, ready to respond to any German effort to relieve the Halfaya garrison. At the same time, the 4th Armoured Brigade would reinforce the 7th Armoured Divsion near Bir Hafid, so that when the expected attack from the west by the 5th Light Division materialized, the Germans would be badly outnumbered. If the German armored force could be dealt sufficient losses to cripple its ability to halt or even interfere with British movements, the way to Tobruk would be open. Despite their own losses and tactical setbacks on the first day of the operation, the British believed that they still had an excellent chance of making *Battleaxe* a success.

The 15th Panzer Division "opened the ball" at about 4:00 A.M. when Neumann-Silkow formed his tanks into two columns and closed on Fort Capuzzo in a pincer movement. They didn't get far: the British had brought forward several 25-pounder field guns during the night, while at the same time digging revetments for the dozen or so Matlidas that remained around Capuzzo. Within six hours two-thirds of 15th Panzer's tanks were out of action, and it was forced to withdraw, taking whatever crippled vehicles that could be easily retrieved. The good news for the Germans was that, despite the losses, Neumann-Silkow's attack drew forces away from Wavell's Coast Force, which made absolutely no progress in its attempt to take Halfaya Pass. It also compelled the 4th Armoured Brigade to abandon its movement westward to reinforce the 7th Armoured Division and instead remain near Capuzzo, sitting idly by while the decisive action of the day would take place on its western flank.

The 5th Light Division began moving south past the west edge of Hafid Ridge at dawn, shadowed by the armored cars and light tanks of the 7th Armoured Division. From time to time the British cruiser tanks would attempt to pick off the "soft-skinned" German transport. Although these intermittent sallies had some success, they proved expensive for the British in the long run, as when they approached the German columns, the Panzer IIIs and IVs, working in careful coordination, first suppressed whatever supporting artillery accompanied the British armor and then counterattacked, or else feigned a withdrawal with the intent of leading the enemy tanks into a waiting antitank gun ambush. By nightfall, the whole 7th Armoured Division, having lost more than half its cruiser tanks, had fallen back behind the Wire at the Egyptian frontier, not far from where they had begun *Battleaxe*.

Rommel accompanied the 5th Light Division when it moved east from Tobruk, but aside from exercising a broad overall command, directing von Ravenstein and Neumann-Silkow as to where and when he wanted their divisions to attack, he had left the tactical decisions to the divisional commanders. Now he took personal command of the battle. Late on the afternoon of June 16 he ordered Neumann-Silkow to leave only a covering force sufficient to contain the British at Capuzzo and bring the rest of the 15th Panzer Division south to take up position on the left flank of the 5th Light. Rommel saw an opportunity to encircle and cut off the 7th Armoured when it began pulling back to the Wire, and at 4:30 A.M., 5th Light and 15th Panzer hit the left flank of the 7th Armoured Division with 75 tanks supported by artillery and antitank guns. Driving straight through the British lines, the panzers almost reached Halfaya Pass before they were stopped. The 4th Indian Division was ordered to withdraw along the coastal road, while the 22nd Guards Brigade was nearly trapped at Fort Capuzzo by Rommel's bold move.

Major General Frank Messervy, commander of the 4th Indian Division, ordered the surviving British armor to form a screen to cover the retreat of the infantry formations. The German wireless intercept unit caught a message from Major General Michael Creagh, commander of the 7th Armoured, to Beresford-Pierse, asking for confirmation of that order. "It sounded suspiciously as though the British commander no longer felt himself capable of handling the situation," Rommel would later remark about this moment. "It being now obvious that in their present bewildered state the British would not start anything for the time being, I decided to pull the net tight by going on to Halfaya." The British tanks fought a tenacious six-hour battle against the two panzer divisions, ably supported by the fighters and medium bombers of the RAF, but their courage could not change the ultimate outcome of the battle. By midday, the 7th Armoured Division could muster fewer than 40 tanks, and Wavell, who had flown up to Beresford-Peirse's headquarters the previous afternoon, chose to forego wasting further men and materiel in what was clearly a lost cause, ordering all of his units to fall back across the Egyptian frontier. The tank battle south of Halfaya gradually petered out as the afternoon progressed, and Rommel was distinctly unhappy ("furious" was the word he used) that the British had managed to escape, albeit without most of their tanks, believing, incorrectly as it turned out, that the 5th Light and 15th Panzer had reached Halfaya in time to prevent the enemy's withdrawal.[128]

Actual losses in the battle were comparatively light for both sides, the British suffering just under 1,000 killed, wounded, or captured; the combined German and Italian casualties numbered around 1,300 (the Italian records are incomplete). Ninety-eight British tanks were written off as total losses, either destroyed or captured, while only a dozen German panzers were actually destroyed—the remainder of the German tanks knocked out during the battle were eventually repaired and put back into service. An additional boon for the Afrika Korps was the large number of British trucks that were captured, and at least a score of British tanks abandoned on the battlefield were easily repaired and put to work for their new masters. The British had suffered yet another defeat, there was no other way to describe the outcome of *Battleaxe*. They had no reserves left, Tobruk was still besieged, and the road to Alexandria lay wide open to the Afrika Korps. Only his critical supply situation would keep Rommel from advancing into Egypt.

CHAPTER EIGHT

CRUSADER

*The mark of a great general is to know
when to retreat, and dare to do it.*
—ARTHUR WELLESLEY,
   1st Duke of Wellington

Ironically—and disappointingly, from Rommel's point of view—hardly
had the world become aware of the defeat he had handed the British in
so thoroughly blunting *Battleaxe* than it was forgotten. A mere five days
after Wavell called off the attack, the titanic offensive known as "*Barbarossa*,"
the Wehrmacht's invasion of the Soviet Union, jumped off in the predawn
hours of June 22, 1941, and for most of the world, the war in North Africa
was immediately relegated to the status of a sideshow. Gripping though it
had been, with tens of thousands of men fighting across hundreds of miles,
it was quickly superceded in the popular imagination at the time—and
largely thereafter—by the spectacle of millions of men locked in mortal
combat across a front of thousands of miles. Hence it was not readily apparent at the time, and has often been overlooked as such in the histories
of the Desert War that would appear in the decades to follow, that *Battleaxe*
was the watershed event of the Desert War. It compelled Churchill and the
British War Cabinet to rethink Great Britain's entire grand strategy, and
triggered the process by which North Africa and the Mediterranean would
for the Allies become a major theater of operations and for the Axis become
a major strategic liability.

For Rommel, his victory in *Battleaxe*—the Germans would know it as
the *Sollumschlact*, the Battle of Sollum—was transformative. *Battleaxe* was
his first real battle, one of fire and movement, where he was variously required to defend, maneuver, or attack, as the tactical and operational situ-

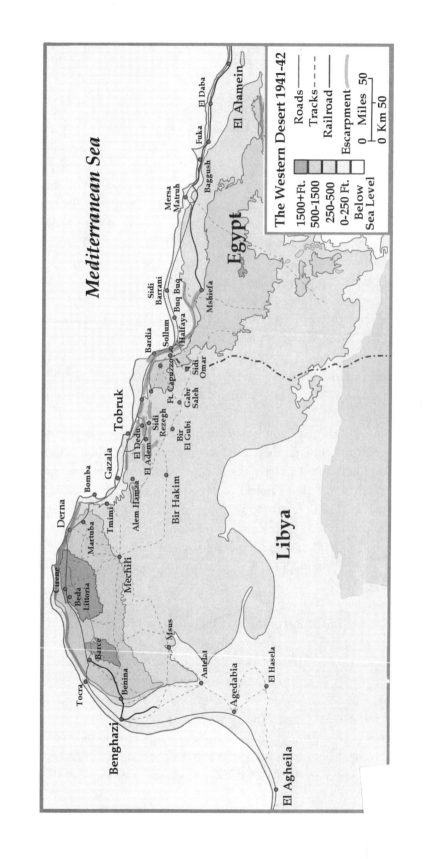

The Western Desert 1941-42

Roads
Tracks
Railroad
Escarpment

1500+Ft.
500-1500
250-500
0-250 Ft.
Below
Sea Level

0   Miles   50
0   Km 50

Mediterranean Sea

Egypt

Libya

El Alamein
El Daba
Fuka
Baggush
Mersa Matruh
Mshiefa
Sidi Barrani
Buq Buq
Sollum
Halfaya
Bardia
Ft. Capuzzo
Sidi Omar
Gabr Saleh
Sidi Rezegh
Bir El Gubi
El Dedim
El Adem
Tobruk
Gazala
Bir Hakim
Alem Hamza
Tmimi
Bomba
Derna
Martuba
Cirene
Beda Littoria
Mechili
Barce
Benina
Tocra
Benghazi
Msus
Antelat
Agedabia
El Hasela
El Agheila

ation dictated, fighting against a determined, disciplined, and organized enemy who possessed his own sound plan of operations. Up to this point it could be fairly said that, no matter how spectacular his achievements, Rommel as a commanding officer had been something of a glorified military opportunist, at heart still the young company commander exploiting the assault on Mount Matajur at Longarone, albeit now writ overly large. *Battleaxe* was his first true test as a corps commander, which he passed with full marks; after *Battleaxe*, Rommel would deploy and move his units with far greater assurance and aplomb than he had previously displayed.

Battleaxe can rightly be said to also mark the beginning of the legend of the Desert Fox. Rommel's letters home to Lucie and Manfred were nothing short of jubilant, mirroring the mood of the officers and men of the Afrika Korps. In a letter written on June 18, he said "The battle today has ended in complete victory. I'm going to go round the troops today to thank them and issue orders." Five days later, he told her how he had "been three days on the road going round the battlefield."

> The joy of the "Afrika" troops over this latest victory is tremendous. The British thought they could overwhelm us with their 400 tanks [Rommel's intelligence section had overestimated the strength of the 7th Armoured Division]. We couldn't put that amount of armor against them. But our grouping and the stubborn resistance of German and Italian troops who were surrounded for days together, enabled us to make the decisive operation with all the forces we still had mobile. Now the enemy can come, he'll get an even bigger beating.[129]

Rommel's mention of the Italians is noteworthy, especially in light of his caustic remarks about their courage and utility—or lack thereof—in action around Tobruk just six weeks earlier. Rommel knew that the gravest problem with the Italian units was not the raw material of their soldiers, but rather the Italian officers, whom he regarded as incompetent, indolent, self-indulgent and unmotivated; they were given command of better men than they deserved. As Bach demonstrated in defending the Halfaya Pass, Italian troops could fight with skill and determination when led by competent officers and NCOs. While they might never be the world's best soldiers, the Italians could be good soldiers, and Rommel knew how to use good soldiers.

Inevitably, Leutnant Berndt, the Propaganda Ministry officer assigned to the Afrika Korps and whom Rommel employed as an aide, made the most of *Battleaxe*. Handsome, articulate, and victorious, Rommel was every propaganda officer's dream; Berndt, who had become a thoroughgoing soldier in his service with Rommel, was still, at heart, a public relations flack, and very good at it, too, so naturally he waxed somewhat overly lyrical in praising Rommel to the German people. Nonetheless, his comments are worth consideration, as they exerted a strong influence on not only how Rommel was perceived by the German people at the time, but also how he would be regarded outside Germany after the war ended.

> He [Rommel] is a master of deception and disguise, and always does what one least expects. If the enemy believe we are particularly strong at one place, then you can be sure we are weak. If they think we are weak and venture close to us, then we are strong. "With your general we just didn't know where we were!"—that's what one British prisoner complained. If he stages attacks coupled with feint attacks, then the enemy virtually always think the wrong one is the real one. If the enemy act on what they regard as the typical signs of feint attacks, then next time it is different and they are wrong again.[130]

What Berndt never spoke of, lest it tarnish the image of Rommel as *le chevalier sans peur et sans reproche*, was Rommel's volatile temperament, his exacting, if sometimes vague, standards of conduct for his officers, and an apparent pettiness, or retributive streak, toward those who angered or crossed him. His dismissal of Streich was regarded by many of his fellow officers as a grave injustice, and indeed, it blighted Streich's career. Rommel believed that Streich had repeatedly been insolent, something which a commanding officer should not and cannot countenance from anyone. And perhaps Streich was insolent, particularly in the actions around Tobruk in April and May—the remark he made to Rommel after the death of von Prittwitz about killing both his divisional commanders in the same day certainly was. Some sort of disciplinary action had to be taken, if only for appearances' sake, but Rommel should have recognized that this was not an instance of a wisecracking private mocking his platoon sergeant in barracks. Streich was an experienced combat officer, who had lashed out in the midst of battle at what he regarded as a patently absurd situation. Rommel should have taken counsel of the kernel of truth in what Streich had implied: that his own rashness was getting good men killed for no purpose. Instead, Sterich went home in disgrace; the harshness of the punishment far exceeding the degree of the offense.

And there were others: General Kirchheim, Colonel Olbricht, Major Köhn, all of them subjected to courts-martial or dismissal for little more than challenging one of Rommel's tactical decisions or operational judgments. Oberstleutnant Count von Schwerin asked to be transferred out of North Africa because he could no longer work under Rommel's command. General Bodewin Keitel, commanding the army's Personnel Department, would record "It is remarkable that in the case of one officer, a battalion commander of the Fifth Panzer Regiment, a recommendation for the Knight's Cross, a cowardice charge, and his dismissal followed one another in the briefest of intervals." Just as it had been in France, not only was Rommel's temper volatile, it was mercurial: at one point he threatened General von Kirckheim with dismissal, then just hours later denied ever having done so. The number of formal complaints reaching Berlin in regard to Rommel's behavior toward his subordinate reached such a point that von Brauchitsch felt compelled to reprimand Rommel, in the bluntest possible language, informing him that he was threatening his own professional future. "I think it my duty to tell you all this, not only in the interest of the Afrika Korps, but in your own personal interest, too."[131]

The source of Rommel's ill temper is difficult to pin down. Not all of the officers who lodged formal complaints against him with O.K.W. can be written off as whiners or overly sensitive souls whose feelings had been hurt. Some allowance can be made for the fact that Rommel was not particularly quick to acclimate to North Africa, and that he felt the effects of the heat more than many other officers. Of course, the reason why that was so stemmed from his own vanity. It would be months after his arrival at Tripoli that he would concede to practicality and begin wearing short trousers and working in his shirtsleeves. Thus for those first months his daily uniform consisted of jodhpurs, riding boots, and a wool uniform jacket (complete with all of his decorations) worn over a uniform shirt, all the while surrounded by men working far more comfortably in shirtsleeves and cutoff trousers. The heat of Rommel's temper may have originated in the fact that he was cooking inside that uniform, a victim of his own ego. Nonetheless, he still had a responsibility as the senior German officer to be more judicious and exercise more wisdom in his relationships with his subordinates. As it was, the Afrika Korps' command structure underwent a thorough housecleaning in the weeks after *Battleaxe*, after which Rommel pronounced himself satisfied with the performance of his officers.

The final British casualty of *Battleaxe* was, in a manner of speaking, Archibald Wavell, who was relieved as Commander-in-Chief Middle East Command on July 1, 1941, and replaced by General Claude Auchinleck. The immediate cause of Wavell's fall from grace was said to be his failure to successfully execute an operation which was thrust upon him against his better judgment, one which he believed had been ill-planned, and was to be carried out by troops he felt were ill-equipped and ill-prepared. More to the point, he was relieved because of Winston Churchill's dislike for him. Churchill, for all his gifts as a politician and a national wartime leader, possessed glaring flaws as a military strategist, and often lost sight of the reality that an army which had the will to stand did not always likewise possess the strength to attack. Given his pugnacious nature, to Churchill the attack was the natural state of affairs in military operations, and any general perceived to be lacking the requisite degree of aggressiveness was suspect in his eyes, and hence expendable.

Wavell was politely "kicked upstairs," taking over the post of the man who replaced him, Claude Auchinleck, as Commander-in-Chief, India, a position he would hold until July 1943, when he was named Viceroy of India. Illuminating the true nature of Wavell's change of command, Auchinleck would later note: "In no sense do I wish to infer that I found an unsatisfactory situation on my arrival—far from it. Not only was I greatly impressed by the solid foundations laid by my predecessor, but I was also able the better to appreciate the vastness of the problems with which he had been confronted and the greatness of his achievements, in a command in which some 40 different languages are spoken by the British and Allied Forces."[132]

Ironically, it was Wavell among all of the British commanders who faced him that Rommel held in the greatest esteem. During the whole of the North African campaign a copy of *Generals and Generalship*, a transcription of a lecture series Wavell had presented at Trinity College published before the war began in 1939, accompanied Rommel everywhere, a distinction not accorded to any work written by a German general. In Rommel's opinion, Wavell, almost alone among the top echelon of British generals, fundamentally understood mechanized warfare and recognized the capabilities as well as the limitations of armored units.

For his part, Wavell's successor, Claude Auchinleck, was no mental bantamweight. Born in 1884, six years before Rommel, and the son of a colonel in the Royal Artillery, Auchinleck was determined from a fairly young age to become an army officer, albeit in the infantry and not with the gunners. Intelligent and affable, he spent the first 30 years of his career with the Indian Army, that peculiar (and fearsome) offshoot of the British Army, where British officers commanded units manned entirely by native Indian rankers. Auchinleck spent the Great War in the Middle East, leading the 62nd Punjabis in some of the fiercest battles fought against the Ottoman Turks. Not one to lead from the rear, he was Mentioned in Despatches and awarded the Distinguished Service Order for his actions in the Mesopotamia campaign, and found himself a brevet lieutenant colonel at the end of the war.

Similar to Erwin Rommel's postwar experience, after the "peace to end all peace" was imposed by the Treaty of Versailles, Auchinleck went through a succession of postings to staff postings, staff colleges, regimental command, and instructor positions with the Indian Army. He saw further combat while successfully leading two punitive expeditions along India's Northwest Frontier, fighting Afghan and Paki rebels, being promoted to major general in the process, and somewhere along the line acquiring the nickname "The Auk." His most outstanding achievement in India, however, didn't come in the field: in 1938 Auchinleck was named chairman of the committee responsible for reorganizing, re-equipping, and modernizing the Indian Army. The quality of the work done by the committee was demonstrated beyond all doubt during the Second World War, when its recommendations allowed the Indian Army to expand from a strength of 183,000 officers and other ranks in autumn 1939 to over 2,250,000 men by the war's end.

When war erupted in Europe in September 1939, Auchinleck initially remained in India, but in early 1940 was abruptly recalled to England, where, in the space of a few months, he was promoted to lieutenant general and given command of the Anglo-French ground forces defending Norway, which had been invaded by the Germans in early April. This posting was a thankless job, for while the strategic concept was sound, the operational execution was thoroughly bungled at the highest levels in London and Paris. A lack of coordinated planning, poor training, and inadequate equipment left Auchinleck and his men "holding the bag," as it were: despite Auchinleck doing his best to stave off the inevitable, Norway was doomed. Evacuated when Norway fell in June 1940, he became General Officer Commanding-in-Chief, Southern Command, where one of his immediate subordinates was Bernard Law Montgomery, then a major general in command of a corps. Not surprisingly, the prickly and self-centered Mongtomery was quick to find fault with the generally affable Auchinleck, Montgomery asserting in his memoirs that "In the 5th Corps I first served under Auchinleck. . . . I cannot recall that we ever agreed on anything."[133]

Nineteen forty-one saw Auchinleck in India once again, this time as Commander-in-Chief, India. In April of that year, when the Iraqi government of Prime Minister Rashid Ali al-Gaylani revolted against its British colonial overlords, it was Auchinleck who ordered a division of Indian infantry into Basra, nominally General Wavell's area of command, to put down the rebellion. General Wavell had been too preoccupied with—and his forces spread too thin by—the rapidly deteriorating situations in the Western Desert and Greece to be able to spare any troops for Iraq, and was grateful for Auchinleck's intervention. Predictably, Churchill had seen Wavell's hesitation as timidity, and from that point forward was ready to sack Wavell as soon as the opportunity to do so presented itself.

As Wavell had before him, Auchinleck, as Commander-in-Chief Middle East, had his headquarters in Cairo; this was not a case of leading from the rear but was necessitated, as it had been for Wavell, by the fact that Auchinleck, in addition to North Africa, was responsible for Persia, Mesopotamia, the whole of the Levant and the Arabian peninsula. This would prove as much of a handicap to Auchinleck as it had been to his predecessor, compelling him to wear too many hats simultaneously, balefully diluting the time and energy he could focus on individual responsibilities. Churchill, though he would never acknowledge it, bore a share of the blame for this flawed command structure, as he would refuse to press for Egypt and the Mediterranean to be organized under a separate command until the summer of 1942. Be that as it may, whatever the realities and handicaps of his command structure might be, Auchinleck was given the unenviable task of effecting the relief of Tobruk while at the same time ejecting Rommel from Libya.

Auchinleck was starkly realistic about how and when that could be accomplished. Though casualties during *Battleaxe* had not been inordinately high, equipment losses were severe, and morale was approaching an all-time low. After-action reports and aerial reconnaissance showed that little more than a dozen German tanks had been destroyed during the battle, while four out of every five British tanks committed to action were either lost or were sitting in the Desert Force's machine shops undergoing major repairs; fully half the British armor strength had to be written off. British cruiser tanks could not stand up to German antitank guns, and even the heavily armored Matilda was vulnerable to the Flak 88. The story goes (it is almost certainly apocryphal, but worth telling nonetheless) that a British officer taken prisoner during the course of *Battleaxe* complained to his captors that it was "unsporting" for the Germans to use AA guns against tanks. A German replied, "Ja! And we think it is unsporting of you to use tanks that only our 88s can stop!" With the Germans now receiving large numbers of a long-barreled 50mm antitank gun (PAK 38) which was nearly as effective as the Flak 88, the tactical advantage would remain decisively with the Germans unless British armor doctrine and tactics were radically revised. For now, the German antitank guns ruled the desert battlefield.

For Auchinleck, the restoration of his soldiers' morale was the first priority, and that would only come about when they were equipped with tanks and guns in which they could have confidence. Infantry weapons were pretty much a wash, although the British rifles and machine guns had a bit of an edge in reliability; the 25-pounder was probably the finest all-round artillery piece on either side, and apart from not being able to function as an antiaircraft gun, it could fulfill any role which the German Flak 88 could take on. That was a start. But the decisions in desert warfare were made by armor, and there was little that could be done at the moment about the under-gunned and under-armored Crusader I. On the other hand, deliveries of American-designed and built M3 light tanks, which the British officially christened the Stuart and were unofficially known as "Honeys" for their speed and reliability, began to arrive in Alexandria in mid-July. By the end of the month, the Desert Force had taken delivery of 84 Stuart tanks, 164 P-40 fighter aircraft, 10 bombers, and two dozen 3-inch antiaircraft guns, along with assorted pieces of field artillery, road-building tools and equipment, and almost 10,000 trucks. More tanks, vehicles, equipment and supplies were arriving weekly; the days when the Desert Force was compelled to tangle with the Afrika Korps in penny packets would soon be a thing of the past. Unruffled, carefully methodical, Auchinleck began drawing up plans for a new offensive that would relieve Tobruk and drive the Axis out of Libya; he expected that it would be ready to go in mid-November — it would be called *Crusader*.

No crystal ball was required for Rommel to understand that the British were far from done with him. Unless he could take Tobruk and then present Auchinleck with a defense in depth along the Egytian frontier that was sufficiently formidable to make the cost of cracking it prohibitive, the Afrika Korps and the Italians were vulnerable. The most pressing question was whether or not Rommel would have the strength to accomplish all this. In the wake of *Brevity*, Halder had dispatched yet another watchdog to Africa, this time in the form of Generalleutnant Alfred Gause. Initially sent with a large staff to act as a liaison officer with Comando Supremo, Gause's mission was a Machiavellian scheme concocted by Halder to rein in Rommel by effectively separating Rommel from active command of the Italian troops, and placing all of the North African supply and support units—Italian *and* German—under Italian control. Counting on Rome's lack of enthusiasm for any further expansion of the war in the Mediterranean, Halder was certain that would put an end to any more adventures on Rommel's part. What this says about Halder is at once intriguing and disturbing: his personal hatred—the sentiment was now too strong to merely call it "dislike"—of Rommel had become so intense that he was prepared to undermine German operations and strategy for the sole purpose of embarrassing Rommel.

To accomplish this, Gause was specifically instructed not to place himself under Rommel's command. But such was the force of Rommel's personality and charm that when Rommel insisted—incorrectly—that command of all Axis troops in Africa had been vested in him, Gause accepted Rommel's claim, despite knowing that it was not true. Gause was strongly influenced in this decision by watching Rommel in action: he arrived at Rommel's headquarters on June 15, the day that *Battleaxe* opened, and was mightily impressed by Rommel's composure and self-assurance in responding to the British attack. While Gause was not blind to Rommel's flaws—in one of his first reports to Berlin, he opined that Rommel was "morbidly ambitious," and he was fully aware of the man's towering ego—at the same time he recognized that he was in the presence of a general with remarkable tactical skills and operational abilities, and that a unique bond of confidence was growing between Rommel and his German and Italian soldiers, one that had the potential to produce results out of all proportion to the forces involved. Also the idea cannot be dismissed that once Gause arrived in North Africa he realized that something other than purely military considerations had been Halder's motive for creating his mission: while he was unquestionably intelligent, Gause by nature was simple, direct, and had no truck with intrigue. Whatever the totality of his reasoning may have been, he turned his entire staff over to Rommel, taking the role of chief of staff for himself. As for Rommel and Gause personally, the two men developed an excellent working relationship that would last for the next two and one half years.

The improvement in command and control which the arrival of Gause's staff gave Rommel allowed him even greater tactical flexibility in his future operations. One thing it did not affect was his penchant for leading from the front: Rommel would always remain the quintessential combat commander who was convinced that his proper place was at the point of engagement; others, subordinates, could stay behind at headquarters, listening to wireless reports, pondering over maps, charts, and tables. Rommel would frequently dragoon Gause into accompanying him to the front, a direct contravention of standing Wehrmacht doctrine, which held that the Chief of Staff's duty was to remain at headquarters in order to function as the commander's deputy if needed. Rommel was fortunate in this case that Gause's staff, now his staff, was already sufficiently experienced—and composed of swift learners who quickly acquired an understanding of their commanding officer's ideas and methods—as to be able to make correct command decisions in Rommel's absence.

One upshot of Gause's unanticipated decision to place himself under Rommel was the immediate functional subordination of all of the Italian troops in North Africa to German command. In order to create a functional command structure, this necessitated the creation of Panzergruppe Afrika and the corresponding promotion for its commanding officer to the rank of *general der panzertruppe* (general of the armored corps), equivalent to American three-star (lieutenant general) or British lieutenant general rank. This was as much Hitler's doing in order to cock a snook at Halder as it was a military necessity; Hitler putting Halder on notice that he was wise to Halder's game. The professional relationship between the Führer and his Chief of Staff had never been particularly good, as can be expected when two fundamentally malevolent personalities are compelled to work together; in the summer of 1941, Hitler and Rommel were still mutually enamored of one another, and Hitler was unwilling to let Halder get away unscathed with his personal vendetta against Rommel.

Naturally, when told that his promotion was in the works, Rommel wrote exultantly to Lucie, telling her that Leutnant Berndt, who had gone to Berlin to confer with Göbbels on how, for propaganda purposes, to best exploit Rommel's latest North African victory, had returned with the news.

> As I have just found out from Lt. Berndt . . . I have only the Führer to thank for my promotion. . . . You can imagine how pleased I am—to earn his recognition for what I do and the way I do it is beyond my wildest dreams. . . . The first congratulations on being promoted to Panzergeneral are coming in. Of course, I've heard nothing official yet, but I understand it's been announced on the wireless.[134]

Rommel's *panzergruppe* included the Afrika Korps, General Crüwell commanding, with its two panzer divisions, the 15th and 21st, and two Italian corps—the XX Armored Corps (the Ariete and Trieste Divisions) and the XXI Corps, composed of four non-motorized infantry divisions. A third German unit, the motorized "Afrika" Division, had been cobbled together out of various odds and sods of smaller units; renamed the 90th Light Division in August, it was strong in firepower but possessed no tanks of its own.

Rommel briefly had hopes of even more forces being at his disposal: with *Battleaxe* so effectively blunted, the British position in North Africa seemed to totter, and the idea was entertained of sufficiently reinforcing Rommel to allow him to deliver a knock-out blow.

> General Roatta . . . informed me that the Italian High Command realized the necessity of considerably reinforcing the Axis forces in North Africa. The German element was to be brought up to four mechanized divisions, and the Italian to an armored corps of three divisions, with a further two or three motorized divisions.

The logistical demands of Operation *Barbarossa* soon put paid to any such largesse in men, equipment and materiel, however, Rommel remarking bitterly that Rome and Berlin's "zeal unfortunately did not last long." Rommel would have to make do with what he had.[135]

It was one of the pivotal decisions in the war and a major blunder, for while the Axis chose not to commit larger forces to North Africa, the British were now committed to making the whole of the Mediterranean a major theater of war. Churchill had taken the failure of *Battleaxe* as a personal affront, and was now determined to commit every available resource to North Africa in order to ensure the Axis defeat. It would take time, but before the year's end, additional divisions from Australia, New Zealand, South Africa, and India, along with a brigade of Polish infantry fighting in exile, would be brought to North Africa and committed to battle. Moreover, no one at the time had the slightest inkling that before 1941 was out the United States of America would have been brought into the war on the Allied side: when the Americans committed their first ground forces to combat in the European Theater, it would be in North Africa. What had begun as a simple rescue operation to save face for the Italians would evolve into a Frankenstein's monster, malevolent and out of control, that would at first alter, then dictate, Axis strategy, fundamentally redirecting the course of the war.

Had Rommel been given men and equipment—and the logistical support to sustain them—sufficient to drive Auchinleck's forces out of Egypt, taking the Suez Canal in the process, the strategic alternatives available to the British (and later the Americans, when they came into the war at the end of 1941) would have been considerably more complex and difficult. As long as the Royal Navy had access to both ends of "the Med" via Gibraltar and Suez, Great Britain could threaten any point on the entire southern coast of Europe. But should the Suez Canal fall to the Axis, the Mediterranean would suddenly once again become what it had been under the Roman Empire: *Mare Nostrum*—"Our sea," an Axis lake. The whole of the Mediterranean coast would be in the hands of the Axis powers, their allies, or countries favorably disposed to them. Indeed, it might even be possible to persuade the Spanish dictator, General Francisco Franco, to seize Gibraltar, something he was loathe to do for fear of antagonizing the British as long as the issue in North Africa remained in doubt. There would have been no need for the sort of fatal dispersion and dilution of Axis forces to protect southern France, Italy, and the Balkans that the rising Allied power in the Mediterranean would eventually demand, allowing an even greater concentration of land and air forces against the Red Army on the Eastern Front. Attempts by the British Empire to reintroduce itself into the Mediterranean via the Persian Gulf and the Levant would have been burdened with logistical and political problems on a nigh-impossible-to-resolve scale. On balance, it's reasonable to conclude that forcing a quick decision in North Africa could well have been a war-winning strategy for the Axis.

Which brings up the much-debated "Plan Orient," or "Great Plan," an invasion of the Middle East by a greatly reinforced Axis army in North Africa and the eventual meeting in the Turkish Caucasus Mountains with Axis forces advancing southward out of the Soviet union. Long the armchair-strategist's ultimate "what if" fantasy, the basic concept has been cobbled together from various disconnected writings, musings and daydreams by Rommel, the Kriegsmarine's Grossadmiral Erich Räder, and the Luftwaffe's Feldmarschall Albert Kesselring, all of whom, at one time or another, entertained something of the basic idea. Rommel, in fact, would go so far as to produce a detailed memorandum in the summer of 1942 outlining in practical terms how such a strategy could be implemented. It was a textbook example of the "perfect plan" which presumes that every operational requirement will be met, every proposed action will be successful, and every consequence of the disruption of existing strategic dispositions it would create would be minimal. It was also predicated on over-optimistic logistic projections, which, given that in the summer of 1941 Germany and Italy were already finding it near-impossible to keep the existing forces in North Africa adequately supplied, further mitigated against it. It was not an impossible plan, but it was a highly impractical one; worse, when Rommel submitted it to Hitler, it came a year too late: by the summer of 1942, the global strategic balance had already shifted against the Axis and the window of opportunity for implementing anything that resembled "Plan Orient" had long closed.

But such was the degree of the British disarray in the wake of *Battleaxe* that had even one more panzer division been to hand for Rommel on the Egyptian frontier, he would have been able to give the task of containing the Tobruk garrison to the Italians and turned all of his German units eastward to tumble the British out of Egypt and functionally deny the British Empire access to the Mediterranean. Admittedly, the presence of another armored division in the Afrika Korps would have created monumental headaches for his quartermasters, as well as the supply and shipping services in Rome, but given the consequences, it would have been a short-term difficulty, hardly insuperable.

As it was, Rommel and Auchinleck were now in a race. Rommel was striving to take Tobruk and be able to redeploy all of his divisions to the Egyptian frontier before Auchinleck could complete reinforcing, reequipping and reorganizing the British forces. Auchinleck had to complete this undertaking and launch a new offensive to relieve Tobruk and drive the Germans and Italians back across Cyrenaica before the Tobruk garrison's position became untenable.

None of his urgency made itself felt in Rommel's letters to Lucie that summer. It's easy to see Rommel regarding his correspondence with his wife as a welcome diversion, a distraction, as it were, from the demands and responsibilities of command allowing a few moments each day to turn his focus to domestic matters—his health, his new-found fondness for a fly swatter, or the progress of Manfred's education. They were a small, welcome slice of normality amidst the sometimes surreal environs of war.

28 June 1941

Dearest Lu:

You need not worry yourself anymore about my health. I'm doing fine. Our place is much healthier, lying 600 feet above sea level. Besides, I've got the advantage of my four walls. Aldinger was sick for a few days, but he's getting better. There's a lot of work.

July 5 1941

I usually spend a lot of time traveling; yesterday I was away for eight hours. You can hardly imagine what thirst one gets up after such a journey. . . .

I was glad to hear Manfred is now getting on in mathematics. It's all a matter of the method of teaching, I'm also very pleased about his other successes in school.

I'm managing, by dint of keeping the place dark and "shooting a lot of them down," to keep my office fairly clear of mosquitoes. I'm even having an occasional bang while writing. . . .[136]

For now, confident that the troops defending the Egyptian frontier, especially those at Halfaya Pass under the command of the fierce and capable *Vater* Bach, could keep the British off his back, Rommel focused on Tobruk, with an emphasis on training the Italian infantry, on whom would fall the larger burden of any attack on the fortress, in assault tactics. The defenders did their best to disrupt the German and Italian preparations, but there were indications that the Australians inside the Tobruk perimeter were running out of steam, as it were. On August 2, two companies of Australian infantry, supported by 60 field guns, attacked Italian positions along the perimeter; both sides took heavy casualties, but the Italians, bearing out the validity of what their comrades had done up in Halfaya Pass during *Battleaxe*, held firm and drove the Australians back.

This was the last effort the Australians would make to retake the positions they had lost three months previously. By the middle of September, the 9th Australian Division was being methodically withdrawn from Tobruk, evacuating at night aboard Royal Navy destroyers sent out from Alexandria. Relieving them was the British 70th Infantry Division, the 32nd Tank Brigade, and the Polish Carpathian Brigade; at the same time that the new troops were arriving, supplies were also being run into Tobruk. Thus the "Siege of Tobruk" was never really a siege at all, in that the defenders were never completely cut off from resupply and reinforcement, but there were limits on just how many men and tons of supplies the British could move at any one time. They were forced to use destroyers because regular transports were too slow to be able to get in and out of Tobruk during the hours of darkness: despite the best efforts of the Desert Air Force, any British transport caught in or near Tobruk in daylight was at the mercy of the Luftwaffe and the Regia Aeronautica—the wrecks littering Tobruk's harbor were mute testimony to the Axis bombers' accuracy.

Axis preparations for the assault on the fortress were proceeding apace, although there were concerns that the supply buildup, especially the artillery ammunition, was taking too long and would impose delays. Rommel was never able to shake his conviction, despite all evidence to the contrary, that the Italians were not doing enough to keep adequate supplies flowing to North Africa, and every time the British sank another supply ship, his suspicions of Italian treachery were renewed. (Rommel, of course, had no more idea of the existence of Ultra than did any other senior German officer—or Adolf Hitler, himself for that matter.) Relations with the Italian High Command remained prickly at best, never more so than after July 12, when the affable and generally cooperative General Gariboldi was replaced by the difficult, autocratic and foul-tempered General Ettore Bastico; Rommel soon had his measure, christening him "Bombastico." The little Italian general immediately sought to put the German upstart in his place: like most Italians in North Africa, he resented the Afrika Korps' presence. It was a standing insult, a constant reminder that Italy's fortunes in Libya had to be rescued by her German ally, and even though Libya was an Italian colony, the Italian Army was relegated to playing a supporting role to Rommel and his panzers. Rommel was dismissive of Bastico, confident that he would, in turn, soon be put in his place, as Rommel would be meeting personally with the Führer in Berlin and the Duce in Rome at the end of the month.

Rommel flew to Germany on July 28, spent two precious days with Lucie and Manfred at Weiner Neustadt, then drove to East Prussia to meet with Hitler at the Führerhauptquartier known as Wolfsschanze—the Wolf's Lair. There Hitler assured Rommel that the German naval forces—U-boats and motor torpedo boats—blockading Tobruk would be reinforced, while the Luftwaffe would be specifically instructed to give their utmost cooperation during the assault on Tobruk, and that strenuous efforts were underway to increase the shipping tonnage available in the Mediterranean to increase the flow of supplies to North Africa. There would be no additional German units for the Afrika Korps, however; when Hitler showed him the situation map of the Eastern Front, where German mechanized columns were ranging far behind Soviet lines and encircling entire Soviet armies, Rommel immediately understood that the Afrika Korps would remain low on the Wehrmacht's list of priorities for a long time to come. Nonetheless, Rommel left the Wolfsschanze feeling revitalized, as he always did after spending time in the Führer's presence. Nearly two more years would have to pass before the power of Hitler's charm finally wore thin enough for Rommel to see through it.

After spending another three days with his wife and son, Rommel met with Mussolini and General Ugo Cavallero, the Italian Chief of Staff, in Rome on August 6, there to brief them on the planned assault on Tobruk. Instead of the expected cooperation, he was initially met with more obstructionism, inexplicable to Rommel, as it was an Italian fortress which was to be liberated. Cavallero began bemoaning the state of the transport and supply services, suggesting that the attack on Tobruk would have to be postponed indefinitely, as it seemed unlikely that the requisite tonnage of artillery shells would ever reach the perimeter around the fortress. Rommel would have none of it: with classic Teutonic exactitude, he described the tactical situation around Tobruk, along with that of the defenses at Sollum and the Egyptian frontier. Then he shamelessly played on the role of the Italian gunners in defending Halfaya Pass during *Battleaxe* (he didn't even have to exaggerate), leaving Mussolini mightily impressed and full of assurances that the necessary supplies and ammunition would reach North Africa, no matter what the effort required.

Rommel returned to North Africa on August 8. Before his departure, he noticed a yellowish pallor developing in his eyes and skin—he was in the early stages of jaundice. Saying nothing lest army surgeons in Rome forbid his return to Africa, he flew back to Bardia aboard a transport that seemed to be plagued by engine troubles. When he heard that particular aircraft crashed on the next leg of his flight, he wrote to Lucie, expressing sorrow at the death of the crew, and remarking with a curious fatalism, "It just goes to show how quickly death can come to you."

Once back in North Africa, it was impossible to hide the symptoms of jaundice, and the Afrika Korps' surgeons prescribed a strict, bland diet and rest. He obeyed the first instruction and defied the second. There was too much to do for the *panzergruppe* commander to spend his days lolling around in bed! He would pay a price for his obstinacy, however: his normally robust constitution weakened, he fell victim through most of August, September, and October to the same sort of gastric disorders that afflicted most of the Germans in North Africa at one time or another, but which he had so far been able to avoid.

28 August 1941

Dearest Lu,

. . . As to my health, I'm feeling absolutely right. Everything's working again. I'm getting on famously with my new Chief of Staff [Gause]—which is of tremendous importance to me. Unfortunately the bugs are still about—four in the last twenty-four hours. But I hope to win that campaign too.

6 October 1941

Unable to write yesterday, my stomach struck work again. We had a fowl the evening before last which must have come from Ramses II's chicken run. For all the six hours' cooking it had, it was like leather and my stomach just couldn't take it.

7 October 1941

My stomach is completely back in order and I'm rushing around in a fine fettle. What do you think of my leave plans? I should be able to get away to Rome for a week at the beginning of November. I have a lot of business to clear up there. I'll have to come back for the battle, of course, and we must hope that supplies work all right, so that we can really get down to it. . . .[137]

In early autumn Rommel's intelligence officer, Major Friedrich von Mellenthin, along with the Abwehr (the German intelligence service) in Berlin, began picking up bits and pieces of information, mainly from radio intercepts, that indicated Auchinleck's organization and planning for the next British offensive in North Africa was beginning to coalesce. By mid-

September, Rommel was beginning to sense that time was running out, and that some sort of preemptive action by the Afrika Korps was necessary. Operation *Sommernachtstraum* ("Summer Night's Dream") was the result. On September 14, he personally led the 21st Panzer Division out of Sidi Omar, first southeast, then east, hoping to find—and destroy—the British forward supply dumps which he was certain were being established in preparation for the attack. After an advance of 60 miles, the strike fell on empty air—forewarned of Rommel's intentions, whether by Ultra or some other means is unknown, Auchinleck simply pulled his forces back far enough that had the Germans advanced far enough to come into contact, they would have run out of fuel. Frustrated and disappointed, Rommel ordered the 21st Panzer to return to Sidi Omar; it was just as the division began its withdrawal that bombers from the Desert Air Force suddenly appeared. There are no exact records of the losses, but several tanks and trucks were hit, including Rommel's beloved Mammut, and some were destroyed outright. The British strike had been carefully staged and coordinated, including the "loss" of "secret" documents which would, upon careful examination, indicate to Rommel's intelligence staff that the expected British attack would not be ready until December. So convincing were these planted documents that Rommel would actually be on his way back from Rome, where he had gone on November 1 to spend two weeks of leave with Lucie when the British attack was sprung.

Rommel and Auchinleck's race now entered its home stretch.

Rommel hoped to be able to begin the assault on Tobruk on or around November 24; as always, the exact date was contingent on the supply situation. The start date for Auchinleck's attack on the Afrika Korps was more firmly set for November 18, although it was always possible that some slippage might creep in and delay it; Auchinleck was sufficiently savvy to keep his planning flexible enough to allow for such an eventuality. In any case, the British attack would be preceded in October and November by a series of commando attacks at widely scattered places and times all along the Libyan coast, their purpose being to create dispersion and confusion, along with striking at a few targets of high strategic value.

On October 28, 1941 Rommel held one last full rehearsal exercise for the assault on Tobruk. In most respects, Rommel's plan of attack was an echo of the last such effort, made back in mid-May. The fundamental differences would be that the preparatory barrage would be of considerably heavier weight and longer duration, and there would be several days of aerial bombardment preceding the actual assault as well. The attacking infantry would this time be throughly briefed on the extent and location of the defensive emplacements—there would be no blindly attacking and hoping for the best results. Not surprisingly, General Bastico was skeptical: he regarded Rommel's determination to take Tobruk with suspicion, thinking it an unhealthy obsession, but then anything involving action against the enemy was, to Bastico, unhealthy and suspect.

No sooner was the exercise concluded than Rommel was dashing off yet another letter, this one to Manfred; Lucie, of course, would be in Rome by the time this arrived in Wiener Neustadt. Nonetheless, writing to his family had become an ingrained part of his daily routine—he almost invariably included some apologetic remark to Lucie when he missed a day—so wherever there was pen, paper, and a postman, Rommel was.

28 October 1941

Dearest Manfred,

We had the Ghibli again today. Sometimes the dust clouds were so thick you could only see two to three yards. It seems to be better today.

It's only a few days now before I take off to fly across the water. I'm very pleased to be seeing Mummy again in Rome and am only sorry that you, young man, can't be with us. It couldn't be helped. I'm certain to get some leave this winter and then we'll have a good prowl round together. There's not much hunting here where I am now. Some of the officers have shot cheetahs, which have their homes in the stony wadis. Occasionally one comes across a bustard, a fox, a jackal, or even a gazelle. The camel-thorn bushes are now growing faintly green and have tiny flowers. Last night the British bombarded us from the sea. Dive-bombers and torpedo bombers have sunk one or two of their cruisers and we've had peace since.[138]

In September, the British forces in the Western Desert had once again undergone a reorganization, being elevated from XIII Corps into the newly minted Eighth Army, under the command of Lieutenant General Alan

Cunningham. XIII Corps, under the command of Lietenant General Reade Godwin-Austen, was now merely a component of the new army, joined by the just-created XXX Corps, commanded by Lieutenant General Willough-by Norrie. Eighth Army would be a far stronger opponent than Rommel's *panzergruppe* had faced in June. XXX Corps fielded one armored division, one infantry division, and one independent infantry brigade; XIII Corps comprised two infantry divisions and a brigade of tanks; one infantry division served as the army reserve. The Tobruk garrison—the 32nd Army Tank Brigade, 70th Infantry Division and Polish Carpathian Brigade—also came under the operational command of Eighth Army. In armored strength, the critical factor in desert warfare after adequate water and gasoline, Eighth Army had 770 tanks in its order of battle. Just over half that number were the new Crusader tanks that had been blooded (in every sense of the word) in *Battleaxe* and which would lend their name to the upcoming offensive; 220 of them were the heavily armored but slow Matildas; the rest were the new but highly popular Honeys.

Facing them would be the 260 panzers of all types the 15th and 21st Panzer Divisions could muster between them, together with 278 Italian tanks, mostly M13/40 models of limited value. Rommel's infantry strength would be almost entirely Italian, with five such divisions available to him. The British had been as assiduous in building up their airpower as they had in accumulating ground forces, and the pilots of the Luftwaffe and Regia Aeronautica would find themselves outnumbered more than two-to-one.

The ball formally opened on the night of November 14–15 when a group of 32 British commandos under the command of Lieutenant Colonel Robert Laycock staged a raid at the coastal town of Beda Littoria, Libya, fully 200 miles west of Tobruk. British intelligence had pinpointed the building where Rommel had his headquarters: this was the target for the commandos' attack, their mission to kill Rommel and as many of his staff as possible. The operation was an utter and abject failure: three German soldiers were killed, as were two British officers, while all but two of the survivors were later captured. The intelligence on which the planning had been based was badly outdated: not only was Rommel in Rome at the time of the attack, but he had spent just two nights in the building in mid-August before moving forward to Gambut, halfway between Tobruk and Sollum.

It would be days before Auchinleck would learn that the mission had failed; by then it made no difference.

Operation *Crusader* began before dawn on November 18, when Eighth Army moved out of Mersa Matruh, Egypt, led by the 7th Armoured Division, and headed west-southwest. It crossed the frontier near Fort Maddalena, almost 60 miles inland, and there turned northwest, taking dead aim on Bir el Gubi. The South African Division protected the column's southern flank, while XIII Corps and the 4th Armoured Brigade moved to a position west of Sidi Omar, ready to meet the expected riposte by the Afrika Korps. Torrential rain during the night of November 17–18 had turned the North African airfields—Allied and Axis alike—into quagmires, utterly incapable of permitting aircraft to be flown off, which turned out to be something of a mixed blessing for both sides. Eighth Army was initially denied the air cover and fighter-bomber support it had been promised for the first day of the offensive, but the weather continued to be dodgy throughout the morning and afternoon, grounding the Luftwaffe reconnaissance flights that would have discovered Eighth Army's advance, letting Auchinleck to steal a day's march on Rommel.

Auchinleck's plan was to have XIII Corps outflank the Axis strongpoints that ran from Sidi Omar to the Halfaya Pass: this would be the anvil. The hammer would be the 7th Armoured Division, which was expected to engage the Afrika Korps somewhere south of Sidi Rezegh. XIII Corps would advance north to Bardia on the coast, and once the German armor had been written down, XXX Corps would continue northwest to Tobruk, where the plan called for it to link up with the fortress garrison, which would launch a breakout attack to the southeast. Even if the Italian infantry contained the garrison, without the Afrika Korps' tanks, it would be essentially helpless against the British armor. The key to the entire offensive was the destruction of the Afrika Korps: Auchinleck understood, unlike far too many British officers in North Africa, that the objective in any desert battle was the enemy's army, not taking and holding meaningless geographic features. Once the Afrika Korps was crippled or eliminated, the Italians would be as good as in the bag. It might not be elegant, and it offered to be bloody, but if properly executed it would work.

It wasn't until the morning of November 19 that the *panzergruppe* headquarters realized the British were attacking, when the left wing of the 7th

Armoured Division ran headlong into the Ariete Division at Bir el Gubi, 35 miles south of Tobruk, and was stopped cold after hard fighting by the Italians. So thoroughly had Rommel been convinced by the evidence from the planted documents captured in September that Auchinleck's attack was still at least a month away that his staff had dismissed earlier reports from Leutnant Seebohm's radio intercept unit that large British formations were on the move. When the entire Eighth Army radio net went silent on the night of November 17, no one paid the incident the slightest heed. Now there was a momentary paralysis in the Axis command structure as it struggled to assimilate a reality it had believed was impossible.

Meanwhile, Eighth Army was well on its way to success as the center and right columns of the 7th Armoured pressed forward to capture the huge airfield complex at Sidi Rezegh, 10 miles from the Tobruk perimeter. Von Ravenstein, after conferring with Crüwell, launched a counterattack into 7th Armoured's right flank with 60 tanks of the 21st Panzer Divison, supported by antitank units and a battery of 88mm Flak guns. Crüwell wanted to pull the 15th Panzer Division back from Tobruk, where it had been positioned to support the upcoming assault on the fortress, and add its weight to von Ravenstein's counterstroke. Rommel, who had finally returned to North Africa late on November 18, disagreed. Still determined that the attack on Tobruk would go in as planned, he argued against overreacting to what may well have been some preemptive stroke by Auchinleck, a British counterpart to his own *Sommernachtstraum*. However, reports of increasingly heavy fighting between Axis forces and large formations of British armor convinced him by the morning of November 20 that this was no mere raid. However reluctant he was to do so, he authorized the indefinite postponement of the Tobruk attack and released the mobile units positioned there to be turned against the advancing British.

Once he had shaken himself free of his stratagems for Tobruk, Rommel began reacting with his characteristic speed and decisiveness. It was not a popular decision in either Berlin or Rome, where, several hundred miles removed from the fighting, strategic and operational realities were not always properly represented by colored pins moved across maps. Men like Franz Halder and Walter von Brauchitsch, traditional commanders in every sense of the word, did not grasp the fundamental reality of desert warfare—as Erwin Rommel, or for that matter, Claude Auchinleck—that the main objective of any operation there was not ground, but the enemy's army. Fritz Bayerlein, Crüwell's new Chief of Staff, would recall that

> Considerable controversy has occurred . . . as to whether Rommel was right in calling off the attack on Tobruk in order to deal with the enemy offensive first. Our covering force might indeed have sufficed to hold the enemy attack until after Tobruk had fallen and this would have been of the greatest advantage for us, for we could then have then operated . . . with far greater ease and freedom than we were, in the event, able to do with the strong Tobruk garrison in our backs. But would the British have allowed us time to capture Tobruk undisturbed? This was not just a matter of audacity and daring; it was a gamble, which General Rommel refused to undertake.[139]

The third day of *Crusader* saw the Ariete Division and the 22nd Armoured Brigade, the 7th Armoured Division's left-flank element, continue to pound away at each other. The Italians justified Rommel's basic confidence in them, and apparently they had learned a few lessons from the Afrika Korps, for despite being handicapped with inferior equipment, they were giving as good as they got, and the battle around Bir el Gubi degenerated into a bloody brawl. Meanwhile, the 4th Armoured Brigade, the 7th Armoured Division's right-flank element, fought a "ducks and drakes" sort of engagement with the 21st Panzer Division, pitting the nimbleness of their cruiser tanks against the hitting power of the German guns. In the center, on the perimeter of the Sidi Rezegh airfield, the 7th Armoured Brigade drove off a strong counterattack mounted by the 90th Light and Bologna Divisions. Casualties, while not yet heavy, were beginning to mount on both sides.

The attack by the Bologna and the 90th Light confirmed the wisdom of Rommel's decision to abandon the Tobruk assault. Both units had been positioned on the fortress perimeter, assigned to the attack; hastily turning about 180 degrees, they struck at Sidi Rezegh. Even though they were unable to drive the 7th Armoured Division off the airfield, they pinned much of the British tank strength in place while the 15th and 21st Panzer Divisions were concentrating. Rommel conceded that for the moment Crüwell had a better grasp of the overall situation, and instructed him to "destroy the enemy battle groups in the Bardia, Tobruk, Sidi Omar area," giving him a free hand in containing the main British armored thrust.[140]

By the evening of November 20, Rommel was confident that he now had the full picture. *Crusader* was not simply an effort to relieve the Tobruk garrison, it was an all-out effort to destroy Panzergruppe Afrika. The Axis positions at the Egyptian frontier—the Halfaya Pass and Sollum—were under heavy, methodical attack; it would be soon be the turn for Bardia, Fort Capuzzo, and Sidi Omar (XIII Corps would, in fact, begin attacking them the next day). Only a fool would expect the Tobruk garrison to sit idly by under these circumstances—and Rommel certainly was no fool. But these were peripheral issues, ones where, in the old Austrian mot, "The situation is critical, it is not yet serious." Rommel was now firmly focused on what had become his primary objective—the airfield at Sidi Rezegh, or more precisely, the enemy armor concentrated at Sidi Rezegh. There the situation was, in the old Prussian mot, "serious but not critical." The British were making a mistake, and if he could exploit it, punish them for it, Rommel could win this battle.

That mistake was in allowing their armor to become separated in three unrelated engagements at and around Sidi Rezegh. Rommel intended to exploit that mistake by doing exactly the opposite: in sheer numbers, the Axis armor was markedly inferior to the British, but by concentrating his panzers, Rommel could achieve a decisive local superiority wherever he chose, giving him the opportunity to defeat the separate British armored brigades in detail. That evening, Rommel took the time to write a hasty letter to Lucie:

20 November 1941

My Dearest Lu,
The enemy offensive began immediately after my arrival. The battle has now reached its crisis, I hope we get through it in good order. It will probably all be decided by the time this letter arrives. Our position is certainly not easy.[141]

It was the Tobruk garrison that struck first. On the evening of November 20, General Sir Ronald Scobie, commanding both the British 70th Infantry Division and the Tobruk garrison, ordered an attack against the Axis units holding the southeast perimeter to begin at first light the following morning. A short but powerful and well-planned bombardment initially stunned the Italians, and several of their strongpoints were overrun as the 70th Infantry Division, supported by 50 Matilda tanks, pressed hard in the direction of Sidi Rezegh. There the 7th Armoured Division, only 10 miles from the Tobruk perimeter, launched an attack of its own, hoping to link up with the Tobruk force. But the Italians' resistance stiffened, and the 70th Infantry's advance slowed, while the 90th Light Division, with Rommel leading in person, contained the 7th Armoured—for the time being. Rommel, though, was under no illusions as to the ability of the 90th Light to hold back the British armor indefinitely—it lacked organic tanks of its own—and so he signaled Crüwell to bring up the Afrika Korps to Sidi Rezegh to prevent the 7th Armoured Division from linking up with the Tobruk garrison. By sundown the two panzer divisions had reached the eastern edge of the airfield and were engaged with the British armor.

Thus far Rommel's tactics were working: British armor was being "written down" at a far faster rate than was German—one British armored brigade had lost all but 28 of its 160 tanks by the end of the day. Now Rommel split his armored force: he had Crüwell move the 15th Panzer to Gambut, from where it could move behind the 7th Armoured, while keeping the 21st Panzer between Sidi Rezegh and Tobruk, the better to guard against simultaneous attacks by the garrison there and the 7th Armoured Division that would link up and raise the siege. Early in the afternoon of November 22, the 21st Panzer attacked Sidi Rezegh and, after a short but fierce fight, captured the airfield, knocking out another 50 British tanks as it did so. In just four days of fighting, Eighth Army's armored divisions had lost 530 tanks; German and Italian losses were around 100. That same day, in Tobruk, General Scobie began preparing for another attempt to break through the Axis perimeter around the fortress.

The Germans and Italians weren't having everything their way, however. To the east, closer to the coast, XIII Corps was mauling the Axis defensive positions. Fort Capuzzo fell on November 22, as did the strong points around Sidi Omar; Sollum and Halfaya Pass would be completely cut off the next day. The fate of their garrisons would depend entirely on the outcome of the battle around Sidi Rezegh. It was during this action that a New Zealander brigade, moving around the west end of the Axis defensive line, stumbled across the headquarters of the Afrika Korps. In a short, confused firefight, almost the entire staff personnel were killed or taken prisoner, only Crüwell and Bayerlein escaping.

Crüwell had already issued his orders to the panzer divisions, however. The 21st Panzer, along with the 90th Light, was holding the escarpment to the north of Sidi Rezegh, under heavy attack by the 7th Armoured Division, which had been reinforced by the South African Division—recalled from the now-superfluous duty of covering the *Crusader* columns' southern flanks. The Italian High Command, acknowledging reality at last, had placed both the Ariete and Trieste Divisions under Rommel's direct command, and now Ariete and 15th Panzer together now moved to strike the British divisions at Sidi Rezegh. This particular November 23 happened to be the *Totensonntag* (Sunday of the Dead), the last Sunday of the ecclesiastical year, the day when *Evangelische* Germans pray for the souls of the departed, and nationally celebrated as the day of mourning for the dead of the Great War; the day would give its name to this battle. Bayerlein's decription of the action is vivid and memorable:

> The Ariete's assault spearheads had meanwhile arrived with 120 tanks and General Crüwell now launched the combined German and Italian armored forces northwards into the enemy's rear, with the object of bottling him up completely and forcing him back against the 21st Panzer Dvision's front at Sidi Rezegh.
>
> The attack started well, but soon came up against a wide artillery and antitank gun screen, which the South Africans had formed at a surprising speed. . . . Guns of all kinds and sizes laid a curtain of fire in front of the attacking tanks and there seemed almost no hope of making any progress in the face of this fire-spewing barrier. Tank after tank split open in the hail of shells. Our entire artillery had to be thrown in to silence the enemy guns one by one. However, by late afternoon we had managed to punch a few holes in the front. The tank attack moved forward again and tank duels of tremendous intensity developed deep in the battlefield. In fluctuating fighting, tank against tank, tank against gun or antitank gun nest, sometimes in frontal, sometimes in flanking, as-

sault, using every trick of mobile warfare, the enemy was finally forced into a confined area. With no relief forthcoming from a Tobruk sortie, he now saw his only escape from complete destruction in a breakout from the ring surrounding him. . . .

The wide plain south of Sidi Rezegh was now a sea of dust, haze, and smoke. Visibility was poor and many British tanks and guns were able to break away to the south and east without being caught. But a great part of the enemy force still remained inside. Twilight came, but the battle was still not over. Hundreds of burning vehicles, tanks, and guns lit up the field of *Totensonntag*. . . .[142]

The outcome of the action around Sidi Rezegh led Rommel to believe the battle was as good as won.

23 November 1941

Dearest Lu,

The battle seems to have passed its crisis. I'm very well, in good humor and full of confidence. Two hundred enemy tanks shot up so far. Our fronts have held.[143]

Lieutenant General Cunningham, Eighth Army's officer commanding, was appalled by his losses, particularly at Sidi Rezegh, where nearly half of the South African Division had been annihilated. With two thirds of his tanks were out of action, he was convinced that *Crusader* had failed, and asked Auchinleck for permission to withdraw and fall back across the frontier. Auchinleck would have none of it, and promptly sacked Cunningham, replacing him with Major General Neil Ritchie, who was given firm, explicit orders to continue the offensive.

On November 24, the surviving German and Italian armor turned east toward Sidi Omar, splitting Eighth Army, XIII to the east, the remnants of XXX Corps to the west, hoping to aggravate Eighth Army's disorganization and confusion. Rommel told Crüwell

The greater part of the force aimed at Tobruk has been destroyed; now we will turn east and go for the New Zealanders and the Indians before they have been able to join up with the remains of the main force for a combined attack on Tobruk. At the same time we will . . . cut off their supplies. Speed is vital; we must make the most of the shock effect of the enemy's defeat and push forward immediately and as fast as we can with our entire force to Sidi Omar.[144]

This operation would become known to the British as "The Dash to 'the Wire.'" Though Rommel would not know it until much later, the Afrika Korps would pass within 4 miles of the main British supply dumps south of Gabr Saleh without catching a hint of their presence—by sheer good fortune, Eighth Army would be allowed to hold on and eventually resume the offensive. A push 15 miles across the frontier yielded nothing but empty desert, and Rommel decided that the time had come to relieve the Halfaya garrison and retake the defensive positions the British had captured earlier. As he did so he would, he was still confident, find those supply dumps.

The following day, he turned the Afrika Korps to the northwest, toward Sidi Azeiz. However when the Desert Air Force discovered and attacked the column, he was forced to pull back. At Sidi Omar, the 5th Panzer Regiment and the 7th Indian Brigade fought each other to exhaustion before the Indians' 25-pounders decided the issue and the panzers called it a day. This was the last hurrah for the Dash to the Wire: for all that he charged to and fro across the desert, Rommel had accomplished nothing decisive. He came perilously close to running the fuel tanks of his panzers dry with no hope of replenishment, and now, like a thunderbolt, came news from his operations officer, Lieutenant Colonel Westphal, that a daring and skillful nighttime attack on the Sidi Rezegh ridge had linked up with a sortie by the garrison of Tobruk. A narrow, vulnerable corridor now connected the Tobruk garrison with Eighth Army. Westphal, in fine "better to seek forgiveness than beg permission" form, on his own initiative ordered the 21st Panzer Division back to Sidi Rezegh in the hope that it still had sufficient strength remaining to sever the link between Tobruk and XXX Corps. Rommel was distinctly unhappy when he learned of Westphal's action, but he knew it had to be done; Westphal's orders were confirmed. The 15th Panzer Division took Sidi Azeiz the morning of November 27, but that was Rommel's last hurrah in the *Crusader* battle. By the early afternoon of November 27, the Afrika Korps was beginning to lose its momentum as a consequence of the exertions and fatigue of four days of almost constant combat around Sidi Rezegh. Rommel managed to convince himself that this was because the battle was almost over, writing to Lucie that evening that "The battle has now been raging in the desert around Tobruk and in front of Sollum since the 19th. You will have heard from the communiqués more or less how it has gone. I think we're through the worst and that the battle will be of decisive importance to the whole war situation. . . ." Ironically prophetic words.[145]

The whole "Dash to The Wire" episode was marked by confusion and bits of surreality. At one point, on his way back to Sidi Omar, Rommel's car broke down in the middle of nowhere as night was approaching. By pure chance, a few hours later, Crüwell, in a big Mammoth bus similar to Rommel's, passed by and gave the errant general a lift. But Crüwell's driver, trying to navigate in the darkness, drove into the Wire by mistake and became lost. Forced to wait until daybreak to get their bearings, the commanders of Panzergruppe Afrika and the Afrika Korps sat huddling in the cold, along with their staffs while columns of British infantry passed by only yards away; the Tommies, noting a British-made vehicle sitting motionless in the darkness, gave the big bus no mind. Later, after Rommel obtained another vehicle, he inadvertently drove into the heart of a New Zealander field hospital, believing it to be German. The informal protocols for such things had already been well established: medical facilities were by tacit agreement neutral ground. So Rommel—visored officer's cap, medals and all—calmly asked the chief surgeon if there was anything he needed, promised to see that medical supplies got through to him, and then with the most perfect aplomb, drove away.

For eight days, from November 29 to December 6, the issue hung in the balance, as both sides licked their wounds, totaled their losses, and engaged in minor attacks in an effort to improve their tactical positions. By December 7, though, Rommel was forced to face the music: the Afrika Korps had fewer than 100 serviceable tanks, the Italians not many more, while the British were bringing forward almost three times that number out of their armor depots. The Axis supply situation could not longer sustain the level of operations required to hold the Tobruk perimeter and a renewed British offensive. The order went out, and the Germans and Italians began abandoning their positions around Tobruk, withdrawing toward Gazala.

9 December 1941

Dearest Lu,

You will have no doubt seen how we're doing from the Wehrmacht communiqués. I had to break off the action outside Tobruk on acount of the Italian formations and also the badly exhausted German troops. I'm hoping we'll succeed in escaping enemy encirclement and holding on to Cyrenaica. I'm keeping well. You can imagine what I'm going through and what anxieties I have. It doesn't look as though we'll get any Christmas this year. It's only a fortnight away.

Auchinleck, meanwhile, officially declared the siege at Tobruk to be lifted on December 10.

Initially, Rommel hoped to be able to hold a position somewhere between Tobruk and Benghazi; the Gazala Line seemed to hold out the best prospect. It was far enough forward that in should the British take a misstep Tobruk would be vulnerable, but far enough west that the British would be unable to slip around behind him and cut him off from Tripoli. He was confident and reassuring when he wrote Lucie on December 12.

Dearest Lu,

Don't worry about me. It will all come out all right. We're still not through the crisis. It'll probably go on for another couple of weeks yet. But I still have hopes of holding on here. I'm now living in a proper house, complete with "hero's cellar" [a dugout]. I spend the days with the troops.

Happy Christmas to you and Manfred. I hope to be with you shortly afterward.[146]

But now Eighth Army set to with a will, although without the same tactical finesse displayed by the Afrika Korps when it was on the attack. The first attack on the Axis line at Gazala took place on December 13—for the next three days, German, Italian, British, Indian, and Polish troops would fight over a hill known as Point 204, the highest point in the whole Gazala Line and the key to the entire position. Casualties were heavy on both sides, but in the end Eighth Army was able to apply too much pressure and Rommel abandoned the Gazala position. Now he set his sights firmly on El Agheila—right back where he had begun his offensive in March. In his judgment, there were no other defensible positions available west of the Gazala ridge. In his letters to Lucie during the withdrawal the depth of his chagrin at being compelled to retreat after having come, as he believed, so close to success, is unmistakable.

20 December 1941

Dearest Lu,

We're pulling out. There was simply nothing else for it. I hope we manage to get back to the line we've chosen. Christmas is going to be completely messed up. . . .

Some supplies have arrived—the first since October. My commanding officers are all ill—those who aren't dead or wounded.

22 December 1941

Retreat to Agedabia![147] You can't imagine what it's like. Hoping to get the bulk of my force through and make a stand somewhere. Little ammunition and gasoline, no air support. Quite the reverse with the enemy. But enough of that. . . .

23 December 1941

Operations going satisfactorily today, so far as it's possible to tell in the morning. It looks as though we'll succeed in extricating ourselves from the envelopment and getting the main body back. It will be a great Christmas treat for me if it does come off. How modest one becomes! It's no good turning to the Italian High Command of course. They would have been roped in long ago with all of their force.

25 December 1941

I opened my Christmas parcel in my caravan yesterday evening and was very pleased with the letters from you and Manfred and the presents. Some of it, like the bottle of champagne, I took straight across to the Intelligence truck where I sat over it with the Chief, the Ia and Ic [Gause, Lieutenant Colonel Siegfried Westphal, and von Mellenthin]. The night passed quietly. But the Italian divisions give us a lot of worry. There are shocking signs of disintegration and German troops are being forced to the rescue everywhere. The British were badly disappointed at Benghazi in neither cutting us off nor finding gasoline and rations. Crüwell has been made a full panzer general. He really deserves it.[148]

There would be nothing in this retreat of the Italian rout of January and February: Eighth Army was never able to outflank Panzergruppe Afrika, and Rommel always covered his movements with a rearguard powerful enough to hurt its pursuers. Despite their diminished numbers, the 15th and 21st Panzer Divisions, along with the Ariete Division, were always handled with great skill, working closely with the inevitable screen of antitank guns which the British armor could not overcome.

The Italian senior officers, in Africa and Rome alike, protested bitterly when Rommel announced his plans to withdraw as far back as El Agheila, but he dismissed them with a figurative wave of his hand. At one point, in a personal meeting with Rommel, the chief of the Comando Supremo, General Ugo Cavallero, insisted that abandoning Cyrenaica would be a catastrophe for Italy; Rommel rounded on him by declaring that losing the whole of Tripolitania would be an even bigger one. All of the Italian generals' combined mutterings, imprecations, pleas, and bluster left Rommel unmoved. He had come to regard his Italian soldiers with something like affection, but of Italian senior officers and government officials he was openly contemptuous. Libya was an Italian colony: many of these same men had been responsible for its loss to the British less than a year before; most of them had been openly obstructionist when he had been trying to retake Libya that spring and summer, and now they were demanding that the *panzergruppe* make a stand against Eighth Army in the same place that the Italian Army had stood the year before, where it could be destroyed in the same manner and for the same operational reasons the Italian Army had been destroyed 10 months earlier. Their protests fell on stone-deaf ears.

Rommel was determined not to let himself get trapped in the bulge of Cyrenaica, hence his decision to abandon Benghazi at the same time he withdrew from the Gazala ridge; for a few days at the end of December he made a stand at Agedabia. General Crüwell's reconnaissance units noted an inviting gap opening up between two British armored brigades, and Rommel, who was at the moment personally commanding the Afrika Korps as Crüwell was bedridden with jaundice, saw an opportunity. On December 27 he turned on his British pursuers and savaged the long-suffering 22nd Armoured Brigade, destroying a third of its tanks in the process. Stunned, Eighth Army halted temporarily, giving Rommel a breathing space to fall back in good order to El Algheila.

By January 10, 1942, the whole of Panzergruppe Afrika, such as it was and what there was of it, was once again on familiar ground. Meanwhile, 450 miles to the east, the last pages of the battle for Tobruk and the Egyptian frontier were being written. The last Axis garrison on the Egyptian–Libyan border, Bardia, had surrendered to the 2nd South African Division eight days earlier. Troops from the same division would take Sollum on January 12. Halfaya Pass, held by a mixed German and Italian force of just over 5,000 infantrymen and artillerymen, including the fighting pastor, Major Wilhelm Bach (he had been promoted while commanding the Halfaya defense) finally capitulated on January 17—but only after all the defenders' supplies were exhausted. Rommel, when communicating the news to Berlin and Rome, made a point of commending the "superb leadership" of the Italian general who had held overall command of the Sollum–Halfaya defenses, Fedele De Giorgis.[149]

That same day, Rommel wrote a particularly cryptic letter to Lucie. Even while still retreating toward El Agheila, Rommel began to spot straws in the wind, telling Lucie on January 17. . . .

The situation here is developing to our advantage and I'm full of plans that I daren't say anything about round here. They'd think me crazy. But I'm not; I simply see a bit farther than they do. But you know me. I work out my plans early each morning, and now often, during the past year and in France, have they been put into effect within a matter of hours. That's how it should be and is going to be in the future.[150]

CHAPTER NINE

DER HEXENKESSEL

> *It has been a damned nice thing—the nearest run thing*
> *you ever saw in your life. . . . By God! I don't think*
> *it would have been done if I had not been there.*
> —ARTHUR WELLESLEY, 1st Duke of
>   Wellington, after the Battle of Waterloo

Nineteen forty-one passed into 1942, and Erwin Rommel found himself, along with his army, standing back on the same ground from which he had begun his North African adventure nine months earlier. A general officer imbued with a more conventional, less imaginative concept of operations and strategy almost certainly would have regarded such a circumstance as a defeat; Rommel most certainly did not. He understood almost from the moment he came ashore in Tripoli that the key to success in desert warfare was not the mere gaining of empty ground. In desert warfare, the primary objective is, with very few exceptions, always the opposing army—the enemy's tanks, troops, communications and supply lines. Those few exceptions involve the holding or seizing of specific, vital geographic locations. These points, whether coastal towns and cities, or dominating geographic features, compel either attack or defense, acting as lodestones to the enemy's forces, and so facilitate, one way or another, the enemy's destruction. There were few such places in Libya and Egypt—the narrow neck between the Mediterranean and the Quatarra Depression at El Alamein, Sollum and the Halfaya Pass, Tobruk, the Gazala Escarpment, and the dunes and ridges around Agedabia.

Rommel had first demonstrated in France, with his free-wheeling, opportunistic handling of the 7th Panzer Division, a clear grasp of how wide-ranging armored columns could severely disrupt a foe's logistics and communications, in the process undermining the enemy soldiers' morale and will to fight, creating confusion and disruption that was utterly out of proportion to the material damage done or the losses suffered on either side. Now, in North Africa, whether on the attack or in retreat, he was thoroughly in his element. Here in the Western Desert, he had schooled the British in the same lesson which they had first taught the Italians in 1940: in the emptiness of Cyrenaica, sheer numbers of tanks, troops, and guns are essentially meaningless—as is merely holding useless ground. It is how those tanks, troops, and guns are employed, and *where*, that makes them decisive. Having already played the headmaster in the spring of 1941, the question tantalizing Erwin Rommel in January 1942 was whether or not he could do it again.

There were straws in the wind which were giving Rommel increased confidence that he would be able to do exactly that. First and foremost was the Allies' supply situation, which now mirrored that of the Afrika Korps just two months earlier. It was the British who were now operating at the end of a 500-mile-long supply line, maintained for almost its entire length on a single roadway. Leutnant Seebohm's wireless intercept wizards were able to tease enough information out of Eighth Army's radio traffic to confirm that the British were diverting ever-increasing numbers of combat units to roadwork and establishing the supply dumps that would be required if Eighth Army were to advance beyond El Agheila. Rommel saw replacements for men and armor begin to trickle in as well: on January 5, 1942, 55 new tanks, all of them the newest Panzer III and IV models, with heavier armor and more powerful main guns than anything the Afrika Korps currently had on strength, arrived at Tripoli.

There had also been a seismic shift in the world's political and military landscape during Rommel's retreat from Tobruk which would directly affect both the Afrika Korps and Eighth Army. On December 7, 1941, the Imperial Japanese Navy launched a crippling air attack on the United States Navy's main Pacific Fleet base at Pearl Harbor, Hawaii. The upshot of the attack was America's declaration of war on Japan; had the situation developed no further, only Eighth Army would have felt the consequences, as within days, sometimes hours, of striking Pearl Harbor, the Japanese launched other attacks, land and naval, on British, French, and Dutch colonial possessions in the Pacific and in Southeast Asia. The British, in an attempt to shore up weak defenses in places like Burma, Singapore, and Hong

Kong, began withdrawing troops from North Africa; at the same time, the Australian government, fearing a Japanese attack on Australia's northern coast, demanded the immediate return of Eighth Army's Australian divisions. To Rommel, it appeared that the situation which had obtained in February 1941 might be repeating itself less than a year later.

But America's entry into the war would have repercussions for Rommel and the Afrika Korps, although they would take longer to manifest. On December 8, America went to war with Japan—there was no corresponding declaration on Germany, however much President Franklin Roosevelt might desire one, given his certitude that the Third Reich posed the greater and more immediate danger for the West than did Japan. Hitler solved the problem for him, however, declaring war on the United States on December 10, the single greatest strategic blunder he would ever commit, doing so, he asserted, out of political necessity, as Germany had to stand by her Axis partner, Japan. What had been a stream of American-supplied tanks, guns, and aircraft supplying Eighth Army would soon become a flood, and by the year's end, American ground and air forces would be fighting in North Africa, adding to the Allies' preponderance of men and materiel. But for now, Rommel was contemplating his next move against Eighth Army, as the straws he was seeing convinced him that Eighth Army might be ripe for a riposte.

AMONG THOSE STRAWS was an intelligence windfall that qualified as an entire bale of hay in its own right, a gold mine which the Germans named *der gutte Quelle* ("the good source") and which Rommel, with sly humor, cryptically christened his "little fellers." It was an operational intelligence coup which has had few parallels in history, for, incredible as it may sound, Rommel's "good source" was a series of official reports about Eighth Army plans and intentions written by the senior United States Army officer in Egypt.

Colonel Bonner Fellers was posted to the American embassy in Cairo as a military attaché in October 1941; his duties required that he make regular reports to Washington DC on Great Britain's military operations in the Middle East. The British gave him *carte blanche* to roam and observe where he chose, after which he would write concise, detailed dispatches about unit strengths and positions, troop movements, convoys, newly arrived reinforcements, Eighth Army's supply situation, and its morale, as well as summaries of plans and pending operations. These reports went directly to the President and the chiefs of staff; they were also being read by Adolf Hitler, Benito Mussolini, and General der Panzertruppe Erwin Rommel.

Colonel Fellers sent his reports by radio, using the U.S. State Department's "Black Code," which had earlier been compromised by Italian spies working at the American embassy in Rome, and then independently broken by the German *Beobachtungsdienst*, or B-dienst. For six months, from December 1941 through June 1942, Fellers' reports were being decoded and read in Berlin and Rome almost before they were read in Washington. From time to time Fellers would express concern that the Black Code might be compromised, and wanted to replace it with a military ciphering system, but he was always assured that the Black Code was secure, so the regular flow of reports continued uninterrupted.

These were Rommel's "little fellers," and they provided not only tactical and operational information for the Afrika Korps, they also provided the German and Italian air forces and navies warning of when Allied convoys were scheduled to sail through the Mediterranean. The consequences were often devastating: in June 1942, for example, two convoys, *Vigorous* and *Harpoon*, one eastbound from Gibraltar, the other westbound out of Alexandria, were almost wiped out as Feller's intercepted signals provided the Luftwaffe and the Regia Aeronautica with their precise sailing times and routes, which resulted in near-incessant air attacks on both.

It would not be until evidence began accumulating in Ultra intercepts that there was a high-level leak in Cairo that the security of Fellers' signals began to be questioned, and it was mid-June 1942 that the suspicions were confirmed. Fellers would promptly change his code and Rommel's *gutte Quelle* would dry up. Until it did, however, it was priceless, as it gave Rommel, O.K.W., and Comando Supremo an astonishing level of insight into British capabilities and planning in North Africa. Standing in his new armored command vehicle, an Sdkfz. 250 half-track nicknamed *Greif* ("Griffin") on January 21, 1941, Erwin Rommel had no idea how long *der gutte Quelle* would last, but while it did, he was determined to make the most of it. Finding only the thinnest of screens in front of him, he concluded that Panzerarmee Afrika possessed the strength to seize the opportunity—if just barely.[151]

The first move of Rommel's riposte against Eighth Army was made that day, when he sent two strong armored columns forward from El Agheila—the 90th Light Division and part of the 21st Panzer on the left, the 15th Panzer and the balance of the 21st Panzer on the right, headed in the direction of El Haseia, a desert crossroads southeast of Agedabia. Once again, the British were caught by surprise, and the Benghazi Handicaps were off and running again. The British had assumed that it would be months before Rommel would accrue the strength necessary to go back over to the offensive, by which time their own attack into Tripolitania would be well underway. A thoroughly green division, the newly formed 1st Armoured, had arrived in North Africa in November 1941, but had not been sufficiently worked up before the end of *Crusader*. Posted forward at Agedabia, where, it was hoped, it could gain a bit of seasoning and finish adapting to the conditions in Libya, the division was mauled by the Afrika Korps, losing 110 of its 150 tanks in a single day as the two wings of Rommel's attack converged on Agedabia. Rommel quickly sensed the same disorder that had marked the Western Desert Force a year earlier, and the likelihood that he could once again tumble the British out of Libya, began to grow with each passing hour. As he had been forced to do the previous March, Rommel had to have a care to minimize his own losses, for while he had a definite local superiority in tanks and men, the full strength of Eighth Army would overwhelm him. Another restraint was at work this time, however, one that had not been as significant a consideration in his previous attack across Cyrenaica, that being his limited stocks of fuel. Every move he made had to be carried out with one eye on his vehicles' fuel gauges; with that in mind, on January 25 he set out for Msus, hoping to bluff the enemy out of the Cyrenaica bulge.

The British scattered like tenpins, Tommies grabbing onto the nearest transport and rushing off in any direction, as long as it was away from advancing panzers. It was not for want of courage: over the course of three years fighting in North Africa British soldiers would prove time and again that whatever else they might lack, it was not that quality. But the various units of Eighth Army were so dispersed and everything was happening so quickly that there was neither time nor opportunity for any level of higher command to impose order on the battlefield. For now, everything was going Rommel's way once again, and the feeling was like a tonic to him. The renewed self-confidence positively oozes from the letter he wrote to Lucie that evening.

25 January 1942

Dearest Lu,

Four days of complete success behind us. Our blows struck home. And there's still one to come. Then we'll go all modest again and lie in wait for a bit. The foreign press opinion about me is improving again. Cavallero arrived and wanted to whistle me straight back on orders from the Duce. But the Duce's directive, which was given to me in writing, reads differently and, at least, left me greater freedom.[152]

It's difficult not to share Rommel's exasperation with—and some of his contempt for—the Italian generals and high command. Once again, their current demands were in direct contradiction of what they had asked Rommel to do only months previously. When Rommel was abandoning Tobruk, they implored him to stand and fight as they had never done, in order to protect Italian citizens and property; then they forbade him to retreat to El Agheila, insisting that he remain at Benghazi. Now, when he was advancing and liberating those citizens and properties and retaking Benghazi, they were demanding that he return to El Agheila. There must have been moments when Rommel wondered just on whose side were the Italian generals.

Their protests were, in truth, mostly bombast and bluster, for the fact of the matter was that Rommel was making them look inept at best, incompetent at worst. Cavallero, along with Bastico, both of whom were nominally Rommel's superiors, were angered as much by the disdain for them Rommel displayed in his actions as they were with the actions themselves. The operational orders for the attack out of El Agheila, for example, had been posted the day of the attack at every German supply dump in Tripolitania: these postings would be the first notice either Bastico or Cavallero had of Rommel's plans. When Cavallero caught up with Rommel in Msus on January 26 and tried to assert his command authority, Rommel cooly informed him that "nobody but the Führer could change my decision, as it would be mainly German troops who would be engaged." That, of course, was nonsense, but Cavallero was hesitant to call his bluff, especially when Rommel received a personal telephone call from Il Duce that evening, during which Mussolini congratulated him on the success of his new attack. Cavallero also knew that Generalmajor Enno von Rintelen, the German military attaché to Rome, was visiting Rommel's headquarters, where Rommel gave him "a glimpse of the battlefield next day. He had spent practically all his time sitting in Rome and I wanted to instill in him some understanding of the needs of this theater." With such allies, Rommel's moral ascendency over the Italian generals was now absolute—it would remain so as long as he continued to be right and they were wrong.[153]

At the same time, along with Rommel's evident dislike of Cavallero, Bastico, and the rest of the Italian high command, there was a strong element of distrust of them. As a rule, Rommel liked his Italian soldiers, who usually fought hard, often bravely, and sometimes ingeniously for him. Once, in an effort to disguise how few of the precious Flak 88s he had—fewer than a dozen at the time—he ordered some of his Italian troops to build dummies and emplace them. A few days later, he was furious to see these irreplaceable guns sitting in the open, being shelled by British artillery. The tables turned on him—they were the dummy guns his Italians had cobbled together, and so convincing were they that the British mistook them for real 88s. Delighted, Rommel told the Italians to make more, and to be sure to bring them along as they advanced—their decoy value was tremendous. But the senior Italian officers were, in Rommel's eyes, a very different kettle of fish. He could understand, perhaps, their lack of enthusiasm for what was at heart Mussolini's war, but he suspected something deeper was at work: treachery.

Rommel's suspicions sprang out of the uncanny success which the Allies experienced in intercepting and sinking the vital supply ships that sailed from Italian ports bound for Tripoli, the ones that carried tanks, ammunition, food, and above all, gasoline. Less than half, and sometimes as little as a third, of the minimum supply needed to sustain Panzergruppe Afrika—a total of 60,000 tons was required every month—was reaching North Africa, the rest lost to Allied aircraft and submarines. Privately Rommel wondered if the Italian generals were somehow transmitting information to the Allies about departure dates for the North Africa-bound convoys, who would then prepare their ambushes. There was no doubt that the Italian navy and merchant marine were doing their best—there is no record of any Italian ship bound for North Africa ever turning back once it departed Italy. The Allies seemed to have inside information, and the only possible source of that information was the Italian high command itself.

Rommel, of course, never knew about Ultra. That was the source of the Allies' "inside information." The best-kept secret of the war, so well kept that its existence remained unknown and largely unsuspected until it was revealed 30 years after the end of hostilities in Europe, Ultra allowed the British to read the operational orders sent to German and Italian air and naval units stationed around the Mediterranean, as well as Berlin's communications with Rommel himself, which gave them a decided advantage in attacking Italian shipping between Italy and North Africa. Of course, it could sometimes be a two-edged sword when the Allies became too heavily dependent on it, especially when a general such as Erwin Rommel was involved. Relying on Rommel to do as he was told by O.K.W., the British had drawn down and dispersed their forces in North Africa, confident that they would have time to once more marshal their strength before Rommel's next attack. That he would once again defy O.K.W. and strike out on his own never occurred to Auchinleck or Churchill. Now Rommel was once more reminding them of why he was becoming known around the world as "The Desert Fox."

27 January 1942

Dearest Lu,

Everything's OK here. We're cleaning up the battlefield, collecting up guns, armored cars, tanks, rations, and ammunition for our own needs. It will take some time. It's chilly again and rainy, though the rain has its advantages, as it prevents the British getting their planes off the ground from their airfields in Cyrenaica.

Gause will be back on February 1. But he'll never be quite the same. It was all rather much at once. I'm more used to such things.

We're getting on with the Italian Corps now. They're very unhappy that they couldn't come along with us. But that's their own fault.[154]

Sometimes Rommel didn't tell Lucie *quite* everything, for rather than taking "some time" to gather up the plunder around Msus, he was off the next day for Benghazi. He wanted to continue his advance to Mechili, much as he had done the year before, but Benghazi was still occupied by the British, and in too great a strength to simply be ignored. So in a swift two-day action Benghazi was surrounded and taken. Inside was a wealth of supplies: artillery, trucks, fuel, rations, uniforms, boots, all of which found new homes with the men of the Afrika Korps, as for the first three months of 1942, Rommel was forced to rely on plundered British supplies and equipment to keep this new offensive going. Tmimi was taken on February 3, and Eighth Army pulled back to the Gazala ridge west of Tobruk, where it began digging in and setting up defensive "boxes" between the Bir Hakim oasis in the south to the Mediterranean coast in the north. This rapidly became known as the "Gazala Line."

For the time being, a sort of equilibrium was reached in the Western Desert as neither side possessed sufficient strength to again go over to the attack. This situation could not and would not last forever. Who moved first would probably decide the war in North Africa, but for now, both Germans and British played a waiting game.

> 7 February 1942
>
> Dearest Lu,
> It's quiet again on our front, which now extends for 300 miles (from the left to the right wing). It's particularly pleasing to have got Cyrenaica back again. I'm hoping the situation will stabilize sufficiently for me to get away for a while. I've been given a new order, by the way (a star on the chest to match the one I've already got round my neck). [This would be the Gold Military Medal of Valor—the other was Colonial Order of the Star of Italy.][155]

The Afrika Korps waited impatiently, for its morale was soaring. Victory is a powerful tonic for any army, and once again the panzers were on the advance. There was a very real sense among these men—Rommel would always fondly call them his "Africans"—that they were an elite, led by an elite general, and while they had suffered a setback in the *Crusader* battles, they believed themselves to be far from defeated. The power which the personality of a charismatic commander exerts on his army cannot and should not be ignored: Wellington, for example, once remarked that the presence of Bonaparte on the battlefield was worth a reinforcement of 40,000 men to the French. There was also something of an "us against the world" attitude shared by Rommel and his "Africans," as every officer and man knew that Panzergruppe Afrika was the German Army's "poor relation," always far down the list of priorities for Wehrmacht planners and supply masters. The distinctive spirit with which Rommel imbued the Afrika Korps was best described by German journalist Hanns Gert von Esebeck in a postwar memoir he wrote recounting his years spent in North Africa as a war correspondent; it is memorable—and effective—for its down-to-earth tone, of which Rommel would have no doubt approved.

> . . . [A]lways there is this strange magic strength that this soldier [Rommel] radiates to his troops, right down to the last rifleman. The privates call him "Erwin"—just that: "Erwin," short and to the point. Not that they intend any disrespect by using his Christian name—it is a mark of profound admiration. Because the men can understand their commander-in-chief: when he talks with them he calls a spade a spade; he doesn't sentimentalize with them, but meets them man-to-man, often uses hard language with them, but also knows how to praise and encourage them and make suggestions, and make complicated subjects easily comprehensible to them. Of course, to start with there were only a few of us—everybody knew everybody else and there was a desert camaraderie: the rifleman saw his general, and for that matter the general his rifleman, eating the same classical Libyan diet of sardines.[156]

Fritz Bayerlein, now a colonel and serving as Rommel's Chief of Staff in Gause's absence, wrote

> The merit and value of a desert soldier can be measured in his physical capacity, intelligence, mobility, nerve, pugnacity, daring and stoicism. A commander of men requires these qualities in even greater measure and in addition must be outstanding in his toughness, devotion to his men, instinctive judgment of terrain and enemy, speed of reaction, and spirit. In General Rommel these qual-

ities were embodied in a rare degree and I have known no other officer in whom they were so combined.[157]

If so much as a single facet of the persona Rommel presented to his men had shone false—and soldiers, no matter in which army they serve, have an unerring instinct for detecting *poseurs*—the entire edifice would have come crashing down. But none ever did, because none ever existed; Rommel never presented himself as a great warrior born, living successive lives of martial splendor, or as a protean, near-Olympian figure set apart from and above the mass of humanity, predestined to lead men to victory. Nor did he claim an artist's temperament, relying on untrained and untutored intuition and inspiration to formulate his strategies and tactics. He was vain, as are most exceptional leaders in one fashion or another. He had a temper, and when provoked was prone to immediately give the provocateur the rough side of his tongue; but he also knew when to make amends and apologize. (Major Heidkamper, late of the 7th Panzer Division, was a case in point: in the closing days of the Battle of France Rommel wrote of him to Lucie, saying "I shall have to have him posted away as soon as I can. . . . I'll have to make a thorough study of the documents so as to put the boy in his place." Two days later, he was informing her that "The Heidkamper affair was cleared up yesterday and has now been finally shelved. I have the feeling that it's going to be all right now.") He had no airs and graces, but he did have his foibles, his quirks: he was always immaculately turned out, no matter what the conditions, and he made his high-peaked officer's hat and a pair of British-issue perspex sand goggles his personal trademark. He was stubborn, arrogant, and undeniably courageous; he was the very embodiment of the "useful soldier" as he had been described 30 years earlier, the genuine article, which his men appreciated and for which they esteemed him.

He was also immensely popular in the Fatherland. When he left North Africa on February 15 for a month's leave, he never expected to arrive in Germany to find his face on the cover of *Illustrierter Beobachter* ("*Illustrated Observer*"), Germany's national news magazine. (He would appear on the cover of *Time* magazine in the United States on July 13.) He also never imagined he would find his desk littered with what in a future generation would be called "fan mail," sometimes hundreds of letters a day, many of them from lovelorn females of all ages, but most especially young women in the throes of unrequited romance. "The newsreels," he quipped to Lucie, "have brought the younger females particularly out of their composure." Göbbels and his minions over at the Propaganda Ministry had turned the handsome, dashing *generaloberst* (Rommel had been promoted on January 24, the same day that Panzergruppe Afrika became Panzerarmee Afrika) into something of a matinee idol, ably assisted by Leutnant Berndt, the officer Göbbels' ministry had foisted on the Afrika Korps. Outgoing, with a ready grin, Rommel was the antithesis of the coldly *korrekt* and aloof Prussian *offizier* of yore and lore which glared at German theater audiences during the newsreels which Göbbels propaganda flacks churned out to glorify the Wehrmacht's feats of arms. That he sprang from stolid yeoman stock rather than being some sprig of a decadent aristocracy also allowed the Propaganda Minister to present Rommel as an ideal of the National Socialist Man, the product of the New Order. There was some measure of truth to this, for Rommel had risen far higher and much faster in the Nazi-spawned Wehrmacht that he could have ever hoped to do in the Reichswehr; at the same time most of that rise was attributable to Hitler's patronage rather than any association with the National Socialist Party, which Rommel never joined and which he continued to scorn. The Nazis might try to take vicarious credit for Rommel's successes, but they could never truly claim him as one of their own.

On February 19, Rommel reported in person to Hitler in Berlin, where he was invited to a private dinner party with the Führer and a few other guests, among them Field Marshal Wilhelm Keitel, the chief of the O.K.W. and effectively Germany's Minister of War; Colonel General Alfred Jodl, the O.K.W. Chief of Staff; and Reichsführer-SS Heinrich Himmler, chief of the SS and the Gestapo. The topics of the ensuing table talk ranged widely, but to Rommel's discomfiture, became increasingly banal and unrealistic, most memorably a long diatribe of abuse heaped on Churchill by Hitler. It was not the nature of Hitler's commentary which disturbed Rommel—he would have hardly been surprised to learn that Churchill on occasion returned the compliment—but rather the sheer pointlessness of it all; he was even more surprised when Hitler's senior adjutant murmured to him in passing to take no note of it, as it was always thus at every meal.

Rommel was grateful to escape back to Wiener Neustadt the following day; he had secured a somewhat equivocal blessing from Hitler for his next offensive against the British—rather than encouraging Rommel to drive hard to take Suez, Hitler had merely enjoined him to tie down as many British divisions as possible in North Africa—along with a promise that Operation *Hercules*, an airborne attack on Malta, à la Operation *Mercury* on Crete in early 1941, would be staged as soon as it was practicable. With that he could now leave Berlin behind and enjoy three weeks together with his wife and son. Manfred, now 13, was going through a growth spurt and would soon, it appeared, be topping out his father. Lucie was thrilled and flattered by all of the attention being showered on her husband in the German press, and related to him how a recent radio concert had featured a series of six classical music selections whose composers' initials, the announcer explained, "spelled out the name of our popular hero, Colonel General Rommel." He enjoyed every moment spent in their company, but when the middle of March approached, he was ready to return to Africa—there was too much to do and now it seemed that there might not be enough time.

Back in Mechili on March 19, Rommel announced that the attack on the Gazala Line would begin at the end of May. The gleanings from his "little fellers" convinced him that Eighth Army's preparations were such that it would not be ready to begin its own offensive until sometime in late June, although there were intermittent reports from other sources that the attack would come much sooner, one putting the start date as Easter Monday, April 6. Rommel, certain that this was in error, went out on a personal reconnaissance that morning, taking only a single Panzer III as an escort. He heard the sound of distant artillery fire, but saw nothing—that is, until shells suddenly started bursting around his command vehicle. The unknown British gunners came within fractions of an inch of ending the Desert Fox's career then and there, as one shell exploded very close by and a splinter struck Rommel square in the midriff. Fortunately for him it was mostly spent, although he was left with a severe bruise the size of a soup plate. In a letter to Lucie written a few days later, he told her about the incident, remarking "It was finally stopped by my trousers! The luck of the devil!" It's doubtful Frau Rommel found it amusing.[158]

Nevertheless, his little foray to the front convinced him that no British attack was pending—his *fingerspitzengefühl*, the "feeling in his fingertips," that uncanny combat sense which he possessed, told him that the British were still far from ready. Even so, the uncertainty as they waited was a source of ever-growing anxiety for Rommel and his staff, for they were well aware that every additional day gave the British more time to prepare the Gazala defenses; Rommel's Ic, his intelligence officer, estimated that the British had already emplaced a half-million mines around the defensive boxes they were setting up along the Gazala Line.

The waiting grated on everyone's nerves, and Rommel sought distraction in the smallest doings back home in Wiener Neustadt. A less-than-stellar school report from Manfred's teachers earned them a broadside from the young man's father, the general. "This pupil does not make the slightest effort to cooperate in the physical exercises. He talks out loud and lacks discipline." Rommel, incensed, fired back: "You expect these teachers to have a grain of common sense. The school ought to be pleased and proud that it can number a son of mine among its pupils." Manfred did not get off scot-free, however: "Your teachers have had cause to complain about you. You must do your duty in all your subjects and behave properly. That is your main task in this war. I'm particularly pleased to hear that your Hitler Youth duty is to your liking. It will be of great value to you in later life." Upon turning 13 Manfred had undergone the mandatory enrollment in the Hitler Jugend; too young to understand the policies of National Socialism, he was more enthusiastic about his new uniform than any other part of the program.[159]

Meanwhile, General Crüwell returned from his convalescence about this time, but although he was reasonably healthy in body, in spirit he was a near-broken man. His young wife, just 34, died quite suddenly just days before he was to leave for Libya, and when he paid a courtesy visit to Frau Rommel before departing, he had, she informed her husband, the look of a man who had no longer had anything to live for save the next battle. Rommel did his best to keep Crüwell constructively occupied, but he, like the rest of Panzerarmee Afrika, had to play the waiting game.

Rommel had no choice but to wait, if his supply situation was to improve to the point where he could not only launch but also sustain a major attack. There was a noticeable betterment in that area after his return from leave: en route back to North Africa he had met with Field Marshal Albert Kesselring, the Luftwaffe's Commander-in-Chief South, who directed the

German air force's operations throughout the Mediterranean, to discuss the island of Malta. Sitting squarely between Italy and Tripolitania, it served as a base for Royal Navy cruisers, destroyers, and submarines, along with Royal Air Force bombers that wreaked havoc on the Italian supply convoys. Unless Malta was suppressed Panzerarmee Afrika could do no more than live hand-to-mouth; there would be no summer offensive.

Kesselring agreed, and soon German and Italian bombers set to with a will, hammering Malta daily, severely curtailing British naval and air operations from the island; almost immediately the number of supply ships reaching Tripoli began to rise, while the much smaller ports of Derna and Benghazi were put to use whenever possible. The Afrika Korps' supply dumps began to grow, though to nothing like the size which Rommel and his logistics staff would have preferred. For the remainder of March and all through April and early May, Rommel's letters to Lucie tell of an endless round of meetings, conferences, and planning sessions: there is a sense of "much sound and fury, signifying nothing." Rommel thoroughly enjoyed seeing his second African spring blossom: for little more than one month each year, the Libyan countryside in the Jebel Akhdar explodes in a profusion of color which has few equals anywhere in the world—such was its beauty that Rommel felt moved to capture it on film and shot several rolls of color movies, which he sent along to Lucie. But by the end of April, it had begun to fade, and the Western Desert again returned to its usual dun, buff, and gray hues. The clock was winding down now, and a sense of anticipation began to come over Rommel and his staff. Rommel himself gave voice to it in a short but thoughtful letter to Lucie written on May 12:

> Dearest Lu,
> Nothing much to report. Heat and lots of dust. The main road is a sea of pot-holes with the amount of traffic on it.
> There's a certain nervousness on our front. The British are expecting us and we them. One day the two forces will measure their strength. You'll hear about soon enough from the papers. We're all hoping that we'll be able to bring the war to an end this year. It will soon have lasted three full years.[160]

On the other side of the hill, Lieutenant General Neil Ritchie, officer commanding, Eighth Army, had problems and anxious moments of his own. The "Gazala Line" wasn't really a line as such, in that it was not a continuous series of trenches, dugouts, strongpoints, and bunkers. Rather, it was a series of "boxes" set up around brigade-strength formations organized for all-round defense, with the approaches to each covered by lengthy—and deep—barbwire entanglements and extensive minefields. The tactical concept was the each "box" would be manned with sufficient infantry and artillery, including antitank guns, to be able to hold off an attacker long enough for mobile reserves—armor and motorized infantry—to arrive and drive off the enemy. The wire and minefields were sited so as to channel any attacker toward these defensive boxes, denying him the opportunity to merely pass them by. In theory it was a sound concept, but to work in practice it required a degree of cooperation between armor and infantry that Eighth Army had yet to master—something the British Army would, in fact, never quite accomplish before the war's end. The right of the line was occupied by the 1st South African Division, while the 50th (Northumbrian) Infantry Division was positioned in the center. The Free French Brigade, which included a detachment of the French Foreign Legion, occupied the southernmost box in the line, at the oasis of Bir Hakim. Behind the line stood the 1st and 7th Armoured Divisions, with the 5th Indian Infantry Division in reserve, and the 2nd South African Division garrisoned Tobruk.

While there remained something to be desired in armor and infantry cooperation, Eighth Army had made great strides in improving the fire coordination between the infantry brigades and the Royal Artillery batteries that supported them. Likewise, Air Vice-Marshal Arthur Coningham, commander of the Desert Air Force, introduced new, more effective methods of calling in air support for ground units. American-built Curtis P-40 Kittyhawks were replacing worn out Hawker Hurricanes, much to the detriment of Fliegerkorps X's pilots and aircraft. Finally, Eighth Army had a nasty surprise for Rommel and the Afrika Korps: the British armored divisions started to re-equip with American-built M-3 "General Grant" tanks, which had a 75mm main gun which was more powerful than even the 75mm gun mounted on the Panzer IV.

Unlike Rommel, General Auchinleck was under considerable political pressure to get his attack underway as soon as possible. For once Churchill wasn't simply meddling in military affairs: it was imperative that Eighth Army drive the Germans and Italians out of Cyrenaica in order to gain some relief for Malta, which was reeling under Kesselring's aerial onslaught. Legitimate doubts were being raised as to whether the island could continue to hold out or would be forced to capitulate—with dreadful consequences for the Allies. The Prime Minister was blunt with Auchinleck, telling him in a cable from London that the loss of Malta ". . . would be a disaster of the first magnitude to the British Empire, and probably fatal in the long run to the defense of the Nile delta." Strategically, should Malta fall, the Germans and Italians would gain absolute aerial and naval supremacy, turning the Mediterranean into an Axis lake. Auchinleck understood this all too well; at the same time he also knew that beginning his own offensive prematurely could easily result in a disaster equal in magnitude to that of the loss of Malta. He pressed General Ritchie and Eighth Army as hard as he could, but he refused to go off half-cocked.[161]

ON MAY 26, 1942 the waiting came to an end when Rommel struck first. Before setting out, he dashed off an intriguing letter to Lucie, one that contained a touch of fatalism, a sense of destiny, and his love for her.

> Dearest Lu,
> By the time you get this letter you will have long heard from the Wehrmacht communiqués about events here. We're launching a decisive attack today. It will be hard, but I have full confidence that my army will win it. After all, they all know what battle means. There is no need to tell you how I will go into it. I intend to demand of myself the same as I expect from each of my officers and men. My thoughts, especially in these hours of decision, are often with you.[162]

At 2:00 P.M., four Italian infantry divisions, along with one brigade of German infantry and a handful of tanks, began moving toward the center of the Gazala Line. The advance was careful and deliberate, giving every indication of being a major attack, while the tanks scurried hither and yon, churning up as much dust as they could. Behind them, out of sight of the

British, spare aircraft engines mounted on truck beds fanned up even larger clouds of dust, which resembled nothing so much as an armored column on the move. It was all, of course, elaborate theater, staged for the benefit of General Ritchie, in an effort to persuade him to draw forces away from the southern end of the line, where on the morrow Rommel's real attack would go in.

Rommel's plan was to stage this feint in the center, then send the Afrika Korps on a long flanking maneuver south of the Bir Hakim oasis and its fortified box; the tanks of the Ariete Division would screen Bir Hakim as the 15th and 21st Panzer Divisions turned to the north to engage the British armored formations and cut off the whole of the Gazala Line from its base in Tobruk. Simultaneously, 90th Light Division was to move northeast, into its old stomping grounds around El Adem, and from there block any enemy effort to reinforce or resupply the British units in the Gazala position. While all of this was taking place, the Trieste Division would clear a route through the minefield north of Bir Hakim in order to open a supply route for the Axis armor. Once that had been accomplished, the combined German and Italian armored strength would take Ed Duda and Sidi Rezegh. The lion's share of Eighth Army would be cut off and trapped, and then could be defeated in detail. It was an ambitious plan, though not as complicated as at first it might sound, with a good probability of success.

A fascinating game of think–counterthink was about to be played out, as between them Auchinleck and Ritchie had decided that Rommel's plan would be the exact opposite of what in fact it was: they believed that any movement in the south would be a diversion while the main Axis attack would come in the center. Ritchie was not as thoroughly sanguine about this conclusion as was Auchinleck, however, and as a precaution he kept the 4th and 22nd Armored Brigades positioned so that they could support each other if in fact the Afrika Korps did make a major offensive move from the south, a decision that would catch Rommel off-guard and put him on his mettle as no one had ever done before.

Rommel got his panzer divisions moving at 9:00 P.M. on May 26, and just around dawn on the 27th, he took personal command of the Afrika Korps, just as it was meeting the first screen of British armored cars south of Bir Hakim. A signal flashed through Panzerarmee Afrika: *Rommel an der Spitze!*—"Rommel is taking the point!" The British scout cars raced to get out of the way of the advancing German tanks, one of them frantically signalling "Enemy tank columns moving toward us. It looks like it's the whole damned Afrika Korps!" Rommel's attack—*Fall Venezia*—was off to a good start. It was also the last part of the operation that went according to plan.[163]

Things started going awry almost immediately after the first contact with the British screening units. The 3rd Indian Motor Brigade, part of the 7th Armoured Division, had, without anyone on the Axis side of the lines noticing, moved into a position 4 miles southeast of Bir Hakim, and proceeded to dig in. Three precious hours were spent overrunning the brigade, which immobilized more than 50 panzers before it was finished, destroying 23 of them. The tanks of the Ariete Division got bogged down in the minefields around the Bir Hakim box, and the artillery of Free French Brigade, some 54 still-potent French 75s, began taking a heavy toll of them. The Ariete's commanding officer, General Giuseppe de Stefanis, continued to push his division forward, however, and drove off elements of the 4th Armoured Brigade and 7th Motorized, completing the encirclement of Bir Hakim. The Free French, who were well supplied with food and ammunition, would hold the oasis for 15 days until, subject to near constant aerial and artillery bombardment, and under attack by no fewer than four Axis divisions, a breakout would be planned for the night of June 10. Most of the Free French Brigade would escape, a significant moral victory, but far too late to influence the ultimate outcome of the larger battle.

While the battle around Bir Hakim was brewing up, the 15th Panzer, which was on the far right of the Afrika Korps' column, ran headlong into the 4th Armoured Brigade, and suffered a nasty shock when unfamiliar-looking British tanks began knocking out panzers at ranges from which the German tanks couldn't begin to reply. This was the Afrika Korps' first experience with the new Grant tanks armed with 75mm guns; they immediately proved to be highly unpopular with the German tank crews. The superior tactical flexibility of the panzer formations allowed the 15th Panzer to envelope the 4th Armoured Brigade, which was able to withdraw in good order nonetheless, falling back to El Adem, where it would spend the rest of the day.

By noon the Afrika Korps had advanced more than 25 miles, but when it ran into the 1st Armoured Division, it was halted in its tracks. The 1st

Armoured was no longer the hopelessly green unit Rommel had so badly mauled back in January, and its tank crews fought like the seasoned veterans they now were. The Grant tanks continued to be problematic, as at medium-to-long ranges it was all but impervious to the main guns of the Panzer IIIs and IVs, save for the handful of the latter that were armed with new, longer-barreled high-velocity 75mm cannons. The Germans' company and platoon tactics were superior to those of the British, which allowed them to offset somewhat the disparity in firepower and protection, but losses were heavy on both sides in this encounter, and for the moment Rommel's attack was stalled.

Echeloned back and to the right of the 15th Panzer was the 90th Light Division, which as the panzers turned northward, headed northeast toward El Adem, only to meet the 7th Motorised Brigade at Retma. It was a "diamond-cut-diamond" moment, as neither unit had any tanks or tracked vehicles, but both possessed enormous firepower. After a short but sharp fight, the 7th Motorised fell back on Bir el Gubi, and the 90th Light continued its advance. Not long afterward it encountered the headquarters section of the 7th Armoured Division, capturing some of its officers and scattering the rest, leaving the division essentially without leadership for two days until its commander, Brigadier Frank Messervy, could regroup his staff. Carrying on, the 90th Light reached El Adem that same day, captured a number of supply dumps, and set up housekeeping, as it were, waiting to drive off any reinforcements that might be coming out of Egypt. The next day, however, the 4th Armoured Brigade tumbled the 90th Light out of El Adem, which retired to the southwest, where it awaited further orders from Rommel.

Rommel, however, was in trouble. Ritchie refused to let himself be rattled by the Axis attack, and as soon as he had a reasonably clear picture of the situation, he began planning his response. His first counterattack began on May 28, and over the next five days he backed the Afrika Korps and the Ariete Division into a tactical and operational corner. Rommel's situation became precarious. He was only intermittently in contact with the rest of his army, cut off from his supply lines, caught between two of the fortified boxes—Sidi Muftah to the west, Knightsbridge to the east—a near-impenetrable minefield to the south, and four British armored brigades pressing hard on the Afrika Korps. General Crüwell's reconnaissance plane was shot down and Crüwell himself taken prisoner. By May 28, Rommel was almost undone by his own success: he had advanced too far too fast, and his supply lines had been cut behind him. Water was in critically short supply; his tanks were running on fumes, food and ammunition were nearly exhausted.

As sunset approached he decided the only course of action available was to concentrate the Afrika Korps in a central position, set up an all-round defensive perimeter, and then go look for the missing supply convoys himself. There were some 1,500 truckloads—almost 3,000 tons of supplies—sitting somewhere southwest of where he was standing; if he could find them, he could lead them through the minefield by following the same route he had taken earlier. He and his ADC, Leutnant Wilfred Armbruster, headed out into the desert in Rommel's Sdkfz 250 command vehicle *Greif* (Griffin), in search of the missing convoys; they found them around 4:00 A.M. With *Greif* in the lead, the convoy headed northeast, now shepherded by tanks from the Ariete and Trieste Divisions, toward the Afrika Korps. At one point the column blundered into a British reconnaissance patrol, which opened fire, but Rommel quickly veered off into the night and broke contact; by mid-morning the entire convoy was safely within the Afrika Korps' perimeter, bringing up enough fuel, ammunition, and rations for perhaps two days.

For the time being Rommel's panzers were back in action, but he was far from being out of the woods. After a quick conference with Gause, Westphal, and Bayerlein, where it was quickly recognized that the expected attack by Crüwell to relieve the Afrika Korps was not going to materialize, Rommel decided to make a virtue out of necessity and repositioned his two panzer divisions so that his southern and western flanks were covered by the British minefields, reducing the frontage his troops would have to cover to only the northern and eastern perimeter. To do so, however, the Afrika Korps would have to overpower the 150th Infantry Brigade, which was holding the Sidi Muftah box, sitting almost squarely in the middle of the Afrika Korps. Rommel set up formidable lines of antitank guns around his outer perimeter to hold off any British attacks and turned his armor and artillery inward. German sappers worked ceaselessly on May 29 and 30 to clear a path through the minefield—on the other side, Italian sappers were doing the same. If they succeeded, the Afrika Korps would have a secure line of supply and the rest of the Italian armor could move up in support.

The greatest weakness, though, in Rommel's current position was a lack of water—there had been no water bowsers in the supply convoy brought forward on May 29. This could well prove his downfall: when one of the prisoners captured in the Afrika Korps' advance, Major Archer-Shee of the 10th Hussars, complained to Rommel about water rations for POWs, Rommel replied that the major and his men were getting exactly the same water ration as the German soldier—Rommel included—exactly a half-cup a day. When Archer-Shee then asserted that if the Germans could not properly provide for captured enemy soldiers as required by the various Hague Conventions, then Rommel should allow Archer-Shee and his men to return to the British lines. Rommel demurred, but after a moment said to the major, "I agree that we cannot go on like this. If we don't get a convoy through tonight I shall have to ask General Ritchie for terms." All that would be necessary to force his capitulation was one more good, hard push by Eighth Army.[164]

It never came. Neil Ritchie had been unable to develop the same degree of coordination and flexibility among the units of Eighth Army that Erwin Rommel had created for first the Afrika Korps and then Panzerarmee Afrika as a whole. There was never that near-intuitive sense of knowing what a superior officer *wanted* to have accomplished as well as what he *needed* to have done. None of Ritchie's subordinates saw the opportunity which presented itself in Rommel's predicament or realized that the moment had come when Eighth Army could deliver a knock-out punch.

Even so, Rommel was now firmly ensconced, even trapped by some definitions, in what quickly became known as *der Hexenkessel*—the Cauldron. This was his "back to the wall" moment in this battle, which would forever define him as a military commander.

It was this point that the Luftwaffe's Field Marshal Albert Kesselring, the Commander-in-Chief South, suddenly appeared at Rommel's headquarters, flying into the Cauldron in his own Storch reconnaissance plane. His mission in North Africa, given to him personally by Hitler, was to see that Rommel got his supplies, something Kesselring's predecessor, Generalmajor Stefan Frölich, had been unable or unwilling to do. He was cheerful, eternally optimistic—some said overly optimistic—and widely known among his soldiers and airmen as "Uncle Albert" (it would be the Allies who would nickname him "Smiling Al" for his wide, ever-present grin). Most people accepted his constant air of bonhommie as genuine, though there were some who considered it to be a well-crafted act. Whatever the case may have been, his sudden appearance at the front had the potential to be both a disruption and distraction which Rommel most sorely did not need.

Instead, at the critical moment of the Afrika Korps' attack, Kesselring voluntarily placed himself and his staff at Rommel's disposal, despite being senior to Rommel, effectively replacing the missing Crüwell as commander of the Afrika Korps itself. He was appalled, though, by Rommel's style of command—rushing from unit to unit, crisis to crisis, leading supply convoys, always trying to be "*an der Spitze.*" Kesselring demanded a personal meeting with Rommel, the two generals coming face-to-face at the headquarters of the Italian XX Corps. Kesselring, who had served in the infantry in the First World War and in the Reichswehr before being transferred to the nascent Luftwaffe in 1934 and thus no stranger to combat, told Rommel that the overall plan appeared sound, but demanded that Rommel get hold of himself, his army, and the battle: this charging to and fro across the battlefield was accomplishing nothing. Rommel, almost in spite of himself, had to agree: he never really warmed to Kesselring, believing him to be a bit too personally ambitious, but in this case, the Luftwaffe field marshal was right.

On May 31, the attack on 150th Brigade's "box" at the center of the Cauldron began again, continuing into the next day. Despite being heavily bombed by the Luftwaffe, the defenders fought hard, often until their ammunition was exhausted, and what artillery they had was used to telling effect—that day General Gause, Rommel's Chief of Staff, and Colonel Westphal, his operations officer, were both badly wounded by mortar shells. Rommel's own description of the action is vivid:

> The attack was launched on the morning of the 31st May. German and Italian units fought their way forward yard by yard against the toughest British resistance imaginable. The defense was conducted with considerable skill and as usual the British fought to the last round. . . . Nevertheless, by the time evening came we had penetrated a substantial distance into the British positions. On the fol-

lowing day the defenders were to receive their quietus. After heavy dive-bomber attacks, the infantry again surged forward against the British field positions. I went forward with them. . . .[165]

The panzer divisions were relentless, and late in the afternoon on June 1, Rommel began to sense that the British had reached the breaking point. He instructed the commander of a *panzergrenadier* battalion to wave white flags to indicate that the Germans were willing to accept the British soldiers' surrender. Rommel was right—the British were through. Singly, then in pairs, then by squads and platoons, the 3,000 survivors of the 150th Brigade put down their weapons, raised their hands, and stepped out of the foxholes and dugouts, exhausted, hungry, thirsty—many were wounded, some seriously. With the elimination of the defensive box at the heart of the Cauldron, a 5-mile wide gap had been torn in the Gazala Line, ready for Rommel's two panzer divisions to go roaring through them on the way to Tobruk.

No one was roaring off anywhere just yet, however: 15th and 21st Panzer needed time to do basic maintenance on their tanks, repair minor damage, replenish their ammunition lockers, and top off their fuel tanks. This was all easier said than done, for the two corridors the Italians had painfully carved out of the minefields to the west of the Cauldron were still within range of several British artillery batteries, who kept up an intermittent, and occasionally heavy, fire that from time to time interrupted the movement of supplies into the Cauldron. It would be three or four days before the Afrika Korps was ready to roll again.

Believing that Rommel was contained and his losses significantly greater than in fact they were, Auchinleck imagined that his fangs were pulled, and pressed Ritchie to bring up the 5th Indian Division forward along the Via Balbia. Together with the 1st South African Division it could strike at the relatively immobile Italian infantry and possibly take Tmimi, even Mechili, completely severing the Axis supply line. Ritchie demurred, wanting to keep the 5th Division where it was. Here he made his first irrecoverable mistake of the battle, for, not realizing just how truly hard pressed was Rommel, his main concern at the moment was protecting Tobruk; instead of sending the 5th Division forward against the Afrika Korps, he set up more additional defensive boxes to cover the approaches to the fortress. It wasn't until June 4 that Ritchie realized Rommel was not going to suddenly lunge out of the Cauldron toward Tobruk, so he authorized the long-overdue attack to begin the following morning. He had waited just that little bit too long, however, for Rommel had not been idle.

While Ritchie was hesitating, the Pavia and Brescia Divisions, on the far side of the western minefield, had succeeded in clearing two routes through the mines, and now, with a reasonably secure supply line, Rommel could meet the British attacks with confidence. Ritchie sent two armored divisions and two independent armored brigades into the attack: they all ran into well-concealed lines of German antitank guns. The handful of Flak 88s still with the Afrika Korps were sufficient to take out the attacking Grants and the few Matildas still in the field; the standard 50mm Pak 38s were more than a match for any Crusaders or Honeys that came forward. The British losses were heavy—114 out of 150 tanks committed to the attack were destroyed, and another 4,000 prisoners were taken. Adding insult to injury, one of Rommel's counterattacks captured the tactical headquarters units of both British armored divisions. In the south, the garrison at Bir Hakim was grimly holding on, but the defenders' courage and tenacity might well be for nought, as in the center, Ritchie was rapidly running out of troops.

(On the second day of the British attack, far away in Wiener Neustadt, Lucie Rommel was opening parcels sent from North Africa with the admonition "Not to be opened until 6 June." This of course, was Lucie's birthday, and Erwin, always the *beau sabreur*, had sent her a collection of bracelets, bangles, and earrings carefully and intricately wrought by Arab craftsmen in Libya. Lucie was, of course, thoroughly delighted.)

When Ritchie's attacks faltered, Rommel counterattacked. The 21st Panzer and Ariete Divisions went east, the 15th Panzer north. Infantry, reconnaissance and artillery units were overrun, as well several headquarters detachments; command and control within Eighth Army began to break down. On June 6, the Trieste and Ariete Divisions, the 90th Light, and the reconnaissance elements of the 15th Panzer began a fresh attack on Bir Hakim; it would not relent until the Free French Brigade evacuated its positions the night of June 10. On June 12 the 2nd and 4th Armoured Brigades once again tried conclusions with the 15th Panzer Division and came off decidedly second best, being pushed back 6 miles from their starting positions and forced to leave all of their damaged vehicles behind, where the Germans and Italians could recover and repair them, and return them to service under new management. The next day it was the turn of the 22nd Armoured Brigade: by the end of the day, British tank strength had been reduced from approximately 300 to fewer than 70. These two defeats decided the outcome of the battle of Gazala, or as Auchinleck later put it, "This unsuccessful counterstroke was probably the turning point of the whole battle." The Knightsbridge box was abandoned by the Guards Brigade after nightfall, and the next morning Eighth Army began its withdrawal from the Gazala Line.[166]

IT WAS AT this point in the battle an incident occurred which shone a stark, revealing light on the character of Erwin Rommel, forever helping define the man for posterity. When the Afrika Korps overran the 150th Infantry Brigade, among a wealth of captured documents was found a copy of an order issued to the 4th Armoured Brigade, directing that no food or water be given to captured Axis soldiers until they had first been interrogated by British intelligence officers. This was a direct contravention of the Hague Conventions concerning the treatment of prisoners of war, and it infuriated Rommel. He instructed his signals section to send a message in the clear, stating that all British prisoners of war in Axis custody would be deprived of food and water indefinitely, or until such time as Eighth Army's order was rescinded. Within hours, a radio broadcast out of Cairo, also in the clear, announced that Eighth Army's order had been withdrawn. Rommel was satisfied; there would be no recurrence of this or any similar incident for the remainder of his time in Africa. Both sides had up to this point fought a clean, almost exemplary, war: atrocities and brutality which were taken for granted in the Balkans or on the Russian Front had no place in Erwin Rommel's war here in the Libyan desert, and he would not countenance their introduction. He recognized that slippery slope for what it was, and refused to take the first step down it—or allow his foes to do the same.

NOW IT WAS a race between the retreating Eighth Army and the Afrika Korps, as one hurried eastward before its line of retreat was blocked, and the other rushed north, trying to interpose itself across that line and prevent the enemy's escape. Meanwhile, the 90th Light Division was making straight for Tobruk. Once again Rommel painted an unforgettable word picture of what transpired:

> During the night of the 13th both divisions of the Afrika Korps were deployed . . . ready for an attack to the north. The Italian Ariete and Trieste Divisions were to act as a screen for their eastern flank. The 90th Light Division moved off to the east to put itself in a position for a quick grab at the Tobruk approaches. Next morning [June 14] the German panzer divisions moved off and rolled northwards. Full speed was ordered, as British vehicles were now streaming east in their thousands. I rode with the tanks and constantly urged their commanders to keep the speed up. Suddenly we ran into a wide belt of mines. Ritchie had attempted to form a new defense front and had put in every tank he had. The advance halted and our vehicles were showered with British armour-piercing shells. I at once ordered the reconnaissance regiments to clear lanes through the minefields, a task which was made easier by the violent sandstorm which blew up towards midday. Meanwhile, I ordered our 170mm guns to open fire on the Via Balbia. The thunder of our guns mingled with the shock of demolitions. The British and South Africans were blowing up their ammunition dumps in the Gazala Line. Late in the afternoon, the 115th Rifle Regiment moved to the attack against Hill 187. In spite of violent counterfire from British tanks, artillery and antitank guns the attack steadily gained ground. Towards five o'clock the British fire, to which my own vehicle had also for some hours been exposed, slowly began to slacken. Enemy resistance crumbled and more and more British troops gave themselves up. Black dejection showed on their faces.[167]

The coastal highway, the Via Balbia, could only support the traffic of a single division, and, given its proximity, the use of the road went to the 1st South African Division. This created a dilemma for the 50th (Northumbrian) Division, however: it could either find another route east to Egypt or wherever Eighth Army finally made its stand, or it could sit tight and wait to be taken prisoner *in toto* by the Italians. In the considered opinion of the division's commanding officer, Major General William Havelock Ramsden, surrender was unacceptable; instead, the division attacked to the southwest, moving out during a duststorm that allowed it to brush by the Brescia and Pavia Divisions. Once past the Italians, the division turned due south, hopped into its lorries and headed into the desert for nearly 50 miles before turning east to eventually catch up to the rest of Eighth Army, which, on Ritchie's orders, was now falling back all the way to Mersa Matruh in Egypt. Being badly understrength and depleted of equipment, the 50th Division would not take the field against the Afrika Korps again until November.

In Rommel's first letter to Lucie after the breakout from the Cauldron, written on June 15, he makes no effort to disguise his satisfaction at Eighth Army's debacle.

> Dearest Lu,
>
> The battle has been won and the enemy is breaking up. We're now mopping up encircled remnants of their army. I needn't tell you how delighted I am. We've made a pretty clean sweep this time. Of course it s cost us some sad losses here and there. Gause and West-phal have been wounded. Gause will be back in three to four weeks, Westphal in a month or two. My health has stuck it all right. I've been living in my car for days and have had no time to leave the battlefield in the evenings. Perhaps we will now see each other in July after all.[168]

Rommel wasted no time in launching his attack on Tobruk, determined that there would be no repeat of April 1941—and there would not. Indeed, almost everything had changed from the circumstances which obtained a year earlier. Lieutenant General William Gott, commanding XIII Corps, gave the task of conducting the defense of Tobruk to Major General Hendrik Klopper, whose 2nd South African Infantry Division was already posted inside the fortress. In addition to his own division, Klopper now had the 201st Guards, 11th Indian Infantry, 32nd Army Tank and 4th Antiaircraft Brigades under command. It remains unclear if Klopper thought he could repeat the nine-month stand made by Tobruk garrison in 1941, but in Auchinleck's opinion the fortress was now more of a strategic liability than an asset, primarily because the Royal Navy was unable to guarantee that it would be able to keep a garrison supplied. Auchinleck and his staff anticipated that Klopper and his men would have to hold out for two months at most, being gradually withdrawn by sea in the same way the Australians had been relieved in autumn 1941. He never imagined that Rommel would take Tobruk in less than two days.

For that matter, neither did Rommel. His window of opportunity, he knew, was narrow: the Luftwaffe bombers which had been providing close support for the Afrika Korps would soon no longer be available, as Kesselring would have to divert them to the upcoming attack on Malta. That support—or lack of it—could well be critical, so Rommel dusted off the plan so meticulously worked out a year earlier for the attack that had been preempted by *Crusader* and put it into motion. The orders went out on June 18 and the troops, tanks, and artillery moved into position the next day. Despite the urgency of the moment, Rommel and his staff had a good laugh that afternoon, when his artillery crews found all of their old positions from the previous year sitting empty and intact, often with stockpiles—thousands of shells—still sitting nearby. All that was necessary was to back the guns into place, dig them in, then sight and register them.

The assault began at first light on June 20, with a furious artillery barrage beginning at 05:30 A.M., followed by wave after wave of Stuka dive-bombers. Once the antitank ditch was bridged, the 15th Panzer Division took the lead through the three defensive lines around the town, Rommel in his *Greif* half-track following close behind, the rest of the Afrika Korps in his wake. The garrison was taken by surprise, Klopper apparently never having thought that Rommel would strike so hard so soon—the official record is unclear but it seems likely that Klopper believed he would have more time to prepare, expecting Rommel to be far more deliberate and methodical, setting up the sort of set-piece battle that had been planned for November 1941.

At 5:00 P.M. the 21st Panzer was on the outskirts of the town of Tobruk itself, and Rommel was standing atop a ridge, looking down into the harbor. Fighting continued throughout the night, but at dawn on June 21, Klopper faced reality squarely and ordered a white flag raised above his divisional headquarters; a total of 32,000 officers and other ranks—19,000 British, 10,500 South Africans and 2,500 Indians—were now prisoners of war. Tobruk had, at last, been taken by the Afrika Korps.

21 June 1942

Dearest Lu,

Tobruk! It was a wonderful battle. There's a lot going on in the fortress area. I must get a few hours' sleep now after all that's happened. How much I think of you.[169]

There was yet another moment, one that accompanied the capitulation of Tobruk, which showed the character of Erwin Rommel in very stark relief. As the 2nd South African Division was being marched into captivity, the white officers and NCOs began to vigorously protest when they learned that they would be compelled to share the prisoner of war compounds with their black soldiers. In their minds the strict rules of apartheid should be maintained no matter what the circumstances. Rommel, at once amused and infuriated, informed the white South Africans that the "blek" soldiers worn the same uniform and had fought alongside their nominal white superiors: to him they were all the same, and would be treated as equals; the matter was closed.

There was always a streak of showmanship in Rommel, but he was never given over to elaborate theatricality. Orders of the Day were the exception rather than the rule in Panzerarmee Afrika—Rommel considered them bombastic and pretentious. Yet there were certain moments when one was not only appropriate, but the occasion all but demanded it, and the capture of Tobruk was one such moment for Rommel and his men. Accordingly, on June 22, he issued a special Order of the Day to his panzer army:

Soldiers! The great battle in the Marmarica has been crowned by your quick conquest of Tobruk. We have taken in all over 45,000 prisoners and destroyed or captured more than 1,000 armored fighting vehicles and nearly 400 guns. During the long hard struggle of the last four weeks, you have, through your incomparable courage and tenacity, dealt the enemy blow upon blow. Your spirit of attack has cost him the core of his field army, which was standing poised for an offensive. Above all, he has lost his powerful armor. My special congratulations to officers and men for this superb achievement. Soldiers of the Panzer Army Afrika! Now for the complete destruction of the enemy. We will not rest until we have shattered the last remnants of the British Eighth Army. During the days to come, I shall call on you for one more great effort to bring us to this final goal.

ROMMEL.[170]

The speed with which Tobruk had been taken astonished everyone, and especially dismayed the British. Churchill experienced a severe political setback, as he had earlier expressed his certainty that no matter what the outcome of the battle of Gazala, Tobruk would stand resolute and defiant, just as it had done in 1941. Instead, the number of soldiers captured at Tobruk constituted the second largest capitulation by British forces in the entire war, exceeded only by those lost in the surrender of Singapore. In the House of Commons a vote of "No confidence" in Churchill's conduct of the war was called; if the motion passed, he would no longer be prime minister. The motion failed, but the message was clear: there must be no more such disasters for Great Britain.

All of Germany was jubilant at the news, of course. Dr. Göbbels and his henchmen immediately set about extracting the maximum propaganda from it, while Hitler, casting about for a way to show his esteem for one of his favorite soldiers, promoted Rommel to the rank of *feldmarschall*. At the age of 49, he was the youngest field marshal in the German Army, and one of the youngest in the entire history of German arms. Naturally, the promotion was meat and drink to Rommel's vanity, but at the same time it was something of a hollow honor. Despite the hopes he expressed in his letter to Lucie, it would be September before he could return to Germany and so be able to receive his marshal's baton from Hitler's hands. When he did so, after the presentation ceremony, his only comment to Lucie would be to murmur, "I would rather he had given me one more division."[171]

CHAPTER TEN

AFRICAN APOGEE

Never let the enemy pick the battle site.
—GEORGE S. PATTON, JR.

T he victory at Gazala followed by the capture of Tobruk was absolutely
exhilarating for Rommel, and electrified the whole of Panzerarmee
Afrika. There were still battles to be fought and much work to be done,
however, and Rommel, being Rommel, was not about to let any desert
scrub grow under his boots. While the temptation to pause, to linger a
moment and savor the triumph was strong, the reality of the situation was
that the Eighth Army was on the run, and the need to maintain the pressure
was paramount. The British could be given no opportunity to pause, catch
their collective breath, and reorganize themselves. On June 24, Axis tanks
rolled through Sidi Barrani, down the coast road, and across the frontier;
two days later a two-pronged attack by the Afrika Korps and the Ariete
Division was surrounding the coastal town of Mersa Matruh even as the
British were evacuating the fortress there.

Mersa Matruh, roughly 100 miles inside Egypt and sitting astride the
coastal road as it ran along the Mediterranean shoreline, was the position
to which General Ritchie had ordered the Eighth Army to fall back when
the Gazala Line fell apart. The border itself was, in his opinion, indefensible: there was too much room to maneuver, and while Rommel's panzers
had suffered serious losses in the Cauldron, the Eighth Army's armored
formations had been reduced to just a few score running tanks, not enough,
in Ritchie's opinion, to conduct a proper defense across a broad frontage—
whatever infantry was actually holding the ground would be defeated in
detail. Worse, the Eighth Army had been forced to leave behind hundreds
of tanks and trucks that had been knocked out but were repairable—or
could at least supply spares for other vehicles under repair—meaning that

the Eighth Army could not turn to its repair shops to make good some of the losses: whatever tanks Ritchie had to hand were all that he *would* have, period. The other side of that coin had all of those abandoned vehicles now in German and Italian hands: the *panzerarmee* was exceedingly grateful for this, as by now almost half its transport was British-built.

It was Ritchie's considered judgment that at Mersa Matruh, where the rough terrain to the south significantly reduced the frontage his forces would have to cover, could be held, presenting Rommel with an obstacle the Panzerarmmee's commander could neither bypass nor overrun. In the 1930s, Mersa Matruh had been developed into a strong defensive position, something of a British reply to Tobruk; there were minefields, antitank obstacles, barbwire entanglements and a ring of strongpoints and bunkers surrounding the coastal town. Ritchie was confident that, even despite having fewer than 100 tanks, he would be able to stop the Axis army, itself steadily weakening, once and for all. Now, however, as the Rommel's two panzer divisions, along with the Ariete, Brescia, and Trento Divisions pushed forward, a confusion of orders caused some British units to stand fast, while others rushed pell-mell eastward, and for a few hours chaos reigned as Allied and Axis units became hopelessly intermingled. British, Indian, and New Zealand infantry battalions, artillery batteries and tank regiments wove around, behind, and sometimes through their German and Italian counterparts in a mad dash toward a railroad siding 60 miles west of Alexandria, the spot where the Eighth Army would make its last stand, identified on the maps as El Alamein.

That the British weren't stopping at Mersa Matruh as originally planned was due to Auchinleck's decision to relieve Neil Ritchie of command of the Eighth Army on June 25. Ritchie's appointment as commander of the Eighth Army was supposed to have been temporary, but in the wake of *Crusader*, he was allowed to retain his post. His plans and deployments on the Gazala Line had been intelligent and realistic, but ultimately needed someone more dynamic to make them successful: at the critical moment in *der Hexenkessel*, Ritchie decided that not losing the battle was more important than winning it, failing to press home a crucial attack in favor of protecting Tobruk. When Prime Minister Churchill publicly declared the loss of Tobruk a "disgrace," time had run out for Ritchie as the officer commanding, Eighth Army.[172]

Rommel, meanwhile, was bristling with energy. This was Matajur all over again, on an epic scale! He had a numerically superior but demoralized enemy on the run, while not 100 miles distant lay the greatest strategic prize in all of North Africa—Alexandria. With "Alex" in the bag, Cairo and the Suez Canal would be as good as taken, and with its loss the entire British strategy for the Mediterranean would come crashing down. In his letters to Lucie during these days, the sense of restlessness, of the need to "get on with it," is unmistakable.

23 June 1942

Dearest Lu,

We're on the move and hope to land the next big punch very soon. Speed is the main thing now. The events of the past weeks lie behind me like a dream. Gause is back again. He still looks thoroughly exhausted, but he just couldn't stick it any longer back at the rear. I'm very well, sleeping like a log.

26 June 1942

Dearest Lu,

We've made a good move forward in the last few days and are hoping to launch our attack on the enemy remnants today. For days now I've been camping out in the car with Gause. Food has been good all the time but washing has suffered. I've had my headquarters by the sea for the past twenty hours and went swimming yesterday and today. But the water doesn't refresh, it's much too hot. A lot to do. Cavallero and Rintelen are coming today, probably to put the brakes on, so far as they can. These beggars don't change!

27 June 1942

Dearest Lu,

We're still on the move and hope to keep it up until the final goal. It takes a lot out of one, of course, but it's the chance of a lifetime. The enemy is fighting back desperately with his air force.

P.S. Italy in July might still be possible. Get passports!

Such was his almost boyish exuberance that even those who came to him with unhappy tidings were infected with his optimism. On June 26 Field Marshal Kesselring and Marshal Cavallero came forward to meet Rommel, the German airman to inform his colleague that, with Tobruk having been taken, the Luftwaffe's air support for the *panzerarmee* would be drastically curtailed as Fliegerkorps X readied itself for the coming invasion of Malta; Cavallero was there to inform Rommel that Mussolini had expressly forbidden him to take Italian units across the Egyptian border. Rommel heard both men out, then dismissed their concerns, not with contempt but with an air of assuredness, telling them, "If my Panzer Army succeeds in breaking through the enemy's line today, by June 30 we'll be in Cairo or Alexandria." So certain did he seem that both Kesselring and Cavallero came away convinced of it. Nor was this merely wishful thinking on Rommel's part, as he had sound intelligence to back up his optimism: one of the last "little fellers" Rommel would receive made it clear that a something very near to panic was overtaking Alexandria. Embassies were being evacuated, coding machines and communications equipment were being destroyed, official documents which could not be removed in time were being burnt, and all non-essential soldiers and civilians—with probably a leavening of essential ones as well—were trying to get out of Alexandria and Cairo.[173]

Rommel wasn't having it all his own way, however. On June 24, just as his division was entering Sidi Barrani, General Ettore Balsassare, one of the few senior Italian officers Rommel truly admired, because the man was a determined fighter and an efficient leader, was killed during a Royal Air Force bombing raid on the town. With the Germans and Italians overrunning its airfields during the battle of Gazala, the Desert Air Force had been rendered pretty much ineffectual, but now that its fighters and medium bombers were operating from airfields inside Egypt, and with the Luftwaffe's attention being increasingly diverted to Malta, the Royal Air Force was making its presence felt once again. The speed of the advance was also taking a toll on the men and machines of the Afrika Korps, along with the handful of Italian motorized units. Of more concern was the dwindling number of tanks and fit men available to him. When Mersa Matruh was taken, the whole of Panzerarmee Afrika had 47 serviceable tanks; there were fewer than 2,500 men fit for duty.

Ultimately even more detrimental to Rommel's fortunes was the degree of his own success. The fall of Tobruk had knocked the Axis strategy for the summer of 1942 into a cocked hat. In March, when Rommel secured Hitler's permission for a summer offensive against the British, he had been adamant that, concurrent with any attack on Tobruk, there had to be an invasion of Malta, so that the single greatest threat to the *panzerarmee's* supply line from Italy could be eliminated once and for time. In this he was firmly seconded by the Luftwaffe commander for the whole of the Mediterranean, Field Marshal Albert Kesselring. Kesselring's endorsement was of no small significance, for while he and Rommel were often able to work together in something akin to harmony, there was no love lost between the two men personally. Kesselring thought Rommel too impulsive and moody, Rommel felt Kesselring to be ambitious and somewhat malleable morally. Both men were, of course, right. But given this background, with Rommel and Kesselring in agreement, Hitler was nearly persuaded; when Grand Admiral Karl Räder, who was still commanding the German navy, added his endorsement to the idea, Hitler had no real option but to agree. Thus Operation *Hercules*—*Unternehmen Herakles*—was born.

Similar in concept to the abortive Operation *Sea Lion*, Hercules was to begin with the Luftwaffe neutralizing the island's air and naval defenses. Then the 7th Fallschirmjäger (Paratroop) Division would secure landing areas for one German and two Italian infantry divisions and a small contingent of tanks. Hitler, though, was never too keen on the entire concept, having been unsettled by the high casualties suffered by the 7th Fallschirmjägers during the invasion of Crete. He repeatedly made excuses to put off authorizing *Hercules*, even though Kesselring and his staff had already completed the planning and the troops designated for the assault had begun training for it. Rommel and especially Kesselring continued to press for the operation to go forward, however, citing the strategic necessity of removing this British threat sitting right astride the shipping lanes between Italy and Tripoli.

But the speed with which the British had been tumbled out of the Gazala Line and Tobruk was taken, coupled with an offhand remark by Rommel to the effect that he had captured enough fuel and supplies to take Panzerarmee Afrika all the way to Cairo, convinced Hitler that there was no longer any need to invade Malta; Kesselring's bombers hammered the island, briefly reducing it to near-impotence, but Operation *Hercules* never materialized. It would prove to be an enormous blunder, for a few months hence, at one of the most critical moments of the entire North African campaign, Allied air- and sea-power based on Malta would intervene to cripple Rommel's panzers.

In the meantime, Claude Auchinleck gathered up the reins of the Eighth Army himself. There would be no stand at Mersa Matruh, as in his considered judgment the front was still too broad and his divisions would be spread too thin to prevent Rommel from punching through them, or else swinging around their southern flank as he had done at Gazala. He fought a series of delaying actions to buy time as the Eighth Army fell back to a new defensive line just west of El Alamein, an unprepossessing railroad siding sitting on the Mediterranean coast. What made the Alamein position so attractive was that just 40 miles inland the bottom of the desert fell out as an impossibly steep 600-foot escarpment gave way to the northern-most reach of the Qattara Depression, a vast, impassable expanse of dry lakes, soft sand, salt marshes, and scrubland. Thus a natural choke point for any army advancing into Egypt from the west was created: it would be impossible to outflank any defensive line which was anchored on the Depression. If Rommel was going to take Cairo, he would have to go *through* Eighth Army, not around it.

Rommel, of course, continued to give Auchinleck reason to want to minimize the Afrika Korps' ability to maneuver. On June 27 the 2nd New Zealand Division and the 50th Infantry Division, just arrived back in the fold after its jaunt across the desert after Gazala, were almost cut off from the rest of Eighth Army by the 21st Panzer and 90th Light Divisions. The officers and other ranks of the 50th Division, who were becoming old hands at this sort of thing, promptly mounted up and drove eastward as fast as they could, slipping the noose before the 90th Light could reach the coast, but the Kiwis were not so lucky. The 21st Panzer was able to swing behind their position at the oasis of Mingar Qaim, almost completely surrounding the 2nd Division. The early hours of June 28 saw a short, sharp melee of rifles, pistols, grenades, and bayonets, as the New Zealanders shot and thrust their way through the 21st Panzer, rejoining the rest of Eighth Army later that day.

Though the action was over in less than 15 minutes, the breakout had unexpected and potentially serious consequences, as a German aid station had been directly in the path of the charging Kiwis. Several German medical personnel and some wounded German soldiers—an accurate number has never been determined—were killed in the rush, some shot, others bayoneted. In a war where both sides routinely demonized their opponents, it was not long before the word spread that the Kiwis had committed a war crime, and Göbbels' propaganda hacks were soon calling them "gangsters." Rommel was furious, in no small part because he felt that such conduct should have been beneath soldiers he had once described as "the elite of the British Army," and threatened reprisals on captured New Zealanders if such practices continued. An explosive situation was eventually defused when Rommel came face-to-face with Brigadier George Clifton, the senior New Zealand POW. Clifton, speaking with a soldier-to-soldier bluntness which Rommel appreciated, regretted that the incident ever occurred, but made the point that it had been a nighttime attack, lit only by muzzle and grenade flashes and the flames of burning vehicles: the New Zealanders could not have known they were attacking a medical unit until it was already too late. Rommel, who had seen his share of nighttime actions go awry, accepted Clifton's explanation and the furor was allowed to gradually fade away.[174]

Though the 50th Infantry Division had escaped when the 90th Light Division reached the coast east of Mersa Matruh, the Germans were now sitting astride the coast road and blocking the retreat of X Corps, composed now of brigade groups from four different divisions. Auchinleck ordered the corps to follow the 2nd New Zealand Division's example and force a way through the Germans, but the brigade movements were poorly coordinated, leading to the 29th (Indian) Infantry Brigade being nearly destroyed, losing more than 6,000 troops and 40 tanks. Huge supply dumps were abandoned at Mersa Matruh, falling, naturally, into the hands of the Germans and Italians, allowing the *panzerarmee* to maintain its momentum a bit longer.

These captured supply dumps were utterly invaluable to Panzerarmee Afrika, as it had completely outrun the capabilities of its supply services for the time being. The Axis effort in North Africa had always operated in a more-or-less hand-to-mouth effort; there is most definitely no record anywhere of Rommel remarking on a surfeit of men, equipment, or materiel— especially fuel. But the additional 400 miles added to the Axis supply line since the fall of Tobruk pushed an already faltering logistical system to its breaking point. Tobruk, Benghazi, and Sidi Barrani would never achieve their full potential as supply ports for Rommel and his men; even had they done so, their capacities were so small that they would have only eased the problem somewhat, rather than eliminated it. In a way reminiscent of Bonaparte's policy of making the enemy pay for his wars, or even, ironically, the Barbary freebooters of the eighteenth century, Rommel was, for the time being, dependent on plundering enemy supplies—he frequently refers to captured "booty" in his diaries and letters—to keep his army in the field and fighting.

The men of the Afrika Korps and the Italian divisions had been in near-constant action now for five weeks. Exhaustion was beginning to take its toll among all ranks, and the sick lists were growing, especially with cases of jaundice and dysentery. The Axis momentum was dwindling, like a pendulum reaching the end of its arc: the moment of stasis was rapidly approaching, though Rommel was doing his best to ward it off. His own drive and enthusiasm never faltered, at least not yet.

> 30 June
>
> Dearest Lu,
> Mersa Matruh fell yesterday, after which the Army moved on until late in the night. We're already 60 miles to the east. Less than 100 miles to Alexandria![175]

So what compelled Rommel push himself and his men so hard? There are several explanations, all of them offered with varying determination over the years, most of them to some degree facile: Rommel's feeble grasp of logistics led him to overstretch Panzerarmee Afrika; Rommel was out of his depth at this command level, still leading his army as if it were a battalion in the Italian Alps; Rommel's vanity fueled his need to accrue personal glory, blinding him to military realities; Rommel was a near-reckless gambler who was unable to rein himself in.

The real answer is supplied by Rommel himself, and works on a much deeper level than any other explanation. In his own words,

> I was determined at all costs to avoid giving the British any oppor-

tunity of creating another new front and occupying it with fresh formations from the Near East. . . . Our intention was to overtake the Eighth Army's formations by a lightning thrust forward and bring them to battle before they had been able to join up with other formations from the Middle East. If we could once succeed in destroying the tattered remnants of the Eighth Army which had escaped from the Gazala battles, plus its two fresh divisions, and this was by no means impossible, then the British would have nothing left in Egypt capable of opposing our advance to Alexandria and the Suez Canal.[176]

"Alexandria and the Suez Canal." Those five words explain everything. They were the glittering prizes of the North African campaign, and Rommel saw that clearly. *Crusader* had demonstrated that merely maintaining Italy's position in North Africa, the mission originally given to Rommel and the Afrika Korps, was irrelevant: the reason why the British had driven the Italians out of Cyrenaica in early 1941 was because three months previously, the Italians had threatened, however ineffectually, the British hold on Alexandria and the Suez Canal. That was why he had been driven across Libya in November and December 1941: it had not been merely to retake essentially useless territory, rather he had been perceived as a threat to the canal, and therefore must needs be repulsed; the British were compelled to honor any threat to the Suez.

Now, incredible as it might seem, Rommel and his army were poised to offer the greatest threat to the canal that had ever been presented. Bonaparte once observed that "In war there is but one favorable moment; the great art is to seize it." Rommel now saw his great moment, an opportunity to hand the British not merely a decisive defeat, but a critical one. Alexandria's port facilities were literally irreplaceable for the British, while denial of access to the Mediterranean via the canal would impose a shift in Allied grand strategy worldwide. It was an opportunity that would never again present itself, Rommel understood this perfectly well: the Allies' capacity to reinforce, re-equip, and resupply far exceeded that of Germany and Italy; Eighth Army could only grow stronger while Panzerarmee Afrika could only weaken. Pausing back at the frontier or at Sidi Barrani to rebuild his strength and restore his forces, as critics then and now have suggested he should have done, would have only accelerated that imbalance. If Rommel was to take Alexandria and the Suez Canal, he had to strike now. He had no other choice—anything less would have been tantamount to an admission not only of defeat, but of purposelessness. Erwin Rommel had already lived through one war where too many men died in the service of a losing cause. He would, if fate permitted, never be part of another.

And that is the deeper level on which rested Rommel's decision to keep attacking even after Tobruk was taken. No truly great commander seeks war in perpetuity, all fight to bring an end to the war at hand: only a madman seeks to make war for its own sake. Erwin Rommel wanted the war with Britain and America to come to an end: his "favorable moment," if he could bring it about, had the power to change the entire paradigm of the war in the Mediterranean and compel the Allies to consider resorting to the negotiating table. It was to this end that he pushed forward every man in the *panzerarmee* to the point of exhaustion, none of them harder than he pushed himself. All that was needed now was one final rush that would put paid to Eighth Army once and for all; the British literally could retreat no further without conceding defeat. The decisive battle of the North African campaign, Rommel was certain, would be fought at El Alamein. He was absolutely right.[177]

EL ALAMEIN WOULD only ever have one moment on the world stage, because, like other places where Churchill's "hinge of fate" also turned, such as Gettysburg, the Mont Saint Jean ridge, Guadalcanal, or the Gallipoli peninsula, El Alamein itself was and would remain thoroughly unremarkable. As the cornerstone of a defensive position, however, the Duke of Wellington himself would have found much to commend it. It sat on the Mediterranean shore, with no right flank to turn, its railroad siding greatly simplified supply problems, while some 10 miles due south sits the 8-mile long Ruweisat Ridge, low, rocky, ideal for covering and concealing large numbers of infantry guns and tanks. The ridge runs almost due east-to-west, and has the natural effect of channeling any attack in its direction to the north or south of it, while any forces positioned in the ridge itself remain poised as a threat to the flank of such an attack. Another 10 miles on into the desert was the Deir el Munnasib depression, not a feature to be held by defenders, but yet another terrain obstacle that by its near-impassability dictated the line of advance to any local attack. Finally, another 10 miles to the south lay the impassable escarpment that marked the beginning of the Qattara Depression. Apart from Sollum and the Halfaya Pass at the Egyptian frontier, no finer defensive position existed anywhere between Alexandria and Tripoli.

Auchinleck was counting on this fact, counting on adding the natural strength of the Alamein position to Eighth Army's, buying him time bring up further reinforcements, reorganize broken divisions, and build up his armored strength in order to turn the tables on Rommel and go over to the attack himself. The defensive potential of the El Alamein line had been recognized by the British Army even before the war began, and some desultory efforts at constructing three large defensive boxes along the line had begun in 1940, one at El Alamein, another southwest of the Ruweisat Ridge, and the third down near the edge of the Qattara Depression, although only limited progress had been made in completing any of them. Now every soldier who could lift a sandbag, swing a pickaxe, or lay a landmine was working like a beaver to finish them. Divisions, brigades, and battalions began arriving willy-nilly from Gazala, the action around Tobruk, and Mersa Matruh, and Auchinleck thrust them into the El Alamein line wherever he could find a slot for them—once he was confident he had a stable front facing Rommel, he began sorting them out. The 10th Infantry Division, 1st South African Division, and 5th Indian Divison—grouped together as XXX Corps—held the right of the line, while the 2nd New Zealand and 5th Indian Divisions—XIII Corps—stood on the left, both corps strongly supported by as much artillery as Auchinleck could muster. It was his armor that caused him the most concern, as both the 1st and 7th Armoured Divisions were at less than brigade strength, with just over 100 tanks between them at the moment, though Auchinleck knew that at least 300 new Sherman tanks, courtesy of the United States Army, were on their way to Alexandria. Faster, more rugged and reliable, better armored and just as heavily armed as any panzer the Afrika Korps had in the field, these tanks promised to be game-changers for Eighth Army, hence Auchinleck's determination to buy time for their arrval.

Rommel understood what Auchinleck was attempting, and as one professional regarding the work of another, he approved:

More and more British tanks and guns were arriving at the front. General Auchinleck . . . was handling his forces with very considerable skill and tactically better than Ritchie had done. He seemed to view the situation with decided coolness, for he was not allowing himself to be rushed into accepting a "second best" solution by any moves we made. This was to be particularly evident in what followed,[178]

"What followed" was that on July 1, the understrength and weary Afrika Korps along with the 90th Light Division carried out Rommel's first attack on the El Alamein line. For once fuel was not a pressing issue, but water and ammunition were, and the limits of both would to some degree dictate Rommel's tactics. The two divisions of the Afrika Korps, the 15th and 21st Panzer, were to move through a gap in the minefields between the defensive box at El Alamein and the Deir el Abyad, a small depression southwest of Alamein. Once past the Abyad, the Afrika Korps would turn right and fall on the rear echelons of XIII Corps, while the 90th Light turned due north, heading straight for the coastal road. As soon as the 90th Light was in position, the division would attack the El Alamein box from the west, driving defenders—in this case the 1st South African Division—straight into the 90th Light's waiting ambush. The Ariete and Trieste Divisions would contain the defenders in the center and southern boxes while the Littorio Armored Division, only recently arrived in North Africa, covered the Afrika Korps' left flank.

Almost from the outset, everything went wrong. Given that Gazala had begun on a similarly discordant note, that might have been seen as a good sign, but it was not to be. The 90th Light moved east as ordered but veered slightly to the north as it did, running into the South Africans and quickly becoming pinned down by enemy artillery. A sandstorm prevented the 15th and 21st Panzers from moving out on time, and when they did begin their advance, they almost immediately came under heavy attack by medium bombers of the Desert Air Force. Kesselring's redeployment of Fliegerkorps X to focus all of its energies on subjugating Malta was now hurting the Afrika Korps; the Royal Air Force had nothing close to air supremacy, but for the moment it was able to achieve local air superiority almost as a matter of course. It might all be worth it if Malta were taken, but by now even

Kesselring began to see how Hitler was using every new success of Rommel's, no matter how minor, as proof that *Hercules* was unnecessary.

When the two panzer divisions finally got rolling, they moved out smartly past the Deir el Abyad as planned. But behind the Abyad was a smaller depression called the Deir el Shein, which was supposed to be unoccupied. Here Germans got their first surprise, running headlong into the 18th Indian Infantry Brigade. Rommel's Ic, Colonel von Mellenthin, had no idea it was there, and understandably so, for the brigade had been rushed to Egypt from Iraq, taking up its position late on June 28. The Indians stood their ground and fought hard, with the remnant of the 1st Armoured Division coming up in support, but eventually the 18th Brigade was overrun and the Deir el Shein taken, though at a cost Rommel could ill-afford: a quarter of the Afrika Korps' remaining armored strength was taken out of action; at the end of the day, the two panzer divisions could muster fewer than 40 tanks between them.

Rommel was getting desperate now. For the next two days he kept up the attack on the western end of the Ruweisat Ridge, but accomplished nothing. On July 5 XIII Corps counterattacked on the Afrika Korps' southern flank, the usual slightly ponderous, overly deliberate attack which the Germans and Italians had been routinely decimating over the previous 20 months: this time they were barely able to bring it to a halt. The near-constant presence of British bombers and fighter-bombers overhead only exacerbated the problems: between July 2 and July 5, the Royal Air Force flew more than 2,000 sorties against Panzerarmee Afrika, continuing to erode Axis strength.

Even the name "Panzerarmee Afrika" began to ring hollow, as between them the German and Italian armored divisions had fewer than 100 operational tanks, while the average infantry strength of each division was just 1,500 effectives. As much as the British, the conditions of the desert were wreaking havoc on Rommel's officers and men: fatigue, poor diet, marginal sanitary conditions, flies in their millions, all were sapping what physical and moral strength remained. Non-battle casualties to dysentery and jaundice, the latter having already once laid Rommel himself low, were equaling losses in combat.

The euphoria that had swept over Rommel after the fall of Tobruk had evaporated, its place taken by a darkening realism. His letters to Lucie in these days stand in stark and startling contrast to those written just a week earlier, showing how far and how rapidly Rommel's situation had unraveled.

3 July 1942

Dearest Lu,

One loses all idea of time here. The struggle for the last position before Alexandria is hard. I've been up in the front area for a few days, living in the car or a hole in the ground. The enemy air force gave us a bad time. However, I hope to manage it. Heartfelt thanks for your many dear letters.

4 July

Unfortunately, things are not going as I should like them. Resistance is too great and our strength exhausted. However, I still hope to find a way to achieve our goal. I'm rather tired and fagged out.

5 July

We're going through some extremely critical days. But I'm hoping to see them through. Gause is in trouble again with concussion (shell burst) and Bayerlein will probably have to replace him for a while. Our buildup of strength is very slow. It's not easy to have to hold on like this, only 60 miles from Alexandria. But it, too, will pass.[179]

But it didn't pass. On July 10, Auchinleck opened a limited attack along the coast road, at a small ridge known as Tel el Eisa, directed specifically at the Italian Sabratha Division, and for the next six days, the fighting along the ridge would be near non-stop, ending only on July 16 with one final lunge to take the ridge by the 26th Australian Brigade. This action dismayed Rommel for two reasons: it marked the beginning of Auchinleck's new strategy of pressing the Italian units as hard as possible, because he was convinced that they were suffering from low morale (not true) and that the Germans alone lacked the strength to hold on to their side of the line at El Alamein (quite true)—"writing down" Italian troop strength would only make the Afrika Korps itself weaker in relation to Eighth Army. Rommel had no way to counter this. More devastating, however, was the loss of Leutnant—now Hauptmann—Seebohm's radio intercept unit in the early hours of the attack. The intelligence which Seebohm had consistently and accurately provided had been literally priceless, and with the loss of See-bohm and his unit, Rommel's single best intelligence source vanished.

The initiative was now, at least temporarily, in Auchinleck's hands, and his next attack on the Italians began on July 14, in the center of the Alamein line, where the Pavia and Brescia Divisions were digging in opposite the west end of Rusweisat Ridge. Bungled communications and poor coordination between armor and infantry left two New Zealand brigades exposed to a counterattack by the Italians, who forced the surrender of one complete battalion that had been stranded on a ridgeline. Auchinleck ordered the 2nd and 22nd Armoured Brigades to move up to support the New Zealanders; General der Panzertruppe Walther Nehring, who had taken command of the Afrika Korps when Crüwell was captured at Gazala, sent in his two panzer divisions to attack the British armor. For three days the fight for the western end of Ruweisat Ridge raged back and forth, until on the evening of July 16, Nehring acknowledged that the Afrika Korps was overmatched and withdrew.

There was a flaw in Auchinleck's new strategy, however, that could have harsh consequences for his soldiers should he press it too hard: assuming that the Italians were demoralized and easy pickings was a mistake, which the 9th Australian Division, the heroes of the defense of Tobruk in 1941, learned to its regret. A night attack against the Trento and Trieste Divisions, after some initial success, was bloodily repulsed, one entire battalion of Australian infantry being overrun in a counterattack by troops of the Trento. It was incidents like these which caused Rommel, who took an almost childish glee in puncturing the pretenses of senior Italian officers and officials, and who would later be accused of blaming all of his ills in North Africa on poor showing of the Italian Army, to most emphatically assert

> . . . that the defeats which the Italian formations suffered at El Alamein in early July were not the fault of the Italian soldier. The Italian was willing, unselfish and a good comrade, and, considering the conditions under which he served, had always given far better than the average. There is no doubt that the achievement of every

Italian unit, especially of the motorized forces, far surpassed anything that the Italian Army had done for a hundred years. Many Italian generals and officers won our admiration both as men and soldiers.[180]

If the Italian Army fought with less competence, assurance, and elan than did the Wehrmacht, it was not, Rommel declared, the fault of the average *soldati*. He was very explicit about where to place the blame:

The cause of the Italian defeat had its roots in the whole Italian military and state system, in their poor armament and in the general lack of interest in the war shown by many of the leading Italians, both officers and statesmen. . . . [T]he Italian command was, for the most part, not equal to the task of carrying on war in the desert. . . . The training of the Italian infantryman fell far short of the standard required by modern warfare. His equipment was so utterly bad, that for that reason alone, he was unable to stand his ground without German help. . . . Rations were so bad that the Italian soldier frequently had to ask his German comrade for food. Particularly harmful was the all-pervading differentiation between officer and man. While the men had to make shift without field-kitchens, the officers, or many of them, refused adamantly to forgo their several course meals. Many officers, again, considered it unnecessary to put in an appearance during battle and thus set the men an example. All in all, therefore, it was small wonder that the Italian soldier, who incidentally was extraordinarily modest in his needs, developed a feeling of inferiority which accounted for his occasional failure in moments of crisis.[181]

The situation that now obtained along the El Alamein line was one of a curious sort of equilibrium. The tactical skill of the Axis forces was insufficient to overcome Eighth Army's numerical superiority, while Eighth Army's advantages in numbers could not counter its enemy's superior tactics. As he had been in the weeks before Gazala, Rommel was once more in a race against time, one which he knew he must ultimately lose if he didn't strike as hard and as quickly as possible. He believed he could muster the strength for one last great attack. Reinforcements had been sent from Germany and Italy—the 164th Light Infantry Division, the Fallschirmjäger-Brigade Ramcke, one of the parachute units originally designated for the now abortive Operation *Hercules*, and the Italian Littorio Division, Italy's last armored unit, which had been thrust into combat within days of its arrival in North Africa and acquitted itself well in the process. But it wasn't enough, Rommel knew, if Auchinleck were allowed the time to bring up *his* new units and begin training them properly in the wiles and ways of desert warfare.

Auchinleck was determined to keep Rommel off balance. The German commander was not confiding his plans to either Rome or Berlin, so Ultra was providing no insights into Rommel's intentions, but Auchinleck knew his man well enough to understand that allowing Rommel to bide his time undisturbed until he was ready to make his move was a very bad idea. In order to keep the pressure on Panzerarmee Afrika, Auchinleck ordered another series of limited attacks, hoping to drive Rommel even farther back from the Ruweisat Ridge while at the same time retaking Tel el Eisa in the north—and inflicting as much damage as possible to the panzers.

The attacks began on July 22; they were hurriedly planned and poorly coordinated, and as a consequence the Eighth Army came out rather second-best on the whole. In the north the Australians were able to eventually retake Tel el Eisa after an extraordinary effort, but in the center the British made no headway whatsoever, and suffered disproportionately heavy losses in the process. By the end of July Auchinleck was ready to admit that Eighth Army was exhausted; offensive operations were postponed indefinitely while the Alamein defenses were further strengthened. Fresh divisions were on their way to Alexandria, along with hundreds of replacement tanks and artillery pieces; there was no need for further penny-packet bickering with Rommel: when Auchinleck deemed his forces sufficiently strong, he would hit Panzerarmee Afrika hard enough to drive it right out of Egypt and across Libya. He had proven once that he could do it: when Eighth Army was ready, he would do it again.

Naturally, Rommel had other ideas, but events would dictate that a rematch *à la Crusader* would not take place. Auchinleck well knew that he was not a favorite of Churchill's, or the Chief of the Imperial General Staff (CIGS), General Sir Alan Brooke. Brooke's disfavor was particularly important, as his position gave him the authority to determine which general officers held commands, and which ones sat on the sidelines. Brooke, one of the more elusive personalities of the Second World War, fancied himself a military genius, which he most manifestly was not—his great wartime talent was his ability to manage Winston Churchill—while in fact being a prime example of the worst effects of the First World War on professional officers' concepts of strategy and operations. A career artillery officer, mentally Brooke was a plodder, haunted by the carnage of the Western Front in the Great War, obsessed with avoiding anything that resembled a repeat of that charnel house. He was better at retreating than advancing, and in retrospect he appears to have been frightened of imaginative, independent-minded officers. This latter proved to be Auchinleck's undoing, as he had insisted back in March that he could not leave Egypt in order to attend a conference in London at Churchill's behest. The prime minister, who liked to fancy that the Army's generals came and went at his beck and call, took exception what he regarded as Auchinleck's impertinence, and even before the Gazala debacle began to consider replacing "the Auk." Brooke fed Churchill's animosity, believing that command of Eighth Army was the perfect posting for one of his own protegés. Auchinleck informed London that in his considered opinion Eighth Army would not be ready for a major offensive until mid-September at the earliest, and no amount of bullying by Churchill and Brooke could persuade him to change his mind and begin the offensive prematurely. The prime minister and the CIGS agreed that it was time for Auchinleck to go. He was relieved as the commanding officer of Eighth Army as well as the Commander-in-Chief Middle East on August 8. That same day, Lieutenant General Bernard Montgomery, Brooke's friend and long-time subordinate, was given command of Eighth Army.

A few days would pass before Rommel became aware of this change of command. In the meantime, he was concentrating his energies on rejuvenating the *panzerarmee*: the German and Italian workshops were doing yeoman duty in repairing damaged tanks, trucks, and armored cars, and the Italians were exerting themselves to make certain that the vital convoys carrying fuel and ammunition reached Tripoli, Cavallero and Kesselring both going so far as to assure Rommel that they would resort to extraordinary measures if need be in order to supply the Axis forces. But the biggest problem at the moment was sickness among the troops, followed closely by the constant harassment by the Desert Air Force.

2 August 1942

Dearest Lu,

All quiet, except for intense air activity against my supply lines. I'm thankful for every day's respite we get. A lot of sickness. Unfortunately many of the older officers are going down now. Even I am feeling very tired and limp, though I have got a chance to look after myself a bit just at the moment. Unfortunately, the railway from Tobruk to the front is not yet in operation. We're waiting for locomotives. Holding on to our Alamein position has given us the severest fighting we've yet seen in Africa. We've all got heat diarrhoea now, but it's bearable. A year ago I had jaundice and that was much worse.

5 August 1942

Trouble with supplies. Rintelen does little in Rome and constantly lets himself be hoodwinked, [believing] the Italian supplies are working excellently.

10 August 1942

Kesselring was here yesterday. We reached agreement over what is to happen. Now it's a question of making full use of the few weeks to get ready. The situation is changing daily to my advantage.[182]

In typical Rommel fashion, he understated the severity of his own condition: he was teetering on the edge of physical and emotional exhaustion, his blood pressure was inordinately low, and the gastric problems which intermittently plagued him most of his life became increasingly severe. He had already decided that the attack on the Alamein line would take place at the end of August, now there was doubt in Africa and Berlin that he would be fit to lead it. Sometime around August 20 he suffered a near-collapse; on Hitler's direct order, a Professor Horster was dispatched to the *panzerarmee* headquarters, where he concluded that while a temporary recovery might be achieved in North Africa if Rommel were to dramatically reduce his workload, but if there were to be a complete recovery, the field marshal needed a prolonged stay in a more moderate climate, i.e. Germany.

24 Aug. 1942

Dearest Lu,

I was unable to write again yesterday. I'm now well enough to get up occasionally. But I'll still have to go through with the six weeks' treatment in Germany. My blood pressure must be got properly right again some time or other. One of the *Führer*'s doctors is supposed to be on his way. I'm certainly not going to leave my post here until I can hand over to my deputy without worrying. It's not yet known who is coming. I'm having another examination today. It's some comfort to know that the damage can probably all be cleared up. At the rate we've been using up generals in Africa—five per division in eighteen months—it's no wonder that I also need an overhaul some time or other.[183]

Leutnant Berndt, the propaganda officer, took it upon himself to be considerably more forthcoming with Lucie about her husband's condition:

26 Aug. 1942

Dear Frau Rommel,

You'll no doubt be surprised at hearing from me from Africa. . . . The reason for my letter is to inform you about the state of the Marshal's health. Your husband has now been 19 months in Africa, which is longer than any other officer over 40 has stood it so far, and, according to the doctors, an astonishing physical feat. After the rigors of the advance, he has had to carry the immense responsibility of the Alamein front, anxiety for which has for many nights allowed him no rest. Moreover, the bad season has come again.

All this has, in the nature of things, not failed to leave its mark, and thus, in addition to all the symptoms of a heavy cold and the digestive disturbances typical of Africa, he has recently shown signs of exhaustion which have caused great anxiety to all of us who were aware of it. True, there is no immediate danger, but unless he can get a thorough rest some time, he might easily suffer an overstrain which could leave organic damage in its train. The Führer has been informed, and it has been agreed that he will receive a long period of sick leave in Europe once the future of this theatre has been decided. Until that time, we will do everything we can to make his life easier and to persuade him to look after himself. We prepare and keep handy everything he needs for his health. I have installed a small kitchen and obtained a good cook. Fresh fruit and vegetables arrive by air daily. We fish, shoot pigeons, obtain chickens and eggs, etc., in order to keep his strength up.

This sort of "mothering" is not of course particularly easy with the Marshal and he has to know as little about it as possible. Being the man he is, he would deny himself any extra rations. . . . There is no cause for worry. All he needs is a lengthy rest in Europe at some time in the fairly near future, and that is already arranged. . . .

As for his personal safety, I shall, in the event of further operations, once again do everything possible to safeguard it, for every one of us, officers and men, would be ready to die for the Marshal. . . .[184]

Rommel rallied to the point where Professor Horstner gave a qualified endorsement to his remaining in North Africa, saying "C-in-C's condition so far improved that he can command the battle under constant medical attention. Nevertheless, essential to have a replacement on the spot." When pressed on this last point, Rommel recommended that General Heinz Guderian be given command of Panzerarmee Afrika in his own absence, but when he sent this request to Berlin, it was denied with a terse, "Guderian unacceptable." That seemed odd to Rommel, but he passed it off, there being so many other matters requiring his immediate attention.[185]

29 Aug. 1942

Dearest Lu,
Tension is growing here. Conferred yesterday with the Commanding Generals. General Värst is back and has taken over his division again. He commanded particularly well and with great dash back in the January fighting. He was, of course, wounded very early in the great May battle. My health is now very good again and I hope

to stand up well to the lively days ahead. Gause will be staying at H.Q. this time and Westphal will come with me. I can't see Gause keeping it up much longer. He's been having constant headaches ever since that day at the beginning of June when the British gave us such a terrible pounding with their bombs and artillery. I hope it will be better for him in Europe.[186]

Rommel's final throw of the dice to break the El Alamein line and reach Alexandria would begin on August 30, 1942. His plan was deceptively simple, as it relied on the much-superior tactical coordination between armor, infantry and artillery the Axis units possessed over their British counterparts. (Whatever senior Italian generals might or might not have done, Italian company- and field- grade officers, as well as their men, had learned a lot while fighting alongside the Germans.) In the north, three Italian infantry divisions, supported by the 164th Light Division, would attack the British defensive box at El Alamein, the strongest and best-sited of the three main boxes in the Alamein line. This attack would pin down the three British divisions in and around El Alamein, and hopefully draw Eighth Army's reserves toward it, for the main thrust of Rommel's attack would be going in further to the south. There the Afrika Korps and the Italian XX Motorized Corps would punch through the British lines, turn north and roll up the rest of Eighth Army.

Eighth Army's new commanding officer, Lieutenant General Montgomery, was content to implement the plans that Auchinleck had created for such an eventuality. The three divisions posted around El Alamein would hold fast, while 2nd New Zealand Division, positioned south of the Ruweisat Ridge, would gradually yield ground as the Axis armor advanced against a deliberately thinned-out screen of infantry further south. Unknown to Rommel, the now-reconstituted 7th Armoured Division and the 8th Armoured Brigade were sitting well back from the front, where they would wait for the Afrika Korps to turn north to outflank the Alamein Line. They would be the hammer—the 22nd and 23rd Armoured Brigades, sitting along the Ruweisat Ridge, would be the anvil. As soon as the German and Italian armor was engaged on the ridge, the hammer would fall.

Before the attack began Rommel took time to post another letter to Lucie; like so many of his letters, this one says much in a few words, and offers an insight into his thoughts and feelings that were never revealed elsewhere. Some of Rommel's old energy and drive had returned to him now that he was advancing again, but for the first time, there is also an acknowledgment that the war in North Africa might not be his to win after all.

30 Aug. 1942

Dearest Lu,

Today has dawned at last. It's been such a long wait worrying all the time whether I should get everything I needed together to enable me to take the brakes off again. Many of my worries have been by no means satisfactorily settled and we have some very grave shortages. But I've taken the risk, for it will be a long time before we get such favorable conditions of moonlight, relative strengths, etc., again. I, for my part, will do my utmost to contribute to success. As for my health, I'm feeling quite on top of my form. There are such big things at stake. If our blow succeeds, it might go some way towards deciding the whole course of the war. If it fails, at least I hope to give the enemy a pretty thorough beating.[187]

Rommel's attack jumped off at nightfall on August 30, with the Italian Littorio and Ariete Armored Divisions, along with the 90th Light Division, screening the left flank of the two panzer divisions. The full moon which was to have provided just enough light to allow the Axis armor to navigate across what was literally a trackless waste instead became a beacon guiding British bombers and fighter-bombers to the columns of German and Italian tanks. The 21st Panzer Division lost its commanding officer, General Georg von Bismarck, killed when he stepped on land mine, just after midnight. The attack fell behind schedule, but late in the morning of August 31, the 15th Panzer and then the 21st Panzer began their attacks on Ruweisat Ridge in a one-two punch. A furious tank battle ensued, which lasted the remainder of the day, with neither side gaining a decisive advantage; at sunset Rommel called a halt to the attack: the Afrika Korps would be back the next day.

British bombers returned during the night, the Axis supply lines their targets this time; the fuel lost in these raids forced Rommel to immobilize the 21st Panzer—he lacked the gasoline to keep both divisions running. At sunrise the 15th Panzer was at it again, but its attack on Ruweisat Ridge was stopped when the 8th Armoured Brigade struck at its right flank. Meanwhile yet another calamity befell Rommel's supply columns, when a squadron of armored cars from the 4th Armoured Brigade, ranging far behind the Axis lines, shot up a convoy of 300 trucks carrying fuel for the panzer divisions. This was the final straw for Rommel, and he called off the attack. Over the next five days the German and Italian troops would fall back to their start line, harassed every inch of the way by the Desert Air Force. Montgomery unwisely tried to counterattack while the Afrika Korps withdrew: two New Zealand brigades suffered heavy losses before Montgomery called them off; after that he was content to let the panzers withdraw unhindered. The drubbing given to the New Zealanders played into Montgomery's intention of continuing the buildup begun by Auchinleck, so that he would eventually be able to attack Rommel in overwhelming force.

Rommel broke the news to Lucie on September 4:

Dearest Lu,
Some very hard days lie behind me. We had to break off the offensive for supply reasons and because of the superiority of the enemy air force although victory was otherwise ours. Well, it can't be helped. Made a quick call at H.Q. for the first time today, even had my boots off and washed my feet. I'm still hoping that the situation can be straightened out. All my wishes to you and Manfred.[188]

Despite the brave face he put on the situation, Rommel knew that this was the end of the line. Panzerarmee Afrika had gone far, well beyond what anyone ever imagined it could, but flesh and blood had their limits, and while Rommel's soldiers, German and Italian alike, had given him everything they could, they had nothing left. They would go no farther.

CHAPTER ELEVEN

EL ALAMEIN

*A commander is not protected by an order from a minister
or prince who is absent from the theater of operations and
has little or no knowledge of the most recent turn of
events. Every commander responsible for executing a
plan that he considers bad or disastrous is criminal.*
—BONAPARTE

Panzerarmee Afrika's defeat at the Alam Halfa ridge just west of El
Alamein triggered a seismic shift in Axis and Allied strategy in the
Mediterranean theater, and Erwin Rommel knew it. The situation
that now obtained would allow for no reprise of the aftermath of *Crusader*:
there would be no opportunity to fall back, regroup, and try again. Rommel
and his army would have to fight where they stood.

Three factors had been key to the Axis defeats in July and September,
and Rommel was certain that they were the shape of things to come: the
ongoing strangulation of his supply lines, the growing power of the Desert
Air Force, and the steadily increasing numbers of Allied troops and equipment opposing him. Not knowing about Ultra, Rommel continued to suspect Italian treachery in the destruction of so many ships carrying supplies
to North Africa, but whatever the causes may have been, what was undeniable was that for the first eight months of 1942, only 40 percent of the total
tonnage needed to sustain his divisions actually reached Panzerarmee Afrika.
A significant amount of the missing tonnage was being siphoned off for the
increasing numbers of reinforcements Mussolini inexplicably kept sending
to the garrison in Tripoli, troops Rommel desperately needed to bring his
depleted Italian divisions back up to something approaching their nominal
strength, but which Il Duce adamantly refused to release for frontline serv-

ice. The Italians could not, of course, prevent German reinforcements and equipment from reaching the Afrika Korps, but those simply were not forthcoming: the massive German offensive in southern Russia, and especially the battle for Stalingrad, had first call on whatever replacements and materiel the Wehrmacht could produce. The supply problem was by no means insoluble, but to effect a solution would require a shift in Germany's strategic priorities which Hitler and O.K.W. were unwilling to make. North Africa had always been a sideshow, and would remain so until the situation was beyond retrieval, no matter what the Wehrmacht might do.

The issue of air power was even more problematic. From the first day of the war the German Army had never fought a campaign in which it did not enjoy air superiority, if not outright air supremacy. Now, in Egypt, the Desert Air Force had not merely contested control of the skies above the battlefield, but actually wrested it away from the Luftwaffe, flying as many as a thousand sorties a day. British bombers staged raids day or night whenever conditions were favorable, while RAF fighter-bombers went hunting daily for targets of opportunity. The casualties from any individual attack were usually light, but the cumulative losses grew into a significant drain on German and Italian manpower and equipment. Additionally, the constant threat of Allied air power inhibited movement by Axis units and soon a simmering level of anxiety began to permeate Rommel's entire command, adding to the strain already inflicted on his officers and men by the harsh desert environment and the stresses of combat.

It also began influencing Rommel's tactical thinking as well, compelling him to recognize that with their movements restricted by Allied air power, his armored and mechanized units could no longer rely on their mobility to increase their effectiveness in bolstering Panzerarmee Afrika's defenses. This created for Rommel what in some circles was characterized as unnecessary pessimism but which was, in fact, a healthy appreciation of the handicaps which would chronically plague the Wehrmacht for the remainder of the war.

Anyone who has to fight, even with the most modern weapons, against an enemy in complete command of the air, fights like a savage against modern European troops, under the same handicaps and with the same chances of success. And since there was no foreseeable hope, with the German Luftwaffe so severely stretched in other theaters, of Kesselring receiving aircraft reinforcements in any way comparable with those flowing to the British, we had to face the likelihood of the R.A.F. shortly gaining absolute air supremacy. . . .

The fact of British air superiority threw to the winds all the tactical rules which we had hitherto applied with such success. There was no real answer to the enemy's air superiority, except a powerful air force of our own. In every battle to come the strength of the Anglo-American air force was to be the deciding factor.[189]

The problem of replacements was at once the thorniest and most urgent of all, for a surfeit of supplies and an ever-victorious Luftwaffe overhead would matter little if Rommel lacked the men and equipment needed to hold the line against the coming British offensive. Rommel's passing mention of "the Anglo-American air force" looms large in its own way: he was sufficiently sharp-eyed to be able to note that not all the low-flying aircraft bombing and strafing his armored columns and troop positions wore the blue-white-and-red roundels of the Royal Air Force. Some of them bore the white stars in dark blue disks of the United States Army Air Force: not only were American-made weapons being brought to bear, but American manpower was now being thrown into the balance against the *panzerarmee*. German manpower was being stretched to its limits everywhere, so there was no chance that Rommel would ever again be able to muster anything approaching parity with the numbers that Eighth Army would put into the field, yet there was a minimum number of troops Rommel would require if there was to be a successful defense of his own Alamein position. He would shortly begin a medical leave in Germany, and while there he would personally present to Hitler his report on Panzerarmee Afrika's situation and demand that it be properly reinforced.

Rommel had mixed feelings about leaving North Africa when the decisive battle of the campaign was clearly approaching. General der Panzertruppe Georg Stumme was scheduled to arrive in mid-September to serve as Rommel's deputy in the field marshal's absence. Stumme was a veteran of the Russian Front and the former commander of Rommel's old unit, the 7th Panzer Division, in its original incarnation as the 2nd Light

Division, and while no one questioned Stumme's competence as a commander, no one imagined him to be a leader of Rommel's caliber.

9 Sept. 1942

Dearest Lu,

My health is now fairly well restored and I hardly think anybody would notice anything. However, the doctor is pressing me hard to have a break in Germany and doesn't want me to postpone it any longer. But Stumme must first arrive and be installed in his job. On the one hand, I'm overjoyed at the prospect of getting away for a while and seeing you, but on the other I fear I shall never be free of anxiety about this place, even though I won't be able to get to the front myself. I know Churchill is supposed to have said that he will only be able to hold Egypt a few months longer, but I'm more inclined to think that he's considering launching a new offensive with superior forces in four to six weeks' time. A victory for us in the Caucasus is the only thing that would stop him.

Now Gause is unfit for tropical service and has to go away for six months. Things are also not looking too good with Westphal, he's got jaundice. Lt-Col. von Mellenthin is leaving today with amoebic dysentery. One of the divisional commanders was wounded yesterday, so that every divisional commander and the Corps Commander have been changed inside ten days.[190]

Rommel did his best to give Stumme whatever advantages he could, and the *panzerarmee* did have some. The same tactical situation at El Alamein which had denied Rommel the opportunity to employ his usual tactics of speed and maneuver in a sweeping flanking move around the southern end of the enemy line now worked in his favor. The relatively narrow front, anchored by the Mediterranean to the north and the Qattara Depression to the south, denied the Eighth Army any chance to outflank the Axis defenses. Any attack on Panzerarmee Afrika would have to go through it, not around it. In order to make this as difficult a proposition as possible, Rommel displayed a hitherto unsuspected talent, one for positional warfare. The same eye for ground that sought out cover and concealment for the movements of his *abteilung* in Romania and Italy in the First World War he now put to work identifying the positions where cover and concealment, along with surprise, would allow his infantry to inflict serious losses on any attacking force while keeping their own casualties to a minimum. He brought considerable imagination in preparing his army for the coming confrontation (certainly more than was being displayed by the new commanding officer of Eighth Army), to the point of developing, with the *panzerarmee's* staff, contingency plans for defeating any amphibious landing on the Egyptian coast that might be mounted simultaneously with the imminent British offensive.

That a coordinated land and seaborne attack at El Alamein might be in the offing was a reasonable conclusion drawn from a series of coastal and inland commando-style raids carried out in September 1942, operations against Axis rear areas as far distant as Benghazi. The purpose of these raids was varied, from disrupting Axis supply lines, to sabotaging German and Italian airfields, to attempts to free Allied prisoners of war. This last was the objective of the largest of these raids, an attack on Tobruk that would, it was hoped, rescue some or even all of the 16,000 British POWs held there. The raid was a monumental failure: the British suffered nearly 800 casualties as well as the loss of a cruiser and two destroyers; the Axis forces suffered just 66 dead and wounded, along with the loss of about 30 aircraft. The audacity of the raid had impressed Rommel, but little else of it did.

> 16 September 1942
>
> Dearest Lu,
> Arrived back last night from Tobruk. You'll no doubt have been pleased to hear the special communiqué about the abortive landing. Everything seems to be under control again now. Stumme is arriving in Rome to-day. I hope to start in a week's time. Kesselring came this morning, after I'd seen and talked to him yesterday in Tobruk. He'd come from the Führer's H.Q. The battle for Stalingrad seems to be very hard and is tying up a lot of forces which we could make better use of in the south. . . .[191]

The Libyan desert was not, of course, the only place where British commandos and similar irregular forces were active. In July 1940 Winston Churchill ordered the creation of the Special Operations Executive, with orders for the new organization to "set Europe ablaze;" in practical terms this translated into espionage, sabotage, and aiding local resistance movements in occupied Europe. Commando units, which carried out some of the same missions, were organized at the same time under the Combined Operations Headquarters; later the Special Air Service (SAS) and the Special Boat Service (SBS), both operating in the Mediterranean, were added to the irregulars' ranks. They proved to be something of a thorn in the flesh to the Axis in Libya, though not quite to the degree which later hagiography would maintain. They were very good at sabotage operations, but other efforts were less than memorable.

> [The SAS] tried again and again to incite the Arabs against us, fortunately with little success, for there is nothing so unpleasant as partisan warfare. It is perhaps very important not to make reprisals on hostages at the first outbreak of partisan warfare, for these only create feelings of revenge and serve to strengthen the partisans. It is better to allow an incident to go unavenged than to hit back at the innocent. It only agitates the whole neighbourhood, and hostages easily become martyrs. The Italian commander shared my view, and so the occasional Arab raid was usually overlooked.[192]

These comments by Rommel must loom very large in any assessment of his character and moral compass, especially in light of Wehrmacht conduct elsewhere in Europe. Upon first reading, they seem to be the realistic, pragmatic reaction of an honorable soldier determined to carry out his duties with that honor intact. Rommel's words assume an entirely new significance when held up against what would become known as the "Commando Order," a personal directive from Adolf Hitler, issued on October 18, 1942, decreeing that any enemy combatant captured while engaged in espionage, sabotage or any other "irregular" activity, whether in uniform or not, was to be summarily executed. Only 12 copies of this order were made, to be individually hand-carried to the Wehrmacht's various Army Group headquarters. By the time Rommel received his copy, he had already departed North Africa for Germany to begin his medical leave, and returned when the long-awaited British offensive at El Alamein began. After the war, the commander of the 3rd Reconnaissance Battalion would state categorically that he watched Rommel burn his copy; in any event, no trace of it would ever be found anywhere among the files, documents, and war diaries of Panzerarmee Afrika.[193]

In any event, while the British desert raiders might be annoying, regardless of whatever Berlin thought of them, they were insignificant in the larger strategic picture Rommel saw. That picture may well have been flawed, for he knew little about the realities of operations on the Russian Front, nevertheless, the point he made to Lucie in his letter of September 16 about the O.K.W.'s tunnel vision toward the war in the Soviet Union was valid. There was a strategic opportunity in North Africa which was being wasted in the growing battle of egos along the Volga between Adolf Hitler and Josef Stalin. By now Rommel had little if any faith remaining in "Plan Orient"—if indeed he had ever seen it as more than an intellectual exercise. Still, all throughout the summer of 1942 there was the possibility of shifting the strategic balance in the Mediterranean decisively in the Axis' favor with the commitment of a fraction of the forces that were destroying Stalingrad to no genuine strategic purpose. If the British were given the time to finish their preparations and launch their attack as they chose, once it began the initiative in North Africa would irretrievably pass to Eighth Army and its new commanding officer. Ironically, given that he would become almost inextricably linked with Erwin Rommel and the Afrika Korps, he was the least of Rommel's concerns at the moment.

Bernard Law Montgomery was the fourth of nine children born to an Anglican minister of Ulster Scots descent. Four years older than Erwin Rommel, he spent the early part of his life in Tasmania before the family relocated to London. His was an unhappy, abused childhood in which he was given frequent (sometimes daily) beatings by his emotionally unstable mother, a sad fact which would account for his bitter, acerbic personality in his adult years and his need to dominate those around him. He was educated at St. Paul's School before attending Sandhurst, the British military academy, graduating in 1908; service in India was followed by a stint as battalion adjutant in the Royal Warwickshires at Shorncliff. Like Rommel, Montgomery went to war in August 1914, and again like Rommel, was wounded for the first time in September. Montgomery's injury was far graver, however, as he was shot through the chest by a sniper; a prolonged convalescence followed, after which he spent the remainder of the war as a staff officer, rising to the rank of temporary lieutenant colonel.

The years between the two world wars saw Montgomery hold a battalion command in a handful of regiments before being appointed officer commanding the 9th Infantry Brigade and then General Officer Commanding 8th Infantry Division. In 1927 he married Elizabeth Carver, and their only child, a son named David, was born a year later. The marriage was, by all evidence, a happy one, but was short-lived: Elizabeth died in her husband's arms in 1937, a victim of septicemia triggered by a botched surgical proceedure; from that point on Montgomery became wholly consumed by his career. In 1938 the 8th Division was posted to Palestine, where Montgomery led a nine-month campaign against Zionist insurgents; July 1939 he was recalled to Great Britain, where he was given command of the 3rd Infantry Division. When Britain declared war on Germany on September 3, 1939 and sent the British Expeditionary Force to Belgium, the 3rd Division went with it as part of II Corps, which was under the command of Lieutenant General Sir Alan Brooke. During the retreat to Dunkirk he handled 3rd Division with considerable skill, and was able to see it evacuated to England with minimal casualties.

Never having been a popular officer before the war began, Montgomery set about making a new set of enemies after Dunkirk, offering to anyone who would listen very detailed critiques of the Chief of the Imperial General Staff, Lieutenant General Sir John Dill, and the commander of the B.E.F., Lord Gort. After being posted to command of V Corps in the south of England, Montgomery began a long-running feud with his immediate superior, Lieutenant General Claude Auchinleck; there doesn't seem to be a clear-cut reason for their dispute, apart from Montgomery's perpetual need for someone with whom he could be at odds. While in command of V Corps, and later XII Corps and then Southeastern Command after Auchinleck's posting to Egypt, Montgomery proved to be a demanding superior, training his men hard and working his officers harder. At the time, the likelihood of receiving a combat command was slim, as Auchinleck appeared to have things well in hand, with Rommel ejected from Tobruk and on the run back to El Agheila.

Then fate took a hand, and Rommel trounced Auchinleck at Gazala then captured Tobruk. Despite having stopped Panzerarmee Afrika cold at El Alamein in the closing days of July and done yeoman work in reorganizing and resuscitating Eighth Army, Auchinleck had lost the confidence of both Churchill and Brooke, who by now was the CIGS. Auchinleck was eased out of command of Eighth Army, kicked upstairs and packed off to India, where he would eventually assume the duties of commander-in-chief of the Indian Army. His place was to be taken by Lieutenant General William Gott, who had performed adequately if not brilliantly at Gazala, but Gott was killed in early August when the transport plane in which he was a passenger was shot down by Luftwaffe fighters. Brooke then pressed Montgomery on Churchill as a substitute for Gott; the prime minister agreed to the appointment and Montgomery was given command of Eighth Army. Why Brooke had such confidence in Montgomery, whose only demonstrable achievement in combat so far was commanding a division in retreat, remains unclear. Perhaps they were simply kindred military spirits, products of the Western Front, methodical, unimaginative, more given to avoid losing battles than they were to attempting to win them; whatever the specifics, they were in almost every way the antithesis of the majority of their German opponents—or, later, many of their American allies.

In any event, Montgomery formally assumed command on August 13, 1942, and as he would later tell the tale, Eighth Army's morale soon soared and its fighting spirit returned. One story has it that he was overheard muttering, "After having an easy war, things have now got much more difficult," and when told to cheer up by a fellow officer, blurted out "I'm not talking about me, I'm talking about Rommel!" Both during and after the war, Montgomery took pains to foster the impression within the British Army and without that he was the source of the dramatic about-face in the morale of Eighth Army in the weeks just prior to the second battle of El Alamein. And the truth of the matter was that in the aftermath of Gazala and the fall of Tobruk, Eighth Army *did* have a serious morale problem: Erwin Rommel.[194]

It seemed inexplicable to the ordinary ranker, and most of his officers as well, that the Germans and Italians, having been so thoroughly walloped in *Crusader*, should in a matter of months, have turned right around and pushed the Eighth Army clean out of Libya and halfway across Egypt. The name "Rommel" was everywhere, on the lips of every prisoner taken, in seemingly every radio signal intercepted, written up in German magazines and newspapers that fell into British hands from time to time. He was "the Desert Fox," who manufactured victories out of defeats and outfought, out-thought, or out-beguiled every British commander sent to face him. He seemed unstoppable! He had even entered the daily vernacular of the average Tommy: doing something especially clever or unexpected soon became known as "doing a Rommel."

It was a problem, and Auchinleck had known it to be so. He also knew that Rommel was in fact nothing more than a very good general who had the wit and skill to improvise as needed and take advantage of whatever luck he could find—and that Rommel *had* been lucky. Auchinleck also understood that for his other ranks, nothing would remove the self-inflicted stigma of defeat save for a victory. For his soldiers to believe that they could win against the Afrika Korps, though, their officers first had to believe it could be done. In early July, just as the First Alamein was heating up, he issued an unusual order to the whole of Eighth Army:

> There exists a real danger that our friend Rommel is becoming a kind of magical or bogey-man to our troops, who are talking far too much about him. He is by no means a superman, although he is undoubtedly very energetic and able. Even if he were a superman, it would still be highly undesirable that our men should credit him with supernatural powers.
>
> I wish you to dispel by all possible means the idea that Rommel represents something more than an ordinary German general. The important thing now is to see to it that we do not always talk of Rommel when we mean the enemy in Libya. We must refer to "the Germans" or "the Axis powers" or "the enemy" and not always keep harping on Rommel.
>
> Please ensure that this order is put into immediate effect, and impress upon all Commanders that, from a psychological point of view, it is a matter of the highest importance.[195]

It is impossible to say at this remove what effect, if any, Auchinleck's order may have had on the officers and men of Eighth Army, but what they accomplished in July 1942 made it irrelevant, as they fought Panzerarmee Afrika to a standstill. It was not a great victory, but the defeats had come to an end. The realization grew that Rommel had shot his last bolt, and that it had not been good enough, after all, to defeat Eighth Army. The action at Alam Halfa in the last two days of August, though by this time Auchinleck was gone, merely added the exclamation point to the statement made by the Tommies a month earlier. Montgomery would disingenuously tell Churchill that when he arrived in Egypt, he discovered that Auchinleck had no plans drawn up save for further retreats: in truth, Montgomery fought Alam Halfa using Auchinleck's deployments, Auchinleck's plans, and troops Auchinleck had trained. In fact, Montgomery's sole contribution to the battle had been to arrange the mauling of two brigades of New Zealand infantry in an ill-advised counterattack on the Afrika Korps as the Germans began their withdrawal.

Soldiers—especially combat soldiers—from the Egyptians Thutmose III led at Megiddo in the fifteenth century BC right up to the present day have always been, by nature, inclination, and experience, a skeptical lot. Brag, bluster, theatrics of any sort, by a commanding officer, particularly a new commanding officer, are greeted with a jaundiced eye at best, derision— sometimes open—at worst. The men of Eighth Army knew who had truly brought them to the point where they were about to turn the tables on the Germans and Italians. The Tommies, South Africans, New Zealanders and Indians would fight well in the months to come, but they would never fight for Montgomery the way that Rommel's "Africans" fought for him. Understandably, the British people were hungry for victories and victors to celebrate, and Montgomery, hungry for an adulation that he had never been able to achieve on his own, along with a desire by men like Churchill and Brooke to burnish their reputations for prescience and wisdom in selecting Montgomery for command of Eighth Army, ensured that the seeds of Montgomery's "legend" would fall on fertile ground.[196] But the Tommies would always know better.[197]

ROMMEL, SUFFERING FROM a liver infection, a duodenal ulcer, low blood pressure and desert sores, finally handed over command of Panzerarmee Afrika to General Stumme on the morning of July 23 and flew to Rome. There he had a tempestuous meeting with Mussolini and Cavallero, insisting that it was incompetence on the part of Comando Supremo and the Italian government that had left the Axis troops in North Africa near-starved for supplies. Mussolini did his best to placate the angry field marshal, who in turn stated in no uncertain terms that if the Italian navy and merchant marine could not properly supply Panzerarmee Afrika, then the time had come to abandon North Africa altogether. This was hardly what Il Duce wanted to hear, but he had come to learn that his bluster and bombast had little if any effect on Rommel, whom he then tried to fob off with assurances that Cavallero would do the very best he could to restore the Axis supply lines.

Frustrated, feeling that he had accomplished nothing in Rome, Rommel departed for Berlin the next day, September 25, where he cooled his heels in Propaganda Minister Göbbels' home until September 30, when he was the guest of honor at a formal reception at Berlin's Sportspalast. It was there that Hitler formally presented Rommel with his *feldmarschall*'s baton, and assured him, far more convincingly than did Mussolini, that North Africa's supply problems would be resolved once and for all. Publicly, Rommel said all of the right things, mouthing the platitudes about where the German soldier sets foot, there he stays, but later, privately, he was far more candid with Hitler, insisting that Panzerarmee Afrika had to have a minimum of 35,000 tons of supplies a month—anything less and it would be impossible, he declared, to stop the British offensive that he and Hitler both knew was coming.

> I quite realize that, with the present strategic sea and air situation in the Mediterranean, a very great effort will be required to ensure a safe and uninterrupted German supply to Africa. It will make the utmost demands of all German and Italian transport services and will require the reinforcement of the transport fleet. But it is only by the fulfilment of the conditions I have stated that the German troops, who are bearing the main brunt of the fighting in Africa, will be able to maintain their hold on this theater against the finest troops of the British Empire.[198]

Not everyone at the conference shared Rommel's sense of realism. Hitler, for one, was convinced that the attack on Alam Halfa had been called off prematurely, for which he chided Rommel. Hitler was also quite confident that when the Afrika Korps once again took the offensive—he had made lavish promises of new weapons, Tiger tanks, *Nebelwerfer* rocket artillery, tank destroyers, and the like—Rommel would sweep the British out of Egypt and deliver the Suez Canal into his hands. Rommel was suddenly aware of the fact that these men in Berlin, who were responsible for directing a war in which Germany was fighting for survival, were disturbingly out of touch with the truth about that war as it existed at the front in North Africa.

> During the conference I realised that the atmosphere in the Führer's H.Q. was extremely optimistic. Göring in particular was inclined to minimise our difficulties. When I said that British fighter-bombers had shot up my tanks with 40mm shells, the *Reichsmarschall*, who felt himself touched by this, said: "That's completely impossible. The Americans only know how to make razor blades" I replied: "We could do with some of those razor blades, *Herr Reichsmarschall.*"[199]

When Göring continued to demur, Rommel produced one of the spent American-made 40mm shells and laid it in front of the *Reichsmarschall*, who promptly fell silent.

Unsettled by the events in Berlin, Rommel hurried down to Vienna and from there to Wiener Neustadt to collect Lucie. The nearby mountain resort of Semmering awaited, where Rommel would take his cure under the watchful eye of Professor Horster. He would be a far from model patient, continually fretting about the situation in North Africa. He had assured Stumme that he would return if the British attacked while he was convalescing, a promise Stumme accepted with somewhat mixed feelings—it was at once a relief to know that he would not have to command such a critical battle himself, and yet it seemed as something less than a total vote of confidence in his ability to do so if need be. Stumme was, in fact, proving to be an able stand-in for Rommel: while he possessed none of the Desert Fox's charisma, tactical cunning, or operational acumen, he was quite conscientious about completing Rommel's defensive plans, from laying new minefields (between them the British and Axis forces would emplace nearly a half-million antipersonnel and antitank mines on the El Alamein battlefield, most of which remain there still), to stockpiling ammunition, to completing specific redeployments of armor and artillery units. Both Rommel and Stumme shared a sense that, given what they had to hand, they had done everything they could to prepare for Montgomery's attack.

There were even moments when Rommel wondered if Montgomery would attack at all, or simply go on building up men, equipment and supplies indefinitely. He had yet to develop the understanding that the British general would not make any offensive move until he had mustered overwhelming numerical superiority and was satisfied that his logistical base was properly organized—improvisation and exploiting unexpected opportunities were utterly unfamiliar concepts to the ever-methodical Montgomery. Even after Alam Halfa, when the Afrika Korps was at its nadir and the Italian infantry divisions were all but immobilized for lack of transport and fuel, he refused to move, declaring that he wished to conserve his forces, leaving Rommel to remark acerbically "If *I* were Montgomery, we wouldn't still be here!"[200]

AS BRITISH WARTIME slang would put it, the balloon went up at 9:40 P.M. on October 23, 1942. More than 900 British artillery pieces, ranging from 25-pounder guns to massive 5.5-inch howitzers opened fire in the single largest "stonk"—a "time-on-target" barrage—in history. A carefully calculated fire plan brought the rounds of all 900-plus guns onto the entire 40-mile front of the El Alamein at the same moment, and proceeded to methodically pound the the battlefield for 20 minutes before shifting to specific targets. As the barrage lifted in the northern half of the front, specially trained infantry units moved forward to clear paths through Axis minefields that had been nicknamed "the Devil's Garden," using man-portable mine-detectors in combat for the first time. Behind the minesweepers came four infantry divisions: their mission was to establish a bridgehead on the far side of the 5-mile deep minefields, through which more than 500 British tanks would rush in order to attack the Axis armored units from the rear.

In the center the 4th Indian Division began advancing from the western end of Ruweisat Ridge, a diversionary attack that would, the British hoped, force the Afrika Korps to move the 15th Panzer and 90th Light Divisions southward rather than "at home," as it were, in the north to meet the advancing waves of Sherman and Grant tanks. A similar effort was underway at the southern end of the front: the 7th Armoured Division and the Free French Brigade were looking to tie up the 21st Panzer and the Ariete Divisions. Neither of these attacks made any significant progress, however, as the Axis minefields and antitank defenses proved far tougher than expected; for the moment, the German and Italian armor remained uncommitted.

In the north, despite the best efforts of the British engineers, progress during the night of October 23 was slow as the mine-clearing proved to be more difficult that expected. By midday on October 24 no comprehensible picture of Eighth Army's attack had yet emerged and Stumme refused to react prematurely. Taking a page from Rommel's own book, he decided he needed to see for himself what was happening: together with his aide, Colonel Büchting, he set out for the headquarters of the 90th Light. He never made it—the next day, October 25, his car was found, Büchting shot through the head, Stumme lying beside it in the sand, dead of an apparent heart attack. Generalleutnant Wilhelm Ritter von Thoma, who just three weeks earlier had taken the reins of the Afrika Korps from the wounded Walter Nehring, was now officer commanding of the whole of Panzerarmee Afrika. Von Thoma kept a cool head, and continued to hold back the panzers, but he did order the Axis artillery to begin lashing the enemy infantry in the north. By the end of its first day, the British attack seemed to have stalled, but von Thoma knew better: in raw numbers alone Eighth Army possessed a clear two-to-one superiority over Panzerarmee Afrika. When comparing British numbers to German, the situation was even worse: in manpower the British outnumbered the Germans six-to-one, in tanks by better than five-to-one. Montgomery literally had men and materiel to burn if necessary to achieve success. If the *panzerarmee* was to survive, it would need a miracle; in short, it needed Rommel.

FIELD MARSHAL WILHELM Keitel, chief of the O.K.W., put in a telephone call to Semmering late in the afternoon of October 24, informing Rommel that the British offensive at El Alamein had begun earlier that day. The situation, Keitel said, was uncertain, but General Stumme was missing. Was Rommel prepared to return to North Africa if needed? Rommel assured Keitel that he was, then waited until midnight before taking a personal call from Hitler, who asked him to fly back to Egypt as soon as possible. Rommel said goodbye to Lucie and Manfred, then flew to Rome, where he discovered that, as he had feared, Comando Supremo had made good on none of Mussolini's promises of adequate supply for the Axis troops in North Africa. This was the final straw: he departed Rome for Benghazi, "[f]eeling that we would fight this battle with little hope of success" and certain that ". . . there were no more laurels to be won in North Africa."[201]

It was late in the day when Rommel arrived back at the front on October 25, but immediately upon arriving he had a signal sent out to every unit, hoping to shore up morale: "I have taken command of the army again—Rommel." It was then that he learned how truly disastrous the situation had become: there was less than three days' supply for the entire *panzerarmee* in the whole of North Africa. The infantry units were beginning to take significant casualties as the British attacks continued, and while the panzers had begun local counterattacks the previous day, the fuel crisis prevented any large-scale riposte against Montgomery's tanks. Frustration set in as Rommel saw a remarkable tactical opportunity had presented itself, one that might well have turned the entire battle in his favor regardless of Eighth Army's numerical superiority: there simply wasn't sufficient fuel to make it a reality.

> Since the enemy was operating with astonishing hesitancy and caution, a concentrated attack by the whole of our armor could have been successful, although such an assembly of armor would of course have been met by the heaviest possible British artillery fire and air bombardment. However, we could have made the action more fluid by withdrawing a few miles to the west and could then have attacked the British in an all-out charge and defeated them in open country. The British artillery and air force could not easily have intervened with their usual weight in a tank battle of this kind, for their own forces would have been endangered.
>
> But a decision to take forces from the southern front was unthinkable with the gasoline situation so bad. Not only could we not have kept a mobile battle going for more than a day or two, but our armor could never have returned to the south if the British had attacked there. I did, however, decide to bring the whole of the 21st Panzer Division up north, although I fully realized that the gasoline shortage would not allow it to return. In addition, since it

was now obvious that the enemy would make his main effort in the north during the next few days and try for a decision there, half the Army artillery was drawn off from the southern front. At the same time I reported to the Führer's H.Q. that we would lose the battle unless there was an immediate improvement in the supply situation. Judging by previous experience, there was very little hope of this happening.[202]

Making the situation worse, the Desert Air Force was operating with near-impunity over the rear areas of the Axis army, specifically targeting German and Italian airfields, often dropping more than 100 tons of bombs in a single raid. That may have been an unimpressive weight of explosives compared to the Royal Air Force raids being carried out against German cities, where thousands of tons of bombs were dropped nightly, but its impact on the already-thin Axis resources belied the numbers. The Luftwaffe, despite the best efforts of Field Marshal Kesselring, was essentially impotent at this point; the Regia Aeronautica was faring no better. Rommel by temperament was not someone who fell prey to despair, but he began to feel something akin to it, as he was confronted every commanding general's worst nightmare: an operational and strategic situation so perilous that admitted of no good solutions, but only allowed the commander to choose what would be, he hoped, the least bad solution.

Initially he tried to put a brave face on the situation for Lucie, writing her on October 26 to tell her that he

Arrived 6:30 P.M. yesterday. Situation critical. A lot of work! After my wonderful weeks at home it's not easy to acclimatize myself to the new surroundings and the job in hand. There's too big a difference.[203]

That morning Rommel ordered a counterattack in the center by the 15th Panzer Division, the 164th Light Division, and units from the Italian XX Corps; British artillery and fighter-bombers effectively broke up the attack before it was properly underway. This was when he decided that it was time to bring the 21st Panzer and Ariete Divisions to the north: his tactical sense was telling him that was where the entire battle would be decided; if they remained in the south, these two divisions would be useless, and in danger of being cut off from the rest of the army.

27 Oct. 1942

Dearest Lu,
A very hard struggle. No one can conceive the burden that lies on me. Everything is at stake again and we're fighting under the greatest possible handicaps. However, I hope we'll pull through. You know I'll put all I've got into it.

Of course, Rommel was not to know that fatigue was hard at work among the infantry and tank crews of Eighth Army as well. The Axis troops were fighting harder and inflicting more serious casualties than Montgomery and his staff had presumed would be the case. The Allied infantry had driven a deep wedge into the Axis defenses in the north, and the British armor was beginning to move through the enemy minefields, but this had been costly, especially among the engineers. There were murmurs at the divisional level that it might be best if the offensive were broken off: some commanders were openly dismayed by Montgomery's seemingly clumsy handling of armored units, using them like bludgeons as opposed to Rommel's rapier-like tactics.

It was not yet a crisis, but the situation was serious, as Montgomery, who had never expected the Axis troops, especially the Italians, to stand firm, had so far been unable to make his preponderance in strength a decisive factor. Recognizing that the attack was losing what little momentum it had, Montgomery changed its direction on October 28, turned the 1st and 10th Armoured Divisions to the north, and gave them new orders: make directly for the coast, cut off the 7th Bersaglieri Division, and open a gap in the Axis lines. The 7th Armoured Division would follow behind them; once the gap was created, it would move up the coast road to take El Daba and Fuka, cutting off Panzerarmee Afrika's line of retreat as it did so.

While Montgomery was preparing this new stroke, Rommel struck at the British armor and infantry massing in the salient carved out of the Axis minefields. First 15th Panzer and the 90th Light, then 21st Panzer, then Littorio and Trieste, all waded into the fight. This was not the calculated riposte which had so tantalized him three days earlier, the counterstroke that could have cut off Montgomery's offensive at the knees, denied Rommel by a lack of fuel. This was a slugfest, more brawl than battle, its sole purpose being to stop the enemy attack in its tracks. The time for finesse had long past.

28 October 1942

Dearest Lu,

Who knows whether I'll have a chance to sit down and write in peace in the next few days or ever again. Today there's still a chance. The battle is raging. Perhaps we will still manage to be able to stick it out, in spite of all that's against us but it may go wrong, and that would have very grave consequences for the whole course of the war. For North Africa would then fall to the British in a few days, almost without a fight. We will do all we can to pull it off. But the enemy's superiority is terrific and our resources very small. Whether I would survive a defeat lies in God's hands. The lot of the vanquished is heavy. I'm happy in my own conscience that I've done all I can for victory and have not spared myself. I realized so well in the few short weeks I was at home what you two mean to me. My last thought is of you.[204]

The Germans and Italians gave better than they got, knocking out two enemy tanks for every one of theirs put out of action, but those were losses Montgomery could afford and Rommel could not. By day's end, the Germans had fewer than 150 tanks still running, the Italians not many more, while Eighth Army's tank strength stood at just over 800, many of them the new American-built Shermans. This was the battle which Rommel had sought to avoid since he first set foot in North Africa, the battle he knew could only have one outcome: the *materialschlact*, the battle of attrition. For 20 months he had used ruse, wile, and guile to avoid being caught in precisely the tactical situation in which he now found himself: fighting a battle without the wherewithal to retreat if necessary. If the Eighth Army broke through up along the coast, the whole of Panzerarmee Afrika would be trapped.

On October 29, having fought each other to a standstill, both sides paused to catch their breath. For the next three days the two armies would bicker back and forth over minor terrain features, but no major actions would be fought. Rommel briefly reflected on what might have been, then turned his mind to the hard choices he now had to make. As he saw it, yet another strategic opportunity was being squandered here: Stumme had done a remarkable job in finalizing Rommel's defensive plans, as evidenced by Eighth Army's inability to punch through the Axis lines despite its numerical and material superiority. It was a pity that Rommel would never be able to thank him for that. Had some of the heroic measures now being put in hand—the Luftwaffe, for example, was daily flying 250 tons of gasoline into Tobruk, a trickle admittedly, but it was better than nothing—begun weeks or even months earlier, Rommel might well have been able to hold the El Alamein line, not indefinitely, but certainly long enough to wake up the incompetents in Rome and Berlin who, Rommel was still certain, lied to the Führer about what could and could not be done for North Africa. Perhaps he might have held the line long enough for some of the manpower and equipment that even now was being squandered, or so he thought, on the Russian Front to be diverted to North Africa, where Rommel could accomplish something useful with them!

What Rommel was not to know of were two factors which rendered any such musings mere daydreams rather than strategic options. He was unaware of Ultra, had no way of knowing how it allowed British submarines to make almost-to-the-minute interceptions of the vital tankers that sailed from Naples or Salerno for Tripoli and send them to the bottom. He was still certain that Italian treachery was to blame—or if not treachery, corruption. (At one point he openly asserted that "It never proved possible to get major Italian naval units used for the protection of convoys or the transport of urgent supplies. Of course, the fuel could not then have been used for the Rome taxis.") It was Ultra that at the end of October enabled the Royal Navy to destroy three tankers, the *Luisiana*, *Prosperina*, and *Portofino*, carrying between them over 5,000 tons of gasoline for the *panzerarmee*, which denied Rommel the ability to conduct a truly effective defense at El Alamein. It is impossible, then, to overstate the value of Ultra to the British in North Africa: when what Rommel accomplished with an under-supplied, under-equipped army is considered, what the Afrika Korps might have done if properly supported can scarce be imagined.[205]

But even had the Allies not possessed Ultra and used it to bring about

Panzerarmee Afrika's undoing, a far more powerful force, at once irresistible and inevitable, would have put paid to any remaining hopes and dreams Rommel might have retained once he had been stopped at El Alamein. What Rommel did not know, indeed what only a handful of Germans at the highest levels of the Nazi regime knew at that moment, was that by the autumn of 1942 Germany had reached the limits of her manpower and her economy. The O.K.W.'s niggardly response to Rommel's pleas for more men and equipment was not due to the senior officers' hostility toward this upstart outsider—at least, not entirely—but rather because there was nothing left to give him: the cupboard was, in fact, quite bare.

The single most enduring myth of the Second World War is that of the awesome German war machine, of matchless technical abilities paired with unparalleled organizational skills. The mighty German industrial juggernaut was actually a canard bruited about by the Allies to exhort their own workers to greater feats of productivity. Germany's economy was never optimized for wartime production, unlike Great Britain and the United States, where vast swathes of the national economies and infrastructure were converted to wartime production, and research, development, and manufacturing were streamlined and rationalized, while the production of consumer goods became secondary. The Soviet Union's reorganization was even more draconian, as the *entire* national economy was subordinated to the military's requirements. In 1936, Herman Göring famously asked the German people "Which would you rather have, butter or guns?" implying that Germany's economy could provide one or the other, but not both. The problem was that the Nazis tried to produce guns *and* butter even after the war began, with the result that the whole of Germany's manufacturing capacity was never devoted to military production. It would not be until 1944, after two years of work by Albert Speer, the minister of Armaments and War Production, that Germany's economy was fully mobilized for war, with production peaking in August of that year, long after Germany's strategic position had become hopeless. Yet even then there were curious anomalies in German production priorities—the Steinbach piano company, for example, was still manufacturing its instruments in April 1945!

Perhaps no single example better illustrates the inherent inefficiency of the German economy, and hence a squandered potential for military might, than a straightforward comparison of the production figures for the mainstay battle tanks of the Wehrmacht, the Allies, and the Soviet Union. The German workhorse of the *panzerkorps* was the Panzerkampfwagen IV, or Panzer IV, of which a total of 8,569 examples of all models were produced from 1936, the year it was introduced, to the end of the war. By comparison, the total production of United States Army's M4 Sherman, in all variants, was 49,234—produced in just five years; the numbers for the Red Army's T-34 reached 84,070 in the same time span. Clearly, there is some merit to the argument of German apologists who assert that the Wehrmacht was never truly outfought, it was simply outproduced.

But on the most basic level, Germany's inability to mobilize her economy as efficiently as did the Allies was due to a fundamental flaw in Adolf Hitler's overall strategy, that flaw being, quite simply, that Adolf Hitler never possessed an overall strategy. He merely lurched from one campaign to another, with no conscious, deliberate connection between them: Hitler had no master plan, no "grand strategy," for going about whatever it was he hoped to achieve, and only vague ideas of what were those goals. Such disjointed strategic "thinking" resulted in operations or even entire campaigns, such as "*Sonnenblum*," Rommel's original mission to North Africa, which had no clearly defined strategic objectives. The consequences could be—and were—disastrous for Germany; in the case of North Africa, what should have been nothing more elaborate than a minor holding action in Libya evolved into an entire new theater of war for the Axis, where they would be catastrophically defeated.

This lack of a grand strategy also meant that Germany's weapon design, development and production was never given a coherent focus or direction until the war was already lost. German technology and engineering could and did produce some remarkably effective, even visionary weapons, but far too many of Germany's research and design programs were given over to producing weapons that, while they were interesting or possessed intriguing capabilities, were not weapons that Germany truly *needed*. By way of contrast, from the outset the Allies formulated a grand strategy for the defeat of Germany, Italy, and Japan: the tanks, aircraft, artillery, ships, and small arms they produced were all designed and built to expedite the accomplishment of that mission.

As disorganized as was Germany's weapons procurement programs, her allocation of manpower was even more absurd. Hitler's eighteenth-century attitudes toward sex and gender prevented German women from ever becoming a significant proportion of the Fatherland's labor pool, which meant that as late as the fall of 1944 there would be several million German men still working at unskilled or semi-skilled jobs that in Allied countries were being more than adequately filled by women. This put a near-crippling strain on the German Army's replacement process, leading the O.K.W. into introducing ever-increasing numbers of foreign-born troops into Wehrmacht units, some of them serving as volunteers, most of them fighting under compulsion. The O.K.W. had to judiciously allocate what manpower it had, carefully prioritizing, and its parsimonious attitude toward North Africa simply indicated that the campaign in the Western Desert was never sufficiently perceived as being vital to the defense of the Reich.

All of this meant that, in the end, even had Rommel been able to hold on at El Alamein in the autumn of 1942, he would have ultimately been driven out under the sheer weight of numbers which the Allies would have brought to bear. In total manpower and industrial capacity, of course, Germany could have never hoped for anything remotely approaching parity with Britain, America, and the Soviet Union combined, even in the most ideal circumstances, but economic decisions made by Hitler and his henchmen at the beginning of the war guaranteed that if Germany could not achieve a swift victory, she would never be able to muster the strength to hold back the Allies long enough to compel any settlement of the war short of an unconditional German surrender.

All of this would only become clear to Rommel in the months ahead, however: on the morning of October 29, 1942, he was focused on extracting as many of the Italian infantry divisions that were manning the El Alamein line as he possibly could; they would fall back to a new line to be established at Fuka, 50 miles to the west along the coast road. By mid-afternoon the order went out for all non-combat troops to begin evacuating to Mersa Matruh, which was even farther west than Fuka. The Afrika Korps and the Italian motorized divisions would do their best to hold back the coming British attack in the north to give the infantry as much time as possible to make good their escape. Not a word of these withdrawal plans were mentioned to either Rome or Berlin.

It was slow going for the infantry, and the southernmost division, Italy's Folgore Parachute Division, was barely a quarter of the way to Fuka when the next storm broke: at midnight on November 2, 1942, another British barrage was underway, and this time Montgomery was determined to force the issue to a conclusion. "Operation *Supercharge*," he called it, a battering-ram of two infantry and two armored divisions tasked with punching through what was left of the Axis defenses, destroying what was left of the Afrika Korps, and cutting off what remained of Rommel's entire army. The Italians began to waver, not surprising as their antitank guns were practically useless against the Eighth Army's Shermans, and the main guns on the Italian tanks were little better. Von Thoma, who still retained command of the Afrika Korps, did his best to stop the onslaught, but the British would not be denied this time. When von Thoma made his report to Rommel that evening, he was able to account for only 30 operable German tanks. For Rommel, that was enough: it was time to go. At 8:00 P.M. on November 2, the order went out to every unit of Panzerarmee Afrika: pull out, begin falling back to Fuka immediately.

It would not be until midnight that Rommel got round to informing Berlin of his decision. When he did so, he sent a detailed signal to the O.K.W., enumerating the reasons for his decision to retreat: exhausted by 10 days of constant fighting, with inadequate supplies of food, fuel, and ammunition, and faced by overwheming enemy numbers on the ground and in the air, the El Alamein position was untenable. Rommel could retreat now and possibly save the Italian infantry, or stand, fight, and accept the destruction of Panzerarmee Afrika. This signal was little more than a formality, as the German military tradition had always been for higher command echelons, accepting that "the man on the spot" would have the best sense of the circumstances which actually obtained where he was, to endorse the tactical and operational decisions that man made.

It was at 1:30 P.M. on November 3—more than 12 hours after Rommel's signal to Berlin—that O.K.W. replied to Rommel, and when they did, it was with a personal message from the Führer himself. It was not at all what Rommel had expected.

To FIELD MARSHAL ROMMEL

It is with trusting confidence in your leadership and the courage of the German-Italian troops under your command that the German people and I are following the heroic struggle in Egypt. In the situation which you find yourself there can be no other thought but to stand fast, yield not a yard of ground and throw every gun and every man into the battle. Considerable air force reinforcements are being sent to Commander-in-Chief South. The Duce and the Comando Supremo are also making the utmost efforts to send you the means to continue the fight. Your enemy, despite his superiority, must also be at the end of his strength. It would not be the first time in history that a strong will has triumphed over the bigger battalions. As to your troops, you can show them no other road than that to victory or death.

(Signed) ADOLF HITLER[206]

This was a watershed moment for Erwin Rommel, for the magic that had thus far kept him spellbound by the Führer was suddenly and irreparably broken. The unspoken bond between a soldier and his commander is never that the commander will not ask the soldier to stand and die, but that he will never ask the soldier to do so needlessly; yet that was precisely what Hitler was expecting of Rommel and his men. The Führer was morally obliged to the officers and men of Panzerarmee Afrika to explain why he was demanding this, if only to encourage them to sell their lives more dearly, but as Rommel suddenly discovered, moral obligation ran in only one direction for Adolf Hitler.

> This order demanded the impossible. . . . We were completely stunned, and for the first time during the African campaign I did not know what to do. A kind of apathy took hold of us as we issued orders for all existing positions to be held on instructions from the highest authority. I forced myself to this action, as I had always demanded unconditional obedience from others and, consequently, wished to apply the same principle to myself. Had I known what was to come I should have acted differently, because from that time on, we had continually to circumvent orders from the Führer or Duce in order to save the army from destruction. But this first instance of interference by higher authority in the tactical conduct of the African war came as a considerable shock. . . . An overwhelming bitterness welled up in us when we saw the superlative

spirit of the army, in which every man, from the highest to the low-
est, knew that even the greatest effort could no longer change the
course of the battle.[207]

His letter to Lucie that night was short, fatalistic, and bitter.

Dearest Lu,
The battle still rages with unspent fury. I can no longer, or scarcely
any longer, believe in its successful outcome. Berndt flies to the
Führer to-day to report.
Enclosed 25,000 lire that I've saved.
What will become of us is in God's hands. . . .

(Even in such dire straits, ever the canny Swabian, Rommel included
a quick postscript, reminding Lucie to "Have Appel exchange the lire. Cur-
rency regulations!")[208]

Despite that momentary assertion of his practical Swabian nature,
Rommel was at once torn by his habitual instinct to obey the orders of a
superior, and furious at the implications of Hitler's directive. He had
pledged absolute obedience to the Führer, and he often demanded the same
from his own subordinates, so it seemed hypocritical to suddenly exempt
himself from the same standard of conduct. And yet the order made absolutely no sense. Walking back and forth outside his command tent with
Major Elmar Warning, an officer on Westphal's staff, Rommel held forth
on Hitler's "victory or death" missive, saying, "If we stay put here, then the
army won't last three days. But do I have the right, as the commanding
officer, or even as a soldier, to disobey an order? If I *do* obey the Führer's
order, then there's the danger my own troops won't obey *me*!" He paused
then blurted out, "My men's lives come first! The Führer is crazy!"

Warming to his subject now, Rommel went on: "Warning, believe me,
Hitler is the greatest criminal whom I know. He will fight not only to the
last German soldier, but to the total destruction of Germany, in his own
selfish interests!"[209]

Giving evidence of his inner turmoil, Rommel's new orders to his
army uncharacteristically temporized: the 90th Light Division, along with
the Pavia, Folgore, Trento, and Bologna Divisions, were ordered to stand

fast, dig in, and hold off the advancing British for as long as possible, thus superficially satisfying Hitler's demand to "yield not a yard of ground," while at the same time the remaining German and Italian units continued to fall back. On the other side of the lines, Montgomery urged the 1st and 7th Armoured Divisions to press hard on the heels of the retreating Axis forces, only to have the 21st Panzer and Ariete give them bloody noses, though by the end of November 3 Ariete was all but spent as a fighting force. The Littorio and Trieste Division surrendered, but the Italian paratroopers of Folgore kept fighting until they literally exhausted their ammunition, putting one last redeeming exclamation point on the career of the Italian Army in North Africa.

That same day, Leutnant Berndt, acting on Rommel's direct orders, flew to Berlin, where he would make Rommel's case directly to Hitler, bluntly explaining that if the no retreat order were obeyed, it would mean the pointless destruction of Panzerarmee Afrika in a matter of days. Berndt, because he was one of the earliest members of the Nazi Party and well as a close associate of Dr. Göbbels, was usually warmly welcomed in Hitler's inner circle. This time, however, he was received with a cold courtesy and his arguments fell on deaf ears. The order would stand.

The fourth day of November was the decisive day for Rommel. His rearguard was disintegrating and there was no point in pretending that he was making any real effort to comply with Hitler's "victory or death" directive. Late that morning he sent one final *pro forma* request for permission to withdraw from El Alamein while at the same time doing his best to accelerate the westward movement of the army. Ritter von Thoma appeared at *panzerarmee* headquarters to report on the state of the Afrika Korps, pronounced Hitler's orders "madness" then drove back to what was left of his panzer divisions. That afternoon he was captured by the British after his own command tank had been immobilized and set on fire. Not long after von Thoma left, Kesselring appeared; the meeting with Rommel was lively to say the least, for Rommel was convinced that overly optimistic reports by Luftwaffe officers—including Kesselring himself—had misled the Führer about the true situation at El Alamein. Kesselring insisted that this was not so, that Hitler was applying the tactical experience of the Russian Front to North Africa, never giving thought to how vastly different were the operational differences between the two. Rommel grudgingly agreed that this was probably the case, then blurted out "He should have left the decision to me!"[210]

Then came the news that the 1st and 7th Armoured Divisions had finally broken through the crumbling Italian rearguard and were now sweeping wide to the west, clearly intent on turning north at some point to cut the coast road near Fuka and complete Montgomery's long-awaited entrapment of Rommel and his army. By any realistic yardstick the decision was now out of Rommel's hands.

> So now it had come, the thing we had done everything in our power to avoid: our front broken and the fully motorized enemy streaming into our rear. Superior orders could no longer count. We had to save what there was to be saved. . . . I issued orders for the retreat to be started immediately. This decision could at least be the means of saving the motorized part of the Panzer Army from destruction, although the army had already lost so much as a result of the 24-hour postponement of its retreat . . . that it was no longer in a position to offer effective opposition to the British advance at any point. . . . Anything that did not immediately reach the road and race off westwards was lost, for the enemy followed us up over a wide front and overran everything that came in his path.[211]

The early winter rain began on November 5, just as Rommel and the remains of the Afrika Korps reached Fuka; there was a short, sharp engagement there between the Axis rearguard and the leading elements of Eighth Army, in which the British came out second best. On November 6 the rain turned into a near-deluge and the landscape became a quagmire, which slowed down the British pursuit and allowed Rommel time to sort out his units as best he could before moving further west to Mersa Matruh. The Eighth Army had for the moment reached the limits of the supplies allocated for *Supercharge*, and Montgomery, not wishing to upset his logistical arrangements, called a halt, save for light mobile units which continued to harass the Axis army. During the night Rommel pulled his forces out of Mersa Matruh and made for Sidi Barrani, where he stopped for two days to rest and reorder his columns; by this time the entire effective strength of Panzerarmee Afrika was barely more than 5,000 men, 20 tanks, and 50 guns.

It was at Sidi Barrani where Rommel was informed that the United States Army had carried out amphibious landings on the North African coast, in French Morocco and Algeria—Operation *Torch*—on November 8. One of the American landings was at Algiers, which placed the US Army closer to Tripoli than was the *panzerarmee* at that moment. This news shifted the entire paradigm of the war in North Africa for Rommel, who saw immediately that this meant Panzerarmee Afrika's days were numbered: his mission now was to get his command to a place where it could be evacuated before it was overwhelmed. Initially Rommel had planned to conduct a staged withdrawal along the Libyan coast, delaying Eighth Army's advance as long as possible; with the news from Morocco and Algeria, that strategy evaporated: delaying the British advance from the east would do no good if the Americans were to take Tripolitania from the west. On the other hand, rushing headlong westward only to have to stop at some point and wait for the British to catch up in order to surrender to them was not a strategy either. Libya's geography dictated that there were no truly defensible positions between Sollum and Mersa el Brega, back where Rommel had begun both of his offensives. Tobruk would have been a rat-trap—the *panzerarmee* would have been as easily bottled up there as had been South Africans in June, and the wherewithal to emulate the Australians from 1941 simply did not exist. Everywhere else in Libya, no matter where Rommel might choose to make his stand, his right flank would always be open, inviting the Eighth Army to swing around behind him in a mirror image of what he had done to them time and again. So what was Rommel to do? For that matter, with the threat it had once posed to Egypt a thing of the past, what strategic purpose did Panzerarmee Afrika now serve? On November 11, Rommel asked Kesselring and Cavallero to meet with him in the hope that between the three of them they could find an answer to the question, but both men declined the invitation, though neither chose to offer an explanation of why they did so. Rommel was vexed: once again, Hitler's lack of a coherent grand strategy was actively hindering Germany's war effort. What purpose was there in having an army in the field when no one could or would present clear instructions as to what was to be done with it?

14 Nov. 1942

Dearest Lu,

Heading west again. I'm well in myself, but you won't need to be told what's going on in my mind. We have to be grateful for every day that the enemy does not close in on us. How far we shall get I cannot say. It all depends on the gasoline, which has yet to be flown across to us.

How are you both? My thoughts even with so much on my mind are often with you. What will become of the war if we lose North Africa? How will it finish? I wish I could get free of these terrible thoughts.

Rommel decided to go straight to the top to get answers, so once again Leutnant Berndt figuratively trudged off to Berlin at Rommel's behest, seeking the counsel of the Führer himself. Hitler proved to be considerably less than helpful, however. It was clear to Berndt, who relayed his thoughts and conclusions to Rommel, that the Führer now regarded the officer commanding Panzerarmee Afrika as a hopeless pessimist who could not endure setbacks and needlessly retreated when he met with the slightest rebuff. However, if Rommel insisted on retreating all the way to Mersa el Brega, then he should, Hitler demanded, concentrate on using that position as the "springboard for a new offensive." The vanguard of an Axis blocking force had been dispatched to Tunisia two days after the Allied landings in Morocco and Algiers; there, it was hoped, it would forestall any Allied advance into Tripolitania. When Berndt asked what advice the Führer had to aid Rommel in coordinating his strategy with the Tunisian force, Hitler snapped back, "*Sagen, der Feldmarschall, sagte ich zu Tunis aus seinen Berechnungen lassen!*"—"Tell the Field Marshal I said to leave Tunis out of his calculations!"

Rommel was not idle while Berndt was in Berlin. Using the 90th Light Division as his rearguard, he deftly fell back across Cyrenaica, snapping at Eighth Army if it got too close or too inquisitive. Montgomery, despite having air superiority and overwhelming numbers of men and equipment, was never quite able to spring the trap on Rommel, who attributed the British general's inability to "finish the job," as it were, to a fundamental timidity. Focused on conserving his manpower and equipment, careful never to overreach his supplies, Montgomery was, in Rommel's words, "overcautious."

He risked nothing in any way doubtful and bold solutions were completely foreign to him. So our motorised forces would have to keep up an appearance of constant activity, in order to induce ever greater caution in the British and make them even slower. I was quite satisfied that Montgomery would never take the risk of following up boldly and overrunning us, as he could have done without any danger to himself. Indeed, such a course would have cost him far fewer losses in the long run than his methodical insistence on overwhelming superiority in each tactical action, which he could only obtain at the cost of his speed.[212]

Astonishingly, the *panzerarmee's* morale remained rock solid—a circumstance due in no small part to the confidence possessed by its soldiers, German and Italian alike, in the man leading them. There was in Rommel none of the questionable bonhommie and avuncular posturing of Kesselring, nor any of the sense of intrinsic privilege which too many senior Italian officers considered to be inherent to their rank. He ate the same rations as his troops, spent just as much time sweating in the sun as did they, slept in his car when necessary, or else in his command vehicle or in a tent most of the rest of the time—the occasions when he had a roof over his head were so infrequent as to be worthy of comment in his correspondence with Lucie. He lived among his soldiers, so that they knew their man: they understood almost implicitly why they couldn't stand and challenge the British to a fight to the finish. Retreating did not come naturally to the men of the Afrika Korps, nor, after being led by Rommel, as easily to the Italians as it once had done; still, they understood why they were falling back across Libya, and while they were unhappy at being compelled to do so, there was none of the sullenness that might have been expected. Instead, a perverse sense of pride manifested itself as they conducted their retreat as skillfully and stubbornly as possible.

During the retreat to Mersa el Brega, Rommel turned contemplative: he had seen and heard a lot during his three weeks in Semmering, before he had to return to North Africa, and he had intuited much, much more. Now he began putting it all together. For the most part, he kept his thoughts to himself, not even confiding them in his letters to Lucie, until an encounter with Hans von Luck, the major commanding 21st Panzer's reconnaissance battalion, turned him unexpectedly voluble. Von Luck was having an interesting war in North Africa: given command of a total of three recon battalions, he led the screening forces that covered the *panzerarmee's* right flank during the retreat from El Alamein. He did so with skill, imagination, and not a little eccentricity: one British unit which von Luck's battalions repeatedly encountered were the Royal Dragoons. So often did the two units cross paths that a certain degree of familiarity sprang up between them, to the point where they would routinely exchange messages about the well-being of recently captured personnel, and established a "gentlemen's agreement" to cease fire at 5:00 P.M. every day for the duration of the retreat.

For all of his quirks, however, von Luck was a soldier's soldier, and together he and Rommel had a long history: he had been one of Rommel's students at the Dresden infantry school in 1931, and when the two men next encountered each other, von Luck was commanding the reconnaissance battalion of the 7th Panzer Division in France in 1940. For most of the campaign, von Luck's unit was leading the division; he impressed Rommel as being brave, intelligent, and very cool under fire. After spending 18 months on the Russian Front, von Luck was transferred to the 21st Panzer Division at Rommel's request; he arrived in North Africa in April 1942. Although von Luck was a Prussian aristocrat with a 700 year-long family military tradition (the full family name was von Luck und Witten), Rommel genuinely liked him, for the young major never affected any of the airs, graces, and pretenses common to the aristocratic officers Rommel found so annoying. It was hardly surprising then, in a way, that it would be to von Luck to whom Rommel would finally open up.

The war was lost, he said. That had become obvious at El Alamein, where Rommel got his first glimpse of the material advantages America would supply to the Allies. Germany must seek an armistice immediately, and force Hitler to abdicate if that was what was required to bring about the ceasefire. Prolonging the war would only assure Germany's destruction: the Wehrmacht was fighting today hundreds of miles distant from the Fatherland, but it would only be a matter of time before the Allies—and the Russians!—were standing on German soil. And if Germany's enemies did not destroy her from without, the Nazis would do so from within; they, too, would have to go. This was a side of Rommel which von Luck had never seen before, and the memory of Rommel's candor and prescience stayed with him for the rest of his life.[213]

On November 24, the same day that Panzerarmee Afrika reached Mersa el Brega, Rommel finally had his conference with Kesselring and Cavallero at the Arco di Fileni, the triumphal marble arch Mussolini had constructed astride the coastal road to mark the border between Cyrenaica and Tripolitania. Neither of them, in his opinion, could truly grasp the reason why the army could not stand at Mersa el Brega: Kesselring, he said, "looked at everything from the standpoint of the Luftwaffe, and thought principally of the consequences which the move would have on the strategic air situation in Tunisia," while Cavallero "lived in a world of make-believe." Rommel opened the meeting by declaring that he thought the Mersa el Brega position was untenable in the long run, because just as with every other position in Libya west of Sollum, the southern flank lay open to the desert, a standing invitation for Eighth Army to swing round it and roll it up. He wanted to continue moving west until he reached Gabes on the frontier between Tripolitania and Tunisia, where the army would have mountains on the right and the sea on the left. There Rommel would be able to make a stand against Montgomery. But both the Führer and the Duce wanted Panzerarmee Afrika to hold the line at Mersa el Brega, and so Rommel would at least make a show of doing so. The question was what would Kesselring and Cavallero do. Kesselring bluntly told Rommel that he would prefer the *panzerarmee* to stand at Mersa el Brega for as long as possible: the defenses in Tunisia were far from ready, and Rommel's army could buy the time needed to complete them. In reply Rommel caustically asked what good would those defenses do if his army, outflanked and overrun, was unavailable to man them. The Afrika Korps had a total of 35 tanks—Montgomery's Eighth Army had over 400. "We either lose the position four days earlier and save the army, or lose both position and army four days later." All of Rommel's subordinates, German and Italian alike, agreed that the *panzerarmee* could not hold back a determined British attack.[214]

Surprisingly, Cavallero agreed with Rommel, at least in his strategic assessment: it was Tunisia which was now the critical Axis real estate in North Africa; Tripolitania was as good as lost, but as long as the Germans and Italians had an army in Tunisia, they could hold the Allies at arm's length from the European continent and even, should circumstances change, go over to the offensive once again at some future date and take back everything that was lost. But, Cavallero insisted, it was imperative that Rommel hold at Mersa el Brega as long as possible in order to finish the defenses of which Kesselring had spoken. When a message from Mussolini arrived on November 26 essentially parroting Hitler's order of November 20 to stand fast at Mersa el Brega and take every opportunity which presented itself to launch local counterattacks against Eighth Army, Rommel realized that drastic measures were needed if the people in Berlin and Rome were to see the realities of the war in North Africa as it now stood.

On November 28 Rommel climbed in his Heinkel 111 transport at Tripoli, and flew to Berlin. The following day he would be in Rastenburg, Hitler's headquarters in East Prussia, where he would fight an entirely different sort of battle than he had ever before fought.

CHAPTER TWELVE

AFRICAN PERIGEE

Theirs not to reason why,
Theirs but to do and die
—ALFRED TENNYSON

n retrospect, Rommel's last four months in North Africa appear to be an anticlimax, a case of "too little, too late," an inevitable end to a once-grand adventure. Yet at the time neither Rommel nor his staff nor his subordinates saw the situation as a forlorn hope. If the Afrika Korps was no longer a threat to the British in Egypt and the Suez Canal, it could still stand as a force to be reckoned with in the counsel of Allied strategy, and Rommel was on his way to Berlin to make certain that it did so in Axis counsel as well.

As a strategist Rommel had grown during his time in North Africa, in both the breadth and depth of his understanding of the widening war and his role—and place—in it as the commander of, successively, the Afrika Korps, Panzergruppe Afrika, and Panzerarmee Afrika. Libya was, of course, about to be written off, as it must be and as it should be, for its strategic value was now nil: the five successive offensives back and forth across Cyrenaica in the previous two years was proof that there was no way to hold Libya—nor in truth was there anything in it worth holding were it possible. Tunisia, however, was another story, as it had the potential to be, for a while at least, an Axis bastion: the terrain was far more rugged, offering far better opportunities for establishing strong defensive positions, the sea route between Italy's southern ports and the city of Tunis was significantly shorter and better protected.

Rommel did not imagine that Tunisia could hold out indefinitely against the Allies: the overwhelming industrial capacity of the United States would, in his considered opinion, assure an eventual Allied victory in any theater where its output could be properly brought to bear. What he was already intuiting—and would see evidence of before his run in Africa was over—was that between them the Americans and the British were bringing not just superior numbers to war, but a more intelligent, sophisticated, and realistic application of their resources than were the Soviets—or the Germans, for that matter. Whereas the Soviets were content with the simplicity of sheer brute force strategy and tactics, and the Germans were depending on their technological superiority to make up for their deficiencies in production capacity, the Allies were building a systematic way of waging war, akin to a machine, one that would, if given sufficient time, integrate formations, units, and weapons types, land, air, and sea into an irresistible force. One that would still be subject to the mental and physical limitations of the flesh-and-blood creatures who had to operate and guide it, but that had been fundamentally designed from the beginning to fight battles in the way the Allies intended to fight them. As Rommel saw it, the Wehrmacht could not defeat that machine, therefore the Gemans must find a way to make it too expensive for the Allies to continue to operate it. That process, he believed, could begin in Tunisia.[215]

The first part of this strategy would be economy of force: throwing more men and materiel into Tunisia was not the solution; doing so would, in fact, only make the situation there worse. Rommel's dash across Libya and into Egypt in the spring and summer of 1942, then the retreat from El Alamein had shown that, however good might be the intentions in Berlin and Rome, sustaining an actual army along the length of the North African coast was beyond the ability of the Axis. In Tunisia, however, a few well-trained, well-equipped mechanized divisions would be able to hold a perimeter near the borders, where mountains, passes, and defiles limited the practical routes along which the Allies could attack; all non-essential personnel ought to be evacuated immediately. As Allied pressure inevitably increased, the remaining units would gradually withdraw, reducing the length of their front, methodically evacuating troops and, when possible, equipment as the perimeter shrank. This process would continue until the Allies finally overran the whole of Tunisia, with nothing to show for their efforts but a handful of prisoners—"and thus be robbed of the fruits of their victory, just as we had been at Dunkirk," as Rommel put it.

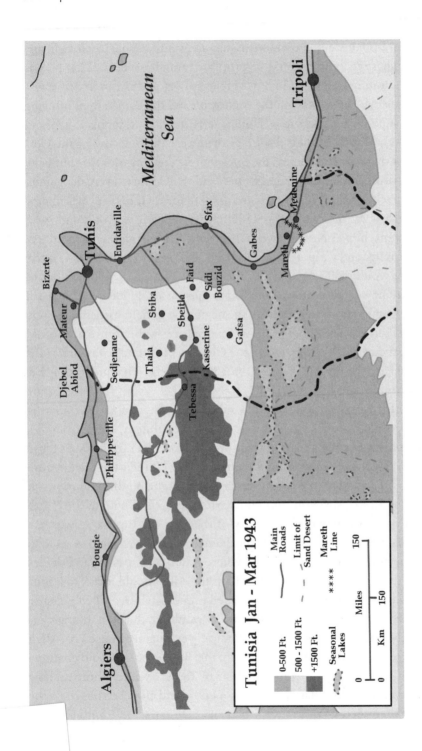

Tunisia Jan - Mar 1943

The troops successfully withdrawn from Tunisia would be a solid core of seasoned veterans, wily to the ways of the British and the Americans, around which would be built the army that would defend Sicily and Italy from the invasions that everyone knew would follow the loss of North Africa.[216]

And so the purpose of his unscheduled flight to Berlin and his sudden appearance at the Führerhauptquartier in East Prussia was to persuade Hitler that there was a viable strategy for Tunisia, one that went beyond merely holding "to the last man and the last round." He was confident, having always been welcomed in the past by the Führer, that this time he would be received at least cordially. He was shocked, then, when brought into the conference room where Hitler was holding court, the first words to issue forth from the dictator's mouth were a shout of, "How dare you leave the theater of your command without my permission!"[217]

It's impossible to tell how much of Hitler's outburst was the product of genuine anger, how much was theatrics, and how much was induced by frustration as he confronted an escalating emergency on the Eastern Front. Just six days earlier the Red Army had encircled and isolated the German Sixth Army at Stalingrad: a quarter-million Axis soldiers were trapped behind Soviet lines, and the situation was still deteriorating. War with the Soviet Union—the National Socialist crusade to rid the world of Bolshevism—had always been one-half of Hitler's overriding compulsion (the other half being the eradication of the Jewish people), and suddenly the spearhead of the crusade, Sixth Army, was facing a military disaster. To Hitler the worth of the campaign in North Africa had always been exceedingly minor, even when Rommel was winning his most smashing victories; Rommel himself was always more useful to Hitler for his propaganda value than for strategic accomplishments. Now, when Rommel came to all but beg for the means to restore Panzerarmee Afrika to a fighting force, all Hitler had to offer was insult and abuse, accusing the men of the Afrika Korps of cowardice, denigrating them for having thrown their weapons away. If Rommel had followed the orders he, Hitler, had issued, the line at El Alamein would have held and there would have been no need for Rommel to come to Rastenburg, to Wolfsschanze to beg for new tanks, guns, and equipment for his men. Rommel, coldly and stiffly correct—no small feat for someone with his temper—told the Führer that the British bombers, tanks and artillery had simply blown the German soldiers' weapons to pieces; it was, he asserted, nothing short of a miracle that anyone had escaped capture. Hitler could not be bothered to listen to the truth.

> . . . there was no attempt at discussion. The Führer said that his decision to hold the eastern front in the winter of 1941–42 had saved Russia and that there, too, he had upheld his orders ruthlessly. I began to realise that Adolf Hitler simply did not want to see the situation as it was, and that he reacted emotionally against what his intelligence must have told him was right. He said that it was a political necessity to continue to hold a major bridgehead in Africa and there would, therefore, be no withdrawal from the Mersa el Brega line.[218]

With that, Hitler made a few vague promises about more supplies and new equipment, then coldly dismissed Rommel; he should have been paying closer attention to what the field marshal was saying, as Rommel had been doing his best to explain how to avert an even greater catastrophe than the one that was unfolding between the Volga and the Don.

Rommel's (wisely well-concealed) anger and resentment at Hitler's refusal to talk constructively about the situation in North Africa was compounded when he learned that he would be traveling to Rome with Reichsmarschall Hermann Göring. The Luftwaffe commander-in-chief had never been one of Rommel's favorites—Rommel very early on detected the underlying malignity of Göring's character—and the feeling was compounded by the memory of Kesselring's condescension and obstructionism—for that is what Rommel saw it to be—for the last six months in North Africa. Rommel found the journey to Rome aboard Göring's specially appointed train uniformly unpleasant, as he was compelled was to

> . . . witness the antics of the *Reichsmarschall* in his special train. The situation did not seem to trouble him in the slightest. He plumed himself, beaming broadly at the primitive flattery heaped on him by imbeciles from his own court, and talked of nothing but jewelry and pictures. At other times his behavior could perhaps be amusing; now, it was infuriating.[219]

Rommel suspected that Göring, who was ostensibly going to Rome as Hitler's plenipotentiary to negotiate new arrangements for supplying Panzerarmee Afrika, had ulterior motives for this excursion. Göring was by nature amibtious—not, as Rommel would have been the first to agree, a bad trait in a man; but he was also ruthless, petty, jealous, and above all amoral. He coveted the influence in the Third Reich which the Waffen-SS gave Heinrich Himmler, its nominal commander-in-chief. He was in the process of creating what was in Rommel's eyes his own Praetorian Guard by organizing Luftwaffe field divisions—mostly infantry units—formed out of surplus Luftwaffe ground personnel. There would ultimately be 20 such divisions—plus the "Hermann Göring Panzer Division"—most of which saw some combat on the Russian Front, where they performed adequately at best; if Göring had hoped they would be the equal of the Waffen-SS he was sadly disappointed. However, he saw an opportunity in North Africa for the Luftwaffe's ground force to make a name for itself, as he regarded the British and Americans as weak and ineffective. Rommel suspected that Göring coveted the post of commander-in-chief in North Africa and was working to bring about Rommel's dismissal. Göring was unquestionably the source of the rumors that Rommel was a sick man whose illness had fostered a pessimism which colored all of his reports to the O.K.W. and the Führer.

> He gave birth to the absurd idea that I was governed by moods and could only command when things went well; if they went badly I became depressed and caught the "African sickness." From this it was argued that since, to win battles, it needed a general who believed in victory and since I was a sick man anyway, it was necessary to consider whether to relieve me of my command. On the subject of the "moods," I should perhaps say that we at the front were naturally not particularly pleased when the situation approached disaster. The Reichsmarschall, on the other hand, sat through it all in his railway carriage. Thus the angle of approach was a little different.[220]

Even as Rommel and Göring rolled toward Rome, the combat elements of the Hermann Göring Division were on their way to Tunisia. Rommel, of course, deplored the entire idea of "private armies," whether they belonged to Heinrich Himmler or Hermann Göring. They created too much competition for limited resources of manpower and equipment, and there was too much duplication of effort in maintaining three separate logisitic organizations. But the Nazi tradition of empire-building, which went all the way back to the days of Ernst Röhm and the SA, was too deeply entrenched, so there was little Rommel could do to stem the rising tide of inefficiency and ineptitude.[221]

On the other hand, Rommel was not entirely ignorant in the ways of using empires other men had built within the Third Reich. If there was any chance for him to remain in command of Panzerarmee Afrika, he could not propose any further withdrawals: Hitler was now enthralled by his own "no retreat" dogma, and Mussolini, if only for political purposes, was echoing the Führer. Defying the two dictators, regardless of how sound the military reasons for such defiance, would all but assure Rommel's dismissal. And yet, for him, it was imperative that he secure permission to begin moving the army all the way back to Gabes, 80 miles inside Tunisia, where the French had built the Mareth Line, a wide, deep belt of prewar fortifications built to hold off any Italian attack out of Tripolitania, before Montgomery began his attack on Mersa el Brega. It would mean the difference between an orderly withdrawal which would save all the men as well as the carefully hoarded vehicles and equipment the army had been able to save from the wreck of Libya, and a hasty, disorganized retreat where some men and materiel would have to be sacrificed to save the lion's share of the army. Rommel knew that whatever plan of operations he put forward in the upcoming conference with Mussolini would automatically incur Göring's opposition. Leutnant Berndt, on the other hand, whose high standing within the Nazi Party and at the Propaganda Ministry gave him a certain cachet with the *Reichsmarschall*, was the perfect emissary for presenting Rommel's proposal for a retreat into Tunisia.

This Berndt did—but not before Rommel added a twist to it that he was certain would play on not only Göring's vanity but on his ambition, as well. This was to disguise the withdrawal to Gabes as a maneuver which would be the prelude to opening an attack to the west, out of Tunisia, against the Americans in Algiers. The *panzerarmee* would fall back *past* the Mareth Line, head northwest and combine with the fresh German units in Tunisia, including the 10th Panzer Division, which had just been dispatched to

Tunis. A lightning-quick blow against the Americans to knock them back on their heels, perhaps even push them farther westward, and then the *panzerarmee* could be back on the Mareth Line to meet any counterstroke by the Eighth Army before Montgomery could finish amassing his troops and supplies.

When Berndt presented this plan to Göring, the *Reichsmarschall,* imagining himself at the head of a conquering army, was openly enthusiastic in his support for it. In fact, when Göring and Rommel met with Mussolini on November 30, Göring attempted to present Rommel's plan as his own. He then went on to imply that Rommel was too sick and exhausted to continue as the senior officer in North Africa—leaving Mussolini to infer that he, Göring, should take Rommel's place. As Mussolini and Cavallero had to assent to Italian forces in Tripolitania being placed under German command, this all but gave them veto power over the appointment of a German supreme commander in North Africa, hence Göring's efforts to sway the Italian dictator. But Göring went too far in trying to make his case, and openly accused Rommel of deliberately abandoning the Italian infantry at El Alamein. Rommel didn't defend himself from Göring's slander—he didn't need to: before Rommel could say a word, Mussolini said, "That's news to me; your retreat was a masterpiece, Marshal Rommel." At that, any chance Göring may have had of gaining the supreme command in North Africa evaporated.

There was one bright spot for Rommel in this excursion to Rome: Lucie had come aboard the *Reichsmarschall*'s train at Munich in order to spend a few days with her husband, who would have neither the time nor the opportunity to visit Herrlingen. All his life, Rommel drew strength and resilience from the bond he shared with his wife, and this time was no exception. Lucie, for her part, gained an even deeper understanding of the fact that not all of the battles fought by her husband were waged against the Allies: she witnessed first-hand Göring's narcissistic prancing, and the antipathy that existed between him and Rommel. There were long private conversations between Lucie and Erwin, of which no detailed recollections survive, but from a handful of oblique references in their letters in the months ahead, it can be inferred that Erwin was being very frank and open with Lucie about the realities of the war and Germany's dwindling chances of victory. For both of them this journey was a pivotal experience: Lucie had for the most part been more enthusiastic about Germany's National Socialist regime—and more vocal in her support of it—than ever was her husband; now she was learning to her dismay that not only was Germany most emphatically not winning the war, the possibility that Germany would lose was growing daily, brought about by Adolf Hitler's growing detachment from reality. Rommel, who had long admired Hitler while being at best mildly contemptuous of most of the rest of the Nazi hierarchy, now saw Hitler's rising sense of infallibility, his reliance on his "intuition," and his belief in his "destiny" as a malign force on the Wehrmacht's ability to defend not only the Nazi empire, but also the Reich itself. Hitler had broken faith with Rommel when he issued the "stand and die" order at El Alamein; he lost any chance of restoring that bond by his outbursts at Rastenburg.

As Rommel expected, very little was actually resolved in Rome: the usual empty promises were made. (Rommel later remarked bitterly that had a fraction of the effort now pledged actually been made a few months earlier, the Axis would not have found itself in its current situation.) Kesselring, citing an increasing threat to his newly established airfields in Tunisia, would have none of the planned withdrawal from Mersa el Brega; for his part Rommel's respect for Kesselring was rapidly diminishing: the Luftwaffe general had yet to fight a ground campaign but regularly delivered himself of oracular pronouncements on how Rommel should conduct his own defense against the Eighth Army. Rommel's antipathy toward Kesselring only grew further when the airman repeatedly hijacked for the Luftwaffe units in Tunisia the supplies and equipment specifically designated for Panzerarmee Afrika, including thousands of tons of gasoline and several batteries of 88mm Flak guns—only on direct orders from O.K.W. was the purloined materiel turned over to Rommel's men.

Rommel was able to secure Mussolini's permission to pull the non-motorized Italian infantry out and sent them back to Buerat, roughly halfway between Mersa el Brega and the Mareth Line, while the remaining motorized and mechanized units held firm. This was, everyone knew, the most transparent of subterfuges, for as soon as the Italian infantry arrived in Buerat, the rest of the *panzerarmee* would begin leapfrogging back to join them, after which the entire army would fall back to Mareth. It was a face-saving gesture, something both men clearly understood, even as Göring gave one final demonstration of how utterly clueless he was as to the true situation in North Africa by demanding that Rommel begin a counterattack against Eighth Army from the Mersa el Brega position. Privately Rommel could only shake his head in mingled dismay and relief that his "Africans" had been spared the leadership of this buffoon.

It was during this series of conferences that Rommel became aware of an increasingly strong undercurrent running through the Italian command, a barely concealed war-weariness that was distinct from the lack of enthusiasm and air of corruption Rommel had sensed and suspected before. For the first time since coming to power in 1922, Mussolini's political position was not entirely secure: there were whispers that the loss of Italy's North African empire might bring about his downfall. The Axis alliance was becoming increasingly unpopular with the Italians as a whole, who resented the spreading perception that Mussolini was little more than Hitler's poodle; Italy was gaining nothing from this war save for growing casualty lists.

The problem with the Axis itself—and there was in fact a great deal of truth in what the typical Italian on the Via Appia believed about it—was, once again, the lack of anything resembling a grand strategy. The Axis had been from its inception no more than a marriage of convenience: Germany and Italy, Hitler and Mussolini, had few if any common goals or objectives apart from the aggrandizement of their respective homelands, and while the military and political support of one for the other at various times was useful, even decisive, their refusal to cooperate and coordinate strategies led to them often working at cross-purposes. By contrast, the Allies, along with the Soviet Union, however fractious their relationships and whatever the specific national goals might be, never lost sight of their larger objective: the defeat of Germany and Italy. As a consequence, the Allied war effort was motivated by a sense of purpose, the like of which the Axis never possessed. That an alliance between Hitler and Mussolini should exist was nearly inevitable—so was the nature of that alliance and the burdens it subsequently imposed on both parties; in some ways Germany and Italy became each other's worst enemy.

MEANWHILE, BACK IN Tunisia, Walther Nehring, now a *general der panzertruppe* and recovered from the wounds he incurred at Alam Halfa, had been sent to Tunisia on November 12, four days after the Allied landings in Morocco and Algiers, to take command of the XC Panzerkorps, which at first seemed to exist only on paper. Within days however, the 10th Panzer Division arrived at Tunis (though it was short most of its artillery regiment), along with two regiments of Fallschirmjäger, the armored components of the Herman Göring Division, and the Division von Broich, so named after its commanding officer, Oberst (Colonel) Friedrich Freiherr von Broich. Originally just a divisional headquarters unit, it was gradually fleshed out with various odds and sods of other units, mostly unassigned replacement battalions, in much the same way the Afrika Korps' 90th Light Division had been created. Also on its way was the Schwere Panzer-Abteilung 501—the 501st Heavy Panzer Detachment: the Allies were about to be introduced to the Panzer VIa—the Tiger tank. This rapid buildup of fresh units, the like of which had never occurred during the whole of the Afrika Korps campaigns in Libya and Egypt, was possible for two reasons: there were two major deepwater ports available, Tunis and Bizerte, both located on Tunisia's northern coast, and they sat close enough to the Italian supply bases on Sicily to allow ships to run in during the night, unload the following day, and return to Sicily under cover of darkness. Tripoli had been the only large deepwater port in Tripolitania, and distant enough from Italy that at least part of the crossing had to be made in daylight, exposing the transports and tankers to attack by the Royal Air Force.

Opportunities to establish strong defenses existed in Tunisia that the flat, open terrain of Tripolitania denied the Axis. Originally a French colony, now ostensibly governed by Vichy, Tunisia was roughly rectangular, measuring 160 miles across from east to west and 500 miles from north to south. The northern and eastern sides of the rectangle were protected—more or less—by the Mediterranean, although now that the Allies were flexing their amphibious muscles, no shoreline could be considered truly inviolate. To the southwest lay the beginnings of the great sand sea of the Sahara Desert—impossible going for any army. To the southeast, inside the border with Tripolitania, lay the Mareth Line, a series of strong defensive works built by the French between 1936 and 1940. Twelve miles wide and 30 miles deep, it included 40 infantry bunkers similar to those built by the Italians to defend Tobruk, along with eight sites for heavy artillery, 15 communication posts and 28 support positions, which included barracks, messes, and storage for supplies and ammunition. It was difficult if not impossible to outflank, and if properly defended could prove as difficult a nut for the Eighth Army to crack as Tobruk had been for the Afrika Korps.

Holding the Mareth Line would be essential to any prolonged defense of Tunisia, as Kesselring's insistence at the Rome conference that Allied air power be kept as distant from possible was not entirely self-serving. At the moment the Allies in Algiers had very few aircraft available, so there was little threat of significant air attacks on the ports of Bizerte and Tunis from the west, but the Desert Air Force had advanced with Eighth Army, and its bombers would present a serious threat to the harbor installations in either port once they were within range. At the moment, the Luftwaffe and the Regia Aeronautica enjoyed air superiority over Tunisia, some 128 Axis fighters having flown into the country within a week of the Allied landings in Morocco and Algiers; how long that situation would last, however, was far from certain.

The taking or the holding of the ports of Bizerte and Tunis then were the keys to any Allied or Axis strategy for Tunisia, and geography would dictate how they were to be attacked—and defended. Both sat on coastal flatlands surrounded by lakes and salt marshes, but it was the Atlas Mountains, which began rising inland from the coast, that would determine the Allies' routes of attack. A handful of rivers flowed through those mountains, and what roads existed followed the rivers: the valleys and passes through the mountains created natural choke points which could be easily held against greatly superior numbers. This of course was not news to the Allies, who hoped to take Bizerte "on the bounce" after their landing in Algiers, moving swiftly enough to deny the Germans the opportunity to set up their defense in the passes. A British task force of two infantry brigade groups and one armored regimental group moved eastward almost immediately along the Algerian and Tunisian coast, but was brought up short on November 17 at Djebel Abiod by a scratch force of 17 German tanks and 400 German paratroopers—ample evidence of how greatly the terrain, if properly used, favored defenders. In the south, an American airborne battalion captured Gafsa the same day that the British attack on Djebel Abiod stalled. Gafsa was important, as it was one of the two major road hubs in southern Tunisia, the other being the coastal town of Sfax, and it was behind and to the west of the defenses of the Mareth Line. At the moment, however, the

Allies, particularly the Americans, hadn't sufficiently reorganized after the *Torch* landings to properly exploit the capture of Gafsa, and for the time being it was contained by Nehring's forces; nevertheless, the Americans' presence at Gafsa could throw a spanner into the works of Rommel's planning for the Tunisian campaign.

Rommel returned to North Africa on December 3, and immediately gave orders to begin pulling the Italian infantry out of Mersa el Brega and packing them off to the Mareth Line the retreat began on December 10. Rommel had left Rome thoroughly discouraged, later writing how he ". . . realized that we were now thrown back entirely on our own resources and that to keep the army from being destroyed as a result of some crazy order or other would need all our skill." In a letter sent off to Manfred just days later, Rommel gave voice to a grim despondency that he had never before articulated, even to Lucie, as he wrote in the manner of a father speaking to a son whom, for the first time, he fears he may never again see.[222]

> 8 December 1943
>
> My Dear Manfred
>
> It's time that I sent you my congratulations on your 14th birthday. My wishes must not arrive too late. The war is very hard and it looks doubtful whether I shall be permitted to return to you. You know what a difficult struggle we're having with the British at present, how great their superiority is and how small our supplies. If it goes on like this, we shall be crushed by the enemy's immense superiority. It is a bitter fate for my soldiers and me to have to go through this at the end of so heroic and victorious a struggle. We will do our very utmost to avoid defeat.
>
> Now, to you, Manfred, dear boy. . . . You're going to be 14, and school will soon lie behind you. You must realize the seriousness of the situation and learn as much as you can at school. You are learning for yourself. It is not impossible that you might soon have to stand on your own feet. The times could become very, very hard for all of us. Be guided by your mother, who always has your best interests at heart. . . .[223]

Rommel's blunt statement that he and his officers were now responsible for not only leading the *panzerarmee* but also keeping it "from being destroyed as a result of some crazy order or other. . ." was a watershed. It was proof of Rommel having realized that his initial reaction to Hitler's "victory or death" order at El Alamein, along with the conclusions which he had drawn from it, could not be dismissed as angry outbursts born of the stress and confusion of a desperate battle. The conference of November 29 had established once and for all for Rommel that Hitler's orders could no longer be treated as wholly rational, and hence could no longer be regarded as inviolate. In the past Rommel had defied, evaded, and constructively construed (or misconstrued, as the case may be) orders when he felt that the superior authority issuing them was lacking either sufficient information or imagination. He had never, ever contemplated the idea that he would be given orders by the Führer himself that demonstrated nothing so much as the fact that Hitler had lost touch with military reality. Nevertheless, that was precisely what had happened.

Realism had always been at the core of the man who called himself Erwin Rommel; it was what made young Lucie Molin once tease her young officer cadet about being "too serious;" it was also what compelled him to his most daring and seemingly outrageously brave acts as a young officer in the First World War; it was what made him an outstanding panzer division and panzer corps commander. He nearly always saw situations and circumstances as they were: he never succumbed to what George S. Patton, Jr. described as an officer's most besetting sin—he did not "take counsel of his fears"; likewise he very rarely made the mistake of "painting pictures," Bonaparte's colorful description of an officer imagining that an enemy was doing exactly what that officer wanted him to do, rather than seeing what was actually being done. That was what made him such an outstanding soldier and combat commander.

Yet at the same time there existed in him an idealism which fed the profound patriotism that created the soldier he was. Some have characterized Rommel as a born soldier—he was not. One observer said that in civilian clothes Rommel resembled nothing so much as a small-time hoodlum, looking shabby and awkward. Without his uniform and medals, it was claimed, Rommel was not one-tenth the man he was with them. Such depictions are rubbish, for Rommel was a soldier by choice, not destiny. A year hence he would be giving almost daily demonstrations of just how keen was his intelligence, in ways that broadly hinted at awesome non-military gifts and talents, to the point that a general who had spent his entire career as an engineer would exclaim, "[Rommel] was the greatest engineer of the Second World War. There was nothing I could teach him. He was my master." To say that Rommel was a soldier because he could be nothing else is to admit to no real understanding of the man.[224]

Because his patriotism was sustained by the idealism in Rommel's character, rather than by mere chauvinistic prejudice, he would not allow it to be compromised by anything. This could—and did—at times fuel the naivety which led him to grave misjudgments, such as his belief that while Adolf Hitler was good for Germany, the Nazis were bad, never grasping how the two were inseparable, how neither one could exist without the other. Still, Rommel's arrogance, vanity, stubbornness, ambition, even his near hero-worship of Hitler in the early days of the war, were never allowed to supercede his devotion to Germany. Even his decision to decline the sort of cash gifts which Hitler routinely presented to many of his other successful generals was taken because such conduct could be construed as compromising his loyalty to *das Vaterland* by leaving him morally indebted to Hitler. He could accept the patronage—the promotions, the plum postings—given to him by Hitler in the role of Germany's head of state, but he would not become Hitler's vassal at the cost of his duty to the Fatherland. For almost 10 years Rommel had never found cause to make a distinction between service to Hitler and service to Germany. Suddenly, in just a few weeks in November and December 1942, all of that changed—permanently.

The change was as profound as it was inevitable: Rommel suddenly understood that the war which Hitler had initiated and for so long had successfully led was not a war which would bring greater glory and security for Germany; Hitler's war was exactly that—Hitler's war, its purpose nothing more than the aggrandizement of Adolf Hitler. Rommel now began turning away from the Führer—in the months to come he would begin to turn *against* him—not because Germany was losing the war, or that Hitler was losing it for Germany, but because of *how* Hitler was causing it to be lost. Hitler would willingly accept no diminution of what he believed he had accomplished, the mere *gefreiter* who never attended a war academy, never held a commission, and knew nothing of strategy but what he had learned from his own erratic reading and through his intuition. The loss of so much as a square meter of ground once conquered by the Wehrmacht was a personal affront to Hitler himself. When in September Rommel had solemnly intoned for the newsreels that where the German soldier set foot, there the German soldier stayed, he had been speaking for the popular consumption of the German public, not articulating strategy. For Hitler, however, where the German soldier set foot, there he stayed indeed, even if it was in his grave, because, in Hitler's fantasies, that conquered territory was now the sovereign property of not the German Reich, but the German Führer. Rommel would have willingly sacrificed his army—and himself—if fighting to the last man and last round was required for the defense of Germany; he was not prepared, however, by inclination or temperament, to make such sacrifices merely to serve what he now understood were Hitler's delusions of grandeur.

And so on the flight from Rome back to North Africa, Rommel decided that, using whatever subterfuges were available, he would take the *panzerarmee* west, first to Sirte, next to Tripoli, then to Buerat, and finally all the way to the Mareth Line, regardless of what orders came from Rome or Berlin. The first Italian divisions began slipping off to the west on December 10, the mechanized units holding the Mersa el Brega line for the time being. Rommel was taking a huge gamble, for this movement would all but exhaust the on-hand stocks gasoline, leaving the remaining mechanized units with just enough fuel to reach Tripoli, but without adequate reserves to maneuver if the Eighth Army attacked. This was one of the reasons for Rommel's fury at Kesselring's high-handed appropriation of fuel specifically designated for the *panzerarmee*: Nehring's 10th Panzer and the Fallschirmjäger regiments already had adequate supplies to accomplish their mission of blocking an Allied advance from the west.

The next day aerial reconnaissance showed that Montgomery was moving his armor to the south, in preparation for precisely the sort of flanking maneuver Rommel had maintained made this position so vulnerable. The Eighth Army's radio discipline continued to be sloppy, and while the near-arcane talents of Hauptmann Seebohm's radio intercept company were still sorely missed, their replacements were gaining skill at divining British intentions from the snippets of signals they could catch. Thus on the evening of December 11, Rommel was informed that the British would be attacking at first light the next morning. When the inevitable artillery barrage began at midnight, the prearranged signal "222" was sent to all Axis units, initiating a well-planned evacuation of the Mersa el Brega line, so that when Montgomery's attack went in, it was a mailed fist swinging futilely at empty space. Rommel noted wryly, "Evidently the enemy has not noted our nocturnal withdrawal." In this he was incorrect, for on December 13 Montgomery, trying to put a brave face on the failure of his "attack" to actually attack anything, wrote to General Alan Brooke saying, "Rommel is very windy and starting to pull out." Apparently Montgomery believed that Rommel was obliged to stay put until such time as Eighth Army and its commander were fully prepared, then dutifully remain in place when the attack finally began. To Rommel, Montgomery's overly elaborate and time-consuming preparations before Mersa el Brega were simply further evidence of a lack of imagination, a shortcoming which Rommel found inexcusable in any general on either side.[225]

In the north, November and December saw the Allies—mainly the Americans—stage a succession of local attacks that the Axis troops easily repulsed with relatively minor losses; by Christmas the Allies had made some gains, but in practical terms were no closer to taking Bizerte and Tunis than they had been in mid-November. The Americans were essentially feeling their way at this point, being utterly inexperienced in actual mechanized warfare and saddled with a cadre of peacetime officers, the majority of whom had been excellent administrators but were inept at leading men in combat. General Nehring, as long as he lasted, handled the American II Corps, as well as the equally green British First Army under General Kenneth Anderson, with aplomb, his earlier stint as commander the Afrika Korps under Rommel as well as his time spent on the Russian Front allowing him to deploy and maneuver his XC Panzerkorps with an easy assurance.

Unfortunately he might have been too good, for even as he was handily keeping the Allies at arm's length, he was strongly critical in his reports of what he regarded as the O.K.W.'s needlessly irresolute strategy for Tunisia. He averred that the Wehrmacht should either make a supreme effort to dispatch at once sufficient men and equipment to Tunisia to take the offensive against the Americans and British, or else should be systematically evacuating the units already there. Sending men and supplies to Tunisia in penny packets, he maintained, was a waste of both: doing so only assured that the

Axis forces in Tunisia remained numerically and materially inferior to the Allies, whose logistical train was much better organized with a greater capacity than the Germans and Italians possessed. In retrospect his point was well made: from mid-November 1942 through the end of January 1943, 243,000 men and 856,000 tons of weapons, ammunition, supplies and equipment were sent to Tunisia—impressive numbers, save that the Allies committed nearly three times the men and materiel to North Africa in the same span of time. In the end, almost all of the Axis troops who had not been killed or wounded, and whatever materiel had not been expended, would be captured by the Allies.

Kesselring, meanwhile, regarded Nehring as needlessly pessimistic, and made the argument to both Rome and Berlin that merely holding Tunisia was sufficient, so long as the Allies were kept away from Sicily and Italy proper. However, Kesselring was not above a bit of empire-building of his own in North Africa, which influenced the advice he gave to his superiors. Maintaining the *status quo* in Tunisia kept the XC Panzerkorps out of Rommel's hands and under Kesselring's command; if the Axis army was reinforced to a strength where it could begin an offensive against the Allies, an army officer would be given that command, with Kesselring at best relegated to that officer's nominal superior; Kesselring's worst nightmare was that such a command would be given to Rommel. On the other hand, a gradual withdrawal and eventual evacuation of Tunisia would mean a reduction in the size of the forces under Kesselring's command, with a corresponding loss of personal prestige. In the end bureaucratic inertia took over and the final determination of Axis strategy in Tunisia was decided in Kesselring's favor when no actual decision was made: no staged withdrawal and evacuation was begun, instead reinforcements would continue to be dispatched to Tunisia, but not in sufficient numbers to allow the Axis to take the offensive. As additional German and Italian units arrived in Tunis and Bizerte, the size of the Axis force in northern Tunisia grew well beyond that of a typical corps, and Kesselring advocated creating a second, separate panzer army, which would be subordinate to him. Berlin agreed and the Fifth Panzer Army was created on December 8, 1942, with command given to Generaloberst Hans-Jürgen von Arnim, a 53-year old veteran of the Russian Front: General Nehring lacked the required seniority for an army command, and so was superceded and placed in reserve.

Although their effect on Panzerarmee Afrika was at the moment slight, Rommel followed the action in the north as best he could, even as Kesselring was being obstinate about keeping Rommel adequately informed: as the Axis perimeter in Tunisia contracted, which Rommel knew it must, the two panzer armies would, at some point, of necessity have to coordinate their operations in order to properly exploit successes and avoid working at cross-purposes; a unified command would have to be created sooner or later. For now, his attention was focused on getting Panzerarmee Afrika out of Tripolitania and into the Mareth Line. In accomplishing this he was receiving an unprecedented degree of cooperation from an unexpected quarter: Marshal Ettore Bastico. When the strutting, pompous little Italian arrived in Libya in July 1941, claiming command authority over the Afrika Korps, Rommel had christened him "Bombastico" and then promptly ignored him. For all of his ego, however, Bastico was not stupid: when he met with Rommel at Buerat on December 17, he listened carefully as the German field marshal recapitulated a screed of figures reckoning fuel consumption, ammunition expenditure, shipping tonnage, shipping losses, and port capacities—in the process giving the lie that Rommel was habitually ignorant of such details—to make his case for abandoning the whole of Tripolitania. Even knowing that it meant the end of Italy's African empire, Bastico could not argue with Rommel's assertion that Tripoli had lost its strategic value once the bombers of the Desert Air Force came within range of the port—it would be suicide for any ship to put in there now—and that without Tripoli, the whole of Libya was worthless. All that mattered now was saving as much of the army as possible.

During the retreat to Tunisia, then, Bastico essentially acted as a buffer between Mussolini and Rommel, mitigating the most absurd of the Italian dictator's demands to stand fast and hold at all costs, echoes of Hitler's "victory or death" decrees, and acting as a brake on what seemed to Bastico, as well as Kesselring along with the O.K.W. and Comando Supremo, as Rommel's near-obsession with rushing headlong to the Mareth Line. However much the Italian dictator might have admired the professional skill shown in Rommel's retreat from El Alamein, he was loathe to give up the whole of Libya: despite his willingness to allow Rommel to fall back from Mersa el Brega, he insisted that the *panzerarmee* make its stand at Sirte, then at Buerat, and finally at Tripoli, each time demanding the position be held at all costs. Bastico, however, had learned the speed and scope of movement that was possible in desert warfare far better than did his superiors in Rome, who frequently gave the impression that they had learned nothing since November 1940. The sort of sweeping attack around an exposed southern flank that Rommel feared Eighth Army could execute, trapping the Axis army as it tried to hold one of those positions, was a very real threat and not, Bastico knew, an excuse for timidity or a lack of resolve on Rommel's part.

Somehow Bastico always found the proper mixture of rational argument and blandishments with which Mussolini could be mollified; Rommel, on the other hand, was not so easily diverted.

The months of December 1942 and January 1943 were, without a doubt, the nadir of Rommel's military career. It is no exaggeration to say that when he left Rome on December 3, he was a thoroughly demoralized man—and as a consequence, for a time his extraordinary capacity for leadership deserted him. He fully expected that, given its dire straits in manpower and equipment—in mid-December Rommel's armored divisions could muster a total of 60 battle-worthy tanks, while Montgomery could field eight times that number—Panzerarmee Afrika would be forced to capitulate to Eighth Army in a matter of weeks. Nowhere else in his letters from North Africa does there appear anything near the despondency he showed in the letter he wrote to Manfred on December 8; three days later he would write to Lucie asking her "I wonder if you could have a German–English dictionary sent to me by courier post. It would come in very useful." He was a man who at that moment regarded the best hope for his future to be a British prisoner-of-war compound. The cause of this sudden collapse of his previously indomitable spirit is not difficult to discern: Erwin Rommel was a sick man, sick at heart and sick in body.

The feeling of betrayal by Hitler weighed very heavily on Rommel; he had imagined himself to be—and by all appearances was—the Führer's fair-haired boy, his favorite general; to be so casually discarded was a sore blow to Rommel's ego. An even greater burden was the realization that not only was he regarded by Hitler as being expendable, but so too was the entire army for which Rommel was responsible—and to no good purpose. He had not brought this army all the way across North Africa from El Alamein to Mersa el Brega only to allow it to be taken like an old badger in a trap.

Having everything for which he and his men had striven and accomplished in the past 20 months so heedlessly dismissed would have been sufficient to dismay the stoutest spirit. At the same time that he was coming to grips with this new reality, Rommel was simultaneously suffering from low blood pressure, insomnia, migraine headaches, fainting spells, and the lingering effects of jaundice. The combination of 10 months of blistering heat every year, the other two months given over to near-torrential rain, the monotonous and unimaginative diet on which Rommel lived—as always he continued to be adamant about eating the same rations as his troops—and the stress and strain of leading an army that was in almost daily combat on some level, all combined to take a physical toll on Rommel, and eventually exacted also a mental toll. Rommel had once written to Lucie jocularly remarking that he was the only senior officer who had stayed in Africa, apart from leave, for the entire campaign; now his time in Africa was rapidly coming to an end.

Given his mental and physical exhaustion, then, it hardly comes as a surprise that Rommel was for a time equally drained of imagination and daring. His determination to save what he could of Panzerarmee Afrika never flagged, however, so it naturally follows that the Mareth Line should become a lodestone for him. It held out the promise of a secure position where he was certain the army would be able to defend against the most determined British attacks while it recovered some measure of its former strength—as he would, he hoped, along with it. Given that there was no place between Mersa el Brega and Mareth where Rommel's army could make a stand, he saw no compelling reason to waste the time or run the risk of being outflanked and trapped that making a protracted withdrawal would present. The critical factor here, as it had been for so much of the retreat from El Alamein, was the availability of gasoline—or, rather, the lack of it. By this time the run from the Italian ports to Tripoli had become so hazardous that Allies were sinking nine out of every 10 ships carrying supplies to Panzerarmee Afrika. Rommel literally did not know from one day to the next if there would be enough fuel available to keep the army moving; and if there was fuel to hand, moving the infantry westward was given first priority. Had Rommel enough gasoline to allow his relative handful of tanks to conduct a proper mobile defense, he might well have been willing to stand at each little settlement or village along the coastal road and make

Eighth Army pay a bitter price for every advance; on the few occasions when the Afrika Korps had fuel and was able to maneuver, the British paid with eight or even 10 of their tanks for every German panzer they took out. As it was, however willing to fight the *panzerarmee's* German and Italian soldiers may have been, the means to do so continued to be denied them.

Given the operational difficulties and the instances where the Axis army was all but immobilized, that Eighth Army did not simply roll up its Axis opponent was due in no small part to the combination of the British force's own supply problems—this time theirs was the army operating at the end of 1,000-mile long supply line—and the plodding, fussy nature of Montgomery's command style, but also to the skill of one of the North African campaign's unsung geniuses, Generalmajor Karl Bülowius. He was a Prussian by birth, with 35 years of service in the German Army, all of them in the engineers. He took command of the Afrika Korps' engineer battalions in late October 1942; when Montgomery's Operation *Supercharge* finally broke the Axis line at El Alamein, Rommel gave Bülowius the task of slowing down the British advance however possible. Bülowius proved to be fiendishly clever at creating dummy minefields, which, because there was always a scattering of real mines among the decoys, had to be cleared as methodically and carefully as a real minefield.

Whenever the Afrika Korps halted, even if only for a day, Bülowius had his engineers busily setting up snares and booby traps to waylay the pursuing Tommies. A crooked picture, a door sitting half-ajar, a tin of peaches on a shelf, an inviting if dilapidated bench, a dropped pistol, a discarded uniform cap, an open book lying face-down, all could serve as triggers for small explosive devices that could kill or wound a soldier incautious enough to disturb them.[226]

Contrary to their sinister reputation, the purpose of such booby traps was not to cause large numbers of fatalities or injuries: it was to delay the advance of an enemy by creating a sense of apprehension and excessive caution among the troops—which naturally translated into slow, even glacial movement on their part: booby traps were snares laid for soldiers who were foolishly unwary. The discovery of the first such trap, whether it was set off or simply found, would immediately introduce a level of apprehension and caution that all but paralyzed every soldier in the vicinity: not knowing where or even if there were other such devices to be found would compel

an infantry unit to move with extraordinary care—and matching slowness—through the locale in which the trap or traps were found, as every
step taken could be potentially lethal. In this way Bülowius often gained
days for Panzerarmee Afrika; not all of the relative slowness of Eighth
Army's advance could be attributed to Montgomery's lack of imagination:
much of it came from the Tommies' well-founded wariness.

Bülowius' gifts for mayhem allowed Rommel to fall back to Buerat in
good order, and by December 18 the whole of the army was in place there,
save for the 15th Panzer Division, which had remained at Sirte to act as a
blocking force. Rommel, though, had no desire to stay there a day longer
than absolutely necessary: there was a broad antitank ditch and several
minefields to deter a frontal attack by the British, but as always, the army's
right flank was open, and Rommel's panzers lacked the fuel to fight a mobile defense. "I was very much afraid," he would later write of Buerat, "that
the British commander might continue in his attempt to outflank us in the
south."[227]

> . . . the Buerat front was strong enough to resist a fair-scale British
> break-through attempt—that is, of course, assuming that they chose
> to attack it frontally. Like almost every other position in North
> Africa, the enemy could make a hook round the south to attack the
> Via Balbia, without even making contact with the fortified line. If
> he decided to throw several divisions into such a move the battle
> would be decided by the motorized forces alone. And in motorized
> forces we were hopelessly inferior quite apart from the fact that
> our gasoline would not possibly run to a mobile battle. . . . Because
> of their lack of speed the enemy can take them on one after the
> other, each time with locally superior forces, and destroy them
> piecemeal without suffering undue casualties himself.
>
> . . . I asked for instructions for such an event. On each occasion
> I received an answer referring me to the Duce's order. Everybody
> in Rome was scared to death of making an independent decision
> and invariably tried to unload the responsibility on to somebody
> else. I decided on no account to let up until I had been given an
> answer which did justice to my question. I had no wish to be the
> scapegoat for the armchair strategists in Rome.[228]

The order from Mussolini, which was endorsed by Cavallero, demanded that Rommel ". . . resist to the uttermost with all troops in the German-Italian Army at Buerat." From Berlin came a message from Göring, expecting that Buerat would be held "at all costs." Rommel despaired.

> I had really done all I could to arouse some understanding of the art of desert warfare in our higher commands and had particularly emphasised that to concern oneself with territory was mere prejudice. The all-important principle was to keep on the move until a tactically favourable position for battle was found and then to fight. In the conditions we were facing, that position was the Gabes line. Nevertheless, orders were once again issued to the troops to "resist to the uttermost." I immediately wirelessed Marshal Cavallero and asked him what we were to do if the enemy outmarched us in the south and simply chose not to do battle with the Buerat garrison.[229]

Cavallero's reply was insulting: if the British did attack, then "the battle should be so conducted so that the Italian troops were not sacrificed again." Rommel immediately went to Bastico and made it clear that he could save the army or he could hold Buerat, but it was impossible to do both—and he adamantly refused to sacrifice his German *soldaten* in order to allow the Italian *soldati* to escape. "If I'm supposed to accept the responsibility," he told the Italian marshal, "then they must leave me free to decide just how I tackle the job." Rommel knew that Bastico was in an awkward spot, as he had his own coterie of enemies in Rome who were looking for any excuse to demand his relief. His letter to Lucie written the same day as the army arrived at Buerat summed up his feelings and his appraisal of the situation in a half-dozen sentences:

18 December 1942

Dearest Lu,
We're in heavy fighting again, with little hope of success, for we're short of everything. One's personal fate fades into the background in face of the bitter fate of the army, and the consequences and ef-

fects it will have. Bastico was also very depressed yesterday. The situation in the west seems to be no better, particularly in the ports. We are hoping to be able to carry on for a few days yet. But gasoline is short, and without gasoline there's nothing to be done.[230]

Ironically, Rommel and his army would remain at Buerat for almost a month, courtesy of Eighth Army and its commanding officer, General Montgomery. The 15th Panzer Division was forced to pull out of Sirte on December 24 when reconnaissance planes caught sight of a large British flanking maneuver to the south of the village, but other German reconnaissance aircraft observed very little traffic on the coast road itself between Sirte and Mersa el Brega: the combination of General Bülowius' minefields and booby traps along with an ever-lengthening supply line had conspired to reduce the British advance to a crawl. One incident that provided a much-needed bit of comic relief among the officers and other ranks of the *panzerarmee* came just before Sirte was abandoned, when a flight of eight American medium bombers landed by mistake at a German airfield: they were carrying not bombs but gasoline for Eighth Army. Some of Montgomery's lead units were running nearly as dry as Rommel's tanks, so Eighth Army came to a halt just beyond Mersa el Brega after Montgomery's abortive attack there on December 12; it would be four weeks before he felt that his supply situation as well as his units had been sufficiently tidied up to warrant continuing the advance.

Eighth Army's difficulties were more-or-less mirrored in the Allies' situation in Tunisia. Christmastime 1942 brought little if any holiday cheer to the headquarters of the Allied commander-in-chief in North Africa, Lieutenant General Dwight Eisenhower. The results of Operation *Torch* had been a mixed bag: the landings in Morocco and Algeria were successful, while the lessons learned about amphibious operations for both the naval and land forces would prove priceless; as a consequence of those landings the Vichy regimes in French North Africa were shunted aside; that was all to the good. But the Vichy commander in Tunis, while eventually coming over to the Allies, had taken his time in choosing which way to jump, so that Berlin was able to rush the 10th Panzer Division, the Fallschirmjäger regiments and over 100 Luftwaffe fighters across the Mediterranean to Tunisia before the Allies could react. Part of the Allied planning for *Torch* had been the hope of taking Tunisia by coup de main—that hope died aborning. Despite a promising start that brought two British brigades to within 25 miles of Bizerte at the end of November, the German resistance stiffened and pushed the British back, while a subsequent series of American regimental- and division-sized thrusts in the center and south of Tunisia were stopped in their tracks. Eisenhower and staff were forced to accept that only coordinated, large-scale, corps-sized attacks, backed by strong air support, were going to crack the German defenses: it would be at least two months before the Americans could be ready for such an undertaking.

Yuletide at the headquarters of Panzerarmee Afrika was actually a somewhat festive affair, with Rommel spending Christmas Eve with his officers and Christmas Day among his soldiers. Among the presents given to Rommel was one that delighted him so much that he would remember it for a long time afterward—it was a miniature fuel can, of the type known as the "Jerry can," which contained not gasoline, but something even more valuable: two pounds of precious ground coffee. Christmas dinner was two gazelles shot by Rommel and his secretary, Leutnant Wilfred Armbruster. The letter he penned to Lucie after returning from the officers' mess, however, was a curious mixture of familiar warmth and personal trepidation:

24 December 1942

Dearest Lu,

Today my thoughts are more than ever with you two at home. To you, Manfred, once more all the best for your 15th year. I expect you will already have received my birthday letter. And I wish you both a very happy Christmas. God will help us as in the past.

. . . I'm going off very early this morning into the country and will be celebrating this evening among the men. They're in top spirits, thank God, and it takes great strength not to let them see how heavily the situation is pressing on us.[231]

Rommel was grateful nonetheless for the comparative inactivity, apart from a few probing raids by the Long Range Desert Group and the Special Air Service, of Eighth Army, as it gave him time to become familiar with the lay of the land between Buerat and Tripoli: if he found himself compelled to fight here, he wanted to know the ground he was fighting on. There was even time for a bit of sightseeing and levity: Rommel spent a day exploring the impressive ruins of the ancient Roman city of Leptis Magna, where his Chief of Staff, Bayerlein, had the opportunity to take a photograph of Rommel's aide de camp, Leutnant von Hardtdegen, who had fallen asleep between two statues of nude females. Even then, though, the unspoken question of when would the British make their next move hung over everything Rommel did, as witnessed by his letter of January 5 to Lucie:

> Dearest Lu,
> Nothing new to report from here. The enemy still doesn't risk an attack. I wonder how long it will be? I wrote to Helene and Gertrud yesterday. [Rommel's sister and his daughter by Walburga Stemmer.] It's still cold and windy. The only time it gets tolerably warm is when the sun comes through for a bit at midday. That's something I'm not used to in Africa. I've had a letter from [Major Eberhard] von Luepke, who was taken prisoner a year ago. He was in South Africa, escaped and trekked north with another man for four months. Finally, a Zulu handed him over to the British again. There's very little post coming through at the moment; most of what comes is from November. There's probably a whole lot at the bottom of the sea. I'm in a slightly better humor again, there being now some hope that we'll be able to make a stand somewhere.[232]

General von Arnim, commander of the Fifth Panzer Army in Tunisia, sent a message to Rommel on January 10, warning of a possible American attack out of Gafsa toward Gabes. Rommel was, of course, unaware of the U.S. Army's command and supply problems in Tunisia, and so saw the possibility of such an attack as posing a most serious threat: if the Americans took Gabes, they would not only deny Rommel the use of the Mareth Line to make a stand against Eighth Army, but the *panzerarmee* would finally be well and truly trapped, with no way to escape. Tripoli was useless for an evacuation—even as Rommel was reading the message, German and Italian engineers were preparing the docks and derricks for demolition. When a copy of von Arnim's message reached Rome, Marshal Cavallero asked

Rommel to send a division back to hold the Gabes defile. Rommel agreed to this and three days later the 21st Panzer Division headed northward—but not before Kesselring got wind of what was happening and accused Rommel of using von Arnim's warning as an excuse to accelerate his own retreat. Rommel neatly turned the tables on Kesselring by ordering the men of the 21st Panzer to leave all of their tanks, artillery, and heavy weapons with the *panzerarmee* at Buerat; they could, he said, be re-equipped from tank and artillery parks under Kesselring's command in Tunisia.

Two days after von Arnim's warning arrived, the Desert Air Force began increasing the intensity of its bombing attacks on the Axis army, the prelude, Rommel knew, to another move by Eighth Army. This was confirmed by the Afrika Korps' wireless intercept section, which also was able to deduce that the British attack would begin on January 15. Rommel immediately issued the orders that got the army moving, the non-mechanized German and Italian infantry going first, back to an intermediate position at the village of Homs, 40 miles west of Buerat and halfway to Tripoli!; by nightfall, before Eighth Army could come to grips with the *panzerarmee*, all of Rommel's troops were on their way to the new line in the sand. His letter to Lucie that day makes it clear that Rommel was pushing himself to his limits.

15 January 1943

Dearest Lu,

Our movement has begun. How fast it will go will depend on the pressure. I'm not feeling too good, for obvious reasons. Berndt has been away again and is expected back to-morrow. Physically I'm well so far. Of course the nervous strain is particularly severe just now and I have to keep a real grip on myself.[233]

The letter is also noteworthy for the mention of Leutnant Berndt being away: Berndt had by now developed a strong personal loyalty to Rommel, and had gone to Berlin on an urgent mission to meet personally with Hitler in order to save his commanding officer's job.

Just before the Buerat line was abandoned, Rommel became aware that Mussolini and the officers of Comando Supremo were planning a coup d'état of sorts, by creating a new Italian First Army once the *panzerarmee* reached the Mareth Line: this would remove the Italian troops—who made up two thirds of Rommel's numerical strength, and who had, by his own admission, been fighting with admirable tenacity when called upon during the retreat from El Alamein—from Rommel's direct command. It would also have the effect of making the Afrika Korps and any other German units under Rommel subordinate to an Italian senior officer. This was to be expected—the Italian generals and marshals in Rome had always been hostile toward Rommel, unlike the Italian generals who actually fought in North Africa, men like Ettore Navarini, who commanded the XXI Italian Corps, or Gervasio Bitossi, Littorio's commanding officer, or even Marshal Bastico, who had come to recognize that Rommel's refusal to stand and fight was not cowardice, but a hard-headed realism dedicated to saving his army.

But now Kesselring was conspiring—there can be no other word for it—with Cavallero to have Rommel dismissed from command of what was now styled the German-Italian Army Group. Tunisia was, in his opinion, simply not big enough for two prima donna German field marshals, and unlike Rommel, Kesselring was prepared to pour honeyed words into the ears of his Italian colleagues in order to have himself named overall ground commander of all Axis forces there. Cavallero, who had long detested Rommel for being as bluntly—even rudely—outspoken as he himself was dissembling and evasive, agreed. "It's quite clear that all he wants is to get to Tunis as fast as his legs will carry him," Cavallero told Kesselring. "We've got to get rid of Rommel."[234]

Matters came to a head once Rommel got the army back in good order to Tripoli; again General Bülowius' infernal devices persuaded the British to be circumspect in their advance, buying the time necessary to evacuate the infantry from Homs while the mechanized units acted as a rearguard should the British become unexpectedly daring. But the halt at Tripoli would last only long enough for the army to figuratively catch its breath while the German and Italian engineers finished wrecking the port facilities in Tripoli in order to deny its use to the Allies. Mussolini, however, demanded that German-Italian Army Group stand at Tripoli and hold the port for at least three weeks—three meaningless weeks in Rommel's opinion, as the ultimate outcome of the retreat out of Tripolitania was, as he saw it, inevitable. Thus the stage was set for Rommel's supersession.

On the morning of January 20, Cavallero sent Rommel a message, endorsed by Mussolini, stating that Rommel's earlier decision to withdraw from Homs and move to Tripoli, was a direct violation of the Duce's instructions. Cavallero was on his way to North Africa to discuss the situation with Rommel in person. That afternoon, four field marshals—Rommel, Kesselring, Cavallero, and Bastico—had a bitter, contentious meeting at Rommel's headquarters outside the village of Azizia. Cavallero, supported by Kesselring, demanded that a stand be made at Homs; Rommel, in turn, demanded to know why—what purpose would it serve when Tripoli was already being wired for demolition? Cavallero offered a vague excuse to the effect that if the army did not stand at Homs, there would not be enough time to finish preparing the Mareth Line, then fell back on the argument that the Duce had given an order, therefore it must be obeyed. Rommel would have none of it, telling Cavallero once again: "You can either hold on to Tripoli a few more days and lose the army, or lose Tripoli a few days earlier and save the army for Tunis. Make up your mind."

Cavallero, however, was resolved to be irresolute: he replied by telling Rommel to hold on as long as possible, but that in the end the army must be preserved. The very next day Eighth Army attacked yet again—had Rommel kept the army at Homs, it would have been encircled and cut off, just as he had predicted. That, however, was not good enough for Cavallero, who returned to Rome determined to rid himself of this turbulent German field marshal.

Meanwhile, Leutnant Berndt returned from Berlin with tidings of great joy: Hitler's faith in Rommel had apparently been magically restored, or at least so Hitler said, assuring Berndt of his unbounded confidence in Rommel. The Führer also promised to resolve the command issues in North Africa by creating a new army group, Heeresgruppe Afrika, with Rommel placed in overall command. The only condition Hitler placed on these promises was that Rommel had to be in sufficiently good health to take on the new responsibilities. Before any of that transpired, however, Kesselring and Cavallero's intrigue to have Rommel removed from North Africa entirely came within a whisker of succeeding.

The attack on Homs that began on January 21 was in fact a major thrust by the now reorganized and resupplied Eighth Army, one which carried it all the way past Tripoli. Rommel gave the order to begin the demolitions and abandon the port on January 23; the British entered the city the following day. But once again Rommel proved cannier than Montgomery: 95 percent of all the supplies and stores stockpiled in Tripoli had already been spirited westward to the Mareth Line, and the Axis army once again escaped. The British victory was symbolic—it had been exactly three months since Montgomery opened his offensive against Rommel at El Alamein—but it was largely hollow in what it achieved materially. By January 26 the whole of the German-Italian Army Group was across the Tunisian frontier, on its way to Mareth.

That same day a signal arrived at Rommel's headquarters informing him that due to his ill-health he would be relieved of command of the army group upon its arrival at Mareth. The exact date he would relinquish command was left to his discretion, but his successor, General Giovanni Messe, a tough-as-nails officer who had commanded the Italian Corps on the Russian Front where it had fought well, was on his way to North Africa. Rommel was not inclined to argue: as he put it, "After my experience during the retreat, I had little desire to go on any longer playing the scapegoat for a pack of incompetents and requested the Comando Supremo to send General Messe to Africa as soon as possible, so that he could be initiated into his new command." Two days later he broke the news to Lucie:

> 28 January 1943
>
> Dearest Lu,
> In a few days I shall be giving up command of the army to an Italian, for the sole reason that "my present state of health does not permit me to carry on." Of course it's really for quite other reasons, principally that of prestige. I have done all I can to maintain the theater of war, in spite of the indescribable difficulties in all fields. I am deeply sorry for my men. They were very dear to me.
>
> Physically, I am not too well. Severe headaches and overstrained nerves, on top of the circulation trouble, allow me no rest. Professor Horster is giving me sleeping draughts and helping as far as he can. Perhaps I'll have a few weeks to recover. . . .[235]

Over the next two weeks, the entire Axis command structure in Tunisia would undergo a dramatic change—but it was not Rommel's head that rolled. Bastico was recalled to Rome on January 31, to be relieved as governor-general of Libya, inevitably, as Libya was no longer an Italian colony; the very next day, though, Cavallero was dismissed as the Chief of Co-mando Supremo. On February 12, the second anniversary of his arrival in North Africa, Rommel decided that he would not give up command of the Afrika Korps or the First Italian Army until and unless directly ordered to do so by the Führer, and so informed Berlin. That prompted the O.K.W., acting on Hitler's instructions, to authorize the creation of a Heeresgruppe Afrika—Army Group Africa—which would include the Afrika Korps, the First Italian Army, and the Fifth Panzer Army, all under the command of a single officer who, as an army group commander, would report and be di-rectly subordinate to the O.K.W.. The administrative work was completed in short order, but the army group was not formally activated and no com-mander officially designated—yet.

Even as all of this was happening, events in southern Tunisia were in-truding on Rommel's attention. Two Allied corps, the Free French XIX Corps and the American II Corps, had been building up their strength just east of Sidi Bouzid: if left undisturbed they could strike almost due east, toward the coastal city of Sfax, cutting Tunisia in two and trapping Rom-mel's forces in the south, or they could move southeast and take Gabes, accomplishing the same thing. An attack on Sfax was, in fact, precisely what Eisenhower was planning, but the American and French units were not yet ready to move. As the 21st Panzer Division had already been sent to von Arnim as a precautionary measure to avert any such move by the Allies, Rommel authorized von Arnim to make use of it in a preemptive attack on the forward French positions in the Faid Pass, just to the northeast of Sidi Bouzid; Faid was the main pass from the eastern Atlas Mountains into the coastal plains, and so was the easiest and most direct route for any army advancing from the west to follow if it was moving to the coast.

Von Arnim brought up the 21st Panzer and three supporting divisions of Italian infantry to attack the French XIX Corps, which was under-strength and poorly equipped, most of its tanks and artillery dating from 1940 or earlier. The French were, understandably, mauled by the German attack, most of XIX Corps being overrun. Frantic requests for reinforce-ments from the American 1st Armored Division went unanswered, and when the American II Corps finally counterattacked, with one combat command, a brigade-sized unit, sent out to do battle with four Axis divisions, it was stopped cold, as the savvy veterans of 21st Panzer were waiting in strong defensive positions. Taking heavy losses, the Americans retired in some disorder to Sbeitla, 30 miles southwest of the Faid Pass. Ten days later it was the U.S. Army's turn, as von Arnim sent four *kampfgruppen* to strike at Sidi Bouzid; the American deployment was amateurish, and two of the three combat commands of the 1st Armored Division were tumbled out of the town with heavy losses. Von Arnim turned northwest, toward Sbeitla, and soon the Americans were abandoning that town as well, finally taking up defensive positions of their own in Kasserine Pass, 40 miles west of Sidi Bouzid and less than 15 miles from the Algerian frontier; the 1st Armored Division lost over 150 tanks and 1,500 prisoners in the two battles. The withdrawal from Sidi Bouzid and Sbeitla also compelled the American forces in Gafsa to retreat as well.

All of this came as welcome news to Rommel, who, as von Arnim's actions to the north were unfolding, was preoccupied with getting the German-Italian Army Group, now properly styled the First Italian Army and Afrika Korps, settled into the Mareth Line. He had first examined the line for himself on January 26, three days after Tripoli had been abandoned, and he had not been impressed by what he found. Apparently he was expecting a scaled-down version of France's Maginot Line, and when he did not find it to be such, he initially pronounced it worthless: his assessment of the line is an example of Rommel at his most pessimistic:

[The line] consisted of antiquated French block-houses which in no way measured up to the standards required by modern warfare. Added to that they had been completely disarmed after the Armistice with France. They could, therefore, serve little purpose in action other than as cover against artillery fire, and the defense proper would have to be fought from field positions lying between the French block-houses. The southern part of the line could be regarded as completely proof against tanks. Its center was given some protection against tanks by a steep wadi, but this obstacle could be overcome by well-trained tank crews. Its northern end was covered to the front by a salt marsh, but most of this was negotiable by vehicles. The siting of the line was also bad, for it lay immediately behind some high ground, which denied any long-range artillery observation to the defense, and at the same time provided the attacking force with excellent opportunities for fire control. So these hills, too, had to be held by our troops, which meant a serious division of our strength.[236]

It is readily apparent, even from Rommel's description, that, while far from being the ideal defensive position Rommel had believed it to be, the Mareth Line had the potential to be a position of significant strength, if adequately and energetically defended; at the same time, reading Rommel's evaluation of the line gives the impression that he expected the position to defend itself. Energy was something which Rommel clearly lacked in February 1943, as witnessed by two letters he wrote to Lucie in the first half of the month:

7 February 1943

Dearest Lu,

Dr. Horster came to see me yesterday and advised me to begin my treatment as soon as possible. My whole being cries out against leaving the battlefield so long as I can stand on my feet.

12 February 1943

It's two years today since I arrived on African soil. Two years of heavy and stubborn fighting, most of the time with a far superior enemy. On this day, I think of the gallant troops under my command, who have loyally done their duty by their country and have had faith in my leadership. I have endeavored to do my duty, both in my own sphere and for the cause as a whole. . . .

We must do our utmost to beat off the mortal dangers which beset us. Unfortunately it's all a matter of supplies. I hope that my decision to remain with my troops to the end will be confirmed. You will understand my attitude. As a soldier one cannot do otherwise.[237]

Naturally then, given that the Mareth Line had turned out to be something of a mirage, Rommel could at least be certain that, as a consequence of von Arnim's actions, the rear of the Mareth position, such as it was and what there was of it, was secure from an Allied attack. Yet even as he read von Arnim's after-action reports, he apparently recalled the bill of goods he and Leutnant Berndt had sold to Hermann Göring at the end of November 1942 in order to secure his cooperation in the planned withdrawal from Tripolitania. In it, they had proposed that Panzerarmee Afrika, as it was then, would fall back *past* the Mareth Line, head northwest and combine with the fresh German units in Tunisia, including the 10th Panzer Division: together the three German panzer divisions would launch a powerful, rapidly moving attack against the Americans holding central and southern Tunisia, pushing as far west as possible. Once that was done, the *panzerarmee* could move back to the Mareth Line before the ever-torpid Montgomery would be able to take advantage of its absence by launching an attack of his own. Now, incredibly, the opportunity to do exactly that suddenly presented itself.

Rommel, whose spirits were somewhat revived by the opportunity of taking the offensive once again, quickly drew up an operational plan and sent it off to Rome on February 17: he proposed a concentrated attack toward Tébessa in French Algeria, as Tébessa at that point was the U.S. Army's major supply base in North Africa. Comando Supremo and Kesselring, however, modified the plan, dividing Rommel's armor and assigning two separate objectives: Kasserine Pass was to be taken by 10th Panzer while 21st Panzer took Sbiba Pass to the north. Rommel was distinctly unhappy with this meddling, as the alterations to his plan put his two panzer divisions (15th Panzer would remain at the Mareth Line) too far apart to be able to mutually support each other, and the axes of their advance were divergent. He was convinced that a single, powerful thrust through Kasserine to Tébessa would compel the Allies to pull back from Tunisia entirely: Rommel, whose strategic talents were so often derided by his colleagues, was thinking in terms of achieving a strategic victory; the plan drawn up in Rome offered only the possibility of tactical success.

Once the attack was authorized, Rommel's staff drew up the operational plans and sent out the necessary orders to all of the combat and support units which would be involved, and the two panzer divisions began moving forward in the early hours of February 19. One last-minute spanner was thrown into the works, however, when von Arnim, rather than dispatching the whole of 10th Panzer, sent only a battle group, deliberately holding back the Tigers of the 501st Heavy Tank Detachment. Rommel combined the *kampfgruppe* with the Italian Centauro armored division to form the Afrika Korps Assault Group, which would attack Kasserine Pass; 21st Panzer would make the attack on Sbiba Pass. Despite the changes made in his original plan, Rommel expected to effectively roll right through the U.S. Army's II Corps: he was openly dismissive of the Americans, declaring that they "had as yet no practical battle experience, and it was now up to us to instill in them an inferiority complex of no mean order."[238]

It came as something of a surprise then when the veteran 21st Panzer Division was stopped in its tracks as it drove on Sbiba: a combination of a previously undetected minefield and carefully sited Allied antitank guns took a heavy toll of the German tanks. The division continued to press its attack all through February 19 and well into the next day, but by sunset on February 20 it was clear that no breakthrough would be achieved at the Sbiba Pass. Whatever success Rommel would have in this attack would come at Kasserine.

The situation that developed at Kasserine on February 19, however, did not seem that far different than the one which obtained at Sbiba: a mixed American and French force was positioned to block the pass, and when Rommel sent the 33rd Reconnaissance Battalion forward to clear them away, it was thrown back. Next a *panzergrenadier* regiment attempted to force its way through the pass, and it too was repulsed. Exasperated, Rommel sent his tanks forward, but they in turn made very little progress; from all appearances, Rommel's estimation of the Americans seemed to be flawed. Part of the explanation for the lack of success at both Sbiba and Kasserine, however, was the lack of experience in fighting in mountains and rough terrain on the part of Rommel's battalion and regimental commanders: Rommel knew mountain fighting, none better, and understood that attacking along the floor of a valley was a recipe for failure. The attack had to be carried to the slopes on either side of valley as well, otherwise the enemy had the luxury of looking—and shooting—down on the attackers with near impunity. Rommel knew this, his subordinates did not, and he had not taken the time to explain to them this simple concept.

When the Germans renewed their assault on Kasserine the next day, the prospects seemed no better than they had been previously. The Allies had moved up reinforcements during the night, a handful of light tanks from the British 26th Armoured Brigade; the Germans were reinforced also, however, in the form of the Italian Centauro armored division. Despite having fought hard and well on February 19 the Allied soldiers holding the shoulders of the pass melted away during the night, and when the panzers went forward again, though the remaining Americans defending the pass held on as long as they could, by mid-afternoon they too were in retreat. As Rommel had hoped, the road to Tébessa was now wide open, or so it seemed.

The American 1st Infantry Division's 16th Infantry Regiment and the already battered Combat Command B of the 1st Armored were rushed forward to the town of Djebel el Hamra, on the road to Tébessa, to block the advance of 10th Panzer and Centauro. The Germans and Americans fought fiercely throughout February 21, causing Rommel to take note of his opponents' "skillful defense" and remark on "the flexibilty and accuracy of the American artillery." It was on February 22 that the issue was decided, when an American counterattack finally pushed the Afrika Korps' *kampfgruppe* back from Djebel el Hamra, ending the threat to Tébessa. Rommel still had one more card to play, however: he saw an opportunity north of Djebel el Hamra to take the town of Thala and in doing so cut the U.S. 9th Infantry Division's supply line while trapping 1st Armored's Combat Command B between the 10th Panzer Division to the north and the Afrika Korps' *kampfgruppe* to the south. But what Rommel saw, Major General Kenneth Anderson, commander of the British First Army, to which the American II Corps was attached, could also see: by the time 10th Panzer and Centauro reached the outskirts of Thala, a screen of British and American armor, well-covered by antitank guns, lay in wait for them.[239]

For a few hours that day at Thala Rommel was once again the Desert Fox of *Battleaxe*, *Crusader*, and the Cauldron: Leutnant Berndt, in a personal letter to Lucie, described how "it was wonderful to see the joy of his troops during the last few days, as he drove along their columns. And when, in the middle of the attack, he appeared among a new division which had not previously been under his command, right up with the leading infantry scouts in front of the tank spearheads, and lay in the mud among the men under artillery fire in his old way, how their eyes lit up." Going forward with the 10th Panzer, he was able to gain a foothold in the town, but was forced to withdraw by the American artillery, at one point taking cover with an infantry unit in a grove of trees on the outskirts of Thala. The Axis armored divisions began to take heavy casualties, and as darkness fell, Rommel ordered a retreat—the last large Axis attack in North Africa was over. At Kasserine, Rommel had won his last victory, a conditional victory at best, because it achieved only local, tactical success without accomplishing anything of strategic value.[240]

In the actions at Kasserine, Sbiba, and Thala, Rommel was given a close look at the future of Germany's war with the Allies, and he was distressed by what he saw:

> Although it was true that the American troops could not yet be compared with the veteran troops of the Eighth Army, yet they made up for their lack of experience by their far better and more plentiful equipment and their tactically more flexible command. In fact, their armament in antitank weapons and armored vehicles was so enormous that we could look forward with but small hope of success to the coming mobile battles. The tactical conduct of the enemy's defense had been first class. They had recovered very quickly after the first shock and had soon succeeded in damming up our advance by grouping their reserves to defend the passes and other suitable points.[241]

That was not all about the U.S. Army that impressed Rommel. He would also note that "The Americans were fantastically well equipped and we had a lot to learn from them organizationally. One particularly striking feature was the standardization of their vehicles and spare parts." Here was the system and method in focusing a nation's intellectual ability, organizational talent, and industrial capacity on the task of winning the war which Germany was so gravely lacking. While German arms makers might continue to produce weapons that, on paper at least, were superior to their Allied counterparts, the British and particularly the Americans would be able to produce their tanks, guns, and aircraft in numbers that German industry could never hope to match, and then deploy and supply them with an efficiency no other nation could hope to achieve. For the first time, Rommel, who had already come to realize that Germany could not *win* this war, now began to entertain the idea that Germany would *lose* it.[242]

In the meantime, there was nothing more to be accomplished in western Tunisia. Rommel would always regret the modifications made by Comando Supremo to his original plan for an attack through Kasserine, convinced that in dividing the attacking force, its strength was fatally diluted, leaving it too weak to achieve a decisive breakthrough at either Kasserine or Sbiba. He was also furious with von Arnim, who had refused to include the Tiger tanks of 501st Heavy Detachment with the 10th Panzer's *kampfgruppe*, despite Rommel's specific request that he do so. Though there were only 19 of them, the 56-ton Tigers were so powerful and so heavily armored (they carried a tank version of the 88mm gun and had 4-inch-thick frontal armor) that they would have been all but invulnerable to the Sherman tanks of Combat Command B—Rommel would remain convinced that their absence was decisive at Thala, where the Tigers' guns would have outranged anything the Allies deployed against them. In any case, it was imperative that he return to the south, where a major assault on the Mareth Line by Eighth Army was expected to begin any day. On February 23, the Axis withdrawal from Thala, Sbiba, and Kasserine began, despite opposition from Kesselring, who imagined that there might still be opportunities for offensive action in western Tunisia. Rommel, however, was adamant: his forces were overextended, fuel and ammunition stocks were low, and reconnaissance flights spotted Allied armor massing near Kasserine for a counterattack. The withdrawal would be carried out as ordered.

That evening, in a classic example of closing the barn door after the horse had bolted, a signal arrived from Rome announcing that "to satisfy the urgent need for a unified command in Tunisia, Heeresgruppe Afrika" was to be activated under Rommel's command. This decision could have been—should have been—made as early as the end of January, in which case the battles at Kasserine, Sbiba, and Thala, would have turned out very differently: Rommel would not have had to request von Arnim's permission to use 10th Panzer, nor would von Arnim have been able to withhold part of the division as well as the 501st Heavy Tank Detachment—Rommel would have been able to simply issue orders for them. But the Italians had reverted to form and dithered about, balking on a meaningless point of national pride at the idea of once again subordinating their forces in North Africa to a German commander, in the process casting away the last opportunity the Axis would have to achieve something from their North African adventures. Rommel's reaction to his elevation to army group command was decidedly mixed: as he later told it, "On the one hand, I was glad to feel that I would again be able to have some wider influence over the fate of my men, General Messe having shortly before assumed command over the Mareth front; on the other hand, I was not very happy at the prospect of having to go on playing whipping-boy for the Führer's H.Q., the Comando Supremo and the Luftwaffe." He did try, after a fashion, to put a good face on the news when he informed Lucie:

24 February 1943

Dearest Lu,

I've moved up a step in command and have given up my army as a result. Bayerlein remains my Chief of Staff. Whether it's a permanent solution is doubtful. I'm tolerably well, although the last few days have been pretty exhausting.[243]

Rommel's health continued to be a source of concern, not only for himself and Lucie, but also for Berlin and Rome as well.

Now more than ever it was obvious that Hitler and Mussolini needed Rommel in Tunisia—given that no other German general had anything like his experience in fighting the British, it became imperative that he remain there. This point was heavily underscored by the abject failure of von Arnim's sole attempt at taking the war to the Allies, the appropriately named "Operation *Oxhead*." Aside from capturing the town of Sedjenane, in the north, the attack accomplished little save to add to the German casualty lists. Particularly galling for Rommel was that 15 of the 19 Tiger tanks under von Arnim's command, the same tanks which could have decisively tipped the balance in favor of the Afrika Korps at Kasserine or Thala, were lost in this offensive—not to enemy action, but because they had become bogged down in a marsh. Kesselring, perhaps feeling chastened when it became obvious that the changes he had urged Comando Supremo to make to Rommel's plan had fatally weakened it, and that he had authorized *Oxhead*, suddenly began pressing Rommel to take the army group command. Rommel finally accepted the post on March 2, though he did so with little enthusiasm.

3 March 1943

Dearest Lu,

I may have the Army Group now, but the worry is no less. Schmundt has written me a very nice letter. The Führer is worried about me. But I can't get away for the moment. I'll just have to go on for a bit. I wouldn't mind having a different job. I'm dictated to by Rome in every single thing, yet the full responsibility is mine. That I find intolerable. I often think my nerves will snap. One is continually having to take paths which lead very close beside the abyss. If it goes wrong, the consequences will be incalculable.

It's spring outside, blossoming trees and meadows, sunshine. The world could be so beautiful for all men. Such infinite possibilities exist to make them contented and happy. There is so much that could be done especially here in Africa with its wide-open spaces.[244]

The second paragraph of this letter is fascinating, as it reveals a thoughtfulness in Rommel that few outside of his immediate circle ever knew existed. It shows him to be more than just a skilled technician of war, with no horizons outside of strategy and tactics, no sense of a future that held anything but yet another battle. Here is a man thinking, speculating—dreaming, even—of how the world might be once the fighting had stopped. For all of its brevity, this paragraph establishes a sense of the breadth of Rommel's character. A little more than a year would have to pass before he would be called upon to demonstrate its depth.

Now that he was well and truly in command in Tunisia, Rommel had to formulate an overall strategy for defending that last Axis bridgehead in North Africa—within whatever constraints were placed on him by Rome and Berlin, of course. The first priority was to buy time, time to allow reinforcements to arrive in Tunis and Bizerte, time to stockpile supplies, time to bring his divisions back up to strength. It was with this objective in mind that he cryptically wrote to Lucie on March 5, saying, "Before I go off on a new and daring operation on orders from above, my dearest love to you and the boy." The "new and daring operation" would be called Operation *Capri*, and it would be the very last attack Rommel would lead in North Africa.[245]

As Rommel was squaring off against the Americans at Kasserine and the British at Sbiba, Eighth Army had begun a probing attack against the screening units of the 15th Panzer Division in front of the Mareth Line. Even though the Allies had not been thrown out of Tunisia by Rommel's attack, it appeared that their advance had for the time being at least been checked, and it was now necessary for Rommel to carry out the second part of his strategy: to return to the Mareth Line and conduct a spoiling attack against Eighth Army, with the purpose of disrupting Montgomery's plans and preparations for his own pending assault on the Mareth position. Rommel's evaluation of the situation was straightforward: "Our whole enterprise was therefore built on the hope that the British would not have had time to complete the organisation of their defenses in the Medenine area. The decision to make the attack at all was based on the realization that we only had two choices open to us, either to await the British attack in our own line and suffer a crushing defeat, or to attempt to gain time by breaking up the enemy's assembly areas."[246]

Eighth Army's main assembly area was around the town of Medenine, near the southern end of the Axis line; posted there were the 51st (Highland) Division, 7th Armoured Division, 2nd New Zealand Division, and 4th Light Armoured Brigade. The terrain was such that Rommel could not expect to achieve either tactical or strategic surprise, instead he would have to depend on superior tactics and the skill of his soldiers to produce a victory. For this attack he would deploy the 10th, 15th, and 21st Panzer Divisions, along with the 90th and 164th Light Divisions; the Italian infantry under General Messe—who had conducted the defense against Montgomery's February 20 attack with a skill and determination which Rommel found pleasantly surprising—would continue to hold the Mareth Line itself.

Once again, however, time was Rommel's enemy: in the time needed for his panzer divisions to pull out of western Tunisia, refuel, resupply, make whatever repairs were required, and move south to their start lines, more than a week passed, allowing the enemy to bring reinforcements forward to Medenine. Montgomery, forewarned by Ultra intercepts, knew precisely where and when Rommel would attack, and in what strength, even though he did not know the details of Rommel's battle plan. Thus when the German attack began in the morning fog of March 6, two additional armored brigades had been added to the British units already in place at Medenine, giving Eighth Army a two-to-one numerical superiority in tanks over the Afrika Korps. Even more critical to the outcome of the battle, over 500 British antitank guns had been dug in at crucial points along the approaches to Medinine.

By 5:00 P.M. it was all over, after nearly half of Rommel's tanks were knocked out of action, half of those totally destroyed, all of them by the British antitank guns and artillery—the British armor was never committed to battle. It was clear to Rommel that his attack had been completely anticipated by Eighth Army, and the initiative was lost: he called off the attack and ordered the panzer divisions to hold their ground while any tanks and vehicles that could be repaired were recovered. By midnight, he decided that trying to hold the ground gained was pointless, and ordered his panzers to return to the Mareth Line. For Rommel, "the cruelest blow was the knowledge that we had been unable to interfere with Montgomery's preparations. A great gloom settled over us all. The Eighth Army's attack was now imminent and we had to face it. For the Army Group to remain longer in Africa was now plain suicide."[247]

Rommel was now determined to make precisely that point to Comando Supremo, Mussolini, the O.K.W., and Hitler himself if necessary. On March 9 he formally handed over command of Heeresgruppe Afrika to von Arnim and flew to Rome. Meeting first with General Vittorio Ambrosio, who had replaced Marshal Cavallero as chief of staff, then with Mussolini, Rommel came away convinced that neither of them truly comprehended that it was impossible to hold Tunisia indefinitely, nor did they understand the value of the soldiers who would be lost to both Italy and Germany when the Tunisian garrison was ultimately forced to surrender. In the course of the conversations, Rommel began to realize that the Italians did not expect him to return to North Africa, believing he would go on sick leave instead. This was something Rommel was not prepared to do, regarding such a course of action as tantamount to deserting his men. There was a surreal quality to these meetings, as if Mussolini and Ambrosio on one hand and Rommel on the other were talking about two entire different fronts in two entirely different wars. Discouraged, Rommel flew to the Ukraine the next day, to meet Hitler at the Führerhauptquartier near Vinnitsya.

If Rommel had been expecting a more realistic appreciation of military realities in Tunisia from Hitler than was offered by Ambrosio or Mussolini, he was sadly mistaken. "[Hitler] was unreceptive to my arguments and seemed to pass them all off with the idea that I had become a pessimist," Rommel would later write of this meeting. "I emphasized as strongly as I could that the 'African' troops must be re-equipped in Italy to enable them to defend our southern European flank. I even went so far as to give him a guarantee—something which I am normally very reluctant to do—that with these troops, I would beat off any Allied invasion in southern Europe. But it was all hopeless." Incredibly, Hitler insisted that Rommel take sick leave, because he would be needed for operations against the Allies in Casablanca. This startled Rommel, who began to understand from this that Hitler was becoming delusional: Casablanca was on Africa's Atlantic coast, far beyond the reach of Germany's ability to launch or sustain operations. Unlike all of his previous meetings with Hitler, Rommel departed with a deep sense of disappointment, despite being awarded the Diamonds to his Knight's Cross, only the sixth such award thus far in the war. His medical leave would begin the following day.[248]

As he flew to Wiener Neustadt, Rommel could only feel a profound sense of failure. "All of my efforts to save my men and get them back to the Continent had been fruitless. . . ." When his sand-colored Heinkel 111 touched down at the huge military airfield outside Wiener Neustadt, Lucie and Manfred were waiting for him. Rommel wrapped his wife in an embrace, then held out his hand to his son. Nothing was said for a moment, then Rommel drew a deep breath and made an announcement.

"The Führer won't let me go back to Africa again," he said. "Von Arnim is taking over the Army Group."[249]

CHAPTER THIRTEEN

THE ATLANTIC WALL

A good general not only sees the way to victory;
he also knows when victory is impossible.
—POLYBIUS

For nine weeks Rommel would chafe and fret in limbo, wondering if, despite the accolades and praise heaped on him by Hitler and his cronies, he had exited Tunisia in disgrace, and he would ever be given a new command. He occupied his time as best he could with organizing and editing his diaries and notes from North Africa, turning them into what he hoped would become a book to be called *Krieg Ohne haas, (War without Hate)*. Lucie typed up the finished notes into a manageable manuscript, while Manfred, now 14 years old, helped detail the maps.

Petty slights multiplied. There were no courtesy calls from senior officers, no communications from the Führerhauptquartier. His letters to the O.K.W. urging that the most valuable German *experten* and officers be evacuated from Africa before it was too late elicited no response. Field Marshal Kesselring, who now made no effort to hide his dislike of Rommel, ordered von Arnim to cease forwarding the regular situation reports which had been going to Rommel since his departure from Tunisia, even though Rommel remained, technically at least, von Arnim's immediate superior. Especially wounding for a man of Rommel's vanity was the absence of any mention in the newspapers of his award of the Diamonds to his Knight's Cross—an incredible oversight, if that's what it was, for the award was far from common—only 27 men would ever hold the Diamonds. According to Manfred, one of the first things his father said to him on his return from North Africa was "I've fallen from grace. I can't expect any important jobs for the time being." To all appearances that was true.[250]

Then came the unexpected call from Berlin on May 8: Rommel was ordered to report to the Führer the next day. The situation in Tunisia was clearly beyond salvation and the curtain was crashing down on Hitler and Mussolini's African adventure; it is likely that Hitler, who could never openly admit to an error, was seeking to mend fences with Rommel. Weeks earlier Kesselring, ever the eternal optimist, had contradicted Rommel's gloomy assessment of the situation, while unconsciously echoing Rommel's earlier pleas for North Africa when he had assured the O.K.W. that if the forces there were properly supplied, Tunisia could be held indefinitely. Hitler, likewise repeating himself, demanded that what was left of Armeegruppe Afrika fight to the last man and the last round. Now, meeting Rommel on May 9, Hitler balefully admitted, "I should have listened to you before."

Even as Rommel and Hitler talked, von Arnim was preparing to formally surrender to Eisenhower. A quarter-million Axis soldiers would become prisoners of war, 150,000 of them Germans. From a military perspective, it was, in some ways, an even greater disaster than Stalingrad. At Stalingrad the Germans lost a battle and an army; at Tunisia, the Germans lost an army group and an entire front. After Stalingrad, the Russians were still 1,100 miles from the Reich itself—after Tunisia, the Allies were less than half that distance away. More ominously for the Axis, the Allies could now establish airfields in North Africa that would bring Italy, southern Austria, and the Balkans within range of the Americans' heavy B-17 and B-24 bombers. Previously untouchable factories and industrial facilities were now threatened; the Luftwaffe, already overtaxed in its efforts to defend the Reich, would be stretched even further. Hitler had more than sufficient reason to regret not paying heed to Rommel.

Meanwhile, the Führer had no immediate assignment for Rommel, though Field Marshal Keitel dropped not-so-subtle hints that Rommel might soon be needed in Italy. It was evident to everyone in the German High Command that things were becoming very dicey indeed for Mussolini; unlike Hitler, he was not an absolute dictator, and he was becoming increasingly unpopular within the Italian government as a consequence of Italy's disastrous showing in this war. If the Allies invaded Sicily—or the Italian peninsula itself—there was a very real possibility of the Duce being toppled from power and the Italians making a separate peace with the Allies.

Delaying either of those eventualities for as long as possible had been, in Hitler's mind, sufficient justification for the sacrifice of 250,000 German and Italian soldiers; now with the invasion of Sicily expected in a matter of weeks, and of Italy sometime in late summer or early autumn, the questions of what to do with the Italians became a pressing issue.

Rommel suddenly became something of a fixture at the Führer's headquarters for the next three months, where Hitler freely and frequently drew on his military expertise. He was present when, on May 15, Hitler rambled through a two-hour monologue that detailed his appreciation of the Allies' intentions, the Italians' likely reactions, and what steps the Germans would take when Italy was invaded. Rommel, who still held deep-seated suspicions of having been betrayed in North Africa by the Comando Supremo and Mussolini's government (he was shortly to discover how valid were those suspicions) repeatedly warned that the Italians would offer little if any resistance when the British and Americans landed in Italy; this time round, his counsel was heeded very carefully.

Hitler announced that four panzer and eight infantry divisions would be withdrawn from the Russian Front to be redeployed in Italy—regardless of the Italian government's wishes—when an invasion began; this would be Operation *Alarich*. Two days later Rommel was told to begin assembling a staff for a new army group headquarters, designated "Army Group B"; Rommel immediately sent for Alfred Gause, his health now much improved, as his Chief of Staff once again. He also met with Fritz Bayerlein, who had stepped in as Rommel's Chief of Staff after Gause had been invalided out of North Africa. Bayerlein was now a *generalmajor* and serving as chief of staff to General Hans Hube, who would command the defense of Sicily, the Allies' next target for invasion. At one point Rommel held forth on what direction he imagined the war would take, saying, "You know, Bayerlein, we've lost the initiative, there's no doubt about it. We've just learned in Russia that dash and high hopes are not enough. . . . For the next few years there can be no thought of resuming the offensive either in the east or in the west. So we'll have to make the most of the advantages that normally accrue to the defense. . . . A few days ago the Führer told me that by the beginning of next year we'll be turning out 7,000 aircraft and 2,000 tanks a month. I no longer see things as blackly as I used to in Africa." It would seem that some of Rommel's old optimism was returning, tempered by a caution born of experience, that is, until he remarked, "but total victory is now hardly possible, of course."[251]

Privately Rommel said as much to Hitler, painting a realistic picture of Germany's true strategic situation as he did so: there could be no doubting that everywhere the Third Reich was now on the defensive. "Hitler listened to it all with downcast eyes," Rommel later told Manfred. "Suddenly he looked up and said that he, too, was aware that there was very little chance left of winning the war. But the West would never conclude peace with him—at least not the statesmen who were at the helm now. He said that he had never wanted war with the West. But now the West would have its war—have it to the end." Rommel did not then take the time to consider the implications of those last words, but later their significance would loom large for him, leading him to make dangerous, even fatal, decisions.[252]

Meanwhile, Rommel was quickly reverting to form, becoming more like his old self—bluff, opinionated, outspoken, brash and sometimes needlessly blunt. He was making enemies at O.K.W. and within the Nazi heirarchy—aside from the curious friendship with Dr. Göbbels, motived in large part by the Propaganda Minister's efforts to promote and burnish Rommel's public image, for otherwise there was little in common between the field marshal and the Third Reich's poison dwarf—none of the senior Nazis liked Rommel. The hostility between Rommel and Göring, for instance, was an open secret at the Führerhauptquartier, particularly after the 40mm shell incident. Even two years earlier, such animosity might have been fatal to Rommel, as Göring had once been the second most-powerful man in the Third Reich, but now the *Reichsmarschall*'s star was beginning to wane, so that while Rommel could not openly show his contempt for "Fat Hermann," he no longer had to pretend it did not exist.

The need to implement Operation *Alarich* increased dramatically on July 10, when 180,000 Allied soldiers, along with 600 tanks and 14,000 other vehicles were landed on the southeast and southwest shores of Sicily. For the better part of a month, the mostly Italian defenders fought hard, though they were inexorably pushed back into the northeast corner of the island, around the city of Messina. There had never been any question of actually holding Sicily, the defenders' mission was to buy as much time for the Axis forces on the Italian mainland to finish their preparation for the inevitable Allied invasion there. Beginning on August 11, the Italian navy was able to carry away more than 100,000 Italian soldiers from Messina while General Hube's four German divisions held the perimeter around the port. Finally they too were extracted, leaving the Allies with what amounted to a strategic draw: they held the island, but they had not inflicted any significant losses of manpower or materiel on the Germans or the Italians; the Axis could look to that as a moral victory at least.

By the time Sicily was in Allied hands, however, Rommel had learned that he had lost his job as commander of Army Group B. "I hear the Führer has been advised not to give me command in Italy as I am adversely disposed towards Italians," he wrote in his diary. "I imagine the Luftwaffe [meaning Göring and Kesselring] is behind this. So my move to Italy is again put right back." Army Group B, he was told, was being reassigned to Salonika, in northern Greece, where Rommel would take command of the defensive operations should the Allies land in Greece or Crete.

What followed has to almost certainly be the shortest army command in history. According to Rommel's diary, this is what happened:

23/7/43

Long discussion with the Führer. I am to report in detail and direct to him on conditions in Greece. Forces there, besides Eleventh Italian Army, include only one German armored division (1st Panzer Division) and three infantry divisions.

25/7/43

Left Wiener Neustadt 8:00 A.M. by air. Arrived Salonika 11:00 A.M.
Terrific heat.

5:00 P.M. Conference with Colonel General Loehr. Loehr described the situation as being dependent upon supplies. . . . General Gause also doesn't take a very rosy view of the situation here.

9:30 P.M. General Warlimont phoned and reported that Eleventh Italian Army will be definitely under my command. I want to get the German divisions directly under my command by interpolating a German Corps H.Q. instead, as was suggested at the Führer's H.Q., of having them under Italian command.

23.15 hours. A call from O.K.W. reversed everything. Duce in protective custody. I am recalled to the Führer's H.Q. Situation in Italy obscure.[253]

There was considerable confusion at the O.K.W. and the Führerhauptquartier: for weeks there had been rumors of a plot to overthrow the Duce and replace him with Marshal Pietro Badoglio, who was far more accomplished at political intrigue than commanding armies in the field; once Mussolini was out of the way, a separate peace with the Allies would be secretly negotiated by the new government. Admiral Wilhelm Canaris, the director of the Abwehr, Germany's intelligence agency, had discounted these rumors, which now turned out to be true, and thus Hitler and the O.K.W., despite their own suspicions, were caught off guard at the moment the coup actually took place. (Canaris, who was actively working in secret to accomplish Hitler's destruction, obviously had his own reasons for downplaying reports of the plot against Mussolini.) But as some sort of betrayal by the Italians had long been accepted as a given, it was not the deed itself that surprised Hitler and his senior officers, only the timing of it.

The Italians continued to proclaim their undying loyalty to the Axis, but everyone on both sides knew better. As Rommel put it, "In spite of the King's and Badoglio's proclamations, we can expect Italy to get out of the war. . . ." It was an absolute imperative that the German divisions already posted in southern Italy, along with Hube's four divisions in Sicily, not be cut off and isolated by the Italians, thus the orders to execute Operation *Alarich* went out almost immediately once it became clear what had happened in Rome. Rommel was given specific objectives, with the seizure of the railway tunnels and roadways through the Brenner Pass between Italy and Austria being the priority, but the exact manner in which they were to be achieved was left to his discretion. In his opinion, it was best if his troops were to act as if this were a "friendly" invasion—an idea not at all farfetched, especially in the Italian Tyrol, where the largely ethnic-German population greeted the Wehrmacht as liberators! Speed, however, was the overriding requirement for *Alarich*: the Italians must be given no time to realize what was actually taking place and move to stop it.[254]

Now the Italians were caught in a cleft stick of their own making: despite Mussolini's dismissal, the Allies were in no hurry to make a separate peace with the new Italian regime, going so far as to announce that no approaches had been made by the Italians to either the British or the Americans. Addressing the House of Commons at the end of July, Prime Minister Churchill held forth with relish, saying, "My advice to the House of Commons and to the British nation and the Commonwealth and the empire and to our allies at this juncture . . . we should let the Italians . . . 'stew in their own juice' for a bit and hot up the fire to accelerate the process until we obtain from their Government, or whoever possesses the necessary authority, all the indispensable requirements we demand for carrying on the war against our prime and capital foe, which is not Italy but Germany." In short, neither side would have the Italians: the Germans expected treachery from them and the Allies were not prepared to accept their surrender.[255]

While the Italians "stewed" they temporized, as all throughout August they played an elaborate, peacock-like dance with the Germans, attempting to work out something that resembled a compromise, one which would allow them to leave the war on their own terms but would not result in an actual German occupation—with all the accompanying police-state apparatus which would attend it—of their country. It was an impossible task, and in early September, events came to a head with an unexpected rapidity.

In addition to the planning for Operation *Alarich*, Rommel had also been given the orders for *Fall Achse*—Case Axis, a contingency plan for responding to an Italian surrender. "Axis" was the code word Hitler would issue for Rommel to immediately descend on the Italian armed forces in northern Italy, disarm them, and take them prisoner. Rommel expected that Axis would be triggered by a major British or American landing at La Spezia, the main fleet anchorage for the Italian navy, that would coincide with the announcement of an Italian surrender—in this scenario the Allies would be in position to attack across the Apennine Mountains and into the Po Valley, cutting off every German unit south of Bologna. As it happened, however, Montgomery was given overall command of the invasion force, and his innate caution compelled him to adopt a strategy which Rommel regarded as inexcusably stupid: multiple, poorly coordinated landings at the very southern end of the Italian peninsula, a plan which then made necessary a long, costly campaign up the length of the Italian boot.

When Rommel's old nemesis, the Eighth Army, landed two divisions at Reggio di Calabria on September 3, he was ordered to report to Hitler the next morning, where he was told to anticipate *Fall Achse* being activated at any time. Some of the old magic that had once held Rommel in thrall remained, at least when Rommel was actually in Hitler's presence: "The Führer gives the impression of being quietly confident. He wants to send me to see the King of Italy soon. He agrees to my Italian campaign plan, which envisages a defense along the actual coastline, despite Jodl's objections." Five days later, at 7:00 P.M., the news was broadcast on Allied radio stations that Italy had formally surrendered. By 8:00 P.M. the code word "Axis" was issued, effective immediately. "Now Italy's treachery is official," Rommel wrote to Lucie the following day. "We sure had them figured out right. So far our plans are running smoothly." Rome was seized by German troops, while Rommel put down Communist-led uprisings in Milan and Turin.[256]

Rommel was taken "out of action," as it were the night of September 9, when he was struck with acute appendicitis. Surgery was performed the next day, and on September 27 he was discharged as fit to return to active duty. There were disconcerting moments as he lay in his hospital bed in La Garda, where he had moved his headquarters in mid-August, particularly on the nights when he could hear the basso-profundo drone of Allied heavy bombers overhead. Wiener Neustadt was no longer immune to air attack, and Rommel had been frankly frightened by what the Royal Air Force and the American Eighth Air Force were doing to Germany's cities—a firestorm created by a massive Royal Air Force incendiary raid had ravaged Hamburg in July, while wide swaths of Berlin were bombed- and burned-out after repeated visits by the British and American bomber commands. The vital Messerschmitt aircraft company had a sprawling works south of Vienna, not far from Wiener Neustadt; Rommel was not prepared to lose Lucie or Manfred to an errant bomb, so he instructed Lucie to begin moving their most valuable possessions out of their house, safekeeping them with friends and relatives who lived in rural areas, far from inviting targets. He also insisted that she begin looking for a new home, preferably back in Württemberg, near Ulm. She would, he knew, be stubborn about the whole idea, but in this instance, he was determined to be even more stubborn; within six weeks Lucie and Manfred were moving into a summer villa in Herrlingen, outside of Ulm, the property of a brewer's widow who no longer used the house. His family once again reasonably safe, Rommel could turn his full attention to the military situation in Italy.[257]

While Rommel was hospitalized, Kesselring, who had overall command of the German forces in the south half of Italy, had been remarkably successful in keeping the Allies confined to their beachheads, much to the surprise of Rommel, who maintained that any attempt to hold Italy south of the Po Valley was doomed to failure. As Rommel saw it, any defensive line across the Italian peninsula was inherently vulnerable, as it could always be outflanked by sea. He found it incredible that none of the Allied generals were imaginative enough to see this. Kesselring, however, was confident that the Allies would never risk an amphibious operation outside the range of their tactical air support, hence a landing in northern Italy simply was not in the cards. Events would ultimately prove Kesselring right, much to Rommel's consternation.

In the meantime, though, both men were called to Rastenburg, where they reported to Hitler on the afternoon of September 30 to present the results of *Fall Achse*. Three quarters of a million Italian soldiers had been interned, a third of them shipped to Germany to serve as prison labor. One million rifles, 2,000 artillery pieces, 400 tanks, and an undetermined number of aircraft in various states of serviceability had been seized, along with substantial stocks of ammunition and supplies—much of it materiel which the Italians had previously claimed was scarce or non-existent. Particularly galling for Rommel was the discovery in a cave near La Spezia of 38,000 barrels—1,650,000 gallons—of fuel, the same fuel which Comando Supremo had insisted was unavailable while Panzerarmee Afrika was sitting immobile and stranded at El Alamein. Finally offered proof that at least some of his suspicions of treachery were valid, Rommel never forgave the Italians.

The strain of the situation in Italy, coupled with a growing crisis in Russia in the wake of the abortive Kursk offensive (Operation *Citadel*) in July was taking its toll on Hitler. Rommel was disturbed to see the Führer bent with fatigue, his speech rambling and sometimes slurred, at times he would uncharacteristically stammer. While to Rommel the emperor was still clothed, his finery was becoming increasingly threadbare. Apparently satisfied with both field marshals' reports on Axis, Hitler asked each in turn to make a case for their respective strategies. When they were finished, he told them, "Every day, every week, every month that we can hold up the enemy down in the south of Italy is vital to us. We must gain time, we must postpone the final reckoning. . . ." No final strategic decision was made, but both Rommel, commanding in the north, and Kesselring in the south, now understood what was expected of them—hold, hold everything, everywhere, to the last man and the last round. It was what Hitler had ordered in Russia, where until Stalingrad it had worked, and because Hitler had ordered it, and it had worked there, once, it would work everywhere, because Hitler decreed it to be so.[258]

Later, Rommel and Hitler would discuss the possibility of a counterattack in Italy, driving the Allies down the boot and into the sea. Privately Rommel thought this pure fantasy, but remained diplomatically non-committal in his replies to the Führer's musings. Hitler indicated that Kesselring was going to be transferred to Norway, which would make Rommel de facto supreme commander in Italy, a position he had hungered after since first reporting to Hitler back in May. There was just one fly in the ointment, from Rommel's perspective: the O.K.W. wanted Rommel to hold the line that Kesselring had already established, roughly a third of the way up the Italian peninsula. At this Rommel hesitated; before agreeing he wanted to inspect the line for himself, and he would have to have, he insisted, clear orders allowing him to conduct the defense of Italy as he saw fit. Though he did not say as much to Hitler, Rommel had already had enough of "no withdrawal, victory or death" strategic thinking. He wanted to keep Germany from losing the war—he had no interest in a *götterdämmerung*.

This was unwise, for Hitler was unaccustomed to being presented with terms and conditions; it was he who made offers, presented compromises—he would dictate, but not be dictated to. He gave Rommel a non-committal response and then dismissed the field marshal. Rommel flew back to his headquarters near Lake Garda on October 19. That evening a call came from Jodl, who informed Rommel that the Führer's order giving him overall command in Italy had been "set aside." Rommel pressed for clarification, but Jodl said no more. Rommel was not to know that after leaving Hitler's presence on October 17, Jodl, sensing Hitler's anger at what he perceived to be Rommel's imperious attitude, had suggested to the Führer that perhaps Rommel was not the best choice for supreme command in Italy. His cynical attitude toward the Italians would make it very difficult for him to work in cooperation with the new Fascist regime set up at Lake Garda.

Two months after he was deposed and arrested on the orders of King

Victor Emmanuel, Mussolini had been liberated in a risky commando operation carried out by German paratroopers; less than two weeks later the former Duce announced the creation of the Italian Social Republic, essentially a Nazi puppet state, in northern Italy. Rommel, whose disdain for Mussolini had grown with every new revelation of Italian obstructionism during the North African campaign, would have been compelled to work with the Duce, a task which would have sorely taxed Rommel's limited capacity for tact and diplomacy—such a situation would, in Jodl's opinion, ultimately prove detrimental to Germany's efforts to hold back the Allied advance in Italy. His ruffled feathers soothed, Hitler agreed and gave the Italian command to Kesselring instead.

A week would pass before Rommel could bring himself to tell Lucie the news:

26 October 1943

Dearest Lu,

The job was not confirmed. By all accounts the Führer changed his mind after all. In any case, he didn't sign the order promulgating the appointment. Of course I know no more than that. Maybe I aroused no great hopes that the position would be held, maybe my delay in taking over command was the cause. There may again, of course, be entirely different reasons. So, for the moment, Kesselring remains. Perhaps I'll be posted away. Anyway, I'll take it as it comes.[259]

The tone of a man struggling to overcome a deep humiliation is very real in Rommel's letter; the element of self-doubt there is extraordinary, if only because it is so unusual. Nevertheless, Rommel *did* feel humiliated by Hitler's decision to give the Italian command to Kesselring. Certainly he regarded it as a personal rejection by someone whom he once deeply admired, however diminished that admiration had now become. The professional rejection, though, Rommel thought was profound, the error potentially catastrophic: he, Rommel, was the man to whom Hitler had confessed he should have listened when warned of the strategic realities of North Africa; it was Kesselring's misplaced optimism that had accelerated the process by which Armeegruppe Afrika had been lost. If Rommel proved to be right and Kesselring wrong, Germany stood to lose yet another army, this one trapped in southern Italy. In the event, it was Kesselring who was proven right, for he had read the Allied commanders correctly and deduced that collectively they were overly cautious and lacking in the strategic imagination to undertake anything but a slow, grinding campaign up the length of the Italian peninsula. Banishing him to Norway would have been a waste of his abilities; instead he was able to redeem himself for his obstructiveness in Tunisia and prove to be something close to a defensive genius as he made the Allies fight for every yard they advanced northward in Italy.

(As events in Italy and France played out in late 1943 and early 1944, a reconciliation of sorts took place between Rommel and Kesselring, and a high degree of mutual respect, if not actual admiration, grew between the two. Rommel recognized a defensive genius at work in Italy when he saw one, while Kesselring, when at last fully confronted by the reality of the Allies' massive material superiority, came to recognize just how brilliant an accomplishment was Rommel's retreat from El Alamein into Tunisia.)

At first, Hitler attempted to mollify Rommel by allowing him to retain the staff he had assembled for "Army Group B," on the pretext that it would serve as a sort of "fire brigade" ready to be posted anywhere in order to handle emergencies. This smacked of make-work to Rommel and at the same time it presented Dr. Göbbels' Propaganda Ministry with a problem: having made something akin to the military equivalent of a matinee idol out of Rommel for the German people, how was it to be explained that their favorite general was now cooling his heels, waiting for a call which might never come? This was not as trivial a problem as it may seem: by the end of 1943 no one in Germany could deny that the war had taken an unexpected turn, and not for the better. The Stalingrad disaster, the loss of North Africa, the invasion and surrender of Italy, the Allied bomber offensive, all were taking their toll on the morale of the German people. They were far from beaten, and, listening to the determined drumming of the Propaganda Ministry, were confident that the British, Americans, and Russians were all suffering in equally great a degree. But civilian morale had to be sustained, and it was Germany's martial heroes who provided that sustenance: Rommel was Germany's avatar of victory, in much the same way Montgomery was becoming to the British, or Eisenhower, Patton, or MacArthur would be to the Americans. It just would not do to have a general who stood as high in the *Volk*'s esteem as did Rommel suddenly appear to have been banished to the sidelines.

The solution came from an unexpected quarter: Colonel General Alfred Jodl, the O.K.W.'s Chief of Operations. On October 30 the Commander-in-Chief West, Field Marshal Gerd von Rundstedt, submitted a report to the Führerhauptquartier which presented an unvarnished—and unpleasant—view of the "Atlantic Wall," the vast and allegedly impregnable system of fortifications which protected Europe's Atlantic coast from Allied invasion. It was the Atlantic Wall—*Atlantikwall* in German—which was to give substance to Hitler's proclamation of a *"Festung Europa,"* a "Fortress Europe," within which no Allied boot would ever be set. Von Rundstedt's report minced no words in declaring the Atlantic Wall to be little better than a hoax, for aside from a few massive fortifications built mainly for propaganda purposes, in the autumn of 1943 the defensive works along the Atlantic coast were limited, and nothing in place was sufficient to stop a cross-Channel landing. Given that the Allies had now demonstrated three times their ability to conduct successful seaborne invasions, the near-pathetic state of the Atlantic Wall could no longer be ignored: everyone, Axis and Allies alike, knew that the decisive battle of the war would be fought on the Atlantic coast.

Jodl saw this as an opportunity to put Rommel to work in a way that got him out of Italy and would be perceived by both Rommel and the German people as useful employment of a general of his talent and skill: assign Army Group B as an inspectorate responsible for expanding, strengthening, and completing the Atlantic Wall defenses. Rommel would be nominally subordinate to von Rundstedt, who was *oberbefehlshaber West*, or OB West— the supreme commander, West—but his own command brief would run along the coast from the northern tip of Denmark south to the Franco-Spanish border. The task was perfect for Rommel, Rommel perfect for the task.

THE ATLANTIC WALL, concept and reality, grew out of a *Führerbefehl*, a Führer directive, this one being Number 40, which was issued by Adolf Hitler on March 23, 1942. Unusually long and detailed compared to the usual Führer directive, which typically consisted of no more than two or three paragraphs, Directive 40 was five pages of closely spaced text which created a uniform defensive doctrine and a rationalized command structure for Wehrmacht, Luftwaffe, and Kriegsmarine units stationed along occupied Europe's long and vulnerable Atlantic coast. The British commandos, along with the S.O.E., the same organization which oversaw the British desert irregulars—the S.A.S., S.B.S., and Long Range Desert Group—which had proven to be a thorn in Rommel's flesh in North Africa, had transformed that coastline into a special operations playground. Not a week went by without a raid of some sort being staged along the coast of Denmark, the Low Countries, or France, ranging from mere "nuisance raids," where isolated sentries were knifed or garroted to increase the anxiety of German guardposts, to full-scale air and sea operations that spirited away entire radar installations; Churchill's directive to the British special forces had been to "set Europe ablaze": this they were doing, and in the process proved that the Third Reich's Atlantic defenses resembled nothing so much as a sieve.

The initial work done in accordance with the instructions laid down in Directive 40 was the construction of fortifications around ports, naval installations, and radar sites, the latter being especially critical as they were vital to the Luftwaffe's defense against the raids of over a thousand bombers which the Royal Air Force's Bomber Command was now routinely sending to Germany.

Most of this work was done by the Todt Organization (*Organization Todt*, or OT), the civil and military engineering arm of the Third Reich. The organization's labor pool had originally been almost exclusively German, but by the middle of 1943 it had been almost completely replaced by conscripted foreign workers, POWs, and, as time went on, increasing numbers of concentration-camp inmates drafted as slave labor, as the Wehrmacht's demands on manpower drew away all of the OT's able-bodied Germans. In February 1942 the Todt Organization became a department of the newly created Ministry of Armaments and Munitions (Reichsministerium für Rüstung und Kriegsproduktion), under Reichsminister Albert Speer. Speer was one of the few high-level Nazis who understood how poorly organized was the German economy for the sort of total war which Hitler had brought about, and once he was confirmed in office set about reorganizing German industry to improve efficiency and productivity. He also reinvigorated the Todt Organization at the same time, though the Atlantic Wall, Führer Directive No. 40 notwithstanding, was still a fairly low-priority project.

It was Hitler himself who gave the Atlantic Wall its first good, hard push toward completion: in August 1942, he informed Speer that he wanted not only the ports, harbors, and fixed military installations on the Atlantic coast protected by defensive works, he wanted the entire coastline converted into a defensive barrier. He mandated the construction of a belt of 15,000 permanent defensive positions constructed on the Dutch, Belgian, and French coastlines. These positions, known as *widerstandsnester* ("resistance nests") would be complex arrangements of trenches, bunkers, dugouts, mortar pits and machine-gun posts. They would be built so that they could offer all-round resistance, placed so that they had interlocking fields of fire and were within mutually supporting distance of each other, and sited so that they could enfilade specific stretches of shoreline. Hitler was confident that a density of 30 such defensive posts per mile, properly manned, would be sufficient to stop any seaborne landing; the total manpower requirement would be roughly a half-million troops. He demanded that the entire construction project be completed by the spring of 1943.

It was an impossible order, and the Todt Organization engineers knew it, but they did their best—one indicator of just how hard they began working their men is that in the wake of Hitler's order, the volume of concrete being poured in Western Europe for defensive works tripled, from 100,000 cubic yards per month to 300,000. Nonetheless, by the time Hitler's deadline arrived the work was only half-finished; the Führer though, by this time, was distracted by the unfolding debacle in Tunisia and then the imminent Allied landings in Sicily. This was hardly unusual: Hitler tended to fixate on one subject at a time, almost to the point of obsession, then when that task was accomplished, move on to whatever next caught his attention. This, of course, was the underlying reason why the Germans as a whole never developed a grand strategy for the Second World War. In any case, prior to the summer of 1943, the question of an Allied invasion of Europe across the English Channel had been problematic at worst: despite the multitude of small-scale raids which the British were carrying out, the Allies lacked the manpower and the seaborne capability to launch and sustain the sort of full-scale, multi-division invasion necessary to establish a permanent bridgehead on the Continent.

That perception changed drastically after Operation *Husky*, the Allied landings on Sicily, in July 1943, which were followed with a swiftness the Germans never expected by the landings at Salerno, Italy—Operation *Avalanche*—at the beginning of September. Now the Allies without question possessed the technical ability along with increasing numbers of landing craft and support ships to stage an operation as ambitious as a cross-Channel invasion; just as important, if not more so, the experience gained in the landings in North Africa, Sicily, and Italy gave them a priceless body of practical knowledge to bring to bear on the challenge of landing on the Continent.

The single most significant factor that would distinguish amphibious operations in the Mediterranean from any potential operation against the Channel coast was the weather: the highly unpredictable, widely—and often wildly—variable, and sometimes violent nature of the weather in the English Channel severely curtailed the "window of opportunity" in which the Allies could land on the Channel coast. The relative lateness in the year of Operation *Avalanche* meant that there would be no cross-Channel invasion before the late spring of 1944—prior to that the weather would be too volatile for the landing to be sustained, even if it were made.

Suddenly the degree to which the Atlantic Wall was ready to confront an Allied invasion acquired a priority and matching urgency that it had never before been accorded. Hitler and the O.K.W. assumed—reasonably and rightly—that the Allies would not attempt a cross-Channel invasion until they had built up their strength in manpower, equipment, aircraft, and ships, including landing craft, as well as the necessary reserves, to a level they believed could not only land successfully and establish a beachhead, but secure one large enough to allow for powerful attacks to be staged out of it when the Allies chose to begin driving on the Reich. The sum of all the strategic issues facing both Allies and Germans could be summed up in a single equation: could the long-neglected Atlantic Wall defenses be shored up and completed before the Allies accrued enough strength to guarantee that their invasion succeeded? When Hitler gave Rommel his new assignment on November 5, 1943, he was explicit in stating just how critical was the success of Rommel's mission: "When the enemy invades in the west it will be the moment of decision in this war," he said, "and the moment must turn to our advantage." This was the challenge that now faced Erwin Rommel; as he had been so many times before, he was once again in a race against time.[260]

FOR ROMMEL TO accomplish his mission, he first had to discover the truth about what defenses, such as they were and what there were of them, had already been constructed, and where. After he had that knowledge, he could go about expanding and improving them. He already had certain ideas about which he would become dogmatic in the months ahead, the first being that any seaborne invasion must be met—and stopped—at the water's edge. In the considered opinion of Field Marshal von Rundstedt, the OB West, and General der Panzertruppe Leo Geyr von Schewppen- burg, the commander of Panzergruppe West, the Wehrmacht's armored re- serve in Western Europe, allowing the Allies to establish a lodgement ashore and expecting to defeat them in a battle of maneuver when they attempted to breakout of their beachhead was the preferred strategy. In Rommel's opinion, this was the height of folly: neither man had fought a battle or di- rected a campaign where they had been compelled to fight an enemy who had absolute air supremacy, as Rommel had been forced to do in Tunisia. All of their presumptions and preconceptions of mobile warfare had grown out of the battles in France in 1940 or in the first two years of the Russian campaign, where the Wehrmacht had either enjoyed air superiority or con- trol of the air over the battlefield was at least contested. Neither man had the slightest conception of the destructiveness of Allied air power, or how severely it curtailed movement. As far as Rommel was concerned, when- ever and wherever the invasion took place, the battle would have to be fought—and won—by the soldiers already in place, using whatever equip- ment they had to hand.

Rommel's second premise was that if Allied air power would deny mo- bility to his forces, then some countervailing measure should be employed to deny mobility to the Allies. For that, Rommel once again looked to North Africa, specifically to the two battles of El Alamein and the Battle of Alam Halfa. He vividly remembered how the vast minefields sown by the Afrika Korps and Eighth Army alike had inhibited the movements of both armored and infantry divisions, and worked to localize and channel attacks. There was no reason the same principles could not be applied to the defense of the Atlantic coastline; mines were to become one of the cornerstones of his overall defensive concept for the Atlantic Wall. Rommel would be, in private, the object of considerable derision among many of his fellow senior officers for his repeated reliance on his experiences in North Africa in guiding his operational and strategic thinking in Western Europe. Their combat experience had been gained on the Russian Front, where fighting was done under far different conditions than those which obtained in the west. They completely missed the fact that North Africa had been, in essence, the laboratory where much of the Allies' operational and tactical doctrines were worked out. They would come to rue their contempt as, after June 1944, Rommel was repeatedly proven right in his conclusions and they were shown to be fatally wrong.

Rommel's "grand tour" of his new command responsibilities began on November 30 in Denmark. With him went Gause, his Chief of Staff, along with Generalleutnant Wilhelm Meise, a career engineer officer upon whom Rommel would come to heavily depend in the months ahead, and Vice-Admiral Friedrich Ruge, his naval advisor who would also become a close friend. The rest of the staff of Army Group B was establishing its headquarters at Fontainebleu, preparing for formal activation on January 15, when it would assume command responsibility for the Netherlands, Belgium, and northern France, including the whole of the Channel coast. The inspection in Denmark was predictable, but the shopping was apparently quite good. Militarily Rommel found what he expected to find— fortifications concentrated around harbors and ports, with little in the way of defensive works constructed elsewhere. Rommel was unconcerned by this, this part of the inspection itself being more-or-less pro forma, as Denmark would never be the site of the Allied invasion of the Continent. The country's geography and location dictated against it: the Danish peninsula was too distant from the British Isles, could be too easily sealed off, any army within it too easily contained, for it to serve as the base for any decisive Allied attack on Germany itself. The stores in Denmark, especially in the capital, Copenhagen, were a marvel, however: luxury goods and foods which had been unavailable in Germany since the beginning of the war were plentiful; of course, Rommel and his fellow officers cheerfully yielded to temptation.

8 December 1943

Dearest Lu,

We're off again today up to the northernmost point. The round trip will be over in a couple of days and then the paperwork will begin. Hard fighting still in the east and south. I need not tell you with what feelings I look on from a distance.

I hear that the call-up is going to be extended to the 14-year-olds. The lads will be sent to labor service or defense according to their size and physique.

11 December 1943

We're now back from Copenhagen. A few days' written work and then the job will continue. You can still buy everything you want here in Denmark. Of course the Danes will only sell to their own compatriots. I've bought a few things for Christmas, so far as the money went. [By regulation, German officers (generals included) were allowed to exchange only limited amounts of Reichsmarks for Danish kroner.][261]

Rommel's reference to 14-year-old boys being called up for national service highlights the manpower shortage that the German armed forces were beginning to experience. Manfred was now eligible for conscription, and a father-and-son talk on the subject that took place a few days after this letter was written, when Rommel was briefly back in Herrlingen, revealed that the once politically naive Rommel was becoming uncomfortably familiar with the realities of the Third Reich. Manfred and his father were discussing which branch of service would be best suited for the young man. Manfred had decided—based on the fact that they were better equipped and had the smarter-looking uniforms—that the SS was for him. Rommel stomped down hard on that idea.

"Absolutely out of the question," he said. "You'll join the same branch in which I've served for thirty years!"

Manfred was startled at the vehemence of his father's response, and Rommel went on to explain: he acknowledged that the SS were good troops, but he did not want his son under the command of a man who, to Rommel's certain knowledge, was guilty of ordering mass executions.

"Himmler?" Manfred asked, his father's revelation taking him by surprise.

"Yes." Then, according to Manfred's recollection of the conversation, "he instructed me to maintain absolute silence about the whole affair. The war was not going at all well and he had heard that people like Himmler were trying, by actions of this kind, to burn the bridges of the German people behind them. I think he was not at all certain at that time whether Hitler knew anything about what was going on, for no mention of the mass executions had ever been made at the Führer's H.Q." Hitler could still inspire momentary bursts of enthusiasm, even something passing for the old loyalty—after being given the Atlantic Wall assignment, Rommel excitedly blurted out to a friend, "What power he radiates! And what faith and confidence he inspires in his people!"—but once away from the Führer's charisma, reality almost instantly replaced adulation. The exchange with Manfred had revealed in just a handful of words what was at the heart of Rommel's determination to go on fighting; being who he was, he could do no other, but now he was fighting for Germany alone.[262]

WHATEVER REMAINING VESTIGES of confidence Rommel might have had in Hitler finally evaporated after he spent six weeks touring the Atlantic coast and inspecting the German defenses, such as they were. Even at this late date, still barely half of the original construction ordered by Hitler was complete, and large tracts of the defensive positions which had been built were already falling into disrepair. Had the Allies invaded, the result would have been much like how the Marhathas recollected the capture of Ahmednagar in 1803: "They came here in the morning, looked at the wall, walked over it, killed the garrison, and returned to breakfast!" Rommel regarded it as a farce, and felt as though he had been duped by Hitler's description of the wall and its state of readiness, blurting out to his staff that it was little more than "a figment of Hitler's '*Wolkenkuckkucksheim*'—'cuckoo land in the clouds'—'an enormous bluff . . . more for the German people than for the enemy . . . and the enemy, through his agents, knows more about it than we do.'" Rommel could, and would, change all of that.[263]

Aboard the train placed at Rommel's disposal to expedite his inspection, he further developed his ideas about how to turn the wall into a reality, and best defend the Channel coastline, especially in light of what was certain to be Allied air superiority, if not actual air supremacy. "When the invasion begins," he told his small entourage, "our own supply lines won't be able to bring forward any aircraft, gasoline, rockets, tanks, guns or shells because of the enemy air attacks. That alone will rule out any sweeping land battles. Our only possible defense will be at the beaches—that's where the enemy is always weakest." Rommel understood that if the Germans made it too costly for the Allies to get ashore in sufficient strength to establish a beachhead, the entire invasion effort would collapse, and it would be a long, long time before they attempted another.[264]

The Allies, then, must begin taking casualties even before the first British or American soldiers set foot on the beaches. Rommel was under no illusion that the Allies would be so cooperative as to choose to land at one of the heavily fortified sections of the coast, where heavy guns and huge concrete bunkers dominated—such installations were imposing, but the sort of weaponry which could defeat or even destroy them swiftly and economically had yet to be invented, so the Americans and British were sure to pass them by. The Allies would land elsewhere, in a more lightly held sector of shoreline, somewhere they could be confident, even certain, that they could bring to bear overwhelming firepower to reduce to impotence whatever German defenses were present. The question then was how to inflict unacceptable losses on the Allied landing forces even in the absence of German heavy artillery, tanks, and deep concrete emplacements. The answer was mines. As Rommel's chief engineering officer, General Meise would be required to translate Rommel's concepts into reality, and he sat enthralled as Rommel described in detail what he wanted to achieve and how he meant to accomplish it. Mines would be the key to Rommel's defense of Festung Europa.

Rommel's inventiveness extended beyond the usual antipersonnel and anti-vehicular mines. He wanted mines that could sink ships and landing craft, mines that would be effective against enemy paratroopers, mines that could be detonated at will by remote control, or set off by trip-wires or electric eyes. Recalling the mine-detection equipment the British had used at El Alamein, he wanted to have mines made of non-ferrous components, virtually undetectable to the British devices. "I want antipersonnel mines, antitank mines, anti-paratroop mines. I want mines to sink ships and mines to sink landing craft," Rommel told Meise. "I want some minefields designed so that our own infantry can cross them, but not the enemy tanks.

I want mines that detonate when a wire is tripped; mines that explode when a wire is cut; mines that can be remotely detonated. Some of them must be encased in nonferrous metals, so that the enemy's mine detectors won't register them. . . ." The keen mind of the teenaged would-be engineer who built his own glider and who tore down and rebuilt his own motorcycle engines was reinvigorated once again. Always handy with a pencil and sketchpad, Rommel frequently drew illustrations and diagrams of the work he wanted done.[265]

Nor did his ingenuity end with mines. Rommel conceived of an entire array of underwater obstacles that would be sited between the high- and low-tide lines which would destroy incoming landing craft: concrete tetrahedrons that had steel blades or antitank mines at their apexes; jagged steel hedgehogs that resembled Brobdingnagian jacks, constructed from girders or steel rails welded at right angles; wooden stakes set in a concrete base that contained a heavy shell—the impact of a landing-craft striking the stake would set off the explosives. His final plan called for four belts of such obstacles, the first placed in 6 feet of water at mean high tide, the second at the 6-foot mark at half-tide, the third in 6 feet of water at low tide, and the last at 12 feet of water at low tide. General Meise, who had been an engineer all his life, could only stand and watch in utter admiration: "Quite apart from Rommel's greatness as a soldier, in my view he was the greatest engineer of the Second World War. There was nothing I could teach him. He was my master."[266]

Rommel's near-obsession with mines, and their impersonal, implacable ability to create casualties and chaos, to intimidate, deflect, and channelize an attacking force, such as he had witnessed at El Alamein, sprang from yet another shortage with which he was confronted: manpower. He lacked sufficient infantry to man the Atlantic Wall in the strength that he believed would be required to stop an Allied invasion. Germany was running out of soldiers fit for combat—in fact, Germany had already run out of them. Hitler still refused to allow German women to join the labor force, so that by the end of 1943, there were at least 5,000,000 fit, able-bodied men working in unskilled and semi-skilled jobs in German factories, men whose Allied counterparts were already in uniform and fighting. (It was this same refusal by Hitler which led directly to one of the most horrible passages in the entire reprehensible history of the Third Reich: the drafting of slave labor—Jews, Slavs, Russian prisoners of war, French, Belgian, and Italian civilians conscripted at random—by the hundreds of thousands, most of whom would be worked to death.) So great was Germany's need for manpower that the Wehrmacht was compelled to accept foreign volunteers— ethnic Germans, Belgians, Czechs, Dutch, Finns, Hungarians, Poles, and Balts, along with Russian prisoners of war—to create new infantry units. They were organized into battalions, which were then integrated into existing infantry divsions; the value of these units can be surmised from the fact that on January 1, 1944, 427,000 Russians and Ukrainians alone were serving in Wehrmacht uniforms: their *Ostbataillone* (Eastern battalions) were the numerical equivalent of 30 divisions.

Nor did the Wehrmacht's ruthless ingenuity stop there. There were thousands of wounded German soldiers whose injuries barred them from the rigors of front-line service in Russia or Italy, but who could still be useful in rear echelon services, as well as in manning fortifications. Organized into what were nicknamed *magen divisionen* ("Stomach Divisions," as chronic stomach problems were the most prevalent ailment), they were ideal for garrison duties. Yet even with such clever expedients, the O.K.W. was convinced that the Allies not only had the Wehrmacht outnumbered—which was true—but had it overwhelmingly outnumbered. And thereby hangs a tale, for Hitler, the O.K.W., and Rommel himself were being systematically deceived by a Allied combined-service intelligence operation known as *Fortitude*.

Operation *Fortitude* was part of a larger operation, *Bodyguard*, which was a vast and complex cover and deception plan created to deceive the Germans as to where, when and in what strength the actual invasion of Europe would take place. *Bodyguard* was actually an umbrella operation, coordinating several smaller—though still significant in size and scope—operations drawn up to accomplish specific missions which built up the whole fabric of *Bodyguard*'s overall deception. *Fortitude* was one of these subordinate operations, its purpose being to supply the German intelligence services with enough seemingly reliable information to cause them to conclude that there existed two, or even three, Allied army groups in Great Britain poised to invade Europe. *Fortitude* was divided into two sections, *North* and *South*. *Fortitude North* was to mislead the Germans into believing that an invasion of Norway was in the offing, which would, it was hoped, divert reinforcements that would otherwise have gone to France or the Low Countries. Based in Scotland, the deception relied primarily on false radio traffic to create the impression that a fictitious British Fourth Army was being built up for the Norwegian invasion. It was a limited success at best.

Fortitude South was an entirely different story. It was developed around the existence of two Allied army groups, 21st Army Group under Montgomery, and 1st U.S. Army Group, or F.U.S.A.G., under the command of Lieutenant General Patton. F.U.S.A.G., which aside from a few hundred men with special duties, was wholly fictional. It was supposedly deployed in southeastern England, directly opposite the Pas de Calais, which Rommel considered the most likely place a cross-Channel invasion would take place. Montgomery's 21st Army Group, which was indeed real and would carry out the actual invasion of the continent, was posted in southern England, opposite Normandy and the Cherbourg peninsula.

A meticulously orchestrated radio deception plan of the sort that the Germans tellingly called a *funkspiel*—a radio game—was carried out to dovetail precisely with the apparent movement of units around southeastern England, where dummy encampments, tanks, vehicles, aircraft, and landing craft were positioned. The Royal Air Force and U.S. Army Air Force, which by this time together owned the skies above Great Britain, would deliberately allow the occasional German high-altitude reconnaissance flight to penetrate the areas where F.U.S.A.G. was supposedly concentrating: the photos those aircraft collected, when cross-referenced with an analysis of the F.U.S.A.G.'s simulated radio traffic, convinced Rommel, OB West, O.K.W., and Hitler that F.U.S.A.G. was real. The cinching argument for many of the high-ranking German officers was the presence of Patton, the one Allied commander whom they had so far come to respect.

Montgomery fully appreciated the value of *Fortitude South*, for he knew that 21st Army Group would field a maximum of 37 Allied divisions, armor and infantry, for the invasion, consolidating the beachhead then expanding it, and breaking out of whatever foothold his forces could create. Rommel would have upward of 60 divisions available, although these would initially be spread out all along the Channel coast. Not that the raw numbers were a true indicator of the balance of strength, as most of the German divisions in France and the Low Countries were significantly understrength, usually underequipped, and some of them were of openly dubious value. Nonetheless, in any attack the advantage always lies with the defender, never more so than in an amphibious invasion: for once Montgomery's slavish devotion to massive superiority in men and materiel would not be misplaced, as he would need a *minimum* of three-to-one odds simply to be confident that the invasion force could get ashore. By inflating the apparent size of the Allied forces arrayed against the German defenders, as well as creating deep uncertainty as to where the actual invasion would take place, it was hoped to entice the maximum possible number of German divisions to "stay home" as it were when the actual invasion hit the Normandy beaches, denying the defenders there the reinforcements they would desperately need.

In this endeavor, the Allies were unwittingly aided by one of the most important German intelligence services, Fremde Heere West (Foreign Armies West), the branch of the Abwehr dedicated to developing an up-to-date order of battle of the British and American forces stationed in Great Britain which would be used in the invasion. So detailed and credible was the evidence, especially the Allied *funkspiel*, which pointed to an unexpectedly massive buildup of American and British forces, that the commanding officer of Foreign Armies West, Oberst Alexander von Rönne, became convinced that the 35 fictitious divisions assigned to F.U.S.A.G. were actually real, and that the British and Americans had or were forming a reserve army of at least another 30 divisions. Thus the intelligence evaluations of Fremde Heere West presented to OB West and Army Group B stated as fact that the combined Allied strength exceeded 100 divisions, when in truth it was less than half that.

Despite this, Rommel's confidence in the ability of the Atlantic Wall—once he was past his initial outrage at its condition and Hitler's duplicity in regard to it—to hold back the coming invasion would grow with each passing month. Something akin to his old optimism, if not cheerfulness, began to assert itself almost as soon as he arrived at his permanent billet in France, a large country house in Fontainebleau.

15 December 1943

Dearest Lu,

Arrived safely yesterday. I've found myself a lovely billet in a chateau which once belonged to Madame de Pompadour. But I won't be here long. I'm already off on a trip tomorrow as today's news announced. It seems that they can't tell the British and Americans soon enough that I'm here. I lunched with von Rundstedt today. He seems very pleased and I think it's all going well, but I must first get a picture of the situation and see how things are. The old chateau is a lovely place. The French built very generously and spaciously for their upper classes two centuries ago. We're absolutely provincial in comparison.[267]

On Christmas Eve he was able to get a telephone call through to Herrlingen—not always an easy feat, as Allied bombers were targeting communications centers in France—and talk with both Lucie and Manfred. He wrote Lucie the next day, of course.

It was grand that the telephone call worked so well last night and that I now know that things are all right with you both. The big news was Manfred's call-up for the 6th January. He is sure to be pleased, but for us, and above all, for you, it's painful to see the youngster leave home, and it will take us a long time to get used to the idea. I wish you both a happy Christmas. Enjoy the time you still have together. . . . I spent yesterday evening with the officers of my staff and afterwards with the men, though it's difficult to be really cheerful at the moment.[268]

Rommel's lack of cheer was understandable, as by this point he had developed a good picture of the Atlantic Wall's shortcomings and the amount of work which would be needed to overcome them. Still, Rommel was the sort of officer—the sort of person—who became bored and disinterested if a task were too easy; the challenge of completing the wall required someone of Rommel's temperament: his penchant for leading from the front in combat, when applied to this task, meant that he wanted to be everywhere, seeing everything, ensuring that the work was actually being done. And he thrived on it.

19 January 1944

Dearest Lu,
Returned today from my long trip. I saw a lot and was very satisfied

with the progress that has been made. I think for certain that we'll win the defensive battle in the West, provided only that a little more time remains for preparation. Günther's going off tomorrow with a suitcase [Lance-Corporal Herbert Günther, Rommel's batman]. He's to bring back my brown civilian suit and lightweight coat with hat, etc. I want to be able to go out without a Marshal's baton for once. . . .

Situation in the East: apparently stabilised. . . .

In the South: severe fighting and more heavy attacks to be met. . . .

In the West: I believe we'll be able to beat off the assault.[269]

As he scurried to and fro across northern France and Belgium, Rommel began to feel the need to get himself back in shape as well. It would not have done for any of his old Goslar *jägers* to see how their former officer commanding, who had been such a stickler for physical fitness, had let himself grow soft during his time in Italy. Always an avid—and skilled—hunter, Rommel stalked the deer, wild boars, and rabbits which made the countryside around the chateau their home. He was not an indiscriminate slaughterer of animals: whatever game Rommel took found its way into the officers' mess Army Group B headquarters.[270]

Back in Herrlingen, Manfred's call-up date came in mid-January; as per his father's stern instructions, volunteering for the SS was right out, but rather than joining the Army, as the elder Rommel had wished, Manfred found himself conscripted into the Luftwaffe, where he would be expected to serve when needed as a "gun bunny" delivering ammunition to an antiaircraft battery. Rommel's letters to his son were now taking on a more man-to-man tone, as the father realized his son was no longer a mere boy—the war was causing everyone to grow up a little faster than they would have otherwise. On the last day of January, Rommel wrote Manfred, saying,

I was particularly pleased with your first letter as a Luftwaffe auxiliary, because you have settled in so well to your new conditions. It is not easy for an "only child" to leave home. Perhaps you'll be getting a few days' leave in February and then you must give us a full report. There's still an endless amount of work here before I'll be able to say that we're properly prepared for battle. People get lazy and self-satisfied when things are quiet. But the contrast between quiet times and battle will be tough and I feel it essential to prepare for hard times here. I'm out on the move a lot and raising plenty of dust wherever I go.

All the best to you and warmest greetings,
Your Father[271]

Rommel's confidence continued to grow as the work on the Atlantic Wall fortifications progressed, but he never allowed confidence to create slackness: he continued to work his officers and men as hard as ever. Mine-laying was the priority, and no matter how quickly it progressed it was never fast enough to satisfy him. In March Generaloberst Hans von Salmuth who commanded the Fifteenth Army, which was responsible for the defense of the Pas de Calais, where Rommel expected the invasion to take place, was pleased to report to Rommel that his men were each laying 10 land mines a day. Rommel's reply was a terse, "Make it twenty a day." Another time, when von Salmuth complained that the working pace Rommel demanded was leaving the Seventh Army's soldiers exhausted, Rommel responded by asking, "Tell me, Herr General, which would your men rather be, tired or dead?" By the time the Allies actually landed in France, the Germans had laid almost six million mines—Rommel's final plan called for a total of twenty million. Existing minefields were extended, with particular attention given to those covering roads or tracks leading from the beaches: the beaches themselves were devil's dens of mines, obstacles, booby traps, barbwire, bunkers, and redoubts. Inland, *Rommels spargel*—"Rommel's asparagus"—began sprouting up in open fields that seemed likely landing spots for airborne troops: these were heavy wooden stakes, with sharpened tops, driven vertically into the ground; barbwire was strung between them. Similar obstacles were to be driven into the sand along the beaches, using fire hoses to excavate the holes hydraulically, as obstacles to Allied landing craft. Not long afterward, some unsung genius in the Seventh Army suggested strapping Teller mines to the top of these stakes: if the stake failed to rip out the bottom of the landing craft, the mine would blow the unfortunate vessel to bits. Rommel immediately endorsed the idea and ordered such obstacles to be emplaced all along the French coast.

Rommel's acerbic dismissal of von Salmuth's complaint that his men were being overworked was a clear-cut demonstration of two vital aspects of the field marshal's command of the Atlantic Wall defenses. First was his renewed singularity of purpose: anything which diverted his attention and energy from the completion of the wall was a needless diversion. This proved to be a source of some minor annoyance to his staff, as evidenced by an entry in Colonel Templehoff's personal journal, where he noted that "On our journeys with the field marshal we always drive straight past the monuments and fine architecture. He's so wrapped up in his job that he's totally uninterested in anything else except the military needs of the moment." The second was the return of the same disregard for personal feelings which had marked his first months in North Africa: he was prepared to run roughshod over any subordinate when and as needed in order to create a command structure on which he could rely to carry out *his* orders and produce the results *he* demanded. General Erich Marcks, one of Rommel's corps commanders and himself no stranger to being short-tempered with subordinates, summed up Rommel to a colleague, saying, "He is a choleric who often explodes and the commanders are terribly scared of him. The first one who has to report to him in the morning receives a chewing-out as a matter of principle."[272]

To speed up the work, Rommel encouraged local commanders to hire French civilians as laborers to work alongside the German troops who were digging trenches and pouring concrete—he was not prepared to countenance the Todt Organization's use of slave labor in his command area. Because he insisted on paying a decent wage, French men and women volunteered by the thousands for this work; to encourage their efforts, he put up notices reminding them that the Allies were least likely to invade a heavily defended area. There was, everyone knew, a trade-off involved, as inevitably there would be members of the French Resistance in the workforce who would happily seize the opportunity to do a bit of sabotage or simply acquire intelligence about the German defensive works which they could pass along to the Allies. For Rommel, however, accelerating the pace of the work was worth whatever minor details about the defenses the enemy might learn in this way: as he had caustically observed earlier, the Allies probably already knew as much about the Atlantic Wall as did the Germans anyway.

Unlike the previous construction efforts, there was nothing haphazard about the work now being done: Rommel had developed an overall plan which would turn the entire Channel coast, from the water's edge to a distance inland of 6 miles, into a death zone for Allied soldiers. He had calculated that a defensive line that extensive and deep would encourage the Allies to give up on the idea of invading at all, or if they had the temerity to invade, breaching it would prove so costly in men and materiel that they would be compelled to withdraw.[273]

31 March 1944

Dearest Lu,
No news of importance. . . . I saw plenty to cheer me here yesterday. Although we've still a lot of weaknesses, we're looking forward full of confidence to what's coming.

On April 15, a newcomer to the headquarters at La Roche Guyon reported for duty: Generalleutnant Hans Speidel, who was replacing Alfred Gause as Rommel's Chief of Staff. Gause and his wife had their home in Berlin destroyed in an Allied air raid in February, and the Rommels had taken them in as houseguests while they found a new home, an increasingly difficult task in the Reich in 1944. As sometimes happens with such guests, they wore out their welcome, irritating Lucie to the point where she not only evicted them, but demanded that Erwin dismiss Gause as his Chief of Staff. Rommel, who rarely stood up to Lucie on anything, chose not to make an issue of the situation and quietly asked for Guase to be reposted, going so far as to write to Colonel Rudolf Schmundt, Hitler's adjutant and still Rommel's good friend, to see to it that Gause was given command of a panzer division as soon as possible.

Rommel may have recognized Speidel when the new Chief of Staff reported to him; Speidel was a fellow Swabian, they had first met the in Argonne Forest in 1915, and later briefly served together in the Thirteenth Infantry Regiment of the Reichswehr. Seven years Rommel's junior, with a doctorate in history, Speidel was bookish and bespectacled—he closely resembled a somewhat distracted owl—well-mannered, erudite, and congenial. Rommel expected to get on well with him; what Rommel did not know was that Speidel brought baggage with him that was not in the valises that were delivered to his quarters: for the past two years he had been part of a growing circle of Wehrmacht officers and influential civilians who were staunch opponents of Adolf Hitler, and whose opposition was beginning to harden into a determination to remove the Führer from power—going so far as to contemplate Hitler's assassination. This, of course, was unknown to Rommel at the time; Rommel would eventually be told some of it, and learn more of it on his own. The one thing which Rommel never imagined was that he had doomed himself by approving Speidel's appointment, for Hans Speidel, five months hence, would implicate Rommel in the plot to kill Adolf Hitler in order to save himself from the hangman's piano-wire noose.

By the end of April, even some of Rommel's old arrogance was beginning to reassert itself.

27 April 1944

It looks as though the British and Americans are going to do us the favor of keeping away for a bit. This will be of immense value for our coastal defenses, for we are now growing stronger every day at least on the ground, though the same is not true for the air. But even that will change to our advantage again some time. My little dog [Rommel had acquired a dachshund from the owners of the chateau] is touchingly affectionate and loves sweet things. He sleeps in my room now, underneath my luggage stand. He's going to be inoculated soon against distemper. Went riding again yesterday, but I'm feeling my joints pretty badly today. . . . The affair with Geyr von Schweppenburg with whom I recently had to be very rough because he would not give way to my plans has all been cleared up now by orders from above and decided as I wanted it.[274]

The last sentence of this letter hints at a story that would profoundly affect and alter the ability of the German forces defending the Atlantic Wall to successfully repel the coming invasion. Geyr von Schweppenburg, was, of course, the officer commanding Panzer Group West, the "affair" was the culmination of a months-long debate over how to best employ the panzer divisions stationed in France to oppose the Allied landings, and Rommel's declaration that everything had been "cleared up" and settled to his satisfaction was misleading. The debate was, in fact, far from over, and the failure of Hitler, von Rundstedt, von Schweppenburg and Rommel to settle it would cripple the Wehrmacht when the Allies finally attacked.

One reason why Army Group B had been assigned the French and Belgian Channel coast as its command area was Hitler's recognition that of all his senior generals—at least those who were not currently behind barbwire in a POW camp somewhere—only Kesselring, now ensconced in Italy, and Rommel had any real experience fighting the British and Americans. Rommel knew this, and all the work he ordered done on the Atlantic Wall, all of the plans drawn up for Army Group B to counter, contain, and drive back into the sea any Allied landings, were based on the experiences of his last year in North Africa. Only a commander who had tried to fight battles under the umbrella of Allied air power could understand how the all-seeing eyes of the Allies' observation planes inhibited movement, or how the attrition wrought by Allied fighter-bombers decimated an army's combat strength. There was nothing comparable to that experience on the Russian front.

Geyr von Schweppenburg disagreed, vehemently. When he first met Geyr, Rommel instinctively bridled, for the man seemed to be the embodiment of everything he despised about the traditional German *offizierkorps*. Tall, lean, thoroughly aristocratic, Geyr came from a Prussian military family, and projected an aura of arrogant omniscience. Transferred to France in the early summer of 1943, he had spent two years fighting on the Russian Front, commanding the XXIV Panzer Corps, and believed that in doing so he had learned all that there was to know about armored warfare. To Geyr, not only did Rommel have nothing to teach him, all of Rommel's experience facing the British and Americans was essentially irrelevant—it was on the Russian Front that *real* tank battles were fought.

Geyr was certain that the only proper way to employ his panzer divisions was to hold them back from the coast by as much as 100 miles, then use them in broad, textbook-like mobile operations to annihilate the Allies when the invasion force attempted to break out of its beachhead. Rommel was appalled by the very idea, for Allied fighters were methodically sweeping the Luftwaffe from the skies above Europe; Allied photo-reconnaissance aircraft already flew more-or-less at will wherever they wished above France and Belgium: once the Allies were ashore, those same reconnaissance planes would be keeping a hawk-like eye on German mobile formations, and the concentration of forces needed for the sort of maneuvers Geyr proposed would never go undetected. He had very carefully articulated this in the formal report he made to Hitler on December 31, 1943, presenting his conclusions on the state of the Atlantic Wall:

> British and American superiority in the air alone has again and again been so effective that all movement of major formations has been rendered completely impossible, both at the front and behind it, by day and by night, and our own air force has only on very rare occasions been able to make any appearance in support of our operations.[275]

When the Allied observation planes spotted a target, the Allied bombers would soon follow, and in northern Europe, these would not be the light and medium bombers of the Desert Air Force. The Allies could, any day they chose, bring the heavies of RAF's Bomber Command and the U.S. Army Air Force's Eighth Air Force to bear on the battlefield; as Rommel saw it, strategic and operational mobility would no longer be an asset in the ledger for the Germans defending Festung Europa. When he tried to drive this point home to von Schweppenburg, the aristocratic *general der panzertruppe* replied condescendingly that Rommel had never led in combat any unit larger than a division (completely ignoring Rommel's two years in Africa), so that he had no true idea of what mobile armored warfare was like; Rommel countered by replying that for all his experience on the Russian Front, Geyr had no idea of what fighting against the British or the Americans was like.

Rommel's concept for employing the panzer divisions was to move them much closer to the beaches, to within a few miles of the water's edge. There, even though it would be impossible to form up large concentrations of armor, battalion- or even company- sized units could prove decisive in the first hours of the invasion. The enemy would be disorganized, their morale (hopefully) shaken, they would be short on ammunition and equipment—especially antitank weapons. The panzer units would retain their tactical mobility and be able to employ it at precisely the moment when it would be most effective—when the Allied forces would be mostly near-immobile infantry. The German tanks would be able to provide fire support for the German infantry holding the *widerstandsnester* even as the Allied armor would be too weak in numbers to be able to effectively do the same for the assaulting Allied infantry. Again, this was a point that he had made as forcibly as possible in his December 31 report:

> . . . It will therefore be necessary, in the worst-threatened sectors, to have heavy antitank guns, self-propelled guns and antiaircraft combat troops standing ready in the forward part of the defense zone, whence they can be rushed up to the coast to engage the enemy while he is still disembarking.
>
> I regard it as urgently necessary to have two reserve divisions held a short distance to the east of the coastal defenses, along the worst threatened stretch of coast between Boulogne and the mouth of the Somme, so that they can intervene in support of the coast-defense divisions, as soon as possible after the main center of the enemy attack has been identified, and thus prevent the creation of any enemy bridgehead. It will be less a question of a formation action than of the piecemeal destruction of the disembarking or disembarked enemy by small combat groups.[276]

Now at the end of April 1944, the issue had to be decided, as time was running out. The Germans still had no idea of exactly when the invasion would take place, but the likelihood that it would take place increased with every passing day as summer approached—further debate on the Wehrmacht's strategy when it actually took place was a luxury the German commanders could no longer afford.

Unfortunately, the man who was Rommel and Geyr's immediate superior, and who should have resolved the issue once and for all time, refused to do so. Field Marshal Gerd von Rundstedt, at 68 years of age, was Germany's senior soldier, born, like von Schweppenburg, into a Prussian family with a long military tradition. He joined the German Army as an officer cadet in 1892 and rose to the rank of *hauptmann* (captain) before the First World War broke out; he would serve as a staff officer for the entire conflict; in point of fact, unlike Geyr or Rommel, von Rundstedt had never experienced combat. After the Armistice, he remained with the Army, a protegé of von Seeckt, and continued to rise in the Reichswehr, ultimately being promoted to *generalleutnant* in 1932. He was able to easily shift his political loyalty to the new National Socialist regime after January 1933; when he retired in November 1938, he had reached the rank of *generaloberst*. Von Runstedt's relationship with Hitler in the years before his retirement were at times rocky, as von Rundstedt saw himself in every way as an officer who must remain aloof from politics. Recalled to active duty when Germany invaded Poland, von Rundstedt protested very vocally when he learned that special SS squads were executing Polish POWs and civilians in the rear areas of his command. He then commanded Army Group B in the campaign in France in 1940, and as a reward for the services rendered by the soldiers under him was one of 12 generals promoted to the rank of field marshal on July 19.

By the time the Wehrmacht invaded the Soviet Union in June 1941, whatever qualms of conscience von Rundstedt may have had in 1939 regarding the treatment of civilians and prisoners of war had vanished, a process helped along no doubt by the several large bribes given to him by Hitler, who rarely went wrong in counting on the venality of his fellow man. (One of Hitler's favorite methods of securing his senior officers' loyalty was the making of large tax-free gifts of cash, little more than thinly disguised bribes, as well as estates seized from their former owners by the advancing Wehrmacht. The list of German officers who willingly accepted these gifts—and often returned to Hitler seeking more—was a surprising number of names from old aristocratic German families. Numbered among the handful of generals and admirals who are known to have refused such offers was Erwin Rommel.) Von Rundstedt was instrumental in the implementation of the infamous Commissar Order and the equally notorious Commando Order. Additionally, no protests about the conduct of the SS Einsatzgruppen (special operations groups—the death squads) ever came out of von Rundstedt's headquarters.

By 1944, having already been sacked and recalled by Hitler, von Rundstedt, though respected, even revered, in some circles within the Wehrmacht, was clearly past his best in terms of ability. He had never really mastered the theory, the "philosophy," of mechanized warfare, and regarded his posting as Commander-in-Chief West to be more of a managerial position than as an active operational command. Comfortably ensconced in

Paris' luxurious Hotel George V, he found his collection of classical music recordings and the contents of his champagne cellar more interesting than the responsibilities of command. When Rommel and Geyr approached him for a resolution to their dispute, he was, to borrow a phrase used in another context by Winston Churchill, "resolved to be irresolute." Von Rundstedt temporized; the matter would have to be settled by Hitler. Eventually Hitler did just that, but with a typically muddled compromise that satisfied no one and neither strategic nor operational doctrine: half of Panzer Group West's armored divisions would be assigned to and deployed by the army groups defending the beaches, while the remainder would be retained in reserve under Geyr von Schweppenburg. This arrangement might have worked out in practice, but then Hitler threw a spanner into the works: the reserve divisions could not be deployed without his direct order, nor could one army group's armor be transferred to another without his permission. It was an unworkable system that would prove fatal for Germany's efforts to defend against the Allied invasion when it finally came.

The other great debate that was raging between the various commands in Western Europe was over the question of exactly where the Allies would land. Rommel was sure the enemy would invade in the Pas de Calais area, the defense of which was the responsibility for von Salmuth's Fifteenth Army, and there were very sound reasons for his conclusion. Paramount among them was that a landing at the Pas de Calais placed the Allied beachhead the shortest distance on the most direct route to the single most valuable and vulnerable strategic target in Germany—the Ruhr, the heart of German heavy industry and arms manufacture. F.U.S.A.G. was poised directly opposite the Pas de Calais, only 19 miles distant; it is a military dictum which any commander ignores at his peril that you must honor a threat, and the threat of an invasion in the Pas de Calais sector was too great for Rommel to discount, because all of the intelligence available gave credence to F.U.S.A.G.'s reality. Unfortunately for the Germans, the concentration of forces in Fifteenth Army came at the expense of other commands, notably its neighbor to the west, Seventh Army, commanded by Generalleutnant Friedrich Dollmann, who repeatedly tried to make Rommel more aware of the vulnerability of the Normandy coast and the relative thinness of the defenses there. Rommel paid heed from time to time, but never made Normandy a priority, focused as he was (and as the planners of *Bodyguard* and *Fortitude* intended him to be) on the Fifteenth Army area.

Ironically, it was Hitler who seemed to be more perceptive to the idea that Normandy would be attractive to the Allies. The distance from shore to shore was greater than at the Pas de Calais, but not decisively so, while the terrain behind the beaches, once past the hedgerow country that immediately backed up the shoreline, was ideal for the sort of full-blooded armored thrusts, backed by powerful air support, that had been the Wehrmacht's *métier* in the glory days of 1940. Isolating first the Cherbourg peninsula, with its premier port, one of France's finest, and then the whole of Brittany would be fairly straightforward once the Allies broke out of their bridgehead. There were no significant river lines west of the Seine to offer a retreating Wehrmacht the opportunity to make a stand, and the liberation of Paris, while strategically not vital, would have tremendous political and psychological consequences for attackers and defenders alike. Hitler would from time to time in April and May return to his theme of Normandy being the Allies' likely choice for the invasion, but because he too was influenced by *Bodyguard* and *Fortitude*, as well as other cover and deception operations, he never insisted that Rommel make Normandy the priority in his defense preparations.

Meanwhile Rommel continued to be confident that if and when the Allies came, wherever they chose to arrive, they would be dealt a major, possibly decisive setback. An Allied defeat on the beaches of France would mean a reprieve for the Germans, by perhaps as much as a year, a year in which Speer could complete his reorganization of Germany's industries; in which German scientists, engineers, and munitions manufacturers could complete the design and testing of new weapons, and finish the defenses of the Western Wall along the German border. The Soviet lunge into Central Europe that everyone was anticipating for the summer of 1944 could be turned into a long, bloody slog against a better-armed and equipped Teutonic foe. And while a defeated invasion might not ensure an ultimate German victory, or even an armistice and a negotiated peace, it would spell death and destruction for millions who were already caught in the grim threshing machines of the Gestapo's *Nacht und Nebel* and the macabre *Endlösung* of the SS. . . .

Consequently, there were many layers of meaning, some of which Rommel was probably unaware, in a sobering observation he made one blustery

February afternoon, standing on bluff overlooking the Pas de Calais. Standing with him was his aide, Captain Helmuth Lang, who was by now a firm friend. Silently looking out over the Channel for some minutes, Rommel abruptly turned to Lang and said, "The first 24 hours of the invasion will be decisive . . . the fate of Germany depends on the outcome. For the Allies, as well as Germany, it will be the longest day."[277]

IN HIS LETTER to Lucie on May 21, Rommel made the most curious comment: "In the afternoon I had a talk with a captured British officer who was quite reasonable." It was a passing reference to one of the most remarkable incidents of Rommel's entire life, the day that Rommel met Lieutenant George Lane.[278]

Lane himself was rather unremarkable, but the circumstances in which a British lieutenant made the acquaintance of a German field marshal are fascinating, as does what the incident reveals about Rommel. Lane was part of a two-man commando mission sent to the French coast to gain information about a possible new German underwater mine, and was captured when he and his companion were surprised by a German patrol while still on the beach. Imprisoned in the cellars at Cayeux for several days, Lane and his fellow captive, Lieutenant Roy Wooldridge, were blindfolded and driven deeper into France, where Lane was eventually introduced to Rommel at Army Group B's new headquarters at the Chateau La Roche Guyon, 30 miles northwest of Paris. The two men hit it off almost immediately, and Rommel invited Lane to sit down at a table laid out for tea.

Using an interpreter, Rommel questioned Lane, who was as evasive as possible in his answers. At one point Rommel commented that Lane was in serious trouble, as there had been problems with gangster commandos in the past, and standing Wehrmacht orders required that captured commandos be shot on sight.

"You must realize that you are in a very tricky situation. Everyone seems to think that you are a saboteur."

"Well, Sir, if you believed that I was a saboteur you would not have done me the honor of inviting me here."

"So you think that this is an invitation?" Rommel asked.

"I do, sir, and I must say I am highly honoured." Rommel smiled at the flattery, and a long conversation followed. At one point he asked Lane, "How's Montgomery doing?"

Lane replied, "Unfortunately I don't know him, but he's preparing the invasion and he'll be here shortly, by the shortest route."

"Oh, so there's actually going to be an invasion?" Rommel said with an obviously feigned innocence.

"So the *Times* tells us, and it's usually pretty reliable about such things."

There was one tense moment for Lane, which came when one of the other officers present asked him why, if he was English, he spoke with a foreign accent. By birth Lane was Hungarian Jew (his real name was Gyuri Lányi) but thinking quickly he replied that his accent was Welsh. None of the Germans present, including Rommel, could tell otherwise, so Lane's fib became part of his permanent record with the Wehrmacht, and probably saved his life in the process. After spending the better part of an hour with Rommel Lane was again blindfolded, and sent to Paris; from there he was incarcerated in an officers' prisoner-of-war compound, rather than having been sent to a concentration camp, which would have been his fate had his Jewish ancestry been discovered. Until his own death in 2010 at the age of 95, Lane remained convinced Rommel's intervention saved his life.[279]

During his time with Army Group B, Rommel carefully studied the Allied landings in North Africa, at Sicily, and in Italy, in the hope of finding an operational pattern which would give a clue as to the solution of one of the two great questions facing him and his command: when the invasion would take place. The more he studied, the more he learned, the more he pieced together, until at last he realized that he had found it. The Allied invasion plans were always coordinated with weather, the phase of the moon, and the tide: when all three fell within a specific range of time or condition, the Allies saw a window of opportunity for their landings. The weather must be good, wind conditions mild to moderate, so as to not scatter the paratroops of any airborne component of the operation too widely. The moon must be full so as to offer maximum visibility to the aircraft carrying the airborne troops to their drop zones, then later to aid those same troops in making their way to their assembly areas. Finally, the tide must be incoming, and at flood when the first wave actually lands on the beach. As May 1944 worked its way toward June, Rommel could look at the calendar with confidence, noting that no such confluence of moon and tide was expected until sometime in August—and even then the weather conditions might prove uncooperative.

The weather would be the key to any invasion attempt: if the English Channel—notoriously fickle at the best of times—was too rough, the Allied landing craft would be swamped and sunk on their run in to the beaches. The waves could be no higher than 6 feet, therefore relatively calm weather was an absolute requisite. In the first days of June, German meteorologists, anticipating a succession of low-pressure waves moving in from the west, predicted that the current rough weather in the Channel would continue well into the middle of the month, well past the full moon that would occur on June 6. Allied weather teams, however, working with better information than that possessed by their German counterparts, saw a coming break in the weather, one that would last no more than 48 hours, beginning around midnight on June 5: if they chose to take it, the Allies would have a window of opportunity that the Germans never suspected was coming. Ironically, both the German and Allied meteorologists were assuring their respective commanders that weather conditions favored their planned undertakings.

This was much to Rommel's liking, as he was hoping to get away from La Roche Guyon and spend a few days back in Herrlingen with Lucie and Manfred at the beginning of June. She would be celebrating her fiftieth birthday on June 6, and Rommel had made a special trip into Paris to purchase a pair of shoes for her as a birthday present. This had been no small sacrifice on Rommel's part, as he despised Paris. To someone with his rather puritanical bent, it was a modern Babylon, where the German soldiers were becoming too accustomed to the soft life of an idle garrison and too fond of the city's bistros, cabarets, and brothels. The thriving black market there, which was officially winked at, even by the Gestapo, was an embarrassment, in his opinion.

But Lucie was Lucie, the love of his life, so the excursion into Babylon was made, and now, early on the morning of June 4, on what promised to be a dull, blustery day, Rommel, his aide, Captain Lang, his operations officer, Colonel Hans-Georg von Templehof, and his driver Daniel were ready to set out for the eight-hour drive to Germany.

IT WAS RIGHT on 7:20 A.M.—6:20 A.M. in France—on Tuesday, June 6, when the telephone rang in the foyer of Rommel's house in Herrlingen. Rommel, always an early riser, was fussing with arranging Lucie's birthday presents on the drawing room table—the handmade Parisian shoes were, of course, the centerpiece of the display. The rest of the house was already filled with flowers, brought in the previous night after Lucie had retired. When he answered the telephone, Rommel was startled to hear the voice of his Chief of Staff, General Speidel, who informed the field marshal that there had been several widely scattered reports of enemy paratroopers landing around Normandy, particularly in the Cotentin peninsula. When Rommel pressed him for details, Speidel could not say for certain if this was some sort of large-scale commando operation or the prelude to the invasion itself.

"Well, find out—now!" Rommel barked, then hung up. After changing into his uniform—he had answered the telephone in his dressing gown—he waited impatiently for almost three hours before the phone rang again. At 10:15 A.M., the call from Speidel came through: deliberately, but with an unmistakable note of tension in his voice, Speidel officially confirmed that, in addition to the British and American paratroopers dropped across the base of the Cotentin peninsula during the night, a major Allied landing was underway on the Channel coast: there were five landing sites, all of which were for the time being reasonably well established. At first Rommel seemed unable to grasp what it was that Speidel was telling him, then the reality of what the Chief of Staff had said set in. The Cotentin meant that the Allies had *not* invaded the Pas de Calais: they were landing in Normandy. Stunned, Rommel informed Speidel that he would set out for La Roche Guyon immediately, then placed the handset back in the cradle. Lucie, roused this time by the telephone's ringing, came and stood silently by her husband's side as, shaking his head, Rommel simply muttered over and over again, "Normandy! Normandy. How stupid of me! How stupid of me. . . ."[280]

CHAPTER FOURTEEN

INVASION AND CONSPIRACY

Speak Truth to Power
—QUAKER PAMPHLET

T he Allies called the grand plan Operation *Overlord*, the actual landings and establishment of the beachheads, Operation *Neptune*. The day itself, June 6, 1944, has come to be commemorated as "D-Day." An immense invasion fleet—6,939 ships in all: 1,213 warships, including six battleships, 23 cruisers and 104 destroyers, 4,126 landing craft of various types, 736 support vessels, and 864 merchantmen—departed ports all along the southern coast of England on June 5, bound for an assembly point in the middle of the English Channel, from whence they sailed south, for France. Incredibly, the movement of this armada went completely undetected: it was not until the fog began lifting on the Normandy coastline, when observers in the bunkers and dugouts along the beaches west of Caen were suddenly confronted with the spectacle of a monstrous fleet that stretched from horizon to horizon that the Germans became aware of its existence.

Equally incredible was that at the exact moment the Allied naval forces off Normandy began their bombardment of the beaches, the entire German command structure was in disarray. Whether by an act of serendipity or the hand of fate, Rommel was, of course, on leave in Germany; his Chief of Staff, Speidel, was completely out of his depth to respond to this emergency: the Knight's Cross at his throat notwithstanding, he was a career staff officer, not a combat commander, and beyond notifying Rommel of the situation, was completely befuddled. Generaloberst Friederich Doll- mann, the commander of Seventh Army, which was responsible for the defense of the Normandy and Brittany coast, was unreachable: he was on his way, along with almost all of his corps and division commanders, to Rennes,

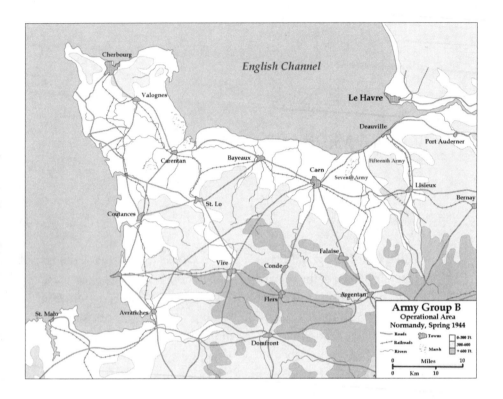

where a series of map exercises—including one of the defense of the Normandy beaches—were scheduled for June 6. In contrast, General Erich Marcks, the commanding officer of the LXXXIV Corps, who had not yet departed his headquarters for Rennes, immediately ordered his troops to go on full alert: he had always believed the invasion would take place in Normandy rather than the Pas de Calais, and now the Allies were landing right in the middle of his command area. In Paris, von Rundstedt, who had been informed of the airborne drops as early as 1:30 A.M., dithered for three hours before sending instruction to Panzergruppe West to "reconnoiter in force into 711th Division sector," well to the east of where any Allied paratroopers had landed.

The situation only grew worse higher up in the German chain of command. At 4:45 A.M., when von Rundstedt finally called the O.K.W. to secure permission to move Panzer Lehr and the 12th SS Panzer Division toward Normandy, Jodl, the O.K.W. Chief of Operations, told the aging marshal that the decision was Hitler's to make, and the Führer had gone to bed less than two hours prior to von Rundstedt's call: Jodl refused to wake him unless von Rundstedt explicitly ordered him to do so. Von Rundstedt in turn was furious: he wanted a decision made by a proper soldier, not that "Bohemian corporal" whom he openly despised, and angrily ended the call. It would be almost noon before Hitler was given the news that the invasion had begun; meanwhile the tanks of Panzergruppe West remained in place, 100 miles and more back from the coast.

It was during these critical hours that Rommel's presence at his headquarters in France was most sorely missed; not for any miraculous maneuver he may have ordered that would have swept the Allies back into the sea, but for his galvanizing—and often polarizing—persona. It is impossible to say what Rommel would have done had he been present, it is undeniable that the acquiescence to inaction displayed by OB West and the O.K.W. would have never been acceptable to him. In North Africa he had become quite the accomplished barrack-room lawyer as he honed his skills at evading inconvenient orders when he was convinced that a particular course of action—which went against those orders—was correct and necessary. He had also developed a particular talent for acting first then seeking permission—or forgiveness, if necessary—later. On the morning of June 6, 1944, his arrogance, rough tongue, and dominating personality could have been expected to mobilize officers who were hesitant or uncertain of what they should be doing—and run roughshod over anyone who barred his way who was not prepared to meet him with equal determination. It is the nature of human beings in a crisis to seek out leadership, to want direction, no matter from whence it comes: Rommel would have provided precisely that missing leadership—never in the whole of his military career is there any record of Rommel passively awaiting orders in a situation which required action. Von Rundstedt declined to request that Jodl awaken the Führer; it is impossible to imagine Rommel not demanding that he do so.

Rommel was out of the house at Herrlingen, with only the tersest of explanations to Lucie and Manfred, within 15 minutes of taking Speidel's 10:30 A.M. call: he and his aide, Lang, were on their way back to La Roche Guyon; there was no time to detour and collect Tempelhof.[281] They stopped at Nancy long enough for Rommel to get a call through to Speidel to confirm that the 21st Panzer Division, the only armored unit close to the Allied beachheads, had begun its counterattack, as per its standing orders. Speidel assured the field marshal that the division had begun moving less than an hour after the Allied landings began.

Speidel was correct—after a fashion. The 21st Panzer, raised again after the original division had surrendered in Tunisia in May 1943, was something of an oddity: essentially cobbled together out of odds and sods, at least half of its tanks and artillery were of obsolete, prewar French design and manufacture, which presented a few tactical problems and was something of a logistical headache. The division commander, Generalmajor Edgar Feuchtinger, was in Paris when the invasion began, but as he had given his regimental and battalion commanders operational guidelines to follow in such an eventuality, this was not the handicap it might have been. By the time Rommel arrived back at La Roche Guyon, 21st Panzer, which had been posted near Caen, one of the Allies' primary objectives on D-Day, had made its attack: dispersed and outnumbered, it had been able to nonetheless push a column of Panzer IV tanks down to the Channel itself, driving a wedge between the Sword and Juno beachheads. But it was not enough: scores of British and Canadian tanks and antitank guns soon took out the panzers, and the remainder of the division's battle groups withdrew.

Materially, the 21st Panzer's attack accomplished little, although it did have unexpected strategic consequences. Suddenly apprehensive about the presence of hitherto-undetected German armored units, General Montgomery, who had overall command of the D-Day landings and subsequent operations in the beachheads, abruptly abandoned his plan to take Caen on D-Day itself; instead he chose to carry out an overly elaborate envelopment of the city that would require two months to complete. The Allies still had their beachheads, but the division had at least bought the Germans time.

It was the Allies' good fortune that the 21st Panzer's attack struck where it did, for if it had gone in just a few miles to the west, their entire plan for the invasion would have come unraveled. The British and American operational concepts for the actual landings differed widely: the Americans favored a brute force approach, expecting to overwhelm the enemy defenses with firepower and numbers. Anticipating that the sheer weight and ferocity of the pre-landing naval and aerial bombardment would leave the German defenders stunned and incapable of effective resistance, the United States Army did not make armored support a priority for the first wave of troops landing on Utah and Omaha Beaches. On Omaha, the two infantry divisions given the task of taking and holding the beach were assigned a total of two battalions of armor—a total of 60 tanks. The British, on the other hand, driven by their own dwindling reserves of manpower, chose finesse over fury: specialized tanks, designed expressly to counter, destroy, or otherwise overcome German defenses and obstacles, were included in the first wave of the landing force from the beginning of the planning phase, along with conventional armor. The whole of the 27th Armoured Brigade was committed to the landing force, with a strength three times that of the American armor committed to Omaha Beach.

The fight for Omaha Beach was the critical battle of D-Day: had the Americans not gained a foothold there, the entire *Overlord* plan would have become unworkable. Essential to the Allies' plan to liberate Western Europe was that the Normandy invasion not merely gain a bridgehead on the Continent, but that it be large enough to allow the buildup of forces in sufficient strength to launch the liberating attacks across France and the Low countries. (This was the actual Operation *Overlord*—the first 90 days of operations against the Germans on the Continent; the name is usually applied—erroneously—to just the D-Day landings.) The Allies had already determined the size and composition of the armies that would be required to break out of the bridgehead: too small a bridgehead would literally mean there would be no place to put all of those units. The initial plan for D-Day called for three beachheads, all to the immediate west of Caen—they would become Sword, Juno, and Gold Beaches in the final plan—but General Montgomery immediately recognized that three beaches were far too small to contain the sort of buildup the Allies anticipated, and demanded that the landing area be enlarged. (While Montgomery was uncomfortable with fluid operations and battles of maneuver, he was the unquestioned master of the set piece.) Thus Omaha and Utah Beaches were added to the invasion plan: once consolidated the resulting bridgehead would meet the Allies' operational requirements for the buildup. Omaha was the lynchpin: if the landing there was unsuccessful, Utah Beach would be isolated, too distant from the British and Canadian beaches to be effectively supported, meaning that the landing force at Utah would have to be withdrawn. The Allies would then be left with the original, inadequate beachhead proposed in the initial *Overlord* planning, leaving them with no viable option but to withdraw from the coast of France entirely—sustaining the existing beachhead while simultaneously trying to plan, organize, and carry out a second landing which would expand the initial foothold would have exceeded the limits of the Allies' resources.

Even as it was, the Germans came closer than they knew to defeating the invasion. The destruction they wrought on the Allies was frightening. Ernie Pyle, arguably the most gifted war correspondent ever to write about human conflict, unforgettably described the carnage he saw on June 7, as he walked along the Normandy beaches:

> The wreckage was vast and startling. The awful waste and destruction of war, even aside from the loss of human life, has always been one of the outstanding features to those who are in it. Anything and everything is expendable. And we did expend on our beachhead in Normandy in those first few hours.
>
> For a mile out from the beach there were scores of tanks and trucks and boats that were not visible, for they were at the bottom of the water—swamped by overloading or hit by shells or sunk by mines.
>
> There were trucks tipped half over and swamped, partly sunken barges, and the angled up corners of jeeps, and small landing craft half-submerged. And at low tide you could still see those vicious six-pronged iron snares that helped snag and wreck them.
>
> On the beach itself, high and dry, were all kinds of wrecked vehicles. There were tanks that had only just made the beach before being knocked out. There were jeeps that had burned to a dull gray. There were big derricks on caterpillar treads that didn't quite make it. There were half-tracks carrying office equipment that had been made into a shambles by a single shell hit, their interiors still holding the useless equipage of smashed typewriters, telephones, office files.
>
> There were LCTs (Landing Craft, Tank) turned completely upside down, and lying on their backs, and how they got that way I don't know. There were boats stacked atop each other, their sides caved in, their suspension doors knocked off.
>
> In this shoreline museum of carnage there were abandoned rolls of barbed wire and smashed bulldozers and big stacks of

thrown-away lifebelts and piles of shells still waiting to be moved.

In the water floated empty life rafts and soldiers' packs and ration boxes and mysterious oranges.

On the beach lay snarled rolls of telephone wire and big rolls of steel matting and stacks of broken, rusting rifles.

On the beach lay, expended, sufficient men and mechanism for a small war. . . .[282]

ROMMEL REACHED LA Roche Guyon at 9:00 P.M., by which time the 21st Panzer's attack was over and its lack of success in driving the Allies back into the sea was confirmed. While he obviously could not have known the details of Allied planning for *Overlord*, and thus the true extent of the opportunity missed, he and his staff understood that the actions of 21st Panzer were proof of what could have been accomplished had Rommel been permitted to position the panzer divisions closer to beaches before the Allies landed, and then given command authority to commit them as needed once the invasion began. The presence of one more panzer division in Normandy in the first 48 hours of the invasion would have been decisive, and the knowledge must have been galling, especially when events simply added the exclamation point to his assertion in the report he had submitted in April to Jodl and the O.K.W.:

> If I am to wait until the enemy landing has actually taken place, before I can demand, through normal channels, the command and dispatch of the mobile forces, delays will be inevitable. This will mean that they will probably arrive too late to intervene successfully in the battle for the coast and prevent the enemy landing.[283]

Rommel would be compelled to fight the Battle of Normandy half-blind, with one hand tied behind his back. While the Allies had an almost embarrassingly detailed knowledge of German troop strength and unit dispositions, Rommel knew next to nothing about the forces confronting him. Allied photo-reconnaissance aircraft flew over the Normandy battlefields with near impunity; so complete was Allied air supremacy over Britain that such German reconnaissance flights as were allowed to successfully penetrate British airspace were carefully shepherded by intercepting fighters so that they would see only what the Allies wanted them to see. The *Fortitude* deceptions continued, which both misled Rommel as to actual Allied strength, but also compelled him to keep the Fifteenth Army in the Pas de Calais to honor what everyone in the German high command continued to believe was a genuine threat of a second invasion. This was arguably *Fortitude*'s greatest contribution to the success of *Overlord*, as it prevented Rommel from reinforcing the Seventh Army while the Allies were building up their forces to break out of the Normandy bridgehead. Rommel was forced to fight the Battle of Normandy with only the troops he had to hand, plus a trickle of reinforcements.

Initially, Geyr von Schweppenburg and von Rundstedt had high hopes for what might be accomplished by the 12th SS Panzer and Panzer Lehr Divisions. Both were large, well-equipped units—SS divisions tended to maintain something much closer to their specified manpower and equipment levels than did normal army units, while Panzer Lehr was organized to teach advanced armor tactics to newly promoted company and battalion commanders, hence its personnel were all combat veterans. Had they arrived at the front intact and on time, they would have wreaked havoc among the invading Allied armies, especially the Americans, for in the first 48 hours of the invasion the landing forces were still somewhat disorganized and under-strength.

Alas for the Germans, it was not to be: both were forced to engage the British and Canadians piecemeal, arriving at Caen late, disordered, and having suffered significant losses, the consequence of constant harrassment by Allied "*jabos*"—*jagdbomber*, fighter-bombers. Von Schweppenburg and von Rundstedt were appalled to discover that Rommel's dire predictions about the effectiveness of Allied air power were all too accurate, as the British and American tactical air forces crippled the ability of the two panzer divisions to advance in daylight. Von Schweppenburg had ordered Panzer Lehr to begin moving into Normandy on June 7, and told the division commander, Fritz Bayerlein, Rommel's one-time Chief of Staff in North Africa, to move the division up in daylight. Bayerlein protested, Geyr insisted, and the movement from Chartres to Normandy, which normally would have been accomplished in a matter of hours, required two days. Bayerlein would remember the roads as "a fighter-bomber race course," and in the near-constant bombing and strafing Panzer Lehr lost five tanks along with a score of half-tracks and armored cars; just as bad was the loss of 150 trucks and fuel tankers. When it tried to move into Caen the 12th SS Panzer fared no better.

Even more problematic for the German defenders was the havoc played on their supply lines by the Allied bombers and fighter-bombers: squadrons of American P-47 Thunderbolts and British Hawker Typhoons ranged over Normandy's roads, seeking out German truck convoys—the destruction they brought to such convoys was crippling on multiple levels: not only were vital supplies being lost, but priceless trucks were destroyed (the Wehrmacht was losing motor vehicles faster than German factories could replace them), and the pool of drivers and logistics personnel was dwindling. Trucks could only move at night; the Luftwaffe was helpless to stop the depredations of the *jabos*, as stocks of aviation fuel were being hoarded for fighters defending the Reich from the Allied bomber armadas: the British and American air forces were flying as many as 10,000 sorties a day, while the Luftwaffe could muster less than a tenth of that number. Compounding the problem was the methodical campaign being carried out by the medium bombers of the US Ninth Air Force against bridges and viaducts in both Normandy and the Pas de Calais (the latter to maintain the fiction of the threat of a second invasion). There were almost no intact rail or road bridges within 100 miles of the French coast, which forced the Germans into tortuous and expensive detours in order to bring up whatever supplies they could by truck or train. After a few weeks, Rommel would be forced to resort to floating barges laden with fuel and ammunition down the rivers flowing into Normandy in order to get even a trickle of supplies to his troops.

Rommel had been right: Geyr and von Rundstedt had never imagined such overwhelming airpower: not even in its finest hour, in France in 1940, had the Luftwaffe been able to so thoroughly dominate a battlefield. Apart from Bayerlein, none of Rommel's subordinates or superiors had yet faced the Americans and the British: only now, too late, were they beginning to comprehend how thoroughly the Allied air forces could interdict the movements of German troops, tanks, and supplies; only now did they understand the truth of Rommel's assertion that Allied air power would deny the mobility on which men like Geyr and von Rundstedt had predicated all of their plans for the German panzer divisions. They had refused to listen when Rommel had warned them:

> Our friends from the East cannot imagine what they are in for here. It's not a matter of fanatical hordes to be driven forward in masses against our line, with no regard for casualties and little recourse to tactical craft; here we are facing an enemy who applies all his native intelligence to the use of his many technical resources, who spares no expenditure of materiel and whose every operation goes its course as though it had been the subject of repeated rehearsal. Dash and doggedness alone no longer make a soldier; he must have sufficient intelligence to enable him to get the most out of his fighting machine. And that's something these people can do, we found that out in Africa.[284]

Geyr would have the lesson driven home very personally and painfully: on June 10, while he was organizing a counterattack on Caen, Geyr's newly established headquarters at La Caine was bombed and strafed by Royal Air Force Typhoons, its location revealed through radio intercepts and Ultra decrypts. Von Schweppenburg's disregard for Allied air power led him to set up his headquarters in an open field: Geyr was wounded while most of his staff was killed in the attack.

Denied the chance to stop the Allied invasion at the water's edge, Rommel now faced the challenge of containing the enemy beachheads, and confining the Allies for as long as possible in Normandy's *bocage* country, ideal terrain for an army weak in armor and limited in mobility defending against a highly mobile enemy whose numbers were steadily growing, and who possessed near-absolute command of the air. The *bocage*—the word means "little forest," a perfect description of the innumerable hedgerows which criss-crossed the most of Normandy and the Cotentin peninsula—would allow him to exploit to the fullest the Germans' superior tactical skills, forcing the Allies to fight for every yard of ground gained.

By June 10 Rommel had correctly divined the Allies' intentions, essential to developing a strategy for containing the beachheads and, should Montgomery or one of his subordinates blunder and present such an opportunity, pushing the Allies back into the Channel. He summed up his conclusions about Allied objectives in a strategic appreciation he submitted to OB West and the O.K.W.:

> The course of the battle in Normandy to date gives a clear indication of the enemy's intentions:
> (a) to gain a deep bridgehead between the Orne and Vire, as a springboard for a powerful attack later into the interior of France, probably towards Paris;
> (b) to cut off the Cotentin peninsula and gain possession of Cherbourg as soon as possible, in order to provide himself with a major port of large landing capacity. (There seems also to be a possibility, as things are developing, that the enemy will dispense with the Cotentin peninsula if the battle is too fierce, and make an early thrust with all his available means, into the interior of France.)[285]

Rommel saw that the tenacity of the German defenders was disrupting the Allies' carefully worked-out timetables for their campaign in Normandy, which offered opportunities to strike back at the Allies with local counterattacks. But lest they start "painting pictures" in Berchtesgaden and Berlin, he pointedly reminded the Führer and the O.K.W. that whatever success the Wehrmacht was able to eke out against the Allies, they would be limited at best as the Allies brought their increasingly superior numbers to bear.

> As a result of the stubborn defense of the coast defense troops and the immediate counterattacks launched by the available major reserves, the enemy attack, despite the strength of his effort, has gone considerably more slowly than he had hoped. The enemy also seems to be committing more forces than he had originally planned. Under cover of his very strong air force, the enemy is visibly reinforcing himself on land, and neither our air force nor our navy is in a position, especially by day, to offer him any hindrance. Consequently, the enemy forces in the bridgehead are growing at a considerably faster rate than reserves are flowing to our front.[286]

Rommel's first priority at this moment was to establish an unbroken front around the Allied beachhead in order to contain it. New units were being thrown into the line piecemeal as they arrived in Normandy, regardless of type or quality, to plug gaps and reduce unit frontages—they could be sorted out later. Admittedly most of the panzers were being sent to the eastern end of the German perimeter, as Montgomery was building up his armored strength for his pending envelopment of Caen, but that did not significantly affect the troops defending the hedgerows: in the *bocage*, tanks were as much a liability as an asset, a lesson the Americans were being taught rather pointedly.

Once again Rommel was in his element, the quintessential combat commander, leading from the front. This time, however, there was none of the exhilaration that had been so evident in the 7th Panzer Division's mad rush across France in 1940, the heady days of the first advance from El Agheila, or the triumph of the Battle of Gazala and its aftermath. This was not a desperate battle, it was a battle of desperation. As at El Alamein, he was engaged in a *materialschlact*, a battle of attrition, one he knew Germany could never win. From the first day of the invasion, when he learned that the Allies had been able to successfully establish their beachheads, Rommel had no real confidence that the patchwork of German infantry, artillery, and armor holding the front in Normandy would prevent the Allies from eventually breaking out of their bridgehead—it was not a question of if but rather when it would happen. For the Allies to be stopped, or even compelled to withdraw from Normandy entirely, would require a miracle.

Rommel was doing his best, trying to extricate armor from the lines to form a mobile reserve that he could keep posted a few miles behind the front for either making local attacks when possible, or for a counterattack should the Allies unexpectedly break through the hedgerows into the open country beyond. Enemy air power was making this difficult, however, as was a factor which Rommel had never considered, having never before encountered it—naval gunfire. The British and American battleships, cruisers, and destroyers posted off the Normandy beaches carried awesome amounts of firepower that were on-call for the Allied soldiers struggling through the hedgerows—the big 15-inch guns of the battleships could range as far as 16 miles inshore, while even the 5-inch guns on the destroyers could strike targets 5 miles inland. The American artillery, shore- and sea-based, was especially dangerous: the most sophisticated fire-control network in the world allowed a single forward observer to request a fire mission that could, if the situation required, bring down the fire of hundreds of artillery pieces, from company mortars all the way through battalion and regimental guns and howitzers, to divisional and corps heavy artillery—and even the offshore guns of the warships—onto a single target within minutes. The Germans' improvised hedgerow defenses were formidable, and often could withstand fire from most Allied field guns, but Rommel's men lacked the time and materials to build dugouts strong enough to withstand heavy naval guns. Thus when the Tommies or GIs had to crack a particularly tough nut, they would whistle up a heavy cruiser or battleship and settle the matter with 8-inch, 14-inch, or 15-inch shells.

Part of the Allies' willingness to use sledgehammers to crack walnuts was due to the overwhelming material superiority possessed by the British and American armies. One of the most frequently overlooked—or worse, glossed over—aspects of the entire *Overlord* plan was the thoroughness with which the Allied command staff had developed the supply and support systems for the beachheads: it did the Allies no good to have troops ashore who could not be properly supported. Thus in the logistics trains for each of the five beaches were more ammunition, rations, uniforms, vehicles, and equipment than the men ashore could possibly expend, stockpiled and ready according to the wisdom of having and not needing rather than needing and not having. This was a consequence of the grand strategy which the British and Americans had formulated in the opening months of the war, the like of which Germany—or rather Hitler, as all of the Third Reich's military policies originated with him—had never possessed. From January 1942 until June 6, 1944, the ultimate objective of Allied strategy, planning, production, training, and operations had been those 90 days allocated to Operation *Overlord*, the 90 days that began on D-Day. The consequences of what Germany might have accomplished had Hitler and the O.K.W. possessed a similar measure of foresight is too terrible to contemplate; the consequences Germany would suffer because the Führer and his flunkies lacked such foresight left Rommel despairing, for there was nothing he could do to avoid ultimate defeat. Three letters written to Lucie in mid-June leave no doubt that Rommel cherished no illusions about how the battle in Normandy would end.

13 June 1944

Dearest Lu,

The telephone line yesterday was really terrible, but it was better than nothing. The battle is not going at all well for us, mainly because of the enemy's air superiority and heavy naval guns. . . . I reported to the Führer yesterday. Rundstedt is doing the same. It's time for politics to come into play. We are expecting the next, perhaps even heavier blow to fall elsewhere in a few days. The long-husbanded strength of two world powers is now coming into action. It will all be decided quickly. We are doing what we can. I often think of you at home, with heartfelt wishes and the hope that everything can still be guided to a tolerable end.

14 June 1944

Very heavy fighting. The enemy's great superiority in aircraft, naval artillery, men and materiel is beginning to tell. Whether the gravity of the situation is realized up above, and the proper conclusions drawn, seems to me doubtful. Supplies are getting tight everywhere.

How are you both? Still no news has arrived.

15 June 1944

Was up forward again yesterday, the situation does not improve. We must be prepared for grave events. The troops, SS and Army alike, are fighting with the utmost courage, but the balance of strength tips more heavily against us every day. Our air force is playing a very modest part over the battle area. I'm well so far. I have to keep my head up in spite of it all, even though many hopes are having to be buried. You can no doubt imagine what difficult decisions we will soon be faced with, and will remember our conversation in November 1942.[287]

These three letters are startling, not merely for their candor in regard to the battle's ultimate outcome, but also because they mark the moment when Rommel articulated the *necessity* of some sort of political settlement to end the war rather than continuing to believe in a military solution which would somehow favor Germany. They mark the penultimate step in a journey of conscience that had begun more than 18 months earlier at

El Alamein. The first step had been compelled by Hitler's breach of faith with his soldiers manifested in the "Victory or death" order; it had progressed during one of the succession of conferences held in Rome with Mussolini and Cavallero—having a chance to spend a couple of days with Lucie during one such, Rommel had confided in her that he had lost his belief in Germany's ability to win the war through military victory. His journey was accelerated during the withdrawal to Tunisia, when he was encouraged, exhorted, and commanded to hold one indefensible position after another, always for no sound military reason but because of the increasingly delusional state of the man in Berchtesgaden. Precisely where was Rommel's point of no return is impossible to say: it may have come as early as the moment in December 1942 when Hitler refused to countenance a methodical withdrawal of Rommel's veteran German and Italian troops—a priceless military asset—from Tunisia. It may not have come until March 1943, when Hitler proposed the patently absurd idea of German operations on Africa's Atlantic coast. It may well not have come until as late as June 7, 1944, when there was no doubting that the Allies were successfully ashore in France and the Germans' best opportunity to throwing them back into the sea had been irretrievably lost.

But whenever that point occurred, what was undeniable was that by mid-June, barely more than a week after the Americans and British came ashore at Normandy, Rommel was convinced that continuing the war could only end in disaster for Germany, and that he had finally lost any remnant of faith in Adolf Hitler as Germany's leader. In May 1943 the Führer, during a rare moment of candor and self-honesty, had confided to Rommel: "I know it is necessary to make peace with one side or the other, but no one will make peace with me." Yet Hitler did not—could not—articulate the inevitable conclusion to which his confession led: if peace was necessary, and he was the obstacle to peace, then he must step down or step aside as Germany's head of state. But if the Allies had been intractable then, now, more than a year later they were implacable. Writing "Whether the gravity of the situation is realized up above, and the proper conclusions drawn, seems to me doubtful" was Rommel's admission of his own realization that Hitler no longer even recognized the need to make peace, let alone a willingness to bring it about no matter how painful the personal price. The final step on Rommel's journey of conscience would be the decision that peace was too important to be left up to someone like Adolf Hitler.[288]

The "miracle" for which Rommel was so desperately buying time came in the form of the *vergeltungswaffen*—vengeance weapons—the V-1, V-2, and V-3. The V-1 was a pulsejet-powered flying bomb that carried a ton of explosives, the V-2 a liquid-fueled ballistic missile, and the V-3 an extraordinarily long-range cannon. All three V-weapons were designed and deployed to be used against Britain, although only the V-1 was operational when Rommel was fighting the battle of Normandy. Launch sites were built in the Pas de Calais region beginning in October 1943, and on June 13, 1944, the first V-1 was fired at London. Nearly 10,000 of these flying bombs— "buzz bombs," Londoners would come to call them, after the distinctive sound made by their motors—would be sent hurtling toward the British capital, killing or wounding almost 23,000 civilians and military personnel while causing almost as much property damage as the "Blitz" of 1940–41, before the last launching site was overrun by the Allies in October 1944. Yet again, though, the V-1 program was one more case of "too little, too late" for Germany: had the flying bomb offensive been unleashed a year earlier—which could have happened had its development not been needlessly delayed—and directed at Britain's Channel ports where the invasion fleets were assembling, the whole *Overlord* plan would have been disrupted and delayed, possibly to such a degree that there might have been no cross-Channel invasion in 1944 at all.

As it was, the V-1 launch sites hamstrung Rommel's effort to contain the Allied bridgehead. He was able to use two divisions of the Fifteenth Army to bolster the extreme right flank around Caen, but could not bring its full weight to bear in Normandy: thanks to Operation *Fortitude*, German intelligence services still regarded a second invasion, this one in the Pas de Calais, where most of the V-1 sites were located, as a viable threat. Fifteenth Army was thus compelled to remain in place at the moment when its strength was needed most in Normandy. *Fortitude*'s fictions would soon become sufficiently threadbare to be seen for what they were, but for five critical weeks they kept an entire German army frozen in place.

On June 17, 1944, near Soissons, Rommel and von Rundstedt met with Hitler, personally briefing the Führer on the situation in Normandy. Rommel gave a vivid, but accurate, description of the conditions under which the German soldiers were fighting—outnumbered, outgunned, with dwindling supplies of ammunition, limited artillery and armored support and no air cover, yet their morale remained high as they were still holding the Allies in check, though for how much longer neither he nor von Runstedt were prepared to guess. Rommel urged Hitler to visit the front to witness first-hand the accuracy of this report, then outlined his plan for more attacks on the Normandy bridgehead: a carefully staged tactical withdrawal from the hedgerow country, far enough to lure the enemy armor into a major attack to break out of the Normandy perimeter. At that point, out of range of the deadly naval guns, a counterattack by a carefully hoarded and assembled panzer corps would strike at the flank of the Allied attack, cutting off the armored spearheads and pushing the supporting infantry back onto the beaches. It could not drive the Allies out of France, but it could deprive them of the units with which they were expecting to overrun France. Later Rommel would confess to Lucie and Manfred that he had never believed the plan had more than a one-in-four chance of success, but it was the best he could have done with what he had; events would intervene, however, which would deny Rommel that one last chance at victory. Hitler meanwhile withheld a final decision on the attack, refusing to contemplate any withdrawal, even to gain tactical or operational advantages, insisting for now that defensive operations continue. Victory, he insisted, would be achieved by "holding fast tenaciously to every square yard of soil."[289]

Meanwhile the British attempted to force a breakout near Caen, at the village of Villers Bocage, on June 12. It was a costly failure, but it kept the bulk of the German armor engaged around Caen, allowing the Americans to strike westward out of the Normandy perimeter and take the Cotentin peninsula, with its vital port of Cherbourg, although a thorough demolition of the port facilities during a surprisingly determined defense led by Generalleutnant Karl-Wilhelm von Schlieben prevented the Allies from utilizing Cherbourg before the end of August. More critically for Rommel, the American advance into the Cotentin further broadened the front his already overstretched forces had to cover, compelling him to thin his lines dangerously, with no armored reserve yet assembled to counter against any fresh Allied thrusts out of the Normandy bridgehead. Worse, the divisions holding that frontage were being bled white: replacements, of both men and equipment, were less than a tenth of losses, while supplies of ammunition were, for whatever reasons, not reaching the troops at what the British sardonically called "the pointy end of the stick." In short, Rommel was being asked to defend more and more with less and less.

It was with this bitter reality in mind that, on June 29, the same day that Cherbourg fell, Rommel, along with von Rundstedt again met with Hitler, this time at Berchtesgaden. On the way to the Führer's mountain eyrie, the two field marshals agreed that the time had come to bluntly tell Hitler that there was no hope of saving the military situation in the West: Germany's only hope was a political solution. Rommel was especially firm in this, declaring that "The war must be ended and I shall tell the Führer so, clearly and unequivocally." They presented concise but detailed reports about the looming debacle in France, insisting that the army be permitted to withdraw behind the Seine, where it was hoped a new defensive line could be established. Hitler, of course, would have none of it, insisting that "fanatical defense" would save the day. Rommel tried to direct the Führer's attention to broader strategic questions, suggesting that the time had come for a political solution to bring the war to an end. Hitler would not hear of it: instead he subjected Rommel and von Rundstedt to one of his interminable military monologues, this one outlining how he intended to turn around the situation in the West.

First, he insisted, the current Allied attacks would be stopped, though how this was to be accomplished he could not say, especially as the two field marshals had just informed him that the means for doing so no longer existed. Next, the Luftwaffe's new wonder weapons, jet fighters and rocket-propelled bombers, would create chaos over the Allied beachhead—again a statement that bore little to no relationship to reality, as very few of the jet fighters and none of the rocket bombers yet existed at this point. Unconcerned with such details, he then declared that 1,000 new conventional fighters would begin operations in the West, temporarily restoring air superiority for the Luftwaffe and reducing or outright eliminating the threat of the Allied fighter-bombers. Again minor details—where would Germany acquire the pilots to fly these new aircraft and the aviation gasoline to fuel them?—were brushed aside: if Hitler desired something to be so, then in his increasingly fractured reality it simply became so. Aiding in the effort to suppress Allied air power, antiaircraft defenses along the roads between Paris and the front would be greatly strengthened; the guns and guncrews needed to make this happen simply did not exist, of course. Efforts at mining the waters off the Allied invasion beaches were to be stepped up, while a dozen *schnelle Boote* (the Allies knew them as "E-boats") and eight submarines would wreak havoc on the support fleet off the Normandy coast—the same fleet protected by nearly 100 Allied destroyers and cruisers.

At the end of this fantastical recital, Rommel simply stared Hitler out of countenance then abruptly asked the Führer if he truly believed Germany could still win the war. When Hitler did not reply, Rommel went on, saying that his own responsibility to the German people required that the dictator accept the truth about Germany's strategic situation, military and political. In response Hitler slammed his fist on the conference table and furiously insisted that Rommel confine himself to purely military matters; Rommel countered by insisting that "History demands of me that I should deal first with our overall situation!" Warned again that he was to speak only about military subjects, Rommel tried once more, attempting to, as he put it, "speak for Germany." At that both Rommel and von Rundstedt were dismissed from the Führer's presence.[290]

Both men left Berchtesgaden convinced that their military careers were over. This turned out to be true in von Rundstedt's case, at least temporarily: the day after the meeting with Hitler, Geyr von Schweppenburg requested permission to withdraw his panzers out of range of Allied naval guns in order to organize a planned attack on Caen, permission von Rundstedt readily gave. Within 24 hours, Hitler had countermanded those instructions, and von Rundstedt telephoned the O.K.W., furiously demanding that his orders to Geyr be allowed to stand. Field Marshal Keitel refused to approach Hitler, fearing yet another of the Führer's near-psychotic temper tantrums. Pleading helplessness, Keitel asked von Rundstedt "What shall we do?" Exasperated, von Rundsteadt barked back "Make peace, you fools!" When word of this outburst reached Hitler the following day, von Rundstedt was dismissed from the command of OB West.[291]

Surprisingly, Rommel retained his post, but it was becoming an increasingly bleak duty. On July 5, in a forest near St Pierre-sur-Dives, Rommel met Geyr von Schweppenburg, who was barely recovered from the wounds he had suffered a month earlier, to deliver official word of Geyr's dismissal. "I've come to tell you that you have been relieved," he told von Schweppenburg. "Rundstedt has been too; I'm the next on the list." Hitler, whose military vocabulary by this time was essentially reduced to "No retreat!"

and "Fight to the last round and the last man!" had taken von Schweppenburg's request to conduct a tactical withdrawal as, all evidence to the contrary not withstanding, a sign of defeatism, and so Geyr had to go. His place was taken by SS Oberst-Gruppenführer Josef "Sepp" Dietrich, a tough, experienced combat veteran, but who lacked Geyr's operational skills. Dietrich would carry out von Schweppenburg's planned attack: under near-constant bombardment while the panzers assembled, the attacking force was poorly organized and the attack badly coordinated, exactly as Geyr had feared; it achieved nothing but a lengthening of the German casualty lists. Rommel, meanwhile, found the task of informing Geyr of his relief an unpleasant one: he had come, in spite of himself, to respect the Prussian aristocrat, and found it increasingly infuriating that the fanatic in Berchtesgaden refused to allow good officers to simply do their jobs. The writing was on the wall for Rommel: Hitler was losing the war and destroying the German Army in the process; before he was finished, he would destroy Germany as well.[292]

Events were now heading to an unforeseen climax for both Rommel and Hitler. Taking von Rundstedt's place as OB West was Field Marshal Günther von Kluge, who had been commanding officer of the Fourth Army in France in 1940 (Rommel had been one of his divisional commanders), and who then led Army Group Center in Russia in 1942 and 1943. Seriously injured in October 1943 when his car overturned on an icy road near Smolensk, he was invalided back to Germany and not pronounced fit to return to duty until mid-July 1944. Even before reaching France, von Kluge had already developed a negative opinion of Rommel, having listened too closely to the gossip flying about the O.K.W. and the Führer's headquarters: Hitler, Keitel, and Jodl had all characterized Rommel as stubborn, insubordinate, and defeatist. Von Kluge, then, arrived in Paris determined to bring the maverick field marshal to heel. It was not long before the gist of some intemperate remarks made by von Kluge reached Rommel, who, always sensitive to slights, real or perceived, demanded that von Kluge explain himself.

5 July 1944

To C.-IN-C. WEST.
HERR GENERALFELDMARSCHALL VON KLUGE.

I send you enclosed my comments on military events in Normandy to date. The rebuke which you levelled at me at the beginning of your visit, in the presence of my Chief of Staff and 1a, to the effect that I, too, "will now have to get accustomed to carrying out orders," has deeply wounded me. I request you to notify me what grounds you have for making such an accusation.

(Signed) ROMMEL
Generalfeldmarschall[293]

Knowing full well where von Kluge's prejudice had likely originated, Rommel had included with his personal letter to the new OB West a copy of the report he had submitted to Hitler on June 17, which detailed the strategic, operational, and tactical details of the situation in France, along with his observations, criticisms and suggestions for properly fighting the battle. It did not take long for von Kluge to discover who was telling the truth and who was spouting fantasy. When it became obvious to him that Hitler and the O.K.W. had knowingly lied about the situation in Normandy—that it was not simply severe, it was an out-and-out crisis—he did a complete about-face and agreed wholeheartedly with Rommel: the battle was lost, which meant that the war itself was lost. The best that they could hope to accomplish was to buy time—but to what end?

Rommel in particular had lost faith in the "wonder weapons." Initially he had been intrigued by the V-1s, their sheer novelty appealing to the engineer in him. But while the "buzz bombs" might influence Allied strategy in France, they had no effect on the Allies' ability to wage war there. As for the V-2s, the jet fighters, the rocket bombers, all of them were, in Rommel's opinion, merely more manifestations of Hitler's *wolkenkuckkucksheim*. Manfred once remarked to his father that perhaps the new weapons would turn the tide in Germany's favor, Rommel replied, "Rubbish! Nobody has any such weapons. The only purpose of these rumors is to make the ordinary soldier hang on a bit longer. We're finished, and most of the gentlemen above know it perfectly well, even if they won't admit it. . . ." Von Kluge and Rommel agreed that simply prolonging the war for its own sake accomplished nothing, save for getting more Germans killed and bringing more destruction down on Germany—and, ominously, allowing the Russians closer to the Reich every day. *Götterdämmerung* was looming, and if "the gentlemen above" refused to acknowledge this to be so and act to ward if off, then other men would have to act as they saw fit to prevent it.[294]

Rommel put forward one last effort to make the Führer and the O.K.W. see reason, drawing up a report—which von Kluge firmly endorsed—in which he hoped the facts would speak for themselves. It is a remarkable document in its stark, straightforward nature—reflecting its author's character—stating not only the situation that exists, but also in accurately predicting what is to come.

C.-IN-C. ARMY GROUP B H.Q. 15 July 1943
The situation on the Normandy front is growing worse every day and is now approaching a grave crisis.

Due to the severity of the fighting, the enemy's enormous use of materiel above all, artillery and tanks and the effect of his unrestricted command of the air over the battle area, our casualties are so high that the fighting power of our divisions is rapidly diminishing. Replacements from home are few in number and, with the difficult transport situation, take weeks to get to the front. As against 97,000 casualties (including 2,360 officers), i.e. an average of 2,500 to 3,000 a day, replacements to date number 10,000, of whom about 6,000 have actually arrived at the front.

Material losses are also huge and have so far been replaced on a very small scale; in tanks, for example, only 17 replacements have arrived to date as compared with 225 losses.

The newly arrived infantry divisions are raw and, with their small establishment of artillery, antitank guns and close-combat antitank weapons, are in no state to make a lengthy stand against major enemy attacks coming after hours of drum-fire and heavy bombing. The fighting has shown that with this use of materiel by the enemy, even the bravest army will be smashed piece by piece, losing men, arms and territory in the process.

Due to the destruction of the railway system and the threat of the enemy air force to roads and tracks up to 90 miles behind the front, supply conditions are so bad that only the barest essentials can be brought to the front. It is consequently now necessary to exercise the greatest economy in all fields, and especially in artillery and mortar ammunition. These conditions are unlikely to improve, as enemy action is steadily reducing the transport capacity available. Moreover, this activity in the air is likely to become even more effective as the numerous air-strips in the bridgehead are taken into use.

No new forces of any consequence can be brought up to the Normandy front except by weakening Fifteenth Army's front on the Channel, or the Mediterranean front in southern France. Yet Seventh Army's front, taken overall, urgently requires two fresh divisions, as the troops in Normandy are exhausted.

On the enemy's side, fresh forces and great quantities of war materiel are flowing into his front every day. His supplies are undisturbed by our air force. Enemy pressure is growing steadily stronger.

In these circumstances we must expect that in the foreseeable future the enemy will succeed in breaking through our thin front, above all, Seventh Army's, and thrusting deep into France. Apart from the Panzer Group's sector reserves, which are at present tied down by the fighting on their own front and due to the enemy's command of the air can only move by night, we dispose of no mobile reserve for defense against such a breakthrough. Action by our air force will, as in the past, have little effect.

The troops are everywhere fighting heroically, but the unequal struggle is approaching its end. It is urgently necessary for the proper conclusion to be drawn from this situation. As C.-in-C. of the Army Group I feel myself in duty bound to speak plainly on this point.

(Signed) ROMMEL[295]

On July 16, reading the maps as Corporal Daniel drove the big open Horsch sedan, Rommel motored up to the outskirts of Le Havre, where the Luftwaffe's 17th Field Division was holding part of the front against the British armor concentrated around Caen. There he met with the divisional staff, including the operations officer, Lieutenant Colonel Elmar Warning, who had for a time served on Rommel's staff in North Africa and who still proudly wore his Afrika Korps cuffband. Confident that he was in the presence of a trusted friend, Rommel was blunt when Warning privately asked him for the truth about the overall situation in Normandy, because, as Warning put it, "we can count the days off on our tunic buttons before the breakthrough comes."

"I'll tell you this much," Rommel said. "Field Marshal von Kluge and I have sent the Führer an ultimatum, telling him the war can't be won militarily and asking him to draw the consequences."

"What if the Führer refuses?" Warning wondered. Rommel's response came with no hesitation.

"Then I'm going to open up the western front, because there's only one thing that matters now: the British and Americans must get to Berlin before the Russians do!"[296]

The following morning, July 17, Rommel, who was clocking as much as 250 miles a day driving between his headquarters at La Roche Guyon and the units fighting at the front, set out for a meeting with Sepp Dietrich, commander of the 1st SS Panzer Corps. While not particularly admirable, Dietrich was an intriguing individual: like Hitler, he was awarded the Iron Cross, 1st and 2nd Class, as an enlisted man in the First World War; he joined the Nazi Party in 1928 and became one of the first commanding officers of the Schutzstaffel, the SS, when it was still only Hitler's bodyguard, later serving as Hitler's personal chauffeur. Given his history, then, his loyalty to the Führer and the Party should have been total and absolute; yet according to Helmuth Lang, after the purely military aspects of the conference with Dietrich were completed, Rommel had the most amazing conversation with the SS general. Well within earshot of Lang, Rommel bluntly asked Dietrich, "Would you always execute my orders, even if they contradicted the Führer's orders?"

"You are my superior officer, *Herr Feldmarschall*," Dietrich replied, offering Rommel his hand, "and therefore I will obey all your orders, whatever it is you're planning."[297]

With that, Rommel's business at Dietrich's headquarters was complete, and within minutes he was on his way back to La Roche Guyon. Dietrich suggested that, given their proximity to the front, Rommel and his men take an ordinary *kübelwagen* rather than the big, conspicuous Horsch, but Rommel waved off the idea—*kübels* were cramped, uncomfortable, and slow. He did accept the SS man's recommendation to stay on side roads rather than the main highways, the better to avoid roving Allied fighter-bombers. Just past 4:00 P.M., Corporal Daniel roared away from St Pierre sur Dives; Rommel sat in front as usual, Captain Lang, Major Neuhaus, and Feldwebel Hoike (who had been brought along specifically as an aircraft spotter) taking their places in the back. As they traveled south, they never went more than a mile—often no more than a few hundred yards— without passing the strafed, often burned-out wrecks of Wehrmacht and SS trucks, tanks, and armored cars that had been destroyed by British or American aircraft. Near Sainte-Foy-de-Montgommery, Hoike spotted a formation of Allied fighters that appeared to be lining up for a strafing run on the road ahead. Rommel ordered Corporal Daniel to take a side road that ran through the village of Sainte-Germaine-de-Montgommery, and it was there that a pair of Royal Air Force Spitfires suddenly appeared. Daniel zigzagged desperately to throw off the British pilots' aim, but a burst of 20mm cannon fire walked across the road and into the car, seriously wounding Daniel, who lost control of the big Horsch. The car skidded for 100 yards before it nosed into the ditch alongside the road, struck a tree and rebounded into the roadway again; everyone in the car was thrown clear by the initial impact. Lang was all but unhurt, Neuhaus and Hoike suffered minor injuries; but Daniel's wounds were fatal—he would lapse into a coma and die a few hours later. Rommel, who had turned to his right to watch the approach of the enemy fighters, was thrown violently against the windscreen pillar, fracturing his skull in three places and suffering massive injuries to the left side of his face before being tossed onto the roadway. Unconscious and bleeding heavily, Erwin Rommel had come to the end of his war.

THREE DAYS LATER, at 12:42 P.M., July 20, 1944, a bomb exploded in the room at the Führerhauptquartier at Rastenburg in East Prussia where Adolf Hitler was having his daily military briefing.

Aside from burns and a perforated eardrum, Hitler survived the blast uninjured—others were less fortunate: four men were killed and two were seriously injured; another five suffered lesser wounds. Predictably, within hours of the bomb detonating, as soon as it became clear that the assassination attempt—the German word is *attentat*—was part of an attempted coup d'état, a *putsch*, by German Army officers, the witch hunts began. The Führer had, with good reason, long been suspicious of the German officer corps—there had been assassination plots and attempts, some of which Hitler had been aware, some of which he knew nothing, concocted by various senior officers as far back as 1938. Hitler and the German *offizierkorps* had always regarded each other as the means to an end; both considered the other as being expendable when those ends were achieved. For Hitler, the tacit approval and cooperation of the *offizierkorps* had provided a cloak of legitimacy and an underpinning of authority as he consolidated his power in the early days of his regime; for the officer corps' part, Hitler resurrected the Germany Army from irrelevance and restored it to a position of international power and prestige. It had been a deal sealed in the blood of the Night of the Long Knives, but neither party to it had any delusions about its permanence; the war prolonged the bargain, but ultimately undermined it. The officer corps viewed Hitler as the rankest of amateurs who after a few strokes of good fortune in the early years of the war was now leading Germany—and more importantly the Army—to defeat, while Hitler saw his senior officers as hidebound reactionaries who were obstacles to his brilliance and hence to victory. The time had come, in the summer of 1944, for Führer and officers alike to be rid of each other.

Enter Claus von Stauffenberg, count, colonel, and Chief of Staff of the Reserve Army. Handsome, intelligent, urbane, educated, aristocratic, and a graduate of the General Staff College, von Staufenberg was not only the complete antithesis of Adolf Hitler, he embodied everything about the German Army Hitler despised most. Von Stauffenberg was also a man highly disillusioned, badly wounded in body and soul, who chose to take action against Hitler when most of his fellows involved in the "German resistance" were content with endless nattering. It was von Stauffenberg who placed the bomb in the Führer's conference room and who, convinced that the monster had died in the explosion, returned to Berlin to lead the *putsch* against the Nazi government apparatus. For this, the young Wehrmacht colonel, who would be executed in Berlin by a makeshift firing squad barely 12 hours after the failed *attentat*, has become widely honored, almost revered, for his courage and determination to take action where other men had hesitated and failed.

All the same, because of this willingness to act when others only talked, von Stauffenberg has been the subject of a great deal of idealizing, even romanticizing, in regard to his character, motives, and objectives in his determination to kill Adolf Hitler. He was not, for example, the passionate anti-Nazi he is frequently depicted to be: though he never formally joined the National Socialist Party, von Stauffenberg was among the Reichswehr officers who publicly celebrated Hitler's ascension to the chancellorship in January 1933, and openly embraced the Nazi ideals of militarism, socialism, and totalitarianism. Moreover, he did not view the elimination of Hitler and the senior Nazi hierarchy as the first great step to ending the war. Rather, he had concocted a list of demands to which the Allies would be required to accede before Germany would make peace with them—this in spite of the declaration at Casablanca by Churchill and the American president, Roosevelt, that only unconditional surrender by Germany would be acceptable to the West. Von Stauffenberg expected that Austria and the Sudetenland would be retained as part of of the Reich, while Germany would simultaneously be allowed to annex most of the Italian Tyrol; Alsace-Lorraine would become autonomous—under close German supervision—while the border with a reconstituted Poland would be redrawn to along the pre-1914 frontiers; and there would be no occupation of Germany in any form by the Allies. In short, von Stauffenberg and his clique of conspirators were prepared to withdraw the German armed forces from southern Italy, France, and the Low Countries in exchange for having removed Hitler and his inner circle of senior Nazis from power.

It is difficult to imagine a concept for a peace settlement more out of touch with the realities of mid-1944. That von Stauffenberg and his fellow conspirators imagined such an offer being palatable to the Allies owed more to their view of themselves and their place in Germany and the world at large than it did to any realistic political and military calculus. Von Stauffenberg held to a near-mystic self-view, that of a latter-day crusader, the embodiment of Christian ideals (he was a devout Catholic, which was the root of his deepest conflicts with National Socialism and its neo-paganism), a Teutonic warrior-poet who, Germany's savior, would usher the Fatherland into a new future which would mystically meld with the myth and legend of Germany's past, racially pure and morally cleansed, guided by the noble paladins of the *offizierkorps*. The great irony of Claus von Stauffenberg was that he sought to abolish Hitler and the Nazis, but not National Socialism: according to his brother, Berthold, Claus "basically approved of the racial principle of National Socialism, but considered it to be exaggerated and excessive."[298]

On some level, and all the evidence indicates that this was not a conscious decision, Rommel understood and rejected all of this. He was never approached by von Stauffenberg directly, although they encountered each other in their professional capacities from time to time in late 1943 and early 1944. Moreover, Rommel was too much the pragmatist to be seduced by von Stauffenberg's romantic nonsense; had the count confided his intentions and ambitions to the field marshal, Rommel would have been quick to chastise the younger man (von Stauffenberg was 36 at the time of the assassination attempt) for being so unrealistic.

In point of fact, von Stauffenberg himself should have known better: by July 20, 1944 he was the veteran of almost four years of combat and had been severely, almost fatally, wounded in an Allied air attack while serving as a staff officer with the 10th Panzer Division in Tunisia in the spring of 1943. Losing his left eye, his right hand, and two fingers on his left hand, von Stauffenberg was invalided back to Germany, where after his recovery he was appointed the Chief of Staff of the Ersatzarmee, the Replacement Army (the central reserve of the Wehrmacht, where new units were created and old, exhausted formations were reconstituted and replenished), which gave him access to the contingency plans for an operation called *Valküre* (*Valkyrie*), which served as the basis for his own planning for the *putsch* he would lead once Hitler was safely assassinated and thus out of the way. Rommel, had he been sought out by von Stauffenberg, would have queried as to what exactly the younger man saw that would lead him to believe that the British and the Americans, who had already thrown the Axis out of North Africa, were handily winning the Battle of the Atlantic, and whose bomber fleets were daily and nightly raining down destruction on the Reich itself, would suddenly simply quit if offered the opportunity to do so through a change of regime in Berlin. Whatever it might have been, Rommel himself saw no trace of it.

This, of course, is one of the fundamental failings of von Stauffenberg's entire plan: he needed Rommel—not merely a senior general of Rommel's stature within Germany, but a general whom the Allies believed they knew and who they undoubtedly respected. That Rommel would have considered von Stauffenberg's goals so much *unsinn*—nonsense—would have left the July 20 conspirators without credibility among the British and American leadership. Thus the most pervasive myth about Rommel and the conspirators who planned and attempted the July 20 *attentat*, that, had he not been severely wounded on July 17 Rommel would have, in cooperation with von Stauffenberg and his co-conspirators in Berlin, announced a capitulation in the West, is rubbish.

As it was, any association, real or imagined, played by Erwin Rommel in the conspiracies against Adolf Hitler began not with Claus von Stauffenberg but with Hans Speidel, Rommel's Chief of Staff beginning in April 1944, who *was* involved in the July 20 *attentat*, but neither so fervently nor as deeply as he would attempt to lead posterity to believe. The source of all "detailed" accounts of Rommel's involvement with the conspirators is Speidel, and as postwar events would demonstrate, Speidel had ulterior motives for offering up Rommel as a key member of the July 20 bomb plot. And thereby hangs a tale, not one of Second World War intrigue, but of postwar politics and personal ambition.

At the end of the Second World War, the four Allied powers, the Americans, British, French, and Soviets, took collective responsibility for the security of Germany, as the Wehrmacht, Luftwaffe, and Kriegsmarine were disarmed and dissolved after the German surrender on May 8, 1945. As the 1940s rolled into the 1950s, tensions grew between the Soviet Union and the West, especially after the Korean War and the formal partitioning of East and West Germany, which led to the idea of a revived German Army, the Bundeswehr, being formed to bolster the newly established NATO, itself a response to perceived Soviet threats to European security. As the idea began to coalesce, the question of who would provide the Bundeswehr's senior leadership became a major political issue in all of the NATO capitals. No one wanted the new German army led by officers who had any ties whatsoever to the Nazi regime, but such officers were in short supply, as most German generals had been tainted, at the very least, either by Hitler's bribes or by association on some level with atrocities carried out by German armed forces, especially on the Eastern Front. Speidel, who had taken up as a professor of modern history at the University of Tübingen, began to quietly but forcefully put his name forward in consideration for a senior officer's posting in the new Bundeswehr. To bolster his credentials as a "politically reliable" officer unblemished by a Nazi past, he let it be known that he had been a part of the July 20, 1944 conspiracy; this much was true. To further enhance his credibility, however, he emphasized his role as Rommel's Chief of Staff, knowing that Erwin Rommel was the one German field marshal whom all of the Western Allies respected, and whom many British and American senior officers openly admired. He then began cultivating Frau Rommel and the field marshal's son, Manfred, simultaneously implying that there had been a close personal as well as professional relationship with his superior while reinforcing the image of Rommel as the "good"—i.e. anti-Nazi—German general. It was a carefully planned and executed campaign, as befitted such a cerebral officer: on November 12, 1955, Hans Speidel was commissioned as *generalleutnant* in the newly constituted Bundeswehr; two years later, he was appointed commander-in-chief of the NATO ground forces in Central Europe, a post that he held until he retired in 1963.

The upshot of Speidel's success, however, is that everything he affirmed regarding Rommel's role or participation in the July 20 plot must be viewed through the prism of how Speidel's words and deeds advanced his postwar career. For that matter, it was not only Rommel's reputation that Speidel worked to burnish: he did his best to enhance his own standing among the von Stauffenberg conspirators, offering up himself as a more dynamic and central participant than in fact he ever was. There is no doubt that Speidel possessed a powerful personal and professional antipathy toward Hitler: his experience on the Russian Front in 1942 and 1943 persuaded him that the Führer's military ineptitude would bring disaster down onto the German Army, while learning of the atrocities committed by the Einsatzgruppen and the SS against civilians in Poland and the Ukraine occupied convinced him of the inherent immorality of National Socialist doctrines. His repulsion did not automatically translate into active participation in the "German resistance," however; instead Speidel was what would have been best described as a "fellow traveler."

He took pains, nonetheless, to offer up the scenario where Rommel specifically requested Speidel's assignment to replace General Gause as Army Group B's Chief of Staff because of Speidel's connections with the conspirators, intending to use him as a conduit to von Stauffenberg, but it is here that Speidel's story begins to unravel. Speidel's utility for Rommel's purposes was far more prosaic than facilitating a conspiracy: Rommel had always displayed a marked lack of enthusiasm for the more mundane details of generalship—generating reports and requisitions, assigning supply priorities, allocating replacement drafts, writing out detailed orders, and so on; it was not that he believed them unnecessary, rather they were the reason why general officers had staffs in the first place—and given Speidel's well-earned reputation for efficient staff work, he was someone to whom Rommel could confidently assign such tasks. Rommel said as much in the very last letter he wrote to Hitler, on October 1, 1944, when he attempted to intervene with the Führer on Speidel's behalf, saying, "[Speidel] took firm control of the staff, showed great understanding for the troops and helped me loyally to complete the defenses of the Atlantic Wall as quickly as possible with the available means. When I went up to the front, which was almost every day, I could rely on Speidel to transmit my orders as discussed beforehand to the Armies, and to carry on all talks with superior and equivalent formations along the lines I required." Rommel, not knowing that his own doom was only days away, had written these words in good faith, and there is no reason to question their veracity or intent.[299]

The truth was that Rommel, had he desired a conduit to von Stauffenberg's conspiracy, did not need Speidel for that purpose: he already had one. While on medical leave in Wiener Neustadt in February 1943, Rommel was introduced by Lucie to Dr. Karl Strölin, the lord mayor of Stuttgart. Actually, it was a reintroduction, as Rommel and Strölin had served together in the 124th Infantry Regiment in the First World War; apart from that shared experience, however, the two men had little in common. After the war, while Rommel continued his military career, Strölin had become immersed in politics, joining the Nazi Party in 1923, while National Socialism was still in its infancy. By 1943, while still holding to the "ideal" of National Socialism, he was convinced that it had become hopelessly corrupted by Hitler and his cronies, and had made common cause with Karl Friedrich Goerdeler, a former senior economist for the Third Reich who had become von Stauffenberg's civilian counterpart in leading the July 20 bomb plot. Goerdeler, "a conservative and a monarchist . . . a devout Protestant, able, energetic and intelligent, but also indiscreet and headstrong . . ." had been "heart and soul in opposition to Hitler" as early as 1937.[300] Strölin often acted as an intermediary for Goerdeler, who was anxious to secure the cooperation and support of a senior Wehrmacht officer who could serve as the military leader for the *putsch* against the Nazi government once Hitler was dead. Strölin was convinced that Rommel was just that officer, and even before the field marshal began his convalescent leave in February 1943 had begun ingratiating himself with Lucie, the better to ease himself, so he believed, into Rommel's good graces.

Rommel, sick and exhausted, had little interest in talking politics with anyone, let alone this Nazi busybody, but to placate Lucie, who had been flattered by Strölin's gifts of flowers, theater tickets, and luxury hotel accommodations for her, her husband, and young Manfred, agreed to hear him out. Strölin immediately launched into what seemed to be a prepared speech denouncing the Nazi regime, urging Rommel to step forward in order to save Germany from destruction. To reinforce his point, he produced a number of documents, some of which detailed crimes and massacres carried out by the SS and Gestapo in occupied territory, especially in the East, and particularly against Jews. (It is quite possible that the irony of Strölin's claims was not lost on Rommel, as Strölin had been personally responsible for the deportation of some 2,000 Jews from Stuttgart, all of whom would perish in Nazi death camps.) When Strölin declared "If Hitler does not die, then we are all lost!" Rommel had enough. "Herr Strölin," he announced, "I would be grateful if you would refrain from speaking such opinions in the presence of my young son!" Recognizing failure when he saw it, Strölin quickly made his manners and left the Rommel household.[301] For Goerdeler's part, the last pieces of the conspiracy fell into place a few months after Strölin's abortive meeting with Rommel, and in doing so obviated the necessity for a senior officer of Rommel's stature to be part of the *putsch*. Meeting Colonel Count Klaus von Stauffenberg shortly after the young officer was posted to the staff of the Replacement Army, Goerdeler found a kindred spirit for his hatred of Hitler and the Nazis, though the two men disliked each other personally. Goerdeler thought von Stauffenberg to be playing at politics, a vain and somewhat superficial romantic socialist who only came to oppose Hitler when Germany began losing the war, and who sought a measure of personal revenge for his maiming. There was an element of truth in all of Goerdeler's misgivings about von Stauffenberg, but at the same time he could not deny the young colonel's courage and determination. Von Stauffenberg in turn saw Goerdeler as a reactionary out of touch with modern political thinking; both men, however, were inclined to make common cause because they recognized that von Stauffenberg's new post presented the conspirators with a unique opportunity: as chief of staff for the Ersatzarmee, he was responsible for developing contingency plans for it, and so concocted *Valküre*—purportedly a plan for suppressing an uprising by the millions of slave laborers working in the Reich, but in reality the cover for toppling the Nazi government in the event of Hitler's assassination. Colonels, lieutenant colonels, and majors would separately lead their units to carry out specific operations which facilitated the *putsch*, without having—or needing to have—any knowledge of the larger plan which they were accomplishing.

Rommel would still have been a priceless asset for the conspirators, a respected and honorable figure who would be the face of the new regime—in the hope that they would not be perceived merely old wine in new bottles—presented to the Allies. With the adoption of the *Valkyrie* plans, however, it would not be necessary for him to take on the role of the provisional army commander-in-chief in the hope that his stature would be sufficient to persuade any hesitant regimental and division commanders to obedience. Instead those officers would simply carry out operational orders which were part of an official Wehrmacht contingency plan, one which had been already been unwittingly approved by Hitler himself. All that remained was for the right opportunity to carry out the *attentat* to present itself; after a handful of aborted attempts, the moment came on July 20, 1944.

And so the deed was done. Von Stauffenberg's bomb exploded, and Adolf Hitler, in a bitter twist of fate, survived. Retribution was swift: goaded into action by Hitler's rage and lust for vengeance, the Gestapo arrested anyone with even the most tangential connection to the core conspirators. The Gestapo's chief, Reichsführer-SS Heinrich Himmler, invoked the ancient German legal principle of *sippenhaft* (literally "imprisoning the family" but in practice blood-guilt) to punish the families of those accused in complicity with the *attentat*. Before the orgy of blood lust ran its course, over 7,000 Germans were arrested, and 4,980 were executed, some by firing squad, most by hanging. And not everyone arrested—or executed—was in fact connected to the July 20 assassination attempt: just as happened a decade earlier in the Night of the Long Knives, there were personal and political scores settled in the Gestapo manhunts.

BUT IF ERWIN Rommel was not part of the July 20 conspiracy did he have any plans of his own to bring about an end to the war—at least in the West? His devotion to Adolf Hitler and the National Socialist regime had clearly been exhausted before von Stauffenberg's bomb exploded, and whatever illusions regarding Rommel the July 20 conspirators might have entertained, he had a different objective than did they, and with it a different agenda which would have employed different methods.

In order to answer the question of Rommel's intentions, the devolution of Rommel's loyalty to Adolf Hitler—and especially his sense of being oath-bound to the Führer—must be understood. Germans of Rommel's generation as a rule took oaths very seriously: they were not mere formalities, to be observed or disregarded as was expedient to the moment, but were instead taken as the measure of a man or woman's character. To be regarded as an oath breaker—*eidesbrecher*—was the worst sort of opprobrium which could be leveled at a German: the word itself, *eidesbrecher*, is in fact far more severe, even violent, than "oath breaker"—it literally means "oath crusher." Indeed, one of the most compelling reasons why the July 20 conspirators were determined to end Hitler's life rather than merely remove him from power was that the Führer's death would remove any remaining moral obligation to the oath of loyalty—the *Fahneneid*—every German soldier, airman, or sailor had sworn to Hitler.

From his letters, diaries, and various conversations with colleagues, subordinates, and family members, it is clear that Rommel came to a far different conclusion: disobedience to the Führer's orders and defiance of his authority did not, in fact, constitute a violation of his oath of loyalty. By the spring of 1944, the *Fahneneid* and any claims it had on the fidelity of German *soldaten* had been thoroughly shredded by Adolf Hitler himself. As Rommel saw it, that process began in November 1942, with Hitler's "Victory or Death!" order at El Alamein; it was accelerated every time some new variation on that theme was offered up in the retreat to Tunisia, as Hitler demanded that the *panzerarmee* stand and die for some meaningless piece of desert waste that Hitler, peering at a map in Berchtesgaden or Rastenburg, had decided must be held at all costs.

In April 1943, when Hitler blithely abandoned Armeegruppe Afrika in Tunisia, consigning 150,000 veteran Axis soldiers, whose combat experience was irreplaceable, to Allied captivity rather than exerting himself to withdraw them to Europe, Rommel's anger became fury. Now back in Italy and so no longer isolated and insulated in North Africa, Rommel quickly learned the truth about Stalingrad, where Hitler denied the soldiers of the Sixth Army any chance to escape the Soviet encirclement, condemning a quarter-million of them to death at the hands of the Red Army, either on the battlefield or as prisoners of war—fewer than 5,000 would ever return to Germany. Such actions on the part of the Führer were a breach of the faith between soldier and leader that was as old as warfare itself, that a soldier would never be sacrificed without meaning.

Rommel also began to hear the stories, often directly from men who had witnessed the events, about the actions of the Sonderkommandos, Einsatzgruppen, and even—particularly shameful to an officer like Rommel—units of the Wehrmacht in Poland, the Ukraine, and Russia; stories of burnings, looting, mass deportations and mass executions of men, women, and children, civilians who were excluded from the racial ideals of Nazi dogma and law, and so were declared *untermenschen*—subhumans. At first Rommel tried to convince himself that such actions were isolated incidents, then later that they were being done without the knowledge or consent of the Führer, but eventually he came to realize that these atrocities were too widespread and carried out on such a scale that it would have been impossible for Hitler not to have known of them—and that in knowing, and refusing to demand that such actions cease and repudiate those who committed them, he at least tacitly approved.

When the officers and men of the Wehrmacht first swore the *Fahneneid* to Adolf Hitler in 1935, no more was asked of them by the Führer than had ever been asked of German soldiers for two centuries: that they obey the head of state and defend the Fatherland, with their lives if need be; implicit in the authority granted by that oath was the pledge made in return that such power would never be abused. Admittedly Hitler had gone a step farther than had even the Prussian kings by conflating the state and his own person, but at the time that seemed to be a mere technicality, and for over six years Hitler honored that unspoken pledge. But by the end of 1941, German soldiers were routinely being bidden to carry out acts of violence and retribution on the helpless and innocent, acts of such inhumanity and immorality that, if they could have done so, millions of ghosts in Prussian blue—*feld blau*—and field gray would have risen from beneath their black crosses in thunderous outrage. The history of German arms was not wholly free from blemish—no nation's history truly is—but from the days of Friedrich the Great the wartime conduct of German officers and other ranks had, as a rule, been more restrained than that of many of their European counterparts. Since 1740 the German soldier had been respected—even feared—for his courage and skill on the battlefield; but now Adolf Hitler was transforming him into the avatar of *schrecklichkeit*—living terror—by making him the instrument of pointless death and needless destruction. It was a transformation in parallel with that of the Führer himself, as Hitler metastasized from a true national leader into a bloodthirsty tyrant little better than a barbarian warlord. The Adolf Hitler of 1944 was so fundamentally changed from the man he had been ten years earlier as to be unrecognizable: in essence the Adolf Hitler of 1934, to whom the officers and men of the new Wehrmacht had sworn their personal loyalty, no longer existed.

The realization that this was so was at the heart of Rommel's final sundering of ways with Hitler: time and again from late 1942, in his diaries, letters and conversations Rommel used words like "crazy," "abnormal," "pathological," and "demoniac" to describe the Führer, a hard contrast to his earlier admiration of the man. When Hitler came to power in 1933, Rommel, along with at least a plurality of countrymen, saw a figure wearing a most-convincing mask of a man wholly dedicated to returning Germany to greatness, and restoring stability, prosperity, and self-respect to the German people. His methods may have been harsh, but they were the ways of authoritarianism, something the Germans—including Rommel—understood and of which they approved. Before ten years had passed, however, the mask had not merely slipped, it had been all but discarded. The only cause Hitler now recognized was his own, the only purpose of Germany's armed forces, her industry, her people, was to serve and preserve himself: Germany and the Germans no longer mattered—indeed, according to Hitler, they no longer were worthy of him: in July 1943 Hitler remarked to Rommel, almost conversationally, that "If the German people are incapable of winning the war, then they can rot." The man to whom the *Fahneneid* was sworn in the summer of 1934 no longer existed, and when that man disappeared, the bonds of the oath of loyalty were broken: for an oath to be binding, there must be both a giver and receiver; absent one or the other, the oath is dissolved.[302]

Rommel recognized this for what it was, a complete abrogation of the

Fahneneid, and understood it as such far sooner than did most of his colleagues. He was also aware that the junior officers and their soldiers, sailors, and airmen, were growing increasingly weary and disillusioned. Hitler and the O.K.W. kept promising miracles if only the men at the front would hold out a little longer, but delivered only more defeat, death and destruction. Whatever threats and exhortations Göbbels and his minions at the Propaganda Ministry might yet be breathing out, only the most dedicated fanatics or hopelessly gullible retained any measure of confidence in the Führer and National Socialism. For the men in uniform, the degree of their loyalty was measured in inverse proportion to their distance from the fighting; by the time the Allies were ashore in Normandy, they were truly fighting only for Germany, in the hope that somehow, some way, the Allies would tire of the war and seek to make peace—who sat in the seats of power in Berlin was immaterial to them. Rommel, having seen first-hand the Allies' overwhelming superiority in materiel and manpower, knew there was no chance of the Allies giving up: it would be the Germans who would have to stop fighting. Given the depth of his vanity, Rommel was most assuredly well-aware that he was more popular, in the proper sense of the word, than Adolf Hitler himself among Germany's soldiers as well as large parts of her civilian population; he also knew that such popularity could bestow a moral authority on him which would be a potent, even decisive, weapon if he were determined to use it.

By 1944 Hitler and the Nazis retained their grip on most Germans through fear and intimidation: the vast majority of Germans had come to understand that it was dangerous to not at least pay lip-service to loyalty to Hitler and the Nazi regime. Rommel himself had done so, in early March 1944, when he added his signature to a document being circulated among the Wehrmacht's most senior officers which affirmed their devotion to the Führer. (The document had been drawn up in response to Hitler's anger at radio propaganda broadcasts being made by German generals—some voluntarily, others under compulsion—captured by the Soviet Army urging Wehrmacht officers and other ranks to stop fighting.) Von Rundstedt signed it, so did Field Marshals Erich von Manstein, Ewald von Kleist, Maximilian von Wiechs, and Ernst Busch; when presented with the document, Rommel signed his name with a flourish.

Yet it was a hollow gesture, something done only as a sop to an increasingly paranoid Hitler rather than as a genuine demonstration of fidelity; Rommel had already made up his mind as to where his true loyalty lay. Germans—and especially Germans of his generation—never confused patriotism with blind loyalty to an individual; the tradition began with Old Fritz himself, when the greatest of the Prussian kings had declared, "A king is the first servant and first magistrate of the state." A successor, Friedrich Wilhelm III, had carried the idea even further: "Every servant of the state has a dual obligation: to the sovereign and to the country. It can occur that the two are not compatible; then, the duty to the country is higher." When, in November 1918, Kaiser Wilhelm II insisted that loyalty to Germany was inseparable from loyalty to himself, he was repudiated not only by the German people at large, but more importantly, for the precedent it set, by the Imperial Army whose fidelity he had taken for granted. And therein lies an essential part of the answer of Rommel's plans—a true German's loyalty was always given to Germany, not to any particular governmental form or leader.

It was just this sort of patriotism which put Rommel at loggerheads with the July 20 conspiracy: like many of the officers who wanted to see Hitler eliminated, the source of von Stauffenberg's anger toward him was that Germany was losing the war, for which he held Hitler responsible. As long as the war progressed in Germany's favor, von Stauffenberg found himself able to rationalize, excuse, or simply overlook the excesses of the Nazi regime, whichever was convenient. When the victories ceased and events turned against Germany, however, then Hitler suddenly became an evil, raving madman who had to be removed from power by whatever means was possible. Rommel, while equally angry that Hitler was losing the war for Germany, was furious at Hitler for *how* it was being lost: the Führer's fanatical insistence on defending every square yard of ground and refusal to even attempt to negotiate a peace, however unlikely an event that might have been, were proof to Rommel that Hitler was only interested in retaining his position and power as long as possible—to the last German soldier and the last German city if need be. Hitler's great crime, in Rommel's eyes, was not losing the war, but the death and destruction he brought down on the Germans and Germany by pointlessly prolonging the losing.

While it is impossible to know in detail what Rommel planned for any move he might have made against Hitler, it can be concluded without fear of effective contradiction that it did not coincide—in scope, timing, or purpose—with the plans of the July 20 conspirators. For all of his later protests as to how deeply and vitally involved he was in von Stauffenberg's plot, Speidel's masterful inactivity at La Roche Guyon the day of the *attentat* when informed that Hitler had been killed in the bomb blast—which should have been his signal to put into action whatever plans for which he was responsible, he did absolutely *nothing*—demonstrates how marginal he truly was to the actual *putsch*. It is also proof that Rommel's plans, whatever they may have been and what there were of them, were not meant to coordinate with those of von Stauffenberg and his clique—including Speidel. There is every reason to believe that when Rommel was incapacitated and almost killed in the strafing attack on July 17, whatever schemes he had concocted were as yet incomplete, and that had he been at his post on July 20 he would have been taken by surprise at the news of the assassination attempt.

It is distinctly possible that Rommel would not have ever created a fully developed plan, at least as the term was understood by most General Staff officers, preferring instead to resort to his command habits from the days in North Africa, when he would have an objective and a vague outline of an operational plan in mind, and would make up the details as he went along. There is a certain essential credibility to this scenario, given how fluid and confusing the situation would be had Rommel been able to act against Hitler: much as he had done in Libya, he would have had to respond with improvisation and inspiration to adapt what would inevitably have been an ever-shifting and volatile situation. In such circumstances, Rommel's name and reputation—and the moral authority which accompanied them—would have been his greatest asset: however ambitious he may have been for professional advancement and public recognition, Rommel was never regarded by his friends or his enemies as a Praetorian—no "man on horseback" with aspirations to political power was he.

Almost as valuable to any plan of Rommel's would have been the open support of Field Marshal von Kluge, the new OB West. Nominally Rommel's superior, he was, according to Fritz Bayerlein, prepared to follow Rommel's lead when the moment to act arrived; the knowledge that the two senior commanders in the West were standing together in open defiance of the Nazi regime would have imbued any orders they gave to units under their command with an air of legitimacy all but impossible to ignore or disregard. So too would have been the knowledge that men like Sepp Dietrich,

Wilhelm Bittrich, and Fritz Bayerlein himself, stood with the two field marshals. Each of them was an experienced, worldly-wise combat commander
in his own right, who inspired tenacious loyalty among their officers and
men; in the case of Dietrich and Bittrich, senior Waffen-SS officers (each
man commanded an SS *panzerkorps*), their presence at Rommel's side
would have shivered the SS, and in doing so eliminated any hope that the
Nazi regime could have mounted an effective resistance to the *fait accompli*
which Rommel intended to present to them.

  But what was it Rommel hoped—intended—planned—to do? There is very
clear-cut evidence, in Rommel's own words, of the broad outlines of his
grand design to end the war in the West and bring down the Nazi regime.
First and foremost, assassination would have played no part in Rommel's
undertaking: unlike, say, the French or the Russians, the Germans have never
regarded assassination as a viable political tool, and, as a result, they have
never been very good at it—witness the several bungled attempts on Hitler's
life from 1938 to 1944. Assassination is a very messy process, which violates
the Teutonic sense of *ordnung*, but more importantly, it violates the political
process, as an attack on the office holder is simultaneously seen as an attack
on the office itself: while Hitler was not the state, he was the head of state,
thus an assault on his person was also an assault on the dignity and integrity
of the state. As Rommel saw it, and declared most emphatically to his son
Manfred in one of the last conversations they would ever have, "The attempt
on Hitler was stupid. What we had to fear with this man was not his deeds,
but the aura which surrounded him in the eyes of the German people." A
dead Hitler would have been a martyr, a rallying point for the fanatical mi-
nority possessed of just sufficient strength to plunge Germany into a civil
war even as she was being assailed east and west by the Soviets and the Allies.
A marginalized Hitler, on the other hand, one deprived of office and power,
would have been a far less potent and moving figure, shown to be so ineffective that he was unable to retain his position or authority.[303]

  That such was Rommel's intent for Hitler and his cronies was made
clear in early July 1944, when Rommel confided to General Heinrich Eberbach, Geyr von Schweppenburg's replacement as commander of Panzer
Group West, that "Germany's only possible hope in getting off reasonably
well lies in doing away with Hitler and his closest associates as soon as possible." Later, again speaking of Hitler, Rommel would tell Eberbach that

"there is nothing else to be done but to make an armistice, at once if possible, and if necessary take steps against his government, in case they weren't sensible enough to give the order." Rommel's choice of verb, *umgelegt*, in this conversation with Eberbach was revealing, for while it does translate as "doing away with," it does so in the sense of setting aside, discarding, or relegating to insignificance a person or thing, rather than an intent to violently dispose of them.[304]

A few months later, Rommel laid out for Manfred what was at the heart of his strategy for making an end of the war in the West. The armistice of which he had spoken to General Eberbach was the first and absolutely fundamental step in the process. "The revolt [against the Nazis] should not have been started in Berlin, but in the West," he told Manfred. "What could we have hoped to achieve by it? Only, in the end, that the expected forcible American and British occupation of Germany would have become an unopposed march-in, that the air attacks would have ceased, and that the Americans and British would have kept the Russians out of Germany. As for Hitler the best thing would have been to have presented him with an accomplished fact."[305]

There it was: Rommel hoped to negotiate a straightforward ceasefire in the West, with nothing like any of von Stauffenberg's demands and preconditions, in order to allow the Allies to overrun Germany and hopefully meet the Soviets while the advancing Red Army was still short of German soil. It was an audacious plan, as bold as any operation of which he had conceived in France or Libya, and yet there was a core element of genius in it that defied rational explanation. For decades the whole idea was derided by historians as unworkable, little more than wishful thinking, the conventional wisdom holding the entire concept as little more than madness, given what was assumed to be the solidarity of the Nazi regime; and yet it may have been an inspired madness, as it is coming to be understood that Nazi Germany was nowhere near so monolithic as was once believed. There is certainly no reason to assume that the sort of *sauve qui peut* deal-brokering, scrambling for personal survival and the salvation of private empires which marked the final collapse of the Third Reich in April 1945 would not have occurred in autumn 1944 had the Allies suddenly flooded across the Rhine and into the Reich. It may well be that Rommel was actually counting on something very like that taking place.

This is not to say that there was not considerable naivety in Rommel's plan. There were certain assumptions he made about the nature of the Anglo-American-Soviet coalition which, while neither unreasonable nor illogical, were nevertheless flawed. The first was that the Allies recognized a distinction between "Germans" and "Nazis." It was a given that, for ideological reasons, the Soviets would regard the two as synonymous, but Rommel had no idea how successful had been the efforts of Dr. Göbbels in presenting to the world the view that all Germans were united behind Adolf Hitler and wholly embraced National Socialism. As a result, the British and American people, and for the most part their governments as well, were fully convinced that Nazism had permeated every level of German society. Experience would prove that such distinctions were real and meaningful, and millions of Germans would come to resent that the Allies did not immediately recognize them as such, but in the summer of 1944 to the Allies the "Germans" and "Nazis" were both "the enemy," and the hair-splitting could wait until the war was won.

The second false assumption was that the Allies would make some sort of common cause with the Germans in keeping the Soviets at arm's length. The British might well have been receptive to the idea, given Prime Minister Churchill's long-standing mistrust of the Soviets and Britain's firm opposition to Bolshevik expansionism since 1919, but President Franklin Roosevelt would have been far more likely to oppose such a proposal, as the Allied demand for Germany's unconditional surrender, first put forward at Casablanca in January 1943, had originated with him, and he might well be loathe to have to repudiate himself. Still, it is difficult to conceive of the British and Americans not rushing at the opportunity to end the war in autumn 1944; there were, nonetheless, a myriad of issues, many of them complex and interrelated, that would have prevented such an undertaking from being the relatively straightforward operation Rommel apparently believed it would be. However it might have turned out, it would not have been a simple process of "opening the floodgates" and letting the Allies roll into Germany, bringing a swift end to the bloodshed and destruction.

Ultimately, of course, none of this ever happened or had an opportunity to take place. Rommel's plan never stood a very good chance of success in any event, as it would have relied on a greater reservoir of goodwill among the Allies than they actually possessed. Rommel might have been respected, even admired, by Allied officers and some Allied politicians, but while he had indeed fought a "war without hate" in North Africa, the rest of the world had not followed his example. There was far too much animosity and mistrust on both sides to overcome for the fighting to have simply ceased as Rommel hoped it would have done. Yet if it showed nothing else, Rommel's plan for a ceasefire in the West demonstrated his determination to see the needless death of Germans and the pointless destruction of Germany come to an end, and in that showed where his true loyalties lay. Germany no longer possessed the ability to win this war, it was Adolf Hitler who was prolonging the conflict, and Erwin Rommel was unwilling to be an accessory to further slaughter. He had unflinchingly spoken this truth to Adolf Hitler, something few other German generals would ever dare to do. Truth, when it was something the Führer did not wish to hear, most especially from the man who was Germany's most popular hero, equated to treason. Though the field marshal had never been part of von Stauffenberg's plot, in Hitler's mind he had acquired the same taint, so that when the Gestapo began its manhunt for the July 20 conspirators, Adolf Hitler would have a score to settle with Erwin Rommel.

CHAPTER FIFTEEN

THE DEATH OF A FIELD MARSHAL

Cowards die many times before their deaths.
The valiant never taste of death but once.
—JULIUS CAESAR, Act II Scene 2

For almost four days following the crash, Rommel lay in a drug-induced fog at the Luftwaffe hospital at Bernay. His survival was considered by expert neurologists to be near miraculous: he had suffered a quadruple skull fracture, an injury so traumatic it would kill most men outright. There was no sign of cerebral hemorrhaging, and in his conscious moments Rommel was lucid and seemed to have full motor control. That was the good news; the bad news was that the lesions on his brain made it impossible for him to open or move his left eye, left him deaf in his left ear, created problems with his equilibrium, and caused him severe, almost debilitating, headaches at night.

On July 22 Speidel and Ruge came to visit Rommel for the first time. Rommel being Rommel, he did his best to convince them both that he was far less severely injured than in fact he was, and that he would soon be fit enough to resume his duties as commander of Army Group B. Speidel, knowing that his commanding officer would have insisted no matter what the doctors advised, briefed Rommel on the situation in Normandy; the news was not good, of course, as the German perimeter around the Allied bridgehead continued to grow ever more brittle with casualties continuing to mount and replacements only a fraction of losses. Despite the field marshal's theatrics, both he and his officers knew he was far from fit, and even if he were there was nothing he could have done to prevent the debacle in France everyone knew was coming.

Rommel was transferred to the much larger hospital at Le Vésinet, just outside Paris, on July 23, where he proved to be a particularly cantankerous patient. Despite his problems with balance and vision, he repeatedly insisted on getting out of bed and trying to walk about; not until one of his surgeons came into his room, produced a human skull, courtesy of the hospital's pathology laboratory, and shattered it with a hammer, remarking that this was the sort of battering Rommel's own skull had undergone, did he subside. He dictated a letter to Lucie the day after his arrival at Le Vésinet, saying

> I'm in the hospital now and being well looked after. Of course I've got to keep quiet until I can be moved home, and that won't be for another two weeks yet. My left eye's still gummed up and swollen, but the doctors say it will get better. My head's still giving me a lot of trouble at night, but I feel very much better in the daytime.[306]

Speidel and Ruge continued to be frequent visitors; they were reluctant to discuss the July 20 assassination attempt with Rommel, although he learned of it just before being transferred to Le Vésinet. Ruge and Hauptmann Lang, both of whom, unlike Speidel, had not known in advance about the plot, were convinced that Rommel, when he was told of the *attentat*, had been just as startled as they.

No official announcement had yet been made about Rommel's injuries, the O.K.W. apparently believing that there was still sufficient potency in his name, both to bolster German morale and encourage caution and hesitation among the Allies, to maintain the fiction that he was still in command in Normandy. A terse, rather impersonal message from the Führer that arrived at Le Vésinet on July 24—"Accept, *Herr Feldmarschall*, my best wishes for your continued speedy recovery"—was the only acknowledgment by Hitler of Rommel's injury. Some may have taken this as an expression of Hitler's displeasure with Rommel, but the fact was that the Führer was utterly preoccupied at that moment with the identification and arrest of the surviving conspirators from the July 20 bomb plot. His attentions—and suspicions—had not yet turned toward Rommel.[307]

Rumors about Rommel were circulating, however: a radio broadcast by the BBC at the end of July announced that Rommel had been gravely wounded in an air attack and might possibly have died as a consequence. This spurred him into calling an impromptu meeting on August 1 with a collection of German war correspondents; having managed to shrug his way into his old Afrika Korps uniform tunic, complete with decorations, he firmly assured the gathered reporters that the rumors of his recent demise had indeed been greatly exaggerated, and that he was going to prove far tougher to kill than the British would like to believe. Even so, he was still a very sick man—the daily briefings and conferences with Speidel, Ruge, Lang, and Templehoff, despite their formality, were merely gestures of courtesy, something the pragmatist in Rommel grudgingly recognized; his doctors insisted that it would be no less than three months before Rommel would be fit for even limited duty. Meanwhile, he was able to keep himself occupied for a time with establishing that his recent injuries entitled him to the rare—and thus highly prized—Wound Badge First Class; the award was confirmed on August 7. Though there was still a deep depression on the left side of Rommel's forehead, his left eye was still swollen shut, and he continued to have problems with balance, there were no indications of permanent brain injury, and thus nothing to be accomplished for his recovery by remaining at Le Vésinet; thus on August 8 he was cleared to be evacuated to Herrlingen, where he would continue to mend.

BUT EVEN AS Rommel was returning to his home, events had been unfolding in Normandy, Paris, and Berlin which would soon overtake, then overwhelm him.

On July 25, the American First Army broke out of the Normandy perimeter at the town of St. Lo, and, exactly as Rommel had predicted in his memoranda to Hitler, the entire Normandy front collapsed like a house of cards. Outnumbered four-to-one in infantry and better than twelve-to-one in tanks, with absolutely no air support, the defenders had no chance of ever stopping the Allied attack: the German reserves had all been committed to holding the Normandy perimeter. Despite several fiercely fought actions, no cohesive defense was possible: by the time Rommel was packed off to Herrlingen, the German Seventh Army had ceased to exist; before the month of August was out, four Allied Armies—two American, one British, and one Canadian—had reached the Seine River. The Seine had been the Allied objective for D+90, that is, 90 days after the D-Day landings; they reached it in 86.

In Paris Field Marshal von Kluge did his best, but he was fighting a battle no general, however skilled and experienced, could have won—the Germans had too many disadvantages. The worst, of course, was Hitler's obsession with holding every square yard of ground—his refusal to acknowledge the wisdom, let alone the necessity, of strategic withdrawals—which played right into the Allies' hands; his demands that the German defenders hold their positions at all costs had not delayed the Allies' advance by so much as one day; instead it needlessly pinned valuable German forces in place, where they could be enveloped, cut off, and eliminated or taken as prisoners of war at the Allies' leisure. What made the situation more difficult still for von Kluge and the other generals in the West who were now trying to salvage something from the wreckage was the knowledge that a cloud of suspicion hung over every senior officer in the Wehrmacht, so that none now dared show the slightest hesitation in carrying out the Führer's orders, or appear to question their wisdom.

Adding to von Kluge's problems was the disarray in his command structure created by the July 20 *attentat*—a disarray compounded in no small part by the growing suspicions in Berlin that von Kluge himself may have been involved. When news of Hitler's apparent assassination reached Paris, the commander of the German occupation forces in France, General Karl-Heinrich von Stülpnagel, ordered the arrest of SS and Gestapo personnel in Paris, a prearranged part of the conspirators' plan to mobilize the German Army in the West in support of their coup. He had previously approached von Kluge, seeking to enlist the field marshal in the *putsch*—how much von Kluge knew, when he knew it, and how much support, if any, he initially offered the conspiracy, is still uncertain. But when it became clear that Hitler had survived the assassination attempt, von Stülpnagel was unable to convince von Kluge to support the conspirators. Instead, the field marshal dismissed von Stülpnagel from his staff, and privately urged him to try to escape to the Allied lines. Rather than take advantage of the confusion at the front and allow himself to be swept up as a prisoner of war, von Stülpnagel tried to brazen it out in Paris, but was recalled to Berlin on July 26; once there, he was certain, he would be arrested by the Gestapo: to prevent this, he attempted suicide near Verdun, but succeeded only in blowing his eyes out of his head. Despite his injury, he was indeed taken into Gestapo custody where, delirious with pain and rambling in semi-coherence, he murmured Erwin Rommel's name. This was the first indication of any possible connection between the July 20 conspirators and Rommel.

The Gestapo grew more suspicious after von Stülpnael's Luftwaffe liaison officer, Oberstleutnant Cäsar von Hofacker, was arrested the same day that his superior departed Paris. Von Stülpnagel's actions the night of July 20 had implicated both of them; when it was confirmed that Hitler had survived the assassination attempt, they knew that arrest, conviction, and execution were all but inevitable. They had not only been involved in von Stauffenberg's plot almost from the beginning, they were key participants in the entire undertaking, von Stülpnagel of course as the commander of the occupation army in France, and von Hofacker as the liaison between the Berlin and Paris branches of the conspiracy. Consequently they were privy to the names of most of the men involved; the two officers did their best to destroy whatever documentary evidence existed, in the hope of protecting other members of the conspiracy.

While von Stülpnagel may have muttered Rommel's name in a pain-induced delirium, hardly admissible evidence even by Gestapo standards, von Hofacker was perfectly lucid when he spoke of the field marshal to his Gestapo interrogators. Exactly what he said and under what conditions he said it is still unclear, as the files and records of both von Hofacker's *and* von Stülpnagel's interrogations vanished late in the war or sometime shortly after the end of the conflict. Second-hand accounts of von Hofacker's ordeal vary wildly, ranging from claims that he was subjected to intense physical torture to assertions that the Gestapo resorted to sophisticated psychological techniques in drawing information out of the Luftwaffe colonel. On the face of it, the latter seems more credible, as von Hofacker, although condemned to death alongside von Stülpnagel by the People's Court—the Volksgerichtshof—on August 30, would manage to survive another four months in Plötzensee Prison before the Gestapo decided that they had wrung out of him every scrap of useful information to be had.

There was one small problem with the information von Hofacker provided—just how useful was it, really? Von Hofacker was a keenly intelligent man, more so than most of his interrogators, who, while not stupid, were unused to matching wits with a clever customer who already knew his life was forfeit. Von Hofacker appears to have been playing a deep game with the Gestapo, offering up names, inferences, red herrings, always providing just enough valid information to ensure that the Gestapo would continue to find him useful, his willing cooperation a ploy to buy time, in the faint chance that he could last long enough for the Allies to overrun Germany and—he hoped—liberate him. If true, it should not be construed to mean that he was lacking in courage: on the contrary, such was a game that only the most courageous—and desperate—men would have dared to play. When led before the Volksgerichtshof, an experience which reduced most defendants to a state of near panic, he was openly defiant and aggressive—a stance which required considerable moral courage.[308]

The Volksgerichtshof—the People's Court—was the ultimate Nazi travesty of justice. It was an extra-constitutional court, that is, it was not bound in its processes or procedures by any legal or constitutional restraints: there was no presumption of innocence, while defendants were denied legal counsel as well as any opportunity to present a formal defense; it was given jurisdiction over cases involving "political offenses," as determined by the Gestapo. Presiding over the Court was Roland Freisler, an indifferent lawyer of no great intellect but a fanatical Nazi, a borderline psychopath who enjoyed offering up from the bench long, vulgarity-strewn harangues of defendants as well as humiliating them personally. Freisler, who alone decided and delivered the verdicts, almost always came down in favor of the prosecution; invariably the penalty for a finding of "guilty" was immediate execution: all of Germany knew the Volksgerichtshof as "kangaroo court."

The trials of the accused July 20 conspirators were Freisler's finest hours: the defendants were brought into the court unwashed and unshaven, dressed in ill-fitting, shabby clothes not their own, denied belts or suspenders for their trousers; in the case of Field Marshal von Witzleben, his false teeth were taken away, allowing Freisler the opportunity to mock the general for his poor diction and ridiculous appearance. By turns derisive, sarcastic, incredulous, raging, Freisler heaped his scorn on the defendants, like a predator playing with its prey, knowing that their fates had been decided before they had ever walked through the doors of the court. (At one point Freisler's conduct became so outrageous that official complaints against him were filed by other German judges, who felt that he was diminishing the overall dignity of German jurisprudence.) Few defendants ever scored points in return on Freisler—most who did were among the July 20 conspirators. Von Witzleben was one of them, bellowing back at the judge that "You may hand us over to the executioner, but in three months' time our disgusted and harried people will bring you to book and drag you alive through the dirt in the streets!" Von Hofacker was another, shouting down Freisler to damn Hitler and declare that he only wished he could have carried out the assassination attempt himself. When the foregone death sentence was handed down, however, instead going straight to the hangman, as had his superior, von Stülpnagel, von Hofacker was remanded back to the Gestapo for further interrogation.[309]

Only one man, short of Hitler himself or the Reichsführer-SS, Heinrich Himmler, could have kept von Hofacker alive at this point: SS-Obergruppenführer Ernst Kaltenbrunner, the chief of the Reichssicherheitshauptamt—the Reich Main Security Office, or RSHA—which was responsible for defending the Reich from all enemies within and without Germany's borders by means of espionage and counterespionage; the Gestapo was one of the office's departments. One of the few German intellectuals to embrace National Socialism, Kaltenbrunner often intimidated many of his fellow Nazis not only with his intelligence, but also with his utter ruthlessness; it was those traits which were now called upon to identify all of the July 20 conspirators, as well as those who had aided and abetted them. Ultimately he proved more than a match for von Hofacker, who finally ran out of stories to tell and so outlived his usefulness, going to the gallows on December 20, 1944. Somewhere in early August, though, the Luftwaffe colonel mentioned the name "Rommel"; in doing so, he set in motion the final chain of events that led to Rommel's suicide.

Because no transcripts, notes, or files of von Hofacker's interrogations survived the war, it is impossible to know exactly what he said regarding Rommel, or in precisely what context. Whatever he offered up lacked any real substance, however, that much can be inferred from what transpired once the information was in Kaltenbrunner's hands. A report was submitted to Himmler on August 14 which contained whatever statements von Hofacker had made about Rommel; Himmler handed the report to Hitler the following day. Intriguingly, the Führer, who was already convinced that General Hans Speidel, Rommel's Chief of Staff, had been deeply involved in the July 20 conspiracy, did not demand immediate direct action against Rommel. The SS began round-the-clock surveillance of the field marshal and his villa in Herrlingen, but nothing further was done.

In the same report Kaltenbrunner had included whatever information von Hofacker had offered up concerning Field Marshal von Kluge and whatever part he may or may not have played in the conspiracy. Whatever was there was sufficient to cause Hitler to immediately relieve von Kluge as *oberbefehlshaber West* and demand his immediate return to Berlin; he was replaced by Field Marshal Walter Model, a defensive genius who had repeatedly saved the German front from disintegration in Russia. Despite the enduring myth that Rommel was Hitler's favorite general, Model had for some time been the new apple of the Führer's eye—known as "the Führer's Fireman," he was expected to work the same sort of miracle against the Americans and British that he had performed against the Red Army.

In taking over von Kluge's command, Model also became the commanding officer of Army Group B, Rommel's former posting, and inherited Rommel's staff. In the same directive dispatching Model to Paris, Hitler also ordered Speidel to return to Berlin, where he would be confronted with the evidence of his complicity in the July 20 *attentat* ("The interrogations prove that he was in it up to his neck!"); Model immediately protested, insisting that Speidel was too useful to be spared for such nonsense: whatever evidence had been produced which incriminated Speidel had to be a fabrication by over-zealous Gestapo agents. Hitler, however, was adamant, sending out General Hans Krebs, another veteran of the Russian Front, as Speidel's replacement.[310]

While informing Krebs of his new assignment, Hitler made a revealing comment about Rommel, saying, "What he did was the worst possible thing a soldier can do in the circumstances: he tried to find some other way out than the purely military. At one time, you know, he was also predicting imminent collapse in Italy; yet it still hasn't happened. Events proved him wrong there and justified my decision to leave Field Marshal Kesselring in charge. . . . I regard Rommel, within certain limitations, as being an exceptionally bold and also a clever commander. But I don't regard him as a stayer, and everybody shares that view." Evidently Rommel had ceased to be Hitler's darling long before any rumors reached the Führer regarding Rommel's possible complicity in the attempted *putsch*. Favoritism, then, would clearly have little, if anything, to do with the fate that in two months' time Hitler would decree for Rommel.[311]

At the same time, the final denouement of Field Marshal von Kluge's personal drama, and Hitler's reaction to it, also spoke to the substance of any evidence Kaltenbrunner and Himmler had against Rommel. When informed of his relief as OB West and his orders to report to Berlin, von Kluge immediately assumed that he was—or soon would be—formally implicated in the July 20 conspiracy. While being driven across France, von Kluge composed a final letter to the Führer, urging Hitler to make peace, as befitting a great man, then, on August 20, near the ancient fortress city of Metz, he bit into a cyanide capsule and died. Upon receiving this news and reading von Kluge's letter, Hitler's only comment was, "There are strong reasons to suspect that had not von Kluge committed suicide he would have been arrested anyway." Eventually sufficient evidence would be gathered to show that von Kluge had not only assured the conspirators of his support once Hitler was dead, but that he had also been involved in a similar but abortive plot in 1943. Yet when he had von Hofacker's information in his hands, Hitler only had "strong reasons to suspect" von Kluge—strong enough to convince him to take the precaution of relieving von Kluge, yet insufficient to convince him of the field marshal's guilt. This from the man who had screamed that he wanted the officers who tried to take his life "hanged like cattle," and whose favorite entertainment until his final days would be watching films of those sentences being carried out. Whatever "evidence" von Hofacker gave Kaltenbrunner, it must have been very thin indeed, otherwise there was no explanation for the comparatively mild reaction: given how completely Rommel had lost Hitler's confidence, together with the Führer's suspicions of Speidel, had von Hofacker offered up anything more than the vaguest hearsay and innuendo about any role Rommel might have played in the conspiracy, Hitler's response would have been swift and brutal.[312]

This is no small point, for von Hofacker's "evidence" has long put forward as the foundation for Hitler's belief that Rommel had been part of the assassination conspiracy, and thus led directly to the Führer's demand that the field marshal make the choice of taking his own life or facing Freisler and the Volksgerichtshof. Instead, the von Hofacker material would do no more than provide the pretext through which, two months later, Rommel would be presented with that choice as a consequence of actions which, to Adolf Hitler, constituted an entirely different form of treason.

NONE OF THIS was known to Rommel, isolated as he was in his villa in Herrlingen. When he arrived there on August 8, Lucie and their butler, Rudolf Loisl, were unable to hide their shock at his appearance; taking a perverse pleasure in their discomfiture, Rommel grinned at them and declared, "So long as I don't have to carry my head under one arm, things can't be all that bad." Captain Herman Aldinger, a lifelong friend of Rommel who had served under him in France and North Africa, was also there to greet him: with a bit of discreet string-pulling he had been posted to Herrlingen as Rommel's aide. Similarly, Manfred was transferred from his duties with a Luftwaffe antiaircraft battery to a temporary "staff" position with his father; when he arrived home, he found the elder Rommel in his study, a black patch covering his left eye, his face still showing evidence of the damage done on July 17. The father decided to be forthright with the son, informing Manfred that he was still unsteady on his feet, suffered from severe headaches, and his left eye was still not working properly. "But it will get better," he assured the young man.[313]

In the days and weeks that followed, Rommel spent endless hours in candid conversations with Lucie and Manfred. He made no attempt to disguise his bitterness at Hitler's repeated interference with the defense against the Allied bridgehead on Normandy, remarking that "My functions . . . were so restricted by Hitler that any sergeant major could have carried them out. He interfered in everything and turned down every proposal we made. . . . If we pulled a division out, Hitler ordered us to send it straight back. Where we ordered 'Resistance to the last round' it was changed from above to 'Resistance to the last drop of blood.' When Cherbourg finally surrendered, they sent us a court-martial adviser. That was the sort of help we got."[314]

Now more than ever it seems, Rommel was convinced that the war must be brought to an end—immediately—telling Manfred, "There is no longer anything we can do. Every shot we fire now is harming ourselves, for it will be returned a hundred-fold. The sooner it finishes the better for all of us." With Model now in command of Army Group B and his command staff broken up, Rommel no longer received the courtesy briefings he had been given in France. Given all that he already knew, however, he found little reason to believe that the situation would—or could—improve in France: as Rommel saw it, the Wehrmacht's collapse was irrecoverable; all that remained to be decided was whether or not Germany would lose the war faster than the Allies could win it. (As events turned out, Rommel underestimated the resiliency of the German Army, at least in the short term. As the Allies began to outrun their supplies in September 1944, their advance slowed, allowing Model time to establish defensive lines on the Rhine River in the north and the Westwall—what the Allies called the "Siegfried Line"—in the south. In the long term, of course, even despite the Ardennes offensive in December, Germany's last great offensive of the war, the Wehrmacht's situation was indeed hopeless.)[315]

Some news of events in France reached Herrlingen, of course, though not always in a timely manner. For some weeks Rommel was aware that von Kluge had disappeared, apparently in mid-August, but it would be close to the end of September before he learned his fellow field marshal's true fate. Manfred found his father sitting in the study, ashen-faced, having read a dispatch just delivered by courier. "Von Kluge is dead," Rommel announced. "We now know what happened to him. Hitler sacked him and gave orders for him to return to the Reich. On the way he poisoned himself in his car. . . ." He never gave any indication to Manfred, however, as to whether or not he saw von Kluge's fate as significant to himself, or if it disturbed him in any way.[316]

Rommel *was* disturbed by the fact that his house was under surveillance, by either the SS or the Gestapo, and he was openly suspicious of their purpose. He was taking daily walks in the woods near his house as part of his rehabilitation; Manfred always accompanied him as his father at times was still unsteady on his feet. It was just before setting out on one of these excursion that Rommel suddenly announced: "Look here, Manfred, it's possible that there are certain people round here who would like to do away with me, quietly and without too much fuss, by an ambush in the wood, for instance. But I don't intend to let it put me off my walk. So for the time being, we'll take pistols. You can have my 8mm. These individuals don't hit anything with their first shots. If shooting does start, the thing to do is to fire blind towards where it's coming from, and they'll almost always go for cover or aim badly." There would be no gun battles in the forest near Herrlingen, but the entire Rommel household was left feeling distinctly uneasy knowing that their every move was being watched.[317]

What Rommel did not know—could not know—was that by the end of September he had fallen completely from Hitler's favor. Rommel had always been noted for being blunt and outspoken in his opinions—after the Allies were securely ashore in Normandy, he became increasingly indiscreet in voicing them, especially his belief in the need to make a separate peace in the West. It was impossible for the Führer to have been unaware of what Rommel was saying—indeed, Rommel had voiced exactly such sentiments directly to Hitler on more than one occasion—and had Rommel not been taken out of action by an RAF fighter he would have soon been relieved as commander of Army Group B, most likely by Model. Rommel's pessimism had been rapidly nearing the point of being out-and-out defeatism, in which case he had to go, lest his attitude begin to permeate his entire command; other generals had already relieved for less blatant offenses. Serendipitously, from Hitler's perspective, the Royal Air Force solved the problem before it became necessary for him to act.

Initially, the Führer saw no reason to take any further steps against Rommel—the severity of the field marshal's injuries had completely marginalized him, and Hitler could always claim that lingering side-effects and complications rendered Rommel permanently incapable of accepting a new command. Jodl offered an indirect confirmation of this when he noted in his diary that "The Führer is now looking for a new Commander-in-Chief West. He plans to question [Rommel] after his recovery, and then quietly order him to retire." But Rommel proved a tougher bird than Hitler had imagined him to be, and as he recovered, there was no doubt that he was lucid and becoming increasingly fit, which presented a problem for the Führer. Even where he to remain assigned only to the pfficers' reserve, a pool of senior officers without a current command assignment, Rommel, by dint of his stature and reputation within the Wehrmacht, would remain a focal point for aggressive, independent-minded officers who, under Rommel's influence, might come to share his pessimism and be inclined to act on it.[318]

By this time, late in the summer of 1944, Adolf Hitler was already deeply lost in an increasingly murky world of delusion and paranoia, where strategic realities no longer signified for him, and he increasingly believed in the validity of his own propaganda. No matter how severe the defeats that were inflicted upon his armies, east or west, he remained convinced that his soon-to-be-unleashed "wonder weapons" would miraculously turn the tide against the Soviets and the Allies and present Germany with ultimate victory. The cause of National Socialism was righteous, and destiny, which was becoming Hitler's new touchstone, would never allow him to go down to defeat. He regarded anyone who did not share in his confidence as having succumbed to *pessimismus und defätismus*—pessimism and defeatism—and increasingly he began to regard both as *verräterischen*—treasonous. Those members of his staff and entourage who were not already utter sycophants quickly transformed themselves into enthusiastic "yes men," while field commanders learned to "adjust" their reports in order to make them more palatable to the Führer—and less hazardous to themselves. For someone who had outlived their usefulness to Hitler, as Rommel evidently had done, repeatedly declaring that the only way to save Germany was to make peace regardless of the political consequences, was downright foolhardy.

Rommel, though, had never been particularly good at keeping his mouth shut, especially where his opinions about Adolf Hitler's strategic decisions were concerned, ever since El Alamein; in Normandy he had become even more outspoken, and now in convalescence, he showed no inclination toward restraint. What Rommel had repeatedly attempted to do was tell Adolf Hitler the truth: that the war was lost, and Hitler's duty as the leader of the German nation was to make the best possible peace, no matter what the personal cost. But by the summer of 1944 truth was something that Adolf Hitler had little if any interest in hearing, let alone accepting; in the last year of the Third Reich, speaking truth to power almost invariably held fatal consequences for the speaker. The same day that Speidel was arrested, September 7, Rommel received an unexpected visitor, Karl Strölin, who had been a key member of von Stauffenberg's plot but whose complicity was never discovered by the Gestapo. Strölin, who of course knew that Rommel had *not* been a part of the conspiracy, was startled to see a pistol sitting on the field marshal's desk, and asked Rommel why it was there. Rommel replied rather cryptically, "I'm not afraid of the English or the Americans, only of the Russians—and the Germans." When Eugen Maier, the local Party boss, called on Rommel a few days later, he confided to the field marshal that the senior SS officer in Ulm had been overheard openly stating that Rommel no longer believed in Germany's ultimate victory.[319]

"Victory?" Rommel was incredulous. "Why don't you just look at the map? The British are here, the Americans here and the Russians here. What is the use of talking about victory?" Maier retorted by saying that what was needed was faith in the Führer. Rommel in reply made no effort to hide his derision.

"That damned fool! You can't have any faith in him at all! Since I saw the Führer in November 1942 I've come to realize that his mental faculties have steadily declined."[320]

Maier begged Rommel to show a little more discretion, saying, "You should not say things like that, Field Marshal—you will have the Gestapo after you, if they are not after you already." Unknown to Rommel, Maier was being disingenuous: when he returned home, he wrote a detailed account of his conversation with Rommel and forwarded it to his boss, Reichsleiter Martin Bormann, Hitler's personal secretary. This incident was, apparently, the last straw for Hitler: the time had finally arrived for him to settle his score with Rommel.[321]

The upshot came on October 4, 1944, when the case of General Hans Speidel was presented to the Ehrenhof der Wehrmacht, the German Army's Court of Honor; while it was Speidel's fate which was supposedly being decided, the appropriate decision by the Court could provide a suitable pretext for Hitler to move against Rommel. A board of army officers, all of *generalleutnant* rank or higher, the Court of Honor was a curious relic of German military tradition and the diabolical deal done by the Reichswehr in the wake of the Night of the Long Knives. Among the conditions laid down in exchange for the pledge of support which the army offered Hitler was a stipulation that, as they had been since the days of Frederick the Great, officers, whether active duty or retired, were subject only to military law, and not to any civilian legal authority—including the Gestapo. In extraordinary circumstances where it was deemed appropriate to consider remanding an army officer to civilian authorities, the Court of Honor would render a judgment of the evidence against the accused officer: if it was sufficiently damning, the accused would be expelled from the army and thus subject to civilian justice. For those officers accused of being complicit in the July 20 *attentat*, expulsion from the army assured that they would stand "trail" in the Volksgerichtshof, with almost certain execution by hanging to follow. A distinctly Nazi twist to these Court of Honor proceedings was that the court was required to consider only evidence against the accused as presented by the Gestapo, but was never permitted to view the evidence itself; the veracity of the Gestapo's evidence could not be questioned, no defense of any kind was permitted, and accused officers were not allowed to appear before the court. Thus the court's only function was to decide if the Gestapo's version of the evidence was sufficient to warrant expulsion of the accused from the ranks of the *offizierkorps* and the Wehrmacht.

Sitting in judgment of Speidel were Field Marshal Wilhelm Keitel, known to his fellow officers as *Lakeitel*—the Lackey—for his fawning devotion to the Führer, Field Marshal Gerd von Rundstedt, Colonel General Heinz Guderian, General Karl-Wilhelm Specht, and Lieutenant General Heinrich Kirchheim. The case against Speidel, presented to them by Kaltenbrunner, hinged on the question of what Speidel knew about the conspiracy and to whom—if anyone—he spoke of it. According to Kaltenbrunner, von Hofacker had met with Speidel on July 9 at Rommel's headquarters at La Roche Guyon and discussed the pending assassination attempt; later that same day, Kaltenbrunner claimed, Speidel spoke with Rommel at length on the subject. When the charge had been put to him prior to the Court of Honor proceedings, Speidel did not deny that either conversation took place; he insisted, however, that he had discharged his moral and legal responsibilities by providing Rommel, his superior, with the information passed on by von Hofacker; the implication, strongly inferred by Kaltenbrunner, was that Rommel, for whatever reasons of his own, had failed to inform Berlin.

The Erhenhof reached its decision fairly quickly, and imparted a curiously Solomonic air to it. The charge of treason—by way of not alerting the Gestapo to his conversation with von Hofacker—was "not proven;" however, that was not, technically, the same thing as an acquittal: while having informed Rommel of what had been said by von Hofacker may have fulfilled Speidel's obligations under army regulations, he had failed in his moral duty to inform Berlin directly. For this, Speidel was discharged, though not expelled, from the army; and though it kept him out of the clutches of Freisler and the Volksgerichtshof, it did not keep him out of Gestapo custody—he would spend the next seven months in prison, eventually being liberated by the advancing Allies at the end of April 1945. For Rommel, however, the consequences of the court's verdict was far more immediate and catastrophic. A message from Keitel was delivered to Rommel on October 7, directing him to report to the O.K.W. in Berlin, where information would be awaiting him of the details of his new command posting; a special train would be laid on to bring him to the capital from Ulm. Upon reading the message, Rommel snorted and said to Manfred, "I'm not that much of a fool. We know these people now. I'd never get to Berlin alive." He said much the same thing to his former naval aide, Admiral Ruge, now in an enforced retirement of his own, who came calling on 11 October: "I should not go to Berlin, I would never get there alive. I know they would kill me on the way and stage an accident." He confided the same thing to his neurologist, Professor Albrecht, who immediately certified Rommel as being unfit to travel.[322]

When he called Berlin to inform Keitel of Dr. Albrecht's determination, Rommel was shunted over to General Wilhelm Burgdorf, the chief of the Army Personnel Office. Burgdorf pressed Rommel to come to Berlin, but the field marshal was adamant. He asked Burgdorf point-blank why it was necessary for him to do so; Burgdorf repeated that it was imperative that Keitel discuss Rommel's new assignment with him personally. Rommel continued to demur and eventually rang off; the uneasiness and foreboding he had first felt when he saw the watchers in the woods grew more sharply defined. On October 13, Rommel and Lucie drove into Ulm to pay a call on Oskar Farny, a longtime friend and comrade from the Great War, and onetime Reichstag deputy. In his own way as outspoken as Rommel about ending the war, Farny expected to be arrested at any moment— indeed two of his closest associates were taken into custody by the Gestapo while he and Rommel talked—but he was certain that Rommel's reputation and popularity would insulate him from any reprisals.

"You're wrong," Rommel told him, "Hitler wants to get rid of me and he'll leave no stone unturned to do it."[323]

As if in confirmation of Rommel's words, when he and Lucie returned home, their butler, Rudolf Loisl, informed the field marshal that in his absence General Burgdorf had called again, with a message that on the morrow, between noon and 1:00 P.M., two general officers from Berlin would be calling on Rommel.

The first visitor to the Rommel household on October 14 was no visitor at all—Manfred, who had returned to duties as a Luftwaffe auxiliary at the beginning of October, had been given a few days' leave from his antiaircraft battery. Rushing back to Herrlingen, he arrived home early in the morning, just as his father was sitting down to breakfast. Rommel, though happy to see his son once again, was characteristically blunt, telling Manfred that "At twelve o clock today two Generals are coming to see me to discuss my future employment. So today will decide what is planned for me; whether a People's Court or a new command in the East."

"Would you accept such a command?" Manfred asked, either having misunderstood the first part of his father's statement, or else choosing to ignore it.

"My dear boy, our enemy in the East is so terrible that every other consideration has to give way before it. If he [Stalin] succeeds in overrunning Europe, even only temporarily, it will be the end of everything which has made life appear worth living! Of course I would go."[324]

Rommel spent the rest of the morning in conversation with Manfred, then later with Lucie, and at one point asked Aldinger to assemble all of the directives and orders issued by Army Group B during the Normandy campaign. Shortly before noon Rommel changed out of his civilian clothes and into his old Afrika Korps tunic, his favorite, carefully pinning on all of his decorations, ribbons, and service badges. Punctually at noon a dark green car pulled up at the front gate: in it were General Burgdorf and Generalleutnant Ernst Maisel, along with Major Anton Ehrnsperger, Maisel's aide, and an SS sergeant named Doose, the driver. The two generals asked to speak to Rommel privately.

Once behind closed doors in the field marshal's study, Burgdorf came straight to the point: Rommel had been accused of being complicit in the attempt on Hitler's life. Burgdorf had with him copies of the interrogations of von Hofacker, von Stülpnagel, and Speidel, along with a letter written by Keitel, ostensibly dictated by Hitler himself. In the letter, the Führer gave Rommel an impossible choice: if he believed himself innocent of the allegations against him, then Rommel must report to Hitler in person in Berlin; refusal to do so would be considered an admission of guilt, his arrest, trial, and conviction would be inevitable. As a final gesture of respect, the Führer had allowed that Rommel be permitted to take his own life; Burgdorf had brought a fast-acting poison with him for that purpose.

There was no mention of Rommel's case first being put to the Wehrmacht's Court of Honor, a curious omission if Rommel were indeed being brought to book as part of von Stauffenberg's conspiracy, less surprising if all Hitler truly sought was to be rid of this troublesome field marshal. Bergdorf's next words to Rommel confirmed the truth: in exchange for Rommel's life, the Führer offered his assurances that Rommel's "treason" would never be made known to the German people, instead the official story would be that he died of complications from his wounds; he would be given a state funeral, Lucie would receive the full pension of a field marshal's widow, and there was to be no application of the *sippenhaft* against Rommel's family or members of his household. There was even talk of a monument being raised to Rommel at some future date. Implicit in Burgdorf's words, however, was the assurance that if Rommel proved uncooperative, the reprisals against his family would be swift, severe, and complete.

At that Rommel understood everything: one way or the other, Hitler wanted him dead and safely out of the way—even if he denied the charges against him, Rommel would never reach Berlin alive. The accusation of complicity in the attempted coup on July 20 was the fiction through which, if Rommel refused to cooperate, his family would be punished. It was the one threat that Hitler could make which he could be certain Rommel would not greet with open defiance. Even so, the field marshal must have toyed with the idea: he spent nearly an hour closeted with Burgdorf and Maisel before excusing himself and slipping quietly into Lucie's bedroom.

Seeing a look on her husband's face that had never been there before, she blurted out, "What is the matter with you? Has something happened? Are you ill?"

"In a quarter of an hour I shall be dead." Rommel said simply; this was not the time or place to mince words. "I'm accused of having taken part in the attempt to kill Hitler. . . . They say that von Stülpnagel, Speidel, and von Hofacker have denounced me. It's the usual trick. I've told them that I don't believe it and that it cannot be true, but the Führer has given me the choice of taking poison or being dragged before the People's Court. They have brought the poison: they say it will take only three seconds to act." At first Lucie begged him to fight back, but Rommel gently refused, explaining that it was all an elaborate theater staged by Hitler: no matter what he said or did, he would never live to reach Berlin. There was time for one final, silent embrace—Erwin and Lucie had been together for 33 years, married for 28, and there were no words for a moment like this. Finally Rommel stepped away and turned to leave the room; Lucie burst into tears behind him. At that moment Manfred, overcome with teenage curiosity and oddly confident that Burgdorf and Maisel had not, after all, come to arrest his father, walked in.[325]

Without preamble, Rommel repeated to Manfred what he had just told the boy's mother. The young man would never forget his father's calm when he declared, "To die by the hand of one's own people is hard. But the house is surrounded and Hitler is charging me with high treason. 'In view of my services in Africa,' I am to have the chance of dying by poison. . . . If I accept, none of the usual steps will be taken against my family, that is, against you. They will also leave my staff alone."

"Do you believe it?" Manfred asked.

"Yes," Rommel replied. "I believe it. It is very much in their interest to see that the affair does not come out into the open. By the way, I have been charged to put you under a promise of the strictest silence. If a single word of this comes out, they will no longer feel themselves bound by the agreement. . . . Call Aldinger, please."[326]

Aldinger, a decorated combat veteran and fiercely loyal to Rommel, wanted to fight it out with Burgdorf, Maisel, and whatever escort had accompanied them, but Rommel dissuaded him, explaining that even if they made their escape from the house, they had nowhere to go: their only hope would be reach the front, and it was too distant for them to have any chance of getting there before they were caught. "Besides," he said, "I have Lucie and Manfred to think of. It's all been prepared to the last detail. I'm to be given a state funeral. I have asked that it should take place in Ulm. In a quarter of an hour, you, Aldinger, will receive a telephone call from the Wagnerschule reserve hospital in Ulm to say that I've had a brain seizure on the way to a conference. Now, I must go, they've only given me ten minutes."

Downstairs, Burgdorf and Maisel were waiting outside by the car. After shrugging his way into the black leather coat which had become his trademark in Normandy, Rommel thrust his hand into an inner pocket in his tunic and withdrew his wallet; the thrifty Swabian to the end, he held it out to Aldinger, saying "There's still 150 marks in there. Shall I take the money with me?"

"That doesn't matter now, *Herr Feldmarschall*," said Aldinger. Rommel nodded, thrust the wallet back into his pocket, settled his peaked officer's hat on his head, then took a firm grip on his marshal's baton. Together, the trio walked through the front door—Lucie could be heard sobbing in her room upstairs. When they reached the waiting car, Burgdorf and Maisel greeted Rommel with the *Hitlergrüsse*, the stiff-armed Nazi salute that by decree had replaced the traditional military salute in all of Germany's armed forces in the days following the July 20 *attentat*. Rommel merely raised the tip of his baton to the brim of his hat, then thrust it under his arm and turned to Manfred and Aldinger, wordlessly offering his hand to each one last time.[327]

Climbing into the back seat of the car, Rommel was joined by the two generals, while Major Ehrnsperger took his place in the front next to the driver. The car quietly drove off from the house, sped up the hill and disappeared round a bend a quarter-mile away. Rommel did not look back; Manfred never saw his father again.

The driver, Sergeant Doose, drove down the lane for perhaps five minutes, then at a signal from Burgdorf, pulled off the road and stopped. Maisel, Ehrnsperger, and Doose left the car at this point, leaving Burgdorf alone with Rommel. Whatever words, if any, passed between the two men in the car at that point remain unknown: there are no records of Burgdorf ever recounting exactly what happened in those moments. After a short time had passed, he waved to his companions, who returned to the automobile, there to find Rommel slumped forward and, in the words of Sergeant Doose, "sobbing." The field marshal was clearly seconds away from death; Doose, unsettled by the indignity of the moment, raised Rommel back into a sitting position and replaced the hat that had fallen from his head. Rommel by now was gone.

What happened next simply continued the charade stage-managed by Hitler, done solely to give the appearance of satisfying the requirements of German law, no more. Burgdorf and Maisel rushed Rommel to the Wagnerschule Hospital in Ulm, where an attending physician, a Dr. Meyer, was directed to attempt reviving the field marshal. The doctor complied, but as he later recalled, "One look at the man and it was obvious he had not died a natural death." Meyer then officially pronounced Rommel dead, and suggested an autopsy; Burgdorf immediately quashed that idea: "Don't touch the body," he said firmly. "Everything is being handled from Berlin."[328]

As Rommel had promised, a telephone call was placed to the house in Herrlingen—the caller was Major Ehrnsperger—where Aldinger took it and was given the news that Field Marshal Rommel had suddenly and unexpectedly died of a cerebral hemmorhage while being driven to the train station in Ulm, where he was to have boarded a special express for Berlin. Ehrnsperger informed Aldinger that he was returning to the house in Herrlingen, and when the major arrived, Aldinger informed him that Frau Rommel was unable to receive visitors. Ehrnsperger, perhaps embarrassed by his part in this travesty, did not insist, and together he and Aldinger drove into Ulm, where Aldinger saw his old chief's body. The following day, he would return, this time with Lucie and Manfred: both wife and son would be struck by the expression of contempt on Rommel's face; Rommel's sister, Helene, who had come down from Stuttgart that morning, would likewise remember the look on her dead brother's countenance. General Maisel, still lurking about in some official function or other, attempted to offer official condolences to Lucie; she pretended not to see him or his outstretched hand.

Rommel's body lay in state in his home for two days, draped in a Nazi flag and guarded by two officers from the garrison in Ulm. While it did so, messages from all over Germany of sympathy and condolence began arriving at Herrlingen. Some were formalities, some were not, some were very different than what might have been expected from the sender. The official communiqué from Adolf Hitler was almost perfunctory, even brusque:

> In the Field
> 16 October 1944
>
> Accept my sincerest sympathy for the heavy loss you have suffered with the death of your husband. The name of Field Marshal Rommel will be forever linked with the heroic battles in North Africa.
> ADOLF HITLER

Field Marshal Model, who had replaced Rommel in France as commander of Army Group B, issued a special Order of the Day, praising Rommel as ". . . one of the greatest German commanders . . . with lightning powers of decision, a soldier of the greatest courage and unequaled dash. . . ." Gastone Gambarra, an Italian lieutenant general who for two years had fought under Rommel's command in Libya, cabled Lucie to say "[Rommel] will always live in the hearts and minds of those who had the honor to see him, as I did, always calm and fearless under fire."[329]

Perhaps the most unusual communication sent to Lucie at this time came from, of all people, Reichsführer-SS Heinrich Himmler, commander of the SS and chief of all the Reich's police and security apparatus, including the Gestapo. Himmler personally sent Alfred Berndt, Rommel's longtime and well-liked companion in France in 1940 and then in North Africa, to pay a call on Frau Rommel. Berndt, by now a *hauptsturmführer* (captain) in the Waffen-SS, conveyed to Lucie Himmler's dismay at her husband's fate: he had no part in it and would have never condoned it had he known what was to happen. Oddly enough, there may be a glimmer of truth in this, given that in six months' time Himmler himself would be attempting to negotiate a separate peace of his own with the Allies—he probably imagined that Rommel would have been very useful in such a situation, not realizing the contempt in which Rommel held him and his minions.

The state funeral that was promised to Rommel did indeed come about, carried out on October 18 in the town hall of Ulm with all of the excess pomp and neo-pagan pageantry at which the Third Reich excelled: flags and banners, wreaths, black-crepe-draped eagles, honor guards, flickering candles, Rommel's awards, decorations, and baton on display. The histrionics reached their crescendo when Field Marshal von Rundstedt gave the funeral oration in the name of Adolf Hitler, who, "as head of the army has called us here to say farewell to his field marshal, who has fallen on the field of honor." This exercise in hypocrisy was only exceeded a few moments later when von Rundstedt, knowing full well where Rommel's true loyalties had always lain, uttered the perfectly ridiculous assertion that Rommel had been a "tireless fighter in the cause of the Führer and the Reich . . . imbued with the National Socialist spirit. . . ." Rommel's heart, von Rundstedt reassured his audience, "had always belonged to the Führer."[330]

Lucie and Manfred, faithful to the pledge of silence extorted from Rommel by Hitler, said nothing to contradict any of this, even though they both knew how far from the truth were any of von Rundstedt's utterances. At the funeral with Lucie and Manfred was Vice-Admiral Ruge, who also knew the truth about Rommel. The occasion was especially bitter for Ruge:

after Rommel's injury in the strafing attack, the admiral had considered urging the field marshal to allow himself remain in the hospital at Le Vésinet, rather than be evacuated to Herrlingen, and so be captured by the advancing Allies; Ruge was certain that Rommel had more to fear from his "friends" than from his foes. "I never plucked up the courage to suggest it," he would later remark. Now as he sat in Ulm's town hall and listened to von Rundstedt's banalities, he wondered if the world would ever know the truth about the fate of the man who had once been his commanding officer—and his friend.[331]

Hitler, as events played out, was as good as his word—almost: Lucie duly collected her pension; she, Manfred, Aldinger, and the remainder of Rommel's household and entourage were not interfered with in any way by the Gestapo, SS, or any other police or security services; and the fiction that Rommel had died of his wounds was carefully maintained, preserving the integrity of his memory and legacy for the German people. Lucie would survive the war and the chaos which followed Germany's collapse and surrender, and live to see a new Germany, the Federal German Republic—popularly known as West Germany—emerge from the wreckage of the Third Reich. She would also see her beloved Erwin become an icon for the new German army, West Germany's Bundeswehr, the exemplar and ideal of the modern German officer, both in ability and conduct; Rommel's stature in the eyes of his former enemies would grow in equal measure: his operations and tactics, both offensive and defensive, would become essential course material in the military academies of both the United States and Great Britain. Lucie would never remarry, and died in Stuttgart on September 26, 1971.

Manfred was discharged from the Luftwaffe a few weeks after his father's death; that was the end of his military "career": after the war he became a lawyer, working for the state of Baden-Württemberg. In 1974 he was elected *oberbürgermeister*—Lord Mayor—of Stuttgart, a post he would hold for the next 22 years. He became a popular figure in Germany, and was noted for his very public—and very genuine—friendships with Major General George S. Patton IV, U.S. Army, and David Montgomery, 2nd Viscount Montgomery of Alamein—respectively the sons of General George S. Patton, Jr., and Field Marshal Bernard Montgomery. Retiring from politics in 1996, Manfred Rommel embarked on a second career as an author, and was always in great demand as a public speaker as well. Manfred died in Stuttgart on November 7, 2013, leaving behind a wife and a daughter.

THE SOLE EXCEPTION to Hitler's assurances to Rommel's family was the promised memorial—it never materialized. It was not until early March 1945 that Lucie was even approached on the subject of a monument to Rommel, by which time, of course, the whole idea was rendered preposterous by circumstances. A letter arrived at her home from the chief design officer for German Military Cemeteries, announcing that

> . . . the Führer has given me an order to erect a monument to the late Field Marshal Rommel, and I have asked a nummber of sculptors to submit designs. I enclose some of them. At this point it would not be possible to erect this monument or to transport it. One can only make a model. . . . I think the Field Marshal should be represented by a lion. One artist has depicted a dying lion, another a lion weeping, the third a lion about to spring. I prefer the last, myself, but if you prefer a dying lion, that too can be arranged.
>
> The slab can be made immediately, as I have special permission from Reichsminister Speer. Generally monuments cannot now be made in stone. But in this special case it can be made and quickly shipped.[332]

The absurdity of the proposal only served to underscore for Lucie the injustice done to her husband; the widow in the house in Herrlingen could never be bothered to respond.

No monuments to Erwin Rommel would ever be raised in Germany. It is very easy to believe that, if he somehow knew of it, Rommel would be pleased by that fact: for all of his vanity, he was never guilty of ostentation. He would be quite satisfied, certainly, with the knowledge that his ashes are buried, as he had wished, in the cemetery at the Community Church of St. Andrew in Herrlingen, and that Lucie rests beside him. They lay together in a shaded, secluded corner of the cemetery. Like all German churchyards this one is immaculately cared for; well-laid paving stones lead a visitor from the street back to the rear of the cemetery, then make a left turn, and descend three steps to where Erwin and Lucie lay. Marking the resting place of Rommel's ashes is a wooden post, topped with an oversize Iron Cross; beneath the cross are carved representations of the Knight's Cross with Oak Leaves, Swords, and Diamonds, along with the *Pour le Mérite*. The inscription is simple, reading only

> General Feldmarschall
> ERWIN ROMMEL
> 1891–1944

THE LEGEND OF THE DESERT FOX

One must not judge everyone in the world
by his qualities as a soldier: otherwise we
should have no civilization.
—Erwin Rommel

Seven decades have passed since Erwin Rommel took his own life, and yet he remains perhaps the most compelling personality of the Second World War. Handsome, dashing, intelligent, charismatic, a brilliant commander and a born leader of men in combat, he came close to being the heroic ideal of the romantic warrior. He was no such thing, of course, and he would have snorted derisively at anyone who suggested that he was. In his own eyes, Erwin Rommel, Field Marshal Rommel, was a soldier; that was all to which he aspired, and for himself he could conceive no higher calling.

What he could not have denied, and would have made no effort to do so, was that if the man was not extraordinary, the life he lived, by any standard, was precisely that. Few men ever fought on so many battlefields, or displayed not only courage, but also intelligence, initiative, and leadership, all to a remarkable degree. His military career spanned four decades and two world wars; in both wars he was awarded his nation's highest decorations for valor; in both wars he was severely wounded. At the height of his career he was the most famous and popular general in the Fatherland, and "Rommel" was a household name around the world. For two years he was the nemesis of the British Empire, and such was his fame and stature that even when his wounds removed him from the battlefield, his name was still used to intimidate the enemy. Yet he was more than just a soldier, the man was not made by the uniform: he was also a loving and devoted husband and father, and a firm and loyal friend; and if pressed would have acknowledged that he was as proud of those accomplishments as he was any of his medals, stars, or ribbons. Such was his life that, as the functionary from the Propaganda Ministry said to him, "*Wenn es auch nicht stimme, wäre es doch gut, wenn es stimmen würde*" ("Even if it is not true, it ought to be!").

As a tactician, Rommel's reputation is secure: he was a born virtuoso, a master of the battlefield—he was only ever restricted by the limitations of circumstances, of logistics or superior orders, never by a lack of imagination. Few generals in history have ever displayed a greater talent for improvisation and invention: Rommel was especially fortunate that his was the imagination of a skilled—even gifted—technocrat. Though his First World War experiences in France, and especially at Monte Matajur and Longarone in Italy, profoundly shaped his concept of operations, the wellspring of Rommel's genius precedes those battles. It can be found in the love of machinery and things mechanical, along with the accompanying ingenuity, which he displayed in his youth. Years later it stirred his adult imagination so that he was able to marry his understanding of machines with the German Army's tactical doctrine of infiltration, and then envision what his mechanized units, with their panzers, armored cars, and half-tracks, and the Luftwaffe in support, could do if unleashed. This set him apart from many of his fellow officers in the Wehrmacht, particularly those of the General Staff, for whom Rommel had only disdain, who never could never quite fully comprehend the capabilities *or* the limitations of the formations of steel behemoths which they commanded, and who would then ask either too much or too little of them. The reverse of this facet of Rommel's character was that while understanding the limits of machines, he was prone at times to forget the limits of what men could endure or achieve, and sometimes asked too much of them.

But what the panzers *could* do was not always the same as what they *should* do, and it was here that Rommel's lack of a higher military education became something of a liability. For all that he despised the General Staff and the arrogant, opinionated officers it produced, he lacked that fundamental understanding of war that transcended combat which was the core of *Generalstab* teaching and doctrine. It can be rightly said that Rommel understood *how* to fight a war—but *why* that war was being fought would probably have eluded him. The upper reaches of strategy, where military operations and political considerations begin to blur together, were always beyond him. Likewise, he could understand the strategic premise behind a particular campaign, but not necessarily see the broader, and longer implications and consequences of that campaign; had he been able to do so, he would have taken the opportunity in 1941, when he was Hitler's favorite, to impose on the Führer and press his case for additional forces in North Africa, where their presence would have exerted a strategic influence on the whole of the war entirely out of proportion to their numbers. It would be precise—and fair—then to say that Rommel lacked an understanding of the "philosophy" of war.

Certainly he was no scholar of military conflict. In the spring of 1944 Lieutenant General George Patton began studying the preparations William the Conqueror undertook in 1066 for the invasion of England, in the hope of discovering what old Roman roads William's soldiers took through Normandy on their way to the coast. Patton believed that, if those same roads still existed, after nine centuries of use they could be counted on to be routes for an army advancing *out* of Normandy. It is impossible to imagine Rommel doing the same thing in an effort to anticipate the axis of the Allied thrust out of the *bocage* country. It simply never would have occurred to him. War to Rommel was a trade, rather than a profession. He was like the builder who could construct an imposing edifice, rather than the architect who could design it.

Yet that did not mean he could not be a craftsman, and at his given trade, Erwin Rommel was very much so. The proof of that assertion lies not in any one of his battles, but rather in the regard in which the men under his command held him. Rommel inspired confidence in his soldiers—some middle and senior officers may have quibbled with his tactics but for the most part the average *soldaten*—the "ground-pounders"—respected and admired him, and because they knew that he rarely threw away their lives foolishly or for no purpose, their trust and confidence in him impelled them to fight harder, take risks, act and think imaginatively and aggressively. To their dying days, thousands of his "Africans" would proudly declare, "I fought for Rommel!" It was a devotion that was more than merely lip service; it paid real dividends in battle. History is replete with commanders, some who have been beloved by their soldiers (Bonaparte, Alexander, Julius Caesar, Lee), others greatly respected (Hannibal, Wellington, Grant, Patton), for whom the ordinary soldier was willing to "try harder." Such soldiers turn their commander into a consistent winner, or at the very least a very tough fighter whom no one wants to cross without having overwhelming strength.

The reverse is true as well: commanders who lack for their soldiers' confidence will tend to be losers unless they have massive numerical superiority (such were most of the British generals in North Africa, for example, including Montgomery, or any of the Italian generals in Libya). Soldiers who do not trust their commanding officers are hesitant soldiers, and soldiers who hesitate at best lose battles, at worst are dead. The bond of trust between Rommel and his soldiers was an essential ingredient to Rommel's success as a military commander.

But if Rommel lacked the academic credentials of a formally trained strategist, this is not to say that Rommel's understanding of strategy did not grow in depth as well as breadth as his career progressed. Quite the contrary: his grasp grew to the point where he could sometimes perceive and comprehend strategic opportunities as well as realities that others missed completely. In France in the summer of 1940, he was the impulsive, thrusting division commander whose eagerness to advance at times imperiled his own command or upset the plans and calculations of his superiors; by the time he took command of the Afrika Korps, he was still as aggressive as ever, but his grasp of the fundamental differences between war on the Continent and war in the Western Desert—where his opponent's army became the primary objective and the mere holding of territory was often irrelevant—was so immediate as to be almost instinctive, and was never matched by any of the British generals who opposed him. He has been taken to task for lacking the strategic foresight to coordinate his operations in Libya in the summer of 1941 with the Wehrmacht's invasion of the Soviet Union, but that was hardly Rommel's fault, as he had been kept ignorant of the existence of Operation *Barbarossa* until it actually began.

Facing defeat at El Alamein, Rommel's strategic horizons expanded even farther, as he immediately understood that once Panzerarmee Afrika no longer presented a threat to Cairo and the Suez Canal its further presence in Egypt—or even in Libya—made it a liability to the overall Axis strategy in the Mediterranean. He kept his under-equipped, overachieving army intact through a retreat of 1,100 miles, disregarding time and again directives, even commands, to stand firm at some intrinsically indefensible position that a self-proclaimed military genius a thousand miles distant decreed be defended to the last man. He halted only when he reached a point where the Panzerarmee Afrika would once again be relevant, where the enemy could not simply pass it by but would be compelled to confront it. Of all the generals, marshals, and national leaders bruiting about their competing strategies for the Axis forces in Tunisia, Rommel's offering was at once the most promising and realistic. He alone seemed to understand that the tens of thousands of veteran German and Italian soldiers under his command would be a priceless military asset in defending Italy against the inevitable Allied invasion—and that squandering such an asset in trying to maintain a meaningless bridgehead in Tunisia was military folly at its most egregious. Meanwhile, fighting a determined delaying action in Tunisia as those troops were gradually withdrawn to Sicily and Italy could have severely disrupted the Allies' strategic timetable for operations on the Continent. It would then be the Axis' sheer good fortune that none of the Allied generals possessed the same degree of imagination as Rommel when the time came to invade the Italian peninsula: they refused to take the sort of risks which Rommel would have regarded as prerequisites to success. The Allied leaders' lack of Rommel's calculated audacity did not automatically invalidate his strategic thinking."

It would be in France, in 1944, that Rommel's true vindication as a strategist would come about, not via brilliant preparation for the cross-Channel invasion, or in dazzling maneuvers against the Allied forces once they were ashore, but rather in how precise and correct he was in anticipating the impossibility of a German victory once the Allies had established their bridgehead. It was Rommel alone who foresaw how Allied command of the air would cripple the operations of the Wehrmacht's mobile forces, or how inexorably the British and American way of war, systematic, methodical, utterly practical and coldly impersonal, would overwhelm the German defenders, no matter how good their individual weapons or how how courageous their individual efforts. It was Erwin Rommel, perhaps the most pragmatic of all of Germany's generals in the Second World War, who alone recognized how the Allies' utterly pragmatic approach to war would ensure Germany's defeat.

Legend has cast Rommel in the role of an overarching genius, which he certainly was not. He was not, for example, invincible, even if his defeats came about more through his enemy's materiel superiority than via brilliant planning. Claude Auchinleck twice proved, during *Crusader* and then at First Alamein, that Rommel could be outmaneuvered and outfought. He can be seen—honestly—as ambitious, somewhat grasping, eager—even anxious—for professional recognition and popular acclaim, even if achieved through the work of others, and sometimes at their expense. While he never took counsel of his own fears, he easily fell into melancholy when events went against him; and he was not above blaming other people for problems that were at least in part of his own making. Yet, even if Rommel cannot be fairly described as *"une chevalier, sans peur et sans reproche,"* what can never be denied is the integrity of Erwin Rommel's moral stature as a man. By turns and sometimes in combination brilliant, generous, petty, jealous, shrewd, headstrong, arrogant, shortsighted, visionary, loving, and dispassionate, he was, at his core, a decent human being. That is no mean verdict, no small epitaph, no damnation by faint praise, for in the moral black hole that was the Third Reich, Rommel alone among the ranks of the Wehrmacht's field marshals never compromised his honor, never chose to conveniently look away, never fell victim to the rationale of "just obeying orders" which ensnared, shamed, and ultimately damned so many of his colleagues, when he confronted the horror and immorality of the Nazi regime and the man who led it.

Which leads directly to the great conundrum of Erwin Rommel's life. Whether bidden or not, the question will eventually rear its ugly head: why did Erwin Rommel serve such an evil master—and serve him so well?

There are those who would condemn Erwin Rommel out of hand simply for the cause he served, the banner he followed. But to paint him with the brush of Nazism is to misunderstand him, along with millions of other Germans like him, who first mistook the swastika as a symbol of hope and change, only to then watch its metamorphosis into a representation of malignant evil. In Hitler's case the devil did indeed assume a pleasing shape, and Rommel took that shape at face value, not only at first, but for years to follow. And this is where any accounting of the life and legacy of Erwin Rommel encounters rocks and shoals, because the very legitimate question arises here as to whether or not through his tacit approval of Hitler Rommel became complicit in the crimes of the Third Reich.

The difficulty in arriving at a meaningful answer to the question lies in maintaining a genuine sense of perspective, never losing sight of the fact that none of the German people, ardent Party members or passionate foes of the Nazi regime or some shading in between, whether soldiers or civilians, were prescient. Thus it is an immense challenge for anyone with a knowledge of the events of 1933 to 1945 but who is two generations removed from them to steer away from exercising flawless hindsight. The Wannsee Conference, the *Endlösung*, the *Nacht und Nebel* decrees, the Sonderkommando and Einsatzgruppen, the death camps, medical experiments, slave labor—all seem inevitable in retrospect, as innumerable decisions and actions, large and small, whether by Hitler, his henchmen, or petty, anonymous Party hacks and bureaucrats, conspired and converged to produce such a monstrous construct. But "inevitability" is a gross oversimplification, a convenient—even lazy—expedient in accounting for Adolf Hitler and the Third Reich. However much the evil of the Nazi regime may appear as given after the fact, the stark truth is that none of it was inevitable before: they were the consequences of the actions of human beings, not outcomes dictated by the laws of nature.

Perhaps the most insidious is the belief, sometimes expressed, other times implied, that the Germans should have recognized the potential for the abuse of power inherent in as authoritative a regime as the Third Reich, should have anticipated that it would happen. But to ask them to have done so is to ask of them powers of foresight such as have never been given to any people, anywhere, at any time in history: any regime in any government, no matter what that government's form, structure, or delimited powers, can be abusive of its power if it is determined to be so. Undeniably the Nazis were an authoritarian regime, and thus potentially more prone to such abuses, but the Germans as a people were comfortable with, even embracing of, living under an authoritarian government as they had never known anything else—aside from the brief experiment of the Weimar Republic, the essence of German government had only ever changed in degree, never in fundamental nature. The Germans followed—obeyed—Hitler and the Nazis because it was their nature as a people to obey: they never had any example, any experience, to follow to do otherwise. Recognizing the truth of the German people's experience does not exonerate them, for the Nazi regime was history's greatest exercise in immorality, and morality is—and must be—based on more than experience; but it does explain them, and so makes them understandable, if not comprehensible.

In the end, it becomes clear that while Erwin Rommel was guilty of a *kolossal* blunder in judging the nature and character of the man who led the Third Reich, in doing so he was simply one of millions of Germans who were deceived by the greatest lie ever told by history's greatest practitioner of the Big Lie. And in the end, Rommel paid a far, far greater price than did the millions of those Germans who had been, if not Hitler's willing executioners, then at least his willing accomplices. And it was a far, far greater price than that paid by many of his colleagues who were accomplices, or at least accessories, to some of the worst excesses of the Nazi regime. It is impossible to imagine Erwin Rommel emulating his one-time rival, Ferdinand Schöner, for example, in ordering the summary execution of German soldiers for mere suspicion of cowardice or desertion, or turning a blind eye, in the manner of von Rundstedt or von Manstein, to the atrocities of the SS that were aided and abetted by men under their command.

From the perspective of Hitler and the Nazis, Rommel's besetting—and ultimately damning—sin was his integrity. Too many of the toadies and sycophants surrounding the Führer were attempting to sugarcoat the bitter strategic realities that came with each new day. They strove to cast the latest defeat, the most recent disaster, as a minor tactical set-back or a strategic move necessitated by the need to buy a little more time in which to allow the much-anticipated wonder weapons to reach the front, where, under the guidance of what was sure to be Hitler's inevitable stroke of strategic genius, the Allies—east and west—would be routed in a *triumph Germaniae*. Ultimately the reason why Erwin Rommel was forced to take his own life was not because he had countenanced tyrannicide—he hadn't—but rather because he chose to commit what was an even greater crime in Nazi Germany in the summer of 1944: he spoke Truth to Power. Erwin Rommel had to die because he chose to tell the truth to Adolf Hitler.

Dulce et decorum est pro Patria mori. So wrote Horace; Conington translated it thus: "What joy, for fatherland to die." And for Erwin Rommel, that is a far more suitable rendering than the traditional interpretation. "Joy" is most often translated into German as "*freude*," but it can also be rendered "*sich freuen*"—"glad." No sane man gladly takes his own life—and Erwin Rommel was one of the sanest men ever to walk the earth—but when confronted with the ultimate choice given him by Adolf Hitler, Rommel must have known a certain gladness, for if he was to die, he would be doing so for the Fatherland which he had served his entire life, at the same time that he was fulfilling the best tradition of *ritter*, *chevalier*, knight, warrior: defending at the last those he loved best—Lucie and Manfred.

———————

IN 1967 GENERALLEUTNANT Ernst Ferber of the Bundeswehr admonished young German soldiers to dismiss the idea of unconditional obedience to the head of state: their duty, he insisted, was to serve the German nation and the German people. Had he heard General Ferber's words, Erwin Rommel would have smiled and nodded in approval, for the general was encouraging those young men to follow the same path of loyalty to which Rommel had devoted his life—that of the true patriot.

He was, after all, a German.

ROMMEL — A TIMELINE

January 21, 1871 — Proclamation of the German Empire, Hall of Mirrors, Palace of Versailles.

November 15, 1891 — Birth of Erwin Johannes Eugen Rommel, Jr.

July 19, 1910 — Rommel joins the 124th Württemberg Infantry Regiment as an officer cadet.

March 1911 — Rommel posted to the *Königliche Kriegschule* (Royal Military Academy) in Danzig, Prussia. While there he is introduced to Lucia Maria ("Lucie") Mollin.

January 1912 — Rommel commissioned as leutnant (Second Lieutenant) in 124th Württemberg Infantry Regiment, posted to Ulm. While there he meets Walburga Stemmer.

January 1913 — Daughter Gertrud Stemmer born to Rommel and Walburga Stemmer.

March 1, 1914 — Attached to the 49th Field Artillery Regiment as a recruit instructor.

June 28–August 1, 1914 — Assassination of Archduke Franz Ferdinand; July Crisis; Germany, Austria-Hungary, France, and Russia mobilize their armies; Germany declares war on Russia. Rommel returns to regimental duties with the 124th Infantry.

August–September 1914 — Rommel's first combat experiences, along the River Meuse on the Verdun Front.

September 24, 1914 — Rommel wounded in the thigh, awarded the Iron Cross Second Class.

January 1915 — Rommel returns to duty with the 124th Infantry Regiment.

January 29, 1915 — Rommel leads an attack on French positions in the Argonne Forest; awarded the Iron Cross First Class.

May 23, 1915 — Italy declares war on Austria-Hungary; a subsequent declaration of war on Germany follows on August 28, 1915.

July 1915 — Rommel suffers a minor leg wound, his second combat wound of the war.

August 27, 1916 — Romania declares war on Austria-Hungary.

September 1915 — Rommel is given command of an infantry company in the II Battalion, 124th Infantry Regiment, and promoted to Oberleutnant (First Lieutenant)later that same month.

October 1915 — Rommel is transferred to the newly-formed *Württembergische Gebrigsbattaillon* (Württemberg Mountain Battalion) as a company commander.

Mid-December 1915–October1916 — Regimental duties with the Mountain Battalion in the Vosges Mountains of France.

October 1916 — The Württemberg Mountain Battalion is transferred to Romania.

November 1916 — Rommel sees his first action against the Romanians.

November 27, 1916 — While on leave, Oblt. Erwin Rommel marries Lucie Mollin in Danzig.

January 7, 1917 — The German attack on Gegesti.

Late January 1917–July 1917 — Withdrawn from Romania, the Mountain Battalion returns to the Vosges Mountains of France.

August 1917–October 1917 — The Mountain Battalion again is deployed to Romania.

August 19, 1917 — Rommel's company leads the successful assault on the crucial Romanian position of Mount Cosna. Rommel is wounded in the arm. For this injury he will be awarded the Silver Wound Badge in January 1918.

October 1917 — The Mountain Battalion is transferred to the Italian Front, where it takes part in the Battle of Caporetto (Twelfth Battle of the Isonzo).

October 24, 1917 — Beginning of the Austro-German assault on the Italian defensive line on Korlovat Ridge.

October 27, 1917 — The infantry *abteilung* led by Rommel captures Monte Matajur, the key to the Italian defense of the Korlovat Ridge.

November 1917 — Austro-German offensive continues, advancing up the Piave River.

November 10, 1917 — Rommel's abteilung captures the town of Longarone, for which Rommel is awarded the *Pour le Mérite* on December 18.

January 11, 1918 — Rommel is promoted to Hauptmann (Captain) and transferred to the Staff of LXIV Corps on the Western Front, where he will remain until the end of the war.

November 9, 1918 — Kaiser Wilhelm II flees to the Netherlands and the German Republic proclaimed.

November 11, 1918 — The Armistice is signed between the Allies and Germany

December 21, 1918 — Rommel is assigned to regimental duties with the 124th Infantry Regiment.

January 1, 1919 — Rommel is assigned to the 13th Infantry Regiment of the new German *Reichsheer* (popularly known as the *Reichswehr*) as a company commander.

August 11, 1919 — The adoption of the new German Constitution, popularly called the "Weimar Constitution," formally establishes the German ("Weimar") Republic.

June 28, 1919 — Under compulsion, Germany signs the Treaty of Versailles

September 1924 — Rommel is assigned to the Staff of II Battalion, 13th Infantry Regiment.

October 1928 — Walburga Stemmer dies of pneumonia.

December 24, 1928 — A son, Manfred, is born to Erwin and Lucie Rommel.

October 1, 1929 — Rommel is posted to the Reichswehr's Infantry School in Dresden as an instructor.

April 1, 1932 — Rommel is promoted to Major.

January 30, 1933 — Adolf Hitler is named Chancellor by President Paul von Hindenburg.

October 1, 1933 — Rommel is appointed commanding officer, 3rd (Jäger) Battalion, 17th Infantry Regiment.

June 30, 1934 — The purge of the SA (*Sturmabteilung*, the Nazi Party's strong-arm paramilitary force) takes place, becoming known as the "Night of the Long Knives."

August 2, 1934 — Upon the death of President von Hindenburg, Hitler combines the Chancellorship with the Presidency into a single position, *der Führer*. All members of the civil government and armed forces are required to swear an oath of personal allegiance (*Fahneneid*) to Hitler.

September 30, 1934 — Adolf Hitler meets Rommel for the first time, at a troop review in Dresden.

March 15, 1935 — Adolf Hitler announces that the German armed forces (Wehrmacht) will reintroduce conscription, his first abrogation of the Treaty of Versailles.

October 15 1935 — Rommel is posted to the Infantry School at the Potsdam War College as an instructor.

March 7, 1936 — In defiance of the Versailles Treaty, Hitler orders German troops into the Rhineland.

September 1936 — Rommel is assigned to command Hitler's military escort at the *Reichspartietag* (the Nuremburg Rally).

October 25, 1936 — The German-Italian military alliance ("Pact of Steel") is created.

February 1937 — Rommel is appointed the officer responsible for the unsuccessful paramilitary training program for the *Hitler Jugend* (Hitler Youth).

Summer 1937 — Publication of Rommel's account of his Great War experiences, *Infanterie Greift an* (*Infantry in the Attack*)

March 1938 — German annexation (*Anschluss*) of Austria.

September 1938 — The Munich Crisis; in response to Hitler's threat of war, France and Great Britain unilaterally cede the Czech Sudetenland to Germany.

October 1938 — Rommel is given command of Hitler's field headquarters during the occupation of the Sudetenland.

November 10, 1938 –Rommel is promoted to Oberst (Colonel) and appointed commandant of the Theresian Military Academy in Wiener-Neutstadt.

March 15, 1939 — Germany annexes the whole of Czechoslovakia, Rommel commands Hitler's military escort into Prague..

August 23, 1939 — German-Soviet Nonaggression Pact is signed, with secret clauses providing for a partition of Poland. Rommel is promoted to *Generalmajor* (Major General) and given command of the *Führerbeglietbrigade*, which guards Hitler's military headquarters.

September 1, 1939 — Germany invades Poland, beginning the Second World War in Europe.

February 15, 1940 — Rommel is given command of the 7th Panzer Division.

May 10, 1940 — Germany begins Fall Gelb (Case Yellow), the invasion of France and the Low Countries.

May 13, 1940 — 7th Panzer Division forces a crossing of the Meuse River, breaching the French main line of defense.

May 15, 1940 — Rommel is awarded the Clasp to the Iron Cross Second Class (indicates a second award).

May 21, 1940 — Rommel's first encounter with the British Army, as the B.E.F. counter-attacks at Arras. After fierce fighting, the British are turned back.

May 26, 1940 — Rommel is awarded the Knight's Cross to the Iron Cross.

May 27–31, 1940 — Battle for Lille; Rommel narrowly escapes death twice during the fighting.

June 10, 1940 — 7th Panzer Division reaches the English Channel at Dalles, near Dieppe, and surrounds the town of Sainte-Valery-en-

Caux, held by the 51st (Highland) Division. Italy declares war on France and Great Britain. Its ammunition exhausted, the 51st (Highland) Division surrenders two days later.

June 19, 1940 — 7th Panzer Division captures the Channel port of Cherbourg. This is Rommel's last action in France in 1940.

June 22, 1940 — France signs an armistice with Germany, bringing the Battle of France to an end.

Rommel and the 7th Panzer Division take up occupation duties.

September 9, 1940 — The Italian Tenth Army in Libya invades Egypt, advancing sixty miles before halting near Sidi Barrani.

December 9, 1940–February 7, 1941 — Operation *Compass*, the British offensive into Libya, which concludes with the surrender of the Italian Tenth Army to the British Western Desert Force at Beda Fomm, 700 miles west of Sidi Barrani.

February 9, 1941 — Rommel is promoted to *Generalleutnant* (Lieutenant General) and given command of two panzer divisions which will be sent to North Africa to reinforce and stabilize the Italians in Libya. These divisions will become the Afrika Korps.

February 12, 1941 — Rommel arrives in Tripoli, along with the lead elements of the 5th Light Division, one of the Afrika Korps' two panzer divisions.

March 20, 1941 — Rommel is awarded the Oak Leaves to the Knight's Cross.

March 25–May 4, 1941 — The Afrika Korps' first offensive against the British Army in Libya, and the first (unsuccessful) assaults on Tobruk.

May 15–16, 1941 — Operation *Brevity*.

June 16–20, 1941 — Operation *Battleaxe*, the first British attempt to relieve Tobruk.

August 15, 1941 — The Afrika Korps and its associated German units are designated *Panzer Gruppe Afrika* (Panzer Group Africa).

September 9, 1941 — Britain's Western Desert Force is re-designated Eighth Army.

November 18–December 10, 1941 — Operation Crusader, Eighth Army's successful attempt to relieve Tobruk. Rommel, the Afrika Korps, and the Italian divisions under his command are driven back to El Agheila, where their offensive had begun in March.

December 10, 1941 — Following the Japanese attack on the United States Navy at Pearl Harbor on December 7, Adolf Hitler, for "political reasons," declares war on the United States.

January 20, 1942 — Rommel is awarded the Swords to the Oak Leaves of the Knight's Cross.

January 21–29, 1942 — Rommel counterattacks out of El Agheila, driving Eighth Army back to the Gazala Line, west of Tobruk.

January 22, 1942 — Panzer Gruppe Afrika redesignated *Panzerarmee Afrika* (Panzer Army Africa)

May 26–June 21, 1942 — The Battle of Gazala.

May 28–June 5, 1942 — "*Der Hexxenkessel*" ("The Cauldron"), the decisive action of the Battle of Gazala.

June 21, 1942 — Tobruk is taken by the Afrika Korps. Within hours of the news reaching Berlin, Rommel is promoted to *Generalfeldmarschall* (Field Marshal).

June 22–July 1, 1942 — Rommel makes his final advance in North Africa, as the Panzerarmee reaches Alam Halfa and El Alamein.

July 1942 — The First Battle of El Alamein, Rommel's first attempt to drive Eighth Army out of the El Alamein Line.

August 30–September 5, 1942 — The Battle of Alam Halfa, Rommel's final (and unsuccessful) attack in the Western Desert Campaign.

September 19, 1942 — Suffering from a variety of health issues, Rommel leaves North Africa, turning over command of the *Panzerarmee* to General Georg Stumme.

October 23, 1942 — The Second Battle of El Alamein begins as Eighth Army attacks all along the El Alamein Line.

October 25, 1942 — General Stumme goes missing (he is later found dead of a presumed heart attack) and Rommel is recalled to North Africa, where he is able to temporarily contain the British attacks.

November 2, 1942 — Operation Supercharge begins: outnumbering the Axis armor by odds of 4 to 1, Eighth Army begins a heavy, set-piece assault on the northern end of the Axis line at El Alamein. Rommel asks Hitler for permission to withdraw to the more easily-defensible Halfaya Pass/Sollum position.

November 3, 1942 — Hitler replies to Rommel's request with an adamant refusal, demanding that the Afrika Korps and the Italian forces stand fast and fight to "the last man and the last round."

November 4, 1942 — Defying Hitler's commands, Rommel orders the withdrawal from El Alamein to begin.

November 8, 1942 — British and American forces land in French North Africa. The Allies are now closer to the main Axis supply base in North Africa (Tripoli) than is the *Panzerarmee*.

November 10, 1942–Janaury 26, 1943 — The Axis withdrawal from Libya and Cyrenaica. Despite overwhelming superiority in numbers and logistics, Eighth Army is unable to cut off Rommel's line of retreat.

January 26, 1943 — *Panzerarmee Afrika* occupies the Mareth Line in Tunisia.

February 19–21, 1943 — The Battle of Kasserine Pass, Rommel's last successful attack in North Africa.

February 23, 1943 — Rommel is given command of *Heeresgruppe Afrika* (Army Group Africa).

March 6, 1943 — The Battle of Medenine, the last battle Rommel would fight in North Africa.

March 9, 1943 — Rommel leaves Tunisia to take a much-needed medical leave in Germany; he never returns to North Africa.

July 10, 1943 — British and American armies invade Sicily.

July 15, 1943 — Rommel is given command of Army Group B and told to plan for a bloodless occupation of Italy should the Italians surrender to the Allies.

July 25, 1943 — Mussolini is deposed by the Italian Grand Council.

July 30, 1943 — Under Rommel's direction, German forces execute Operation Alarich, occupying Italy.

September 3, 1943 — Allied forces invade southern Italy; the Italian government sues for peace five days later.

November 21, 1943 — Rommel and his Army Group B headquarters are transferred to France, where he is placed in charge of completing the Atlantic Wall.

June 6, 1944 — The Allied invasion of Europe, Operation *Neptune*, begins with the British, Canadians, and Americans landing divisions on five beaches in Normandy.

June 6–July 17, 1944 — Rommel conducts the defense of Normandy.

June 29, 1943 — Rommel has what will be his final conference with Hitler, demanding that the Führer make peace with the Allies before Germany is destroyed. Hitler rebuffs him.

July 17, 1944 — Rommel is severely injured when Royal Air Force Spitfire fighters strafe his automobile near Sainte-Germaine-de-Montgommery.

July 20, 1944 — A bomb, placed by Wehrmacht officers engaged in an anti-Hitler conspiracy, explodes in the Führerhauptquartier (Führer's Headquarters) in East Prussia. Hitler is injured in the blast, but survives.

Early August 1944 — After two months of near-constant attacks by the Allies, the German front in Normandy disintegrates. Rommel is transferred from a hospital at Le Vésinet to his home in Herrlingen.

October 7, 1944 — Under suspicion of being complicit in the attempt to assassinate Hitler, Rommel is ordered to report to Berlin. Citing health reasons, he declines.

October 14, 1944 — Rommel, on the orders of Adolf Hitler, in order to avoid reprisals against his family, takes a quick-acting poison, and dies outside Herrlingen, Germany.

October 18, 1944 — Rommel's state funeral in Ulm.

September 26, 1971 — Lucie Rommel dies in Stuttgart, and is buried beside her husband in Herrlingen.

November 7, 2013 –Manfred Rommel dies in Stuttgart.

ENDNOTES

CHAPTER ONE: THE BIRTH OF A SOLDIER
1. Tuchman, *The Guns of August*, 8.
2. Irving, *The Trail of the Fox,* 10, 11.
3. Because the Imperial German Army was organized around the armies of the four kingdoms of the German Empire (Prussia, Bavaria, Saxony, and Württemberg), its organizational nomenclature was a bit complicated. The first number of any unit designation was its standing in the Imperial Army organization, the second, parenthetical number identified the unit's place in the order of battle of its parent kingdom. This numbering system was applied at the corps, division, and regimental level.
4. A corresponding tradition in the British Army at the time held that "Lieutenants can not marry, captains should not marry, majors may marry, and colonels *must* marry!"
5. Churchill, *The World Crisis, vol. 1*, 4.

CHAPTER TWO: THE GREAT WAR
6. Rommel, *Infantry in the Attack/Infantry Attacks*, 11.
7. Ibid, 11.
8. Ibid, 16.
9. Ibid, 20.
10. Ibid, 50.
11. Ibid, 54.
12. Ibid, 56.
13. Ibid, 51.
14. Ibid, 74–75.
15. Ibid, 80.
16. Ibid.
17. The *kampfgruppe* concept would utilize company- or battalion-sized units taken as needed from larger armor, infantry, or artillery units to create a combined-arms force whose organization and equipment were tailored to a specific operation or mission. In Romania and elsewhere, the Germans were groping toward this sort of operational doctrine at the same time they were developing their *Stosstrupptaktik*, or infiltration tactics. When the two concepts were combined, as they would be in 1939, the results were devastating for the enemy.
18. Rommel, *Infantry in the Attack/Infantry Attacks*, 121.

19. Ibid, 94.
20. Young, *Rommel The Desert Fox,* 23; Werner quoted in Irving, *The Trail of the Fox,* 17.
21. Rommel, *Infantry in the Attack/Infantry Attacks*, 102.
22. Ibid, 127.
23. Ibid, 137.
24. Ibid, 148.
25. Ibid, 150.
26 There is more than a bit of what old soldiers know as a "pissing contest" involved in the spat between Major von Bothner, Major Sprösser, and Oberleutnant Rommel. The Bavarian Life Guards were a self-proclaimed "elite," and like Guards regiments everywhere, had a tendency to look down their collective nose at "mere" line units. Given that the Württemburgische Gebirgsbataillon possessed a combat record every bit as distinguished as that of the Bavarians', Sprösser no doubt felt justified in putting the arrogant von Bothner in his place.
27. Rommel, *Infantry in the Attack/Infantry Attacks*, 159.
28. Like Rommel, Ferdinand Schörner would attain the rank of *feldmarschall* in the next war. Unlike Rommel, he would not be remembered as an honorable man: he would be tried and convicted of war crimes by both the Soviets *and* the Germans. The Soviet charges were for the most part the usual trumped-up rubbish through which Stalin exacted his vengeance on German officers (there is no evidence, for example, that Schörner ever aided and abetted the SS *Einsatzgruppen* in occupied Russia, as other German generals had done), but the German charges were far more serious. On page 50 of his book *The End*, historian Ian Kershaw describes Schörner as "a fanatical Nazi loyalist" who pandered to Adolf Hitler's wildest delusions in the closing days of the Third Reich, and who cheerfully carried out summary executions of German soldiers who were deemed as having left their posts without orders, the usual penalty being hanging rather than a firing squad. Schörner was also something of a coward: when captured by the US Army on May 11, 1945, he was wearing civilian clothing, having deserted his post as commanding officer, Army Group Center. When he died in 1973, the last German field marshal, the West German government forbade any official recognition of the man or his passing.
29. Rommel, *Infantry in the Attack/Infantry Attacks*, 179.
30. Ibid, 183–184.
31. Ibid, 185–185.
32. Ibid, 203.
33. Rommel, *The Rommel Papers*, 201.
34. Rommel, *Infantry in the Attack/Infantry Attacks*, 214.

CHAPTER THREE: AN OFFICER OF THE REICHSWEHR
35. Manchester, *The Arms of Krupp*, 306.
36. Fest, *Hitler—Eine Biographie*, 175.
37. Wette, *The Wehrmacht*, 145.
38. Ibid, 144.
39. Von Seeckt, "The Remarks of the German Chief of the Army Command Based on His Inspections during 1921," in *United States Military Intelligence Reports: Germany, 1919–1941* (Frederick, MD: University Publications of America, 1983), microfilm

reel XV, frames 73–150, 3–4.

40. Fraser, *Knight's Cross: A Life of Field Marshal Erwin Rommel,* 86.

41. Lewin, *Rommel As Military Commander*, 1.

42. Manfred Rommel, quoted in Irving, *The Trail of the Fox*, 32.

43. Rommel, *The Rommel Papers*, 241; Rommel's Personnel File 6/5, Bundesarchiv—Abteilung Militärarchiv, Freiburg im Breisgau.

44. Intriguingly, throughout his career, General George S. Patton, Jr., when emphasizing the necessity of frequent, intense training, would remark to his soldiers that "A pint of sweat saves a gallon of blood." Both men, the best-known armor commanders of the Second World War, deeply understood the truth of Flavius Josephus' commentary on the Romans: "Their drills are bloodless battles, and their battles bloody drills."

45. Rommel quoted in Irving, *The Trail of the Fox*, 28.

CHAPTER FOUR: THE THIRD REICH

46. Wheeler-Bennett, *The Nemesis of Power: The German Army in Politics 1918*–1945, 726.

47. Evans, *The Third Reich in Power*, 26.

48. Höhne, *The Order of the Death's Head: The Story of Hitler's SS*, 117.

49. Fest, *Hitler—Eine Biographie*, 470, Klemperer, *I Will Bear Witness: The Diaries of Victor Klemperer*, 73–74, Fraser, *Knight's Cross: A Life of Field Marshal Erwin Rommel*, 115.

50. Irving, *The Trail of the Fox*, 30.

51. Fest, *Hitler—Eine Biographie*, 469.

52. Manchester, *The Arms of Krupp*, 365.

53. Irving, *The Trail of the Fox*, 31.

54. Mitcham, *Triumphant Fox*, 16.

55. Irving, *The Trail of the Fox*, 32.

56. Ibid, 35–36.

57. It has been said the Swabians are the German Scots—thrifty, hardworking, mechanically gifted, and terrific fighters. As the author has a Scots heritage, he concedes that there could well be some substance to that comparison.

58. Hitler quoted in Bullock, *Hitler: A Study in Tyranny*, 135.

CHAPTER FIVE: BLITZKRIEG

59. Text of the Treaty of Versailles, from The Avalon Project website: http://avalon.law.yale.edu/imt/partiii.asp.

60. Text of the Treaty of St. Germain-en-Laye, from the Australian Treaty Series website, http://www.austlii.edu.au/au/other/dfat/treaties/1920/3.html.

61. Rommel quoted in Irving, *The Trail of the Fox*, 39.

62. Fraser, *Knight's Cross: A Life of Field Marshal Erwin Rommel*, 134–135; Irving, *The Trail of the Fox*, 39.

63. BBC Archive, "Chamberlain Addresses the Nation on His Negotiations for Peace," September 27, 1938.

64. Irving, *The Trail of the Fox*, 40.

65. Hitler quoted in *Time* magazine (2 October 1939).

66. Irving, *The Trail of the Fox*, 45.

67. Ibid, 44.

68. From the title of Goldhagen's book, *Hitler's Willing Executioners* (Knopf Doubleday, 2007).

69. Irving, *The Trail of the Fox*, 46.

70. Ibid, 49.

71 Pzkw: *Panzerkampfwagen*—"Armored Fighting Vehicle" or tank, usually reduced to simply "Panzer."

72. Rommel, *Infantry Attacks*, 128.

73. Rommel, *The Rommel Papers*, 6.

74. For a thorough examination of von Manstein's *Sichelschnitt* plan and its evolution, see Robert Allan Doughty's *The Breaking Point: Sedan and the Fall of France, 1940*, and Karl-Heinz Frieser's *The Blitzkrieg Legend: The 1940 Campaign in the West.*

75. Leutnant Braun, National Archives, T 84/277.

76. Leutnant Braun, National Archives, T 84/277.

77. Rommel, *The Rommel Papers*, 22.

78. Ibid, 24.

79. Shirer, *The Rise and Fall of the Third Reich*, 720; Churchill, *History of the Second World War: Vol. 2 Their Finest Hour*, 43–51.

80. Rommel, *The Rommel Papers*, 30–32.

81. Ibid, 34.

82. Ibid, 39–40.

83. 7th Panzer Divisional History, National Archives, T 84/277.

84. Irving, *The Trail of the Fox*, 64.

85. Rommel, *The Rommel Papers,* 43.

86. Ibid, 44.

87. Ibid, 49.

88. Ibid, 66–67.

CHAPTER SIX: AFRIKA KORPS

89. Throughout the North African campaign Great Britain deployed troops from several nations in the Empire and Commonwealth, including Indian, Australian, New Zealand, and South African divisions, along with units of the British Army itself. For the sake of brevity, the author has chosen to use the term "British" when referring to these forces as a whole. Unit nationality is distinctly identified when specific reference is made to it. Later references to "the Allies" are meant to include the British and American armed forces; Soviet forces are mentioned separately, unless otherwise noted.

90. Playfair et al, *The Mediterranean and Middle East, Volume I–IV*, 265.

91. Schofield, *Wavell: Soldier and Statesman*, 206.

92. Ciano, *The Ciano Diaries 1939–1943*, 297.

93. Rommel, *The Rommel Papers*, 103–104.

94. Ibid, 198.

95. "Flak" was the German abbreviation for *Flugzeugabwehrkanone*—antiaircraft gun.

96. Lewin, *Rommel As Military Commander*, 33.

97. Rommel, *The Rommel Papers*, 111.

98. Ibid, 110.

99. Ibid, 112.

100 Irving, *The Trail of the Fox*, 82, taken from General Streich's unpublished memoirs.

101. Hans von Luck, Hans, *Panzer Commander*, (Praeger, New York, 1989), 82.

102. Rommel, *The Rommel Papers*, 116.

103. Ibid, 118.

104. Ibid, 119.

105. Lewin, *Rommel As Military Commander*, 143.

106. Irving, *The Trail of the Fox*, 82.

107. Streich, Lecture notes, Institut für Zeitgeschichte, University of Munich.

CHAPTER SEVEN: TOBRUK

108. He wasn't alone in such a circumstance. Major General George S. Patton, Jr., in what was unquestionably the most tactically inelegant battle of his career, was frustrated for three months before the walls of the ancient French fortress city of Metz in the autumn of 1944. His Third Army eventually took the city through sheer brute force, Patton being able to draw on resources of materiel and men on a scale of which Rommel could only dream. It's interesting to note how two of the Second World War's best-known armor generals, remembered for their mastery of mobile warfare, were so stymied by fixed fortresses.

109. So well executed would be Morshead's defense of Tobruk that it is still presented in military academies and war colleges, including the US Army Command and General Staff College at Fort Leavenworth, Kansas, as an example of how a largely infantry force can successfully conduct an in-depth defense against superior armored forces.

110. Both sides could—and did—fight ferociously in actual combat, but by a mutual, unspoken agreement, they also understood that there were lines to be drawn and respected even in warfare. No mention is made in either German or Australian records of any attempt by the Australians to hinder the German soldiers in taking away their dead and wounded comrades. Already being set was the tone of what would, in harsh contrast to the war without quarter on the Eastern Front, become known as the "war without hate."

111. Rommel, *The Rommel Papers*, 124.

112. Streich, Lecture notes, Institut für Zeitgeschichte, University of Munich.

113. Coombes, *Morshead: Hero of Tobruk and El Alamein*, 121.

114. Rommel, *The Rommel Papers*, 126.

115. Ibid, 126.

116. Ibid, 129.

117. Ibid, 131.

118. Halder, *War Diary*, Vol VI, 41, 64, 71, 81.

119. Streich, Lecture notes.

120. Rommel, *The Rommel Papers*, 134.

121. Paulus, of course, is best remembered as the German commander of the Sixth Army during the battle of Stalingrad, where a quarter-million German soldiers were killed or captured, and who surrendered to the Soviet Red Army there on January 31, 1943. Hitler, in an effort to encourage Paulus to fight to the last man and last round, promoted him to the rank of field marshal on January 29, 1943, with the pointed reminder that no Prussian or German officer of that rank had ever been captured alive by the enemy. Paulus refused to take the hint and commit

suicide, and instead surrendered his command the next day, eventually collaborating with the Soviets to oppose the Nazis. His actions were, at the time, regarded as a disgrace to the reputation of the German Army.

122. Rommel, *The Rommel Papers*, 137–138.
123. Ibid, 139.
124. Streich, Lecture notes.
125. Wavell quoted by Churchill, *The Grand Alliance*, 304.
126. Rommel, *The Rommel Papers*, 139.
127. Ibid, 144.
128. Ibid, 145.

CHAPTER EIGHT: *CRUSADER*
129. Rommel, *The Rommel Papers*, 146.
130. Berndt, "*27 Monate Kampf in Afrika.*"
131. Keitel and von Brauchitsch quoted in Irving, *The Trail of the Fox*, 132.
132. Auchinleck, "Despatch on Operations in the Middle East From 5 July 1941 to 31 October 1941," 4215.
133. Montgomery, *Memoirs*, 71.
134. Rommel, *The Rommel Papers*, 148–149.
135. Ibid, 148.
136. Ibid, 148–149.
137. Ibid, 150–151.
138. Ibid, 152–153.
139. Bayerlein, quoted in *The Rommel Papers*, 159.
140. Fraser, *Knight's Cross: A Life of Field Marshal Erwin Rommel*, 282.
141. Rommel, *The Rommel Papers*, 160.
142. Bayerlein quoted in *The Rommel Papers*, 161–162.
143. Rommel, *The Rommel Papers*, 162.
144. Bayerlein quoting Rommel, *The Rommel Papers*, 163.
145. Rommel, *The Rommel Papers*, 168.
146. Ibid, 173–174.
147. In the original letter Rommel actually used only the first character of the town's name.
148. Rommel, *The Rommel Papers*, 175–176.
149. Ibid, 178.
150. Ibid, 179.

CHAPTER NINE: *DER HEXENKESSEL*
151. Colonel Fellers left Egypt at the beginning of July and returned to the United States, where he was awarded the Distinguished Service Medal and promoted to brigadier general in recognition of the work he had done in Egypt. He had been in no way responsible for the security failure, his concerns about a possible compromise of the Black Code being summarily overruled by his civilian superiors. He would go on to serve with the OSS and then in the Pacific on the staff of General Douglas MacArthur. He retired from the US Army in 1946, after 30 years of service, and died in 1973.

152. Rommel, *The Rommel Papers*, 182.
153. Ibid, 182.
154. Ibid, 182.
155. Ibid, 183.
156. von Esebeck, *Afrikanische Schicksalsjahre: Das deutsche Afrikakorps unter Rommel*, 148.
157. Bayerlein quoted in *The Rommel Papers*, 185.
158. Rommel, *The Rommel Papers*, 187.
159. Irving, *The Trail of the Fox*, 166.
160. Rommel, *The Rommel Papers*, 188.
161. Lewin, *Rommel As Military Commander*, 109.
162. Rommel, *The Rommel Papers*, 204
163. Fraser, *Knight's Cross: A Life of Field Marshal Erwin Rommel*, 319.
164. Young, *Rommel The Desert Fox*, 135.
165. Rommel, *The Rommel Papers*, 212.
166. Ibid, 216.
167. Ibid, 222–223.
168. Ibid, 224.
169. Ibid, 231.
170. Ibid, 232.
171. Ibid, 232.

CHAPTER TEN: AFRICAN APOGEE

172. Churchill, *The Hinge of Fate*, 344.
173. Irving, *The Trail of the Fox*, 226.
174. Rommel, *The Rommel Papers*, 240.
175. Ibid, 241.
176. Ibid, 233.
177. Ibid, 241.
178. Ibid, 248.
179 Ibid, 249–250.
180. Ibid, 261.
181. Ibid, 262.
182 Ibid, 263.
183. Ibid, 270.
184. Ibid, 270–272.
185. Quoted by Bayerlein, in *The Rommel Papers*, 271.
186. Rommel, *The Rommel Papers*, 271–272.
187. Ibid, 275.
188. Ibid, 282.

CHAPTER ELEVEN: EL ALAMEIN

189. Rommel, *The Rommel Papers*, 285–286.
190. Ibid, 290.
191. Ibid, 291–292.
192. Ibid, 292.
193. The full text of the Commando Order can be found in The Avalon Law Project's

website containing full transcripts of the indictments handed down by the International Military Tribunal for Germany, Nuremberg, 1945–46, specifically the section "Nazi Conspiracy and Aggression," Volume 2, Chapter 15, Part 7: http:// avalon.law.yale.edu/imt/chap15_part07.asp

194. Churchill, *The Hinge of Fate*, 420.

195. Lewin, *Rommel As Military Commander*, 245–246.

196. "Legend" is used here as defined in the intelligence community, i.e. a well-prepared synthetic identity.

197. See Jonathan Fennell, "'Steel my soldiers' hearts': El Alamein Reappraised" in the *Journal of Military and Strategic Studies* (Volume 14, Issue 1, Fall 2011) for an in-depth examination of the morale problems experienced by Eighth Army in the summer and early autumn of 1942. Fennell presents an excellent original analysis of the mood and temper of Eighth Army's soldiers, as well as the root causes of the army's crisis of confidence in those months, but errs in significantly overestimating the speed with which Montgomery would have been accepted by the Tommies as not only a proven combat general but a winning one as well.

198. Rommel, *The Rommel Papers*, 294–295.

199. Ibid, 295.

200. Behrendt, *Rommels Kenntnis vom Feind im Afrika Feldzug*, 208.

201. Rommel, *The Rommel Papers*, 304, 305.

202. Ibid, 308.

203. Ibid, 308.

204. Ibid, 310.

205. Ibid, 288.

206. Ibid, 321.

207. Ibid, 321–322.

208. Ibid, 322.

209. Irving, *The Trail of the Fox*, 279; Peter Hoffman in Denton, *The Limits of Loyalty*, 118.

210. Rommel, *The Rommel Papers*, 324.

211. Ibid, 325–326

212. Ibid, 360–361.

213 Von Luck, *Panzer Commander*, 129–130.

214. Rommel, *The Rommel Papers*, 362.

CHAPTER TWELVE: AFRICAN PERIGEE

215 Rommel, *The Rommel Papers*, 360–362.

216. Ibid, 362.

217. Irving, *The Trail of the Fox*, 245.

218. Rommel, *The Rommel Papers*, 365–366.

219. Ibid, 366.

220. Ibid, 367.

221 Bayerlein in *The Rommel Papers*, 366.

222. Rommel, *The Rommel Papers*, 369.

223. Ibid, 371.

224. Generalleutnant Wilhelm Meise, in a private letter to William W. James; the original

resides in the archives of The Citadel, Charleston, South Carolina.

225. Irving, *The Trail of the Fox*, 250; Fraser, *Knight's Cross: A Life of Field Marshal Erwin Rommel*, 395.

226 Bülowius would become a prisoner of war in early May 1943, and subsequently be sent to a POW camp in the United States. There are stories that suggest some sort of mental instability on his part, but the details remain unknown. On 27 March 1945, Bülowius committed suicide.

227. Rommel, *The Rommel Papers*, 377.

228. Ibid, 378–379.

229. Ibid, 377.

230. Ibid, 376, 377; Irving, *The Trail of the Fox*, 254.

231. Rommel, *The Rommel Papers*, 379.

232. Ibid, 383.

233. Ibid, 385.

234. Irving, *The Trail of the Fox*, 254.

235. Rommel, *The Rommel Papers*, 391–392.

236. Ibid, 392.

237. Ibid, 394.

238. Ibid, 398.

239. Ibid, 406–407.

240. Berndt, quoted in *The Rommel Papers*, 411.

241. Rommel, *The Rommel Papers*, 407.

242. Ibid, 404.

243. Ibid, 407, 409.

244. Ibid, 412.

245. Ibid, 412.

246. Ibid, 414.

247. Ibid, 415–416.

248. Ibid, 419.

249. Ibid, 425.

CHAPTER THIRTEEN: THE ATLANTIC WALL

250. Manfred quoting Rommel, *The Rommel Papers*, 425.

251. Bayerlein quoting Rommel, *The Rommel Papers*, 451.

252. Rommel, *The Rommel Papers*, 427–428.

253. Ibid, 431.

254. Ibid, 432.

255. *Vital Speeches of the Day*, Vol. IX, 646.

256. Rommel, *The Rommel Papers*, 445.

257 The surgery removed Rommel's appendix, but not his sense of humor. When Lucie made a passing remark about the zipper-like scar left by the appendectomy, Rommel smile wryly and said "Well, you'll just have to look the other way, won't you?"

258. Irving, *The Trail of the Fox*, 307–308.

259. Rommel, *The Rommel Papers*, 447.

260. Irving, *The Trail of the Fox*, 313.

261. Rommel, *The Rommel Papers*, 461.

262. Ibid, 429; Irving, *The Trail of the Fox*, 313

263. Longford, *Wellington: The Years of The Sword*, 92; Ryan, *The Longest Day*, 23, 28.

264. Rommel, *The Rommel Papers*, 468.

265. Irving, *The Trail of the Fox*, 315.

266. Meise, in a private letter to William W. James; the original resides in the archives of the Citadel, Charleston, South Carolina.

267. Rommel, *The Rommel Papers*, 461.

268. Ibid, 461–462.

269. Ibid, 462.

270. Rommel's old command would come to a sad end: the Goslar Jäger Battalion would be all but annihilated by the Soviet Army in January 1945; very few of the *jägers* were captured alive and of those only a handful would survive long enough to return to Germany in the mid-1950s.

271. Rommel, *The Rommel Papers*, 463.

272. Beckett, *Rommel: A Reappraisal*, 120.

273. Ryan, *The Longest Day*, 25.

274. Rommel, *The Rommel Papers*, 463–464.

275. Ibid, 455.

276. Ibid, 456.

277. Ryan, *The Longest Day*, 27–28.

278. Rommel, *The Rommel Papers*, 465.

279. There are several interations of the encounter between Rommel and Lane, all of which agree on the significant aspects, and differ only in the details. This recounting is taken from George Lane's obituary in *The Daily Telegraph*, (London), 26 March 2010.

280. Mitcham, *The Desert Fox in Normandy*, 79.

CHAPTER FOURTEEN: INVASION AND CONSPIRACY

281. As if to add insult to injury, the hand-made shoes Rommel purchased in Paris for Lucie's birthday did not fit properly.

282. Pyle, *Brave Men*, 390–391.

283. Rommel, *The Rommel Papers*, 470.

284. Ibid, 467–468

285. Ibid, 474–476.

286. Ibid, 476.

287. Ibid, 491–492.

288. Wheeler-Bennett, *The Nemesis of Power: The German Army in Politics 1918–1945*, 604.

289. Rommel, *The Rommel Papers*, 479.

290. Showalter, *Patton and Rommel: Men of War in the Twentieth Century*, 356.

291. Messenger, *The Last Prussian*, 197.

292. Geyr von Schweppenburg, *Die Verteidigung des Westens*, 200.

293. Rommel, *The Rommel Papers*, 481.

294. Ibid, 496.

295. Ibid, 486–487.

296. Fraser, *Knight's Cross: A Life of Field Marshal Erwin Rommel*, 507.

297. Messenger, *Hitler's Gladiator*, 212.

298. Fest, *Hitler—Eine Biographie*, 961.

299. Rommel, *The Rommel Papers*, 500–501.

300 Shirer, *The Rise and Fall of the Third Reich*, 372.

301. Shirer, *The Rise and Fall of the Third Reich*, 372.

302. Rommel, *The Rommel Papers*, 428.

303. Ibid, 496.

304. Rommel, quoted in Hansen, *Disobeying Hitler: German Resistance After Valkyrie*, 54, 56.

305. Rommel, *The Rommel Papers*, 429, 486, 496.

CHAPTER FIFTEEN: DEATH OF A FIELD MARSHAL

306. Rommel, *The Rommel Papers*, 493.

307. Ibid, 493.

308 Hansen, *Disobeying Hitler: German Resistance After Valkyrie*, 63.

309. Hoffman, *History of the German Resistance, 1933–1945*, 526.

310. Irving, *The Trail of the Fox*, 430.

311. Ibid, 430.

312. Shirer, *The Rise and Fall of the Third Reich*, 1077, 1393.

313. Rommel, *The Rommel Papers*, 495.

314. Ibid, 495.

315. Ibid, 496.

316. Ibid, 499.

317. Ibid, 497.

318. Jodl diaries, National Archives, film T84/149.

319. Young, *Rommel The Desert Fox*, 251.

320. Irving, *The Trail of the Fox*, 436.

321. Young, *Rommel The Desert Fox*, 252.

322. Ibid, 254.

323. Rommel, *The Rommel Papers*, 502.

324. Ibid, 502.

325. Young, *Rommel The Desert Fox*, 255.

326. Rommel, *The Rommel Papers*, 503.

327. Ibid, 503–504.

328. Marshall, *The Rommel Murder: The Life and Death of the Desert Fox*, 158.

329. Young, *Rommel The Desert Fox*, 261.

330. Ibid, 263.

331. Brighton, *Masters of Battle: Monty, Patton and Rommel at War*, 318.

332. Young, *Rommel The Desert Fox*, 270–271.

SOURCES AND BIBLIOGRAPHY

ARCHIVAL MATERIAL

National Archives, Washington DC

Primary Rommel sources and related documentation: T77/858; T84/273–278, 282.

Records of the German General Staff: T78/324-326.

War Diary of the Oberkommando des Wehrmacht (O.K.W.): T77/780.

Diaries of Col-Gen. Alfred Jodl, the Chief of Operations for the O.K.W.: T84/ 149, 268.

War diaries of the Afrika Korps, Panzerarmee Afrika, Heeresgruppe Afrika: T314/2, 15, 16, 18, 21, 23; T313/416, 423, 430, 467, 471–475, 480.

War Diaries of Army Group B and Component Units: T314/1263, 1264, 1270, T315/2371.

Fifteenth Army: T312/534, T312/509, 514, 516.

Seventh Army: T312/1564.

Panzer Group West/Fifth Panzer Army: T313/420.

LXVII Corps: T314/1533.

LXXXI Corps: T314/1589.

LXXXII Corps: T314/1601.

LXXVIII Corps: T314/1620.

War Diary of the German Army Personnel Branch: T78/39.

Bundesarchiv—Militararchiv, Freiburg-am-Breisgau

Rommel's personnel file: BA-MA Pers. 6/5.

War Diaries of Oberbefehlshaber West: BA–MA RH19-IV/8,9,10, 11, 27, 31, 33, 39, 88, 89.

Unpublished manuscript: BA-MA N 20/2.

The Citadel
Correspondence between Generalleutnant Wilhelm Meise and Mr. William W. James

PRINTED WORKS

Almásy, László. *With Rommel's Army in Libya*. Bloomington: 1st Books Library, 2001.

Atkinson, Rick. *An Army at Dawn: The War in North Africa, 1942–1943, Volume One of the Liberation Trilogy*. New York: Holt Paperbacks, 2007.

Auchinleck, Claude. "Despatch on Operations in the Middle East From 5 July 1941 to 31 October 1941," *The London Gazette (Supplement)* no. 37695, 20 August 1946, 4215–4230.

Barnett, Corelli. *The Desert Generals*. London: William Kimber, 1960.

Beckett, Ian F. *Rommel: A Reappraisal*. London: Pen and Sword, 2013.

Behrendt, Hans Otto. *Rommels Kenntnis vom Feind im Afrika Feldzug* [*Rommel's Intelligence in the African Campaign*]. Freiburg im Breisgau: Romberg, 1980.

Berndt, Alfred. *"27 Monate Kampf in Afrika."* Broadcast script, May 1943.

Bierman, John; Smith, Colin. *The Battle of Alamein: Turning Point, World War II*. New York: Viking Press, 2002

Brighton, Terry. *Masters of Battle: Monty, Patton and Rommel at War*. New York: Penguin, 2009.

Bullock, Alan. *Hitler: A Study in Tyranny*. London: Oldhams, 1962.

Carrell, Paul. *Invasion! They're Coming!: The German Account of the D-Day Landings and the 80 Days Battle for France*. 1994, London: Schiffer Publishing Ltd., 2004

Carell, Paul. *The Foxes of the Desert*. New York: Dutton, 1960.

Churchill, Winston S. *The World Crisis, Volume 1, 1911–1914*, New York: Scribners, 1928.

Churchill, Winston S. *The Second World War, Volume 2: Their Finest Hour*. Cambridge: Houghton Mifflin, 1949.

Churchill, Winston S. *The Second World War, Volume 3: The Grand Alliance*. (first ed.). Boston: Houghton Mifflin Harcourt Mariner Books, 1953.

Ciano, Count Galeazzo. *The Ciano Diaries 1939–1943*. Mudderidge Ed. London: 1947.

Coggins, Jack *The Campaign for North Africa*. New York, Doubleday & Company, 1980.

Conington, John (translator). *The Odes and Carmen Saeculare of Horace*. London: George Bell and Sons, 1882.

Connell, John. *Auchinleck: A Biography of Field-Marshal Sir Claude Auchinleck*. London: Cassell, 1959.

Coombes, David. *Morshead: Hero of Tobruk and El Alamein*. Australian Army History Series. South Melbourne: Oxford University Press, 2001.

Cooper, Martin. *The German Army 1933–1945: Its Political and Military Failure*. New York: Bonanza Books, 1984.

Crisp, Robert. *Brazen Chariots*. New York: W. W. Norton and Co., 2005.

Denton, Edgar (ed.). *The Limits of Loyalty*. Waterloo, Ontario: Wilfrid Laurier University Press, 1980.

Doughty, Robert A. *The Breaking Point: Sedan and the Fall of France, 1940*. Mechanicsburg: Stackpole, 2014.

Ellis, John. *Brute Force: Allied Strategy and Tactics in the Second World War*. New York, Viking, 1990.

von Esebeck, Hanns Gert. *Afrikanische Schicksalsjahre: Das deutsche Afrikakorps unter Rommel*. Munich: Limes Verlag, 1950.

Evans, Richard. *The Third Reich in Power*. New York: Penguin Group, 2005

Fest, Joachim. *Hitler—Eine Biographie*. Berlin: Propyläen Verlag, 2004.

Forty, George. *The Armies of Rommel*. London: Arms and Armour Press, 1998.

Fraser, David. *Knight's Cross: A Life of Field Marshal Erwin Rommel*. New York: Harper Collins, 1994.

Frieser, Karl-Heinz. *The Blitzkrieg Legend: The 1940 Campaign in the West*. Annapolis: Naval Institute Press, 2005.

Geyr Von Schweppenburg, Leo. *Die Verteidigung des Westens*. Frankfurt: Verlag Friedrich Rudl, 1952.

Goldhagen, Daniel. *Hitler's Willing Executioners: Ordinary Germans and the Holocaust*. New York: Knopf Doubleday, 2007.

Greene, Jack; Massignani, Alessandro. *Rommel's North Africa Campaign: September 1940–November 1942*. Conshohocken: Combined Books, 1994.

Halder, Franz. *War Diary of Franz Halder,* Volumes III–VII. United States Army, 1947.

Hamilton, Nigel. *Monty: The Making of a General*. London: Hamish Hamilton Ltd., 1981.

Hansen, Randall. *Disobeying Hitler: German Resistance After Valkyrie*. Oxford: Oxford University Press, 2014.

Hesketh, Roger Fleetwood. *Fortitude: The D-Day Deception Campaign*. New York: The Overlook Press, 2002.

Hinsley, F. H.; Thomas, E. E.; Ransom, C. F. G.; Knight, R. C. *British Intelligence in the Second World War: Its influence on Strategy and Operations, Volume Two*. London: HMSO, 1981.

Hoffman, Karl. *Erwin Rommel*. London: Brassey's, 2004.

Hoffman, Peter. *History of the German Resistance, 1933–1945*. Montreal: McGill-Queens University Press, 1996.

Höhne, Heinz. *The Order of the Death's Head: The Story of Hitler's SS*. New York: Coward-McCann, 1970.

Howard, Michael. *Strategic Deception in the Second World War: British Intelligence Operations Against the German High Command*. New York: W. W. Norton & Co., 1995.

Irving, David. *The Trail of the Fox*. New York: Avon Books, 1978.

Jentz, Thomas L. *Tank Combat in North Africa: The Opening Rounds: Operations Sonnenblume, Brevity, Skorpion and Battleaxe February 1941–June 1941*. Atglen: Schiffer Military History, 1998.

Keegan, John. *Six Armies in Normandy: From D-Day to the Liberation of Paris; June 6–Aug. 5, 1944*. New York: Penguin, 1994.

Kelly, Orr. *Meeting the Fox: The Allied Invasion of Africa, from Operation Torch to Kasserine Pass to Victory in Tunisia*. New York: J. Wiley, 2002.

Kitchen, Martin. *Rommel's Desert War: Waging World War II in North Africa, 1941–1943*. Cambridge: Cambridge University Press, 2009.

Klemperer, Victor. *I Will Bear Witness: The Diaries of Victor Klemperer.* New York: Random House, 1998.

Kriebel, Rainer; Gudmundsson, Bruce I. *Inside the Afrika Korps: The Crusader Battles, 1941–1942*. London: Greenhill Books, 1999.

Latimer, Jon. *Alamein*. Cambridge: Harvard University Press, 2002.

Latimer, Jon. *Tobruk 1941: Rommel's Opening Move*. Oxford: Osprey Publishing, 2001.

Lewin, Ronald. *Rommel As Military Commander*. New York: B&N Books, 1998.

Liddell Hart, B.H., *The German Generals Talk*. New York: Morrow, 1948.

Longford, Elizabeth. *Wellington: The Years of The Sword*. New York: HarperCollins Publishers, 1971.

von Luck, Hans. *Panzer Commander: The Memoirs of Colonel Hans von Luck*. New York, Dell Publishing, 1991.

Manchester, William. *The Arms of Krupp*. New York: Little, Brown and Company, 1968.

Marshall, Charles F. *The Rommel Murder: The Life and Death of the Desert Fox*. Mechanicsburg: Stackpole Books, 1994.

Messenger, Charles. *Hitler's Gladiator: The Life and Times of Oberstgruppen-führer and Panzergeneral-Oberst Der Waffen SS Sepp Dietrich*. London: Brassey's, 1988.

Messenger, Charles. *The Last Prussian: A Biography of Field Marshal Gerd von Rundstedt 1875–1953*. London: Pen & Sword, 2011.

Mitcham, Samuel. *The Desert Fox in Normandy: Rommel's Defense of Fortress Europe*. New York: Greenwood Group, 1996.

Mitcham, Samuel. *Triumphant Fox: Erwin Rommel and the Rise of the Afrika Korps*. New York: Stein and Day, 1984.

von Mellenthin, Friedrich. *Panzer Battles: A Study of the Employment of Armor in the Second World War*. New York: Cassell, 1956.

Montgomery, Bernard Law. *The Memoirs of Field-Marshal Montgomery of Alamein*. London: Pen & Sword, 1958.

Moore, John. *Quotations for Martial Artists: Hundreds of Inspirational Quotes to Motivate and Enlighten the Modern Warrior*. Boston: iUniverse, 2003.

Moorehead, Alan. *Desert War: The North African Campaign 1940–1943*. New York: Penguin Books, 2001.

Moorhouse, Roger. *Killing Hitler: The Third Reich and the Plots Against the Führer*. London: Random House, 2007.

Playfair, Major General I. S. O. with Commander G. M. S. Stitt, R.N., Brigadier C. J. C. Molony, and Air Vice-Marshal S. E. Toomer; J. R. M, Butler (ed.). *The Mediterranean and Middle East, Volume I–IV*; United Kingdom Military Series. London: Naval & Military Press, 2004.

Pyle, Ernie. *Brave Men*. New York: Henry Holt and Co., 1944.

Ralf, Georg Reuth. *Erwin Rommel: Des Führers General*. Munich: Piper Verlag, 1987.

Reuth, Ralf Georg. *Rommel: The End of a Legend*. London: Haus Books, 2006.

Rommel, Erwin. *Infantry Attacks (Infantrie greift an)*. San Francisco: Presidio Press, reprint edition, 1990.

Rommel, Erwin; Liddell Hart, B. H. (ed). *The Rommel Papers*. New York: Da Capo Press, reprint edition, 1987.

Ryan, Cornelius, *The Longest Day*. New York: Simon and Schuster, 1959.

Schaulen, Fritjof. *Eichenlaubträger 1940–1945 Zeitgeschichte in Farbe III Radusch—Zwernemann* [*Holders of the Oak Leaves 1940–1945 Contemporary History in Color, volume III: Radusch – Zwernemann*]. Germany: Selent, Pour le Mérite, 2005.

Scherzer, Veit. *Die Ritterkreuzträger 1939–1945 Die Inhaber des Ritterkreuzes des Eisernen Kreuzes 1939 von Heer, Luftwaffe, Kriegsmarine, Waffen-SS, Volkssturm sowie mit Deutschland verbündeter Streitkräfte nach den Unterlagen des Bundesarchives* [*The Knight's Cross 1939–1945 The holders of the Knight's Cross of the Iron Cross in 1939 by Army, Air Force, Navy, Waffen-SS and Volkssturm allied with German armed forces according to the documents of the Federal Archives*]. Jena, Germany: Scherzers Miltaer-Verlag, 2007.

Schofield, Victoria. *Wavell: Soldier and Statesman*. London: John Murray, 2006.

Schraepler, Hans-Joachim; Schraepler, Hans-Albrecht (ed.). *At Rommel's Side: The Lost Letters of Hans-Joachim Schraepler*. London: Frontline Books, 2009.

von Seeckt, Hans. "The Remarks of the German Chief of the Army Command Based on His Inspections during 1921," in *United States Military Intelligence Reports: Germany, 1919–1941*. Frederick, MD: University Publications of America, 1983.

Shirer, William L. *The Rise and Fall of the Third Reich*. New York: Simon and Schuster, 1960.

Showalter, Dennis. *Patton and Rommel: Men of War in the Twentieth Century*. New York: Penguin, 2006.

Speidel, Hans. *Invasion 1944: Rommel and the Normandy Campaign*. Chicago: Henry Regnery, 1950.

Stegemann, Bernard. *Germany and the Second World War—Volume III—Part IV and V*. Oxford: Clarendon Press, 1995.

Thomas, Franz. *Die Eichenlaubträger 1939–1945 Band 2: L–Z* [*The Oak Leaves Bearers 1939–1945 Volume 2: L–Z*]. Osnabrück, Germany: Biblio-Verlag, 1998.

Tuchman, Barbara. *The Guns of August*. New York: MacMillan, 1962.

Toland, John. *Adolf Hitler: The Definitive Biography*. New York: Doubleday, 1976.

Van Creveld, Martin. *Supplying War: Logistics from Wallenstein to Patton*. Cambridge: Cambridge University Press, 1977.

Wette, Wolfram. *The Wehrmacht*. Cambridge: Harvard University Press, 2006.

Wheeler-Bennett, John. *The Nemesis of Power: The German Army in Politics*

1918–1945 (2nd edition). London: Palgrave Macmillan, 2005.

Windrow, Martin. *Rommel's Desert Army*. New York: Osprey Publishing, 1976.

Young, Desmond. *Rommel The Desert Fox*. New York: Harper & Row, 1950.

WEB RESOURCES

The Australian Treaty Series, http://www.austlii.edu.au/au/other/dfat/treaties/1920/3.html

The Avalon Project, http://avalon.law.yale.edu/

INDEX

(Officers are listed according to their highest rank attained by war's end or time of their death.)